How to Teach Reading to Elementary and Middle School Students

How to Teach Reading to Elementary and Middle School Students

Practical Ideas from Highly Effective Teachers

Robert B. Ruddell

University of California, Berkeley

PEARSON

and

Boston   New York   San Francisco
Mexico City   Montreal   Toronto   London   Madrid   Munich   Paris
Hong Kong   Singapore   Tokyo   Cape Town   Sydney

Executive Editor: Aurora Martínez Ramos
Series Editorial Assistant: Kara Kikel
Executive Marketing Manager: Krista Clark
Production Editor: Annette Joseph
Editorial Production Service: NK Graphics
Composition Buyer: Linda Cox
Manufacturing Buyer: Megan Cochran
Electronic Composition: NK Graphics
Interior Design: NK Graphics
Cover Administrator: Linda Knowles
Cover Designer: Elena Sidorova

For related titles and support materials, visit our online catalog at www.pearsonhighered.com.

Between the time website information is gathered and then published, it is not unusual for some sites to have closed. Also, the transcription of URLs can result in typographical errors. The publisher would appreciate notification where these errors occur.

ISBN-10: 0-205-62542-8
ISBN-13: 978-0-205-62542-0

Library of Congress Cataloging-in-Publication Data

Ruddell, Robert B.
  How to teach reading to elementary and middle school students : practical ideas from highly effective teachers / Robert B. Ruddell.
       p.   cm.
  Includes bibliographical references and index.
  ISBN-13: 978-0-205-62542-0 (alk. paper)
  ISBN-10: 0-205-62542-8 (alk. paper)
 1. Reading.   2. Effective teaching.   3. English language—Composition and exercises—Study and teaching.
4. Classroom management.   I. Title.
  LB1050.R83 2008
  372.4—dc22
                                   2008032442

Printed in the United States of America

10 9 8 7 6 5 4 3 2 1 BR 12 11 10 09 08

Credits appear on page 471, which constitutes an extension of the copyright page.

Allyn & Bacon
is an imprint of

To my love and companion in life—Sandy.

And to those highly effective literacy teachers who will make a difference in the lives of their students.

About the Author

Bob Ruddell has been a reading teacher for over four decades. His research has examined the characteristics of reading teachers who are highly effective and influential in the lives of their students. The ideas and instructional strategies for teaching reading found in this book are a distillation of these teaching experiences and research findings.

Bob has successfully combined his work in public schools with his university teaching and research, and has worked with students and teachers in schools ranging from the inner city to rural areas. He has also lectured and conducted workshops for teachers in each of the fifty states, as well as in England, Sweden, Germany, Australia, Canada, and the Ivory Coast. He has taught a wide range of courses in reading and language development working with teaching credential students and M.A., Ed.D., and Ph.D. students at Berkeley. He is Professor Emeritus of the Language, Literacy, and Culture Faculty Group at the University of California, Berkeley.

Dr. Ruddell received his M.A. degree from West Virginia University and George Peabody College for Teachers and his Doctorate from Indiana University. He is the recipient of the International Reading Association's (IRA's) William S. Gray Citation of Merit recognizing lifetime achievement and leadership contributions to the field of reading and literacy development. He received the Oscar S. Causey Research Award from the National Reading Conference recognizing his research on effective and influential teachers. Bob also received the Crystal Apple Award from the California Reading Association for his high-quality teaching and research work. He has been President of the IRA's Reading Hall of Fame, and has served on the IRA Board of Directors. He is senior editor (with Norman Unrau) of *Theoretical Models and Processes of Reading* (International Reading Association). Professor Ruddell's articles have appeared in *Reading Teacher* and *Language Arts,* as well as in a variety of research journals and yearbooks. His research and teaching interests focus on the study of comprehension and critical thinking, word identification skills, reader motivation, and the ways in which highly effective and influential teachers develop these skills with their students.

Bob and his wife, Sandy, enjoy traveling throughout the United States and internationally. They especially enjoy visits from their three grandchildren—Rebecca, Grace, and Madeline. Bob delights in conversation with his former students, and he relaxes with suspense and mystery novels, and a good round of golf.

He can be reached at rruddell@berkeley.edu.

BRIEF CONTENTS

CONTENTS

CHAPTER 3

Understanding Early Reading and Writing Development 49

CHAPTER 4

Increasing Word Recognition Knowledge and Word Identification Skills 84

CHAPTER **5**

Using Instructional Strategies to Develop Reading Comprehension   121

CHAPTER 8

Developing Reading and Writing in Content Areas   217

CHAPTER 9

Assessing Students' Progress in Literacy Development   250

CHAPTER 10

Instructing Delayed Readers in a Regular Classroom Setting 282

**Sandra McCormick, Professor Emeritus
The Ohio State University**

CHAPTER 11

Understanding Language Diversity, Cultural Diversity, and Special Needs 307

CHAPTER **12**

Examining Instructional Approaches to and the Organization and Management of Literacy Learning   345

CHAPTER 13

Continuing Your Professional Growth as a Highly Effective and Influential Literacy Teacher   381

the Highly Effective Teacher

Research and Evidence-Based Practice

Did You Know?

How to Do . . .

continued on following page

How to Do . . . *continued from previous page*

Strategies in Use

continued on following page

Strategies in Use *continued*

the Highly Effective Teacher on Technology and . . .

Professional Standards for the Classroom Teacher

Professional Standards and . . .

*The flame of literacy serves to illuminate
the darkness of ignorance.*
Robert B. Ruddell

To the Student

Welcome to the world of literacy instruction. Your effectiveness as a teacher of reading and other literacy skills will become one of the most important gauges used to measure your teaching success. My central purpose in writing this book is to assist you in *becoming a highly effective and influential literacy teacher.* The ideas, teaching strategies, and content of this text come from my years as a classroom teacher, reading supervisor, university professor, and lecturer throughout this country. I have been privileged to observe, discuss, and examine the teaching of highly effective and influential teachers at all grade levels, including the college and university levels. From these experiences, I have distilled the very best literacy teaching ideas for this text. I have attempted, with the help of editors, designers, and artists, to create a text that presents and communicates these ideas to you in a clear and concise manner—in a manner that can be used effectively in your classroom teaching.

Text Themes That Support Your Teaching

The first of the central themes of this book is *how to become a highly effective and influential literacy teacher.* Highly effective literacy-teaching practices and strategies are integrated throughout the text. Many of these are identified by the **Highly Effective Teacher** margin note over a star, and a **Highly Effective Teacher graphic organizer** at the end of each chapter. This organizer provides a chapter overview and a synthesis of instructional strategies and practices within and across chapters.

The second theme that guided the development of the text is the *identification and introduction of research and evidence-based practices.* This theme highlights the importance of using those highly effective instructional practices and decisions that are based on sound research and theory. You will find that each chapter reviews the latest research, evidence, and theory base that supports the instructional strategies and practices presented. Side-margin notes on **Evidence-Based Practice** appear throughout the book and identify key research and evidence-based practices. In addition, each chapter contains a **Research and Evidence-Based Practice** box presented in a "Did You Know?" format with key literacy-teaching findings related to the chapter topic. These findings will be of great value to your teaching.

The third theme is the *application of instructional strategies and the research and evidence-based practices in the classroom.* The strategies and teaching ideas are applied to literacy teaching through examples, instructional strategies, and illustrations—all designed to guide and support you as you work toward your goal of becoming a highly effective literacy teacher.

EVIDENCE-BASED PRACTICE

Text Features That Support Your Learning

A variety of special learning devices have been designed for this book and integrated throughout to help you understand and use the text content in your own teaching.

Each chapter opens with two **selected literacy quotes** from well-known individuals or literacy specialists and are intended to encourage you to think about and create positive mental associations with the chapter topic. The chapter-opening **vignette** follows and introduces the chapter's subject.

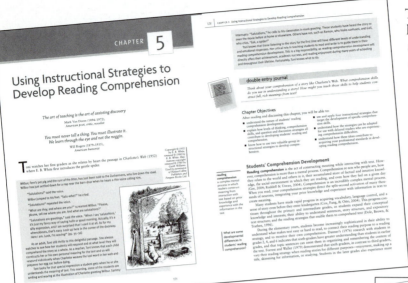

The vignette may present, for example, a real-life classroom situation, a teacher's memory of a childhood literacy experience at school, or a dialogue between two teachers who are working on a cooperative-teaching venture. As you read each vignette, recall your own past experiences that may be similar.

The first part of a **Double Entry Journal (DEJ)** also appears at the beginning of each chapter. The DEJ includes questions to stimulate your thinking about the vignette and the chapter topics, based on your previous experience and personal knowledge. As a follow-up, the second part of the DEJ appears near the end of each chapter to allow you to combine your

previous knowledge with the new ideas and strategies you learned by reading the chapter. The idea is to encourage you to reflect on and record your responses to the journal questions both before and after reading as an aid to your learning.

How to Teach Reading to Elementary and Middle School Students: Practical Ideas from Highly Effective Teachers contains **marginal annotations** throughout each chapter. Some annotations serve as *topical reference guides* to help you locate and review material. Other annotations provide definitions of *key terms and concepts* printed in boldface in the text narrative. Still other annotations ask critical-thinking questions or *content-review questions* to help you apply theory to practice and prepare for course exams.

Chapter objectives identify the specific knowledge, strategies, and instructional practices that you should be able to acquire or do after reading and discussing the chapter content. The objectives help to focus the intent of your reading and, in turn, your comprehension of the content.

Other practical text features include **How To Do . . .** features in Chapters 3 through 13, which provide practical step-by-step summaries of the specific classroom teaching strategies presented in the chapter. Each How To Do offers a quick and convenient review of what you need to plan, prepare for, and consider in order to use an instructional strategy successfully with your students. The *How To Do* features are listed on the inside front cover of the book, along with the *Strategies in Use* features which provide an instructional model for the *How To Do* features.

The **Strategies in Use (SIU)** features, also found in Chapters 3 through 13, model many of the *How To Do* teach-

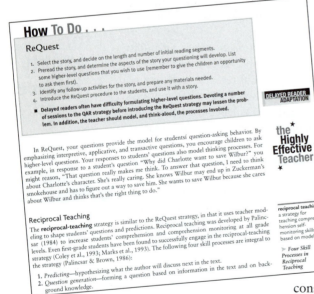

ing strategies in authentic contexts. Strategies in Use present real-life situations or teaching scripts of interactions between highly effective teachers and their students. These instructional models directly apply research and theory to literacy teaching and demonstrate literacy learning in action. Each SIU closes with a series of **Critical Thinking** questions to help you further apply the model strategy in your own understanding and teaching. As noted above, there are identifications on the inside front cover of the book.

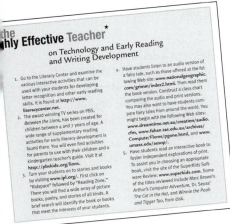

A special **delayed reader adaptation** feature has been developed for this text. This adaptation is inserted in each How To Do and is designed to help you adjust the instructional strategy to meet the needs of those readers who are experiencing reading difficulty. These adaptations were developed by Dr. Sandra McCormick, Professor Emeritus, The Ohio State University, who is a national expert on teaching delayed readers and is the author of Chapter 10.

The importance of technology in the classroom is emphasized in **The Highly Effective Teacher on Technology** boxes found in each chapter. These ideas and Web sites are designed to help you use and integrate technology into your literacy teaching. Ideas range from the creative use of software to exploration of high-interest Web sites on the Internet. The Internet addresses have also been expanded and updated.

The **Research and Evidence-Based Practice** box, found in each chapter and mentioned earlier, provides a summary of key research findings related to the chapter topic. These findings are developed in a form that will be of value to you in understanding students' literacy growth and in making instructional decisions in your classroom.

A special feature in this text is the **Professional Standards for the Classroom Teacher.** The five major standards and the specific elements for each, developed by the International Reading Association (2004), are found in Appendix C. These standards and the related elements are presented near the end of each chapter and are applied to the chapter content under study. You must become aware of the recent standards movements and the performance expectations for you as a classroom-teacher candidate.

Applications: Bridges to the Classroom are found near the end of each chapter. They invite you to choose from a variety of interesting applications and activities that will extend your knowledge and facilitate your professional development as a highly effective teacher. Applications and activities link specific chapter content to the classroom and include suggestions for classroom observations, interviews, assessments, research, lesson plans, and artifacts for your teaching portfolio.

You will find the **Additional Research and Practice** section located at the end of each chapter. These sections present carefully selected recommended readings, which are annotated to assist in your selection. Two of the references provide extended practice for your students, while the third provides research and literacy instruction findings of value to your teaching.

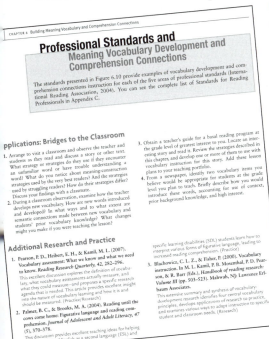

Text Content That Supports Your Literacy-Knowledge Acquisition

Each of the thirteen chapters is based on the latest research and evidence-based practice. The **Bookshelves** feature, figures that identify key pieces of literature that can be used in your classroom, are found in Chapters 3, 7, 8, 10, and 11; Chapter 4, Increasing Word Recognition Knowledge and Word Identification Skills, has detailed sections on word identification, word recognition, and fluency. Chapter 9, Assessing Students' Progress in Literacy Development, introduces the assessment topic using concepts developed in Chapters 1–8. A brief description of the content of each chapter follows.

Chapter 1, Becoming a Highly Effective and Influential Literacy Teacher, introduces the concept and characteristics of the influential and highly effective literacy teacher and provides a snapshot of reading instruction in U.S. schools today, followed by an overview of the three major approaches to teaching reading: the basal reader, literature-based, and language-based approaches. This foundational chapter concludes with a brief historical overview of reading and writing instruction from colonial times to the present.

Chapter 2, Understanding the Reading and Writing Process, establishes the theoretical and developmental foundations for the remaining chapters by developing your understanding of the reading and writing process and its connection to children's language development. The focus of the chapter is sociocognitive theory, which explains how new concepts and language and literacy growth are connected to students' social and cognitive development. Chapter 2 also develops an explanation of the reading comprehension process—how it is built on purposeful meaning construction and meaning negotiation between teachers and learners.

Chapter 3, Understanding Early Reading and Writing Development, focuses on early reading and writing development in preschool, kindergarten, and grade 1. It emphasizes the importance of using instructional strategies to develop the language of instruction, picture and print awareness, letter recognition, phonemic awareness, representation of thoughts and ideas in print, sense of story and narrative, positive attitudes toward reading, and observation and recording of children's progress. This chapter also explains how to organize the classroom environment and the school day.

Chapter 4, Increasing Word Recognition Knowledge and Word Identification Skills, presents solid suggestions for helping students develop an automatic word recognition vocabulary. It also explains the role of phonics and other decoding strategies in developing reading fluency. Word learning is the key to transforming print into language and meaning. This chapter identifies strategies for teaching phonics and other specific word learning skills in meaning-based contexts, thereby fostering students' reading independence, fluency, and ability to construct meaning from narrative and expository text.

Chapter 5, Using Instructional Strategies to Develop Reading Comprehension, develops your understanding of instructional strategies that build students' comprehension and promote higher-level thinking throughout the elementary and middle school grades. An instructional framework is presented for integrating specific comprehension skills and questioning strategies in order to develop four levels of thinking using a wide range of comprehension strategies.

Chapter 6, Building Meaning Vocabulary and Comprehension Connections, emphasizes the critical role of vocabulary knowledge in the comprehension process. Principles of meaning vocabulary instruction and specific vocabulary-development strategies are introduced. This chapter emphasizes encouraging students to construct meaning by "reasoning with words" as they use key vocabulary strategies.

Chapter 7, Using Literature, Reader Response, and Engagement to Enhance Motivation and Comprehension, shows how to use children's and adolescent literature and responses to enhance positive attitudes and motivation toward reading and how to use various instructional strategies to engage students' active comprehension. Chapter 7 also shows how the teacher's instructional stance is instrumental in successful teaching of all literary genres.

Chapter 8, Developing Reading and Writing in Content Areas, stresses the importance of meaning construction in content area reading and writing, especially for older students. The chapter presents a wide range of reading and writing strategies to guide and enhance students' literacy development across the curriculum.

Chapter 9, Assessing Students' Progress in Literacy Development, emphasizes the development of your observational skills in authentic learning situations and your proficiency in using informal assessments to plan for and meet students' instructional needs. Formal assessment is discussed, and the values and limitations of standardized achievement testing are explored. This chapter also provides guidelines for effective communication with parents.

Chapter 10, Instructing Delayed Readers in a Regular Classroom Setting, provides ten key principles for helping underachieving students in your classroom. The discussion illuminates the causes for delays and explains how to effectively meet the needs of delayed readers. Topics include assessment, word recognition and identification, comprehension, and motivation. This chapter was written by Dr. Sandra McCormick, Professor Emeritus, The Ohio State University. Dr. McCormick has conducted extensive research on delayed readers, has written articles and textbooks on this topic, and has many years' experience directing a university reading clinic.

Chapter 11, Understanding Language Diversity, Cultural Diversity, and Special Needs, discusses specific classroom-based strategies and activities that have been used effectively with bilingual learners and students from diverse language and cultural backgrounds. This chapter also emphasizes the important role that you will play in inclusive classrooms with exceptional learners and students with special needs.

Chapter 12, Examining Instructional Approaches to and the Organization and Management of Literacy Learning, suggests ways to modify and combine the three major approaches to reading instruction (basal reader, literature-based, language-based) for a balanced, comprehensive approach to literacy learning. This chapter also develops instructional strategies for using computer-based technologies, including Internet resources, in literacy instruction.

Chapter 13, Continuing Your Professional Growth as a Highly Effective and Influential Literacy Teacher, encourages you to remain open to new ideas and the process of professional growth and development, to develop a personal support network, to participate actively in professional organizations and staff-development programs, and to reflect on your professional practice.

Several very useful appendixes appear at the end of this book. The first two include lists of award-winning books that can play an important role in your classroom reading program. Appendix A lists the Newbery Medal Books, an honor awarded each year for distinguished contributions to children's or adolescent literature; Appendix B lists the Caldecott Medal Books, awarded annually for the most distinguished illustrated book. Appendix C contains the complete set of *Standards for Reading Professionals* and is applied to the content of each chapter at the chapter's conclusion. Appendix D presents a location summary of references to children's and adolescent literature, technology, and teacher resources used throughout this text and categorized by content area with page locations.

The General References section provides a complete list of all professional references used in developing this book and will prove useful to you in locating original sources for support papers you might write. The Name and Subject Index is a quick reference source for locating professional authors (see boldfaced listings) and their contributions and children's and adolescent literature authors (not boldfaced) and their books. The Name and Subject Index is very detailed and has been specially prepared to provide an easy reference location system for you in finding concepts, strategies, and resources in the text.

I hope that you find this book interesting, informative, and useful as you develop your instructional repertoire and move toward the goal of becoming a highly effective and influential literacy teacher.

To the Instructor

Organization and Content Features in This Text

The most recent research and evidence-based information has been included to support literacy practices, while at the same time discussion of "hot" topics has been included. The book contains thirteen chapters, four appendixes, and a complete set of general references. A name index for professional authors and children's literature authors combined with a detailed subject index provide convenient and easy reference location.

The text organization and special features are those that follow:

1. **Research and Evidence-Based Practice** boxes relate to the content of each chapter. This feature uses a "Did You Know?" format and summarizes key literacy-development and instructional findings based on solid research and evidence-based support. Side-margin notes for **Evidence-Based Practice** are identified throughout the text.

2. A special figure in each chapter identifies **Professional Standards for the Classroom Teacher** using the International Reading Association's *Standards for Reading Professionals*—Revised 2003. These standards and related elements highlight professional performance expectations through examples, using the content of each chapter. Appendix C presents the entire set of standards and standard elements.

3. The importance of effective instruction for children who are experiencing reading difficulty is found in the **delayed reader adaptation** inserted in each **How To Do ...** strategy summary throughout the book. This insertion, created by Dr. Sandra McCormick, Professor Emeritus, The Ohio State University, provides for highly effective instruction by showing how to adapt each How To Do to achieve success with the struggling reader. Dr. McCormick, a national authority on teaching delayed readers, also wrote Chapter 10.

4. **A strategic chapter order is found in the placement of Chapter 9.** This chapter introduces assessment concepts before the student encounters two of the most advanced instructional chapters—Chapter 10, Instructing Delayed Readers in a Regular Classroom Setting, and Chapter 11, Understanding Language Diversity, Cultural Diversity, and Special Needs. Chapter 9 was not introduced earlier in the book because of the need to have developed basic instructional concepts and strategies in areas such as word recognition and word identification (Chapter 4), comprehension (Chapter 5), vocabulary (Chapter 6), literature (Chapter 7), and content area reading (Chapter 8), in order to understand how to use the assessment strategies in identifying student needs in these areas.

5. **Chapter 4, Increasing Word Recognition Knowledge and Word Identification Skills,** emphasizes *implicit and explicit phonics* as well as structural analysis directly related to the instructional needs of the student. Strong emphasis is placed on the importance of immediate word recognition and fluency in the reading process, particularly as these skills relate to wide reading and effective comprehension.

6. **The Highly Effective Teacher on Technology** includes high-interest Web sites related to the content of each chapter. Instructional tips and the Internet sources provided are designed to help integrate technology with literacy instruction in the classroom. Internet resources given in the form of URLs are current at the time of this book's publication. However, Web sites are dynamic, and it is a good practice to check their availability before making them a part of your assignments and curriculum.

7. **The importance of literature in reading instruction is emphasized in the text as evidenced by the extensive Bookshelf references** in Chapter 3, Understanding Early Reading and Writing Development; Chapter 7, Using Literature, Reader Response, and Engagement to Enhance Motivation and Comprehension; Chapter 8, Developing Reading and Writing in Content Areas; and Chapter 11, Understanding Language Diversity, Cultural Diversity, and Special Needs. Appendix D, References for Children's and Adolescent Literature, Technology, and Teacher Resources, has been designed to assist students in quickly finding children's literature related to a specific literacy content area with location and page reference provided.

8. **The five areas that served as the academic cornerstones of the Reading First legislation are emphasized in various chapters.** These areas and the degree of emphasis in each chapter are identified in the chart on the facing page.

I hope your use of this book in your classroom will establish a three-way partnership among author, instructor, and student that will help develop highly effective and influential reading and writing teachers. I ask for your support in the form of comments on features of the book that work well for you and features that can be improved. You may write to me directly at the following e-mail address:

Dr. Robert B. Ruddell
University of California, Berkeley
rruddell@berkeley.edu

Reading First Cornerstone Areas

The following chapter list from *How to Teach Reading to Elementary and Middle School Students: Practical Ideas from Highly Effective Teachers* indicates which of the five Reading First Cornerstone Areas are emphasized within each chapter as well as the degree of emphasis.

Chapter 1	Becoming an Effective and Influential Literacy Teacher	P	V	C		
Chapter 2	Understanding the Reading and Writing Process	PA	P	F	V	C
Chapter 3	Understanding Early Reading and Writing Development	**PA**	**P**	**F**	V	C
Chapter 4	Increasing Word Recognition Knowledge and Word Identification Skills	**PA**	**P**	**F**	V	C
Chapter 5	Using Instructional Strategies to Develop Reading Comprehension	**F**	**V**	**C**		
Chapter 6	Building Meaning Vocabulary and Comprehension Connections	**F**	**V**	**C**		
Chapter 7	Using Literature, Reader Response, and Engagement to Enhance Motivation and Comprehension	**F**	**V**	**C**		
Chapter 8	Developing Reading and Writing in Content Areas	**F**	**V**	**C**		
Chapter 9	Assessing Students' Progress in Literacy Development	**PA**	**P**	**F**	**V**	**C**
Chapter 10	Instructing Delayed Readers in a Regular Classroom Setting	PA	P	**F**	V	C
Chapter 11	Understanding Language Diversity, Cultural Diversity, and Special Needs	PA	P	F	V	C
Chapter 12	Examining Instructional Approaches to and the Organization and Management of Literacy Learning	P	F	V	C	
Chapter 13	Continuing Your Professional Growth as a Highly Effective and Influential Literacy Teacher	F	V	C		

Reading First Key Skills: *Note:* Bold indicates *major* emphasis within the chapter; not bold indicates emphasis within the chapter.

PA Phonemic Awareness
P Phonics
F Fluency
V Vocabulary
C Comprehension

Supplements

For the Instructor

Instructor's Resource Manual and Test Bank includes the following:

- Alternative course syllabi and student-evaluation options as planning aids
  - Chapter-specific teaching suggestions and resources
  - Suggested answers for the Critical Thinking questions in the Strategies in Use features
  - More than fifty handouts and transparency masters
  - Test items in a variety of formats, including short answer, essay, and multiple choice
  - Suggested answers to test items and answer feedback
- **PowerPoint™ Presentations** of lecture outlines and electronic images to support your classroom presentations for each chapter.

For the Student

VideoWorkshop for Reading Methods CD-ROM Package Available free when packaged with the textbook, the CD-ROM contains nine modules of digitized video clips, featuring snapshots of teachers and students in real classroom settings. The VideoWorkshop CD comes with a Student Study Guide, containing all the materials needed to help students get the most out of this exciting media product. With questions for reflection before, during, and after viewing, this guide extends classroom discussion and allows for more in-class time spent on analysis of material. An Instructor's Teaching Guide is also available to provide ideas and exercises to assist faculty in incorporating this convenient supplement into course assignments and assessments. (Visit www.pearsonhighered.com/videoworkshop for more details.)

ACKNOWLEDGMENTS

I would like to acknowledge and thank a number of key individuals whose support, influence, and encouragement have made this book possible. A number of students from my early years of teaching were in my thoughts as I wrote this text. Some of these students still live in a small coal-mining town just outside of Charleston, West Virginia, in the Allegheny Mountains near the location of the one-room schoolhouse where I started teaching, while others are found along the Eastern seaboard, the Midwest, and the West Coast. I have maintained contact with a number of these special "kids" over the past several decades. I owe them a great deal and wish to express my appreciation to them—especially Neil Blount and Nancy Gill—for what they taught me during my novice years of teaching.

I have been most fortunate in having had a number of highly effective and influential teachers in my own life. These patient, nurturing, and motivated teachers shared their vision, which helped me shape a career in literacy education. Two of these teachers were my own parents, Nellie Hogshead Ruddell—a teacher of children—and Byron Burnette Ruddell—a kind and gentle man. Both provided unqualified love and support and were role models who emphasized the importance of motivation, drive, and persistence in doing a job well. I vividly remember two of my teachers from my small, rural high school—Mrs. Louise Massey, my demanding math and chemistry teacher, and Mr. Charles Allen, science teacher and coach, who always presented a positive and optimistic view of the future.

My influential university professors include Dr. Eddie Kennedy at West Virginia University, who encouraged me to pursue my master's degree and, later, my doctorate; Dr. Robert Gates at George Peabody College for Teachers, who provided a vision of education in the computer and space age; Dr. Ruth Strickland, my doctoral thesis advisor at Indiana University, who conducted hallmark research on children's language development and was a demanding and fair taskmaster; and Dr. Leo Fay, also at Indiana, who was my shadow advisor through my doctorate and who supported graduate students through his presence and his concern for rigorous research design. The influence of these individuals can be found in this text.

I wish also to recognize my own credential, master's, and doctoral students—present and past—who have contributed in important ways to this book. Their questions, insights, and responses have been invaluable. They have listened, commented, and provided helpful suggestions in completing this book. You will find selected examples of their teaching and conversations from their classrooms in various parts of the book.

The editorial staff at Allyn and Bacon has been most supportive in facilitating the completion of this book. Aurora Martínez Ramos, Executive Editor for Literacy, ESL, and Bilingual Education, has also provided excellent support and encouragement in the development of this book.

I would also like to acknowledge my family and several close friends. They include, first, my immediate family: my wife, Sandy Ruddell, whose love, thoughtfulness, professionalism, trust, and sharp editorial eye is unparalleled; my children, Amy Gault, a project manager at a northern California University, her special husband, Paul, and their precious tiny daughter, Rebecca; Rob Ruddell, an influential fourth- and fifth-grade teacher in a northern California school district, his lovely wife, Diane, and their beautiful little daughters, Grace and Madeline; Cecile Ruddell, a special aunt with unusual insight into people and world events; Jim Heavener, a cousin who is like a brother, and Jim's wife, Una. And, second, my "next-to-kin" family: David Ruddell, Hal and Joan Herber, Ed and Kathy Fry, and Marsha and Hal Wilson. These special individuals have greatly enhanced the support climate in which the writing of this book took place.

Thank you all. Your caring support has been most important.

Robert B. Ruddell
University of California, Berkeley

Becoming a Highly Effective and Influential Literacy Teacher

One looks back with appreciation to the brilliant teachers, but with gratitude to those who touched our human feelings. The curriculum is so much necessary raw material, but warmth is the vital element for the growing plant and for the soul of the child.

Carl Jung (1875–1961),
Swiss psychologist, psychiatrist

I touch the future. <u>I teach</u>.

Christa McAuliffe (1948–1986),
American teacher, first teacher in space

In a bright, colorful, literature-rich classroom at Hidden Valley School, Joyce Burke observes her second graders as they read "Ramona's Book Report" in *Ramona Quimby, Age 8* (Cleary, 1981).

It's a class favorite. Advertisements for the book—artwork with writing created by the children in their reader-response groups—decorate the bulletin boards. Other Beverly Cleary titles, including *Henry Huggins* (1950) and *The Mouse and the Motorcycle* (1965), are among the many books in the classroom's Reading Center, which also features stories on audiotape and story-related activity centers for integrating the curriculum.

Joyce prepares to read the part where Ramona and her classmate partners put on cat masks they made and report on *Left-Behind Cat*. Joyce enjoys reading aloud to the students, both as a way to provide motivation and as a way to model reading, just as she was read to by her second-grade teacher—the exciting, demanding, and sometimes mysterious Ms. Wolters. That special influential teacher, above others, inspired Joyce to read, and to become a teacher herself. She looks forward now to laughing with the students over Ramona's antics. She also treasures their reactions when they discover that they, too—like Ramona—will "sell" books, but, she hopes, with both verve and truth in advertising.

"Read along with me," Joyce invites.

After arithmetic, Mrs. Whaley called on several people to come to the front of the room to pretend they were selling books to the class. Most of the reports began, "This is a book about . . ." and many, as Beezus had predicted, ended with ". . . if you want to find out what happens next, read the book." (p. 154)

Joyce interrupts to ask, "If someone were trying to sell you a book, what would you look for before you bought it?" To continue reading, Joyce eventually has to interrupt the lively discussions that ensue.

Then Mrs. Whaley said, "We have time for one more report before lunch. Who wants to be next?" Ramona waved her hand, and Mrs. Whaley nodded.

Ramona beckoned to Sara and Janet, who giggled in an embarrassed way but joined Ramona, standing behind her and off to one side. All three girls slipped on their cat masks and giggled again. Ramona took a deep breath as Sara and Janet began to chant, "*Meow,* meow, meow, meow. *Meow,* meow, meow, meow," and danced back and forth like the cats they had seen in the cat-food commercial on television. (pp. 154–155)

Joyce sings the "meow, meow" song, to her students' amazement and delight. She asks if anyone has ever seen a commercial like that on television, and instantly the classroom fills with other jingles as the students share their experiences. Later they will compose and lyricize music as theme songs for the books they "sell" to the class.

"*Left-Behind Cat* gives kids something to smile about," said Ramona in a loud clear voice, while her chorus meowed softly behind her. She wasn't sure that what she said was exactly true, but neither were the commercials that showed cats eating dry cat food without making any noise. "Kids who have tried *Left-Behind Cat* are all smiles, smiles, smiles. *Left-Behind Cat* is the book kids ask for by name. Kids can read it every day and thrive on it. The happiest kids read *Left-Behind Cat. Left-Behind Cat* contains cats, dogs, people—" Here Ramona caught sight of Yard Ape leaning back in his seat, grinning in the way that always flustered her. She could not help interrupting herself with a giggle, and after suppressing it she tried not to look at Yard Ape and to take up where she had left off. ". . . cats, dogs, people—" The giggle came back, and Ramona was lost. She could not remember what came next. ". . . cats, dogs, people," she repeated, trying to start and failing. (pp. 155–156)

Joyce stops to ask if anyone has ever gotten the giggles the way Ramona did. When their giggles subside, she poses questions: "What do you think will happen next? How do you think the chapter will end?" The students make various predictions and then Joyce continues with the story.

. . . All she could remember was the man on the television who ate the pizza, and so she blurted out the only sentence she could think of, "I can't believe I read the *whole thing!*"

Mrs. Whaley's laugh rang out above the laughter of the class. Ramona felt her face turn red behind her mask, and her ears, visible to the class, turned red as well. (p. 158)

After they finish reading, the students discuss their chapter-ending predictions and consider other ways that Ramona could have ended her book report. Joyce asks, "Do you think Mrs. Whaley will like Ramona's book report? And do you think the students will choose to read the book because of Ramona's report?"

The students then discuss how to give livelier book reports that are both honest and informative. Joyce provides copies of *Left-Behind Cat* for her students to read together on their own in their groups. Their assignment is to suggest specific ways to improve Ramona's book report and to draft a new script. Joyce makes a mental note to e-mail her Canadian professional partner in the collaborative curriculum network her school has joined. Later her students will share their scripts via e-mail with their distant classmates in Saskatchewan, who are also reading "Ramona's Book Report" in *Ramona Quimby, Age 8.*

In later years, many of Joyce Burke's students will remember her as an influential teacher, one who made a major difference in their lives as learners. And because of the solid foundation she is giving them in reading, Joyce will also be remembered as a highly effective teacher.

double entry journal

Reflect on your school experiences from kindergarten through grade twelve, and identify one or more teachers who were especially important to you academically or personally or both. Recall the names of these influential teachers, the grade levels and subject areas they taught, and their personal appearance and characteristics. How were these teachers influential in your experience? Considering them now as fellow professionals, can you describe what made them highly effective teachers?

Chapter Objectives

After reading and discussing this chapter, you will be able to:

- identify the characteristics of influential and highly effective teachers.
- distinguish between three of the most effective reading programs used across the United States.
- understand a historical context for literacy instruction and related instructional implications.
- confront the personal challenge of becoming a highly effective and influential teacher.
- understand the role of professional standards in literacy instruction.

Characteristics of Influential Teachers

An **influential teacher** is one whom you recall in a vivid and positive way from your academic experience—kindergarten through college years—and who had a major influence on your personal or academic success (Ruddell, 2004; Ruddell, Draheim, & Barnes, 1990). You probably can identify at least one such teacher, and possibly as many as five or six. In most cases, you will remember not only the names of your influential teachers but also the grade levels they taught and even their personal attributes, physical characteristics, and teaching styles.

> **influential teacher** a teacher at any grade level who has a major impact on a student's academic achievement or personal development

Well-known children's novelist Beverly Cleary had an influential teacher. Cleary, author of books you may remember from your own childhood (including *The Mouse and the Motorcycle; Henry Huggins; Ribsy; Ramona and Beezus*), describes Professor Benjamin Lehman, in her autobiography, *My Own Two Feet, a Memoir* (1995). Professor Lehman was an English professor who "was a short, slightly stooped man who entered the classroom at the last minute, faced the class from behind the lectern, and delivered fascinating lectures on novels . . ." (p. 151). Mrs. Cleary recalls two ideas from Professor Lehman's teaching that had a marked influence on her writing: the first, "The proper subject of the novel is universal human experience" and the second, the importance of "the minutiae of life" that give reality to fiction (p. 151). Influential teachers such as Professor Lehman and those in our own lives not only influence our academic and personal lives but also serve as important role models for our own teaching.

Research (Ruddell & Unrau, 2004a, p. 954; Taylor Pearson, Peterson, & Rodriguez, 2005) reveals that influential teachers

> ➤ *Research on Influential Teachers*

- show that they care about students.
- help students understand and solve their personal and academic problems.
- manifest excitement and enthusiasm about what they teach.
- adapt instruction to the individual needs, motives, interests, and aptitudes of students and have high expectations for them.
- use motivating and effective strategies when they teach, including clarity in stating problems, use of concrete examples, analysis of abstract concepts, and application of concepts to new contexts.
- engage students in the process of intellectual discovery.

Believing in Influential Teaching

In-depth interviews with influential and highly effective teachers at all grade levels, including the university level, indicate five common features that these teachers believe are important to their work (Ruddell & Kern, 1986). These features can be nicely represented by the acronym TEACH (teaching, excitement, attitude, caring, helping) and are presented in Figure 1.1. (See page 4.)

> What beliefs listed in Figure 1.1 are similar to those of your influential teachers?

Between kindergarten and grade 12, high achievers have an average of 3.2 influential teachers, while low achievers have only 1.5 such teachers. Nevertheless, research reveals that high achievers and low achievers perceive the characteristics of influential teachers in almost identical ways (Ruddell, 2004):

> ➤ *How Students Perceive Influential Teachers*

- Influential teachers use clearly formulated instructional strategies with clearcut instructional goals, plans, and monitoring for student feedback; these features are readily apparent and are used consistently throughout their teaching lessons.

FIGURE 1.1

Shared Beliefs of Influential and Highly Effective Teachers about Teaching

1. **T**eaching: Quality of Instruction
   - makes material personally relevant
   - stresses basic communication: clear writing, comprehension of text material, and critical thinking
   - uses logical and strategy-oriented teaching methods:
     (a) clearly states problem
     (b) uses familiar concrete examples
     (c) extends to more abstract examples
     (d) analyzes abstract concepts involved
     (e) applies concepts to new contexts
   - identifies issues that should be considered before conclusions are reached
   - engages students in the process of intellectual discovery

2. **E**xcitement: Personal Characteristics
   - shows energy, commitment, and passion
   - is warm and caring
   - is flexible
   - has high expectations of self

3. **A**ttitude: Attitude toward Subject
   - exhibits enthusiasm
   - creates intellectual excitement
   - considers alternate points of view

4. **C**aring: Understanding of Learner Potential
   - is sensitive to individual needs, motivations, and aptitudes
   - understands student's current level of learning
   - places high demands on learners

5. **H**elping: Life Adjustment
   - is concerned with the student as a whole person
   - is attentive to both academic and personal problems

- Influential teachers have in-depth knowledge of reading and writing processes as well as content knowledge, and they understand how to teach these processes effectively in their classrooms.
- Influential teachers frequently tap students' internal motivation by stimulating students' intellectual curiosity and desire to solve problems, exploring their self-understanding, and using aesthetic imagery and expression. They place little emphasis on external student motivation, such as achievement pressure to please the teacher.

Recognizing Highly Effective Teaching and Professional Standards

Teaching effectiveness can be measured by qualitative means such as observations of teacher-student interactions in the classroom to quantitative analysis of student performance on achievement tests. Within the last decade, a major standards movement has swept across the United States and has recently taken two forms. These standards and the form they take are very important to you because they influence how the achievement growth of your students and your teaching effectiveness may be measured and evaluated.

The first form consists of performance standards for students and has received a major boost from the 2001 *No Child Left Behind* legislation. This legislation is intended to ensure that all students will be reading on grade level by the year 2014, with progress measured by prescribed and sometimes controversial assessments. An important component of this legislation is the Reading

First program. The essential components of the program consist of explicit and systematic instruction on phonemic awareness, phonics, vocabulary development, fluency, and comprehension. More information can be found at www.ed.gov/print/programs/readingfirst/index.html/.

The second form presents professional standards for teachers. These standards provide criteria for developing and evaluating professional-development programs for teachers. In the literacy field, such standards are found in *Standards for Reading Professionals—Revised 2003* (International Reading Association, 2004) and describe expected performance at the end of a preparation program. You can see the complete list of Standards for Reading Professionals in Appendix C. This document presents the five major standards with competencies identified for paraprofessionals, classroom teachers, reading specialists/coaches, teacher educators, and administrators. These standards and an example for each in the classroom teacher category are shown in Figure 1.2. We will revisit various forms of these standards in the Professional Standards near the conclusion of each chapter of this text.

Influential teachers are also highly effective teachers. The characteristics of highly effective teachers, measured by standards such as those shown in Figure 1.2, are similar in many ways to those that make teachers influential. Highly effective teachers use instructional strategies with clear goals, plans, and assessment; they have in-depth knowledge of both content and teaching processes; and they foster students' motivation to explore, discover, and succeed.

These common characteristics of influential and highly effective teachers represent the bedrock of good teaching. This book emphasizes these characteristics and presents classroom-tested instructional strategies designed to help you understand critical reading and writing processes and *teach these processes effectively* in your classroom. Each chapter of this book traces the process of becoming a highly effective teacher through a summary graphical feature called The Highly Effective Teacher. In addition, the "Highly Effective Teacher" icon in the margins of this and subsequent chapters identify portions of the text that relate to these common characteristics. The goal is to help you to become a highly effective and influential literacy teacher.

FIGURE 1.2

Professional Standards for Classroom Teacher Candidates

Standard	Example
1. Foundational Knowledge	**Element 1.1** Knows foundational theories of reading and writing processes and instruction; e.g., knows foundational theories related to reading practices and writing processes and instruction and materials they use in the classroom.
2. Instructional Strategies and Curriculum Materials	**Element 2.2** Ability to use a wide range of instructional practices, approaches, methods, and curricular materials for instruction; e.g., matches instructional grouping options to specific instructional purposes that take practices, approaches, and methods into account to accommodate the developmental, cultural, and linguistic differences among students.
3. Assessment, Diagnosis, and Evaluation	**Element 3.1** Effective in using a variety of assessment tools and practices to plan and evaluate effective reading instruction; e.g., selects and administers appropriate formal and informal assessments including technology-based assessment.
4. Creating a Literate Environment	**Element 4.1** Uses students' interests, reading abilities, and backgrounds as foundations for the reading and writing program; e.g., uses an informal interest inventory to assess individual student interests and plan instruction to account for these interests to create high motivation.
5. Professional Development	**Element 5.2** Continues to pursue the development of professional knowledge; e.g., indicates knowledge of and holds memberships in some professional organizations related to reading and writing.

Part 2 from IRA. (2004). Professional Standards and Ethics Committee, International Reading Association. *Standards for reading professionals—revised 2003.* Reprinted with permission of the International Reading Association. All rights reserved.

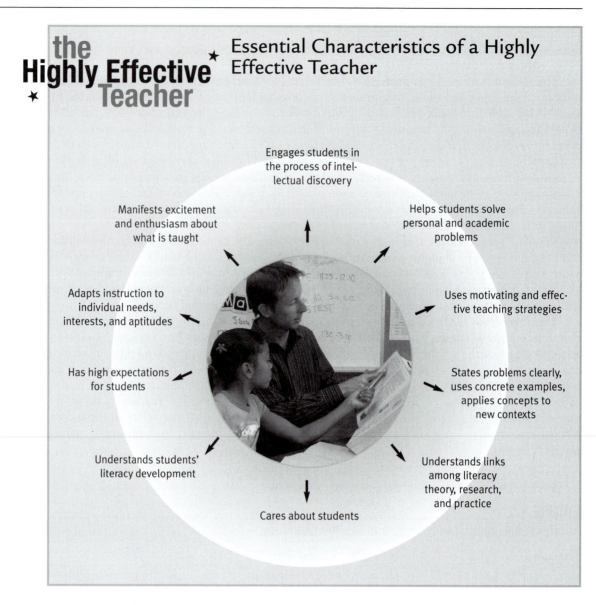

the Highly Effective Teacher

Essential Characteristics of a Highly Effective Teacher

- Engages students in the process of intellectual discovery
- Manifests excitement and enthusiasm about what is taught
- Helps students solve personal and academic problems
- Adapts instruction to individual needs, interests, and aptitudes
- Uses motivating and effective teaching strategies
- Has high expectations for students
- States problems clearly, uses concrete examples, applies concepts to new contexts
- Understands students' literacy development
- Understands links among literacy theory, research, and practice
- Cares about students

The following statement from a teacher expresses the enthusiasm, vitality, and caring that are so important in becoming a highly effective teacher:

> I've been teaching for 15 years, and each year gets better and better. I want to be where I am. I love the students. I think that they are the best show in town, and I tell them that over and over again. I keep my youth and optimism because of them. They contribute far more to my life than anybody can possibly imagine. What I give, I'm sure, is minimal next to what I receive. Teaching for me is an avocation, not a vocation. I feel that people who are burnt out ought to get out. They don't belong with children. Children are the best that any society has. They are the future, and they deserve the best of everything. If we, as teachers, can't give them that, then we should find other work to do. The salaries certainly don't compensate for the commitment involved—but, I am a teacher. (Anonymous, 1978)

Understanding Links among Literacy Theory, Research, and Practice

literacy
the knowledge and skills necessary to read and write

A thorough grasp of the most recent theories and research findings about **literacy** will be critical for the daily decisions you make as you teach your students. Contrary to the popular belief that theory and practice are separate and incompatible entities, the fact is that we all use our own (and others') theories daily as we go about our lives. Theories are merely informed hunches about how things work. Theories help us make sense of the world and inform our actions—our practice.

Research and Evidence-Based Practice

Understanding Literacy Development

Did You Know?

- Influential teachers increase their understanding of students' reading development by observing their oral and written language use (Rogers, Marshall, & Tyson, 2006; Tabors & Snow, 2004).

- Influential teachers view their students as hypotheses testers and meaning makers as they explore their world (Dyson, 2004; McIntyre, Kyle, & Moore, 2006; Ruddell, 2004).

- Students are constantly examining their surroundings and testing ways in which events in their world fit into their already developed understandings (Dyson, 2004; Piaget, 1952).

- Students work to understand environmental print such as signs, logos, and words like *exit* as they experiment with new language forms (Cox et al., 2004; Ehri & McCormick, 2004; Sulzby & Teale, 1991; Vygotsky, 1978).

- Students construct and reconstruct meaning as they talk with adults at home and with teachers and peers at school (Forman & Cazden, 2004).

- Students acquire oral language that supports their reading and writing development (Nagy & Scott, 2004).

This relationship between theory and practice holds true in the classroom; that is, your theories of how children acquire and develop literacy directly influence your classroom practice. As you explore current language and literacy theory and research in this book, you will have opportunities to construct personal views (or, theories) to guide your own classroom practice.

> *Relationships among Theory, Research, and Practice*

The knowledge base in language and literacy today is vastly different from what we had to rely on in the past. Studies in psycholinguistics, sociolinguistics, cognitive science, and the anthropology and sociology of language have provided a wealth of information with valuable implications for reading and writing instruction (Bloome, 1991; Kamil et al., 2000; Menyuk, 1991; Ogbu, 1983; Ruddell & Unrau, 2004). This work has led to many new understandings of the way people think, process information, organize and retain knowledge, and generate new knowledge. For example, current theories of literacy development show how schemata, knowledge modules, and mental categories help individuals assimilate, store, and retrieve new and old information (Anderson, 2004; Schallert, 1991; Spiro et al., 2004). Current theories also suggest how readers and writers comprehend and effectively interact with text (Rosenblatt, 2004) and how teachers translate theoretical knowledge into practical instructional strategies in classrooms (Beck & McKeown, 1991; Langer, 1994).

Research also highlights the important influence of family language patterns and cultural interaction styles on students' responses—or lack of responses—in the classroom (Au, 2000; Heath, 1982a; Purcell-Gates, 2000; Stokes, 1997). We now have instructional knowledge, strategies, and materials readily available to help students from diverse language and cultural backgrounds to succeed in the classroom (Hiebert & Martin, 2004; Moll, 1994; Tierney & Readence, 2005).

The NAEP Reading Report Card

One source of research information is government agencies devoted to education. For example, you can get a quick impression of fourth-grade student national reading achievement across the years from the **National Assessment of Educational Progress (NAEP).** Table 1.1 shows the reading achievement test results from 1992 to 2005. These findings indicate that average reading achievement for all fourth-grade students has increased slightly over the past ten years.

A summary of findings from this research (Figure 1.3) focuses on the reading achievement and interests of fourth-grade students and the instructional approaches and reading skills emphasized in their classrooms. These NAEP results show that the reading achievement scores have remained relatively stable over the years.

National Assessment of Educational Progress (NAEP) studies nationwide assessment of students in grades 4, 8, and 12 in reading and content areas

TABLE 1.1

Average Reading Achievement Scale Scores of Fourth-Grade Students on the National Assessment of Educational Progress (1992–2005)

	Year						
	1992	1994	1998	2000	2002	2003	2005
National average	217	214	217	213	219	218	219
European American	224	224	225	224	229	229	229
African American	192	185	193	190	199	198	200
Hispanic American	197	188	193	190	201	200	203

http://nces.ed.gov/nationsreportcard/pubs/main2005/reading

Do these NAEP findings surprise you? Why or why not?

Responses to the NAEP Findings

The NAEP findings show the close connection among the students' reading success in the classroom, their home literacy experiences and socioeconomic conditions, and instructional practice in schools. It thus becomes very important to recognize and address the specific instructional needs of children from varied cultural backgrounds and socioeconomic conditions. Although the fourth-grade teachers appear to use various instructional approaches to emphasize comprehension, word analysis skills, and vocabulary development, it is clear that they still rely heavily on workbooks and worksheets.

The 1992 NAEP study (Mullis, Campbell, & Farstrup, 1993) indicates that teachers are emphasizing greater integration of reading and language processes by encouraging students to write about their reading. However, an earlier nationwide study (Langer et al., 1990) suggests that higher-level reasoning activities, such as discussing and analyzing what students have read, receive minimal emphasis. The results from that NAEP report show that 40 percent of fourth-grade students are not performing at the basic level that demonstrates the ability to make connections between text and their experiences and the ability to make simple inferences based on the text. Experts agree that students need opportunities to develop higher-level reasoning skills and to participate in small-group and teacher-directed discussions involving reading and writing experiences. In addition, the NAEP studies highlight the need to build strong reading interest and motivation so that students maintain the desire to read across all grade levels.

➤ *Students need more opportunities to develop higher-level thinking skills.*

Using Effective Instructional Strategies

The theoretical and research knowledge based on literacy guides the creation and use of strategies and approaches that will become your tools of instruction. As an influential reading and writing teacher, you will integrate current language and literacy theory into your personal theories and beliefs about language and literacy development, and you will apply this knowledge base in your own classroom practice. Whether you realize it or not, you already have a rather elaborate belief system about the nature of teaching and of reading and writing instruction. Your belief system has been formed from many sources—early home learning experiences, learning experiences throughout your schooling, and influential teachers you were fortunate enough to meet in your career as a student.

The instructional practices you use in your classroom will be influenced by the following factors:

➤ *Your Personal Belief System as a Teacher*

➤ *Factors That Influence Your Instructional Approach*

- your knowledge and personal beliefs about the most effective ways to develop and implement reading and writing instruction.
- your personal experience in using particular instructional approaches, which tempers and refines your knowledge and beliefs.
- your willingness to devote the time and energy required to develop a particular approach and shape it to fit your students' needs and your own knowledge and belief system.
- your school district's philosophy regarding literacy instruction and assessment, which includes the textbook-adoption process, flexibility and willingness to use a variety of instructional approaches, and financial support for the purchase of materials and supplies.

FIGURE 1.3

Findings of the National Assessment of Educational Progress—Fourth Grade, 1992–2005

Achievement Differences

1. Significant achievement differences were found across ethnic groups and communities, with European American and Asian American students achieving higher than African American, Hispanic American, and Native American students. The scores for all groups increased between 1992 and 1995.
2. Girls were found to achieve a higher reading level than boys.
3. A slight decline in achievement scores was found between 1992 and 1994, but it was not significant; a slight increase was noted between 1994 and 2005 for each ethnic group.
4. Students who had access to reading material in their homes, such as books and magazines, had higher reading proficiency than students who did not have such access.*
5. Students who watched television four hours or more per day (44 percent) were found to have the lowest average reading proficiency.
6. Higher-achieving fourth graders reported home environments that emphasized academic achievement, reflected in higher levels of attendance at preschool and kindergarten, more time spent on homework, and more required reading.

Reading Interest

7. Interest in reading decreased as students progressed through the grades. Forty-four percent of the fourth-grade students reported reading for fun almost every day, but this was the case for only 25 percent of the eighth and twelfth graders.
8. Students were found to prefer television to books, with 60 percent of the fourth graders watching three or more hours of television each day. Only 44 percent reported reading for pleasure on a daily basis.

Instructional Approaches

9. Instruction for 85 percent of fourth-grade students was based in part on a basal reader approach, with 36 percent of the classrooms relying solely on this approach.
10. Some aspect of language-based instruction was used with 82 percent of the students.
11. Literature-based instruction received moderate emphasis in 88 percent of the classrooms.

Skills Emphasis

12. Sixty-one percent of the classrooms placed moderate (50 percent) or heavy (11 percent) emphasis on phonics.
13. Fifty percent of the fourth-grade students received daily comprehension skill emphasis, 28 percent received word analysis skill emphasis, 40 percent received vocabulary instruction, and 38 percent had the opportunity to read aloud.
14. Fifty-seven percent of the teachers reported that they read daily to their students.
15. According to the fourth-grade teachers, two-thirds of the students read silently and were provided time to read self-selected books almost daily.
16. For reading instruction, 79 percent of the fourth graders were assigned to ability-based reading groups. Approximately one hour was spent each day in reading instruction and about 30 minutes in small groups. Even so, 28 percent of the students were never or rarely asked to discuss their reading in small groups.

* Items 4 through 16 are based on the 1992–2003 test results.

National Assessment of Educational Progress

An Overview of Highly Effective Instructional Approaches

The point of view and ideas developed in later chapters have been designed to equip you with an array of effective instructional strategies that will enable you to achieve the balance you need in your literacy teaching to become a highly effective teacher of reading and writing for all students. You will develop an understanding of the basal reader approach, the literature-based approach, and the language-based approach, all of which are introduced in this chapter. You will find each of these approaches developed in detail in Chapter 12. The major goal of this book, however, is to provide instructional understandings and specific strategies that will help you design and implement a *balanced* skills curriculum, whatever general approach you eventually adopt.

The Basal Reader Approach

The **basal reader approach** is the approach most widely used for literacy development in the United States (Allington & McGill-Franzen, 2004). Current estimates indicate that basal readers are the chief instructional tool in 75 to 85 percent of elementary classrooms, and in large numbers of middle school classrooms, as well. Although basal reading programs differ, the underlying philosophy is that students can best be taught to read through systematic instruction in a predetermined sequence of skills, using selections in a student text, guided by recommendations in a teacher's guide, and reinforced through practice activities in a student workbook. The basal philosophy also recognizes the need to go beyond these materials to include full-length literature selections and to integrate skills instruction with other areas of the curriculum, such as social studies, mathematics, and science. Features of the basal reader approach are shown in Figure 1.4. (See below.)

The Literature-Based Approach

The **literature-based approach** gained popularity during the late 1980s and is still popular in some school districts today. This approach grew in part from the belief that students were not receiving adequate exposure to full-length quality literature. The general goals of the literature-based approach include the development not only of literacy skills but also of children's intellectual and aesthetic growth, sense of citizenship and rootedness in American society, and ethical responsibility (Ruddell, 2006). These goals are traditional in American education, and most teachers share them, whatever instructional approach they use. A literature-based approach, however, offers a unique opportunity to systematically develop these goals with literature selections.

basal reader approach
a framework and materials for literacy instruction based on graded readers and a predetermined scope and sequence of skills

literature-based approach
a framework and materials for literacy instruction based on exposure to literature with strong emphasis on child-development goals

What about the basal reader approach appeals to you? What don't you like about it?

FIGURE 1.4
Instructional Features of the Basal Reader Approach

1. Students are taught literacy skills that follow a *predetermined skill sequence.*
2. Instruction relies on the student *basal text,* containing narrative and expository selections. Stories and other reading material in the student text are organized in *unit themes,* such as animals in the wild or inventions, that weave the selections together.
3. Instruction is supported by a *teacher's guide* that provides *lesson plans* and detailed suggestions for teaching each selection.
4. Skills development is organized around specific *instructional strands* (such as phonics and word analysis, comprehension, vocabulary, language, literature, content area reading, and study skills) and relies heavily on activities in the *student workbook.*
5. The predominant group reading strategy is the *Directed Reading Activity* (*DRA*), which follows the steps of introducing the selection and motivating students, introducing vocabulary, guiding silent reading, checking end-of-story comprehension, rereading, discussing, and following up with activities to reinforce and extend skill development.
6. The *reading difficulty* of student texts is adjusted to approximate grade level based on perceived difficulty established through review recommendations and, frequently, the use of readability formulas.
7. The *word analysis skills* and *vocabulary items* are carefully controlled in the early grades in an attempt to provide decodable text.
8. The *student workbook* is designed to support the skills taught and provide opportunities for practice and reinforcement. Other instructional aids such as picture and word cards and "big books" are frequently provided for the early grades.
9. Evaluation of student progress is determined by *end-of-unit tests* that assess skills taught in that particular unit and/or check maintenance skills taught earlier in the program. Informal teacher observation is also encouraged.

A literature-based program uses literature in the classroom in at least three ways:

1. A core set of books provides shared literary experiences for students at each grade level.
2. The literature selections are extended by supplementing and enriching the curriculum in such areas as social studies and science.
3. The use of literature is based primarily on individual student interest and motivation.

> *Uses of Literature in the Literature-Based Approach*

Using a literature-based approach requires strong commitment and knowledge on the part of the teacher of both literacy and literature teaching. Selected aspects of this approach are still used widely throughout the United States to supplement the basal reader approach. Figure 1.5 shows the main instructional features of the literature-based approach.

The Language-Based Approach

The **language-based approach** is grounded in the belief that reading and literacy skills can be developed most effectively by providing children with "rich, authentic, developmentally appropriate school experiences" (Goodman, 1991a, p. 4; Temple, Ogle, Crawford, & Freppon, 2008). This approach is based on a philosophy of language acquisition and literacy processing that calls for highly integrated learning experiences in the classroom.

language-based approach
a framework and materials for integrated literacy instruction based on developmentally appropriate, active, authentic learning experiences

The key ideas that underlie the language-based philosophy explain this approach's instructional goals and strategies. The language-based approach acknowledges the following characteristics of language and literacy development (Cambourne & Turbill, 1987):

> *Characteristics of Language and Literacy Development*

- Students are active participants in their own language and literacy development; they build theories and test hypotheses as they construct meaning about their world.
- Students' perception of print and their production of oral and written language follow rule-governed, coherent behavior that reflects their current understanding of how print and language work.
- Students enter school with a high degree of language competence; their reading and writing development progresses throughout the elementary and middle school grades in a parallel and interactive manner.
- Students' reading and writing acquisition is influenced by their language, culture, and world knowledge; their social interactions; and their literacy environment, including available language models (from family, teachers, and peers), language and literacy routines, and opportunities to use language in meaningful interactions.
- Students' family and community language and their literacy environment, interactions, and routines strongly influence their reading and writing development; close home–school linkage is important to their language and literacy growth.

FIGURE 1.5
Instructional Features of the Literature-Based Approach

1. Literature-based programs tend to be highly *individualistic* and rely heavily on *teacher initiative* and teacher decisions on skills selection, sequencing, and development.
2. Class or group sets of core *literature books* are used so that students are reading and responding to the same book at any given time. Students work in small *reading-response groups,* in which four or five students form an independent working group to read and respond to literature. Students' *self-selection* into reading-response groups is often allowed, based on their book choices.
3. The teacher guides reading-response groups by providing *reading or discussion prompts* for them to use in their discussions. Prompts are designed to access students' (a) background knowledge (how their experiences relate to the text); (b) ideas derived from text (how students construct meaning); and (c) ideas that go beyond the text (how students interpret or react to the text) (O'Flahavan, 1989).
4. Students maintain *individual response logs, or journals,* throughout the reading-response group experience.
5. *End-of-book summary and synthesis activities,* such as plays, puppet shows, murals, reports, and reader's theatre, are often used.
6. *Informal teacher observation* is used to assess student progress.

What about the literature-based approach appeals to you? What don't you like about it?

The language-based approach shares with the basal reading and the literature-based approaches the common goal of developing students' reading and literacy skills to their highest potential. In instructional approach and strategies, however, the language-based approach is more closely related to the literature-based approach because it uses full-length literature selections, focuses on a naturalistic response to literature, and integrates reading and writing development.

Specific instructional goals focus on integrated skills development in areas such as word analysis, comprehension, vocabulary, language, written expression, literature, study skills, and thinking processes. The language-based approach to developing these skills differs significantly from the basal reader approach of preselected skills development. Instructional features of the language-based approach are presented in Figure 1.6.

Technology-Based Instruction

Technology has begun to play an important support role in classroom literacy instruction. More computers have become available in many schools, although availability is limited to a small number in most classrooms. Some schools also have a computer center that provides opportunities for use by an entire class.

Technology support can take many forms, including the instructional medium for story writing, e-mailing, and Internet research on special topics. A wide variety of software programs are available that can provide special instruction in word identification (e.g., *Reading Blaster, Beginning Reading*), vocabulary (e.g., *Writing Advantage*), and comprehension development (e.g., *Storybook Theatre*). Other software programs are available that provide skill-and-drill games for some students with special needs. The importance of technology in literacy instruction is reflected in The Highly Effective Teacher in Technology feature found in each chapter of this text. We will devote special attention to integrating technology in the classroom in Chapter 12.

Characteristics of Exemplary Reading Programs

The highly effective teacher is the key to good reading instruction, regardless of the instructional approach or method used. The International Reading Association (2000a) has developed a position statement that identifies essential components of exemplary reading instruction (Figure 1.7).

FIGURE 1.6

Instructional Features of the Language-Based Approach

What about the language-based approach appeals to you? What don't you like about it?

1. The *teacher assumes major responsibility* as the instructional decision maker who creates the instructional goals and objectives, plans the instructional activities, and creates the learning environment.
2. Specific instructional goals focus on highly *integrated skills development* in areas such as phonics and word analysis, comprehension, vocabulary, language, written expression, literature, and study skills.
3. Students are *immersed in language*—from print to personal sharing of home and school events.
4. Students are *actively involved* in meaningful demonstrations of language in action—from predicting to discussing.
5. Language and literacy are used for *real-life purposes*—from writing letters to pen pals to writing stories based on a field trip.
6. Students are encouraged to *assume responsibility for their own learning*—from self-selecting books to deciding on their use of free time.
7. Teachers and parents hold the *expectation that all students will learn*—based on an understanding of developmental learning differences, goal setting, and conferencing.
8. *Approximation to the targeted reading and literacy skill* is encouraged—from story predictions to writing revisions.
9. *Ongoing informal teacher observation* constitutes the main form of evaluation and learner feedback and may range from analysis of children's responses during story discussions to periodic portfolio evaluation.

FIGURE 1.7

Components of Exemplary Reading Programs

1. Teachers adapt various methods of early reading instruction to meet individual students' needs.
2. Instruction helps students develop solid repertoires of advanced comprehension strategies, as well as study skills.
3. Programs are planned and taught by teachers who are not only initially well prepared but are also up-to-date as a result of continual participation in professional development programs.
4. Because students who read *more* read *better*, teachers provide wide access to books and encourage voluntary reading in school, as well as out of school.
5. Reading assessment identifies both students' weaknesses and their strengths—a major purpose of testing in these programs is to assist teachers in determining instructional activities that will foster literacy learning.
6. Students who evidence delays in reading development receive intensive instruction from individuals specifically and intensively prepared to teach reading.
7. Students' reading growth is enhanced by the participation of parents and by the involvement of community groups such as organizers of library programs, volunteer tutors, and policymakers.
8. Students are provided literacy instruction that makes meaningful use of their first-language skills.
9. Students have access to technology that supports reading instruction.
10. Students attend a school that optimizes learning opportunities—for example, with appropriate student-teacher ratios, adequate instructional materials, credentialed teachers, and disciplined behavior in classrooms.

Paraphrased from *Making a difference means making it different* (2000a), Newark, DE: International Reading Association.

A Historical Context for Literacy Instruction in the United States

A brief overview of the history of literacy instruction in the United States enables us to gain perspective on the enormous progress that has been made in literacy instruction, materials, classroom facilities, and teacher preparation (Chall, 2000; Chall & Squire, 1991; Smith, 2002; Venezky, 1991). The greatest progress has occurred over the past half-century.

Table 1.2 (page 14) presents an overview of historical events, key influences on education, materials used, curricular content and the classroom environment, instructional emphasis, and teacher preparation for four different time periods from 1607 to 2006.

Reading and Writing from Colonial Times to the Modern Era, 1607–1910

The **hornbook** was used at the time of the Jamestown settlement in 1607 and was one of the most commonly used reading materials of the colonial period. At that time, the primary reason for learning to read was to be able to read and understand Biblical scriptures. This was made very clear in the "Old Deluder Satan Law," passed in Massachusetts in 1647, which pronounced the right of individuals to read the scriptures for themselves (Smith, 1974). The hornbook, the basic tool of literacy, was a paddle-shaped hardwood board covered by a thin sheet of transparent horn that protected one page containing the alphabet, a few letter-pattern combinations, and the Lord's Prayer.

The ***New England Primer*** (Figure 1.8, page 15), the first schoolbook other than the Bible, was originally published about 1690 and was reprinted in many editions over the next hundred years. The primer contained a speller, moralistic sayings of the time illustrated by woodcuts, and a catechism. Some three million copies of this short text were printed. Its emphasis on teaching reading and spelling consisted of developing letter-name knowledge, spelling out a word, and then pronouncing the word. Oral reading, "spell downs" (a form of today's spelling bee), and memorization of Biblical selections consumed a significant portion of the school day.

The **McGuffey Eclectic Readers** (McGuffey, 1836/1920) were the first widely used set of materials that organized literary selections according to different reading levels, gradually increasing the difficulty across the grades. The readers were a mainstay in U.S. education for

hornbook
a wooden board with text protected by a transparent sheet of animal horn

New England Primer
the first colonial schoolbook, originally published about 1690

McGuffey Eclectic Readers
a series of graded readers based on vocabulary and moral teachings, originally published in 1836

TABLE 1.2

Historical Perspective on Reading and Literacy Instruction

1607–1840

Historical events	Settlement at Jamestown; Declaration of Independence; War of 1812
Key influences on education	Religious views; patriotic views; acclimation to new life in new country
Materials used	Hornbooks; Bible; *New England Primer* (speller, moral sayings, catechism); *Webster's Blue-Backed Speller*
Content and classroom	Religious and patriotic content; benches; poor lighting and heating
Instructional emphasis	Letter-name knowledge; pronunciation; oral reading; "spell downs"; memorization of Bible; letter-sound relations; art of elocution valued in democracy
Teachers	Individuals with good moral character who are able to read and write, usually male

1840–1910

Historical events	Gold Rush; westward expansion; Industrial Revolution; railroads; Civil War; electricity; telephone; radio; population 70 percent rural; beginning of urban movement
Key influences on education	Expanding nation; growth of technology; rural society; schools needed and school districts formed; European influence emphasizing oral instruction and object teaching (Pestalozzi); developmental view of children; beginning of scientific movement in education
Materials used	McGuffey Eclectic Readers; illustrated texts; materials became more available
Content and classroom	Moralistic and literary content; emphasis on history and geography; beginning of grade levels based on age; desks fastened to oil-treated floor
Instructional emphasis	Phonics and syllable work in isolation and in context; oral reading; recitation of memorized passages; handwriting and copying; little composition; beginning of achievement test use
Teachers	Graduates of one- and two-year normal schools; women entered teaching in large numbers for first time

1910–1960

Historical events	World War I; Great Depression; World War II; television; Korean War; launch of Sputnik; jet air travel; large urban populations
Key influences on education	Expanding world view; scientific research in education; child-centered curriculum (Dewey); literacy awareness; World War II induction testing; advancements in technology and communication; lay critics of education (Flesch & Trace); educational publishing industry; urban center needs
Materials used	Basal reading programs; language programs; teacher manuals developed to guide instruction
Content and classroom	Broadening curriculum; more flexible seating arrangements; greater concern for lighting and comfort of students
Instructional emphasis	Word analysis and comprehension; usage; reading groups by ability; increased use of testing; concern for the individual student
Teachers	Graduates of four-year teacher colleges and universities; school district inservice workshops introduced; advanced training encouraged; teaching professionalized; state teacher certification introduced

more than forty years and continue to be reissued from time to time. For many Americans in the nineteenth and early twentieth centuries, the McGuffey Readers provided their only access to literature (Smith, 1974). The sample from *McGuffey's Second Eclectic Reader* shown in Figure 1.9 (page 16), a moralistic story about two boys at a circus, is typical of the series. Repetition of new words was used to develop a recognition vocabulary. Note the emphasis on factual-level comprehension and moral development in the concluding exercises.

The readers' upper-grade materials included literary selections and social science selections, emphasizing areas such as history and geography. The German-Pestalozzian movement (named after Swiss educational reformer Johann Heinrich Pestalozzi) strongly influenced the development of the graded materials that appeared in several reading programs during the nineteenth century (Smith, 1974).

TABLE 1.2 (continued)
Historical Perspective on Reading and Literacy Instruction

1960–2008

Historical events	Civil Rights Movement; War on Poverty; Vietnam War; feminist movement; moon landing; federal government support of education; computers; Persian Gulf War; end of the Cold War; global interdependency; HIV/AIDS and other public health concerns; increased immigration to United States; technology; *No Child Left Behind* legislation; standards movement
Key influences on education	Racial integration; federal funding for special programs; movements for equality and justice for women and minorities; dramatic increase in cultural diversity; educational applications of computer-based and telecommunications technologies; environmentalism; use of technology in classrooms; emphasis on performance-based primary-grade reading; strong stress on assessment of student progress
Materials used	Basal reader, language-based, and literature-based programs; supplementary and technology-based instructional programs
Content and classroom	Reflection of racial, cultural, and gender diversity in story content; movable seating and modular classrooms; greater attention to the classroom as a learning environment
Instructional emphasis	Word analysis and comprehension based on story context; integration of oral and written language; informal evaluation for instructional planning; teachers' role in developing and implementing the curriculum; use of computers and Internet; extensive use of assessment and testing
Teachers	Graduates of five-year preparation programs; more opportunities, funding, and encouragement provided for continuing higher education for teachers and for their participation in professional organizations; specialization encouraged in special education and other education fields; inservice work on technology in the classroom; standards movement influenced student assessment and competence-based teacher-preparation programs

FIGURE 1.8
Sample Pages from the *New England Primer* (ca. 1690)

Good Boys at their Books.

HE who ne'er learns his A,B,C,
Forever will a Blockhead be;
But he who to his Book's inclin'd,
Will soon a golden Treasure find.

Children, like tender Trees do take the Bow,
And as they first are fashon'd always grow,
For what we learn in Youth, to that alone,
In Age we are by second Nature prone.

abcdefghijklm
nopqrſstuv
wxyz&
Vowels.
AEIOUY a e-i o u y.
Confonants.
bcdfghjklmnopqrſstvwxz
Double Letters.
ff ffſt fi fi ſh fl fl ffi ſſi ffl &
Italick Letters.
Aa Bb Cc Dd Ee Ff Gg Hh Ii Kk
Ll Mm Nn Oo Pp Qq Rr Ss
Tt Vv Uu Ww Xx Yy Zz
Italick Double Letters.

FIGURE 1.9

Sample Pages from *McGuffey's Second Eclectic Reader* (1836)

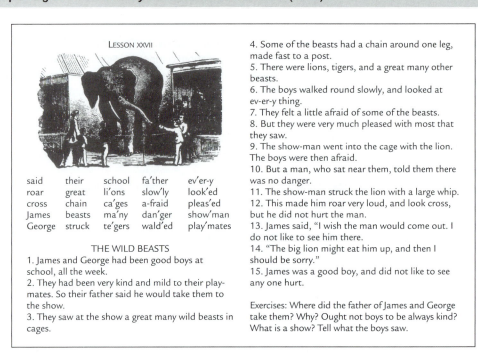

LESSON XXVII

said	their	school	fa′ther	ev′er-y
roar	great	li′ons	slow′ly	look′ed
cross	chain	ca′ges	a-fraid	pleas′ed
James	beasts	ma′ny	dan′ger	show′man
George	struck	te′gers	wald′ed	play′mates

THE WILD BEASTS

1. James and George had been good boys at school, all the week.
2. They had been very kind and mild to their play-mates. So their father said he would take them to the show.
3. They saw at the show a great many wild beasts in cages.

4. Some of the beasts had a chain around one leg, made fast to a post.
5. There were lions, tigers, and a great many other beasts.
6. The boys walked round slowly, and looked at ev-er-y thing.
7. They felt a little afraid of some of the beasts.
8. But they were very much pleased with most that they saw.
9. The show-man went into the cage with the lion. The boys were then afraid.
10. But a man, who sat near them, told them there was no danger.
11. The show-man struck the lion with a large whip.
12. This made him roar very loud, and look cross, but he did not hurt the man.
13. James said, "I wish the man would come out. I do not like to see him there.
14. "The big lion might eat him up, and then I should be sorry."
15. James was a good boy, and did not like to see any one hurt.

Exercises: Where did the father of James and George take them? Why? Ought not boys to be always kind? What is a show? Tell what the boys saw.

Reading and Writing in the Twentieth Century to the Present Time

The period from 1910 to 1960 brought new emphasis on reading readiness, silent reading, and phonics instruction that developed sound-letter relationships in context. The preprimer was introduced by the publishing industry at this time. The concepts of language growth and emergent literacy developed from a child-centered curriculum emphasis enhanced by the early efforts of progressive reformer John Dewey (Crosby, 1964). The progressive viewpoint emphasized enriched and direct experiences that drew on children's personal knowledge and background. Oral dramatization, creative writing, and spelling were encouraged and often based on unit study intended to integrate content areas.

Figure 1.10 (page 17) shows the table of contents from *Days and Deeds*, a fifth-grade reader from the Curriculum Foundation Series published in 1947 (Gray & Arbuthnot). This series, commonly known as the **Dick and Jane Readers,** was used throughout the United States. Dick and Jane (and their dog Spot) are the fictional characters in the primary-grade books of the program. The *Days and Deeds* table of contents reveals the impact of new communication ("The Mail Must Go Through," "SOS by Wire") and transportation ("Bob Becomes a Railroad Man," "Glint of Wings"). Reading material content broadened significantly during the mid-twentieth century and included stories from other countries, folktales, biography selections, and poetry. Teacher guides and workbooks also were introduced for the first time.

After the 1950s, curricular changes reflected the Civil Rights Movement, the Cold War, and awareness about poverty and public health. Increased awareness of social injustices led to nationwide school-integration efforts and new federally supported educational programs. For the first time, ethnic-minority characters were represented in basal readers, gender roles began to diversify in illustrations and stories (Hamlin, 1982), and characters with disabilities were included in publisher-produced stories. Instructional materials also reflected new scientific knowledge about how children learn. In response, teacher preparation programs underwent reform, some shifting to five-year programs to provide additional time and greater focus on theory and practice (National Commission on Teaching & America's Future, 1996).

The sample pages shown in Figure 1.11 (pages 18–19) from *Ramona Quimby, Age 8* (Cleary, 1981), which is recommended for the second half of third grade, appear in the teacher's

Dick and Jane Readers
a series of graded readers based on child development and social relevance, originally published in the early 1930s

➤ *Curriculum Reforms after the 1950s*

FIGURE 1.10

Table of Contents from *Days and Deeds,* a Fifth-Grade Reader

Contents

Young Citizens of Today

Moving Westward

3

Wonders of Today

Story-Land of Here and Now

Young Citizens of Other Lands

The Great Outdoors

4

edition of *Horizons: Smart Solutions* (Cooper & Pikulski, 2005). These pages contain detailed suggestions for a five-day lesson sequence that ranges from background building, vocabulary introduction, and purpose setting on day one to the development of comprehension and information and study skills on day five. The lesson plan also provides suggestions for whole-class and small-group instruction using teacher-led discussion, individual work, and special provision for English-language learners. Follow-up suggestions are presented to encourage the integration of spelling, writing, and language arts. The program also has practice and skill books to accompany the colorful children's reader and a variety of supplementary materials for teaching.

The second half of the twentieth century and the early twenty-first century were characterized by a proliferation of curricular materials for literacy and a stronger emphasis on authentic full-length literature selections, process writing, the integration of reading and writing instruction, and the instructional use of computer-based technologies. More options enabled teachers to select and design instruction for students who have a wide range of achievement and learner characteristics (Alexander & Fox, 2004; Allington & McGill-Franzen, 2004).

> ➤ *List five outcomes of changes in literacy instruction since the 1950s.*

Literacy Trends and Implications

Literacy progress over the years can be measured in part by the degree of literacy achieved by the general population. It has been estimated that at the time of the signing of the Declaration of Independence in 1776, only 15 percent of the population was literate. This figure rose to 45 percent during World War I and 65 percent by World War II (R. Tyler, personal communication, July 14, 1973). Today, 85 to 95 percent of the U.S. population possesses sufficient literacy skills

FIGURE 1.11

Teacher's Edition Pages for *Ramona Quimby, Age 8,* from a Modern Reader

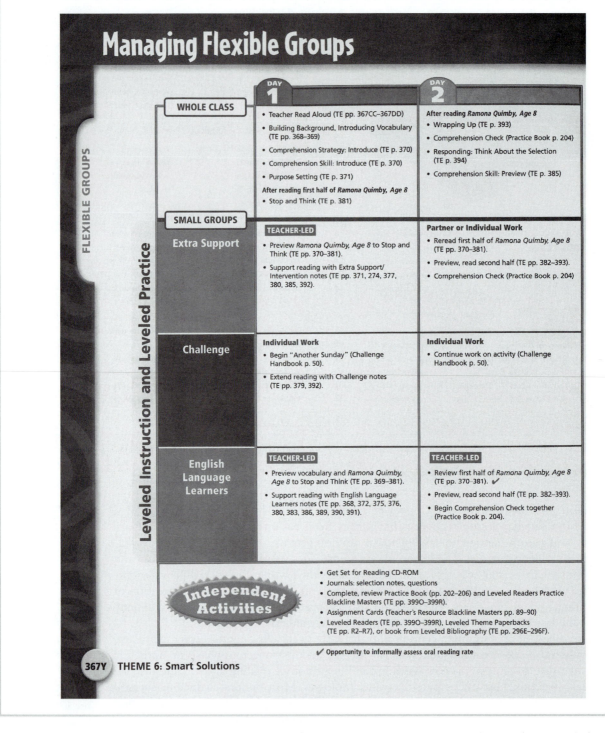

Excerpts from HORIZONS Teacher's Edition: Smart Solutions, Level 3, Theme 6 in HOUGHTON MIFFLIN READING by J. David Cooper and John J. Pikulski, et al. Copyright © 2005 by Houghton Mifflin Company. Reprinted by permission of Houghton Mifflin Company. All rights reserved.

DAY 3

- Rereading: Lessons on Writer's Craft (TE pp. 387)
- Comprehension Skill: Main lesson (TE pp. 399A–399B)

TEACHER-LED
- Reread, review Comprehension Check (Practice Book p. 204).
- Preview Leveled Reader: Below Level (TE p. 399O), or read book from Leveled Bibliography (TE pp. 296E–296F). ✔

TEACHER-LED
- Teacher check-in: Assess progress (Challenge Handbook p. 50).
- Preview Leveled Reader: Above Level (TE p. 399Q), or read book from Leveled Bibliography (TE pp. 296E–296F). ✔

Partner or Individual Work
- Complete Comprehension Check (Practice Book p. 204).
- Begin Leveled Reader: Language Support (TE p. 399R), or read book from Leveled Bibliography (TE pp. 296E–296F).

DAY 4

- Reading the Drama Link (TE pp. 396–399): Skill lesson (TE p. 396)
- Rereading the Link: Genre Lesson (TE p. 398)
- Comprehension Skill: First Comprehension Review lesson (TE p. 383)

Partner or Individual Work
- Reread the Drama Link (TE pp. 396–399).
- Complete Leveled Reader: Below Level (TE p. 399O), or read book from Leveled Bibliography (TE pp. 296E–296F).

Individual Work
- Complete activity (Challenge Handbook p. 50).
- Complete Leveled Reader: Above Level (TE p. 399Q), or read book from Leveled Bibliography (TE pp. 296E–296F).

TEACHER-LED
- Reread the Drama Link (TE pp. 396–399) ✔ and review Link Skill (TE p. 396).
- Complete Leveled Reader: Language Support (TE p. 399R), or read book from Leveled Bibliography (TE pp. 296E–296F). ✔

DAY 5

- Responding: Select from Activities (TE pp. 394–395)
- Information and Study Skills (TE p. 399H)
- Comprehension Skill: Second Comprehension Review lesson (TE p. 391)

TEACHER-LED
- Comprehension Skill: Reteaching lesson (TE p. R12)
- Reread Leveled Theme Paperback: Below Level (TE pp. R2–R3), or read book from Leveled Bibliography (TE pp. 296E–296F). ✔

TEACHER-LED
- Evaluate activity and plan format for sharing (Challenge Handbook p. 50).
- Reread Leveled Theme Paperback: Above Level (TE pp. R6–R7), or read book from Leveled Bibliography (TE pp. 296E–296F). ✔

Partner or Individual Work
- Reread book from Leveled Bibliography (TE pp. 296E–296F).

FLEXIBLE GROUPS

Ramona Quimby, Age 8

- Responding activities (TE pp. 394–395)
- Language Center activities (TE pp. 399M–399N)
- **Fluency Practice:** Reread *Pepita Talks Twice; Poppa's New Pants; Ramona Quimby, Age 8* ✔
- Activities relating to *Ramona Quimby, Age 8* at Education Place www.eduplace.com

Turn the page for more independent activities.

to function effectively in society. This dramatic increase in literacy may be attributed to new reading materials, new instructional programs, the greater availability of literature to the general public, a wider variety of reading material, and the proliferation of mass media. A significant portion of the credit for increased literacy, however, must be given to effective teachers, who have helped countless millions of students to learn to read and write.

> *A Summary of the History of Literacy Development*

A historical perspective on reading and literacy development can be summarized as follows:

1. Historical events and political influences in society contribute to and shape story selection, the content of materials used for literacy learning, the instructional approaches emphasized, and the preparation of teachers.
2. A shift in emphasis has occurred across the years in educators' perceptions of the way students develop reading and writing skills. The early reading readiness and isolated skill-and-drill approach has yielded to the present view of students' emergent literacy as a skill-balanced, integrated, and active process of meaning construction.
3. Instructional materials and technology of the twenty-first century differ dramatically from those of the past in complexity, availability, appropriateness, interest, and breadth of content.
4. Teachers' abilities to choose materials and instructional approaches are much greater and more encompassing today than in earlier periods.
5. Greater care and concern than ever before are now given to identifying students' instructional needs through informal observation and meeting these needs through skill balance in reading and writing instruction.
6. More emphasis is placed on formal assessment using achievement tests.
7. Heightened sensitivity to students' developmental, linguistic, cultural, and achievement diversity represents a major step in meeting all students' learning needs.

What do you expect to get out of reading this book? How might your current beliefs and theories about reading and writing instruction change as a result of reading this book?

8. Professional programs of teacher preparation are more theory and strategy driven and provide a broader range of teaching experiences than ever before. Teachers are encouraged to continue their professional development through inservice workshops and advanced-degree work.
9. Standards-based instruction has strongly influenced student assessment and teaching at the district, state, and national levels as well as teacher-preparation programs. This movement is controversial because of teacher concern that testing may not measure what is being taught by the classroom teacher; that the extensive testing time takes up valuable classroom instruction time; and that tests will start to dictate what is being taught and will erode local school control.

The Challenge of Becoming a Highly Effective and Influential Literacy Teacher

Table 1.3 contains a checklist, "Identifying My Personal Belief System: Teaching Reading and Writing Skills." Take a few minutes to complete this checklist, indicating your agreement (1 means strongly agree) or disagreement (5 means strongly disagree) with each item. Your decisions will initiate the process of defining your personal belief system about reading and writing instruction and teaching.

As you read this book, expect your current belief system (i.e., your theories) to change and grow. As they do, you will find that your ideas about classroom practice will likewise change. To guide you in this process, this book covers major topics on literacy development, such as emergent literacy, word-analysis skills, reading comprehension, reader motivation, writing development, and classroom organization for literacy learning. Each section includes specific, classroom-based teaching strategies

Are you ready to define your own personal belief system about reading and writing instruction and teaching? How might you initiate this process?

grounded in current theory and research and highly effective classroom practice. These selected strategies have a clear instructional goal or goals, a plan for implementation, opportunity for instructional evaluation, and opportunity for the development of self-directed monitoring by your students. These teaching strategies and tools are designed to assist you in creating comprehensive reading and writing instruction.

TABLE 1.3
Identifying My Personal Belief System: Teaching Reading and Writing Skills

	Agree				Disagree
1. Teaching reading is, for the most part, helping students understand the relationship between letters and sounds.	1	2	3	4	5
2. It is important to make reading material personally relevant to each student.	1	2	3	4	5
3. Students' reading motivation is highest when it is based on internally driven interest rather than external teacher direction.	1	2	3	4	5
4. Students' comprehension can be greatly enhanced by engaging students in the process of intellectual discovery.	1	2	3	4	5
5. Using family and life experiences of the student is very important in helping students comprehend text.	1	2	3	4	5
6. Reading and writing are two very different skills and should not be taught in conjunction with each other.	1	2	3	4	5
7. Students who speak a second language will have greater difficulty learning to read than students who speak only English.	1	2	3	4	5
8. Monitoring and feedback on students' reading and writing responses are important for students' success.	1	2	3	4	5
9. Students' nonverbal responses deserve little consideration in small-group discussion.	1	2	3	4	5
10. Clear, definite teaching goals and plans are critical for good reading and writing instruction.	1	2	3	4	5
11. High achievement expectation is important if students are to achieve at the optimal level.	1	2	3	4	5
12. Exhibiting a positive attitude toward reading and writing and the skills being taught is the mark of a good teacher.	1	2	3	4	5

Summary and Classroom Applications

double entry journal

Review your Double Entry Journal notes at the beginning of the chapter about characteristics of influential and highly effective teachers you remember. How have these teachers influenced your personal beliefs about teaching effectiveness? To what extent and in what ways are they role models for characteristics you wish to demonstrate as a classroom teacher?

Chapter Summary

This chapter introduces the concept of the highly effective and influential teacher and identifies key characteristics of these master teachers. Searching for such teachers in your past educational experience will enable you to relate personally to this concept. Becoming a highly effective teacher involves understanding children's language development and the important connections among literacy theory, research, and practice. The NAEP Reading Report Card, for example, strongly suggests the need to emphasize higher-level reasoning skills and to involve students actively in the meaning construction process by using highly effective teaching strategies. The brief introduction to the three major approaches to reading instruction— basal reader, literature-based, and language-based— provides an idea of the options you will have. A historical overview of reading and writing instruction from colonial times to the twenty-first century offers an important perspective on literacy development over the past 500 years.

the Highly Effective Teacher ★

on Technology and Professional Growth

1. There are many ways to enhance your professional and personal growth as a highly effective literacy teacher. One of the best ways is to understand the links between literacy theory and practice. Some useful Web sites that make this connection visible include the following: **www.readingonline. org, www.ncte.org/teach, www.ncss. org,** and the Web resources provided by the International Reading Association at **www.reading.org/resources/index.html.**

2. Read about ideas for beginning teachers at: **www.sitesforteachers.com.**

3. Interview local teachers who have taught in your district in the past. Use technology to broaden your access and hear teachers' stories and read about different educational issues on the following Web site: **www.teachers.net.**

4. Visit online sources to read articles and opinions that surround technology in our schools and society. A good source is the U.S. Department of Education's home page: **www.ed.gov.**

5. Consider how technology can support your instructional goals as a highly effective literacy teacher. You may want to participate in mailing lists such as **listserv@h-net.msu.edu** or **listserv@vms.cis.pitt.edu** to share your thoughts, concerns, and struggles.

6. To explore the latest state- and nationwide achievement test results for grades four, eight, and twelve, go to the NAEP Web site at **http://nces.ed.gov/nationsreport-card/reading/results.** And to find recent updates on *Standards for Reading Professionals, Revised 2003,* which includes those for the classroom teacher, go to the Web site for the International Reading Association at **www.reading.org/resources/issues/reports/professional_standards.html.**

Professional Standards and Literacy Instruction

You were introduced to standards earlier in this chapter. But how can these standards be applied to you? Let's begin by recalling the first standard in Figure 1.2 (page 5). This Foundational Knowledge Standard (1.1), "Knowledge of foundational theories of reading and writing processes and instruction," means that you are knowledgeable about basic theories related to practices and materials that you will use in your teaching.

It is important for you to recognize that you already have a foundational theory about the reading and writing process. At this point let us focus on reading only. So, now develop a statement about your personal "theory" that will explain how children acquire reading skills. Take into account your own experiences in learning to read. What role did your influential teachers play? Your family? After completing your statement, share it with a colleague or classmate and refine it based on that discussion. Chapter 2 will be devoted exclusively to understanding this process. Please keep your statement and expand on it as you move through the remainder of your course.

Applications: Bridges to the Classroom

1. Review the key characteristics of the basal, language-based, and literature-based programs. Develop questions about each type of program and then interview a K–6 teacher you know or have observed. List some strengths and limitations of each approach.

2. Think about the changes in reading instruction that occurred in the twentieth century. Locate a basal reader published between 1910 and 1960 for the grade level you plan to teach and a reader published within the last ten years for the same grade level. Compare and contrast the readers with attention to story content, story interest, cultural and gender diversity, and skill emphasis. What influences and events might account for the differences you find (see Table 1.2)? Which reader would you prefer to use? Why?

3. Review and share with a class partner your response to each item in the "Identifying My Personal Belief System" checklist (see Table 1.3). Record and discuss your reasons for agreement or disagreement on each item. How do your responses relate to your general teaching philosophy?

4. Draft a statement that expresses your personal teaching philosophy as it relates to reading and writing instruction. Take into account the impact made by your influential teachers, the beliefs of your family, and your personal schooling experiences. After drafting your statement, identify the teaching characteristics that you believe to be most important in implementing your personal philosophy. Place these documents in your portfolio.

5. Start collecting news clippings and professional articles on innovations and trends in reading and writing instruction. Identify key professional journals that you can use on a continuing basis during your teaching career as sources for research on reading and writing. You may want to check the Web site for the International Reading Association (www.reading.org) or that of the National Council of Teachers of English (www.ncte.org) as a starting point. Add information about these resources to your portfolio, and share the information with your class partners.

Additional Research and Practice

1. *Making a difference means making it different: Honoring children's rights to excellent reading instruction* (2000), Newark, DE: International Reading Association.

   This position statement on the development of excellent reading instruction identifies and briefly discusses ten key principles that can be used to evaluate classroom practice and administrative policy. (Practice)

2. Fitzgerald, J. (1999). **What is this thing called "balance?"** *The Reading Teacher, 51,* 100–107.

   This article addresses the issue of a balanced approach to reading instruction using expert knowledge and philosophy and explores the benefits to teachers derived from examining their own instructional outlook. (Practice)

3. Fresch, M. J. (Ed.) (2008). *An Essential History of Current Reading Practices.* Newark, DE: International Reading Association.

   This book explores the history of several facets of instruction related to reading, one chapter per facet, written by an author with expertise in that area. Topics include guided reading, fluency, comprehension, phonics/phonemic awareness, literature, content area reading, vocabulary and spelling, remedial and clinical reading, family literacy, teacher education in reading, and others. (Research)

Understanding the Reading and Writing Process

A child's mind is like a shallow brook which ripples and dances merrily over the stony course of its education and reflects here like a flower, there a bush, yonder a fleecy cloud . . .

Helen Keller (1880–1968),
American writer

. . . that is what learning is. You suddenly understand something you've understood all your life, but in a new way.

Doris Lessing (1919–),
British writer

Y ou are an expert reader. In becoming an expert reader, you have developed specific literacy competencies that enable you to construct meaning from print.

What are these competencies? That is, what processes and strategies do you use as you read to make sense of passages? Try to describe the processes you use to make sense of the following passage for the purpose of answering the questions that follow it.

The Wimmy Wuggen and the Moggy Tor

Once upon a time, a wimmy Wuggen zonked into the grabbet. Zhe was grolling for poft because zhe was very blongby.

The wimmy Wuggen grolled and grolled until zhe motted a moggy Tor.

Zhe glind to the moggy Tor, "Ik am blongby and grolling for poft. Do yum noff mehre ik can gine some poft?"

"Kex," glind the Tor, "klom with ne, wimmy Wuggen. Ik have lodz of poft in ni bove."

So the Wuggen womt with the Tor to hiz bove. Dhem the Wuggen glind to the Tor, "Vhat kimd of poft do yum habt?"

And the moggy Tor glind, "Yum Wuggen zar excellent poft!"

Now, respond to the following questions:

1. Where did the wimmy Wuggen zonk?
2. Why was zhe grolling for poft?
3. Did the moggy Tor help the Wuggen? Why do you think so?
4. Would you have womt with the moggy Tor had you been the wimmy Wuggen? Why or why not?

How did you do on the questions about the wimmy Wuggen and the moggy Tor? Because answering questions was given as the purpose for reading the passage, you may have looked at the questions before reading it. Then you read the passage with that goal in mind. In doing so, you were using a comprehension strategy, one competency of expert readers. You developed this competency when you learned to read, but how?

double entry journal

Think about your early schooling experiences from kindergarten through grade three. What do you remember about learning to read? What do you remember about your first experiences with children's literature—for example, fairy tales? Can you identify any beginning reading competencies or strategies that you used as a child?

Chapter Objectives

After reading and discussing this chapter, you will be able to:

- identify six expert reader competencies.
- understand the nature of children's oral language development.
- explain the progression in children's emergent literacy and literacy development in the elementary and middle school years.
- identify key factors that influence oral and written language development.

- explain the sociocognitive theory of language and literacy development and how it helps us understand how we learn to read and comprehend printed text.
- understand and explain the nature of the reading comprehension process.

Expert Reader Competencies

Educators, philosophers, psychologists, and others have long been interested in how students learn to read and write. A century ago, Huey (1908/1968) called reading the "most remarkable specific performance that civilization has learned in all its history" and challenged researchers and theorists to explain what people actually do when they read and comprehend language. Since Huey produced his pioneering work, we have made important progress toward understanding key **expert reader competencies**—using word identification, meaning clues, story schemata, motivation, hypothesizing, various comprehension strategies, and other competencies.

> Are you feeling blongby today?

expert reader competencies knowledge and processing skills needed for reading fluency and comprehension

Word Identification

Because you are an expert reader, the word identification skills you used with "The Wimmy Wuggen and the Moggy Tor" to transform the print to sound and meaning were largely automatic. You moved swiftly from left to right across the page, activating your well-integrated knowledge of letter-sound and letter pattern–sound pattern relationships (Ehri & McCormick, 2004). You easily processed the print in the words, using your familiarity with English spelling patterns. Capital letters and sentence markers (such as commas and periods) were also processed at an automatic level (Samuels, 2004) to identify meaning-bearing units, as were quotation marks signaling conversational units.

> *Readers transform print to meaning automatically through word recognition and word identification.*

Meaning Clues

You also were highly effective in using two types of **meaning clues** from your expert language background. The first clue comes from relational meanings; for example, the words *a* and *the* signal that a noun will follow, and the suffixes *-ed* and *-ing* signal a verb. The second clue involves sentence context; your knowledge of syntax, or sentence structure, allows you to grasp word

meaning clues relational and contextual clues to the meaning of text meaning. From the sentence "Zhe was grolling for poft because zhe was very blongby," you were able to infer that *grolling* is a verb and *poft* is a noun. It is possible that you also may have inferred that *grolling* could mean "looking" and *poft* could mean "food," at least as a hypothesis (Nagy & Scott, 2004). You may have tested this hypothesis as you continued reading.

Story Schemata

story schema
concept of what a story is and how a story narrative is organized

The story title "The Wimmy Wuggen and the Moggy Tor" activated your background knowledge of a **story schema.** A story schema is the concept of what a story is and how a story narrative is organized. (The word *schemata* is the plural of schema.) The title suggests the possibility that this is a story narrative (as opposed to an informational article or essay, for example) and that it involves two main story characters, the wimmy Wuggen and the moggy Tor. This assumption is reinforced by the opening words "Once upon a time . . ." These words triggered the expectation of a folktale schema, with story features such as simple characterization (for example, good versus bad) and linear plot (Anderson, 2004; Kintsch, 2004). In fact, this story structure may have brought to mind the old favorite folktale "The Fox and the Chicken." If it did not, it became necessary for you to use your general folktale schema to predict the possible story outcome.

Motivation

What was your motivation for reading "The Wimmy Wuggen and the Moggy Tor"?

Your motivation for constructing meaning for "The Wimmy Wuggen and the Moggy Tor," which provided for persistence and will to succeed, came from two sources. The first is the internal motivation of intellectual curiosity—to see if you really could make sense of the story. The second is external motivation, which may be driven by the expectation that your instructor and/or your peers will read the story and be ready to discuss the questions, so you need to do the same (Ruddell & Unrau, 2004b).

Hypothesizing

Readers test hypotheses about text until they achieve meaning closure.

The interactive nature of reading and language processing is evident in your use of various aspects of your language background to form tentative hypotheses. Some of these hypotheses concerned words in the story—for example, *grolling, poft*—and some were about entire sentences—"Ik have lodz of poft in ni bove." Others had to do with the story schema—its folktale characteristics. These hypotheses were tested as the meaning-making process continued (Anderson, 2004; Goodman & Goodman, 2004; Spiro, 2004). Eventually, you reached some level of meaning closure for the text.

Comprehension Strategies

Finally, responding to each of the four questions involved the use of different comprehension strategies. Each question required a different level of comprehension processing and thinking. You also monitored your responses to the questions by testing their "correctness" against the information in the passage and against your story expectations, which were based on your background knowledge (Adams, 2004). Figure 2.1 summarizes six expert reader competencies.

Oral Language Development

Expert readers have developed the art and skill of meaning making through years of print, language, and literacy experience. But what level of reading and writing expertise can be expected of students in kindergarten through grade 8? Their level of expertise depends on a variety of factors, ranging from the literacy environment in students' homes and communities to instructional experiences that students have encountered at school. Whatever the influence of such factors, however, you can be sure that your classroom will contain pupils with widely varying literacy abilities and achievements. Your challenge will be to adjust your instructional program to meet

FIGURE 2.1
Six Key Expert Reader Competencies

1. Expert readers like you recognize almost all words they encounter in print automatically and accurately. In the few circumstances when a word is unknown, they use word identification strategies skillfully.
2. Expert readers use their knowledge of language (for example, their relatively unconscious knowledge of sentence structures) to help them infer meaning from written text.
3. Expert readers have had prior experiences in reading and hearing stories and informational text, and they use this experience to make educated guesses about characters, characters' actions, vocabulary associated with certain story types or informational text types, and about probable logical outcomes and meanings.
4. Expert readers possess both internal and external reading motivation, which supports their will and persistence in working to understand material.
5. Expert readers combine sources of information (for example, knowledge about language, knowledge about story or informational text types, and others) to gradually build a sense of what a passage, story, or informational piece means. This is referred to as "meaning construction."
6. Expert readers are effective in drawing on comprehension strategies that enable them to use different levels of thinking (from simple recall to high-level inference) and monitor meaning construction in light of background knowledge, text meaning, reading objective, and expected outcome.

the learning needs of each student. One requirement to meet that challenge is to understand oral language development.

Reading is a language-based activity. As such, as a teacher of reading you need to know something about how an individual learns language.

Acquiring language is one of the most complex tasks human beings will ever accomplish, yet experienced adult language users have little or no memory of how they accomplished it. Despite its complexity, the process is well under way in infancy (Tabors & Snow, 2004).

> Students have widely varying literacy abilities and achievements.

> Language Acquisition

Mastering Phonology

Phonology refers to the *sounds* of language. By the time children enter school, they have mastered most of the sounds that comprise the **phonological system** of their native language (Ervin & Miller, 1963; Templin, 1957). The vowel sounds are acquired first. In fact, most vowels and several initial and final consonants, such as /m/, /n/, /p/, /t/, and /f/, have developed by age three. A few consonants, such as /v/ and /th/, develop as late as age 6 or 7 (Templin, 1957). Most native speakers of English, however, can produce the great majority of English sounds by age 5 or 6.

phonological system units of sounds produced in a language

Mastering Grammar

In this context, *grammar* refers to something a bit different from what a high school English teacher means when she or he admonishes students not to say "ain't," but to "use good grammar." Instead, in reference to oral language development, the term **grammar** refers to language factors such as the rules of language, for instance, use of word forms consistent with those generally used in a particular language (for example, in English we say *geese* to mean more than one *goose*, but not "meese" to mean more than one *moose*).

Like mastery of the sound system, children's grammatical sense is also well along by the time they enter the early grades. The learning process in early language development seems to include some degree of imitation. More importantly, it includes the ability to generalize—to apply language principles to whole categories of language structures—as a child must do, for example, to learn how to create plural nouns. In the process, children overgeneralize when dealing initially with irregular English language forms (Fromkin & Rodman, 1993). After learning to form the plural *blocks* from *block*, children generalize to *toys* and *dogs*; some weeks later, they overgeneralize to "foots" for *feet*, "mans" for *men*, and "sheeps" for *sheep*. Once they begin to use the past tense of regular verbs, such as *walked* and *watched*, children subsequently overgeneralize,

grammar language factors such as rules of language, consistent use of word forms and structures

Why do young children say "mouses" for mice and "seed" for saw?

using irregular verb forms such as "breaked" for *broke* and "runded" for *ran* (Fromkin & Rodman, 1993; Miller & Ervin, 1964).

> *Order of Acquisition of Grammar*

The order of acquisition of grammar appears to be highly consistent as children progress through four developmental stages (Fromkin & Rodman, 1993). These stages are (1) little or no use of a particular word form, (2) sporadic use of the form, (3) overgeneralization, and (4) adult-like use of the form (Anderson & Freebody, 1985; Brown, 1973; Cazden, 1968; DeVilliers & DeVilliers, 1973). Children's ability to generalize and to extend those generalizations in order to create other language forms is basic to language learning, and overgeneralization is a natural part of this process.

Mastering Syntax

syntax
sentence structures and patterns

telegraphic speech
a syntactic pattern in early oral language development in which pivot and remainder words are used to convey meaning

syntactical control
development of complexity in sentence construction and use

Syntax refers to sentence structures and patterns. Control of language patterns progresses rapidly at the preschool and primary grade levels. Children at these levels not only comprehend complex sentences but also produce expanded, elaborated, and transformed sentences (Chomsky, 1969; Fraser, Bellugi, & Brown, 1963; Loban, 1976).

By the age of 4 or 5 years, children have progressed from their earlier single word utterances ("doggie") to telegraphic speech ("See doggie") to a high degree of control ("Ooh, look at the doggie"). **Telegraphic speech**—such as "Where Mommy?" "Want cookie," "No bib," and "See doggie"—illustrates normal syntactic patterning in early language development (Fromkin & Rodman, 1993).

Following the development of two-word utterances, children's telegraphic speech expands rapidly, so that within one or two years they have control over prepositions, conjunctions, plural forms for nouns, and verb tenses. They use questions, negatives, and infinitives (Miller, 1967).

Development of **syntactical control**, however, extends well into and even beyond the elementary grades (Chomsky, 1969; Menyuk, 1963). For example, even in first grade, some patterns—such as *if* and *so* clauses—and perfect tenses are still in the process of development, and students' syntax continues to evolve from multiple conjoined sentences such as "I have a cat and he's black and he likes hot milk" to the embedded form "My black cat likes hot milk" (DeStefano, 1978). Even in middle school years, new and more complex syntactic structures are being added to students' language repertoires.

> *Order of Acquisition of Oral Language Syntax*

The developmental sequence for oral language syntax moves from simple constructions and run-on forms to more complex subordination-type patterns (O'Donnell, Griffin, & Norris, 1967). The developmental process for syntactical control, like that for grammatical control, appears in stages. Menyuk (1984) suggests three stages of syntactic development: (1) acquiring the ability to comprehend and produce sentences, (2) judging the correctness of sentence forms, and (3) making corrections based on intended meaning.

Developing Vocabulary

An individual's vocabulary grows at the phenomenal rate of 2,700 to 3,000 words per year—about seven words each day—from preschool through the early adult years (Beck & McKeown, 1991; Nagy, Anderson, & Herman, 1987; Nagy & Scott, 2004; Shu, Anderson, & Zhang, 1995). This progression in the early years is shown in Table 2.1. See page 29.

The motivation to learn new vocabulary is driven by the dual factors of intellectual curiosity and the social nature and use of language (Blachowicz, Fisher, Ogle, & Watts-Taffe, 2006). This is evident in studies of conditions that influence independent word learning. Haggard (1980) identified four specific conditions associated with elementary school students' acquisition of new lexical items in their vocabularies (*lexical item* is a term used by linguists to mean "words").

> *Four Conditions That Influence Acquisition of Vocabulary*

1. The word has an appealing sound or is perceived to be an "adult" word (for example, "I learned the word *fickle* because it rhymed with *pickle*").
2. The word first occurred in an incident involving strong emotion, such as embarrassment stemming from mispronunciation (for example, *centrifugal* pronounced "cen-tra-fu-gal").
3. The word has immediate personal usefulness (for example, *room mother, appendectomy*).

TABLE 2.1
Major Steps in Language Acquisition

Approximate Age	Major Language Development
8 months	Can identify words in speech stream
1 year	Babbles, uses intonation pattern similar to adult speech; beginning of speech
13 months	Can understand about 50 words but not produce them
18 months	Can speak about 50 words
2 to 4 years	Progresses from single words to telegraphic speech to language production using rules of grammar such as plural forms
3 years	Can produce vowel sounds and several initial and final consonants
5 years	Can produce the great majority of English sounds; major progress in acquiring syntactical control, although control of complex forms will extend even beyond the elementary grades
6 years	Knows about 10,000 words and acquires about 3,000 words each year through early adult years

4. The word is common in peer-group usage (for example, *wretched*, from a class of children who called one child "Wretched Ritchie").

Another finding of Haggard's (1980) study emphasizes the importance of social interactions in vocabulary development: Once learners determine the meaning of a new word, they rehearse using it in safe environments—among family and friends or in a classroom where word learning and exploration are valued. The social nature of language learning is thus a strong motivating factor in language acquisition. This social motivation to engage in language interaction with others, combined with mental maturation, leads to the rapid acquisition and control of language.

> *Social interactions are key motivators in language acquisition.*

Oral Language Development and Reading

Using what they know about oral language when they attempt to read provides students with important assistance to word recognition and to comprehension. Indeed, when reading, most students use their knowledge of language sounds, sentence structures, and vocabulary meanings they learned as they developed oral language. Some of this knowledge is consciously used and some used rather unconsciously. Other students, however, do not intuitively call upon their oral language knowledge to help them read—delayed readers, for example, may have to be encouraged and shown how to make use of this language information. Later chapters in this book will give you some ideas for helping students capitalize on oral language information.

Emergent Literacy and Literacy Development in the Elementary School Years

Emergent literacy is defined as the early writing and reading behaviors that signal the beginning of children's development of conventional writing and reading processes (Sulzby & Teale, 1991). This early level of literacy progressively develops into the writing and reading conventions associated with the elementary school years.

emergent literacy early reading and writing behaviors that signal the beginning of literacy processes in children

Emergent Writing

Our knowledge of written language acquisition has increased enormously over the past two decades. The development of children's writing awareness has been the subject of research that now serves as a foundation for classroom practice (Dyson, 2004; Dyson & Freedman, 1991; Morrow, 1993).

Children's writing moves progressively through developmental stages from writing as art (or marks that represent a story); through messages in which scribbling represents real and specific

What is the relationship between young children's art and the development of writing?

meanings to the child (the child can "read" back these scribblings to you), the discovery of key writing principles, and the invention and reinvention of written forms through discovery; to the mastery of conventional writing forms (Gunning, 2008). This maturation process is illustrated in Figure 2.2. (See below.)

Preliterate youngsters produce writing that is contextually appropriate, such as vertically aligned grocery lists and paragraphed letters to a grandparent. Research has demonstrated that children's writing and print awareness develop before formal schooling, much earlier than previ-

FIGURE 2.2

Stages in Children's Development of Written Expression

1. Writing as Art, or Marks That Tell a Story

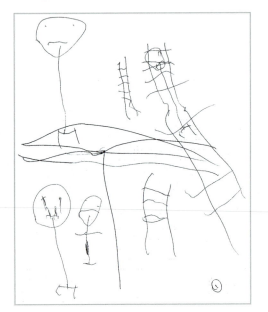

The child's description: "There is all the firemen and this is the fireman on the ladder. This is the little ladder and the fireman again. [When asked about the horizontal lines in middle of page] That's the flag. This is all the guys putting out the fire with the hose."

2. Scribbling That Represents Real and Specific Meanings to the Child

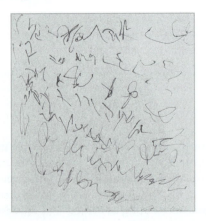

3. Discovery of Principles That Govern Writing Forms

Recurrence: Writing consists of recurring shapes and strokes.
Generativity: An unlimited number of words can be generated from recombinations of a limited number of letters.
Flexibility: The same letters may be written in different ways.

4. Invention and Reinvention of Written Forms through Discovery, Including Invented Spelling for Letter-Sound Relationships

> Andrew and the paydid house
> One day Andrew giet paet
> and. wiete to paet the house
> he giet mise. wien he wes
> dien. the house wes mise
> to. but he like it. his
> paris dient tike it. but
> Lest he Lrnd hiw to pate
> sied Dad but Mom sied
> not a vare god Jib but Andrew
> sied but I like it. but
> lest I paet it. do you like
> it.

The child's description: "Andrew and the Painted House. One day Andrew got paint and wanted to paint the house. He got messy. When he was done the house was messy too. But he liked it. His parents did not like it. 'But least he learned how to paint,' said Dad. But Mom said, 'Not a very good job.' But Andrew said, 'But I like it. But least I painted it. Do you like it?'"

5. Mastery of Conventional Writing

ously thought (Harste, Burke, & Woodward, 1982). Children's scribbling and looking at books are now understood as early literate behaviors. The separation of oral language development from written language development is an artificial one; literacy must be viewed as part of a continuum of speech acts. Thus, children's oral language development provides the foundation for their emergent literacy development.

On the basis of their extensive study of preschool children's written production, Harste, Burke, and Woodward (1982) conclude that (1) written language, like oral language, is learned naturally; (2) children in literate societies are involved at an early age in understanding and controlling print; and (3) children's perceptions of print are organized, systematic, and identifiable.

> *Conditions of Emergent Writing*

Invented Spelling and Patterns of Spelling Development

Another facet of the work on emergent literacy is the study of children's invented spelling. For a delightful example of one young child's invented spelling, see Figure 2.2, item #4. **Invented spelling** is typical of children at the preschool and kindergarten levels and extends well into the early grades as students gain control over the spelling system. Some people prefer the term *temporary spelling* to emphasize the transitory nature of invented spelling (Gillet & Temple, 1990). Invented spelling is systematic, rule governed, and consistent (Bear & Templeton, 1998). Many invented-spelling rules grow directly from children's attempts to map and connect speech to print (Henderson & Beers, 1980).

invented spelling
spelling in which children systematically apply their own spelling rules for the purpose of connecting speech to print

Children use five different patterns of invented spelling as they progress toward conventional spelling—prephonemic, phonemic, letter-name, traditional, and derivational spelling (Temple & Gillet, 1989). Literacy instruction must be designed to recognize these patterns and to assist children in moving through the invented-spelling stages.

The first pattern is **prephonemic spelling** (illustrated in Figure 2.3), in which letters and letterlike forms are arranged in horizontal lines, indicating awareness that words are made from letters. This pattern is typical of kindergartners and many first graders.

prephonemic spelling
spelling using letterlike forms in horizontal rows

FIGURE 2.3

An Example of Prephonemic Spelling: "Phillip's Story"

From Jean Wallace Gillet & Charles Temple, *Understanding Reading Problems: Assessment and Instruction,* 3e. Published by Allyn & Bacon, Boston, MA. Copyright © 1990 by Pearson Education. Reprinted by permission of the publisher.

phonemic spelling
spelling in which letters and letter-like forms appear in short consonant strings

letter-name spelling
spelling in which letters' names represent sounds

transitional spelling
spelling close to conventional spelling but less fluent

derivational spelling
spelling close to conventional spelling but less sophisticated

The second pattern is early **phonemic spelling** (see Figure 2.4 below), in which letters and letterlike forms appear in short consonant strings, indicating discovery of the alphabetic principle. This pattern is typical of kindergartners who are beginning to read and most first graders.

The third pattern is **letter-name spelling**, in which letters' names are used to represent sounds in words. For example, *h* may be used to represent "ch" because it is the only letter in the alphabet with /ch/ in its name (that is, "aich"). This form of spelling indicates awareness of a symbol-sound relationship but without a clear understanding of the full extent of that relationship. This pattern, illustrated in Figure 2.5 (page 33), is typical of beginning readers, most first graders, and many second graders.

The fourth pattern, **transitional spelling**, is typical of more advanced readers who are still not fully fluent. Letters are used to represent all sounds, and long and short vowel sounds are represented correctly (for example, *ham, pig; cake, bake*), indicating that the spelling system is near completion.

In the fifth pattern, **derivational spelling**, letters reflect rule-governed spelling patterns for vowel marking (for example, *pin* and *pine; mat* and *mate*) and consonant doubling (for example, *run* and *running*). However, spelling still shows a lack of awareness of relational patterns among words derived from the same base, as seen in more mature spelling (for example, *extreme* and *extremity*). Derivational spelling is typical of students and adults who have some fluency but who have not read widely.

FIGURE 2.4

An Example of Early Phonemic Spelling: "I Love My Mother"

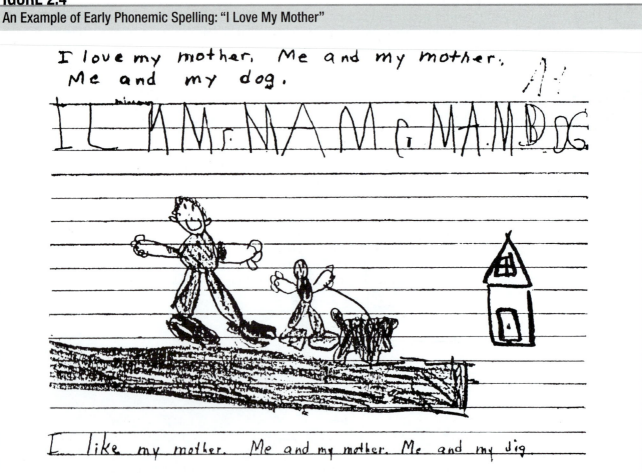

From Jean Wallace Gillet & Charles Temple, *Understanding Reading Problems: Assessment and Instruction,* 3e. Published by Allyn & Bacon, Boston, MA. Copyright © 1990 by Pearson Education. Reprinted by permission of the publisher.

FIGURE 2.5

An Example of Letter-Name Spelling: "My Teeth"

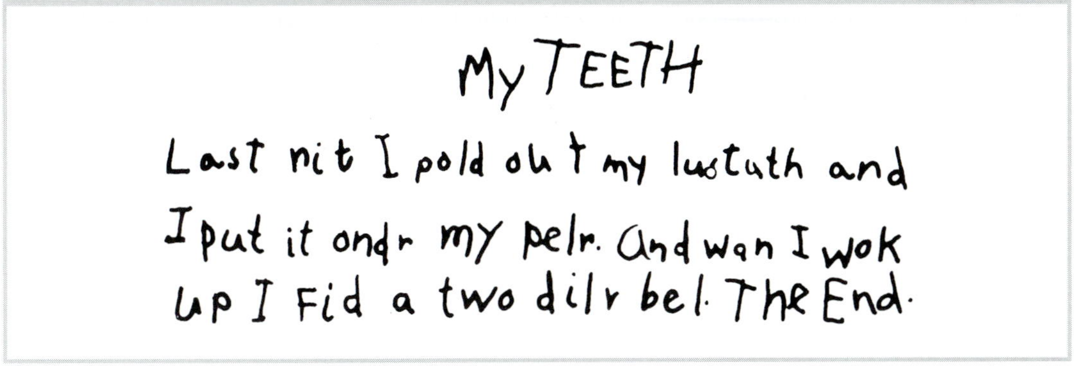

> My TEETH
>
> Last nit I pold oht my lustuth and
> I put it ondr my pelr. And wan I wok
> up I Fid a two dilr bel. The End.

From Jean Wallace Gillet & Charles Temple, *Understanding Reading Problems: Assessment and Instruction*, 3e. Published by Allyn & Bacon, Boston, MA. Copyright © 1990 by Pearson Education. Reprinted by permission of the publisher.

Writing Development

An extensive research review by Danielewicz (1984) indicates that children progress through four stages of writing development. In the first stage, they unify spoken and written language, making few distinctions between the two. In the second stage, they distinguish between spoken and written language by reducing the use of coordinating conjunctions, such as *and* and *but,* in their writing. In the third stage, children strip features of spoken language from written production. In the fourth and last stage, they add features typically associated with written language.

Although the stages of development are not sharply defined, a clear progression is noted in children's awareness of differences between spoken and written language, syntactic complexity, the functions and uses of writing, story elements and sense of story, and voice and audience.

Writing in the Primary Grades

Students' writing development increases steadily throughout the elementary school years, with early writing bearing close resemblance to spoken language (Hunt, 1970; Loban, 1976; O'Donnell, Griffin, & Norris, 1967). The content of kindergarten and first-grade children's writing is egocentric, focusing on the social self, family, friends, and their environment (Calkins, 1986). Dyson (2004) expresses the view, based on her extensive observations, that students are constantly in the process of negotiating meaning in the context of the classroom and that the "writing world" is only one of many worlds that students are actively constructing. Writing involves meaning negotiation with teacher and peers within the social context of the classroom.

How do young children construct their "writing world"?

Stories written by students in the primary grades move from simple descriptions to simple narratives characterized by chronology (Calkins, 1986). Gradual change occurs in story complexity, as students move from writing all they can remember about a topic to simple characterization and plot.

Writing in the Intermediate and Middle School Grades

During the intermediate and middle school grades, students demonstrate increased awareness of characterization and plot in their writing, develop the ability to revise, and use narration and description effectively (Calkins, 1986). As with oral language development, written language control becomes more complex. Students move from multiple sentences connected by *and* and *but* to sentences that combine these meanings into one sentence through subordination and embedding. Students also begin to think through a story idea before expressing it in writing. Many students in grades five through eight start to develop a writer's voice and an awareness of audience (Calkins, 1986).

How do older students elaborate their "writing schemata"?

Reading Acquisition in the Primary Grades

What do many children know about reading and writing by the time they enter kindergarten?

Language background knowledge is closely allied with reading acquisition, as students encounter print in picture books and storybooks and throughout their environment (e.g., traffic signs, fast-food logos, toothpaste containers). Many students develop a strong sense of print and meaning awareness based on their experiences with storybooks, comic strips, cereal boxes, television advertisements, and the like (Dyson, 2000). When they enter kindergarten or first grade, some children can print and read their own names, write the letters of the alphabet, and recognize a limited number of words that carry special meaning for them, such as I, my, birthday, while others are reading conventional print.

In kindergarten and grade 1, they extend their understanding of the relationship between print and its oral language counterparts. Refining the idea that print represents language—and, in turn, meaning—is critical to early reading acquisition. This concept enables beginning readers to make fairly accurate guesses at what some print says using the language knowledge they already possess. They come to understand that the print is arranged from left to right on the page and that words are represented by printed letters separated by blank spaces.

Phonics and Other Word Identification Skills in Grades K–3

word identification skills
procedures for deciphering or decoding printed words into oral utterances

phonics
a word identification skill based on letter-sound and letter pattern/ sound pattern relationships

phonemes
discrete units of sound

phonemic segmentation
the process of separating the units of sound, or phonemes, in spoken words; an important prerequisite for matching specific phonemes with specific letters in printed forms

As students progress through the primary grades, they learn to use phonics and other **word identification strategies** that help them decipher print into its oral counterparts and meanings. **Phonics** involves understanding letter-sound relationships (c-a-p, /kăp/), as well as larger letter pattern/sound pattern relationships, such as the final e marker that signals a different sound for the previous vowel (c-a-p-e, /kāp/). The opportunity to use word analysis skills in a natural language context, either oral or written, is critical at this stage (Ehri, 1997). Students integrate word identification skills into the sentence context and test deciphered words for meaning (e.g., "The wind was cold so the boy put the cap on his head" in contrast to "The man waved the red cape at the angry bull").

Recent study of the word identification process indicates that successful early readers learn to separate the units of sound, or **phonemes,** in spoken words to assist them in finding a match between the sounds and letters or letter patterns in printed words (Blachman, 2000; Bryant & Bradley, 1985; Ehri, 1997; Ehri & McCormick, 2004). This process of **phonemic segmentation** is a prerequisite for further word identification. As students move through the primary grades, they develop word identification generalizations that follow English spelling patterns and apply these generalizations in identifying new words—for example, vowel-consonant pattern (at), consonant-vowel-consonant pattern (mat), consonant-vowel-consonant-e pattern (mate) (McCormick, 2007).

Changes in language function also influence students' word identification process. For example, words such as hafta, gonna, and wanna, which are functional when used in informal conversational settings, are usually written as have to, going to, and want to (Lindsay, 1969). These more formal representations occur with some frequency in primary-grade texts as the language function shifts from an informal personal exchange ("Look out—he's gonna come down the slide.") to a more formal informational text form ("Look out—he is going to come down the slide.").

Students also learn to recognize many words automatically, quickly, and accurately during grades 1 to 3; thus their reading becomes more fluent since they do not have to pause to apply word identification strategies to those known words.

How do changes in language function influence students' word identification process?

How do young students comprehend stories?

Comprehension in Grades K–3

Children entering the early grades already have made enormous progress in developing concepts, word knowledge, syntactical or sentence structure knowledge, and story or text structure knowledge. Most use picture clues and can comprehend stories presented orally. Their understanding of story progresses from unorganized lists of information to sequences and simple narratives. Children also develop a sense of story chronology, using a chain of related events that reflects a general sense of story plot (McNeil, 1987). Their sense of story becomes further refined as they encounter narrative reading in their classrooms.

Story Reading in Grades K–3

As students gradually acquire word recognition and word identification abilities in the first and second grades, they shift from focus on correct identification of words to the use of sentence structure and story sense to create meaning. At this stage, children make predictions and develop meaning expectations using the background knowledge they have acquired in oral language interactions.

Reading interests of students in the primary grades include picture books, highly repetitive and predictable books, fairy tales, folktales, modern fantasy, and humor. Students at this level have special interest in story characters their own age and in family- and animal-oriented narratives. Individual students' interests may vary, however, depending on their background experiences and personality traits. A good way to determine interests is to administer an interest inventory. An appealing one for primary grade students is seen in Figure 2.6. One suitable for any grade level is found in Chapter 9.

Reading Development in the Intermediate and Middle School Grades

Students' knowledge of and familiarity with the syntactical, vocabulary, and text structure elements directly influence their success in comprehending text in the intermediate and middle school grades. Along with their background language knowledge, this knowledge of and familiarity with different text forms will be of critical importance in forming and testing predictions and constructing meaning from narrative and expository text. Both home and school environments exert strong influence on students' literacy acquisition by providing experiences in comprehending various text forms and in establishing the importance and value of literacy.

FIGURE 2.6

An Interest Inventory to Use with Primary Grade Students
The teacher may administer this orally, writing in students' answers. Or, slightly older students may write in their responses themselves.

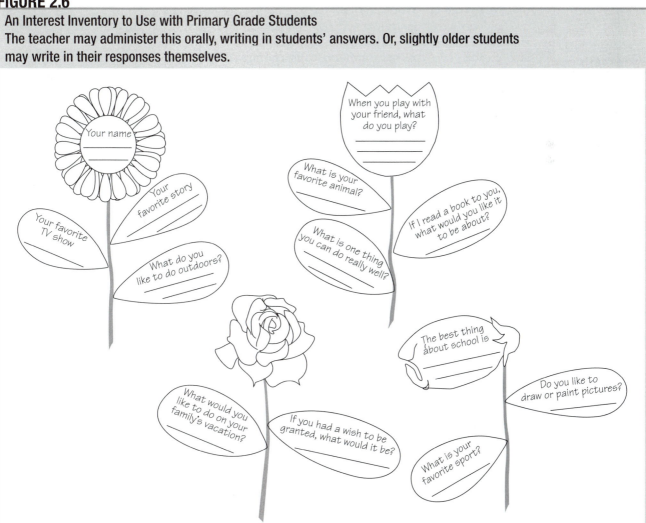

Word Identification in Grades 4–8

How do older
students achieve
reading fluency?

As students progress into the intermediate and middle school grades, they develop the ability to analyze larger words into pronounceable units, using syllable generalizations. This complex process requires visual analysis of the word to locate the pronounceable units (e.g., *bas-ket*, or *wo-ven*), then the blending of these units into the oral representation of the word. The use of meaningful context is important, as the word is tested for meaning in the context of the sentence and the text (e.g., "The beautiful *basket* was *woven* from reeds of many colors") (Ehri, 1991; Ehri & McCormick, 2004).

Many students have become fluent readers by grade 3 and have reached a stage of near-automatic word recognition, requiring little conscious thought. Some students, however, have not reached a high level of reading fluency even at grades 4 through 8. Because of the heavy reading requirements in these grades in content area textbooks, these students experience major reading difficulty unless given special attention (Kuhn & Stahl, 2004).

Story Comprehension in Grades 4–8

*How do older
students develop
complex story
comprehension
strategies?*

In the intermediate and middle school grades, many students develop a more refined sense of narrative, including expectations of characters, story setting, and problems and goals. They are interested in episodes forming the story plot, attempts to resolve problems, and story resolutions. A strong predictive sense develops in narrative reading.

Reading interests of students ages 9 through 13 focus on narrative adventure and fantasy, while their expository interests may include space exploration, computers, sports, and biography. At these ages, reading interests are strongly influenced by peers' recommendations and continued reading of a favorite author.

Students also begin to connect their purpose in reading to an appropriate reading strategy. For example, they may read to locate specific story information or to better understand the story plot. Readers also are more attuned to evaluating their strategy use through comprehension monitoring, a form of **metacognitive awareness**. Metacognitive awareness can be defined as knowledge individuals have about their own thinking. In regard to comprehension monitoring, after reading a particular passage, for example, a student might say to himself or herself (consciously or unconsciously) something like, "I didn't 'get' that. I'd better reread it." Teachers should encourage students to do this type of monitoring, and should introduce them to strategies for doing so in an efficient way. Chapter 5 will describe such strategies that you can teach your students (and use in your own reading and studying!).

**metacognitive
awareness**
awareness and
control of thought
processes; the ability to systematically apply
strategies and
monitor comprehension

Content Area Reading in Grades 4–8

The role of expository, that is, informational, reading in science, social studies, and other areas expands dramatically for students in the intermediate and middle school grades. Students develop an understanding of text organization that differs markedly from the familiar narrative text structure. Text organization patterns in **expository text** include description and information, cause and effect, problem and solution, and comparison and contrast. These new patterns become important organizational guides for intermediate grade and middle school readers as they recognize and use one or more of them in creating meaning from expository text. Understanding the new patterns, however, presents a challenge to many students (Meyer & Poon, 2004).

expository text
text, often found
in content areas,
whose organization pattern differs
from that of narrative text

Accompanying new text structures in content area reading in the intermediate and middle school grades is a rapidly expanding vocabulary load, especially in science, social studies, and mathematics. Students need to acquire words of Latin origin such as *vertebrate* and semantically related vocabulary items such as *mammal*, *bird*, *fish*, *amphibian*, and *reptile*. The teacher's role includes helping students connect these new concepts to their related background knowledge.

Factors That Influence Oral and Written Language Development

*What environmental factors
influence literacy
development?*

Many variables influence students' oral and written language development—for example, the opportunity for verbal interaction with adults. Cazden (1965) found in her studies with two- and three-year-olds that children's grammatical development increased when adults responded to their telegraphic speech using full grammatical sentences. In another classic study, higher-achieving first graders were found to have had more conversations with adults than had lower-achieving children (Milner, 1951). Other environmental variables that influence literacy development pertain to the home, community, culture, and school. Students' individual abilities, attitudes, and motivations to use language also influence their oral and written language development.

Motivation and Engagement in Literacy Learning

Students' motivation to learn language and to use it effectively at home and in school is social (Ruddell & Unrau, 2004b; Vygotsky, 1986). The desire to engage in social interaction is inherent in children from their earliest years. This desire provides high motivation for children to develop and use background knowledge to communicate with parents, siblings, and peers. In the family unit, language plays an important social interaction function, conveying a sense of belonging, love, and self-esteem (Mathewson, 2004). Central to the social desire to use language is the importance of "making meaning"—understanding and sharing ideas with other human beings. This social aspect of communication is critical in forming positive attitudes toward reading and literacy use.

This same motivation drives students as they enter school and encounter their teacher and other youngsters of similar age and interests. The social environment of the school, however, is distinctly different from that of the home for many students. Now the student is one of many, and the attention of the teacher is spread across the class. New rules are present, as demanded by the organization of the classroom. New language functions must be learned, such as how to engage in a discussion with small and large groups of peers. And new concepts are encountered, ranging from understanding the role of community helpers to developing reading and writing skills.

Highly effective teachers understand students' dual motivations: (1) the need to engage in social interaction and (2) the desire to communicate, to understand, and to make sense of school experiences (McIntyre et al. 2006). A central objective of instruction is to support and maintain these motivations in the classroom.

> What are students' motivations in literacy learning?

internal motivation
acting on the basis of a self-selected purpose or learning objective

external motivation
acting on the basis of a purpose or objective selected by another

Research and Evidence-Based Practice

Motivation and Engagement in Learning to Read

Did You Know?

- A prime motivation for a student's participation in reading instruction is the social dynamics of the classroom (Dyson, 1998; Guthrie et al., 1996).

- Literacy instruction is most effective when a student experiences a high degree of social and intellectual engagement with the new concept or topic (Brown, Pressley, Van Meter, & Schuder, 2004; Ruddell, 2004; Wang & Guthrie, 2004).

- A student's background knowledge is more easily activated and engaged when the objective and expected use of the literacy learning experience is clearly established and understood (Guthrie, Wigfield, Metsala, & Cox, 2004).

- A critical instructional role that the teacher must play is to ensure that the literacy learning objective is established whether this be **internally motivated** and student determined or **externally motivated** and teacher directed (Many, 2004; Ruddell & Unrau, 2004a).

- High motivation and positive attitudes toward reading are critical to a student's learning success (Mathewson, 2004).

- Highly effective teachers use motivating teaching strategies, understand where students are in the learning process, make material personally relevant, and use a process approach to intellectual discovery (Brown et al., 2004; Langer, 2004).

the Highly Effective Teacher

Learning the Functions of Language

An important aspect of language learning for children is the acquisition of a wide range of **language functions,** to serve different purposes in various environments. Speakers use language for a variety of functions, depending on their intentions. Types of functions include the following (Halliday, 1978):

> *Seven Types of Language Functions*

- *Instrumental* ("I want"): satisfying material needs
- *Regulatory* ("do as I tell you"): controlling the behavior of others
- *Interactional* ("me and you"): getting along with other people
- *Personal* ("here I come"): identifying and expressing the self through linguistic interaction
- *Heuristic* ("tell me why"): learning and exploring both internal and external reality
- *Imaginative* ("let's pretend"): creating a world of one's own
- *Informative* ("I've got something to tell you"): communicating content and new information

How do the different social environments of the home and the school affect literacy learning?

Flexibility and effectiveness develop as children acquire different language functions, learning what subjects are appropriate—how, when, and with whom to discuss them—and what speech patterns to use. Within the school setting, language appears to have at least three functions in the classroom: informal personal exchange, formal information exchange, and literary exchange (Ruddell, 2006); examples are shown in Table 2.2.

Students from language- and book-enriched backgrounds appear to achieve control over a wider range of language functions earlier than do students from less enriched backgrounds. Teachers must be sensitive to the influence of home and culture on students' language use and understand that homes and communities often are language- and literacy-rich in diverse ways and in ways that may differ from classroom norms (Moll, 1992; Purcell-Gates, 2000). Teachers' awareness of these differences enables them to plan learning experiences that support students' language and literacy achievements and help them develop effective control over language functions important to classroom success.

Influence of Home, Community, and Classroom

How can socio-economic differences influence literacy learning?

Students' attitudes and motivations with respect to literacy learning are forged in the home, community, and classroom, where many social and cultural factors affect the literacy learning environment (Au, 2000; Garcia, 2000). For example, socioeconomic differences in lifestyles and parenting styles affect students' social opportunities to acquire the language experience backgrounds that promote literacy. Studies have long shown that students more readily acquire such backgrounds in nonauthoritarian middle-class homes where parents encourage their children to be verbal and use questioning routines ("See the cow? What is the cow doing?") to give children information and teach concepts (Brown, 1973; Gallimore, Boggs, & Jordan, 1974; Ward, 1971). Other researchers (Clay, 1979; Durkin, 1966) have shown that children who have been read to before they enter school are more likely to succeed earlier in learning to read. These children already know story structure and the language of text.

TABLE 2.2

Classroom Language Functions

Function	Oral Form	Written Form	Intention
Informal Personal Exchange	Greetings Communication of feelings Control of others' behavior	Personal notes to friends Unedited written experiences Memos and directions	Interactional, personal Instrumental, interactional, personal Instrumental, regulatory
Formal Information Exchange	Classroom discussion Classroom lectures Public talks	Edited experience stories Edited reports School textbooks	Informative, heuristic Informative Informative
Literary Exchange	Drama and theater	Poetry, narrative, drama	Imaginative, informative, heuristic

FIGURE 2.7

Influences on Oral and Written Language Development

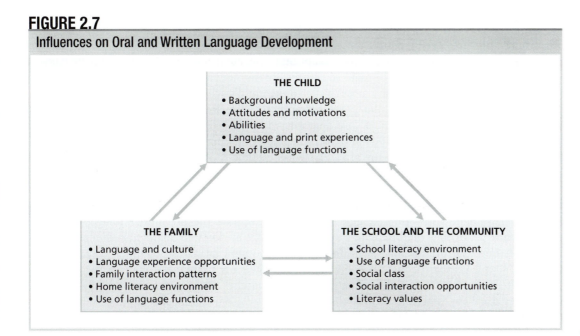

THE CHILD
- Background knowledge
- Attitudes and motivations
- Abilities
- Language and print experiences
- Use of language functions

THE FAMILY
- Language and culture
- Language experience opportunities
- Family interaction patterns
- Home literacy environment
- Use of language functions

THE SCHOOL AND THE COMMUNITY
- School literacy environment
- Use of language functions
- Social class
- Social interaction opportunities
- Literacy values

Heath (1982a, 1983) studied children from three different communities, which she labeled Gateway (a diverse urban community), Roadville (a white mill community), and Trackton (a black mill community). She found that children from these communities held vastly different attitudes toward written language and they transferred their community and home literacy patterns to learning behaviors at school. Gateway children received early initiation into books and experienced written and oral narratives, book-reading behaviors, and questioning routines. Roadville children were expected to accept the power of print through association with alphabet letters and workbook-like activities. Trackton children lived in a highly oral community where storytelling and verbal attention-getting skills were prized, and few children's books and book-reading activities were found in the home. Heath concluded that Gateway children entered school familiar not only with book-reading routines, but also with well-developed comprehension strategies.

> Where might you have lived in Heath's classic study?

Students' background language knowledge thus serves as the foundation for reading comprehension and literacy success. Their home, community, and school environments provide continual opportunities to form new concepts, develop understanding of story sense, build explanations of how things work, and see and use written language in many informal and formal settings. These opportunities serve to expand and enrich students' linguistic knowledge (Cazden, 1994) and have a strong influence on their literacy development. Figure 2.7 (see above) summarizes the sources of influence on oral and written language development.

> ➤ *Home, community, and school determine the structure of opportunity for literacy development.*

The Sociocognitive Theory of Language and Literacy Development

Experts have proposed theories about how individuals learn to read. Familiarity with theories can give teachers clues about what is best to do to help students accomplish the marvelous feat of becoming literate. One theory that presently is widely accepted is called a **sociocognitive theory.** The "socio" part of this word has the same root as "social" and refers to the importance of *interactions* with others to a student's learning—interactions with teachers, parents, peers—and with authors of textbooks through their writings. The "cognitive" part of the word refers to "cognition" or, in other words, *thinking*—an obvious part of learning. The basis for the sociocognitive theory of language and literacy development rests on the works of Jean Piaget (1967), Lev Vygotsky (1978), and schema theory (Rumelhart, 1981).

sociocognitive theory
a theory that social interactions and cognitive development jointly influence language and literacy learning

Piaget's Theory of Cognitive Development

According to Piaget (1967), people are born with tendencies toward (a) organization (arranging thoughts coherently) and (b) adaptation (adapting to the environment). Because of their tendencies toward *organization,* people create structures for thinking about things, called *schemes,* and these schemes often change over time. A very young child's scheme for the meaning of *reading,* for example, may change from believing this simply to be the turning of pages of a book, to (later in school) believing *reading* means sounding out words based on letter-sound associations, to (still later as an adult) the effortless understanding and enjoying of a novel.

➤ *According to Piaget, cognitive development occurs through mental processes of organization, adaptation, assimilation, accommodation, and equilibration.*

Because of their tendencies toward *adaptation,* people do two things—they assimilate and accommodate. People assimilate new learning into existing schemes, change their schemes to accommodate new learning that does not fit into existing ones, and even create new schemes to reorganize their thoughts and behaviors. For instance, young children with their first dinosaur picture book might apply their doggie scheme to assimilate the unfamiliar image, naming a dinosaur *doggie,* or they might create a new scheme such as *diney* to distinguish dinosaurs.

In what sense is learning a process of construction and reconstruction?

Piaget said that organizing, assimilating, and accommodating are complex balancing acts in which people search for mental balance between their own schemes for things versus information from the environment, which sometimes matches their preconceived schemes, but sometimes does not. There is mental conflict whenever a particular scheme does not work to make sense of the world (Piaget & Inhelder, 1969). Piaget used the term *equilibrium* to describe the changes in thinking and behavior that restore balance. People continually use assimilation and accommodation to maintain a balance between their understanding of the world and the information the world provides. Seen this way, learning is a process of developing (or building) meanings (often referred to as *meaning construction*) and sometimes later, *reconstruction.*

➤ *Piaget's Four Stages of Cognitive Development*

In addition to theorizing about these basic tendencies in our thinking, Piaget also hypothesized four general stages of cognitive development that relate to maturation. In the *sensorimotor stage* (ages birth to 2 years), children rely on their sensory experiences, especially taste and touch, for information about the world. In the *preoperational stage* (ages 2 to 7), children gradually develop use of language. Children's thinking is one-directional and egocentric in this stage. In the *concrete operations stage* (ages 7 to 11), children's egocentrism is reduced, and they can use logic and cause-and-effect reasoning in concrete problem situations. At the *formal operations stage* (ages 12 and higher), they are able to understand principles of the scientific method, use abstract language and concepts, see another person's point of view, and develop concerns about social issues and personal identity.

Practical Implications

developmentally appropriate practice matching instruction to children's stages of cognitive development

One educational concept based largely on Piaget's work is referred to as **developmentally appropriate practice.** This concept asserts that we should assess a student's developmental stage and present instruction accordingly. As just one example, in this view, implications for teaching reading and writing to *preoperational-stage* students might include using concrete props and visual aids to represent concepts; using actions as well as words when giving instructions; avoiding long explanations about others' points of view; inviting students to explain the meanings of their invented words; providing cut-out letters with which to build words and other hands-on practice with skills that serve as building blocks for reading comprehension; and providing a wide range of experiences to build a foundation for concept learning and language.

Vygotsky's Theory and the Zone of Proximal Development

Although Piaget focused on a learner's thinking in terms of stages of cognitive development linked to biological maturation, Vygotsky (1978), focused on thinking in relation to learning in social contexts, that is, in interactions with others. According to Vygotsky, students' concept development depends on adults, older students, and more competent peers who model new or more advanced thinking and behavior, which students then imitate or test. In this view, opportunities to interact verbally with other people are, thus, crucial to cognitive development. As one example, verbal interaction with competent speakers provides learners with chances to test hypotheses about word meanings.

Practical Implications

Vygotsky theorized that this type of learning best takes place in the individual's *zone of proximal development (ZPD)*, the area of challenge and opportunity between what a learner can do independently and what he or she can do with a little assistance at the right time in the learning process. Assistance might be in the form of instruction or in the form of opportunities for observation of others. For instance, a student can test whether he is making the right sounds for a letter during a phonics lesson by observing the teacher model the sound or after a classmate receives positive feedback from the teacher for successfully making that sound. In Vygotsky's theory, it is through the modeling of parents, teachers, and more competent peers that students come to understand. Instructional strategies with names like *cooperative learning, scaffolding support,* and *cross-age tutoring* are based on Vygotsky's concept of learning in the ZPD. You will learn how to use these important teaching strategies later in this text.

> *According to Vygotsky, cognitive development occurs through socially mediated processes in the learner's zone of proximal development.*

EVIDENCE-BASED PRACTICE

Schema Theory

Piaget's and Vygotsky's theories have helped establish a foundation for studying thinking. Expanding on Piaget's ideas of schemes (or schema), proponents of schema theory also incorporate into their hypotheses additional ideas from cognitive science about how thinking takes place in the brain (Rumelhart, 1981).

Schema theory suggests that schemata (plural for schema) can be thought of as "packets of information" in the brain that have been formed from direct personal experiences, as well as from learning as a result of interactions with others. Schemata usually contain what could be called *overarching* information—for example, the "reading a poem" schema for one person may include information that conveys thoughts of reading a literary form characterized by certain types of style, meter, and rhyme. In addition, the information packet (the schema) usually includes other knowledge subsumed under the overarching information, and this all appears to be arranged sequentially or hierarchically, like an outline. For example, below the general concept "reading a poem," there may be a more specific schema, such as reading an epic poem or reciting a haiku. If this particular person's brain were outlining his or her schema for "reading a poem," it might begin something like this:

schema theory
a theory that knowledge is organized, stored in memory, and used to make sense of the world

READING A POEM
I. Reading a literary form that has certain types of style, meter, and rhyme
   A. Reading an epic poem
   B. Reciting a haiku

Like Piaget's ideas, schema theorists view thinking, comprehension, and learning as "constructive" processes with the learner organizing, building, and reorganizing information—a process in which knowledge structures are formed in memory and new information is incorporated as a result of new experience. A related hypothesis, referred to as **cognitive flexibility**, accounts for our ability to be flexible in using the schemata from our previous experiences to solve new problems never before encountered, suggesting that we tailor old schemata to fit the new situation (Spiro et al, 2004).

What is another example of the hierarchical organization of schemata?

cognitive flexibility
a theory that prior knowledge can be adapted, or used in a novel and creative way, to solve new problems

Practical Implications

Schemata are the background information that learners have formed over time and use to construct new knowledge about their personal experiences and the world. New information is added to schemata by connecting that information to the overarching conceptual framework. (For example, one of your students might connect "performances" to his or her "reading a poem" schema after you have shown to your class a DVD of poetry readings by a children's author.)

Readers also use schemata (that is, their background information) to infer information that is not directly and explicitly provided in a text or in a real life situation. Helping students expand their background information is important to literacy development, and, indeed, to all learning. It is also critical to note that students learn best when new information is connected to old information they already have in their prior knowledge base. Highly effective teachers consider many ways to make these connections throughout the school day.

> *Background knowledge is key to comprehension.*

Sociocognitive Theory: A Synthesis

The sociocognitve theory of language and literacy learning draws upon the preceding theories to explain students' development of increasingly complex language and reading/writing skills. This theory provides practical implications for teachers. Sociocognitive theory contends that learning is influenced by:

1. intellectual development
2. specific types of social interactions (from which students can learn)
3. the learner's store of background experiences.

Knowing this, highly effective teachers understand the importance of matching reading and writing instruction to the student's intellectual development, and in doing so, not only consider (a) what is easy for a student to do and (b) what is too hard for real learning to occur, but also importantly, (c) what the student could do with the interaction and assistance of others.

A related, important principle of sociocognitive theory is that real learning involves much more than a teacher simply going before a class and conveying information that he or she knows to students who do not know that information. Interactions with peers (for example, through cooperative learning activities), as well as interactions with teachers (for example, so the teacher can model good responses and strategies), all facilitate learning. In fact, the highly effective teacher keeps in mind the several contributors to learning that are illustrated in Figure 2.8: interactions among individual readers, the teacher, the students in the classroom as a whole, and the information conveyed by the author of a text, which can all contribute to the learning of information or skills. Note that Figure 2.8 also includes the phrase "Meaning Negotiation." That may be a new vocabulary term for you. This term is one often used by experts on literacy learning. **Meaning negotiation** is defined as an interactive process which integrates the background knowledge of the teacher, the student, and the classroom community to reach a shared understanding of a text (or classroom event).

In addition, according to sociocognitive theory, planning daily instruction to help students enlarge their fund of background information also is important to literacy learning (for example,

---

the ★ Highly Effective Teacher ★

meaning negotiation
an interactive process which integrates the background knowledge of the teacher, the student, and the classroom community to reach a shared understanding of a text (or classroom event)

FIGURE 2.8

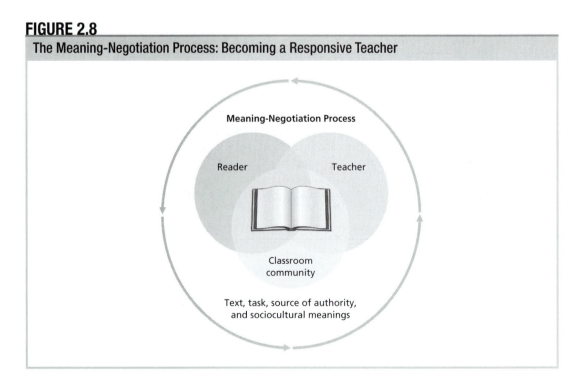

The Meaning-Negotiation Process: Becoming a Responsive Teacher

Meaning-Negotiation Process

Reader   Teacher

Classroom community

Text, task, source of authority, and sociocultural meanings

From Ruddell, Robert B., & Unrau, Norman J. (2004b). The role of responsive teaching in reader motivation. *Theoretical Models and Processes of Reading,* Robert B. Ruddell and Norman Unrau (Eds.). Newark, DE: International Reading Association. Copyright © 2004 by the International Reading Association. Adapted with permission.

important to reading comprehension, word identification, development of meaning vocabulary, and to other reading related areas, as well). Furthermore, sensitive teachers are aware that background experiences not only shape a student's stored knowledge, but also have *affective* consequences, that is, consequences that influence feelings or emotions. As two examples of the latter, prior experiences can (a) affect motivation to read, or, (b) cause a student to interpret text in a particular way because of an emotional response to its content. Individual students may understand certain things differently if they have different backgrounds, including cultural backgrounds. During their planning for a lesson, highly effective teachers take into account the differences in knowledge levels and cultural beliefs that exist in a classroom.

The sociocognitive theory of learning underlies many of the teaching ideas in this book. A graphic summary of the sociocognitive theory of language and literacy development, and the theories that support it, is found in Figure 2.9 (S. McCormick, personal communication, April 30, 2000). Take a moment to read over this figure, which may simplify for you the rather complex information found in the preceding section.

FIGURE 2.9

Instructional Implications from the Sociocognitive Theory of Language and Literacy Development

Schema Theory
- Schemata are knowledge structures in memory that help organize our experiences.
- Children experience things, store information about this in their brains, and later use this background knowledge to understand new things.

A SOCIOCOGNITIVE THEORY OF READING DEVELOPMENT

Learning is influenced by:
1. Intellectual development.
2. Specific types of social interactions.
3. Background knowledge.

INSTRUCTIONAL IMPLICATIONS

1. It is important that instruction be matched to a child's cognitive development.
2. We must be aware not only of what is easy for a child to learn and what is too hard but also—most importantly—of what the child likely could do with teacher or peer assistance.
3. Cooperative learning among students is important.
4. Teacher modeling of responses can greatly facilitate learning.
5. Providing opportunities for students to build background knowledge about a wide array of topics helps them understand what they read (i.e., aids their reading comprehension).

Piaget's Theory of Cognitive Development
- Children create structures (schemata) for thinking about things.
- These structures change throughout development.
- Intellectual development occurs in stages.

Vygotsky's Theory
- Learning occurs through interactions with adults and peers.
- Assistance and instruction needs to be geared to the child's zone of proximal development (ZPD).

the Highly Effective Teacher

on Technology and Understanding Meaning Making

1. Identify one or two ideas from this chapter that you would like to explore in greater detail. Identify several words that describe this idea and Google them in an Internet search. Then follow your interest, e.g., reading motivation, reading comprehension, children's oral language development, invented spelling, or other Chapter 2 topics. Create one or two questions from your search for follow-up discussion with your classmates and professor.

2. For a wide range of highly motivating lesson plans or student activities for literacy development go to the following Web site: **www.reading.org/** and click on "Teaching Tools," followed by "Lesson Plans for K–12" or "Student Materials."

3. You may want to do further reading on social constructivism and the works of Vygotsky and others. The following Web site is a good place to start: **www.stemnet. nf.ca/~elmurphy/emurphy/cle.html.** Or to enhance your understanding of the readings in this chapter, you may want to visit the Jean Piaget Society Web site at **www.piaget.org.**

4. The following book will help you gain insight on translating theory to practice through the use of technology: *Teaching with the Internet: Lessons from the Classroom,* by D. J. Leu and D. D. Leu. (2000) Norwood, Massachusetts: Christopher-Gordon.

5. The following Web sites give examples of how technology and literacy have been used together on the Internet: **www.kn.pacbell. com/wired/BHM/AfroAm.html, www. thirteen.org/wnetschool/origlessons/ savage/index.html, www.worldtrek.org/ odyssey/teachers/perulessons.html, www.education-world.com/a_curr/ curr195.shtml.**

the Highly Effective Teacher

Helping Students Develop Expert Reader Competencies

One of your most important roles as a highly effective teacher is to assist students in the development of rapid word recognition/identification and meaning-construction strategies. You are central in defining instructional objectives with concern for motivation and expected outcomes. You will communicate objectives to the students using your own background knowledge, teaching strategies, and attitudes toward both the content and individual students.

The students, in turn, will interpret the objectives, including the expected outcomes, and have objectives and expectations of their own. Students will use this information to activate their background knowledge schemata. Your instruction must facilitate this process to ensure that activated prior knowledge is linked to text content and discussion as students begin the meaning-construction process. Negotiating meaning between you, the students, and the text is a vital aspect of teaching (Hall, 2006). You direct the instructional experience. And you provide instructional monitoring and feedback for the students through discussion.

To ensure students' successful development of the meaning-construction process, you must take into account student characteristics, instructional goals, and learning resources as you negotiate meaning through interaction with your students. The dynamics of this process are shown in the figure titled Highly Effective Teacher: Interactions with Students in the Meaning-Construction–Meaning-Negotiation Process (see page 46).

The reading process thus involves the following elements:

➤ *The Reading Comprehension Process*

- Purposeful reading guided by internally and externally motivated objectives and expected use ("the will")

- Mobilization of attitudes and values related to the text content and expected use of the constructed meaning ("the use")
- Activation of background knowledge content, including word recognition/identification and vocabulary, syntactic, and story structure schemata ("the what")
- Activation of background knowledge processing strategies for effective word reading and meaning construction ("the how-to")
- Activation of conditional knowledge to determine when to apply the word recognition/identification, background knowledge, and processing strategies ("the when")
- Activation of monitoring strategies to check the word recognition and meaning construction as directed by the objective ("the check")
- Interactive use of these processes to construct meaning

In an expert reader, these processes require little conscious thought. Recommendations for establishing these processes in elementary and middle school students are presented in Figure 2.10.

FIGURE 2.10

Teaching Recommendations for Literacy Development

1. Build instruction on what the student already knows about oral language, reading, and writing. Focus on meaningful experiences and meaningful language rather than solely on isolated skill development.
2. Respect the language the student brings to school, and use it as a base for language and literacy activities.
3. Ensure feelings of success for all students, helping them to see themselves as people who enjoy exploring both oral and written language.
4. Provide reading experiences as an integrated part of the communication process, which includes speaking, listening, and writing, as well as art, math, and music.
5. For young students, encourage students' first attempts at writing, without concern for the proper formation of letters or correct conventional spelling.
6. Encourage risk-taking in first attempts at reading and writing, and accept what appear to be errors as part of students' natural growth and development.
7. Use reading materials that are familiar or predictable, such as well-known stories, as they provide students with a sense of control and confidence in their ability to learn.
8. Present a model for students to emulate. In the classroom, teachers should use language appropriately, listen and respond to students' talk, and engage in their own reading and writing.
9. Take time regularly to read to students, no matter their age, from a wide variety of poetry, fiction, and nonfiction.
10. Provide time regularly for students' independent reading and writing.
11. Foster students' affective and cognitive development by providing them with opportunities to communicate what they know, think, and feel.
12. Use developmentally and culturally appropriate procedures for evaluation, ones that are based on the objectives of the program and that consider each student's total development.
13. Make parents aware of the reasons for a broader language program at school, and provide them with ideas for activities to carry out at home.
14. Alert parents to the limitations of formal assessments and standardized tests of pre–first graders' reading and writing skills.
15. Encourage students to be active participants in the learning process rather than passive recipients by using activities that allow for experimentation with talking, listening, writing, and reading.

"Recommendations" from *Literacy Development and Early Childhood (Preschool through Grade 3)*. (1987). A joint statement prepared by the Early Childhood and Literacy Development Committee of the International Reading Association.

Summary and Classroom Applications

double entry journal

Reread your notes on your memories of learning to read and early experiences with children's literature. What reading competencies have you developed since that time? How do your early experiences reflect the model of reading presented in this chapter?

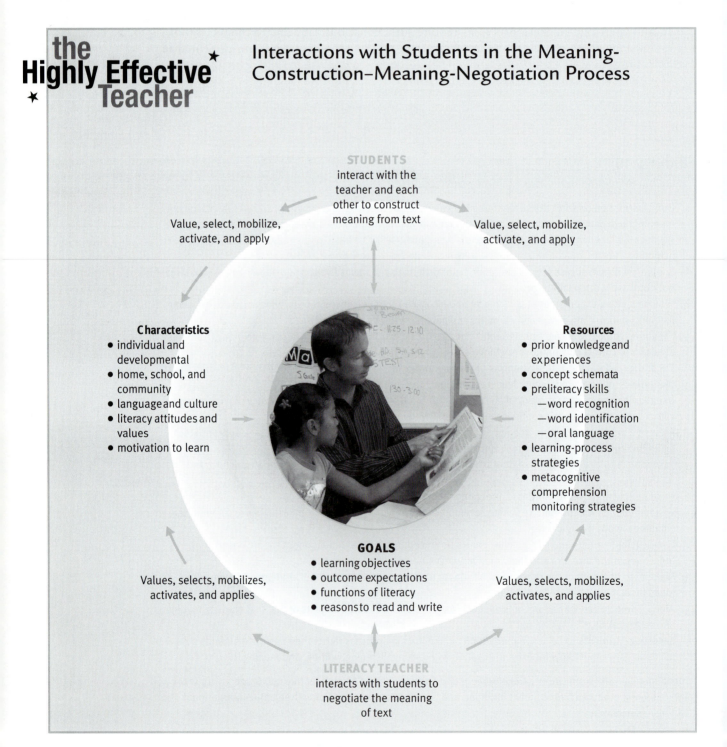

the Highly Effective★ ★ Teacher

Interactions with Students in the Meaning-Construction–Meaning-Negotiation Process

STUDENTS
interact with the teacher and each other to construct meaning from text

Value, select, mobilize, activate, and apply

Value, select, mobilize, activate, and apply

Characteristics
- individual and developmental
- home, school, and community
- language and culture
- literacy attitudes and values
- motivation to learn

Resources
- prior knowledge and experiences
- concept schemata
- preliteracy skills
  - word recognition
  - word identification
  - oral language
- learning-process strategies
- metacognitive comprehension monitoring strategies

GOALS
- learning objectives
- outcome expectations
- functions of literacy
- reasons to read and write

Values, selects, mobilizes, activates, and applies

Values, selects, mobilizes, activates, and applies

LITERACY TEACHER
interacts with students to negotiate the meaning of text

Chapter Summary

Expert reader competencies range from word recognition/identification and use of meaning clues to hypothesis building and sophisticated comprehension strategies. Our understanding of the reading process and its connection to language development has increased significantly over the past four decades.

By age 6, most children have developed a high level of expertise in oral language, including mastery of phonology, grammar, syntax, and enormous vocabulary growth. Children's productions of oral language are systematic and organized even when overgeneralizations create language forms that do not conform to conventional English.

Emergent literacy encompasses children's movement from pictorial representations of meaning through writing and reading stages associated with the primary, intermediate, and middle school grades. Initially, children make little distinction between oral language and written expression. Later, students' written language forms take into account characterization, story plot, and—eventually—a writer's voice and awareness of audience.

Reading acquisition starts with the early understanding that print represents language and meaning. Primary-grade instruction develops phonemic awareness and word identification strategies. Comprehension skills and reading interests also develop at this time. The driving force behind much of this extraordinary growth is the need and strong desire to construct meaning—to make sense of the world.

Influences on oral and written language development include students' motivation to learn and the operation of the learning functions of language. Students' language acquisition and literacy development also are strongly influenced by opportunities for interaction with adults. Their understanding of various language functions and their attitudes toward literacy are shaped by social and cultural factors in the home, community, and classroom. Congruence between home and school language and literacy experiences increases students' opportunities for success in learning to read and write.

The sociocognitive theory attempts to explain how both language learning and concept development are acquired in social settings as children interact with their peers and adults. The work of Jean Piaget and L. S. Vygotsky and the subsequent schema theory provide a foundation for our understanding of the acquisition of concepts, language, and literacy growth in relation to social and cognitive development.

Students are active participants in their own language and literacy development. They are expert hypothesis testers and use their experiences in their social world (home, community, and school) to construct meaning. A critical role played by the teacher is to facilitate students' meaning-construction process by activating background knowledge, introducing monitoring strategies, and developing expert reader competencies. The reading comprehension process involves purposeful meaning construction and meaning negotiation, which are guided by the students' and teacher's objectives and intended use.

Professional Standards and
Foundational Knowledge

Figure 2.11 (page 48) focuses on Standard 1, Foundational Knowledge, from the *Standards for Reading Professionals—Revised 2003* (International Reading Association, 2004) and identifies instructional knowledge critical to the understanding of the reading and writing process. You can see the complete list of Standards for Reading Professionals in Appendix C.

Applications: Bridges to the Classroom

1. Select a favorite cartoon, such as *Dennis the Menace* by Hank Ketcham or *The Far Side* by Gary Larson, and use your understanding of schema theory to explain its humor. Share your ideas with a class partner. How can background knowledge schemata help explain the difficulty that students from a different culture may have in understanding American humor?

2. Reread "The Wimmy Wuggen and the Moggy Tor" and the four comprehension questions at the beginning of this

chapter. Briefly explain how you would use this passage with students to activate background knowledge, build higher-level thinking, and motivate the study of vocabulary. Discuss your responses with a group of classmates.

3. Request a morning or an afternoon observation of an elementary or middle school teacher and his or her students in a classroom at your favorite grade level. Identify and briefly describe examples of teacher-student or student-student interactions that illustrate students' strong motivations to

FIGURE 2.11

Professional Standard 1: Foundational Knowledge Essential for Understanding Meaning Making and the Reading and Writing Process Instruction

Professional Standard	Example
1. Knowledge of psychological, sociological, and linguistic foundations of reading and comprehension process	**Element 1.1** Understands the application of sociocognitive theory of language and literacy development, including the work of Piaget, Vygotsky, and schema theory, to the reading instruction that serves to explain the development of reading comprehension.
2. Knowledge of reading research and histories of reading	**Element 1.2** Can describe the development of reading acquisition in the primary, intermediate, and middle school grades and the research that supports this development.
3. Demonstrate knowledge of language development and reading acquisition and the variations related to cultural and linguistic diversity	**Element 1.3** Can describe the acquisition of phonology, grammar, syntax, and vocabulary and the connection between these linguistic factors, home environment, and reading acquisition.
4. Demonstrate knowledge of the major components of reading and how they are integrated in fluent reading	**Element 1.4** Understands how phonemic segmentation, word identification, vocabulary, background knowledge, motivation, and comprehension all contribute to reading fluency and expert reader competencies.

Part 2 from IRA. (2004). Professional Standards and Ethics Committee, International Reading Association. *Standards for reading professionals—revised 2003*. Reprinted with permission of the International Reading Association. All rights reserved.

(1) engage in social interaction and (2) communicate, understand, and make sense of their classroom experiences. How can instruction be designed to use these motivations to foster students' literacy development?

4. Based on the discussion in this chapter and your personal insights, write a brief (one to two pages) definition of the reading process. Be sure to account for the role of comprehension as well as attitudes and motivation in your definition. After completing your definition, share your key ideas with a class partner. Keep your definition in your notebook and add new ideas to it as you progress through your readings and class discussions.

Additional Research and Practice

1. Squires, D., & Bliss, T. (2004). Teacher visions: Navigating beliefs about literacy learning. *The Reading Teacher 57* (8), 756–763.

   This insightful article describes how teacher beliefs about reading instruction influence classroom instruction and encourages the reader to use visioning to help surface deeply held instructional beliefs and clarify these to work toward effective instructional practice. (Practice)

2. Waldbart, A., Meyers, B., & Meyers, J. (2006). Invitations to families in an early literacy support program. *The Reading Teacher,* 59, 774–785.

   This discussion describes the development of an early literacy support program which bridges home and school for low-income families. Parents and family members of the students are directly involved in the development of emergent literacy skills. The importance of teacher patience and persistence is highlighted in this article. (Practice)

3. Shanahan, T., & Neuman, S. B. (1997). Literacy research that makes a difference. *Reading Research Quarterly,* 32 (2), 202–210.

   This discussion identifies research studies that have most influenced literacy instruction—ranging from reading comprehension to story grammar—during the last half of the twentieth century. (Research)

Understanding Early Reading and Writing Development

*My heart is singing for joy this morning. A miracle has happened!
The light of understanding has shone upon my little pupil's mind,
and behold, all things are changed!*

Annie Sullivan (1866–1936),
American teacher of the deaf, including Helen Keller

*Language is a wonder, of course, but learning is what language
allows us to do, and learning is what we need most as a species.*

Lewis Thomas (1913–1993),
American physician

On a Tuesday morning in early September, Jenny Sirell (T) engaged the students (S) in her new kindergarten class in a discussion about "what good readers do." Let's join their conversation.

T: What do you think makes someone a good reader?

S1: They know how to read the words, and they read a lot.

S2: They tell funny stories.

S3: They look at the words and sound them out.

S4: They think about reading.

T: How?

S4: I don't know—they just think about the story they're reading and stuff.

T: Do you know a good reader?

S1: My mom's a good reader. She reads all the time . . . so does my dad.

T: So good readers read a lot! What do they read?

S1: I don't know—stuff like newspapers, magazines . . .

S5: My dad always reads in the bathroom.

T: How do you think good readers learned to read?

S4: They went to kindergarten.

T: Yes, that's true, but what do you think they learned in kindergarten when it came to reading? [Begins listing children's ideas on chart paper.]

S5: They learned how to sound out words.

T: What else?

S1: They looked at the pictures.

S4: They guessed. They made up a story.

T: Good—anything else?

S2: They read the story over 'til they memorized it.

S3: They learned their stories from their moms and dads and practiced.

T: Wow! You guys know a lot about what it takes to be a good reader. Now, I have another idea. What do you think your brain is doing when you read? I mean, is it sending messages to your body? Are your eyes doing something? Are your lips doing something? Are your ears doing something? Is your nose doing something? [Children laugh.] Are your hands doing something?

S1:   Well, your eyes are looking at the words so your brain is saying, "Hey, these are words." And your lips are moving, telling your brain what the words are, and your ears are listening to the words.

T: Do your hands move?

S3:   Yeah, to turn the page, silly.

T: Oh, so your brain tells your hands when to turn the page?

S3:   Yeah.

S5:   Sometimes I point at the words I say when I read.

T: Why?

S5:   'Cause that way I remember what word I'm on.

T: So it sounds like your brain is doing a lot of important things. What I'd like you to do is draw a picture of your brain reading. Think of all the things that you just told me it takes to be a good reader and all the things your brain does while you're reading. You can draw pictures inside your brain or write words if your pictures aren't saying enough.

(From J. Sirell. Reprinted by permission.)

In this delightful interchange, not only did Jenny's students learn from one another, but also Jenny learned about the students' perceptions of the reading process and had the opportunity to extend these perceptions. Children come to school expecting to become literate. This expectation is so universal that if you were to poll a group of children getting ready to start school, chances are the first thing they would tell you they were going to do when they got to school was "learn to read." In fact, many children expect to become fully literate on their first day of school.

double entry journal

Working with a partner, brainstorm and prioritize a list of concepts that you believe students need to know to learn to read.

Chapter Objectives

After reading and discussing this chapter, you will be able to:

- specify general principals for highly effective teaching in any classroom setting.
- identify seven optimal conditions for literacy learning in the classroom.
- understand basic early reading and writing concepts and know how to develop these using key instructional strategies.
- organize and manage instruction in the early literacy classroom.
- effectively assess and record students' progress.

General Principles for Highly Effective Teaching

Most of Chapter 3 is devoted to identifying many *specific* ideas you can use in your own classroom for helping students who are in early stages of reading and writing development. There are, however, some very critical *general* ideas that you need to consider, first—ideas that can help you to be a highly effective teacher in any type of literacy instruction. These ideas are crucial whether students are beginning readers, in the mid-level stages of learning to read and write, or at more advanced levels (as is typical for many middle school students, for example). In fact, these ideas are important to any kind of teaching (for instance, teaching math, or social studies, or home economics or science).

Several general principles for highly effective teaching were introduced in Chapter 2: for example, the importance of taking into account students' (a) background knowledge, (b) zone of proximal development, and (c) interactions with others (teachers, peers, parents, experts through their writing in textbooks) in order for the most favorable learning environment to exist. Other principles that should be considered in all instructional settings are listed in Figure 3.1. As a prospective teacher these principles are important for you to know. Following Figure 3.1 is an equally important section of special interest to the teacher of reading on optimal teaching/learning conditions to ensure high-quality literacy learning.

FIGURE 3.1

Instructional Recommendations for Highly Effective Teaching

1. Develop clear purposes and instructional plans.
2. Emphasize activation and use of students' prior beliefs, knowledge, and experiences.
3. Incorporate higher-level thinking questions, questioning strategies, and sensitivity to students' responses in conducting instruction.
4. Orchestrate instruction using a problem-solving approach and encourage intellectual discovery by posing, exploring, and resolving problems.
5. Monitor students' thinking, use verbal feedback, and ask subsequent questions that encourage active thinking.
6. Understand the importance of text, task, source of authority, and sociocultural meanings in negotiating and constructing meaning.
7. Involve students in meaning negotiation based on the text by encouraging interaction between the students, yourself as teacher, and the classroom community of learners.
8. Share teacher authority in discussions to encourage student thinking, responsibility, interaction, and ownership of ideas.
9. Understand the importance of using internal reader motivation to enhance student interest and authentic meaning construction.
10. Develop sensitivity to individual student needs, motivations, and aptitudes, but hold appropriate and high expectations for learning.

Optimal Conditions for Literacy Learning

Two Australian language educators, Cambourne and Turbill (1987), have identified seven optimal conditions for literacy learning. According to Cambourne and Turbill, classrooms that provide optimal conditions for learning are those in which the following factors exist:

1. *Students are immersed in language.* Written text is everywhere—on signs and bulletin boards and in books, magazines, and papers. Their drawing and writing are displayed on classroom bulletin boards. The classroom day is filled with story-reading time, sharing time, and many other language-rich activities.

2. *Students and teachers are actively involved in meaningful demonstrations of language in action.* The classroom is filled with the buzz of conversations as work and play progress. Classroom activities and events are alive with working noise. Teachers and students alike are active questioners, and teachers use questions to activate background knowledge and encourage predictions, both during and after reading.

3. *Language is used for real-life purposes,* providing opportunities for children to use literacy for personal, social, and school needs. Cooperative planning of class events (a class birthday party or field trip), recording plans on wall charts, and following up with necessary action are commonplace. Students (and teachers) keep diaries, logs, and journals. Calendars, weather records, seating charts, and all manner of other useful documents and charts are displayed throughout the room.

4. *Students assume responsibility for their own learning.* Students have many opportunities to work cooperatively in creating, planning, and carrying out both large and small projects; self-selecting books they want to read and topics they want to write about; and participating in classroom centers. Students are personally accountable for using free time productively.

5. *Adults hold expectations that all students will learn.* The prevailing attitude is that everyone will succeed. Teachers—and other adults in the classroom and school—set clear expectations for students' accomplishments and provide a supportive environment in which they can meet these expectations.

6. *Approximation is encouraged,* for perfection is not the issue here. Language learners of all ages need positive reinforcement as they acquire more sophisticated language forms and achieve literacy. For example, in storytelling teachers encourage children to predict story outcomes and to revise and refine their predictions as the story progresses. This process

> *Optimal Conditions for Literacy Learning*

provides a psychologically safe setting for children to approximate and to keep trying with planned instructional support. Approximations in such an environment are not wrong; they are a step toward being right.

7. *Ongoing feedback is given to the learner.* Language learners need lots of feedback in order to evaluate their progress, draw new or revised conclusions, and move forward. Students in classrooms need feedback from teachers, other adults, and their peers.

These seven conditions for literacy instruction define the optimal environment for reading and writing classrooms, and they guide learning events in those classrooms.

the ★ **Highly Effective Teacher** ★

➤ *Stages in the Development of the Linguistic Repertoire*

Early Reading Development

The study of young students' early literacy experiences has yielded extraordinary insights into how they become literate (Mansell, Evans, & Manilton-Hulak, 2005). Sulzby (1985), for example, focused on young students' early reading of favorite storybooks. Sulzby's findings demonstrate that they progress from picture reading to independent reading. Sulzby conceptualizes these reading patterns as the "linguistic repertoire" that students acquire and move in and out of on their way toward conventional reading, refining old patterns and adding new ones in the process. This repertoire includes picture-governed story attempts, in which young students treat the picture as the main source of the story meaning, and print-governed story attempts, in which they consider the printed language as the story's meaning source. Figure 3.2 (page 53) shows the variety of patterns that children use on their way to conventional reading.

In her discussion of conventional reading, Sulzby (1985) makes the following comment:

> [Children] also seem to show a particular knack for mimicry of a whole activity, of "acting as if" they were accomplished performers when clearly they still lack certain skills or accomplishments of their elders. They seem to use their social sense of what linguistic usages and forms "work" in a particular social context. (p. 284)

Thus, our observations of children must take into account their ability to "act as if" and not overestimate their literacy abilities. At the same time, "acting as if" can be an effective support strategy or scaffolding for acquiring new skills and behaviors.

Instructional Concepts and Strategies for Early Reading and Writing

➤ *Children use pictures and text to create meaning as they move toward conventional reading.*

The linguistic (that is, language) repertoire proposed by Sulzby (1985) suggests that children use pictures and text to create meaning as they move toward conventional reading. This process is greatly enhanced by home and school learning environments where they have opportunities to participate in storytelling and story reading and where adults and older siblings demonstrate a strong interest in and place value on reading and literacy use (Purcell-Gates, 1988; Soderbergh, 1977). For example, Durkin (1966) found in her classic research on children who read before they entered school that between 47 and 83 percent of their parents reported that reading materials, paper, pencils, and chalkboards were readily available at home. By contrast, only 14 to 23 percent of parents of preschool-age nonreaders reported that such materials were available in the home. A logical connection is found between early picture and print experiences and reading as children draw pictures, label and title their pictures, and learn to write their own names, the alphabet, and beginning stories.

➤ *Reading Conventions and Concept*

Children entering kindergarten vary greatly in their understanding of the "conventions of reading," as well as the "arbitrary rules that govern the act of reading (e.g., knowing that one reads from left to right [in English], that punctuation is important, and what spaces between letters mean)" (Mason, 1984, p. 511). There is significant variation in young students' understanding of labels and concepts used in reading instruction. Research on young students' knowledge about printed text—including alphabet knowledge, letter-name identification, the ability to use

FIGURE 3.2

Sulzby Classification Scheme: Storybook Reading for Preschool and Kindergarten Children

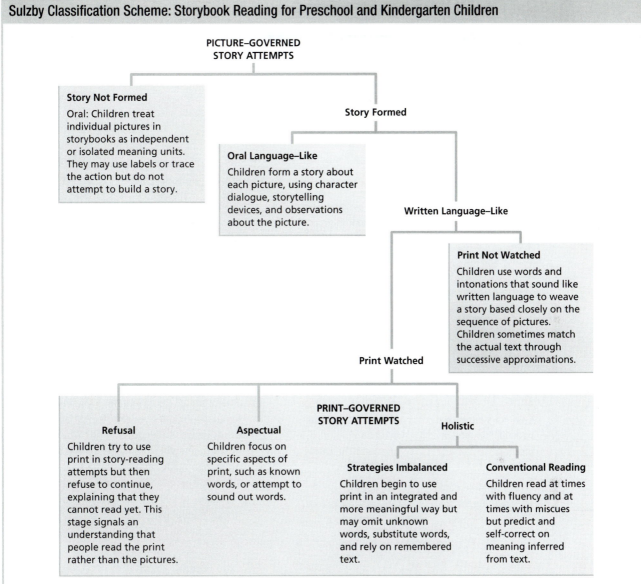

rhyming words, and knowledge of locational terms such as *top* and *bottom*—reveals marked growth during the kindergarten year (Hardy, Stennett, & Smythe, 1974).

Students of this age also need to develop concepts such as syllable, word, and sentence. Because of the dominance of oral language in the child's life, a spoken sentence, for example, may represent a single meaning unit in the child's mind—in effect, one long word.

Just as important are their understandings about what constitutes literate acts. Classic studies (Johns, 1972; Kita, 1979; Reid, 1966) have shown that many young students associate reading solely with school or with doing workbook exercises, sounding out words, or reading aloud. Other children think meaning resides in pictures; still others simply don't know what reading is about. Figure 3.3 lists six instructional goals for developing children's literacy awareness.

Strategies in Use
Identifying Children's Language Repertoires

From the time Jennifer was a year old, she was read to regularly by her mother. At three years, three months of age, Jennifer was visited by a researcher (R), who asked her to read *Are You My Mother?* (Eastman, 1967), a book that had been read to her many times. In an enthusiastic manner and with a reading intonation, she read the entire book, a portion of which follows:

Jennifer	Text
Out pop the baby birdie.	Out came the baby bird.
He says, "Where is my mother?" [Aside to R] He's looking for it.	"Where is my mother?" he said. He looked for her.
Looked up; did not see her.	He looked up. He did not see her.
And he looked down; he didn't see it.	He looked down. He did not see her.
So he said he's gonna go look for her.	"I will go and look for her," he said.
Came to a kitten and he said, "Are you my mother?"	He came to a kitten. "Are you my mother?" he said to the kitten.
"N . . ." and he didn't say anything. He just looked and looked.	The kitten just looked and looked. It did not say a thing.

Then he came to a hen and he said, "Are you my mother?" "No."

The kitten was not his mother, so he went on. Then he came to a hen. "Are you my mother?" he said to the hen. "No," said the hen.

From Teale, William H. & Sulzby, Elizabeth. (1989). Emergent literacy: New perspectives. *Emerging Literacy: Young Children Learn to Read and Write,* Dorothy S. Strickland and Lesley Mandel Morrow (Eds.). Copyright © 1989 by William H. Teale and the International Reading Association.

CRITICAL THINKING

1. Examine Jennifer's responses to the two portions of *Are You My Mother?* In terms of Sulzby's categories (see Figure 3.2), describe Jennifer's linguistic repertoire as she responds to the text. What stage of development does she exhibit?
2. Briefly speculate on Jennifer's reading and language experiences at home. What experiences would you expect to find? Why?
3. What do Jennifer's responses to text tell you about her picture and print awareness?
4. What do her responses to text reveal about her ability to self-correct and her comprehension development?

FIGURE 3.3

Six Instructional Goals for Early Literacy Instruction

➤ *Instructional Goals for Developing Literacy Awareness*

1. Develop children's understanding of the conventions of reading, the language of instruction, concepts about literacy, and group participation conventions that will enable them to participate effectively in individual and group instructional activities.
2. Develop children's awareness and understanding of picture and print concepts that form the basis for early reading and writing.
3. Develop children's phonemic awareness (the understanding that words are composed of sounds) and their knowledge of phonemic segmentation (the understanding of how sounds are separated and come together in words), which are important steps in their grasping the relationship between sounds and letters.
4. Develop children's sense of observing, recording, and writing with the aim of building understanding of how thoughts and experiences can be represented in print.
5. Develop children's sense of story and narrative features, which will serve as the basis for their understanding of narrative text.
6. Develop positive attitudes in children toward early reading and writing through shared book and story experiences.

Teaching Conventions of Reading

Specific language of instruction and group-participation concepts that need to be developed in kindergarten and first grade include the following:

- *Direction words,* such as *left* and *right, top* and *bottom, over* and *under, into* and *out of,* and *beside* and *between*
- *Ordering words,* such as *front* and *back; beginning, middle,* and *end;* and *first, second,* and *third*
- *Color words,* such as *red, green, orange, yellow, blue, black,* and *white,* and *geometric shape words,* such as *circle, square, triangle,* and *rectangle*
- *Instructional directions,* such as "make a circle around," "draw a line under," and "draw a picture of"
- *Feeling- and sensory-based words,* such as *happy* and *sad, sweet* and *sour, soft* and *rough, bright* and *dark,* and *quiet* and *noisy*
- *Group participation, attention, and task-sequencing directions,* such as "All eyes look at me"; "Now listen carefully; next we will . . ."; "Find your favorite book"; and "Put your materials away"

Most young students develop many of these conventions in the natural context of classroom events. Some students, however, do not understand seemingly basic concepts. Highly effective teachers carefully observe students who have difficulty understanding instructional tasks that include basic conventions. These teachers use every opportunity in all areas of instruction to develop and use these concepts in meaningful high-interest classroom activities.

Directional Concepts

Directional concepts can be readily developed through game and play activity. For example, the concepts of *right, left, in,* and *out* may be developed in a group game using the old folk song "Here We Dance Looby Loo" (another version of this song is known as "The Hokey-Pokey"). The children hold hands in a circle, sing the song together, and follow the song's directions ("I put my right foot in, I put my right foot out, I put my right foot in and I shake it all about").

You also can use directional terms when working with individuals and small groups. As you discuss a picture during story sharing, point to an object in the illustration and ask "What is that at the top [bottom, left, right] of the page?" This type of informal learning can be used to develop a wide variety of literacy concepts inductively. Another idea is to involve students in planning a directional trail through the classroom (up the steps, across the rug, around the aquarium, and under the table). After the route has been determined, they follow it, identifying the points on the trail and recording each point on a chart as they name it. You may then help the students make and attach tagboard signs for points on the trail and use string to trace the trail as the signs are read.

Geometric Shape Language

Awareness of geometric shape language can be developed by having young students trace and cut two or more large paper circles, squares, rectangles, and triangles from different-colored construction paper. They can then create familiar objects and paste these on art paper. After the geometric pictures are completed, each child can describe the object to the rest of the class, using the geometric shape vocabulary—for example, "This is an ice cream cone. The brown triangle is the cone. The red circle on top is the strawberry ice cream."

Class-Participation Rules

Group cooperation can be greatly enhanced early in the school year by identifying and discussing classroom-participation rules that are important to everyone. A final list, such as the one shown in Figure 3.4, can be recorded on chart paper and displayed in the room. Referring often to the agreed-on list will remind children of the importance of cooperation in group sharing. Students need to understand how to enter into, take turns during, and share ideas in discussions.

What reading conventions do students develop in the K–1 years?

the Highly Effective Teacher

What other activities might help children learn directional concepts?

What other activities might help young students learn geometric shape language?

Language of Instruction

You will find attention-direction strategies helpful as you introduce, explain, and conclude instructional activities. These include phrases such as "All eyes look at me" and "Now listen carefully; next we will . . ." Frequent opportunity exists throughout the school day for developing these oral signals for group directions.

Many language of instruction concepts can be developed in an exciting and enjoyable way through story sharing and individual exploration, using a variety of books. The books listed in Figure 3.5, for example, are especially designed for introducing new concepts to young students.

What verbal and nonverbal instructional language will you teach your students?

Teaching Picture and Print Knowledge

The development of picture and print knowledge goes hand in hand with the development of young students' concepts about reading and writing and the language of instruction. Most pupils enter school with rich picture and print experiences from their environment—from television, movies, home computers, magazines, newspapers, comic books, cereal boxes, billboards, and so forth. Many young students also have experience in observing adults and older siblings writing and reading. Although most students already have picture and print awareness, teachers should not assume that all children have this background.

Concepts about Pictures and Print

Specific concepts related to early picture and print knowledge include the following:

1. *Picture knowledge.* Pictures (drawings, illustrations, photographs) represent ideas and meaning; they may be used in sequence to tell a story or to explain new ideas.
2. *Print knowledge.* Print represents ideas and meaning through written language. Each word is made up of letters that represent or stand for sounds. Print is organized by words identified by the blank spaces between them. Each line of print (English) is read on the page in a left-to-right direction; the lines of print themselves are read from top to bottom on the page. Special punctuation marks are used to indicate the end of sentences (.), to ask questions (?), to provide special emphasis (!), and to show that someone is talking ("/").
3. *Page knowledge.* Pages have top and bottom positions, and when two pages are side by side, the left page is read first.
4. *Book knowledge.* Books have fronts and backs. Pages are organized from left to right in a book. Pictures and print in books can be used to tell a story or explain new ideas.

FIGURE 3.4

Example of Classroom Rules

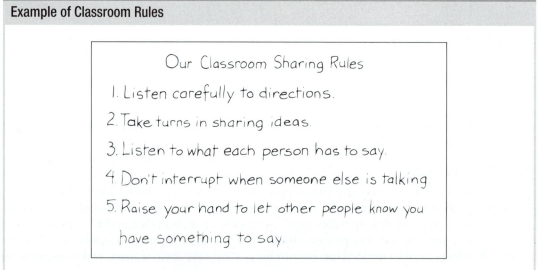

FIGURE 3.5

Bookshelf: Concept-Development Books

Carle, E. (1969). *The Very Hungry Caterpillar.* New York: Philomel/Putnam.

Cole, J. (1995). *In the Haunted Museum: A Book about Sound.* New York: Scholastic.

Davenport, Z. (1995). *Animals.* New York: Ticknor & Fields.

———. (1995). *Garden.* New York: Ticknor & Fields.

Falconer, I. (2002). *Olivia's Opposites.* New York: Atheneum.

Gerth, M. (2000). *Ten Little Ladybugs.* Los Angeles: Piggy Toes Press.

Good, E. E. (1995). *It's Summertime.* Intercourse, PA: Good Books.

Hoban, T. (1972). *Count and See.* New York: Macmillan.

———. (1976). *Big Ones, Little Ones.* New York: Greenwillow.

———. (1978). *Is It Red? Is It Yellow? Is It Blue?* New York: Greenwillow.

———. (1985). *Is It Larger? Is It Smaller?* New York: Greenwillow.

Jeunesse, G., & Delafosse, C. (1992). *Musical Instruments.* New York: Scholastic.

Maestro, B., & Maestro, G. (1985). *Where Is My Friend? A Word Concept Book.* New York: Crown.

Parr, T. (2005). *Otto Goes to School.* New York: Little, Brown.

Reiser, L. (2006). *Hard Working Puppies.* Orlando, FL: Harcourt.

Rockwell, A. (1982). *Boats.* New York: Dutton.

———. (1986). *Things That Go.* New York: Dutton.

Rosen, M. (1992). *How Animals Got Their Colors.* New York: Harcourt Brace Jovanovich.

Tafuri, N. (1986). *Who's Counting?* New York: Greenwillow.

Wildsmith, B. (1965). *Brian Wildsmith's 1, 2, 3.* New York: Franklin Watts.

Williams, S. (2001). *Long Train.* (K. Wilson-Max, Illus.). New York: Scholastic.

Marie Clay (1979), a New Zealand educator, developed the Concepts about Print Test, which is used to evaluate young students' early print awareness. Any small book that has both print and pictures may be used. As the examiner reads from the book, the student is asked to "help." Questions identify the child's print awareness related to the book, sentences, and words. For example, as the book is handed to the student with the spine of the book facing the student, the examiner says "Show me the front of this book." Then the examiner opens the book to a place where print is on one page and a picture is on the other and says "Show me where I begin reading." Other tasks require the child to show where on the page one begins reading, how one moves from the top to the bottom of pages, and what words and letters are. Throughout, the examiner observes and records the student's responses and notes the strategies used in responding to the questions. Valuable instructional information regarding students' book and print awareness can be obtained through similar observations using storybooks or specially prepared print in your classroom.

> *Clay's Concepts about Print Test*

Many picture- and print-awareness and knowledge concepts are developed through environmental print in the classroom-language experience charts, big book reading, oral storytelling using picture book illustrations, and direct hands-on book experiences. Extensive use and display of environmental print in the classroom is very important in developing the concept that letters create words, which, in turn, create sentences that form a story. The How To Do gives suggestions for creating a print-rich learning environment.

Wordless Picture Books and Picture Storybooks

A good beginning for connecting picture-awareness knowledge to meaning is the **wordless storybook,** in which illustrations alone tell the story. Early on, young students are able to infer and create the story by relying on the illustrations. Examples of excellent books of this type are found in Figure 3.6. (See page 58.)

wordless storybook
a book in which illustrations alone tell a story

Picture storybooks, which use pictures and text to tell a story, are valuable in developing characterization, setting, and plot. These stories would be incomplete without the pictures. Some examples of picture storybooks are presented in Figure 3.7. The importance of pictures in these books is clearly evident—for example, if the text states "He waited," the picture may portray the waiting individual's excitement, fear, or loneliness, as intended by the author.

picture storybook
a book in which illustrations and text tell a story that would be incomplete without the pictures

FIGURE 3.6
Bookshelf: Wordless Storybooks

Anno, M. (1977). *Anno's Journey*. New York: Philomel Books.
Fleischman, P., & Hawkes, K. (2004). *Sidewalk Circus*. Cambridge, MA: Candlewick Press.
Graham, A. (2003). *Full Moon Soup*. Flat Rock, NC: Chrysalis Books.
Hutchins, P. (1968). *Rosie's Walk*. New York: Macmillan.
Keats, E. J. (1973). *Skates*. New York: Franklin Watts.
Sis, P. (2000). *Dinosaurs*. New York: Greenwillow.
Wiesner, D. (1991). *Tuesday*. New York: Clarion Books.

Big Books and Oral Story Reading

big book
a giant-sized re-
production of a
standard-sized
storybook

➤ *Instructional
Uses of Big Books*

Big books provide another opportunity for young students to develop concepts about books and knowledge of pictures and print in a meaningful language context. **Big books** are giant-sized reproductions of standard-sized books. The illustrations and print are large enough for children to see as you work in both large and small groups.

As you introduce a big book, you can draw attention to the concepts of *front* and *back, left* and *right,* and *top* and *bottom.* You can also highlight the roles of illustrations and printed text in telling the story. The large print in big books enables you to direct students' attention by tracking the print with a pointer or your hand. In this way, the concepts of left-to-right organization of print, organization of lines of print from the top to the bottom of the page, special punctuation marks, and print as representation of meaning are all embedded in a meaningful story context.

Many big books are readily available from publishers. Some big books that teachers and young students especially like are found in Figure 3.8.

Language-Experience Charts

➤ *Recording
language
experiences helps
children realize
that print
represents
meaning.*

Language-experience charts that record students' home and school experiences develop print-awareness knowledge and the understanding that print represents meaning (Juel & Minden-Cupp, 2004; Ruddell, 2002). The great advantage of this instructional activity is its flexibility. You and your students can create a written record of any experience, using large chart paper and a marker pen. For example, after a walk around the school, a field trip to the zoo or aquarium,

FIGURE 3.7
Bookshelf: Picture Storybooks

Ahlberg, A. (1992). *The Ghost Train*. New York: Mulberry Books.
Brown, M. W. (1947). *Goodnight Moon*. New York: Harper.
Cole, J. (1995). *In the Haunted Museum: A Book about Sound*. New York: Scholastic.
Cowley, J. (2004). *Chameleon, Chameleon*. New York: Scholastic.
Crume, M. (1995). *Do You See Mouse?* Englewood Cliffs, NJ: Silver Burdett.
Emberly, E. (1967). *Drummer Hoff*. Englewood Cliffs, NJ: Prentice-Hall.
French, V. (1995). *A Song for Little Toad*. Cambridge, MA: Candlewick Press.
Galdone, P. (1968). *Henny Penny*. New York: Houghton Mifflin.
Kellog, S. (2001). *A Penguin Pup for Pinkerton*. New York: Dial Press.
Koontz, R. (1988). *This Old Man: The Counting Song*. New York: Dodd, Mead.
London, J. (1993). *Hip Cat*. San Francisco: Chronicle Books.
Mosel, A. (1968). *Tikki Tikki Tembo*. New York: Holt.
Rathmann, P. (1994). *Good Night Gorilla*. New York: Putnam.
Repchuk, C. (2002). *The Race*. (A. Jay, Illus.). San Francisco: Chronicle Books.
Rohmann, E. (2002). *My Friend Rabbit*. Brookfield, CT: Roaring Brook Press.
Stevens, H. (1987). *Fat Mouse*. New York: Viking.
Taback, S. (2004). *The House That Jack Built*. New York: Puffin.

FIGURE 3.8
Bookshelf: Big Books

Gomi, T. (1989). *My Friends*. New York: Chronicle Books/Scholastic.

Martin, B. (1983). *Brown Bear, Brown Bear, What Do You See?* New York: Holt.

Slobodkina, E. (1996). *Caps for Sale* (Big Book Edition). New York: HarperCollins. (Originally Published in 1940 by Wm. Scott, Inc.)

Wadsworth, O. (1985). *Over in the Meadow*. New York: Viking.

Wildsmith, B. (1982). *Cat on the Mat*. New York: Oxford.

———. (1988). *Toot, Toot*. New York: Oxford.

Wood, D., & Wood, A. (2003). *The Little Mouse, the Big Red Strawberry, and the Big Hungry Bear*. (D. Wood, Illus.) Sydney, Australia: Child's Play International.

or a half-hour in the class's garden area, you can create a chart that lists the key events in the experience as revealed in their discussion. Here is one example.

Our Trip to Marine World
We went to marine world.
We saw dolphins and killer whales.
We went on the elephant ride.
We saw tigers in the water.
We then went to the ski show and there was a man skiing on bare feet!
We had a good time.
Then we rode the bus back to school.

Activities to further develop picture- and print-awareness knowledge include the following:

- Have each student draw a picture of his or her favorite experience during the event and then dictate a title for the picture or a sentence about it. Record the title or sentence, and display the picture on the classroom bulletin board.
- Have individual students identify specific letters or words on the experience chart story by cupping their hands around the letter or word.

How To Do ...

A Print-Rich Learning Environment

1. Place large alphabet posters in a location easily visible to the students.

   - **Because of its abstract nature, learning letter recognition often is particularly difficult for students who have a low aptitude for reading. A *variety* of and *many* specific activities will likely be necessary, in addition to the incidental posting of letters (McCormick, 2007).**

   DELAYED READER ADAPTATION

2. Print word labels on tagboard and tape them to familiar objects in the classroom, such as desks, the chalkboard, bookcases, doors, the piano, and the aquarium.

3. Print the name of each child on tagboard and place it on the child's desk. Have small groups of students compare their names, noting the different letters that are used in each.

4. Use newspaper photographs or poster-sized illustrations with high-interest content, such as community helpers in action, animals, or a playground scene, as the basis for oral language discussion. Then develop written word labels for individuals, animals, or objects in the pictures and discuss these. Mount the pictures and word labels on the classroom bulletin board.

5. Ask the students to draw a picture of a family member or a special pet. Label each student's picture using the name provided by the child and display it on the bulletin board.

6. Surround the students with and immerse them in environmental print and language of all types.

> *Describe a language experience activity you might use to teach print awareness.*

■ Make tagboard cards for individual words, specific letters, and punctuation marks (e.g., *We, dolphin, s, tiger, . , !*). Have individual students match the words, letters, and punctuation marks on the cards with those in the chart story as you and the rest of the class read sentences together.

Letter-Recognition Knowledge

Quite a few children have learned to recognize and name the letters of the alphabet before they enter school. Many parents teach their children the alphabet. And programs such as *Sesame Street, Reading Rainbow,* and *Reading Between the Lions* provide valuable letter-recognition exposure. In all probability, however, children will have learned only capital letters (Nurss, 1979).

Learning both uppercase and lowercase letters is not an easy task. Letters are abstract and require a specific orientation. Each of the twenty-six letters must be recognizable in uppercase and lowercase manuscript print in its specific visual orientations (e.g., B-b, D-d). In later grades, two more letter sets are added as students learn uppercase and lowercase cursive writing.

Research indicates that beginning readers identify letters by analyzing their individual features, such as orientation, line segments, and line curves. This information, stored in memory, is used in the scanning and recognition process (Gibson et al., 1962). Visual discrimination of letters accounts for recognition of the following features:

> Left-right orientation: b-d, p-q
> Top-bottom orientation: n-w, n-u, m-w
> Presence of extension: i-j, q-a, d-a, n-h
> Direction of line extension: b-p, d-g, d-q
> Line-curve presence: U-V, P-F, u-v

Researchers such as Pick (1965) and Beck and McCaslin (1978) have found that the presentation of such letter pairs is useful in instruction if familiarity with the first letter in the pair is thoroughly developed through instruction before the second letter in the pair is taught. The value of teaching pairs is to help children recognize the relevant contrasting features. However, remember that letter reversals by young readers and idiosyncratic letter forms are commonplace and represent their understanding of how print works.

Adams (1990a) has the following recommendations for developing letter-recognition knowledge:

> *How to Develop Letter Recognition*

1. Teach the letter names first so that students will have a "conceptual peg" on which to hang their perceptions and observations.
2. Use highly motivating activities with rhyme, rhythm, and song in teaching the letter names (e.g., "The Alphabet Song"). Then provide instruction in recognizing letters and connecting names with letters.

How can you use big books like Bread, Bread, Bread *to develop children's picture and print awareness? What picture-, print-, and story-awareness concepts must children learn?*

3. Help students avoid confusing letter names with sounds by teaching the letter-sound relationships after they have developed solid familiarity with letter names.

ABC books are excellent for developing letter-name knowledge and initiating the connection between letters and sounds. Most of these delightfully illustrated books display uppercase and lowercase letters with high-interest illustrations and printed words that begin with the letters being displayed (Yopp & Yopp, 2000a). For example, in *Dr. Seuss's ABC* (1963a), Theodore Geisel develops the letter *b* in the following way:

> Alphabet books help children develop letter-name knowledge.

BIG B little b (p. 6)
What begins with B? (p. 7)

After turning the page, students see the words *Barber, baby, bubbles,* and *bumblebee* (p. 8), with whimsical illustrations on the opposite page (p. 9). This type of book not only develops letter-name knowledge but also begins to develop initial consonant sound–letter relationships. Examples of alphabet books are found in Figure 3.9.

Displaying alphabets prominently in primary classrooms will help students learn letter names and associate them with the letter sounds in word context. Classroom alphabet posters or cards also serve as a printing-writing reference for them.

Teaching Phonemic Awareness Knowledge

Phonemic awareness is the basic understanding that *spoken* words are composed of different sounds. The development of this skill is essential to children's mastery of the skill of using grapheme-phoneme relationships in words as they learn to read (Ehri & McCormick, 2004). In 2000, at the request of the United States Congress, a National Reading Panel was formed by the National Institute of Child Health and Human Development (NICHD) to conduct a comprehensive review of research findings related to several literacy issues, including phonemic awareness. Several conclusions of the panel regarding the instruction of phonemic awareness are presented in the Research and Evidence-Based Practice feature.

phonemic awareness
the understanding that spoken words are composed of sounds

A significant number of young students at the kindergarten and beginning first-grade levels are not aware of the concept of phonemic awareness. They appear to move through several stages in developing this concept. Initially, they tend to think of a word as the smallest unit of language (e.g., *cat, kitten, neighborhood*). Next, they become aware of syllable breaks in words. Syllable breaks are apparent when the teacher taps out the number of sound units in a word (e.g., *cat*: one tap, *kit-ten*: two taps, *neigh-bor-hood*: three taps). Then they become aware that syllables often have a beginning sound and a rhyming ending (e.g., *c-at, k-it t-en, n-eigh b-or h-ood*).

EVIDENCE-BASED PRACTICE

The beginning and ending of the syllable have special labels that are used by linguists and psycholinguists. The beginning part is known as the **onset** (e.g., the *c* in *cat*) and the ending,

onset
in a syllable, the beginning sound, usually an initial consonant

FIGURE 3.9
Bookshelf: Alphabet Books

Agard, J. (1989). *The Calypso Alphabet.* New York: Henry Holt.
Azarian, M. (1981). *A Farmer's Alphabet.* New York: Godine.
Baker, L. (2003). *The Animal ABC.* New York: Henry Holt.
Ehlert, L. (1989). *Eating the Alphabet: Fruits and Vegetables from A to Z.* San Diego, CA: Harcourt Brace Jovanovich.
Geisel, T. (1963). *Dr. Seuss's ABC.* New York: Random House.
Kitchen, B. (1984). *Animal Alphabet.* New York: Dial.
Martin, B., & Archambault, J. (1989). *Chicka Chicka Boom Boom.* New York: Simon & Schuster.
Metropolitan Museum of Art. (2002). *Museum ABC.* New York: Little, Brown.
Mufford, S. (2004). *Dinosaur ABC.* (J. Rigg, Illus.). New York: St. Martin's Press.
Onyefulu, I. (1993). *A is for Africa.* New York: Dutton.
Steig, J. (1992). *Alpha Beta Chowder.* New York: HarperCollins.
Wood, J. (1993). *Animal Parade.* New York: Bradbury.
Ziefert, H. (2006). *Me! Me! ABC.* Maplewood, NJ: Blue Apple Books.

Research and
Evidence-Based Practice

Phonemic Awareness and Learning to Read

Did You Know?

- A student's ability to use phonemic awareness is critical to learning to read and spell (Ehri et al., 2001; National Reading Panel, 2000).

- Some students enter kindergarten and first grade with little or no understanding of phonemic awareness (McCormick, 2007; National Reading Panel, 2000).

- Students' phonemic awareness skills have been shown to be strong predictors of reading achievement (Ehri & McCormick, 2004; Sweet, 1993; Vellutino & Scanlon, 1987).

- Many students initially think of words as the smallest language units, but they must learn that words are composed of syllables and these are composed of sounds or phonemes, the smallest language units (Ehri & McCormick, 2004; Ruddell & Unrau, 2004a).

- Phonemic awareness can be developed in a variety of ways, such as focusing on rhyming words through poetry and rhymed stories, e.g., reading Dr. Seuss books, categorizing pictures by rhyme, using riddles that focus on sound units in words, and identifying syllable and word patterns (Ball & Blachman, 1991; Juel, 1991; McCormick, 2007; Yopp, 1992).

- Effective phonemic awareness instruction involves helping students: (1) identify sounds in words and connect these sounds to written letters, (2) focus on one or two types of phonemic manipulation, and (3) practice in small-group settings (Hohn & Ehri, 1983; National Reading Panel, 2000; McCormick, 2007).

- Phonemic awareness instruction should be carried out as part of a larger, well-balanced reading program (National Reading Panel, 2000).

---

rime
in a syllable, the ending sound, usually a vowel and a consonant

which includes a vowel and consonant ending, is known as the **rime** (e.g., the *at* in *cat*). (Think of the terms *rime* and *rhyming ending* as interchangeable in the following discussion about alphabet and rhyming books.) The recognition of onset and rime appears to develop before students can identify individual sounds or phonemes (Nation & Hulme, 1997; Trieman, 1985). The skill sequence for the development of phonemic awareness is shown in Figure 3.10. It is helpful to keep this developmental sequence in mind as you observe and work to develop students' phonemic awareness.

Developing Phonemic Awareness

How can you develop phonemic awareness through onset and rime?

An excellent way to develop phonemic awareness is by reading familiar nursery rhymes and poetry to children (Nikola-Lisa, 1997). Mother Goose rhymes have special appeal for kindergarten and first-grade students, in part because many students are already familiar with these rhymes. For example, "Little Boy Blue" and "Tom, Tom, the Piper's Son" provide wonderful opportunities to use familiar, meaningful text to teach and reinforce onset and rime. By focusing

FIGURE 3.10

Skill Sequence for the Development of Phonemic Awareness

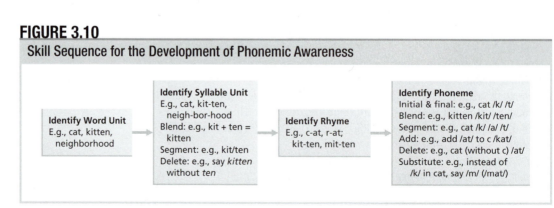

FIGURE 3.11

Bookshelf: Poetry Anthologies Useful for Developing Rime and Phonemic Awareness

Brown, M. (1980). *Finger Rhymes.* New York: Dutton.

Cullinan, B. (Ed.). (1996). *A Jar of Tiny Stars: Poems by NCTE Award-Winning Poets.* Honesdale, PA: Boyds Mill Press.

Kennedy, C. (2005). *A Family of Poems, My Favorite Poetry for Children.* New York: Hyperion.

Kuskin, K. (2003). *Moon, Have You Met My Mother?* (S. Ruzzier, Illus.). New York: HarperCollins.

Larrick, N. (1983). *When Dark Comes Dancing: A Bedtime Poetry Book.* New York: Philomel/Putnam.

Prelutsky, J. (2002). *The Frog Wore Red Suspenders.* (P. Mathers, Illus.). New York: Greenwillow Books.

Rosenthal, B. R. (2004). *My House Is Singing.* (M. Chodos-Irvine, Illus.). San Diego, CA: Harcourt.

attention on the rimes in *horn* and *corn, sheep* and *asleep,* and *eat* and *beat,* you can help children learn how words are alike and different. Many favorite rhyming words are found in poetry collections, such as those listed in Figure 3.11.

In addition, books such as Dr. Seuss's *The Cat in the Hat* (1957) and *Hop on Pop* (1963b), Martin's *Brown Bear, Brown Bear, What Do You See?* (1983), and *Five Little Chicks* Tafuri's (2006) include rhymes and recurring word patterns that develop phonemic awareness by focusing attention on the sounds of language and sound-letter relationships. As students notice how rhyming words are similar and different, they begin to incorporate phonemic awareness knowledge into their language theory.

> *Rhymes and recurring word patterns are a basis for learning letter-sound relationships.*

Phonemic Segmentation

Phonemic segmentation involves the ability to direct and focus attention on the separate sounds in a word. This ability becomes important as young students begin to establish the connection between sounds and letters using the alphabetic features of our writing system (Blachman, 2000). The beginning reader must understand that sounds in words can be separated out and then blended together to form words. Phonemic segmentation may be demonstrated by asking students to do the following:

phonemic segmentation the ability to recognize separate sounds in a word

1. Tap out the number of sounds they hear in a word (e.g., *d-o-g*: three taps).
2. Tell what word or sound sequence remains after a sound is removed from a word (e.g., *cat* without the /k/, or *mill* without the /m/).
3. Blend sounds (e.g., /m/ + /at/, /k/ + /at/, /r/ + /at/).

The ability to segment and blend individual sounds signals students' understanding of the sound system and of relationships between sounds and letters.

> *Children's ability to segment and blend sounds is a basis for using letters to represent sounds.*

Teaching Observation and Writing Awareness

Students' curiosity and social nature provide a good opportunity for you to encourage them to pursue their observations through discussion. This, in turn, leads to helping them begin to compose and record their ideas. With your guidance, they come to understand how their observations and thoughts can be represented in written language. As a highly effective teacher, your objectives include the following:

- To help students understand the use of vocabulary to create descriptions of people, animals, objects, and events
- To develop their understanding that events occur in a time sequence, which they can show by the order in which they present their ideas in writing and by using special words such as *next, then, after that,* and *finally*
- To build students' familiarity with conventional ways to record ideas in written form, using titles, capital letters, and punctuation

the
**Highly
Effective
Teacher**

Expression through Art

An effective way to engage kindergarten and first-grade students at a high level of interest is to encourage expression through art forms, which can serve as a basis for composing and recording ideas (Ernst, 1994; Olshansky, 1994; Yopp & Yopp, 2000b). For example, finger painting, brush painting, and drawing provide ways of representing self, a family member, a pet, or a favorite storybook character. Encourage each student to develop the topic through a picture, which the child then shares by describing it to classmates. The student may dictate a title, which can be written on a piece of lined tagboard and affixed to the picture.

Descriptive Language from Observation

What observation activity might you use for developing descriptive language?

Many opportunities for descriptive writing can be developed from a visit to a nearby park, children's animal farm, or zoo. After a field trip, students can talk about their observations, perhaps reflecting on an animal's size, color, shape, and distinguishing features and how the animal might feel to touch. Individually or collectively, students can create a large picture of a favorite animal and dictate a description. Have them observe as you write the description on the drawing.

Descriptive Language from Sensory Experience

The "mystery box" activity is effective in developing descriptive language. Prepare closed cardboard boxes with circular holes cut in opposite sides. The holes should be large enough for a student's hands, but small enough so that no one can see the object inside. In each box, place an object that can be easily identified through touch—for example, an apple or a pencil. Students take turns putting their hands into the holes, describing the shape and feel of the object, and trying to guess what it is. They may also try to guess the name of an object on the basis of its physical description alone.

Strategies in Use

Teaching Phonemic Segmentation: How Words Are Made Up of Sounds

Geraldine Smith prepares 3-inch-by-3-inch pieces of cardboard and outlines the edges using a black marker. She counts the number of squares needed to represent each sound in the words *dog* and *book*. Three squares will be needed for each. Geraldine plans to use these words with Artie in her instruction on phonemic segmentation.

Geraldine invites Artie to choose a set of counters from the classroom collection of game pieces and buttons. By the time he has chosen, she has located her file pictures of dogs and books. She has Artie place three blank squares before him in a row beside his handful of red buttons.

Next, Geraldine lets Artie select a picture of a dog. "What is this animal?" she asks. After listening to Artie's pronunciation, she pronounces *dog* slowly for him, taking care not to exaggerate sounds unnecessarily or distort pronunciation. She asks Artie to pronounce the word just as she has done.

Then Geraldine demonstrates how Artie will put a red button on a square for each sound he hears when a word is said. She models this pro-

cedure on the chalkboard, pronouncing /d/ŏ/g/ slowly and drawing a button in each of three squares as she articulates each sound in the word.

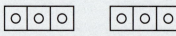

Artie is flushed with the pleasure of "counting" sounds using game pieces. When all the sounds are counted out, Geraldine asks him to use the word in a sentence. Artie practices the procedure again. Geraldine repeats the game using pictures of books. Next time, she will invite Artie to choose the words he will sound out.

CRITICAL THINKING

1. What do beginning readers learn through the process of phonemic segmentation?
2. What materials could you use to focus children's attention on the sound and letter parts of each word?
3. Using *dog* and *book,* how could you adapt this counting-out game to develop a beginning understanding of sound-letter associations?

FIGURE 3.12

Recording Descriptions from Sensory Experience

Our Mystery Box Objects

	My Description	My Mystery Object
Amy	rough, round, pointed end	pine cone
Mike	smooth, long, sharp end	pencil
Marcus	soft, fuzzy, thin, round	felt circle
etc.		

To encourage the use of descriptive language, include familiar objects with rough, smooth, and soft textures, such as a pine cone, a seashell, a small rock, an orange, and a piece of fabric. These and similar objects also encourage shape and size descriptions, such as *square, round, long, short, big, small, soft,* and *hard.* Record students' mystery box descriptions on chart paper, as shown in Figure 3.12.

Using descriptions based on visual and auditory awareness is an effective way to develop students' observation skills and to build cause-and-effect relationships. A favorite activity is the "listening observation" walk around the school, playground, block, or nearby park. Before the walk, encourage your students to predict what sounds they think they will hear and to record their predictions on the chalkboard or chart paper. During the walk, the students should listen and try to observe the sources of the sounds they hear. After returning to class, encourage them to discuss their observations and compare them with the predictions they made before the walk. To help the students develop a sense of time sequence, encourage them to reconstruct the order in which they heard the sounds. Number each sound to show its order of occurrence during the walk, as illustrated in Figure 3.13.

Why are multi-sensory aware-ness activities important for literacy develop-ment?

Language-Experience Stories

The listening observation walk activity can be extended easily into a **language-experience story** using vocabulary that shows a time sequence. Students create a story about the listening walk by using each observation in a sentence in the order recorded on the chart, as in Figure 3.14.

language-experience story a chronological written record of students' language experiences

FIGURE 3.13

Using Descriptive Language to Build Cause-and-Effect Relationships

Our Listening Walk Around Our School

Sounds We Heard	What Made the Sound
(3) buzzing	a lawn mower
(5) hammering	a carpenter
(2) barking	a dog
(1) banged shut	our classroom door
(4) chirping	birds

FIGURE 3.14
A Language-Experience Story

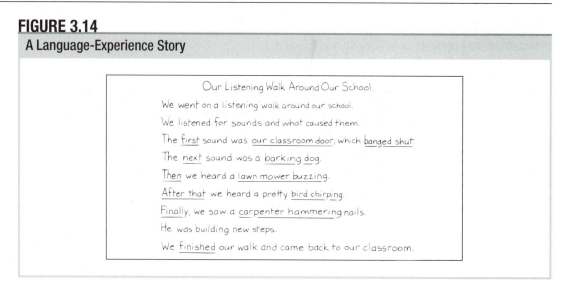

Our Listening Walk Around Our School

We went on a listening walk around our school.

We listened for sounds and what caused them.

The <u>first</u> sound was <u>our classroom door</u>, which <u>banged shut</u>.

The <u>next</u> sound was a <u>barking dog</u>.

<u>Then</u> we heard a <u>lawn mower buzzing</u>.

<u>After that</u> we heard a pretty <u>bird chirping</u>.

<u>Finally</u>, we saw a <u>carpenter hammering</u> nails.

He was building new steps.

We <u>finished</u> our walk and came back to our classroom.

Collecting and Recording Words and Images

word banks
children's collections of written words they have encountered

Your students can become more independent and confident in their early writing and spelling by developing individual **word banks.** Words that they encounter are written on strips of lined paper and stored in their personal word banks. File boxes make perfect containers for word banks and file cards may be used instead of strips of cut paper. Students will accumulate a growing collection of words they know and are able to spell conventionally.

Throughout kindergarten and first grade, young students frequently request help in writing descriptions and stories. Shift gradually from initial language experience activities in which you

How To Do . . .

A Language-Experience Story

1. Begin a language-experience story by saying, "Let's write a story about our listening observation walk. How should our story begin?" Accept whatever opening sentence the students provide.
2. Continue eliciting the students' participation with prompts like "Okay, what should go next?" and "Now what do we want to say?" Be sure to record exactly what they say and allow them to negotiate among themselves to arrive at the final wording or content of a sentence.
3. After the story is recorded, say, "Now I'm going to read the story back to you. After I'm finished, tell me if you'd like to make any changes or additions." Allow them ample time to discuss and evaluate their ideas for revisions.
4. Read the story again after the revisions have been made, and check to make sure that the story in its final form meets with class approval.
5. Focus the students' attention on the key concepts of time sequence and cause and effect by reading the story aloud and inviting the class to choral read along with you. Point to the words as you read, inviting students to identify any words they have difficulty with.

   ■ **To increase the likelihood of a successful rereading experience on the next day, select three to five words for specific attention. Write these on the chalkboard and have students pronounce them; if appropriate, discuss the words' meanings; ask students to write the words themselves and to pronounce them again; have them spell the selected words with magnetic letters and pronounce them; and so on. Reread the story to return to contextual practice of the words.**

6. Following these activities, the students may illustrate the story. The next day (or soon thereafter), distribute a typed, "real print" version of the story to each student.

DELAYED READER ADAPTATION

How To Do . . .

Spelling Instruction

1. Say to a student, "Spell it the way you think it should be spelled" or "Spell it as best you can." This encourages invented spellings but also may create discomfort or frustration for a child. Some may refuse to attempt any spelling.
2. If a student persists in requesting help with spelling or refuses to attempt spelling, say the word (without exaggeration) and ask, "How do you think the spelling starts? What letter would you use?" Then accept whatever letter the student proposes. Say "Good—what letter comes next?" This reduces frustration and helps convince the student that attempting to spell is not risky in this classroom.
3. Later, write the conventional spelling above or below the student's spelling and say "Here's how we usually spell. Look how close you came." This gives students information about conventional spelling that allows them to continue moving toward it.
4. Convert invented spellings to conventional ones during revision and polishing stages of the writing process. This practice shows students how writers attend to conventional spelling in any writing that moves beyond early drafting stages.
5. Each week, select five to ten words that the students want to learn and know more about. These may be kept in a special "word bank" that becomes their spelling list as they learn to use conventional spellings.

■ If possible, arrange the environment so that words to be learned for reading lessons, and those to be targeted for conventional spelling at this stage, are the same words. Many studies show that beginning readers and delayed readers learn best the words they have been exposed to the most (e.g., Ehri, 1991; Gough, Juel, & Roper-Schneider, 1983; McCormick, 2007).

DELAYED READER ADAPTATION

do the writing to activities in which the students assume greater responsibility for writing their own accounts. As they collect words, encourage them to try spelling on their own and to move from invented spelling to conventional spelling of words. The How To Do provides suggestions.

Children's books are also a wonderful source of imagery in illustrations and descriptive language. As you share literature with students, encourage them to identify illustrations, words, and expressions that are rich in description of character, setting, and action. Figure 3.15 lists some favorite picture books and storybooks that contain image-evoking descriptions.

The development of students' sense of observation, composing, and recording heightens their descriptive language ability. It also reinforces the understanding that their thoughts and ideas can be recorded through drawing and writing.

> *Remember that children begin writing by using invented prephonemic and letter-name spellings.*

Teaching Concepts of Story and Narrative

Many children have developed some sense of story by the time they enter kindergarten or first grade. This story sense has been developed in part through story reading and story listening with parents, other adults, and siblings (Galda et al., 2000; Galda & Beach, 2004). Students' experiences in watching favorite movies and television shows may also contribute to a sense of story. They are aware that characters interact with each other, and they have a general sense that a story plot will lead to some outcome or resolution, which is usually positive. The following concepts are basic to the development of a sense of story and narrative:

> *Basic Concepts of Story Sense*

■ The idea that stories have characters, settings, events, and a plot
■ A sense of sequence as story events unfold
■ The ability to make simple inferences and predictions about story events and story outcomes
■ The ability to retell and create simple stories through dictation, drawings, or writing and sharing these stories with other children

FIGURE 3.15

Bookshelf: Some Children's Books That Are Rich in Imagery

Aliki (1984). *Feelings*. New York: Greenwillow.

Angelou, M. (1994). *My Painted House, My Friendly Chicken, and Me*. New York: Clarkson N. Potter

Bandes, H. (1993). *Sleepy River*. New York: Philomel.

Bemelmans, L. (1939). *Madeline*. New York: Viking.

Blegvad, L. (1985). *Anna Banana and Me*. New York: McElderry.

Canon, J. (1993). *Stellaluna*. San Diego, CA: Harcourt.

Craft, K. Y. (2002). *Sleeping Beauty*. New York: Sea Star/North-South Books.

de Angeli, M. (2000). *Thee, Hannah!* New York: Herald Press.

Florian, D., (1997). *In the Swim*. New York: Harcourt Brace.

Holabird, K. (1983). *Angelina Ballerina*. New York: Crown.

Kuskin, K. (2003). *Moon, Have You Met My Mother?* New York: Harper Collins.

Lamorisse, A. (1957). *The Red Balloon*. New York: Doubleday.

Lionni, L. (1967). *Frederick*. New York: Pantheon.

———. (1969). *Alexander and the Wind-Up Mouse*. New York: Knopf.

Maris, R. (1983). *My Book*. New York: Puffin.

McCloskey, R. (1941). *Make Way for Ducklings*. New York: Viking Penguin.

Rey, H. A. (1941). *Curious George*. Boston: Houghton Mifflin.

Scarry, R. (1968). *Richard Scarry's What Do People Do All Day?* New York: Random House.

Seuss, Dr. (1957). *The Cat in the Hat*. New York: Beginner Books.

Steptoe, M. (1987). *Snuggle Piggy and the Magic Blanket*. New York: Dutton.

Tompert, A. (2002). *The Pied Piper of Peru*. (K. Kasparavicius, Illus.). Honesdale, PA: Boyds Mills Press.

Shared Book Experiences

shared book experience
a literature-based strategy for teaching story concepts to groups of students

An excellent instructional strategy for developing sense of story and narrative is the **shared book experience** (Lynch, 1986). This strategy introduces the concept of story through high-interest literature and develops active thinking through the social dynamic found in small-group interaction. Stories are introduced in a secure, nonthreatening, motivating environment that encourages optimal exploration and learning.

The central instructional tool in the shared book experience is the big book, which can be seen clearly from ten to fifteen feet away. Criteria for selecting big books for your class include high student interest, a predictable story line, high-quality illustrations, and variety in language, ranging from repetitive patterns to simple narrative. The Strategies in Use illustrates a shared book experience using *Brown Bear, Brown Bear, What Do You See?* (Martin, 1983).

Predictable Books

predictable books
storybooks that develop a repeating, or predictable, pattern

Predictable books like *Brown Bear, Brown Bear, What Do You See?* help young students develop a story sense and the ability to predict and draw inferences. The key to their use is (1) developing the predictable pattern through shared oral reading, (2) involving them in using and responding to the pattern, and (3) extending the book experience to retelling the story or creating a new story using the same pattern. Several of the books listed in Figure 3.9 are among students' favorite predictable books. These predictable books encourage active participation and involvement in the reading experience.

The Directed Listening-Thinking Activity (DL-TA)

Directed Listening-Thinking Activity (DL-TA)
an instructional strategy for developing story sense through predictions and inferences

Another strategy for developing a sense of story through predictions and inferences is the **Directed Listening-Thinking Activity (DL-TA)** (Stauffer, 1976), which is suitable for small or large groups of students. In the DL-TA, the teacher reads a story to the class, stopping at planned points to ask the students to make predictions about the story and comment on what has happened thus far. Using a DL-TA requires that you read the story carefully (or already know the story well) before using it with your students. Identify stop-points where you will pause in your reading to ask students to make predictions and support their predictions with information in the story and their own knowledge base. These stop-points usually occur (1) after the title, (2) after

Strategies in Use

Using *Brown Bear, Brown Bear, What Do You See?* in a Shared Book Experience

Carmel chooses the delightful big book *Brown Bear, Brown Bear, What Do You See?* for a shared book experience with her first graders. The book is written by Bill Martin Jr. (1983) and contains brilliant illustrations by Eric Carle. It is a cumulative patterned story, starting with the title question "Brown Bear, Brown Bear, what do you see?" The beginning of the patterned response is "I see a redbird looking at me." The question is repeated with each new animal: "Redbird, redbird, what do you see?" Redbird responds, "I see a yellow duck looking at me." The story continues with blue horse, green frog, purple cat, white dog, black sheep, goldfish, mother, and children. The ending poses the question "Children, children, what do you see?" followed by a reiteration of all the characters presented and the patterned refrain "That's what we see."

CRITICAL THINKING

1. How can Carmel begin the shared book experience so that the children will feel safe responding to and participating in the story?
2. How could you use this story as a shared book experience to develop the idea of story characterization?
3. How could you use this story to develop the idea of story sequence?
4. Using other strategies described in this chapter, how could you use this story to teach observation and writing awareness? For example, how could you combine shared book experience with language experience, pantomime, and word collecting activities?
5. How could you use this story to launch students' own story writing?

"BROWN BEAR, BROWN BEAR, WHAT DO YOU SEE?"

"I SEE A REDBIRD LOOKING AT ME."

From "Brown Bear, Brown Bear, What Do You See?" by Bill Martin Jr., illustrated by Eric Carle, © 1967, 1970 by Harcourt Brace & Company, copyright renewed 1995 by Bill Martin Jr. Illustrations © 1992 by Eric Carle. Reprinted by permission of Henry Holt and Company, LLC.

the story introduction (usually a paragraph or two), (3) at one or two points of high interest or suspense in the story, and (4) just before the story ending.

The main questioning pattern is quite simple: After reading the story title, you ask, "With a title like that, what do you think this story will be about? Why do you think so?" After the stop-points during the story, you ask, "What do you think will happen now [next]? Why do you think so?" And at the final stop-point, you ask "How do you think the story will end? Why?" Note that these questions are deliberately open-ended to allow students freedom to think about the story in their own ways. These questions encourage speculation, prediction-making, and discussion about individual interpretations. It is very important that you accept your students' predictions and inferences as long as they can provide some logical justification for them.

The DL-TA provides an excellent opportunity to use the social dynamic of the group. As children make and justify different story predictions, new ideas and possible story outcomes will emerge from the group. As different predictions develop, it will be helpful to ask the group questions, such as "Which of these predictions do you agree with?" This kind of questioning encourages your students to consider various plot options and outcomes and reexamine their own predictions. The DL-TA also is valuable as a springboard to other activities.

> **How could you apply a DL-TA to a story you plan to share with children?**

> ➤ *Recall that literacy learning occurs in social contexts.*

Teaching Positive Reading and Literacy Attitudes

As you orchestrate instructional experiences in the classroom, remember that there should be a place and time for students simply to enjoy stories and share their reactions. Opportunities to experience good literature through story listening, story reading, and story sharing help students build positive attitudes toward literacy development. Positive attitudes create the desire to

How To Do . . .

Story Reading and Sharing

1. Examine and read the book you select in advance. How will you present the story? What stop-points will you use?
2. Practice using expression when you read so that your voice fits the dialogue and characters.
3. Use pacing to emphasize suspenseful parts and build interest as the story progresses.
4. Slow down your reading presentation. Think of the mental images you are creating in the minds of the students through the language of the story.
5. Be sure all students are seated comfortably and can see the storybook pictures that you are sharing.
6. Use storytelling aids to heighten interest. For example, you might bring a small toy mouse to class when you share a book such as *Alexander and the Wind-Up Mouse* by Leo Lionni (1969). A felt board or puppets may also be used to develop actions of key story characters or to retell a story.
7. Help students understand that books are written and illustrated by real people. Encourage writing to the author or illustrator through the publisher, enclosing a self-addressed, stamped envelope for the author's convenience in responding.
8. Use questioning strategies to encourage students to interact with the story content during or following the story.

■ **Daily story-reading time can also be used to develop concepts about print for students still lacking those concepts. Each day ask about or point out a different concept, such as "Who can show me where I should begin reading on a page?" or "Who can point to a *word?*" or "Who can point to a *letter?*" (See the section titled Teaching Picture and Print Knowledge, page 56, for additional pertinent questions.)**

9. Create an atmosphere of informality and enjoyment for your students during book sharing time.

How To Do . . .

A DL-TA

1. Select the story to be read. Preread the story (even if you already know it). You may even wish to practice reading it aloud.
2. Determine stop-points. Stop first after the title. Stop again after the opening (one or two paragraphs). Stop one or two more times during the story at points of high interest or suspense. Stop just before the story end or resolution is reached.
3. Prepare questions to ask at stop-points ("With a title like that, what do you think this story is about?" or "Now what do you think will happen?"). Be sure to ask, "Why?" or "What makes you say that?" after students make predictions or draw conclusions.
4. At the last stop-point, ask, "How do you think the story will end?" and "Why?"

- **In listening activities such as this, delayed readers often reveal their strengths. Because of other failures, however, they may be cautious about participating. Be certain that all students are asked to respond in every session—and do provide encouraging and patient "wait time" if a student appears shy or hesitant.**

DELAYED READER ADAPTATION

explore the world of books, as they pursue topics of special interest and share their reactions to the books they read. Positive reading and literacy attitudes can be developed as follows:

> *Building Positive Attitudes toward Reading*

- Create a special place in your classroom for storytelling, story sharing, and independent book exploration.
- Select books that are of special interest to your students, taking into account their background knowledge and level of maturity.
- Establish a daily book sharing and story experience time.
- Read to the children every day.
- Demonstrate your enthusiasm and love of reading to the children by reading to them daily and sharing your favorite books and your personal reading interests.

Organizing Early Literacy Classrooms

Our current understanding of how young students continue their development toward fluent literacy during kindergarten and first grade includes the following beliefs and assumptions:

> *Children's Literacy Development in the K–1 Grades*

- Students learn the language of written text by hearing and seeing written text and by experimenting with written text themselves.
- Students acquire and develop picture and print concepts, a sense of story structure, and theories about how written language works as they invent and reinvent oral and written text forms, test current language hypotheses, and successfully negotiate meanings with text.
- Students' language and literacy learning are mediated by social interactions and transactions with peers and literate others.

These beliefs and assumptions suggest that the following experiences and events must be present in kindergarten and first-grade classrooms to promote your students' language and literacy development:

- Ample time and space for drawing, reading, writing, and illustrating written work
- Opportunities for rich language interactions during and after play and lessons, including time for sharing experiences, elaborating ideas, and exploring and making sense of new experiences and events
- A literate environment, where many different forms of written text can be experienced in many different circumstances

- Many opportunities for shared reading and writing
- Being read to every day

How might you organize a kindergarten or first-grade classroom?

Organization of K–1 Classrooms

Kindergarten and first-grade classrooms should be large enough to accommodate a number of defined areas in the room, as in the organizational plan shown in Figure 3.16. Evidence of literacy should be everywhere: signs, books, posters, paper, writing utensils, magazines, labels, lists, displays of children's writing, and all manner of written messages.

Strategies in Use   Using *One Fine Day* in a DL-TA Lesson

Nonny Hogrogian's (1971) *One Fine Day* is a beautifully illustrated Armenian folktale that tells of a sly, thirsty fox who steals milk from an old woman. The woman chops off the fox's tail and demands that her milk be returned in exchange for it. The story progresses in a cumulative problem-solving plot. The fox must journey to the cow for milk, to the field for the grass the cow needs to make milk, and to the stream for the water the field needs to grow. He must go on to the maiden for the water jug, to the peddler for the maiden's blue bead, to the hen for the peddler's egg, and to a kind old miller for the chicken's grain. All ends well as the old woman sews the fox's tail back in place, and he joins his friends on the other side of the forest. The discussion that follows uses *One Fine Day* in a DL-TA lesson.

Jackson Lee reads the title to introduce the book and then asks "With a title like that, what do you think this story will be about? And tell me why you think that."

"Good things will happen," Jenny suggests.

"The sun will be shining and it won't be too hot or too cold," offers Fahd. "That's what a 'fine' day is."

"Somebody will be lucky that day," Min says.

Jackson reads the story to the point where the fox has lapped up most of the milk; then he pauses to ask, "What do you think will happen now, and why do you think so?"

The students make mostly dire predictions, but not as dire as the story's actual plot. Jackson decides to remind the students that in folktales punishments can be drastic and impossible things can happen. The students begin to catch on.

"He blows up and squirts milk all over the place," Bruce exclaims.

Jackson reads on to the point where the old woman chops off the fox's tail. The students murmur appreciatively. The old woman says, "Give me back my milk, and I'll give you back your tail." Jackson asks, "Now what do you think will happen? Why?"

Jackson repeats these questions at stop-points in the story. As the story pattern becomes clear, the pupils happily contribute solutions to the fox's dilemma. As the fox reaches the kind miller and begins to cry, Jackson asks the students how they think the story will end and why. They take a poll; those students who think the fox will get his tail back outnumber pessimists two to one. To conclude the story, Jackson rereads the final cumulative episodes with the students reading along in chorus. Afterwards they discuss how they might express the story in a puppet play or dramatic production.

CRITICAL THINKING

1. What value do you see in the prediction and inference questions Jackson used?
2. What social dynamic of the DL-TA in Jackson's lesson intellectually engaged the students?
3. Recall the predictable storybook *Brown Bear, Brown Bear, What Do You See?* or another patterned story. How would you use that story in a DL-TA lesson?
4. What other strategies for literacy learning could you use with DL-TA lessons? How could you incorporate props and movement into Jackson's DL-TA lesson?

FIGURE 3.16

Physical Organization of the Classroom: Early and Beginning Readers

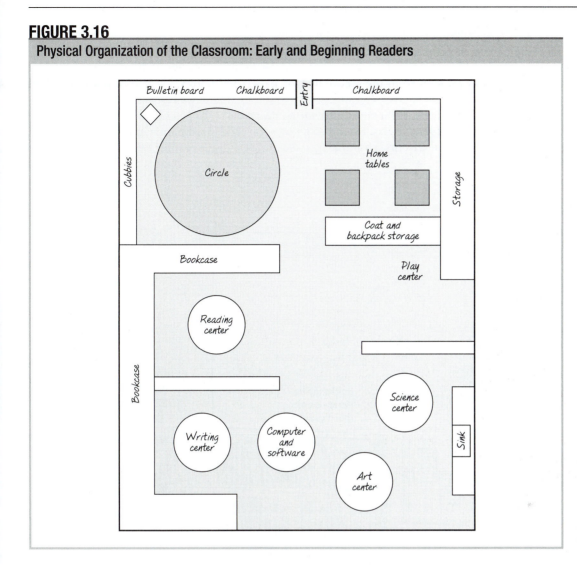

Home Tables

At "home tables" or at their own desks, young students are free to read and write on their own. In some classrooms, the chairs at home tables are the only places that students have to hang sweaters and coats. In others, a home table may be designated to store writing materials and other personal possessions. Home tables provide a place in the room where each student has personal space. These tables or desks may be used as part of a space rotation; while some students are working or playing in centers, others may be working individually or in groups at the home-table cluster.

Circle-Area Tables

The circle area is a multipurpose area where the class gathers for large-group discussions. Students generally sit on the floor, and the teacher sits in a low chair. The circle area may host many events: daily opening and closing routines, sharing time for the writing workshop, the teacher's reading to the students, and presentations by guest speakers.

What else might you include in a circle area?

To define the circle area and make the floor more comfortable, provide a carpet remnant or an area rug large enough so that the students can sit comfortably without crowding. Designate an area next to a bulletin board or chalkboard and near storage shelves to hold materials (e.g., writing paper) that students commonly carry away from circle discussions. If possible, locate their individual cubbies or baskets nearby to facilitate the distribution and return of papers. The chair or chairs at the front of the circle should be low rather than standard height so that you don't tower over those sitting on the floor.

Reading-Center Tables

The reading center, or book corner, is where students go to browse, choose new books to read, and spend some time reading for pleasure. Stock the book corner with all manner of reading materials—books on loan from the school library, paperback books, big books, books children have written and made, magazines, comic books, maps, charts, newspapers, and any other reading materials your students might enjoy. Provide comfortable seating, such as an old easy chair or sofa from home or beanbag chairs, oversized pillows, or child-sized patio chairs (see Figure 3.17 below). Suggested initial selections for kindergarten and first-grade reading centers include the following types of books:

FIGURE 3.17
Creating a Reading Center

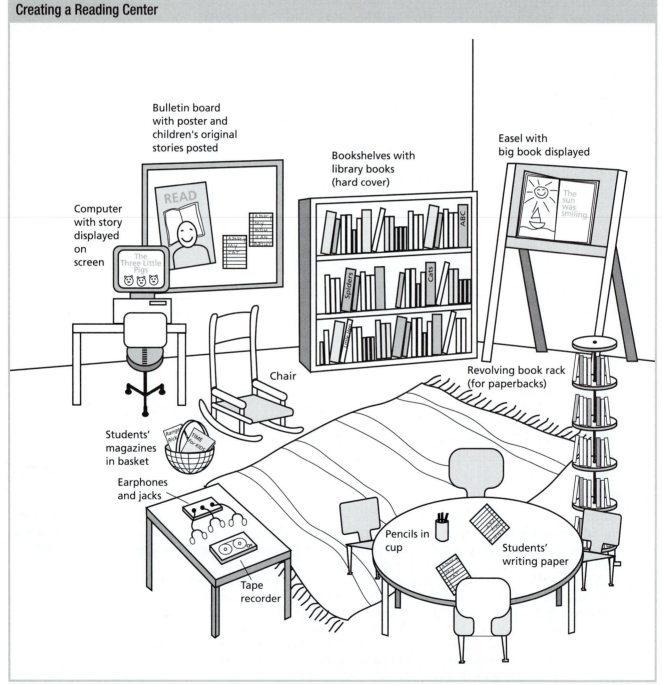

- Alphabet picture books that include letters and illustrations of objects with names that begin with each alphabet letter
- Concept and informational books that describe objects, colors, shapes, and abstract ideas such as sizes and textures
- Nursery rhyme and poetry books that contain traditional, favorite poems and nursery rhymes with illustrations
- Storybooks that use illustrations to tell the story without words
- Predictable books with repetitive and highly structured patterns
- Easy-to-read books with limited vocabulary and creative story lines
- Picture storybooks that develop story through pictures and print
- Fairy tales and folktales that use pictures and print
- Narrative storybooks that use high-interest story lines with few illustrations

> *Books for the K–1 Reading Center*

Trelease's (2006) *The New Read-Aloud Handbook,* Lipson's (2004) *The New York Times Parent's Guide to the Best Books for Children,* and Freeman, Martinez, Yokota, & Temple's (2006) *Children's Books in Children's Hands: An Introduction to Their Literature* have many suggestions, ideas, annotations, and categorized book lists that will enhance your teaching. As you look for books that match students' interests, keep in mind the following topics: adventure, animals, bedtime, behavioral problems, boys, cats, dancing, death, dinosaurs, divorce, dogs, family problems, fantasy, fear, friendship, girls, grandparents, growing up, health, history, holidays, humor, manners, mice, music, pigs, rabbits, science, siblings, and sports.

What other topics might interest students in the age group you plan to teach?

The reading center also might have a tape player, headphones, and books on tape; CD player and books on disk; and special collections of literature and print. Decorative posters and a bulletin board with literature-related art and writing, such as book illustrations and students' letters to authors, complete the ideal reading center.

Technology is an important addition to the reading center. At least one computer, and hopefully three or four, should be available for easy kindergartener and first-grader access. Instructional software should be provided for high-interest work, ranging from letter recognition to word meaning and story development (e.g., *Reading Blaster, Beginning Reading, Franklin's Reading Work,* and *Storybook Weaver*).

Writing Center

Locating the writing center next to the reading center reinforces the concept that reading and writing are closely related. It also allows readers easy access to reading and writing materials and computers. The writing center should be stocked with many different writing media (pens, pencils, markers, etc.), different paper types and sizes, one or more computers or word processors

What role does technology play in the K–1 classroom?

How does this activity support emergent literacy? What other activities should be accommodated or encouraged in an effective early literacy classroom?

and a printer, dictionaries and other reference aids, bookmaking and book-binding materials, and related supplies. Writing software such as *Kidworks 2, Kid Pix 2,* and *Orly's Draw a Story* should be available. Students can take lap desks to the circle area to do free writing. Their writing folders or journals may be stored in the writing center.

Art, Activity, and Play Centers

➤ *Activity centers should include writing materials so that students can record their experiences.*

The art center is where students draw, paint, and use chalk and other media to create works of art, illustrate their writing, or explore art media for fun during supervised sessions. Stock the art center with easels, paints, brushes, colored chalk, colored markers, crayons, left- and right-handed scissors, glue or gluesticks, papers of many colors and textures, wooden craft sticks, and other age-appropriate materials for producing art. Designate an area in or near the art center for displaying students' work.

Two or more other centers in the K–1 classroom can display content-area materials for activities relating to integrated or thematic units. For example, you might have a science center that houses weather-charting materials, leaf collections, beans sprouting in paper cups, and equipment with which children can experiment and explore their physical world. Nearby, you might have a math center stocked with Cuisenaire rods, blocks of various sizes, activity cards, an abacus, and various other manipulatives. Or you might customize activity centers as needed for instructional plans. Activity centers should always include reading and writing materials. If play areas do not have a specifically designated theme, you may wish to keep on hand dress-up and pretend boxes, filled with costumes, accessories, tools, and other props that students can use for dramatic play. Puppet theaters are nice to have in play areas, with supplies available for creating puppets, writing scripts, and producing puppet plays.

the Highly Effective Teacher ★

on Technology and Early Reading and Writing Development

1. Go to the Literacy Center and examine the various interactive activities that can be used with your students for developing letter recognition and other early reading skills. It is found at **http://www.literacycenter.net.**

2. The award winning TV series on PBS, *Between the Lions,* has been created for children between 4 and 7 years of age. A wide range of supplementary reading activities for early literacy development is found there. You will even find activities for parents to use with their children and a kindergarten teacher's guide. Visit it at **http://pbskids.org/lions.**

3. Turn your students on to stories and books by visiting **www.ipl.org/.** First click on "Kidspace" followed by "Reading Zone." There you will find a wide array of picture books, poetry, and stories of all kinds. A brief search will identify the book or books that meet the interests of your students.

4. Have students listen to an audio version of a fairy tale, such as those offered at the following Web site: **www.nationalgeographic.com/grimm/index2.html.** Then read them the book version. Construct a class chart comparing the audio and print versions. You may also want to have students compare fairy tales from around the world. You might begin with the following Web sites: **www.dreamtime.net.au/creation/audio.cfm, www.fahan.tas.edu.au/archives/Compute/Flores/pgone.html,** and **www.umass.edu/aesop/.**

5. Have students read an interactive book to foster independent explorations of print. To assist you in choosing an appropriate book, visit the site of the SuperKids Software Review: **www.superkids.com.** Some of the titles reviewed include Marc Brown's *Arthur's Computer Adventure,* Dr. Seuss' *The Cat in the Hat,* and *Winnie the Pooh and Tigger Too,* from disk.

TABLE 3.1
Organization of the Half-Day Preschool or Kindergarten

8:30–9:00 A.M.	**Centers**—reading, writing, science, mathematics, art, play. Children choose a center and stay in that center for a full half-hour. Circle rug available for reading-center children to use.
9:00–9:15	**Clean up/settle down**—necessary cleanup is done; students go to their home table as cleanup is completed.
9:15–9:35	**Circle**—attendance, morning song, daily helpers appointed, calendar, weather chart, sharing, story/poetry.
9:35–10:05	**Snack and recess**
10:05–10:40	**Group projects**—dramatic play, construction blocks, puppet theater, literature discussion circles, writing workshop.
10:40–11:10	**Music and movement/art projects/seasonal projects**—alternate singing, instrumental music, dance, music interpretation, papier-mâché projects, murals, finger painting, holiday plays and projects.
11:10–11:25	**Clean up/settle down**
11:25–11:35	**Circle**—reflections on the day, story/poetry.
11:35	**Dismissal**

Organization of the Kindergarten Day

Most preschool and kindergarten classroom days are approximately half the regular school day. Some kindergarten days are shortened full days, in contrast to a regular full school day for first grade. Kindergarten days include time spent at play and work centers, on group projects, in class meetings, in opening and closing routines, in sharing time, in reading time when an adult or peer reads to the class, in motor play and movement, in music and drama, and at snack and recess.

> *Kindergarten Activities*

Plan the day so that you have large blocks of time for extended activities that alternate with motor activities and whole-class meetings for sharing and discussion. Table 3.1 presents a typical half-day preschool or kindergarten schedule and Table 3.2 suggests a whole-day kindergarten or first-grade schedule.

TABLE 3.2
Organization of the Full-Day Kindergarten or First Grade

8:15–8:30 A.M.	**Settle in**—put folders in cubbies, store snacks and lunches, go to home tables.
8:30–8:45	**Journal writing and special words**—students share special words to go into their word banks. Everyone writes in her or his journal.
8:45–9:15	**Circle**—calendar, weather, attendance, sharing, story/poetry.
9:15–10:00	**Reading and language arts**—basal readers and literature, story dictation, literature circles, story illustration, journal writing, computer lab (Thursday)
10:00–10:15	**Morning snack and recess**
10:15–11:00	**Math, science, and social studies projects**—six tables with manipulatives and experiments/projects. Students choose a table and stay in one center for the forty-five-minute time block.
11:00–11:30	**Music** (music teacher three days a week)
11:30–11:45	**Clean up/settle down**
11:45–12:30	**Lunch and recess**
12:30–1:30	**Quiet time**—free reading, writing, and art or nap; quiet sharing of books, writing, or art with a partner.
1:30–2:00	**Physical education/Spanish/eighth-grade buddies**—physical education, Monday and Wednesday; Spanish, Tuesday and Friday; eighth-grade buddies, Thursday (physical education and Spanish teachers).
2:00–2:30	**Free play**—dramatic play, construction blocks, puppet theater, play centers.
2:30–2:45	**Circle**—reflections on the day, story/poetry.

Managing the Classroom

Classroom management is simple when the environment is organized for efficiency and order. As you decide on the physical arrangement of the room, consider how and when materials and equipment will be used, distributed, and stored. Find, buy, or build sufficient storage bins and shelves to accommodate the full range of materials, equipment, props, and supplies you plan to use and place them so that you have quick, efficient access to them.

▶ Lesson Planning

Also plan your own organizational needs for daily instruction. Think ahead to identify all the materials and equipment you'll need for a given day, and have them ready for use. Lack of planning may lead to unsuccessful lessons and behavior management problems. When teachers are not well organized and activities are not well thought out in advance, discipline problems may result.

Establishing Rules and Routines

For classrooms to be safe and orderly, young students must understand and abide by certain rules. On the first day of class, the classroom community should begin discussing rules, roles, and expected conduct—and you should continue this discussion throughout the school year. Begin with one or two rules that you believe are important and have the students add others. Rules of general deportment might include "Listen when others are talking," "Be considerate of others' belongings," "Treat books with care," and "Do not disturb others when they are working." Special rules are required for activities with high spill and slosh rates (painting, planting seeds, cooking) and potentially dangerous materials or equipment (scissors, thermometers, Cuisenaire rods, hot plates). Post general classroom rules where children can see them.

What routines do you regard as most helpful in teaching students?

Routines are patterns of action teachers use consistently to manage movement and activity in the classroom. For example, you might establish a routine for dismissal in which the last event of every class day is a chant or a song in the circle area, followed by the distribution of take-home folders as the students depart. Another routine is the teacher's signal for attention when the room is busy with working noise—a raised hand, the ringing of a bell, or a tone sounded on a musical instrument. Routines reduce uncertainty about what students are supposed to do and when, thus creating a sense of stability and order in the classroom.

Many K–1 teachers find it helpful to have other adults working with them in the classroom. Special educators often work collaboratively with classroom teachers. Such assistance allows close supervision of multiple activity and play centers in the room and provides students with easy access to adult help when they need it. Paid classroom aides, parents, and volunteers also work in classrooms. For arrangements to work well, you will need to prepare aides and parents for their responsibilities and roles. To do so, you should (1) explain your classroom, curriculum, and instructional approach; (2) clarify classroom rules and routines; (3) assign and coordinate activities and duties; and (4) handle any problems that arise. Keep in mind that aides and parents bring their own interests, abilities, and talents into the classroom; their expertise can be a rich resource for you and your students.

Showing Students How to "Do" School

▶ Students need to learn the pragmatics of "doing" school.

A major aspect of the kindergarten and first-grade years is children's learning the pragmatics of how to "do" school (Harris et al., 2004). In kindergarten, children come to understand school routines and expectations, language and literacy tasks, group membership roles, the language and materials of learning, interpersonal relationships, the cultural and language backgrounds of other students, and myriad other facets of the human ecology of classrooms and schools. One of your biggest challenges is realizing the wide range of experiences and knowledge about school life that students bring to your classroom.

Some children arrive in kindergarten after two or more years of organized day care; these students already know a great deal about many school routines and expectations. Other children have played "school" with older siblings and friends and thus have considerable knowledge about school. Yet others have little or no knowledge about school, other students, and what happens in classrooms. Even simple routines, such as lining up or raising hands, may be unfamiliar. And some students are suddenly immersed in a country, culture, and language different from their own when they enter school. Your planning must take this wide range of life experiences and background knowledge into consideration (Strickland & Morrow, 2000).

the Highly Effective Teacher

Conditions and Contexts for the Meaning-Construction–Meaning-Negotiation Process

LITERACY TEACHER
negotiates many types of meaning with students in a literacy-rich learning environment

Plans, organizes, creates, provides, and shares

Plans, organizes, creates, provides, and shares

CURRICULUM
· authentic learning tasks
· literacy for real purposes
· meaning of classroom tasks
· reading conventions

Classroom
· print-rich language immersion
· home tables
· circle area
· reading center
· writing center
· computer and media center
· art and activity areas
· play areas
· story time
· rules and routines
· group participation

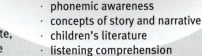

Instruction
· active learning and involvement
· predicting and questioning
· cooperative learning
· student's responsibility to learn
· high/positive expectations
· successive approximation
· many opportunities to succeed
· safe/low-risk learning contexts
· opportunities to observe and write
· ongoing feedback and evaluation
· storytelling and story sharing

· language of instruction
· concepts about literacy
· picture and print awareness
· phonemic awareness
· concepts of story and narrative
· children's literature
· listening comprehension

Plan, organize, create, provide, and share

Plan, organize, create, provide, and share

STUDENTS
develop literacy awareness and linguistic repertoires in a literacy-rich learning environment

Assessing Students' Progress

assessment
evaluating stu-
dents' progress as
a guide to instruc-
tional planning

Included in organizing the K–1 classroom and day is making provisions for attending to the important task of assessment. The purpose of **assessment** is twofold: (1) Assessment provides information on students' progress and (2) it suggests ways to adjust instruction to meet the needs of individual students.

In past years, formal readiness tests played a central role in group placement and achievement testing in kindergarten and first grade. These tests, designed to be used at the beginning and at the end of the school year, place major emphasis on print and sound awareness and are limited in the skills and background knowledge evaluated. At best, they provide some insight into students' visual recognition of letters, sounds, and comprehension of sentences.

Today, assessment practices emphasize a broader array of reading and writing concepts within the learning environment of the classroom and rely more on teachers' observations (Shepard, 2004). Assessment informs instruction and takes place in the natural context of daily instruction as students participate in reading and writing events.

➤ *Classroom-based teacher observation is one of the most important forms of assessment.*

Highly effective teachers observe the following principles of observational assessment:

the ★ Highly Effective Teacher ★

1. Understand the importance of frequent observation-based assessment.
2. Be sensitive to the multiple opportunities in the classroom day for observing students' literacy abilities.
3. Identify the concepts and knowledge to be assessed, based on instructional goals.
4. Develop systematic ways to observe and record your students' progress.
5. Identify ways to use this assessment information in planning and implementing curriculum and instruction to meet students' needs.

➤ *Principles of Observational Assessment*

Every instructional event presents an opportunity to note some aspect of your students' progress. The assessment may be as simple as observing whether a student understands directions essential to completing a learning task, or as complex as determining a child's understanding of a story plot. The checklist in Figure 3.18 (pages 80–81) is based on five instructional goals and includes specific reading and writing concepts and the behaviors associated with them. Complete the checklist for each student, selecting three or four students to observe each day. In this way, you will be able to note the progress of all students in your classroom over a two-week period. More information on assessment is presented in Chapter 9.

Summary and Classroom Applications

double entry journal

Reexamine your list of conventions and concepts students need to know to read and write from the Double Entry Journal at the beginning of the chapter. Revise your list on the basis of the information you learned in this chapter. Add a list of what K–1 children need from their learning environment for optimal literacy development.

Chapter Summary

The following four areas are critical to early reading and writing development: (1) the creation of optimal reading and writing learning conditions in the classroom, (2) the development of literacy awareness and the implementation of instructional goals through a variety of activities and strategies, (3) the organization of the classroom and the school day, and (4) ongoing assessment, based on daily observations of children's progress.

Understanding the way students negotiate meaning is critical to helping them understand and actively participate in learning experiences. Instruction also must develop students' ability to negotiate meaning by teaching them how to "do" school. Pragmatics include learning the language of instruction, knowing how to participate and work cooperatively in small groups, developing a rich concept of literacy processes, understanding how to carry out instructional tasks, and recognizing the unique features of printed text that contribute to meaning.

Early literacy development involves the following six building blocks: (1) understanding the language of

FIGURE 3.18

Early Reading and Writing Assessment Checklist

Student Name _____ **Grade** _____

Dates Observed _____

Instructions: Circle the appropriate letter to assess your student's progress: R = rarely; O = occasionally; U = usually.

1. Understands Language of Instruction and Group Participation **Activity Observed**

a. Knows direction words, ordering words, color words, feeling- and sensory-based words R O U _____

b. Can follow instructional directions R O U _____

c. Can participate and cooperate in group activities and is tolerant of other children's viewpoints R O U _____

d. Understands how to ask questions to clarify a task-meaning or text-meaning problem R O U _____

e. Understands how to ask questions to clarify a personal or group problem R O U _____

2. Has Picture- and Print-Awareness Knowledge **Activity Observed**

a. Knows that pictures and print represent ideas and meaning R O U _____

b. Understands that pictures used in sequence can tell a story R O U _____

c. Knows concept of letter, word, and sentence and role of special punctuation marks R O U _____

d. Recognizes alphabet letters and has developed phonemic awareness and phonemic segmentation knowledge R O U _____

e. Knows that print is read in left-to-right direction, that lines are read from top to bottom, and that pages have top and bottom positions and are organized from left to right R O U _____

f. Understands that picture and print can be used to tell a story and explain ideas R O U _____

3. Knows How to Use Observing, Recording, and Writing Knowledge **Activity Observed**

a. Understands that thoughts and ideas can be recorded through drawing and writing R O U _____

b. Writes fluently to produce stories and descriptions R O U _____

c. Can use written conventions such as story titles and capital letters R O U _____

d. Understands specific vocabulary that reflects order and sequence of events R O U _____

e. Can use ideas to create or recreate experiences based on classroom and field-trip experiences R O U _____

---

instruction, developing concepts about reading and writing, and becoming adept at group participation; (2) developing picture and print awareness knowledge; (3) teaching phonemic awareness and phonemic segmentation knowledge; (4) knowing how thoughts and ideas can be represented in print through observing, recording, and writing; (5) developing a sense of story and narrative; and (6) building positive attitudes toward reading.

Successful literacy instruction in kindergarten and first grade depends, in part, on an appropriate instruc-tional environment, including, for example, home tables, a circle area, and reading and writing centers. Your careful organization of the school day is also important, as you establish rules and routines and help children understand how to "do" school.

Assessment of students' progress will be based to a great extent on your observations in real learning situations in relation to your knowledge of your students and the meanings they bring to school.

FIGURE 3.18 (continued)

Early Reading and Writing Assessment Checklist

4. Demonstrates Sense of Story and Narrative   **Activity Observed**

a. Understands that a story has characters, settings, events, and plot	R	O	U	_____
b. Can follow and understand events in story sequence	R	O	U	_____
c. Can develop inferences and predictions about story events and outcomes and support these using story content or background knowledge	R	O	U	_____
d. Can comprehend and retell a story to other children or the teacher	R	O	U	_____
e. Can and does read, conventionally or otherwise	R	O	U	_____

5. Demonstrates Positive Attitude toward Reading and Literacy Activities   **Activity Observed**

a. Enjoys story-reading and story-sharing time	R	O	U	_____
b. Shows enthusiasm about exploring picture and storybooks	R	O	U	_____
c. Likes to share personal stories and books with a friend or small group	R	O	U	_____
d. Enjoys small-group discussion of ideas related to books that have been shared or read during story sharing	R	O	U	_____
e. Enjoys creating new stories based on a shared story	R	O	U	_____

Professional Standards and
Early Reading and Writing Development

The standards found in Figure 3.19 provide examples from early reading and writing instruction for each of the five standards found in the *Standards for Reading Professionals—Revised 2003* (International Reading Association, 2004). The standards reflect a number of the teaching competencies that are essential in becoming an effective literacy teacher. You can see the complete list of Standards for Reading Professionals in Appendix C.

Applications: Bridges to the Classroom

1. Review Cambourne's and Turbill's (1987) list of seven optimal conditions for literacy learning that was presented earlier in this chapter. Observe a K–1 classroom during reading and language-arts instruction, and identify classroom experiences and events that reflect those optimal conditions. If some conditions are not present, speculate on the reasons why they are not.

2. Apply the Directed Listening-Thinking Activity (DL-TA) comprehension strategy to a children's story of your choice. As you read the story, identify "prediction stop-points." Then present the story to primary-grade students at the appropriate level, and observe students' predictive responses. (You may find it helpful to tape-record the session.) What insights can you derive from the students' responses? What changes might you make in using this story again with the DL-TA strategy?

3. Observe a kindergarten or first-grade student working in his or her classroom reading center. How does the student select a book? What strategies does the student use in exploring and reading the book selected? Ask the teacher about her or his beliefs concerning the way a reading center contributes to literacy development. Are those beliefs consistent with your observations?

4. Arrange an observation in a kindergarten or first-grade classroom during reading and language-arts instruction. With the teacher's assistance, select one student to observe for the entire period, using the Early Reading and Writing Assessment Checklist in Figure 3.18. Report on your experience, and discuss your instructional recommendations for the student you observed in terms of the checklist categories.

FIGURE 3.19

Professional Standards and Early Literacy Instruction for the Classroom Teacher

Professional Standard	Example
1. Foundational Knowledge	**Element 1.4** Demonstrates knowledge of the major components of reading such as phonemic awareness, vocabulary and background knowledge; e.g., explains how phonemic awareness is essential to mastering the skill of using grapheme-phoneme relationships in learning to read; demonstrates understanding of how the language of instruction concepts are basic to teaching students to read.
2. Instructional Strategies and Curriculum Materials	**Element 2.1** Uses instructional grouping options, such as individual, small-group, and whole-class, as appropriate for accomplishing a given purpose; e.g., understands how to organize the early literacy classroom where rich language interactions can take place, where different forms of written text can be experienced, and where instruction strategies can be employed and adjusted to meet the needs of individuals, small groups, and the entire class.
3. Assessment, Diagnosis and Evaluation	**Element 3.3** Uses assessment information to plan, evaluate, and revise effective instruction that meets the needs of all students; e.g., can describe early language and reading connections and benchmarks such as language of instruction and stages of storybook reading, and can assess students' progress and needs in these areas and design instruction to meet these needs.
4. Creating a Literate Environment	**Element 4.4** Effectively plans and implements instruction that motivates readers intrinsically and extrinsically; e.g., understands how to use children's literature to teach concepts of story and narrative through such activities and strategies as shared book experiences, predictable books, and the Directed Listening-Thinking Activity; can describe and demonstrate a variety of ways to build positive reading and literacy attitudes through special-interest books, daily book sharing, and sharing your own favorite children's books and personal reading interests.
5. Professional Development	**Element 5.1** Displays positive dispositions related to reading and the teaching of reading; e.g., works with families and communities to support students' literacy learning through parent and community volunteers who can assist in literacy tutoring as well as sharing their expertise and talents in students' literacy development.

Part 2 from IRA. (2004). Professional Standards and Ethics Committee, International Reading Association. *Standards for reading professionals—revised 2003*. Reprinted with permission of the International Reading Association. All rights reserved.

Additional Research and Practice

1. Yopp, R. H., & Yopp, H. K. (2000). **Sharing informational text with young children.** *The Reading Teacher, 53*, 410–423.

   This article focuses on the use of informational alphabet books and offers before-, during-, and after-instructional strategies easily adapted for primary-grade classrooms. (Practice)

2. Harris, P., Trezise, J., & Winser, W. N. (2004). **Where is the story? Intertextual reflections on literacy research and practices in the early school years.** *Research in the Teaching of English, 38*, 250–261.

   This discussion reports on insights and classroom implications derived from a three-year longitudinal study (kindergarten through grade 2) that tracked two groups of students to identify the nature of teacher-class interactions and intertextual conflicts that occur as texts are read and discussed. (Practice/Research)

3. McIntyre, E., Kyle, D., & Moore, D. H. (2006). **A primary-grade teacher's guidance toward small-group dialogue.** *Reading Research Quarterly, 41*, 36–66.

   This study describes how one primary grade teacher promoted small-group dialogue about books and literacy concepts for poor and working class students. This study confirms the importance of a classroom culture which promotes a problem-solving environment for students in the effective construction of meaning. (Research)

Increasing Word Recognition Knowledge and Word Identification Skills

I always begin at the left with the opening word of the sentence and read towards the right and I recommend this method.

James Thurber (1894–1961),
American writer and humorist

To the layperson, recognition of words seems to be the basis of reading. And it is! Word recognition is a necessary, although not sufficient, condition for understanding text.

Sandra McCormick,
distinguished literacy educator, professor emeritus, The Ohio State University

As an expert reader, you respond to print differently than do kindergarten and first-grade students. Your text processing is more automatic because of your familiarity with word and text structure. What happens, however, when you encounter text in an unknown alphabet? This is what print is like for beginning readers. Read the cartoon caption on page 85, and answer the following comprehension questions.

1. What is your interpretation of the caption? What word identification strategies did you use in translating the caption?
2. What meaning did you construct for the cartoon? What meaning strategies, picture and text, did you use in deriving the meaning of the cartoon?
3. How long did it take you to read and comprehend the cartoon?

Perhaps you used some of the following strategies in rapid succession:

- Picture interpretation: application of familiar schema (e.g., bedtime story schema)
- Cartoon schema: use of title, familiar cartoonist, familiar characters, expectation of humor
- Letter-sound relationships: transformation of the new alphabet (e.g., ⌐ = *i;* ⊤⌐ = *to*) and association of frequent letter symbols with sounds (e.g., ∟ = *e,* as in He's, asleep, comes)
- Letter pattern–sound pattern relationships [e.g., s-*ee* (consonant, vowel), *th-i-s* (consonant, vowel, consonant)]
- Rhyming ending: observation of familiar letter patterns (e.g., asleep)
- Sentence context: use of context clues from word sequence (e.g., ". . . how this *story* comes out")

- Rapid recognition of a word after having completed part of the word in sentence context (e.g., "I just w . . . [want] to see . . .")

Your rapid application of these strategies probably enabled you to make meaning of the cartoon and caption in two or three minutes. You worked interactively from "part to whole" and "whole to part," inferring missing information by holding a general bedtime story schema in mind and using bits of information to complete the meaning.

double entry journal

Reflect for a moment on your experience in deciphering the cartoon's caption to transform print into meaning. List the word identification strategies you used in this experience. What knowledge and associations do you have about phonics, phonics instruction, and word identification skills?

Chapter Objectives

After reading and discussing this chapter, you will be able to:

- grasp an understanding of the five developmental stages that students progress through in acquiring word knowledge.
- identify key goals and objectives that will guide your word identification instruction.
- know instructional strategies for teaching automatic word recognition.
- understand the heated controversy that often surrounds phonics instruction.

- understand how to effectively use a wide variety of instructional strategies for teaching phonics, syllable identification, compound words, affixes and roots, context clues, and fluency, as well as how to use wide reading in achieving your goals and objectives.
- use word knowledge skills to support effective meaning construction from text.

A Teacher's Introduction to Word Learning Concepts and Goals

This chapter will help you know how to develop word recognition knowledge and word identification skills with your students.

Word Recognition and Word Identification

Word recognition refers to the ability to recognize a word *at sight* without "sounding it out," guessing it from context, or using other strategies. In these cases, the reader sees a word and almost instantly knows what it is.

word recognition
the ability to recognize a word at sight

word identification
circumstances
where a learner
needs to figure out
a word

Word identification, on the other hand, is the term used to indicate those circumstances where a learner does not automatically recognize a word, and therefore, purposely uses a strategy (or more than one strategy) to "figure it out." This is sometimes called *decoding* the word. Some strategies helpful for word identification are phonic analysis (usually called *phonics*), structural analysis, and, sometimes, use of context clues.

Students need instruction in both word recognition and word identification. To conceptualize your teaching goals for word knowledge development, consider this outline. Doing so will help you organize your thinking as you read this chapter.

> **WORD LEARNING**
> I.   Word recognition knowledge
> II. Word identification skills
>   A. Phonic analysis
>   B. Structural analysis
>   C. Use of context clues

Developmental Stages in Word Learning

Research suggests that children progress through developmental stages as they gain word knowledge (McCormick, 2007; Ehri & McCormick, 2004; Ehri, 1991; Frith, 1985; Mason, Herman, & Au, 1991; Morris, 1993). Children's rate of progress through these stages depends heavily on their experiences with print and books at home and in the early grades. Ehri and McCormick's (2004) extensive research review supports the five stages of word learning, shown in Figure 4.1.

**pre-alphabetic
stage**
a stage of word
identification
based on visual
cues

In the **pre-alphabetic stage** of word learning, children rely on visual contextual or graphic features to read words. For example, they may read a word by remembering a logo (e.g., the golden arches with the word *McDonald's*), a visual cue (e.g., the flashcard with the word *elephant* happens to have a smudged thumbprint), or a special typographic connection (e.g., the "tail" on the end of the word *monkey*). Students in the pre-alphabetic stage may depend on specific semantic connections to letter shapes or other cues to prompt memory; may attempt to read words by looking only at the gross shape or length of the word; and, if letters are used as cues, may attend only to certain ones. Some functional knowledge about print may be developed, but word reading continues to rely on visual and nonphonological (nonsound) cues. Most students remember a word only after an unusually large number of exposures to it.

FIGURE 4.1

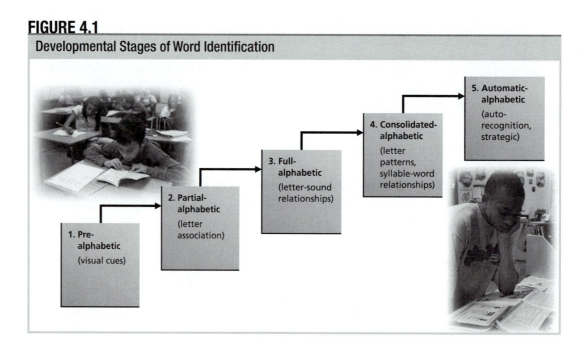

Developmental Stages of Word Identification

1. **Pre-alphabetic** (visual cues)
2. **Partial-alphabetic** (letter association)
3. **Full-alphabetic** (letter-sound relationships)
4. **Consolidated-alphabetic** (letter patterns, syllable-word relationships)
5. **Automatic-alphabetic** (auto-recognition, strategic)

Kindergartners, entering first graders, and severely delayed older readers frequently rely on a pre-alphabetic system to read environmental print and to read a limited number of words at sight. Children's understanding of the alphabetic nature of printed language is only beginning to develop at this stage. Awareness of the **alphabetic principle** is important for reading an alphabetic language like English. This is the principle that the letters in written words have an approximate match to the sounds heard in those words when we speak.

During the transition to the **partial-alphabetic stage**, students begin to shift from visual context and specific letter associations to the alphabetic principle. They begin to associate some letters in a word's spelling with sounds in its pronunciation. For example, the initial sound /d/ in the word *dog* is associated with the letter *d*, or the "two sticks" in the middle of the word *yellow* become associated with the "el" sound in the word. In this transition stage, students start to connect the printed letters to sounds and pronunciations. While these readers are able to use letter-identification knowledge and beginning associations with sounds, they are still largely limited to reading words at sight, because the alphabetic principle is only beginning to develop. Many kindergarten, first graders, and sometimes older delayed readers are in this transition stage.

The **full-alphabetic stage** is characterized by the ability to read words using letter-sound, or grapheme-phoneme, relationships. During this stage, students move from rather slow sounding-out and blending of sounds to rapid application of alphabetic principles. As children attempt to read new words, their oral reading responses range from processing hesitancy to word substitutions to rapid reading. Reading speed begins to increase as strategies become more automatic and sight vocabulary develops from reading practice. Analogy begins to be used more often (e.g., reading *beak* by analogy to *peak*). Some beginning first graders are well into the alphabetic stage, while others have not yet entered this stage. Even in the second and third grades, some delayed readers will function only at the beginning levels of the alphabetic stage.

In the **consolidated-alphabetic stage**, students use alphabetic principles but make efficient use of predictable letter patterns and groups that are larger than letter-sound, or grapheme-phoneme, correspondences (e.g., *-ed, -ing, -est*). These patterns and groups are established in memory, just as the letter-sound units are during the alphabetic stage (Ehri, 1991). Larger letter units help in analyzing multisyllabic words, reduce the number of units needed in memory, and speed up the process of reading words (Juel, 1991; Juel & Minden-Cupp, 2004; Venezky & Massaro, 1979). These units become highly functional in "orthographic neighborhoods," where words share letter sequences and stand for consistent pronunciations (e.g., m*ade*, w*ade*, f*ade*) or for inconsistent pronunciations (e.g., st*eak* cr*eak*, w*ave* h*ave*, m*ost* c*ost*) (Glushko, 1979, 1981). The consolidated-alphabetic stage emerges as students grasp the alphabetic principle and rhyme-based patterns. The word identification efficiency of this stage can be seen in the following example. The word *interesting* contains ten letter-sound correspondences (including *-ng* representing one sound) but only four graphosyllabic units (Ehri & McCormick, 2004). Sensitivity to pattern consistency starts to appear in first grade; sensitivity to pattern inconsistency begins to be seen in second grade.

By the end of the consolidated-alphabetic stage, which may not occur until the fourth or fifth grade or later, children have developed the ability to use analogy to read new words. For example, they generalize from the *-ain* in r*ain* to read the new word tr*ain*. They also are able to separate letter strings of multisyllabic words into root words and affixes or into syllables. Children then convert these to pronunciations and blend them into known and recognizable words (Ehri, 1991). Context becomes an important meaning-based pronunciation check.

The most advanced stage is the **automatic stage.** This phase is characterized by the ability to recognize most words in text automatically by sight. The reader is able to apply various strategies to identify unfamiliar words, including technical and foreign-derived words. Multiple word identification and meaning sources are used to recognize and maintain a high level of reading accuracy. This stage is found in the mature reader.

Individual Variability in Word Knowledge Development

Highly effective teachers understand that students' skills may not match their grade levels, because students within each grade often vary significantly in word knowledge development. For example, many children entering kindergarten understand how print works and are already at

alphabetic principle
letters in written words have an approximate match to sounds in spoken words

partial-alphabetic stage
a stage of word identification based on letter associations

full-alphabetic stage
a stage of word identification based on letter-sound relationships

consolidated-alphabetic stage
a stage of word identification based on alphabetic principles and predictable letter patterns

EVIDENCE-BASED PRACTICE

➤ *Generalization, syllabication, and blending are hallmarks of the automatic-alphabetic stage.*

automatic-alphabetic stage
a stage of word identification characterized by the ability to recognize most words automatically by sight

the beginning of the full-alphabetic phase. Some are able to read text with fluency and understand that reading is a meaning-construction process prompted by printed text and illustrations. Other children, who have had limited experience with print and books, may be at the pre-alphabetic stage, barely beginning to connect print to sounds and familiar meanings. However, unless students have developed a solid foundation in word reading skills and meaning construction by the end of third grade, they will have difficulty reading the content area material that is prevalent in grades 4 and 5, and even greater difficulty reading middle school materials. (National Reading Panel, 2000).

Students with reading difficulty in the intermediate and middle school grades often have not learned to use well letter-sound relationships, blending, predictable letter patterns, visual identification of syllables, context clues, and sight recognition of frequently used words. Most important, some of these students do not understand that reading is a meaning-construction process; they do not enter text with the expectation of making sense. Students depend on their teacher to help them develop needed word recognition and word identification skills in a meaning-based context (Juel & Minden-Cupp, 2004; National Reading Panel, 2000).

Instructional Goals and Objectives to Facilitate Students' Word Learning Knowledge and Skills

Why do some children experience reading difficulty?

Your teaching of word recognition and word identification skills must address two basic goals. The first goal is to assist students who depend on school for word learning and literacy skill development to learn to read and comprehend printed text. The second goal is to enable them to enter a story or an expository text and construct their own meaning (Ruddell & Unrau, 2004a). The following specific objectives are critical for any instructional program:

➤ *Objectives*

1. Develop *print awareness* and *letter recognition* to assist children in the transition from the pre-alphabetic to the full-alphabetic stage of word-learning development.
2. Develop *phonemic awareness* (awareness of separate sounds in words) and *phonemic segmentation* (how sounds are separated and come together in words) as an important step in grasping the relationship between sounds and letters.
3. Provide opportunities to develop *automatic recognition* of words.
4. Build an understanding of and an ability to use *phonics skills*, including letter-sound relationships and blending as students develop key principles in the full-alphabetic stage and read words independently, and use *letter patterns and rhyming endings* as children enter the consolidated-alphabetic stage of word learning.
5. Develop an understanding of structural analysis, using word- and letter-pattern clues to read multisyllabic words in meaning context.
6. Develop an understanding of the use of *context clues,* in coordination with previously developed word identification skills, to read and confirm meaning.
7. Encourage each student to read, read, read, using high-interest reading material to develop *reading fluency.*
8. Provide opportunities for students to read extensively at their independent reading level to develop high level *skill application and automaticity* for word-learning skills and strategies leading to *meaning construction.*

Instruction in word identification should lead to students' automatic and near-automatic use of the various word identification skills (Samuels, 2004). Some students, through wide reading of both narrative and expository texts, will arrive at their own word identification system with minimal guidance. Others will depend heavily on your instruction and guidance to learn to read. In both cases, it is important that students read often and widely to reinforce, apply, and practice the word recognition and word identification skills developed in the classroom.

The instructional principles presented in Chapters 2 and 3 are critical to successful word-learning instruction. These principles state that students are active theory builders and hypothesis testers, that the driving force behind their questions and explorations is to make meaning, that their language performance and social interaction are directly connected to the classroom learning environment, and that their oral and written language development is directly connected

to their reading acquisition. These principles translate into the following four conditions for effective instruction:

➤ *Conditions for Effective Instruction*

1. Develop word recognition knowledge and word identification strategies through activities that have meaning for students.
2. Use students' own curiosity, interests, and background knowledge.
3. Let students know that you expect them to be successful in the instructional activity.
4. Provide positive response and feedback, based on your observations, as students participate in instructional activities.

These principles will be used in developing the following instructional strategies for teaching phonics, syllable identification, compound words, affixes and roots, context clues, fluency, and skill application through wide reading—all of which are critical to each student's reading success.

Common Teaching Emphases in Word Learning Programs

The five stages of word learning provide a developmental context for an instructional program. Regardless of the methodology used in teaching word skills, students appear to progress through these stages in acquiring reading independence. A common teaching emphasis, with associated grade levels, is found in Table 4.1. The first two entries in the table—print awareness and phonemic awareness/phonemic segmentation—were discussed in Chapter 3. The remainder of this

TABLE 4.1

Common Teaching Emphases and Placement of Word-Learning Skills, Grades K–8

Word Identification Skill	Grade Level								
	K	1	2	3	4	5	6	7	8
1. Print Awareness									
Print organization	xxx	xx	x						
Page organization	xxx	xx	x						
Book organization	xxx	xx	x						
Letter recognition	xxx	xxx	x						
2. Phonemic Awareness;	xxx	xxx	xx	x					
Phonemic Segmentation	xxx	xxx	xx	x					
3. Phonics									
Letter-sound relationships									
Consonants	xxx	xxx	xxx	xx	x	x	x	x	x
Vowels	xxx	xxx	xxx	xx	x	x	x	x	x
Letter patterns and rhyme	xxx	xxx	xxx	xx	x	x	x	x	x
4. Syllable Identification/ Structural Analysis									
Pattern clues to breaks		xxx	xxx	xxx	xxx	xxx	x	x	x
Consonant cluster breaks		xxx	xxx	xxx	xxx	xxx	x	x	x
Compound words	xx	xxx	xxx	xxx	xxx	xxx	xx	x	x
Affixes (prefixes & suffixes) and roots	xx	xx	xxx	xxx	xxx	xx	x	x	x
5. Context Clues (+3 +4, above)	xxx	xxx	xxx	xxx	x	x	x	x	x
6. Automatic Word Recognition		xxx	xxx	xxx	xx	xx	xx	xx	xx
7. Reading Fluency			xxx	xxx	xx	xx	x	x	x
8. Skill Application through Wide Reading		xxx	xxx	xxx	xxx	xxx	xxx	xxx	xxx

Key: xxx Major emphasis: high probability of learning and development
    xx Minor emphasis: continued development
    x Maintenance: reinforcement through wide reading

chapter will emphasize word recognition and word identification skill development for the other skills in Table 4.1, from letter-sound relationships to skill application through wide reading.

Instructional Strategies for Teaching Automatic Word Recognition

word recognition
the immediate identification of a word at sight

As indicated elsewhere in this chapter, **word recognition** is recognizing a word *at sight,* without "sounding it out," guessing it from context, or using other such strategies.

Learners use sight recognition of words in the beginning of their development as readers, during their development, and later as mature readers. In the *beginning*, while in the pre-alphabetic phase, students *must* use sight recognition because they do not yet have the skills for using sound-symbol relationships or for using structural components of words such as syllables, affixes, and roots. *During* their development as readers, after they have identified a word many times through use of phonics or other analyses, learners begin to remember that word—at which point they no longer need to use these word identification skills because they can now recognize the word at sight. *Mature readers* (such as you) recognize almost all words they encounter at sight; to check that assertion, look over this page and count the number of words that you had to sound out (in most cases, the number will be zero or, at least, very, very few).

When you teach phonics and structural analysis to your students, not only does this provide an important temporary route to reading words, it also furnishes a critical component for building a sight vocabulary. Chapter 3 also contributed suggestions for teaching sight vocabulary. Return briefly to Chapter 3 and review the information on the use of Big Books (page 58); the use of language-experience charts, including tagboard word cards (pages 58–60); how to display word labels around the room (page 59); and the use of word banks for spelling, writing, and reading (page 66). All of these provide ideas you can use to help students build their sight vocabularies. A How To Do box in Chapter 10 (page 293) presents a list of principles for developing sight word recognition with delayed readers, highly useful principles that also have practical application with average students as well.

word wall
an area in the classroom for displaying high-frequency words and special words encountered in students' reading

A **word wall** is another instructional strategy used by highly effective teachers for building students' sight word recognition (Cunningham, 2005). A word wall is comprised of nicely displayed words, large enough for students to see from their desks, posted on all walls of the classroom (or on a large bulletin board reserved for this purpose). This display grows over time, throughout the year, as more words are added. Usually the words fit a preselected theme—such as *high-frequency words* or simply *special words encountered in our reading lessons*. The specific words that are chosen to be displayed are important words likely to occur often in reading material, as well as "tricky" words that are phonetically irregular or difficult in some other way. A number of steps are taken so that these words become part of a student's sight vocabulary: The words are referred to often, are pointed out when confusion arises, and are the basis of various word-learning activities. The goal is that students gain automatic recognition of these specially targeted words. Word walls can be used at any grade level. Figure 4.2 shows one first-grade classroom's partially developed word wall.

A Web site with good ideas for making and using word walls is www.k111.k12.il.us/lafayette/fourblocks/word_wall_grade_level_lists.htm.

Several additional activities for promoting gains in sight word recognition, which are both instructionally sound and appealing to students, are found in the Strategies in Use box, Developing Activities for Automatic Word Recognition (pages 92–93).

automaticity
mastery of word skills, such as rapid recognition of high-frequency words, at such a high level that they can be used automatically

Ultimately, the goal is that readers will recognize almost *all* words at sight. Although this principle is true for any word, one group of words—high-frequency words—deserve special mention. As the label implies, these words occur very frequently in *all* written material. For example, the word "the" occurs as about every tenth word in children's text. Many of these high frequency words play a basic role in English sentence structure. Some nouns, verbs, and adjectives occur so often that a central objective is to develop high-speed, automatic recognition of them (Allington & Cunningham, 1996; Samuels, 1994). This **automaticity** enables students to focus on the primary goal of reading—comprehension of text.

FIGURE 4.2

A Word-Wall Example, Taken from a First-Grade Classroom Halfway through the Year

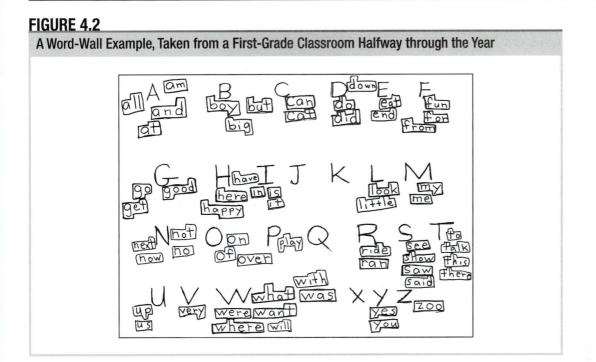

From Patricia M. Cunningham. *Phonics They Use: Words for Reading and Writing,* 2e. Published by Allyn & Bacon, Boston, MA. Copyright © 1995 by Pearson Education. Reprinted by permission of the publisher.

Teachers sometimes use word lists to determine which words occur most frequently. A number of word lists have been constructed based on counts of "running words" in various types of reading material (Dolch, 1936; Durr, 1973; Kucera & Francis, 1967; Walker, 1979). Interestingly, although these researchers have examined different kinds of texts (e.g., easy and hard; narrative and expository; children's and adult), the first couple of hundred words on all of their lists—that is, the most frequently occurring—are almost the same! This is because there are basic function words that "glue" together our English sentences and, thus, have to occur repeatedly in any text—words like *the, and, a, that, is, these, but, he, she, one, you, they, may, this, are, see, in, of, be, there, been, on, like, to, have,* and others. Check this very page and see how many of these high-frequency words you find in just this one small section.

Fry (1977a) developed a list of high-frequency words that is especially functional for teachers. He called the list "Instant Words," implying that, because of their recurrent use, they should be learned to the point where they would be recognized automatically and rapidly—that is, instantly. As is generally the case, the words Fry identified as most commonly occurring are similar to those included on the other well-known lists; in addition—and helpful for teachers—Fry gave approximate grade-level recommendations for use. The complete list is printed in Table 4.2 (pages 94–95). Although development of word-recognition skills must be based on a teacher's observations and knowledge of individual students (for example, some students develop an extensive rapid-recognition vocabulary early in the primary grades, while others need assistance into the intermediate grades), Fry's "Instant Words" list identifies a core of words that should ultimately be developed to high-speed recognition.

Instructional Strategies for Teaching Word Identification

Word identification strategies are helpful when students do not recognize a word automatically. The major word identification strategies are *phonic analysis* and *structural analysis*. If used in conjunction with these first two strategies, use of *context clues* also can, at times, be helpful.

Strategies in Use

Developing Activities for Automatic Word Recognition

Activities for developing rapid-recognition vocabulary develop meaning for these words through a picture context, written sentence or story context, or oral language context. These activities must create high motivation and active involvement of students in individual, partner pair, or small-group settings. Here are five such activities.

SPIN A WORD

Search through old magazines for pictures that represent high-frequency vocabulary. These should include nouns (e.g., *mother, father, girl, boy, house, book, people, tree, eyes,* and *water*), verbs (e.g., *jump, fly, ride, eat, drink,* and *wash*), and adjectives (e.g., *red, blue, yellow, little,* and *funny*). Paste the pictures in a large circle on tagboard, and attach a tagboard pointer in the center of the circle with a paper rivet. Use a felt-tip pen to prepare a set of tagboard word cards with the words representing the pictures.

Each student spins the pointer and notes the word represented by the picture. He or she then quickly sorts through the word cards, locates the word that matches the picture, and uses the word in a sentence. The student's score is the number of words correctly identified. A stopwatch or other timer can be used to set a time limit (e.g., 20 seconds) for each turn in a round and to add higher motivation for acquiring rapid word recognition.

WORD TRAIN

Find and cut out age-appropriate comic strips or cartoons that use a variety of high-frequency words in context. Make up a brief story of three or four sentences to accompany the strip or cartoon, and print each sentence on a strip of tagboard. For example, three strips of tagboard might contain the following three sentences:

> Dennis threw the ball to his friend.
> It smashed the big picture window.
> Mr. Wilson looks very angry and is talking to the boys.

Next, cut apart the words in each sentence (e.g., *Dennis / threw / the / ball / to / his / friend*), and clip them together.

Using a timer, see how fast a student or small group can organize each sentence to form a story representing the action in the strip or cartoon. Partner pairs work well for this type of activity.

Phonic Analysis

Phonic analysis is more often simply called "phonics" by the lay person and the lay press—and even by some teachers. Many individuals, incorrectly, believe that phonics skills are all students need in order to become good readers. The following sections discuss the important—and "hot"—topic of phonics and provide accurate information on ways phonics knowledge can contribute to literacy development.

Phonics: A History of Controversy

Word identification skills are critical to your students' reading success (Hiebert, 1996; Perfetti & Zhang, 1996; Stahl et al., 1998; Taylor, 1996; van den Broek, 1996). These skills are the key to transforming printed text into meaning. Effective word identification enables readers to understand the relationships among printed or written letters, letter patterns, and contextual clues and their familiar counterparts in students' oral language. A teacher's major instructional goal is to assist students in the development of these skills. Their automatic use frees students to focus on the primary purpose of reading—to construct meaning and develop personal interpretations.

The instructional approach used in teaching word identification skills has become one of the most controversial educational topics of this new century and the last (Adams, 1990a, 1990b; Alexander & Fox, 2004; Chall, 2000; Flesch, 1955; Hiebert & Taylor, 2000). Heated debate has centered around the issue of phonics versus whole-word instruction. During the 1920s and 1930s, reading instruction emphasized **reading readiness** and language growth. The materials used ranged from teacher-pupil experience charts, which drew heavily on children's background knowledge and experiences, to publisher-produced reading programs. Publishers introduced the

➤ *Word identification skills are a key to reading success.*

reading readiness preparedness for reading instruction, developed through preprimer skill training

FLASH CARDS

Prepare a set of flash cards by printing high-frequency words on the front of 5-by-8-inch cards. On the back of each card, paste a small picture clue to the word's identification and meaning. Expose each word card for a few seconds to individual students or partner pairs, and have them name the word. Complete a meaning check by using the picture clue on the reverse side. This activity may be varied by having individuals or partner pairs refer first to the picture clue and then, after giving the pronunciation and meaning of the word, trace the word with the index and middle fingers. This approach ensures careful attention to the distinguishing features of the word.

WORD FISHING

Write high-frequency words on tagboard strips. On the reverse side of each strip, use the word in a sentence or add a picture meaning clue. Affix a paper clip to each card, and place the cards in a small bowl or box. Provide each partner pair with a short stick that has a string and magnet attached. Each student fishes a word card out of the container, places the card word side up on the desk, and attempts to read it. If the student has difficulty reading the word, the card is turned over and the picture clue is used, but the "fish" must be thrown back. New word cards are drawn from the container until the student is successful. Each correct pronun-ciation "lands" the fish and scores one point. The game may be played again using a timer to increase motivation.

SIGHT-WORD HUNT

Students are given a short amount of time (e.g., five to ten minutes) to locate in the classroom as many of their targeted sight words as they can. Encourage students to skim through their books and other classroom resources to find the words. Students may work individually or in pairs. The success of the word hunt is shared as a whole group by reading the words and telling where they were found. (Adapted from a suggestion by Joan C. Fingon, personal communication, April 23, 2004).

CRITICAL THINKING

1. What is the value of these activities for students?
2. Which of the above activities would you select for use in your classroom? Why?
3. Turn to Table 4.2 (pages 94–95). How would you determine which of these words would be of greatest value to your students?
4. Develop another high-frequency vocabulary activity you could use with students.
5. How could you adapt the rapid word recognition activities for use in content area instruction with older students?

preprimer with the intent of providing an initial whole-word recognition vocabulary for children. **Phonics instruction,** defined as the teaching of alphabetic principles and conventions of written language, was introduced gradually over several grade levels within the context of basal reader vocabularies. Teacher's guides contained detailed scope and sequence suggestions for the gradual development of word identification and comprehension skills based on the content of the reader.

The concept of **language growth** emerged from a child-centered curriculum and was enhanced by the efforts of John Dewey and his followers. The central idea was to provide enriched direct experiences through oral dramatization and creative writing in a content-oriented unit that related to children's own experiences. Instruction in correct usage was still viewed as an important part of the curriculum. Spelling words were derived from unit activities, and a spelling text was commonly used in classrooms.

During the 1940s, World War II induction testing indicated that new armed forces personnel were unable to read and follow detailed instructions in either oral or written form. The instruction and literacy levels of America's youth were deemed inadequate. The armed services proceeded to offer literacy courses to raise performance levels of new inductees. In the late 1940s, public schools across the country began to provide **remedial-reading instruction** on a wide scale.

Basal reading programs during this period emphasized immediate word recognition and context clues, with the gradual introduction of phonics and other word identification skills. Initial instruction, however, still focused on the development of a sight vocabulary (the whole-word emphasis) through frequent repetition of words in basal readers. These readers had broader literary selections than did those published earlier in the century.

By the 1950s, the stage was set for an angry protest movement. This movement was triggered

phonics instruction
the teaching of alphabetic principles and conventions of written language

language growth
a child-centered, developmental, experiential approach to word identification skills

remedial-reading instruction
teaching of word identification and other skills in an effort to help students overcome reading difficulties

TABLE 4.2
Fry's List of "Instant Words" for Automatic Recognition

First 100 Words (Approximately First Grade)				Second 100 Words (Approximately Second Grade)				Third 100 Words (Approximately Third Grade)			
Group 1a	Group 1b	Group 1c	Group 1d	Group 2a	Group 2b	Group 2c	Group 2d	Group 3a	Group 3b	Group 3c	Group 3d
the	he	go	who	saw	big	may	fan	ask	hat	off	fire
a	I	see	an	home	where	let	five	small	car	sister	ten
is	they	then	their	soon	am	use	read	yellow	write	happy	order
you	one	us	she	stand	ball	these	over	show	try	once	part
to	good	no	new	box	morning	right	such	goes	myself	didn't	early
and	me	him	said	upon	live	present	way	clean	longer	set	fat
we	about	by	did	first	four	tell	too	buy	those	round	third
that	had	was	boy	came	last	next	shall	thank	hold	dress	same
in	if	come	three	girl	color	please	own	sleep	full	tell	love
not	some	get	down	house	away	leave	most	letter	carry	wash	hear
for	up	or	work	find	red	hand	sure	jump	eight	start	yesterday
at	her	two	put	because	friend	more	thing	help	sing	always	eyes
with	do	man	were	made	pretty	why	only	fly	warm	anything	door
it	when	little	before	could	eat	better	near	don't	sit	around	clothes
on	so	has	just	book	want	under	than	fast	dog	close	through
can	my	them	long	look	year	while	open	cold	ride	walk	o'clock
will	very	how	here	mother	white	should	kind	today	hot	money	second
are	all	like	other	run	got	never	must	does	grow	turn	water
of	would	our	old	school	play	each	high	face	cut	might	town
this	any	what	take	people	found	best	far	green	seven	hard	took
your	been	know	cat	night	left	another	both	every	woman	along	pair
as	out	make	again	into	men	seem	end	brown	funny	bed	now
but	there	which	give	say	bring	tree	also	coat	yes	fine	keep
be	from	much	after	think	wish	name	until	six	ate	sat	head
have	day	his	many	back	black	dear	call	gave	stop	hope	food

TABLE 4.2
Fry's List of "Instant Words" for Automatic Recognition (*continued*)

Second 300 Words (Approximately Fourth Grade)

Group 4a	Group 4b	Group 4c	Group 4d	Group 4e	Group 4f	Group 4g	Group 4h	Group 4i	Group 4j	Group 4k	Group 4l
told	time	word	wear	hour	grade	egg	spell	become	herself	demand	aunt
Miss	yet	almost	Mr.	glad	brother	ground	beautiful	body	idea	however	system
father	true	thought	side	follow	remain	afternoon	sick	chance	drop	figure	line
children	above	send	poor	company	milk	feed	became	act	river	case	cause
land	still	receive	lost	believe	several	boat	cry	die	smile	increase	marry
interest	meet	pay	outside	begin	war	plan	finish	real	son	enjoy	possible
government	since	nothing	wind	mind	able	question	catch	speak	bat	rather	supply
feet	number	need	Mrs.	pass	charge	fish	floor	already	fact	sound	thousand
garden	state	mean	learn	reach	either	return	stick	doctor	sort	eleven	pen
done	matter	late	held	month	less	sir	great	step	king	music	condition
country	line	half	front	point	train	fell	guess	itself	dark	human	perhaps
different	remember	fight	built	rest	cost	hill	bridge	nine	themselves	court	produce
bad	large	enough	family	sent	evening	wood	church	baby	whose	force	twelve
across	few	feet	began	talk	note	add	lady	minute	study	plant	rode
yard	hit	during	air	went	past	ice	tomorrow	ring	fear	suppose	uncle
winter	cover	gone	young	bank	room	chair	snow	wrote	move	law	labor
table	window	hundred	ago	ship	flew	watch	whom	happen	stood	husband	public
story	even	week	world	business	office	alone	women	appear	himself	moment	consider
sometimes	city	between	airplane	whole	cow	low	among	heart	strong	person	thus
I'm	together	change	without	short	visit	arm	road	swim	knew	result	least
tried	sun	being	kill	certain	wait	dinner	farm	felt	often	continue	power
horse	life	care	ready	fair	teacher	hair	cousin	fourth	toward	price	mark
something	street	answer	stay	reason	spring	service	bread	I'll	wonder	serve	president
brought	party	course	won't	summer	picture	class	wrong	kept	twenty	national	voice
shoes	suit	against	paper	fill	bird	quite	age	well	important	wife	whether

In what ways are the media influencing literacy instruction today?

largely by critic Rudolph Flesch's (1955) widely read book *Why Johnny Can't Read*. Flesch argued for phonics instruction that would teach children the names of letters and the sounds those letters represent. This argument was not new, but his appeal made a political connection between phonics and democracy through such statements as "Equal opportunity for all is one of the inalienable rights, and the word method interferes with that right" (p. 130).

Closely following the publication of Flesch's book, Russia launched Earth's first satellite, Sputnik I, thus increasing public concern about education in the United States. Criticism of the teaching of reading in U.S. schools was clearly evident in Arthur Trace's (1961) *What Ivan Knows That Johnny Doesn't*. As a result of popular books like those by Flesch and Trace, the general public developed an oversimplified view of reading instruction. They perceived a polar dichotomy between whole-word and phonics instruction. Actually, such a dichotomy never existed. Neither approach had been the exclusive means of word-learning instruction in any major basal reading series. Rather, reading programs differed in what was emphasized and what was taught first: letter sounds (phonics) or words (whole word). The true issue was relative emphasis and sequence. Nevertheless, the either-or viewpoint of the phonics versus whole-word method persists today in the minds of many members of the general public and some educators.

Research on Beginning Reading and Phonics

Research in the 1960s led to works such as Jeanne Chall's (1967/1983) *Learning to Read: The Great Debate*. This analysis of early reading instruction was based on the study of publisher-produced programs, observations in primary-grade classrooms, and an extensive review of reading research to date. Chall concluded that systematic phonics instruction, used with connected and meaningful reading, resulted in higher reading achievement for some students.

The First Grade Studies
federally funded nationwide research on literacy instruction in the 1960s

During the mid-1960s, a nationwide, federally funded, cooperative research program, known as **The First Grade Studies** (Bond & Dykstra, 1967), was launched to examine various approaches to beginning reading instruction. This research involved twenty-seven research centers that used identical achievement tests and measures to attempt to determine the best method of early reading instruction. Findings revealed that combined approaches—those using *both* systematic phonics and emphasis on connected reading and meaning—produced superior results. However, with every instructional approach, some students achieved well and some did not.

The best predictor of reading success proved to be the students' ability to recognize and name uppercase and lowercase letters of the alphabet at the beginning of first grade. This finding supports the importance of print awareness, understanding the relationships between letters and sounds, and early literacy development at home (Dykstra, 1968). By the end of third grade, few differences were found favoring any of the approaches, combined or otherwise. In effect, critical word identification skills were learned in all programs by grade 3 and were reinforced through application in reading children's literature.

the Highly Effective Teacher

In some of The First Grade Studies, greater variation was found in students' achievement levels between different teachers' classrooms than between the kinds of reading programs used. This finding supports the importance of effective teaching, regardless of the instructional emphasis. Both high quality teaching and instructional programs that combine word identification with connected meaningful reading contribute to students' reading achievement.

Follow-Through Program
federally funded nationwide research on children's achievement gains in the primary grades in the 1970s

The 1970s saw the implementation of the federally supported **Follow-Through Program**, which studied students' achievement gains in the primary grades through twenty-two instructional approaches. All approaches emphasized one of three areas: (1) basic academic skills, (2) cognitive and conceptual development, and (3) child-centered activities focusing on development. Like The First Grade Studies, the Follow-Through Program showed that approaches emphasizing basic academic skills through highly structured word identification produced the greatest gains for grades 1 and 2. Few differences were found by grade 3, and almost no differences could be discerned by grade 4 (Adams, 1990b). By grades 5 and 6, however, students in the group receiving direct instruction in basic academic skills had the highest achievement levels (Becker & Gersten, 1982). These students were involved not only in a more structured program of word identification but also in reading and interpreting stories from the beginning of first grade. Again, the findings support the importance of balanced, integrated instruction that emphasizes both word identification and interpretation of meaningfully connected reading (Chall, 1967/1983).

Reading Instruction and Phonics Today

The phonics and meaning controversy has not yet been fully resolved (Farstrup & Samuels, 2002). In the 1980s, as a result of numerous reports on education and literacy education (see, for example, Anderson et al., 1985), the late Senator Edward Zorinsky of Nebraska sponsored legislation to commission a major study and report on phonics instruction. This resulted in the publication of *Beginning to Read* by Marilyn Adams (1990b), which covered educational, psychological, and sociolinguistic research on reading since the early 1970s. The work has generated significant controversy (Adams, 1994). Some phonics advocates believe it is too meaning-based, and natural-language advocates think it emphasizes teaching print-sound systems too early. Adams (1990b) calls for the development of print awareness, use of invented spelling in word identification instruction, systematic instruction in word identification, instruction using meaning-based text, and opportunities for children to develop near-automatic word identification skills through wide reading. As Adams notes in the book's conclusion,

> Written text has both method and purpose. It is time for us to stop bickering about which is more important. To read, children must master both, and we must help them. In the interest of developing not just their reading skills but their own personal intellectual and productive potential, we must further encourage them to read frequently, broadly, and thoughtfully. (p. 424)

➤ *Students must master both method and purpose.*

➤ *Chapter 1 introduced and defined these basic approaches to literacy instruction.*

During the past decade, publishers have continued to produce reading programs with detailed teacher's guides and support materials such as workbooks. However, a noted shift in emphasis has occurred, as word identification skills are introduced in the earlier grades in a more concentrated way and more in the context of meaningful text. At the same time, comprehension development has continued to be emphasized and greater emphasis has been placed on content area reading.

The debate about word identification undoubtedly will continue, fueled by the writings of lay critics, sensational media coverage, and nationwide advertising of programs such as *Hooked on Phonics*. The critical issue is not whether teachers emphasize phonics or whole-word instruction but whether they recognize that word identification skills play a critical role in developing reader independence and that they teach these skills systematically, in a well-planned, meaning-based context. This viewpoint is most recently evident in the phonics instruction recommendations presented in the Research and Evidence-Based Practice feature on Phonics and Other Word Identification Instruction.

Important Information About Teaching Phonics

Chapter 3 already has presented several instructional strategies for teaching beginning word identification. The basic print awareness and phonics skills developed there include the following:

EVIDENCE-BASED PRACTICE

1. Print awareness knowledge to understand that print, picture, page, and book organization represent meaning
2. Letter-name and -recognition knowledge to understand that words are composed of letters
3. Phonemic awareness knowledge to understand that spoken words are composed of sounds
4. Phonemic segmentation knowledge to understand that words consist of separate sounds and that letters correspond to sounds

Two basic approaches, or combination of approaches, are used to help students learn letter-sound relationships in phonics. The first approach is **implicit-phonics** (also called *analytic-phonics*) instruction (McCormick, 2007). This approach teaches letter-sound relationships in the context of the word in which it is found. For example, you would write the words *bat, ball,* and *boy* on the chalkboard and say, "The sound of *b* is the one we hear at the beginning of *bat, ball,* and *boy.*" You might then underline the *b* in each word as the word is pronounced by the children. The sound at the beginning of each word is emphasized by underlining it and some sound emphasis, but the target sound is not isolated. The words would then be used in a sentence context, such as *The small boy hit the ball with the big bat.* This implicit approach supports the viewpoint that letter sounds should be presented only in the context of a word and then a sentence to enhance meaning and avoid the sound distortion that may occur when some sounds are isolated. For example, the sound represented by the letter *b* is pronounced /*buh*/ in isolation. This distortion may confuse the learner when applied to decoding a new word. At times basal readers have subscribed to this approach, which has developed effective word identification skills for many readers. (See How To Do, Letter-Sound Relationships: Implicit and Explicit Phonics, page 99).

implicit phonics an instructional method in which letter-sound relationships are taught in the context of the words in which they are found

Research and Evidence-Based Practice

Phonics and Other Word Identification Instruction

Did You Know?

■ Systematic phonics instruction is beneficial to reading and spelling for students in grades K–6, as well as for delayed readers (Report of the National Reading Panel, 2000, White, 2005).

■ To use letter-sound associations successfully, students must have developed some level of phonemic awareness (Report of the National Reading Panel, 2000).

■ Reading instruction should not focus only on letter-sound associations. Students must have opportunities to practice putting these associations to use (1) in identifying real words through *blending* sounds to read them and (2) in *separating* spoken words into their sounds to write them (*Author's note:* Sometimes referred to as practice in "making and breaking words") (Clay, 1985; Juel & Minden-Cupp, 2004; Report of the National Reading Panel, 2000).

■ Phonics instruction can be implemented in a vibrant, creative, entertaining manner, and it is more likely to stimulate motivation if presented in this way (Report of the National Reading Panel, 2000).

■ Children progress through five phases of understanding as they master the alphabetic system in word reading:

(1) the pre-alphabetic phase, (2) the partial-alphabetic phase, (3) the full-alphabetic phase, (4) the consolidated-alphabetic phase, and (5) the automatic-alphabetic phase. Instructional effectiveness can be enhanced through careful observation, determining a student's phase of development and matching instruction to meet the student's needs in that phase (Ehri & McCormick, 2004; McCormick, 2007).

■ Children entering first grade with minimal reading skills appear to have greatest success when teachers model word-recognition strategies by chunking words into syllables or onset/rime units, identifying little words in big words, as well as actively modeling the blending of individual letters and phonemes into word chunks that make sense (Juel & Minden-Cupp, 2004).

■ The purpose of phonics instruction is to develop accurate word identification to support the main reason for reading—comprehension of text. Furthermore, phonics instruction is only one part of a larger, well-balanced reading program (Report of the National Reading Panel, 2000; Ruddell & Unrau, 2004).

---

explicit phonics
an instructional method in which letter-sound relationships are taught by articulating the sounds in isolation

The second approach is known as **explicit phonics** (also called *synthetic phonics*) (McCormick, 2007). This approach teaches letter-sound relationships by articulating the sound in isolation. Proponents of this approach point out that many letter sounds are distorted when pronounced in isolation (these are known as consonant continuants, e.g., /m/, /n/, /s/, and will be discussed shortly). Using the explicit phonics approach, you would write the letter *m* on the chalkboard, along with the words *mat, may,* and *mother.* Then say, "The sound of *m* is /mmm-mmm/. Let's say the sound together (as you point to the letter *m*) /mmm-mmm/. This is the sound that we hear at the beginning of the words *mat, may,* and *mother* (as you underline the *m* in each word). Let's say the sound together again, /mmm-mmm/." This approach has the value of providing students with phonemic details about letters that enable them to effectively learn letter-sound associations and to blend these (Adams, 1990a). This may be especially important for those delayed readers who are experiencing reading difficulty (Leppanen, Niemi, Aunola, & Nurmi, 2004).

The approach recommended in this text is that the highly effective teacher must understand and be aware of both implicit and explicit approaches. Instructional examples presented in this chapter illustrate how these two approaches can be effectively combined. The following discussions identify phonics-instruction strategies using both approaches for developing consonants, vowels, and letter-pattern recognition through rime/rhyme.

letter-sound relationships
regular correspondences between letters in the written alphabet and sounds

The English alphabetic system *generally* has regular **letter-sound relationships** and predictable letter patterns. A summary of letter-sound principles follows:

1. Single consonants in the initial positions of words are highly regular (e.g., *b* as in *bat*). As noted in Table 4.3, there are a few exceptions, such as *c* as in *can* (/k/) and in *city* (/s/), *g* as

How To Do . . .

Letter-Sound Relationships: Teaching Implicit and Explicit Phonics

1. Develop letter-sound relationships in a meaning-based context.
2. Use discussions, activities, and reading material that will actively involve and interest students.
3. Help students understand that letters and letter patterns stand for sounds and sound patterns—not that "letters make sounds," which leads to confusion.
4. Use the following instructional sequence for teaching *implicit phonics:*
    a. Introduce the new letter-sound relationship, or concept, in the context of known vocabulary (e.g., *m* /m/—*mat*).
    b. Develop visual association with the new letter or letter pattern in the context of the written word (e.g., underline the letter *m* as you say the word *mat*. Have your students say the word *mat* as you point to the letter *m*).
    c. Provide a range of word examples using the new letter-sound concept in the same position and direct attention to the new concept in these examples (e.g., *mat, mother, man*).

■ **Also articulate the sound of the targeted letter(s) in isolation. Have students practice the sound(s) both in isolation and in the context of words. Research indicates that *explicit phonics* instruction, such as this, is more productive for delayed readers, with students finding it easier to learn separate sounds and easier to learn to blend them (Adams, 1990a, 1990b; Anderson et al., 1984; Johnson & Baumann, 1984; U.S. Department of Health and Human Services, 2000).**

DELAYED READER ADAPTATION

EVIDENCE-BASED PRACTICE

    d. Contrast the new letter-sound concept with a different letter-sound concept substituted in the same position to form a new word or words (e.g., *mat, bat, cat*).
    e. Encourage students to identify the name of the letter that stands for the sound at the beginning (or middle or end) of the words developed in the discussion (e.g., ask your students what letter stands for the sound at the beginning of the word *mat*).
    f. Use the word examples in meaningful sentence context.
5. Use the following instructional sequence for teaching *explicit phonics:*
    a. Introduce the new letter-sound relationship, or concept, using known vocabulary (e.g., *m/mmm-mmm/—mat*).
    b. Develop the visual association with the new letter by writing the letter (e.g, *m*) on the chalkboard.
    c. Provide a range of word examples using the letter in the same position in each word (e.g., *mat, mother, man*) and direct attention to the new letter in each word.
    d. As you direct attention to the new letter in each word, say "/*mmm-mmm*/. This is the sound that we hear at the beginnings of the word *mat* /*mmm-mmm*/, *mother* /*mmm-mmm*/, and *man* /*mmm-mmm*/." (As you say the sound, underline the letter *m*).
    e. Encourage the students to say the sound together, /*mmm-mmm*/, as you point to the letter *m*.
    f. Use the word examples in a meaningful context.

in *get* (/g/) and in *gym* (/j/), and *s* as in *sit* (/s/) and in *sure* (/sh/). Note, however, that there are only two variations for each of these exceptions.

2. **Consonant digraphs,** two letters standing for one sound, are also highly regular, as is evident in Table 4.4 (e.g., *ch* as in *chip*, *kn* as in *knit*).
3. **Consonant blends,** two letters representing different sounds but blended together, likewise are very regular, as noted in Table 4.4 (e.g., *bl* as in *blue*, *tr* as in *tree*).
4. Short vowel sounds, represented by the letters *a, e, i, o,* and *u,* have a much lower level of predictability when considered in isolation, as shown in Table 4.5 (e.g., *a* as in *bat* and *talk*).

consonant digraphs
two letters that stand for one sound

consonant blends
two letters that represent different sounds but are pronounced together

TABLE 4.3
Consonant Patterns: Letter-Sound Relationships and Frequency of Occurrence*

Consonants		Example of Major Pattern Use	Rank Order	Frequency	Varied Pattern Use
b	/b/	bat	20	2,242	tuba, cab
c	/k/	can	6	3,452	
	/s/	city	5	4,599	racer
d	/d/	doll	12	1,067	soda, mad
f	/f/	fit	9	1,580	heifer, life
g	/g/	get	11	1,178	tiger, rag
	/j/	gym	14	647	margarine
h	/h/	hat	13	762	ahead
j	/j/	jaw	22	218	pajama, rajah
	/w/	Juan	—	—	
k	/k/	kitten	16	601	baker, break
l	/l/	lake	4	4,894	sailor, metal
m	/m/	man	7	3,302	tamer, ham
n	/n/	nut	3	7,452	finer, hen
p	/p/	picnic	8	3,296	piper, drip
q	/k/	queen	23	191	liquor, opaque
r	/r/	run	1	9,134	bearer, car
s	/s/	sit	5	4,599	pets, pastel
	/sh/	sure	18	398	passion
	/z/	has, cars	15	640	
t	/t/	time	2	7,528	meter, hit
v	/v/	voice	10	1,485	mover, wave
w	/w/	work	17	578	shower, rower
x	/ks/	box	19	245	
	/z/	xylophone	—	—	
y	/y/	yard	24	53	Sawyer
z	/z/	zoo	21	229	blazer, jazz
	/zh/	azure	—	—	

*The letter-sound-relationship frequencies found in Tables 4.3, 4.4, & 4.5 are based on a study published by Edward Fry (2004). These frequencies are interesting in identifying the potential utility of consonant and vowel letter-sound correspondences. For example, a quick inspection of Table 4.3 shows a relatively high frequency of occurrence for consonant correspondences such as b /b/, bat (2,242); c /k/, can (3,452); c /s/, city (4,599); l /l/, lake (4,894); r /r/, run (9,134); and t /t/, time (7,528); and the relatively low occurrences for consonant correspondences such as g /j/, gym (647); j /j/, jaw (218); and y /y/, yard (53). Table 4.5 shows short and long vowels and their frequency of occurrence. The short-vowel correspondences, as might be expected, have a much higher frequency than the long-vowel correspondences. For example, the frequency of the short a /ă/, cab (4,192) and the short i /ĭ/, nick (5,346) correspondences far outdistance the frequency of the long a /ā/, made (790) and the long i /ī/, mice (555).

Fry's frequencies were derived from research that examined and counted every grapheme-phoneme correspondence in the Thorndike & Lorge 17,310-word vocabulary list (Hanna, Hanna, Hodges, & Rudorf, 1966). This list of different words was selected from the Thorndike-Lorge *Teacher's Word Book of 30,000 Words* (1944). One could question the word database published in 1944; however, new words tend to have a lower frequency than the more common structure words such as "is," or common base words like "run." Fry also expresses the view that even new words would be expected to use the same more common correspondences and thus would not substantially change the frequency order of the correspondences.

Based on data from E. Fry. (2004). Phonics: A large phoneme-grapheme frequency count revised. *Journal of Literacy Research, 36* (1), 83–96.

TABLE 4.4
Digraph and Blend Patterns and Frequency of Occurrence*

Digraphs (Two Letters Stand for One Sound)			Rank Order	Frequency
ch	/ch/	chip, porch	3	313
	/k/	chasm, archangel	7	142
gh	/g/	ghost	10	10
	/f/	tough	—	—
ph	/f/	photo	5	242
ck	/k/	bucket, rack	4	290
kn	/n/	knit	9	41
wh	/h/	who	—	—
sh	/sh/	ship	2	398
th	/th/	thin	1	411
th	/th/	then	6	149
wr	/r/	wreck	8	48

Blends (Two Letters Stand for Two Blended Sounds)		
bl	/bl/	blue
cl	/kl/	close
fl	/fl/	fly
gl	/gl/	glass
pl	/pl/	please
sl	/sl/	slow
br	/br/	brick
cr	/kr/	crawl
dr	/dr/	draw
fr	/fr/	fry
gr	/gr/	great
pr	/pr/	pretty
tr	/tr/	tree
st	/st/	start
str	/str/	string
sk	/sk/	skate

*See note following Table 4.3

Based on data from E. Fry. (2004). Phonics: A large phoneme-grapheme frequency count revised. *Journal of Literacy Research, 36* (1), 83–96.

5. Short vowel sounds, however, have a relatively high level of predictability in the consonant-vowel-consonant (C-VC) letter pattern, as shown in Table 4.5 (e.g., *a* as in *d-ad*). The same is true of the consonant-vowel-consonant-consonant (C-VCC) pattern (e.g., *a* as in *s-and* and *b-ank*).
6. Long vowel sounds, represented either singly or in some combination of *a, e, i, o, u, y*, and *w*, have a lower level of predictability in isolation, as illustrated in Table 4.5 (e.g., *a* as in *said, aisle, Paul, law*).
7. Long vowel sounds, however, have a much higher predictability in the consonant-vowel-consonant-final *e* (C-VC*e*) letter pattern, as shown in Table 4.5 (e.g., *-ake* as in *b-ake, m-ake*, and *t-ake*). The same is true for the consonant-vowel-vowel (C-VV) pattern (e.g., *-ay* as in *b-ay* and *h-ay*) and the consonant-vowel-vowel-consonant (C-VVC) pattern (e.g., *-ain* as in *r-ain* and *p-ain*).
8. **Diphthongs,** which are complex vowel sounds formed by shifting from one vowel sound to another, are regular in the consonant-vowel-vowel (C-VV) pattern (e.g., *-aw* as in *l-aw* or *p-aw*) and in the consonant-vowel-vowel-consonant (C-VVC) pattern (e.g., *-oi* as in *b-oil* and *s-oil*), as noted in Table 4.6.

diphthong
complex sound formed by shifting from one vowel sound to another

TABLE 4.5
Short and Long Vowels in Major Letter Patterns*

Short Vowels		Patterns C-VC and C-VCC (e.g., *d-ad, s-and*)							Rank Order	Frequency
a	/ă/	-ab	-ack	-ad	-ag	-am	-amp	-an	2	4,192
		-and	-ang	-ank	-ap	-ash	-ask	-at		
e	/ĕ/	-eck	-ed	-ell	-en	-end	-ent	-ess	3	3,316
		-est	-et							
i	/ĭ/	-ick	-id	-ig	-ill	-im	-in	-ing	1	5,346
		-ink	-ip	-ish	-it					
o	/ŏ/	-ob	-ock	-og	-op	-ot			5	1,558
u	/ŭ/	-ub	-uck	-uff	-ug	-um	-ump	-un	4	1,923
		-ung	-unk	-ut						

Long Vowels		Pattern C-VC*e* (e.g., *b-ake*)							Rank Order	Frequency
a-e	/ā/	-ace	-ade	-ake	-ale	-ame	-ane	-ate	1	790
e-e	/ē/	-ese							11	62
i-e	/ī/	-ice	-ide	-ike	-ime	-ine	-ive		2	555
o-e	/ō/	-oke	-one	-ope					4	370
u-e	/ū/	-use							5	290

Long Vowels		Patterns C-VV and C-VVC (e.g., *d-ay, b-oat*)			Rank Order	Frequency
ay	/ā/	-ay			9	131
ai		-ain			8	208
ea	/ē/	-ea			7	245
ee		-eep	-eet		6	249
ie	/ī/	-ie			3	555
oa	/ō/	-oat	-oast		10	126

*See note following Table 4.3

Based on data from E. Fry. (2004). Phonics: A large phoneme-grapheme frequency count revised. *Journal of Literacy Research, 36* (1), 83–96.

TABLE 4.6
Diphthongs and *r*-Controlled Vowels

Other Vowels or Diphthongs		Patterns C-VV and C-VVC (e.g., *b-oy, b-oil*)	
oi	/oi/	-oi (boil)	
oy		-oy (boy)	
oo	/o͝o/	-ook (book)	
oo	/o͞o/	-oo (too)	-oom (boom)
ow	/ou/	-ow (cow)	
ou		-ound (sound)	-ouse (mouse)

R-controlled vowels		Patterns C-V*r* and C-V*r* C (e.g., *c-ar, b-ark*)			
ar	/är/	-ar (far)	-ark (bark)	-arm (harm)	-art (part)
air	/âr/	-air (fair)			
are		-are (dare)			
ear		-ear (bear)			
eer	/ĭr/	-eer (sneer)			
ore	/ōr/	-ore (core)			
orn		-orn (born)			

9. **R-controlled vowels,** as noted in Table 4.6, are highly predictable in the consonant-vowel-*r* (C-V*r*) pattern (as in *c-ar* and *f-ar*) or the consonant-vowel-*r*-consonant (C-V*r*C) pattern (as in *b-ark* and *h-arm*).

You can see from this summary that the alphabetic system functions in a highly predictable way for single-consonant letters, consonant digraphs, and consonant blends. The predictability of single vowels and vowel-consonant combinations increases dramatically when they are viewed in predictable letter-pattern contexts. The patterns for diphthongs and *r*-controlled vowels also hold a high level of predictability. Children will use these patterns nearly automatically as they progress through the consolidated-alphabetic stage of word identification. The How To Do (page 99) provides general guidelines for teaching letter-sound correspondences, and the Strategies in Use (page 105) models a lesson using those guidelines.

Developing Use of Consonant Sounds

Although letter-sound relationships for consonants are highly predictable, consonants produced with a continuous flow of air—**consonant continuants**—are especially good candidates for early introduction. When words in which they appear are pronounced slowly, the consonants can be pronounced easily without distorting the sounds. Note, for example, that you can prolong the /m/ (a continuant) in *mat* without distorting the sound. In contrast, if you try to prolong the /b/ in *bat,* you will find that you are really saying "buh" in the initial position. Consonant continuants include /f/, /l/, /m/, /n/, /r/, /s/, /v/, and /z/. Introducing these consonants helps you establish the idea that letters stand for sounds in our alphabetic system.

An added value of introducing consonant continuants early is their use in teaching blending of sound units. As students learn letter-sound relationships and begin to apply this knowledge independently, they must learn how to blend sounds together. For example, in reading the word *mother* in the sentence "My mother baked a cake for my birthday," the initial consonant sound /m/ can be prolonged to blend with the vowel to pronounce the first syllable in *mo-ther* or to blend with the rhyme ending in *m-other* to pronounce the word. Using continuants to teach the blending process prevents students from distorting sound values, which can lead to confusion.

A commercially published reinforcement activity for the initial consonant *n* is shown in Figure 4.3 (page 104). Note that the activity builds and reinforces the letter-sound relationship through printing of the letter in word context. Teacher-designed activities are just as useful for reinforcing consonants. For example, after instruction in or discussion of a target consonant (e.g., *n*), have students go through their word banks or vocabulary journals and find all the words that begin with the letter *n*. Or, have the students look for words that have *n* in the middle or that end in *n*. This same exercise can be used with students' individual writing, class-generated language-experience charts, or a book or story the students just read.

Not all consonants are continuants. Some, such as the *b* example given above—often called *stops*—are more difficult for readers to hear, pronounce, or use in isolation. Some teachers find a workable solution by having students whisper the sound, resulting in much less distortion. Others use an approach such as the one illustrated in the Strategies in Use box titled "Introducing Initial Consonant *b,* /b/."

The use of **consonant substitution** prompted by context is a more advanced word identification skill. It requires students to generalize word-ending sounds from one word to another.

One way to provide practice in consonant substitution is to prepare a series of sentences, each of which uses a word containing one of the consonants you wish to emphasize. Sentences may be taken from language-experience stories or other writing that students have done. Create a new word for each sentence by substituting another consonant at the beginning of the original word. Identify the original word and the new word in parentheses at the end of each sentence, and insert a blank space in the sentence for the original word; examples follow:

1. The _____ was eating the foot-long hot dog. (toy, boy)
2. The girls had fun playing _____. (tag, bag)
3. The clown has a big red _____. (mall, ball)
4. The paper was very _____. (thin, shin)

Ask students to read each sentence and identify the correct word to complete the sentence using the sentence context.

---

r-controlled vowel vowel whose sound is controlled by the r or consonant-r at the end of the word

consonant continuant consonant that can be pronounced slowly without distortion

Why should you begin instruction in letter-sound relationships with consonant continuants?

consonant substitution advanced word identification skill, involving the generalization of word-ending sounds through analogy and context

FIGURE 4.3

Developing the Initial Consonant *n* through Meaning Context and Printing

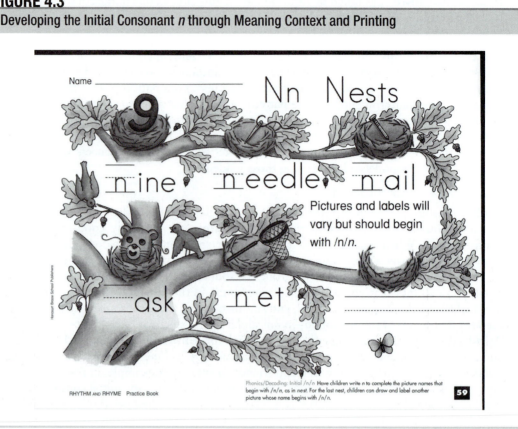

Excerpt from *SIGNATURES, RHYTHM AND RHYME,* Practice Book, Teacher's Edition, Graded K/1. Copyright © by Harcourt, Inc. Reprinted by permission of the publisher.

Developing Use of Vowel Sounds

> *Vowels may be taught in any order.*

the ★ Highly Effective Teacher ★

Why should students acquire a "set for diversity"?

How might the development of writing relate to the development of word identification skills?

The sequencing of vowel letter-sound concepts is largely arbitrary. In some publisher-developed programs, short vowels are taught before long vowels, whereas the reverse is true of other programs. Teaching students to expect one-to-one letter-sound consistency for vowels may inhibit their ability to transfer word identification knowledge to new words with vowel letters that do not fit the expected pattern. Students thus should be introduced to variable but predictable letter patterns, which will encourage them to try various pronunciations when they encounter different vowel-letter patterns. For example, you might first introduce students to the short *i* sound, /ĭ/, in *bit* and *kit* and teach this concept thoroughly. Next, you might introduce the corresponding /ī/ sound for the long-vowel concept, as in *bite* and *kite.* You would then contrast the short *i* and the long *i* letter-sound relationships, emphasizing the letter patterns in *bit* (-*it*) and *bite* (-*ite*) to develop the understanding that the letter pattern influences short and long vowels. In this way, you teach a "set for diversity" as students begin to anticipate optional and predictable letter-sound relationships for vowel letters used in specific letter patterns.

After introducing the vowel using known vocabulary in context, focus attention on the visual association of the letter-sound relationship. Use the new vowel in a variety of meaningful word examples, contrast the new vowel with a different vowel substituted in the same position, refocus attention on the name of the key vowel letter used in words from the discussion, and use the word examples in sentence context. See the Strategies in Use box titled "Introducing Short Vowel *a*, /a/" (page 108) to follow one teacher's vowel lesson.

Figure 4.4 (page 106) shows commercially published reinforcement activities for the letter *u*, representing the short *u* sound. Again, note that the activity uses printing to reinforce the relationship between letter and sound. Consider also the many possible reinforcement activities available using vocabulary logs or journals, word banks, and language-experience charts. Long-

Strategies in Use | Introducing Initial Consonant *b*, /*b*/

In September, Ms. Garcia introduced the initial consonant *b*, /*b*/, to first graders, using the following strategy. She displayed a picture card to six of her students in a small-group circle. The picture card showed a large inflatable ball, with red and green stripes, and the word *ball* printed below the picture. She read the word and developed a brief discussion to explore the students' experience with this type of ball, after which she asked the students to use the word in a sentence. She then wrote the word *ball* on a large piece of chart paper taped to the chalkboard. Next she presented word cards created from magazine pictures with objects whose names started with the initial consonant *b*—*bat, book, baby,* and *balloon.* The students were asked to identify each object and to listen for the initial sound in each picture word. As the words were pronounced, she wrote each one on chart paper (so that it could be saved for later use in reviewing the concept) and asked the students to use each word in a sentence. Her enthusiasm in teaching this lesson was evident in her intonation, her presentation style, and her praise of the students' responses.

Ms. Garcia then directed the students' attention to the word chart and the letter *b*, pointing to the letter as she pronounced each word. She asked the students to identify the name of the first letter and pointed out that the letter *b* stands for the first sound in each word. She encouraged the students to think of other words that begin with the same consonant sound. They provided *bear, boat, beet,* and *bird,* and she added these to the list. Each student in the group was asked to go to the word chart, select a word, draw a line under the initial consonant *b* in the word, pronounce the word, and use it in a sentence. She provided assistance as needed.

Ms. Garcia concluded the lesson by quickly printing the words on blank tagboard cards using a felt-tip marker. She held the tagboard word cards in her hand and, by pointing to the letter *b*, directed the students' attention to the initial consonant in each word as it was read. She asked the students to identify the letter that stood for the sound at the beginning of each word.

CRITICAL **THINKING**

1. Identify the key steps in the instructional sequence that Ms. Garcia used in introducing the initial consonant *b*. What type of phonics instruction is this example?
2. How did Ms. Garcia develop interest and motivation in this lesson?
3. How did she develop the concept that letters stand for sounds?
4. How did she provide for reinforcement and review in the lesson? How would you change this lesson to another type of phonics instruction?

vowel letter-sound relationships are developed following the same instructional sequence just described and illustrated in Figure 4.5.

Teaching Letter-Pattern Recognition Through Rime/Rhyme

As previously discussed, short and long vowels are highly predictable and stable if they are within the letter patterns that stand for rhyming endings for words (see Table 4.5, page 102) or for syllables in multisyllabic words (e.g., *-at* as in *bat, bat-ter,* and *bat-tery*). As students move into the consolidated-alphabetic stage of word learning, rapid recognition of these letter patterns is essential to increase rapid word identification. **Rime pattern** identifies a word family sharing the same letter pattern that stands for the same vowel and ending-sound sequence, for instance, *bat, hat, cat,* or *make, cake, lake.* (Caution: Note that *rimes* usually produce words that *rhyme.* Although *rime* and *rhyme* are pronounced the same, they not only have different spellings, they also have different meanings—a *rime* is a letter pattern and a *rhyme* is a sound pattern.) The use of rime patterns is of great value to the reader because of the predictability of vowels in the rime letter pattern and the ease with which students learn them. The following letter sequences define four key rime patterns:

1. Vowel letter(s) + consonant (e.g., *-at* as in *bat, pat, catalogue*).
2. Vowel letter(s) + consonant group (e.g., *-and* as in *sand,* *-ound* as in *pound*).

rime pattern
sequence of words sharing the same letter pattern, representing the same vowel and ending-sound sequence

➤ *Four Key Rime Patterns*

3. Vowel letter(s) + consonant or consonant group + final *e* (e.g., *-ate* as in *mate*, *-edge* as in *ledge*).

4. Vowel letter(s) + consonant or group + final *y* (e.g., *-oggy* as in *foggy*, *-unny* as in *funny*).

> *The concepts and uses of onset and rime were introduced in Chapter 3.*

Initial consonants, consonant digraphs, and consonant blends, which represent the onset, or beginning, of a word, can be substituted in the same rime to make a variety of different words—

FIGURE 4.4

Developing Letter-Sound Relationships for the Letter *u* and the /ŭ/ Sound

From *HELLO/SHARE LITERACY ACTIVITY BOOK* in *HOUGHTON MIFFLIN READING: INVITATIONS TO LITERACY* by J. David Cooper and John J. Pikulski et al. Copyright © 1996 by Houghton Mifflin Company. Reprinted by permission of Houghton Mifflin Company. All rights reserved.

FIGURE 4.5

Developing the *a-e* Letter Pattern for the /ā/ Sound

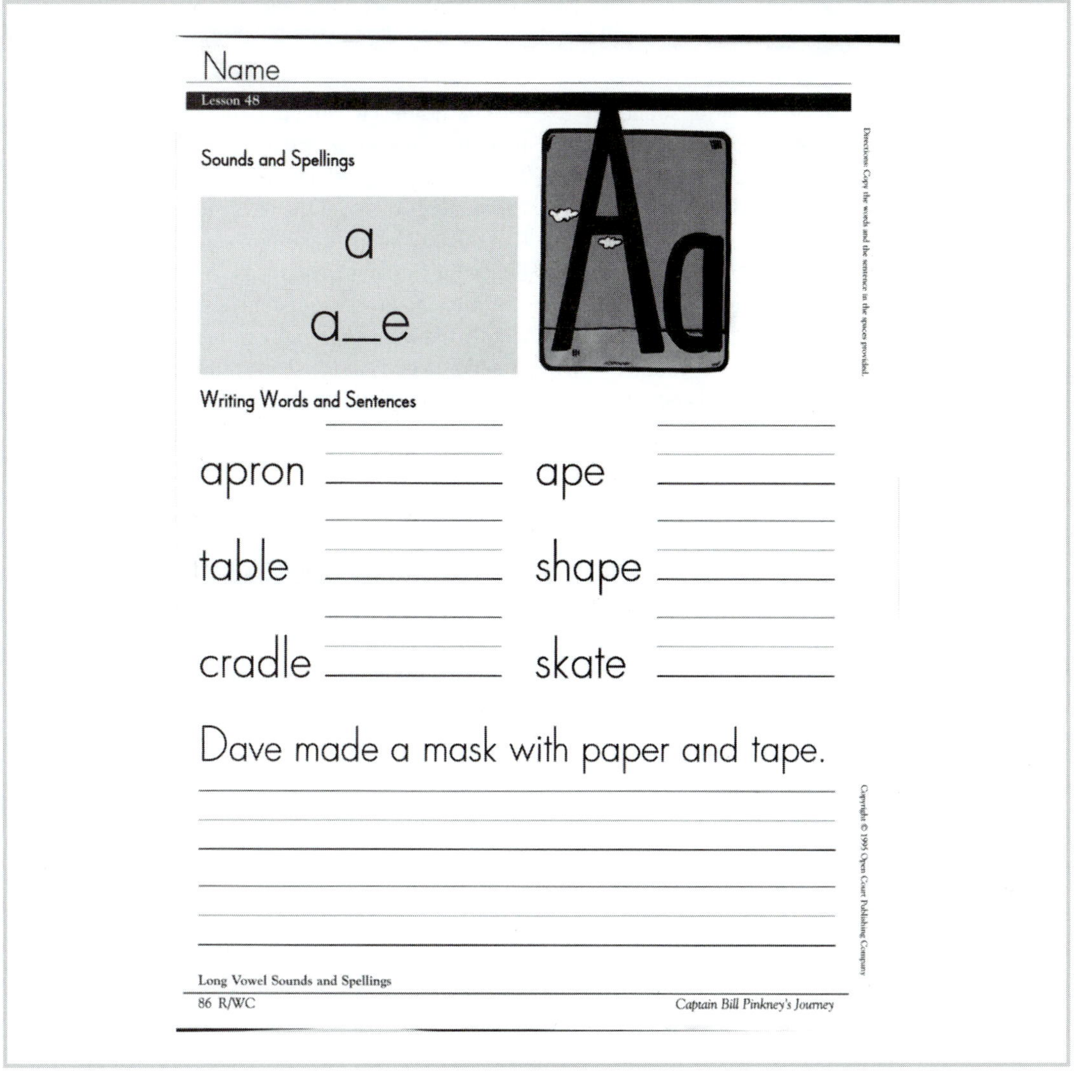

Name

Lesson 48

Sounds and Spellings

a

a_e

Aa

Writing Words and Sentences

apron _____   ape _____

table _____   shape _____

cradle _____   skate _____

Dave made a mask with paper and tape.

Long Vowel Sounds and Spellings

86 R/WC   *Captain Bill Pinkney's Journey*

for example, *b-at*, *m-at* (initial consonants); *th-at*, *ch-at* (digraphs), and *fl-at*, *sl-at* (blends). To develop letter patterns using rime, select, from a story or an expository text used with your students, several words with a common letter-pattern rime (e.g., *-ite* as in *kite*, *bite*, and *site*). Write these words in a list and ask students to read them. Provide assistance as needed and briefly discuss the meaning of the words to ensure that they are in the students' working vocabulary.

> *Developing Letter Patterns Using Rime*

Then ask the students to examine the group of words carefully to note similarities in the sequence of letters. The obvious similarities are that all the words end in *-ite* and rhyme. Ask the students to pronounce each word. As they do, point to the letter *i*, noting that each of the three words contains the long *i* vowel sound, /ī/, represented in the letter pattern *-ite*.

Ask students to think of other words that end in the same letter pattern and stand for the long *i* vowel sound (e.g., *mite*, *write*). Conclude the discussion by pronouncing the words and focusing attention on the rhyming letter pattern *-ite*, which contains and represents the long *i* vowel sound, /ī/.

Figure 4.5 illustrates a commercially published lesson for development of the *a-e* pattern, which stands for the long *a* sound. Word-bank and vocabulary-journal searches for specific letter

Strategies in Use

Introducing Short Vowel *a*, /ă/

In late September of the school year, Ms. Garcia introduced her first graders to the letter-sound relationship for the letter *a* and the short *a*, /ă/, vowel sound. She used the word chart that she had developed to introduce the initial consonant *b* (see the Strategies in Use, Introducing the Initial Consonant *b*, /b/). She reviewed the words and directed the students' attention to the initial consonant *b* in each word. She then developed the lesson emphasizing the short *a*, /ă/, sound by using initial consonant substitution and rhyming endings.

Here's how she did that. Ms. Garcia wrote the word *bat,* from the original list, at the top of a new piece of chart paper. Under the letter *b,* she wrote the letter *h* and asked the students what letters would be needed to create a new word that would rhyme with *bat*. The students immediately responded with *at* to form the word *hat*. She wrote the letters *at* beside the letter *h* to create the word *hat*.

Ms. Garcia then asked the students to pronounce the words *bat* and *hat,* pointing to the letter *a* in each word as the words were pronounced. She emphasized that the letter *a* stands for the short *a*, /ă/, sound. The students were encouraged to provide other words that rhymed with *bat* and *hat*. They responded with *cat, mat,* and *fat,* and these words were added to

the chart. Each student was then invited to go to the chart, select a word, underline the letter *a,* pronounce the word, and use it in a sentence. Ms. Garcia conveyed her enthusiasm in helping her students discover the letter-sound connection through her presentation style and warm praise for students' responses.

Ms. Garcia concluded the lesson by quickly writing the words *bat, hat, cat, mat,* and *fat* on blank tagboard cards using a felt-tip pen. She asked the students to pronounce each word and use it in a sentence and provided assistance as needed. She directed their attention by pointing to the letter *a* as each word was read.

CRITICAL THINKING

1. How are the processes of introducing initial consonants and short vowels similar? How are they different?
2. What motivation did the teacher use in this lesson?
3. How would you evaluate the students' responses in this lesson to determine what additional instruction was needed?
4. How is phonemic segmentation related to students' development of initial consonants and vowels in word identification?
5. How might you further extend this lesson?

patterns are just as useful as searches for individual letters. Because letter patterns create rhymes, having students read and write charts and poems is also good reinforcement.

Structural Analysis

structural analysis
a word identification strategy that focuses on meaningful word parts

syllabication
the ability to recognize, blend, and transfer syllables that make up words

➤ *Guidelines for Identifying Pronounceable Units*

Structural analysis is a word identification strategy that focuses on meaningful word parts. When students use phonics, attention is given to letter sounds, but with structural analysis, attention is often on larger word units like syllables, prefixes, suffixes, and even whole words (for example, when compound words are studied).

One critical structural analysis skill is **syllabication**—breaking a multisyllabic word into syllables that can be pronounced and blended to identify the unknown word. Learning syllabication involves developing an awareness of and sensitivity to pronounceable spelling patterns and units in words. The goal is to pronounce these units, blend them into the word, and check the meaning of the word on the background knowledge and the context of the sentence. The use of spelling patterns and rhyme contributes to the identification of pronounceable units in long words.

Using Pattern Clues for Syllable Identification

Teach students the following guidelines for identifying syllable breaks and pronounceable units in words. It is important to provide students with direct instruction in these syllable identification strategies.

1. See if the word is a compound word made up of two or more words that you know. If so, pronounce each word, blend the words together, and check the meaning of that word in the sentence (e.g., *playmate = play + mate*).
2. Look for prefixes (or word beginnings), root word parts, and suffixes (or word endings) (e.g., *defense, de-* and *-fense; slowly, slow-* and *-ly*). Look for other word parts you can pronounce (e.g., *-ceps* as in *biceps*). When you find these parts, divide the word by removing that part and pronounce the rest of the word. Blend the parts together to form the word, and check the meaning of the word in the sentence.
3. Look in the middle of the word for consonant pairs. If the consonants are the same letter, divide the word between the consonants, pronounce each part of the word, and blend the two parts together (e.g., *bellow, bel-low*). If the consonant letters are different and each has a separate sound, divide the word between the consonants, pronounce each part, and blend the parts together (e.g., *basket, bas-ket*). If the consonant letters are different but stand for one sound (consonant digraph), divide the word after the consonants, pronounce each part, and blend the parts (e.g., *bushel, bush-el*). Check the meaning in the context of the sentence in each case.

   It is important to note that the goal here is to identify pronounceable units that can be blended to form the word. Avoid confusing this process with dividing words according to the precise syllable breaks found in dictionaries. It does not matter if children break the word *basket* into *bas-ket* or *bask-et* as long as pronounceable units can be identified and blended to form the word in the sentence context.
4. If there are no consonant groups (blends or digraphs) in the middle of the word, look for parts of the word you can pronounce. First, divide the word after a vowel and consonant, pronounce the parts, blend, and check the meaning (e.g., *lizard, liz-ard*). Second, divide the word after the first or second vowel, pronounce the parts, blend, and check the meaning (e.g., *tiger, ti-ger; raisin, rai-sin*). After you pronounce and recognize a word, always check whether it makes sense in its context.

> **Are pronounceable units and dictionary syllables the same thing?**

Using Consonant Clusters to Identify Pronounceable Units

The value in teaching **consonant clusters,** which occur in the middle of words, is to help students quickly identify word breaks for pronounceable units. These consonant clusters consist of consonant groups, such as *-sp-* and *-nt-* in *whisper* and *centered,* which stand for two different sounds; and consonant digraphs, such as *-th-* and *-ck-* in *brother* and *bucket,* which stand for one sound (see Tables 4.3 and 4.4 on pages 100, 101).

> **consonant cluster** predictable group of consonants that stand for two different sounds

The key point is to develop rapid recognition of these consonant groups and digraphs in the middle of words. The location of these consonant groups, however, requires a shift of focus to the medial position. The following strategy will help you teach students to rapidly identify consonant clusters and use them in locating pronounceable word parts. It assumes that you have developed with your students a basic understanding of consonant groups and consonant digraphs.

> ➤ *Using Median Consonant Groups to Pronounce Words*

1. Look at the word and find the consonants in the middle of the word (e.g., *whisper* or *centered*). If the consonants stand for two different sounds, divide the word between the two consonants (e.g., *whis-per* or *cen-tered*). Pronounce each part to yourself. Put the two parts together and read the whole word. Check the word for meaning in the sentence.
2. Look at the word and find the consonants in the middle (e.g., *brother* or *bucket*). If the consonants stand for one sound, divide the word after the consonants (e.g., *broth-er* or *buck-et*). Pronounce each part to yourself. Put the two parts together and read the whole word. Check the word for meaning in the sentence.

Discussions and independent activities can be developed using words drawn from daily reading. Ask students to underline consonant groups in words like *napkin, cactus, summer, bottle,* and *middle* and then to divide the word, pronounce the parts, blend the parts, and pronounce the word. The same procedure is followed for words containing consonant digraphs, such as *bucket, pickle, jacket, fashion, cushion,* and *bushel.* After underlining the consonant digraphs, the students should divide the word after the digraph, pronounce the two parts, blend the parts to pronounce the word, and conduct the meaning check.

> **What are some other examples of consonant clusters? Of consonant digraphs?**

How To Do . . .

Syllable Identification (Structural Analysis) Using Letter-Pattern Clues

1. See if the word is a compound word made up of two or more words that you know—pronounce each, blend them, and check the meaning in the sentence.
2. Look for prefixes (word beginnings), root word parts, and suffixes (word endings)—pronounce the word parts, blend the parts, and check the meaning.
3. Look in the middle of the word for consonant pairs. If the consonants are the same letter or if the consonant letters are different and each has a separate sound, divide the word between the consonants, pronounce the parts, blend the parts, and check the meaning. If the consonant letters are different but stand for only one sound (consonant digraph), divide the word after the consonants, pronounce the parts, blend the parts, and check the meaning.
4. If there are no consonant groups (blends or digraphs) in the middle of the word, look for parts of the word you can pronounce, blend the parts, and check the meaning.

■ **Delayed readers may have difficulty using all or some of the syllable rules (for example, rules 3 and 4). Focusing, instead, on frequent spelling patterns and familiar word parts (rule 2) often is a solution. As such, it is important for delayed readers to learn common prefixes and suffixes—and to practice using them in words.**

Instructional Strategies for Teaching Compound Words

compound word
word composed of two independent words

The recognition of **compound words** relies on vocabulary students already know. *Classroom, sidewalk, airplane,* and other words made up of familiar words can be written on the chalkboard or chart paper. A search for the independent component words can then be conducted to identify recognizable words and syllable breaks that will assist pronunciation (e.g., *class-room, side-walk, air-plane*) (Carlisle & Stone, 2005). Your discussion of these compound words should lead students to the conclusion that they contain two known words. Each word contributes to the meaning of the compound word in a specific way—for example, a *classroom* is a room where one has a class. Model for the students how to separate an unknown compound word into its component word parts, pronounce each, blend the parts back into a whole, and then check for meaning in context.

➤ *Activity for Forming Compound Words*

To teach students to form compound words, place two columns of words on the chalkboard and invite students to match a word in the first column with a word (or words) in the second column to form a new word. Use words from the students' reading material; the following list is from *Tar Beach* (Ringgold, 1991).

roof	light
flood	scraper
sky	top
neck	where
pea	lace
some	nut

Write the new words on the board as they are given. Then draw a line between the individual words in the compound words the students create. Ask the students to pronounce each word, blend the two words to form the compound word, and use the new word in a sentence. Spend time talking about the relationship of the component words to the meaning of the compound word.

As you encourage students to search for known words in compound words, avoid characterizing this activity as "looking for little words in big words." Otherwise, students might begin searching for non-meaning-based "little words" that are common sound units in larger words. For example, in *anyone* and *somewhere*, the identification of the little words *an, on,* and *me* pro-

the
**Highly
Effective
Teacher**

vides inappropriate meaning and pronunciation clues. Students need to search for larger word units and other pronounceable units (e.g., *any-one* and *some-where*). Focus on meaning and the contribution of the component words to the overall meaning of the compound word.

Instructional Strategies for Teaching Affixes and Roots

The basic idea in teaching **affixes**—prefixes and suffixes—and **root words** is to help students develop the strategy of identifying syllable breaks in order to locate pronounceable units (Carlisle & Stone, 2005). Instruction focuses attention on finding these parts, pronouncing the parts, blending, and then testing the meaning of the word. For example, the words *delay* and *renew* contain

affixes
prefixes and suffixes

root word
independent word whose meaning can be modified by affixes

Strategies in Use
Encouraging Word Identification with Compound Words

Mrs. Schmidt's third-grade class is working on compound words using a game board the teacher has designed and word cards displaying compound words. To start the game, the deck of word cards is shuffled and placed face down in the middle of the board. Each student draws a word card from the top and attempts to pronounce it. Each compound word has been rated for difficulty; this rating is reflected by a number in the bottom-left corner of the card. Easy words are worth one move; the hardest words are worth up to five moves on the board.

[James (S1) has just drawn a word card.]

T: Let's see what James has.
S1: [James looks at the word card in his hand.] Summertime.
T: Great! You are getting better and better every minute. OK.
S1: Summer and time.
T: OK.
S1: Wow! I even pass here [pointing to a "return to square #3" space on the game board].
T: [Laughing] You were lucky to miss that one. You'd have had to go all the way back to three.
S2: Now make a one and you'll be to the castle.
T: Maybe. All right; let's see what Mike's going to get. James, it's Mike's turn. OK.
S2: [Mike picks up the word *skyscraper*.] Sky.
T: That's really a tough one. That might even have been a five. [The word's rating is three—that is, it's worth three moves.]
S3: I know it.
T: Don't tell. [To Mike] Would you like a hint?
S2: That's "er." [Mike points to the end of the word.]
T: Yes, it is. You found the ending.
S2: And . . .

T: Now you have a problem. Would you like a hint? James, can you think of a hint that you can give without telling what the word is? So far Michael has the beginning and he has the ending, but he has a problem in the middle. Show him your card, Mike, so he can see where your problem is.
S3: I know what it says.
S2: Sky . . . scroap . . . scraper.
T: Good, you have the right "sc" sound. What are the two words?
S2: Sky . . . scraper.
S2: But there are three kinds—sky . . . scrape . . . er.
T: All right, *sky* and *scraper,* and *scrape* is a word, but if you use *scrape* as a word, then is *er* a word by itself at the end?
S2: No.
T: So we have to call it that. OK?
S2: Scraper . . . skyscraper.
T: Great, Mike! Now can you use it in a sentence to tell us what it means?
S2: A skyscraper is a big, tall building with offices and stuff in it.
T: Yeah. The tops of the big tall buildings look like they "scrape," or touch, the sky. That's good, Mike!

CRITICAL THINKING

1. How does Mrs. Schmidt develop motivation in this instructional experience?
2. What insight do you gain about Mike's word identification strategies as he works with the word *skyscraper*?
3. How does Mrs. Schmidt assist in Mike's effort?
4. What suggestions do you have for designing the next word identification activity for Mike?
5. How could you adapt this game to teach the other key word identification skills?

prefixes that can be separated (e.g., *de-lay* and *re-new*) to identify the pronounceable units. This instruction may be extended to develop the meanings associated with commonly used prefixes. For example, *de-* can mean "away from" or "off," as in *delay* or *deport*. This prefix can easily be contrasted with *re-*, meaning "back" or "again," as in *relay* or *report*.

> *Activity for Teaching Prefix Awareness*

To develop awareness of prefixes, ask students to add *de-* or *re-* to each of the following word parts, then read each word and identify its meaning.

de-	re-
lay	turn
frost	pair
cay	new

The students then match the words with the following definitions.

Words beginning with *de-*
a. To remove the frost
b. To rot
c. To put off

Words beginning with *re-*
a. To mend
b. To go and come back
c. To begin again

> *Word Wheels*

You can design word wheels to reinforce understanding and rapid identification of prefixes, suffixes, and roots. Simply fasten tagboard circles of two different sizes together with a paper rivet. To develop suffixes, for example, print root words, such as *jump* and *open,* on the edge of the smaller top circle. Print appropriate suffixes, such as *-s, -ed,* and *-ing,* on the edges of the larger bottom circle. To play the suffix game, one student spins the top circle and reads the word that is formed, and a second student uses this word in a sentence. Word wheels also can be prepared for prefixes. Prefixes, suffixes, and Latin roots that occur with high frequency are found in Table 4.7.

Instructional Strategies for Teaching Context Clues

> **context clues**
> units of meaning that aid in word identification

Context clues serve as a word identification resource from two perspectives. First, they provide a meaning check after the new word is pronounced in the context of the sentence or story; second, they are a source of information that children can use in combination with other word identification skills. Your instruction should emphasize the importance of the following key questions that students need to keep in mind:

- Does the pronounced word make sense in the context of the sentence?
- Does the word fit the meaning of the story?
- Does the word seem appropriate to the context of the story illustrations?

These questions will confirm or reject a tentative pronunciation of the word.

> *Three Forms of Modified Cloze Procedure*

A simple but effective procedure for developing context clues is the Modified Cloze procedure. The Modified Cloze procedure can take three basic forms:

1. Context with initial consonant clue.

   Lad, the d_____, wagged his tail.
   The boy threw the ball h_____ into the air.

2. Context designed with varied meaning possibilities.

   The little _____ ran into the barn.
   The _____ sank one of our ships.

3. Context with narrowed meaning intent.

   The little _____, which was three days old, ran into the barn to find the mother cow.
   The deep-running _____ sank one of our ships.

> *Activities for Developing Context Clues*

In addition to the Modified Cloze procedure, try using the following activities for developing context clues:

TABLE 4.7

Common Prefixes, Suffixes, and Roots Useful for Rapid Word Pronunciation and Meaning

	Meaning	Example
Prefix		
a-	in, into, on, in the act of	aboard, ashore, ablaze
be-	around, make, affect by	beset, bewitch, befriend
de-	away from, off, down	depart, decline, depress
ex-	from, out of	expel, exempt, exert
in-, im-	in, into, not	infer, invade, impale, incapable, impeach
pre-, pro-	before in time, in front of	prewar, precede, prophet
post-	after in time, later, behind	postgraduate, postpaid
re-	back, again	repay, react, retell
sub-	under, below, division into smaller parts	submarine, subgroup
super-	over, above, on top of	supervisor, superimpose, superhuman
trans-	across, over, beyond	transcontinental, transcend
un-	not, lack of, opposite of	unknown, unemployed, unhappy
Suffix		
-able	capable of being	debatable
-al	pertaining to	educational
-er, -ian	performer of	grader, musician
-ist, -or	performer of	pianist, tailor
-ful	full of	playful, thankful
-ly, -y	in the manner of	slowly, funny
-sion, -tion	act of	provision, redemption
Root		
fac, fact	to make or do	factory
fer	to bear or carry	refer, transfer
mot, mov	to move	motion, movement
port	to carry	report, transport
sta, stat	to stand	stable, statue
tend, tens	to stretch	extend, extension, tension
ven, vent	to come	convene, convention, prevent
vid, vis	to see	video, television, revision

■ *Connect the sentence.* Select several sentences from the reading material used in your class-room, and separate each sentence into meaning-bearing units. Place the sentence parts in two columns. Have students use the sentence context to form the original sentence by draw-ing a line to connect the two parts.

Mike plays	a dog house.
Amy likes to ride	with his pet squirrel.
Rob built	her new bicycle.

■ *Identify the words.* Select a group of sentences from your reading material, and delete sev-eral letters in key meaning-bearing words. Ask the students to identify the partial words, using sentence context.

The p_____ drew their covered wagons into a large cir_____ for protec-tion at night.

Both astro_____ stepped onto the moon's surface.

The s_____ caught the wind, and the crew cheered as the b_____ sped _____y toward the finish line.

the Highly Effective Teacher *

on Technology, Word Recognition, and Word Identification

1. One school system created an excellent program to develop word recognition and word identification skills. Activities range from emphasis on high frequency words using a "Word Wall" to "Word Patterns" to help read and write new words. Go to **www.k111.k12.il.us/lafayette/fourblocks/** to find practical suggestions and understand how this program works.

2. Practice on word identification and word recognition can be motivated by using easy to read books. The following Web site provides an excellent list of annotated high interest books for early readers. Go to **http://www.superkids.com/aweb/pages/reviews/vocab/**. Then click on "Market Place," followed by "Reading Corner," and then "Books for Pre and Early Readers."

3. You will find the following Web site using short film clips, story books and songs helpful in working on word recognition, word identification, and fluency. **http://pbskids.org/lions.**

4. Have your students visit the following Web site to learn about drawing cartoons: **http://unclefred.com.** Encourage them to make a cartoon and give it a title that contains a rhyme, e.g., after following the directions to draw a "bunny" the title might read, "My funny bunny." Have fun.

5. Use a software program such as Davidson's Word Blaster to explore different dimensions of print and letter-sound connections. Have the students work in pairs or small groups and allow them time to explore and experiment.

■ *Choose the missing word.* Create a sentence using vocabulary from students' reading material. Delete a key word in the sentence, leaving a blank space. Provide the key word with another word to form a multiple-choice-type question. Ask the students to circle the appropriate word, based on the sentence context.

John's _____ is to clean out the garage.
   respectability
   responsibility

Maria slipped and fell _____ into the water.
   backward
   upward

The _____ helped the boys find the racing book.
   politician
   librarian

In addition to these grammatical and logical context clues, help students understand how to use the following four clues that often occur in reading both expository and narrative text:

How do children's meaning negotiations aid in word identification?

1. *Definition in context.* The word is defined in the sentence context. For example, "John experienced *claustrophobia,* a strong fear of confined space, when he entered the elevator."
2. *Contrast and comparison.* The word is defined through a direct contrast in the sentence. For example, "Unlike his friend Bill, who had something to say about every topic, Mike was *laconic.*"
3. *Example-illustration.* The word is defined by the example or illustration accompanying the word. For example, "Henry *monopolized* the conversation; no one else could get a word in edgewise."

4. *Prefix or suffix*. An important clue to the word is found in the affix. For example, "The *transcontinental* railroad was completed in 1869 as the Union Pacific and Central Pacific laborers met at Provost, Utah [*trans = across*, as in *across the continent*]."

Many opportunities for using context can be found throughout the reading and literacy activities of the day. Encourage lots of paired, small-group, and whole-class discussions so that students have access to each other's thinking during the process. This interaction allows the logic of context use to become explicit and therefore available to all (e.g., "It has to be the name of something because *the* is right before it" or "It's gotta be *calf* because it's only three days old and it's looking for the mother cow"). By combining this meaning aspect of word identification with other word identification skills, students can become highly effective in self-monitoring tentative pronunciation—and understanding—of new words.

Instructional Strategies for Developing Reading Fluency

Fluency is important for successful reading. To read fluently, the reader must recognize at sight—both quickly and accurately—most of the words in any given passage. This allows for more text to be covered—a significant factor because text coverage is a critical contributor to reading growth. Fluency also permits greater attention to the message, rather than the mechanics, of reading and therefore is conducive to good comprehension (Schwanenflugal, Kuhn, Strauss, & Morris, 2006).

Nonfluent reading is typical in some phases of learning to read. Clay (1967) described the following now widely accepted stages through which most beginning readers progress:

1. In initial stages, reading sounds fluent; however, the child makes many word-recognition errors as she or he approximates the actual text. This is often called "pretend reading," in which some aspects are consistent with what is in the book, but others are skillfully invented by the child (Sulzby, 1985).
2. The reader becomes conscious of the need to match his or her responses exactly with the words in the book. As the student points to each word, reading is slow and decidedly nonfluent.
3. As a next step, even though the student no longer finger-points, nonfluent word-by-word reading is still evident as the student consciously grapples with the new task of word recognition.
4. The student recognizes larger numbers of words automatically, allowing her or him to attend more to meaning and to read in phrase units. Nonfluent reading subsides.

In early phases of learning to read, nonfluent reading is a normal developmental behavior. Teachers, however, can do much to help students progress appropriately through those stages and on to fluent, mature reading. McCormick (2007) reminds us of a critical point: A first requirement of fluent reading is the placement of students in reading material at the correct level; that is, the *independent reading level* if the student is to handle the material alone or the *instructional level* if the teacher is to be actively involved in the reading lesson and is available to provide assistance. If placed in inappropriate material where the reader meets an excessive number of difficult words, then reading will be slow and halting. Word recognition must be accurate before it can be automatic or fluent. Placement of students in material that is too hard for them—that is, material at their frustration level—dooms them to nonfluent reading.

Another instructional goal to help students realize fluency is to assist them in the development of automatic use of word identification strategies. Using phonic analysis and structural analysis is critical to reading progress, but only when these skills have been practiced enough to be used quickly can students move from nonfluent reading to fluency. Furthermore, for this practice to encourage fluency, the practice must not be limited only to isolated skills work, but must also include use of the skills within the context of real, connected reading material—under direct teacher guidance.

A third crucial point is this: The more words that can be read at sight, the more fluent the reading. Automatic word recognition is the very basis of fluency. In general, teachers should help students to progress in accurate word recognition to automatic recognition to rapid recognition.

To assist most students in moving through the normal developmental stages from nonfluency to fluency, the teacher may need to do no more than (1) ensure correct reading-level placement,

(2) provide adequate practice with word identification strategies (including the very important contextual practice), and (3) establish the goal that, at least eventually, most words will be recognized automatically at sight.

Although these three prerequisites for fluency development may be in place, there may be students who lack expected fluency growth. Rasinski and Padak (2000, p. 105) offer general guidelines for determining if students are exhibiting typical reading rates (that is, words per minute read) at various elementary grade levels. Note the word "approximately" for each grade level specification indicated here because, in reality, a reasonable *range* of rates centered around those specifications would still be within the norm. Rasinski and Padak suggest that the following might be anticipated by the *second* semester of each year: (a) first grade: approximately 80 words per minute (wpm); (b) second grade: approximately 90 wpm; (c) third grade: approximately 110 wpm; (d) fourth grade: approximately 140 wpm; (e) fifth grade: approximately 160 wpm; and (f) sixth grade: approximately 180 wpm.

When students' fluency rates are markedly below the norm, not only will they be able to read less text and experience impaired comprehension, but a lasting avoidance of reading may set in as they come to dislike the plodding laboriousness of the task. Special attention to fluency instruction is then necessary. In such cases, an often-used intervention is *repeated readings*.

Repeated readings is a technique that requires just that—students are asked to repeatedly read the same material orally until they reach a predetermined goal for reading rate. Originated by Samuels (1979), this technique has become popular because of its simplicity and effectiveness. Students are given short selections to read and their reading is timed and graphed. If they have not reached the preset criterion for words per minute, they read the selection again, either during that session or at the next. A half dozen readings may be necessary to meet the goal early in the intervention, but fewer usually are needed as more practice takes place. When students do reach the criterion, they move to a different reading selection. Eventually, the criterion is raised as the students progress in their fluency. The guidelines suggested by Rasinski and Padak (2000) should be helpful in setting the criterion for individual students. Characteristically, repeated readings result in improved fluency, more accurate word recognition, and heightened comprehension. To take into account the comprehension as well as word-practice effects, it is usual to graph both. (Figure 4.6 shows this type of graphing. See page 117.)

Other interventions include **teacher modeling**, with the teacher reading one page orally and the student reading the next, alternately throughout a text; and **simultaneous reading** in which the teacher and the student read the same page orally at the same time, with the teacher reading very slightly faster than the student, in effect "pulling the student up" to a more fluent pace. Reading written plays has merit in achieving fluency, because a play can legitimately be read and reread many times as one practices his or her part. Students also respond well to **paired reading** in which individuals of like ability work together reading a story or an informational selection orally until it can be read fluently. **Choral reading** can be constructive if pupils of similar abilities practice the selections in unison. Finally, using commercially prepared read-along tapes of simple children's literature is an effective technique for promoting fluency.

See Figure 4.7 for a brief summary from the Report of the National Reading Panel (2000) regarding fluency.

Skill Application through Wide Reading

The development of automatic recognition of vocabulary, as well as the skillful use of phonic-analysis and structural-analysis strategies, requires time and opportunity to read. Providing easy access in your room and in the school library learning center to a wide range of high-interest reading materials at students' independent reading levels and at their instructional reading levels is very important. In addition to many chances to read, read, read, also furnish many opportunities to write. Chapter 7 suggests additional ways to enhance students' word learning and their fluency through the use of high-quality literature. A positive cyclical effect takes place: Automatic word recognition and automatic use of word identification strategies increase interest in reading, and reading extends word learning further.

repeated readings a reading strategy used to increase reading rate and fluency

teacher modeling one page of text is read orally by the teacher to model reading and the next page is read by the student and they alternate throughout the text or story

simultaneous reading text is read at the same time by teacher and student with the teacher increasing the reading rate slightly to enhance student fluency

paired reading the grouping of students at similar reading levels to read text orally and develop fluency

choral reading having students at similar reading levels read a text or script orally together

What effect does wide reading have on reading-skill application?

FIGURE 4.6

Sample Graphs Showing Rate and Comprehension for Fourteen Lessons

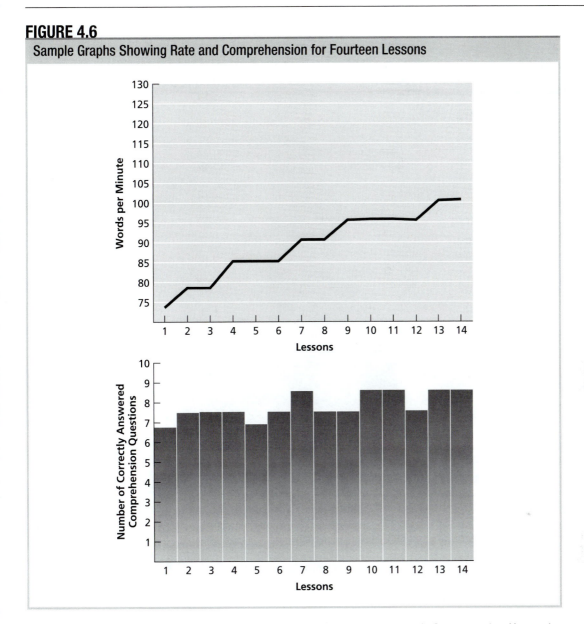

McCormick, Sandra, *Instructing Students Who Have Literacy Problems*, 4th Edition. Copyright © 2003. Reprinted by permission of Pearson Education, Inc., Upper Saddle River, NJ.

Summary and Classroom Applications

double entry journal

Try to recollect the turning point when you were learning to read, perhaps when you read your first "real" book. How old were you? What word identification skills had you mastered at the level of near automaticity? What did you do to help yourself keep on reading?

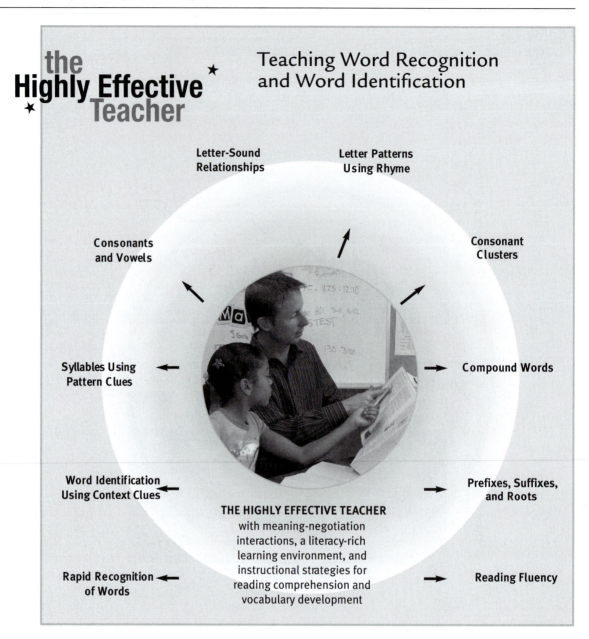

the
Highly Effective
Teacher

Teaching Word Recognition
and Word Identification

Letter-Sound
Relationships

Letter Patterns
Using Rhyme

Consonants
and Vowels

Consonant
Clusters

Syllables Using
Pattern Clues

Compound Words

Word Identification
Using Context Clues

Prefixes, Suffixes,
and Roots

THE HIGHLY EFFECTIVE TEACHER
with meaning-negotiation
interactions, a literacy-rich
learning environment, and
instructional strategies for
reading comprehension and
vocabulary development

Rapid Recognition
of Words

Reading Fluency

FIGURE 4.7

Fluency

A. *Oral reading instruction*. Repeated oral reading of the same texts, undertaken with guidance, has positive effects on word recognition, fluency, and comprehension for students in regular classrooms and in special-education programs.

B. *Silent reading instruction*. Research in this area is lacking. Studies that do exist suggest that independent, silent reading, alone, is not sufficient for the development of fluency or other reading strategies, especially for those who have not yet built up good word-reading skills.

Paraphrased from the *Report of the National Reading Panel: An Evidence-Based Assessment of the Scientific Literature on Reading and Its Implications for Reading Instruction*. (2000). Washington, D.C.: U.S. Department of Health and Human Services.

Chapter Summary

Automatic word recognition and skillful use of word identification strategies are the key to transforming print into familiar language counterparts and meaning.

Research on developmental stages of word learning reveals that children first use a pre-alphabetic system, relying on visual or graphic features to read words. They then move through a partial-alphabetic stage to the beginning use of the full-alphabetic system, as they use initial letters that stand for sounds to recognize words. In the full-alphabetic stage, students develop the ability to use letter-sound relationships to unlock and read words. The consolidated-alphabetic stage enables students to take full advantage of the alphabetic principle and predictable letter-pattern sequences. This stage relies on word families, orthographic neighborhoods that share common letter sequences, and word analogies. Finally, in the automatic stage the mature reader uses and integrates the many features from the preceding stages, to read with a high degree of fluency, possessing strategies that can be used to rapidly unlock new words. Expect wide developmental differences among students in your classroom, and plan to teach and reinforce automatic word recognition and word identification skills throughout the primary, intermediate, and middle school grades.

Historically, the controversy surrounding the whole-word versus phonics debate has shed more heat than light on the issue of reading instruction. Although it is important to understand the nature of this conflict, it is of paramount importance to teach word identification skills in a meaning-based context.

Strategies and activities for word learning should include: developing phonics skills through print awareness, letter recognition, phonemic awareness, and phonemic segmentation, letter-sound relationships, and letter patterns using rhyming endings; identifying syllable units using word- and letter-pattern clues; using context clues; developing automatic recognition of high-frequency vocabulary, and skill application through wide reading. Students' knowledge of these strategies is critical to their success as independent readers.

Students need opportunities to apply their word identification skills in real reading situations using children's or adolescent literature and high-interest expository material. The dual goals in teaching word recognition and word identification skills are to develop reader independence, which will enable students to transform print into meaning, and to enable readers to enter the story or the expository text and construct their own meaning.

Applications: Bridges to the Classroom

1. Briefly review the ideas you identified in the Double Entry Journal at the beginning of the chapter about phonics, phonics instruction, and word identification, and add new ideas from this chapter. Use these ideas to formulate your philosophy and approach for teaching word identification in your classroom. Express this philosophy hypothetically in a talk with (or a note to) parents.

2. Arrange to observe a kindergarten or first-grade classroom during reading instruction. Before visiting the class, review the five stages of word identification development (pre-alphabetic, partial-alphabetic, full-alphabetic, consolidated-alphabetic, automatic). Then observe a single student or a small group of students to identify the developmental level(s) of the student(s). Record some examples that support your conclusion.

3. How would you respond to parents who complained that phonics or whole language should be the method of choice in reading instruction?

4. Choose one word learning skill (e.g., letter recognition, phonemic segmentation, letter-sound relationships, letter patterns, syllable identification, context clues, rapid word recognition) that you believe is particularly important for students at the grade level you plan to teach. Why is this skill important at that level? Develop an instructional example illustrating how you would teach this skill.

5. Working with a partner, develop a proposal and sample materials for supplementary software for a first-grade reading program.
   a. Identify the first six letters you would present and explain why.

Professional Standards and Word Learning Instruction

The professional standards found in Figure 4.8 (page 120) provide examples from word recognition and identification instruction for each of the five major standards found in the International Reading Association's *Standards for Reading Professionals—Revised 2003* (2003). These examples reflect key teaching competencies essential for teaching effective word skills. You can see the complete list of Standards for Reading Professionals in Appendix C.

FIGURE 4.8

Professional Standards and Word Recognition/Identification Development for the Classroom Teacher

Professional Standard	Example
1. Foundational Knowledge	**Element 1.4** Demonstrates knowledge of the major components of reading, such as phonemic awareness, word identification, and phonics; e.g., explains how phonemic awareness, word identification, and phonics are developed and how these features are integrated during fluent reading.
2. Instructional Strategies and Curriculum Materials	**Element 2.2** Uses a wide range of instructional practices and methods appropriate for students at different stages of development; e.g., uses a variety of word identification strategies, such as development of letter-sound relationships, letter patterns using rhyme, syllable identification, context clues, and rapid word recognition appropriate for students at each of the five developmental stages of word identification.
3. Assessment, Diagnosis, and Evaluation	**Element 3.3** Uses assessment information to plan, evaluate, and revise instruction for students at each of the five developmental stages of word identification; e.g., uses observational information from word-identification strategy instruction, such as letter-sound relationships, letter patterns, syllable identification, context clues, and rapid word recognition to evaluate student progress and adjust and plan further instruction.
4. Creating a Literate Environment	**Element 4.1** Uses students' interests, reading ability, and backgrounds as foundations for the reading program; e.g., knows how to collect information on students' developmental reading level and helps them select materials that match their reading levels, interests, and linguistic backgrounds to develop reading fluency.
5. Professional Development	**Element 5.2** Continues to pursue the development of professional knowledge; e.g., identifies specific instructional questions related to the improvement of word identification skills; demonstrates ability to develop strategies to find answers to these questions; participates in local school workshops and subscribes to a professional journal to continue to increase knowledge of word identification instruction.

Part 2 from IRA. (2004). Professional Standards and Ethics Committee, International Reading Association. *Standards for reading professionals—revised 2003*. Reprinted with permission of the International Reading Association. All rights reserved.

b. Create a beginning vocabulary using those letters.
c. Write a brief story using this vocabulary, adding simple illustrations as necessary.
d. Indicate the word identification skills you would teach from the story.
e. Develop an activity for teaching one of these word identification skills.

Additional Research and Practice

1. Yopp, H. K., & Yopp, R. H. (2000). **Supporting phonemic awareness development in the classroom.** *The Reading Teacher, 54* (2), 130–143.

   This article provides a detailed discussion of the role of phonemic awareness in the reading process and includes activities and games to develop sound manipulation and identification of three different linguistic units—syllable, onset-rime, and phoneme. (Practice)

2. Morrow, L. M., Kuhn, M. R., Schwanenflugel, P. J. (2007). **The Family Fluency Program.** *The Reading Teacher. 60,* 322–333.

   The importance of fluency for the reader and how to involve parents in helping develop fluence is developed in this study.

   Practical ideas such as echo reading, choral reading, partner reading, and repeated reading are discussed. Excellent suggestions are provided on how to develop a family fluency reading program (Practice/Research).

3. Juel, C., & Minden-Cupp, C. (1999–2000). **One down and 80,000 to go: Word recognition instruction in the primary grades.** *The Reading Teacher, 53* (4), 332–335.

   This article reports important findings from a study that examined language-arts instruction in the classrooms of four experienced first-grade teachers for the purpose of identifying instructional practices that best fostered learning to read words for students who entered school at different readiness-preparation levels. (Practice/Research)

CHAPTER 5

Using Instructional Strategies to Develop Reading Comprehension

The art of teaching is the art of assisting discovery

Mark Van Doren (1894–1972),
American poet, critic, novelist

*You must never tell a thing. You must illustrate it.
We learn through the eye and not the noggin.*

Will Rogers (1879–1935),
American humorist

Toni watches her first graders as she relates by heart the passage in *Charlotte's Web* (1952) where E. B. White first introduces the gentle spider.

Wilbur, Fern's pet pig and the runt of the litter, has just been sold to the Zuckermans, who live down the road. Wilbur has just settled down for a nap near the barn door when he hears a thin voice calling him.

"Salutations!" said the voice.

Wilbur jumped to his feet. "Salu-*what?*" he cried.

"Salutations!" repeated the voice.

"What are *they,* and where are *you?*" screamed Wilbur. "Please, please, tell me where you are. And what are salutations?"

"Salutations are greetings," said the voice. "When I say 'salutations,' it's just my fancy way of saying hello or good morning. Actually, it's a silly expression, and I am surprised that I used it at all. As for my whereabouts, that's easy. Look up here in the corner of the doorway. Here I am. Look, I'm waving!" (pp. 35–36)

As an adult, Toni still thrills to this delightful passage. She always watches to see how her students will respond and at what level they will comprehend the story as a whole. As a teacher, Toni knows that each child constructs her or his own personal meaning for the text and so will respond individually when Charlotte weaves the last word in her web and prepares her egg sac before dying.

Toni looks for that special expression a student gets when he or she understands the meaning of text. This morning, some of the students are smiling and waving at the illustration of Charlotte greeting Wilbur. Sammy interrupts: "Salutations," he calls to his classmates in mock greeting. These students have heard the story or seen the movie before at home or elsewhere. Others have not, such as Ramon, who looks confused, and Gail, who cries, "Eek, a spider!"

Toni knows that those listening to the story for the first time will have different levels of understanding and emotional responses. Her critical role in teaching students to read and write is to guide them in their reading comprehension development. This is a big responsibility, as reading comprehension development will directly affect their achievement, academic success, and reading enjoyment during many years of schooling and throughout their lifetime. Fortunately, Toni knows what to do.

double entry journal

Think about your comprehension of a story like Charlotte's Web. *What comprehension skills do you use in understanding a story? How might you teach those skills to help students construct full, rich meanings from text?*

Chapter Objectives

After reading and discussing this chapter, you will be able to:

- understand the nature of students' reading comprehension development.
- explain how levels of thinking, comprehension skills, and question and discussion strategies all contribute to developing students' reading and comprehension.
- know how to use two valuable group instructional strategies to develop comprehension.

- use and apply four instructional strategies that target the development of specific comprehension skills.
- understand how the strategies can be adapted for use with delayed readers who are experiencing comprehension difficulties.
- understand how these ideas contribute to acquiring your professional standards in developing reading comprehension.

Students' Comprehension Development

reading comprehension
a complex mental process in which readers construct meaning from interaction with text based on prior knowledge and experience with the information in the text

Reading comprehension is the act of constructing meaning while interacting with text. However, comprehension is more than a mental process. Comprehension reflects who people are, how they relate to the world and others in it, their accumulated store of factual and intuitive knowledge, the social environment in which they are reading, and even how they feel on a given day (Gee, 2004; Ruddell & Unrau, 2004). Comprehension is an incredibly complex mental process. When you read, your comprehension strategies direct the split-second activation of many thousands of neurons, integrating your prior knowledge and experience with information in text to create meaning.

Many students have made rapid progress in acquiring vocabulary, language control, and a sense of story even before they enter kindergarten (Cox, Fang, & Otto, 2004). This progress continues throughout the primary and intermediate grades, as students expand their conceptual knowledge and interests; their ability to understand sentences, story structure, and expository text structure; and the reading strategies that enable them to comprehend text (Dole, Brown, & Trathen, 1996).

What are some developmental differences in students' reading comprehension?

During the elementary years, students become increasingly sophisticated in their ability to understand what makes text easy or hard to read, to connect their reading purpose to a reading strategy, and to monitor their own comprehension. Danner's (1976) research with students in grades 2, 4, and 6 indicates that sixth-graders have greater understanding than students in earlier grades, and that topic sentences can assist them in organizing and remembering the content of the text. Forrest and Waller (1979) demonstrated that sixth graders, in contrast to third graders, vary their reading strategy when reading stories for different purposes—enjoyment, making up a title, skimming for information, or studying. Students in the later grades also experience more success in monitoring their comprehension than do younger students (Myers & Paris, 1978). For example, younger readers do not appear to possess comprehension "fix up" strategies, even when they are aware of a comprehension problem (Myers & Paris, 1978). These findings suggest that reading instruction in the elementary and middle school grades should emphasize self-monitoring of comprehension and building clear connections between reading purpose and strategy use (Alexander & Jetton, 2000; Beck et al., 1997).

The National Reading Panel (2000), discussed in Chapter 3, reviewed and analyzed a broad body of experimental and quasi-experimental research on comprehension instruction. Figure 5.1 summarizes some of their findings.

Comprehension Instruction in the Classroom

A highly effective teacher knows that his or her goal is to help students develop the reading comprehension abilities that will enable them to construct, interpret, apply, and transform meaning using narrative and expository text (Ruddell, 2004). Instruction should emphasize active meaning negotiation and comprehension processing and provide students with a wide variety of opportunities for social interactions that are directly connected to their reading experience. Interactions of this kind provide higher-level comprehension processing, interest, and motivation.

The Teacher's Role in Comprehension Instruction

The comprehension objectives, summarized in Figure 5.2 (page 124), define a teacher's role in comprehension instruction. These objectives clearly demonstrate that development of comprehension relies heavily on involving students actively in the thinking process (Beck et al., 1997; Brown et al., 2004; Fresch, 1995; McIntyre et al., 2006). Teachers involve students by activating background knowledge, building and using text processing strategies, and modeling how to monitor one's own meaning constructions (Temple, Ogle, Crawford, & Freppon 2008). The teaching model you present to students as you use various questioning strategies, as you respond to their questions, and as you engage them in discussions is important in shaping their reading comprehension (Taylor et al., 2005).

Engaging students in **active thinking** stimulates higher-level comprehension processing that goes beyond the factual recall of information. Research on higher-level questioning reveals that in the primary and intermediate grades approximately 70 percent of teachers' questions are at the factual or literal comprehension level (Durkin, 1979; Guszak, 1967; Ruddell, 2004). When teachers ask open-ended questions, most can be answered by yes or no (e.g., "Did you like this story?") (Guszak, 1967). This kind of factual approach to discussion may actually lead students away from complex understanding of events, interactions, and ideas in narrative and expository text.

Dolores Durkin's (1979) extensive, and classic, observational study of teachers using basal readers indicated that most questions teachers use are factual and serve to test and assess children's recall of story content, rather than to instruct. Durkin characterized the teachers she studied as

the **Highly Effective Teacher**

the **Highly Effective Teacher**

EVIDENCE-BASED PRACTICE

➤ *The Comprehension Objectives*

active thinking
higher-level comprehension processing

What are some examples of open-ended questions?

FIGURE 5.1

National Panel Recommendations on Text-Comprehension Instruction

- Instruction that helps students develop a *variety* of text-comprehension strategy types is most effective.
- Well-developed comprehension strategies can help students (a) recall details, (b) answer and/or generate questions, and (c) summarize main ideas of text. Furthermore, when students use a combination of strategies, standardized test performance can be improved.
- Teaching comprehension strategies within the context of expository materials (e.g., those used in social studies or science classes) can be effective.
- Greater attention should be given in teacher-training programs to the teaching of comprehension strategies because this type of instruction can be complex.

Adapted from the *Report of the National Reading Panel: An evidence-based assessment of the scientific literature on reading and its implications for reading instruction*. (2000). Washington, DC: U.S. Department of Health and Human Services.

➤ *National Reading Panel Recommendations*

FIGURE 5.2

The Teacher's Role in Comprehension Instruction

EVIDENCE-BASED
PRACTICE

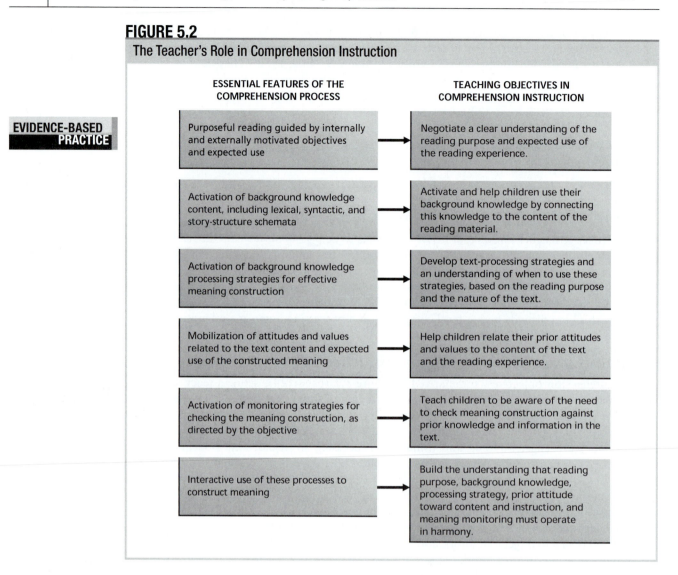

ESSENTIAL FEATURES OF THE COMPREHENSION PROCESS	TEACHING OBJECTIVES IN COMPREHENSION INSTRUCTION
Purposeful reading guided by internally and externally motivated objectives and expected use	Negotiate a clear understanding of the reading purpose and expected use of the reading experience.
Activation of background knowledge content, including lexical, syntactic, and story-structure schemata	Activate and help children use their background knowledge by connecting this knowledge to the content of the reading material.
Activation of background knowledge processing strategies for effective meaning construction	Develop text-processing strategies and an understanding of when to use these strategies, based on the reading purpose and the nature of the text.
Mobilization of attitudes and values related to the text content and expected use of the constructed meaning	Help children relate their prior attitudes and values to the content of the text and the reading experience.
Activation of monitoring strategies for checking the meaning construction, as directed by the objective	Teach children to be aware of the need to check meaning construction against prior knowledge and information in the text.
Interactive use of these processes to construct meaning	Build the understanding that reading purpose, background knowledge, processing strategy, prior attitude toward content and instruction, and meaning monitoring must operate in harmony.

"interrogators" and "mentioners." John Goodlad (1984) found from his nationwide study of over one thousand classrooms that "frontal teaching," in which the teacher stands or sits in front of students and talks, is the norm in classrooms at all levels. He concluded that students are rarely engaged in actively learning from one another or in using higher-level thinking in productive interactions with their teachers.

Four Levels of Thinking

Read the following passage from *Charlotte's Web* for the purpose of answering the questions that follow it. As you read, try to keep track of your thinking and comprehension processes as directed by the questions. In this excerpt from Chapter 11, "The Miracle," Charlotte is gravely concerned about Wilbur, and she decides to act.

The next day was foggy. Everything on the farm was dripping wet. The grass looked like a magic carpet. The asparagus patch looked like a silver forest.

On foggy mornings, Charlotte's web was truly a thing of beauty. This morning each thin strand was decorated with dozens of tiny beads of water. The web glistened in the light and made a pattern of loveliness and mystery, like a delicate veil. Even Lurvy, who wasn't particularly interested in beauty, noticed the web when he came with the pig's breakfast. He noted how clearly it showed up and he noted how big and carefully built it was. And then he took another look and he saw something that made him set his pail down. There, in the center of the web, neatly woven in block letters, was a message. It said:

Research and Evidence-Based Practice

Developing Comprehension through Active Thinking

Did You Know?

- Students' comprehension is greatly enhanced when clear and purposeful reading objectives have been developed and monitoring and feedback strategies are used (Ciardiello, 1998; McKeown & Beck, 1988).

- Students' comprehension development relies heavily on the teacher's ability to actively use their background experiences and knowledge through questions and discussion—a sort of *cognitive commerce* (Brown, Pressley, van Meter, Schuder, 2004; Ciardiello, 1998; Fielding, Anderson, & Pearson, 1990; McIntyre et al., 2006; Taba, 1965).

- By connecting students' prior attitudes and values to reading content through active teacher and peer discussion, reading motivation and interest is increased (Jewell & Pratt, 1999; Mathewson, 2004; Rogers et al., 2006).

- Increased motivation and interest in reading content heightens attention and in turn reading comprehension (Ruddell & Unrau, 1994; Ruddell & Unrau, 2004).

- Developing students' monitoring and self-correction strategies leads to improved comprehension (Hacker, 2004; Ruddell & Unrau, 1994).

- Highly effective teachers are highly successful in actively engaging students across a range of thinking levels in story-based discussion (Ruddell, 2004; Taylor et al., 2005).

EVIDENCE-BASED PRACTICE

➤ *Cognitive Commerce*

the Highly Effective Teacher

SOME PIG!

Lurvy felt weak. He brushed his hand across his eyes and stared harder at Charlotte's web. (p. 77)

Now, briefly respond to the following questions:

1. What was written in Charlotte's web?
2. Why did Lurvy, the hired hand, feel weak?
3. How would you have reacted, had you been the very first person to see the words in Charlotte's web that morning?
4. How do you think Charlotte felt as she observed Lurvy examining the web that morning?

Do you find that each of these questions requires different mental processing as you respond? The answer is obviously yes. These questions have been designed to represent the following four levels of thinking:

1. The **factual level,** illustrated in the first question, involves memory and recall of information directly from the text. Because this information is stated explicitly in the text, answering the question involves "reading the lines" and recalling information from the lines (i.e., "SOME PIG!"). No higher-level mental processing is required. The comprehension skill of identifying details is used in this question.

2. The **interpretive level,** illustrated in the second question, requires inference and the manipulation of text-based information. Because this information is implied in the text, processing it might be thought of as "reading *between* the lines"—for example, "Lurvy was surprised to see words written in the web because he had never seen words in a spider's web before." Responding to this question involves the comprehension skill of associating cause and effect.

3. The **applicative level,** illustrated in the third question, involves integrating text-based information with personal-knowledge schemata. This information and knowledge establish a personalized meaning that requires "reading *beyond* the lines," illustrated in such possible

> What levels of thinking do these questions require?

factual level
a level of thinking involved with memory and recall of information from text

interpretive level
a level of thinking involved with inference and reorganization of information from text

applicative level
a level of thinking involved with integrating text with prior knowledge

responses as "I might call Mr. Zuckerman to see if he sees the same thing that I do" or "We could call a newspaper reporter and a photographer to write a story on this web." This question involves the comprehension skill of predicting outcomes.

4. The **transactive level**, illustrated in the fourth question, involves the use of text-based knowledge, personal-knowledge schemata, and values (Rosenblatt, 2004; Ruddell, 2004). The reader is encouraged to empathize or identify with a character and more fully enter the story. In narrative text, this process can be thought of as "reading the character." In expository text, the transactive level is reached when the reader transforms the text in a personal way that creates a strong internal response to text. Responses at the transactive level may include "I think Charlotte was happy to see that Lurvy was so surprised when he read the words in her web" or "She thinks her plan to save Wilbur is going to work." This question involves the comprehension skill of valuing.

transactive level
a level of thinking involved with affective response to text

Using the Four Levels of Thinking in the Classroom

As you consider the emphasis you wish to place on these four levels of thinking, you will find that it is very easy to create factual-level questions (i.e., questions that require identifying details). This is one reason why teachers rely heavily on questions at this level and why these questions are so common in basal reader teacher's guides—they simply ask for story information in question form. Factual questions also can be answered quickly. Unfortunately, they provide limited opportunity for developing discussions that build higher-level thinking. Emphasis on questions that require active mental processing of story-based information and personal schemata at the interpretive, applicative, and transactive levels is of paramount importance in teaching. Figure 5.3 presents findings from a study on levels of questioning used by highly effective influential versus noninfluential teachers (Ruddell, 1997).

The instructional framework presented in Table 5.1 (page 127) is intended to assist you in building your own mental conceptualizations of levels of thinking in the comprehension process (Ruddell, 1978, 2004; Ruddell, Draheim, & Barnes, 1990). This instructional framework identifies the four levels of thinking in relation to seven frequently used comprehension skills. The four levels of thinking and the seven comprehension skills operate in concert; that is, a given comprehension skill can be developed through each of the four levels of thinking. For example, a child understands the comprehension skill of associating cause and effect at a factual level of thinking if cause-and-effect relationships are stated explicitly in the text and require only recall. Cause-and-effect relationships that require thinking at the interpretive level involve the child in making inferences from text-based information and personal background knowledge.

Why do many teachers rely heavily on factual questions?

How can this instructional model help you plan instruction?

FIGURE 5.3

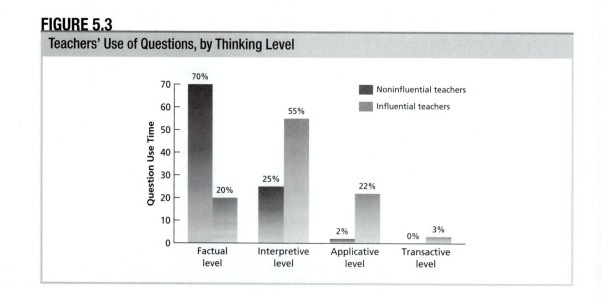

Teachers' Use of Questions, by Thinking Level

TABLE 5.1

An Instructional Framework for Comprehension Development

	Levels of Thinking			
Comprehension Skills	Factual	Interpretive	Applicative	Transactive
1. Identifying details	✓ ⟷	✓		
2. Establishing sequence of events	✓ ⟷	✓		
3. Associating cause and effect	✓ ⟷	✓	✓ ⟶	✓
4. Determining main idea	✓ ⟷	✓	✓ ⟶	✓
5. Predicting outcomes	✓ ⟷	✓	✓ ⟶	✓
6. Valuing	✓ ⟷	✓	✓ ⟶	✓
7. Problem solving	✓ ⟷	✓	✓ ⟶	✓

How could the seven comprehension skills be developed in a lesson on *Charlotte's Web*?

Seven Comprehension Skills

Although the comprehension skills identified in Table 5.1 are, to some extent, self-defined, a definition of each follows, with examples based on our excerpt from *Charlotte's Web*. The purpose is to show in more detail the relationship between each comprehension skill and the level of thinking involved.

1. **Identifying Details.** Students are **identifying details** when they recall specific information from the text. This skill involves using either memory or visual scanning for text-based information to answer such questions or directives as "What was Lurvy doing in the barnyard that morning?" or "Read the first page of the story to find out what was written in the web." Such questions and directives involve the factual level of thinking. They may serve to troubleshoot when a student is unable to respond at a higher level because specific details are not understood. However, a child's understanding of the story may not be revealed if you use only identifying details rather than higher-level thinking questions.

2. **Establishing Sequence of Events.** Determining the order in which ideas or actions occur in the text is **establishing sequence of events.** This comprehension skill is used in building factual and interpretive levels of thinking. The interpretive level of thinking is elicited by the question "What do you think Lurvy will do now?" which requires the reader to make inferences using the information presented to this point in the story.

3. **Associating Cause and Effect.** The comprehension skill of **associating cause and effect** requires explanation of causes of story events and outcomes. If the causal information is stated directly in the text, the factual level of thinking is used in information recall, as in answering the question "What made Lurvy set his pail down?" The association of cause and effect can be used to develop any of the higher levels of thinking. Questions at the higher levels will frequently start with *what, why,* and *how.* The interpretive level of thinking is elicited by the question "Why do you think Charlotte wrote the words 'SOME PIG!' in her web?"

4. **Determining Main Idea.** **Determining the main idea,** or the central thought, of the text requires synthesis and interpretation of information. This skill may be used with each of the four levels of thinking. If your question is based on the main idea stated in a topic sentence, as is often the case in science and social studies material, a student may simply recall this information and respond at the factual level. However, a main-idea question at the interpretive level—"Why do you think this chapter is called 'The Miracle'?"—requires the student to integrate story content and synthesize it in relation to the central thought of the text. Main-idea questions can develop the interpretive, applicative, and transactive levels of thinking.

5. **Predicting Outcomes.** The skill of **predicting outcomes** requires thinking that integrates story details, character traits, and sense of story plot to consider immediate and long-range story event outcomes. This comprehension skill can be used to develop interpretive, applicative, and transactive levels of thinking. The question "What would you have done if you had been the first person to see the words in Charlotte's web?" is at the applicative level of thinking. Responding to this question requires use of text-based information and personal background knowledge to explain how you would have reacted, and why.

identifying details
a comprehension skill based on recalling information

establishing sequence of events
a comprehension skill of ordering information chronologically

associating cause and effect
a comprehension skill of explaining story causes and outcomes

determining main idea
a comprehension skill of synthesizing and interpreting information to arrive at the central idea of the text

predicting outcomes
a comprehension skill based on integrating and projecting information

valuing
a comprehension
skill based on
applying personal
attitudes, beliefs,
and values

6. **Valuing.** The skill of **valuing** involves the use of personal attitudes and values in interpreting character motives and traits and, eventually, identification of the author's motive. Valuing questions can be used to develop interpretive, applicative, and transactive levels of thinking. For example, "Why did Charlotte want to help Wilbur in our story?" is a valuing question at the interpretive level. This question requires the integration of information to define Charlotte's character and connect this character to Wilbur's predicament. "Why do you think Charlotte selected the specific words 'SOME PIG!' to write in her web?" is an applicative-level question.

At the transactive level, you might ask, "Pretend for a moment that you are Charlotte. What words would you have selected to write in the web, and why?" This question encourages the student to take Charlotte's role and perspective, empathize with her situation, think of Wilbur's position in the story and the story events to this point, and integrate this information with personal values to identify the word or words for the web.

problem solving
a comprehension
skill that involves
manipulating and
transforming infor-
mation

7. **Problem Solving.** Active manipulation and transformation of information results in **problem solving.** This complex skill utilizes all the other comprehension skills, ranging from identifying details to valuing. To use the problem-solving skill, the student must identify the problem and relevant information, formulate hypotheses, test these hypotheses and search for solutions, and develop explanations and conclusions. This comprehension skill builds interpretive, applicative, and transactive thinking levels. In a sense, reading, discussing, and understanding *Charlotte's Web* is a problem-solving process.

Questioning and Discussion Strategies

Questioning and discussion strategies are of critical importance to orchestrate the development of the seven comprehension skills and the four levels of thinking just discussed. These strategies provide maximum opportunity for you to focus your students' thinking; extend, clarify, and raise their thinking levels; and develop the seven comprehension skills. The use of question and discussion strategies provides your "window on the mind" as you observe how an individual student responds to questions through discussing ideas, generating new questions, and summarizing text.

Your role as teacher places you in a key position to identify one or more of the seven comprehension skills (e.g., main idea) and the level of thinking (e.g., interpretive) that you wish to develop with students in your classroom instructional program. The ten questioning and discussion strategies listed and described in Figure 5.4 can be used to direct and develop the selected skill and level of thinking.

It is also very important to understand how you respond to your students as you receive, control, and ignore responses from them. Finally, the effective use of wait time, the three to five seconds of productive thinking time after asking a question, can provide huge benefits to students' reflection and higher-level thinking.

Group-Reading Approaches for Comprehension

**group-reading
approach**
an instructional
strategy used with
groups to develop
students' compre-
hension

A **group-reading approach** is an instructional strategy that can be used with an entire story, book chapter, or content area text to develop comprehension with a small or large group of students. Group reading requires clear instructional objectives and a plan for implementing the objectives that leads to meaning construction. Group reading also provides the opportunity for observation and evaluation during instruction and makes provision for follow-up skills instruction. Two valuable group reading approaches you can use in your classroom are the Directed Reading Activity (DRA) and the Directed Reading-Thinking Activity (DR-TA). Each of these strategies can be effectively used to develop the four levels of thinking and seven comprehension skills just discussed. The eight questioning and discussion strategies, however, must be carefully orchestrated if you are to provide for maximum comprehension development with your students.

EVIDENCE-BASED
PRACTICE

FIGURE 5.4

Ten Key Questioning and Discussion Strategies for Developing the Seven Key Comprehension Skills and Four Levels of Thinking

Questioning and Discussion Strategies	Examples
1. **Focusing**—a questioning strategy used to initiate or redirect a discussion by activating background knowledge and developing a clear reading purpose.	"Charlotte is really worried about Wilbur's ending up in the Zuckerman's smokehouse. What do you think she might do to help him?" (Focusing strategy question using predicting outcome comprehension at the applicative thinking level)
2. **Extending**—a questioning strategy used for eliciting additional information on a topic at the same level of thinking.	"Is there anything else you could say about that?" "Who has another thought about this idea?" "Keep going; that sounds interesting." (Extending strategy at the interpretive, applicative, or transactive thinking level.)
3. **Clarifying**—a questioning strategy for eliciting further explanation and refinement of a response at the same or lower level of thinking.	After a vague response: "Could you explain your point again?" or "Oh, I see what you mean; it could have been . . ."
4. **Raising**—a questioning strategy for eliciting a response to a topic at a higher level of thinking.	After asking the factual-level question, "What was written in Charlotte's web?" You could then "raise" to the interpretive thinking level by asking, "Do you think Charlotte's plan will save Wilbur? Why do you think so?"
5. **Summarizing**—a discussion strategy used to identify the most important idea to a given point in the text.	"Charlotte's words in the web will help the Zuckermans understand that Wilbur is a very special pig."
6. **Question Generation**—creating a question based on information in the text and background knowledge.	"How did you feel when Charlotte's pet pig was sold to the Zuckermans?" "How do you think Wilbur felt?"
7. **Receiving**—a discussion strategy acknowledging a response, without elaboration. This strategy can be positive, involving eye contact, a nod of the head, or a smile; or it can be negative, involving a verbal or nonverbal response.	"Right—good thinking." An excellent idea." OR "That's wrong!" "You need to work harder."
8. **Controlling**—a strategy for dominating discussion, which often discourages verbal interaction.	"That was a really good story, wasn't it? I think Charlotte's plan will work, don't you?" "Who would you like to be in this story? Would you like to be Templeton?"
9. **Ignoring**—a strategy of purposefully not responding to or receiving a question or comment.	May be due to limited time to receive, a negative attitude toward a child, or lack of skill in conducting a discussion.
10. **Wait time**—a discussion strategy using silence to stimulate student response.	After asking a question, provide three to five seconds of reflection time before continuing discussion.

The Directed Reading Activity (DRA)

The **DRA (Directed Reading Activity)** is the primary instructional approach used in basal reading programs (Betts, 1946). The main purposes of the DRA are to remove barriers to comprehension by preparing students for reading, to develop word-recognition and comprehension skills, and to guide students' reading through selected text. Instruction that uses questioning and answering instruction has been shown to improve information-location skills in text and lead to deeper text processing (McKeown & Beck, 2003). You probably were taught to read in your elementary school years by a teacher who relied on a basal reader teacher's guide that used the DRA approach.

DRA (Directed Reading Activity) a group-reading approach to remove comprehension barriers

Strategies in Use

Developing Comprehension through Questioning Strategies and Levels of Thinking

Two sessions involving classroom dialogue follow. Carefully examine each, and respond to the questions that follow. Session A is between Juanita (T), an influential teacher, and her first-grade students (S); Session B is between Marcy (T), a less-experienced teacher, and her students (S) at the same grade level. Both teachers have just concluded reading aloud *Alexander and the Wind-Up Mouse* by Leo Lionni (1969). This story, as you may recall, expresses the theme of friendship and caring as Alexander, a real mouse, becomes concerned about his friend Willy, a toy mouse, who is broken and about to be thrown away.

Session A begins as Juanita and her students examine the story illustration collage showing Alexander and Willy at the end of the story.

SESSION A

A student asks, "Which one is Willy?"

T: Can't you tell? [Focusing, factual level, identifying details]
S1: No.
T: I don't know. It's hard to tell. How could you tell them apart? [Focusing, interpretive level, identifying details]
S1: Because he's a wind-up mouse.

T: Anything else about them that was different? [Extending, interpretive level, identifying details]
S2: Yes, he had a key.
T: Yes; anything else? [Extending, interpretive level, identifying details]
S3: Round wheels.
T: Yes, maybe.
S4: Kind of like an egg.
T: Sort of.
S4: His ears were like two drops of tears.
T: Well, that's a good description. Can you think of anything else about the way Mr. Lionni chose to make the mice? [Wait time, five seconds.] Here's Alexander. Here's Willy [shows picture of each]. [Extending, interpretive level, cause and effect]
S3: One's rounder.
S2: One of them is smooth, and the other one's rough.
T: Why do you suppose one's smooth and one's rough? [Raising, applicative level, associating cause and effect]
S3: Because one's a toy.
T: Which one would that be, the smooth one or the rough one? [Clarifying, interpretive level, associating cause and effect]
S2: The smooth one.

Five Steps of the DRA

The DRA group-reading approach consists of five steps.

How could you use the five steps of DRA with "Slipstream"?

1. *Preparation for reading.* This step includes activating students' prior knowledge related to the story, introducing new vocabulary and concepts, and building interest and motivation to read the selection.
2. *Guided silent reading.* The teacher provides a purpose-setting statement or question to guide students' reading. The teacher may encourage students to read the entire selection, guided by the purpose-setting question or statement, or may use guided-reading questions provided in the teacher's guide to direct discussion on a page-by-page basis.
3. *Comprehension development and discussion.* This step starts with a restatement of the purpose-setting question or questions from the previous step, followed by discussion questions that promote more in-depth understanding of story characters, plot, or concepts.
4. *Purposeful rereading.* The purpose of this step is to give students frequent opportunities for oral reading after they have read the text silently. Rereading often occurs naturally as students support answers to questions ("It says right here . . ."), or teachers may direct students to read aloud a favorite part of the story, a passage that describes a character, or a particularly interesting conversation in the story.

T: That's probably the one I would choose, because I would think of a toy—

S4:   [interrupts.] Because a real mouse would have fur.

T: And so he wouldn't be very smooth, would he? [Extending, interpretive level, associating cause and effect]

S3:   No, he would be rough with hair sticking out.

Marcy is also in the process of concluding the story discussion with her students. She initiates the following discussion.

SESSION B

T: What did you like about the story? [Focusing, interpretive level, valuing]

S1:   I liked the part where he found the pebble.

T: You like where he found the pebble. Where did he find it, Timmy? [Extending, factual level, identifying details]

S1:   By a box.

T: Where? [Extending, factual level, identifying details]

S1:   By a box.

T: By a box. What were some of the things that were in the box? [Extending, factual level, identifying details]

S2:   Dolls—

T: [interrupts.] There were old toys in that box. Why had they been placed there? [Extending, factual level, associating cause and effect]

S3:   Because they were old and couldn't work.

T: And they couldn't work. What did they plan to do with them, Henry? Henry, what did they plan to do with the old toys? [Extending, factual level, establishing sequence of events]

CRITICAL THINKING

1. In terms of questioning levels and the instructional framework (see Table 5.1, page 127), what are some differences between Juanita's dialogue with her students (Session A) and Marcy's discussion with her students (Session B)? Which session was more effective in the use of questioning strategies and the development of higher-level thinking? Why?

2. In Session B, note that Marcy's question "What did you like about the story?" allowed for an interpretive response, but the student answered at the factual level. How could Marcy have stimulated interpretive thinking at that point in the discussion?

3. How could Marcy have used clarifying and raising to help students develop higher-level thinking? Rewrite the dialogue in Session B to show how the questioning strategies of clarifying and raising might affect students' thinking-comprehension levels.

5. *Follow-up activities and skill extension.* Skills may include word analysis, vocabulary, comprehension, literature concepts, or writing development. Activities introduce skills or provide practice. In basal reading programs, the follow-up activities often are in workbook or skillbook formats for students who are reading at a similar ability level.

A DRA Lesson Plan

The lesson plan in Figure 5.5 for the story "Slipstream," reprinted from a basal reader teacher's guide, illustrates the key steps in the development of the DRA approach. First read the story in Figure 5.6 (pages 137–138) and then carefully examine the lesson developed in Figure 5.5 (pp. 133–137) in the basal reader's Teacher's Guide. Note that in this lesson plan step one, *preparation for reading,* consists of the sections titled "Instructional Materials," "Lesson Objectives," "Story Summary," "Background Information," and "Key Words and Meanings" while step two, *guided silent reading,* is identified as "Motivation and Key Reading Purpose," and "Answers to Questions on Student Text Page 112." The "Key Reading Purpose" could easily be formulated into a question such as "How could you explain the mysterious occurrences in Captain Armitage's flight?" Step three, *comprehension development and discussion,* uses the key reading purpose followed by discussion questions, such as those found in "Follow-up Discussion After Reading," that focus on important story information and understandings (e.g., questions 1, 2, and 8). Step four, *purposeful rereading,* provides opportunities for locating and sharing infor-

the ★
Highly
Effective
Teacher
★

How To Do . . .

A DRA

1. Select the story and estimate the number of days you'll need to complete the preparation for reading, guided silent reading, and follow-up extension activities.
2. Choose the vocabulary words to be presented, and prepare materials for presentation (sentence strips for pocket chart, duplicated handout, sentences written on board, etc.).
3. Determine the purpose-setting question or statement (use or adapt the one from the teacher's guide).
4. Decide what comprehension questions to use (choose from those in the teacher's guide or write your own).

DELAYED READER ADAPTATION

■ **When working with delayed readers, it usually is best to plan to intersperse your questions frequently throughout their reading, rather than waiting until they have read the entire selection.**

5. Identify skills to be developed and activities for developing those skills, and prepare materials or equipment necessary for activities (choose from activities in the teacher's guide or develop your own).
6. Determine extension and follow-up activities (choose or adapt from the teacher's guide).
7. Prepare any handouts, materials, or equipment needed.

mation after silent reading, exemplified by questions found in "Follow-up Discussion After Reading" (see questions 3, 4, 5, 6, 7, and 9). The final DRA step, *follow-up activities and skill extension,* is identified as "Activities for Skill Development and Evaluation" in the lesson plan.

How would you adapt the lesson plan shown in Figure 5.5 for your teaching of "Slipstream"?

Highly effective teachers are adept at choosing appropriate questions and activities from those provided in basal reading programs. The suggested DRA lessons are developed by authors and publishers for nationwide markets without specific knowledge about individual teachers and their students. This results in extensive, detailed activities for each selection. If you used every activity, you could easily spend two or three weeks on only one story, which is not practical or productive for you and your students. You have the freedom and the responsibility to adapt lesson plans to effectively communicate your instructional philosophy and meet the needs of your students.

Strategies in Use | Exploring the DRA Lesson Plan

Carefully examine the DRA lesson plan in Figure 5.5 and respond to the following questions.

CRITICAL THINKING

1. What parts of the lesson plan illustrate the first step of the DRA, preparation for reading?
2. What parts of the lesson plan illustrate the second step of the DRA, guided silent reading?
3. What parts of the lesson plan illustrate the third step of the DRA, comprehension development and discussion?
4. How would you use the fourth step of the DRA, purposeful rereading, with this lesson?
5. What parts of the lesson plan illustrate the fifth step of the DRA, follow-up activities and skill extension?
6. What extended resources for students would add to the lesson?
7. Compare this DRA lesson plan with the DR-TA lesson plan. What are the similarities and differences between these two group reading approaches?

FIGURE 5.5

DRA Lesson Plan

SLIPSTREAM

Text pages 107–112
Workbook pages 32–33
Lesson Activity Master 8

INSTRUCTIONAL MATERIALS

map of British Isles, showing the English Channel
and the Channel Islands
any recording of Glenn Miller's music, especially
any with cuts of "Moonlight Serenade" or "In
the Mood" (optional)
encyclopedias and other references
duplicator master prepared by teacher (optional)

LESSON OBJECTIVES

The student should be able to:

1. identify sequence of events at the interpretive
   level (Comprehension)

2. locate information in encyclopedias and other
   references (Research and Study Skills)

3. demonstrate fluency in the invention of solutions to an open-ended story (Creativity)

STORY SUMMARY

Captain Armitage, charter pilot, is flying a
group from England to a jazz festival in the Channel Islands when foggy weather makes it impossible to land. He is ordered to return to base. The
return flight goes smoothly, but, as the plane approaches the runway, he sees another aircraft
parked directly across his path. Fortunately, he
pulls his plane up and overshoots the parked
plane. The control tower doesn't understand what
is happening and orders him to try another approach. It happens again. Armitage and his co-pilot try to land at several other fields only to have
the same experience. They recognize the aircraft
that blocks each runway as an American plane
dating from the Second World War. Furthermore,
from time to time, both men hear faint sounds of a
familiar jazz tune, sounds not coming from a radio
aboard the aircraft. When the fuel is gone, Captain
Armitage crash-lands in the English Channel. Fortunately, everyone is picked up unhurt. During the
investigation that follows, the salvage party reports a structural defect in the plane which would

have caused it to be blown apart if the plane had
landed on dry land. Armitage decides that they
were saved by his instinct. His co-pilot, however,
remembers the jazz tune, does some research, and
discovers that an American jazz musician disappeared over the Channel at Christmas many years
ago. He is not convinced that Armitage is correct
in his explanation of the incident.

BACKGROUND INFORMATION

Students may be interested to learn that the
famous orchestra leader Glenn Miller disappeared
on a flight during the Second World War. Miller
was famous for his "big band" sound though he
was not really noted as a jazz musician. The reference to a jazz musician in the story may refer to
him. Students interested in music, especially
bands, may want to do some research on Glenn
Miller.

KEY WORDS AND MEANINGS

*Some of the words listed below will be familiar to
most students through library books, textbooks,
and other media. Present to your students only
those words that you believe they will not be able
to read independently.*

adverse	light aircraft
calculated risk	obsolete
charter	overshooting
diverting	salvage
grammar school	slap
hallucination	syncopated
indifferent	technology

Introduce the Key Words by duplicating and
distributing Lesson Activity Master 8. Ask the students to read the words aloud. After each word
has been pronounced, ask students to volunteer
ideas about the meaning of the word. Tell them
that they may use the Glossary for any clues that
give them difficulty. Then let them complete the
activity independently. Answers are in parentheses.

SLIPSTREAM (107–112)

89

From Teacher's Edition of *Wingspan* of PATHFINDER—Allyn and Bacon Reading Program, © Copyright, 1981, by Allyn &
Bacon, Inc. Used by permission of Silver Burdett Ginn Inc.

FIGURE 5.5

DRA Lesson Plan *(continued)*

Find the definition for each of the following words. Then put the letter for that definition in the space in front of the word it defines. The first one is done for you.

WORDS		DEFINITIONS	
(h)	adverse	a.	to save
(j)	calculated risk	b.	to rent or hire
(b)	charter	c.	the study of the mechanical arts
(k)	divert	d.	go beyond the target
(f)	grammar school	e.	no longer in use
(m)	hallucination	f.	elementary school
(i)	indifferent	g.	a slang term meaning suddenly straight, directly
(n)	light aircraft	h.	unfavorable or harmful
(e)	obsolete	i.	not caring
(d)	overshoot	j.	a chance
(a)	salvage	k.	turn away from a direction
(g)	slap (slang definition)	l.	in an irregular rhythm used in jazz music
(l)	syncopated	m.	something that is seen or heard that really isn't there
(c)	technology	n.	a small plane

MEANINGFUL READING

MOTIVATION AND KEY READING PURPOSE

You might introduce the selection by showing the students a map of England, the English Channel, and the northern coast of France. Ask a student to locate the English Channel and the Channel Islands. Then ask students to imagine a light aircraft caught in a heavy fog over the Channel Islands. The pilot has been ordered to return to England. The plane moves on through the thick fog, seeming to be the only thing alive in the sky. Ask students what thoughts and feelings they would have if they were flying the plane. Finally, ask them what they think might happen to them while up in the sky in this situation.

Key Reading Purpose: Tell the students to read the story to find out what strange experiences the pilots of a small plane have and what explanations are given for their mysterious adventure.

ANSWERS TO QUESTIONS ON STUDENT TEXT PAGE 112

Correct answers are provided for factual questions. Suggested responses are provided for those questions and activities that are open-ended.

1. As Armitage approached the glide path he saw a light aircraft parked across the runway. He abruptly lifted the plane up and circled the field. He switched over to his instrument-landing system and made a second attempt. As he approached the runway, he saw the aircraft again and was forced to lift his plane.

2. Students might suggest that Captain Armitage and Chris David saw the ghost of an American musician who disappeared over the Channel during World War II at Christmas time.

3. Students might suggest a scene such as the one that follows.

Investigator:	Captain Armitage, why did you refuse to land after receiving ground clearance?
Armitage:	Because I saw an aircraft parked across the airfield.
Investigator:	You saw this aircraft both times you approached the airfield?
Armitage:	I did.
Investigator:	And you, Mr. David? What did you see as Captain Armitage approached the runway?
David:	I didn't see anything, sir.
Investigator:	Then why did you refuse to land at Keston?
David:	Because I saw the same plane that Captain Armitage had seen.
Investigator:	Did either of you consider the possibility of a mirage? You know, it's quite possible Mr. David, that after Captain Armitage told you what he thought he saw. . .
David:	I know sir, the power of suggestion is great. We did discuss this possibility; and we both came to the conclusion that even though we might be hallucinating, it still wasn't worth chancing a crash.
Investigator:	As it turned out you still made a crash landing in the Channel.
Armitage:	But that was because we had run out of fuel, sir.

90

UNIT 2—A BIT OF SKY

FIGURE 5.5

DRA Lesson Plan *(continued)*

Investigator: Well gentlemen, this is quite a story you have told me. I can't say it is very believable. However, you were extremely lucky. The report from the salvage party says you had a serious fault in your undercarriage. If you had come down on dry land instead of the Channel, you would have blown apart.

FOLLOW-UP DISCUSSION AFTER READING

When students have read the selection choose questions from the following to guide a discussion.

1. Why do you think the author included a description of misty, foggy weather at the beginning of the story? (valuing—author's motive identification, interpretive)

2. Was Captain Armitage the kind of person who would enjoy telling about his mysterious experience? Why or why not? (valuing—character trait identification, applicative)

3. What happened the second time Captain Armitage tried to land the plane? (He saw the same aircraft across the runway that he had seen when he tried the first landing.) (identifying details, factual)

4. Why was the charter flight bound for the Channel Islands? (The passengers were on their way to a jazz festival.) (identifying details, factual)

5. Why was the destination of the passengers important in the story? (main idea, interpretive)

6. How did Captain Armitage react the first time he saw the aircraft across the runway? (valuing—character trait identification, interpretive)

7. How did Armitage react when his co-pilot saw the same plane across the runway at Keston? Why do you think he changed? (cause and effect, interpretive)

8. What role did the sound of jazz music play in this story? Why is it important? (main idea, interpretive)

9. Which man, Captain Armitage or Chris David, do you think had the most likely answer for the strange happenings? Why? (valuing—personal judgment, interpretive)

ACTIVITIES FOR SKILL DEVELOPMENT AND EVALUATION

From the suggestions below, choose activities to meet the needs of your students. Evaluate student achievement throughout the lesson. Activities marked with **[E]** *are especially suited for evaluation. Activities marked with* **[I]** *may be completed independently.*

Objective 1: Comprehension: To identify sequence of events at the interpretive level.

Activity. [I] Discuss the term *flight log* with the students. Ask them how a flight log might be kept and why it might be useful. Explain that a flight log is one of the first things investigators look for when a plane crashes or makes an unusual landing. Tell the students that the flight log often gives some idea of what might have caused the problems. Then duplicate and distribute the following lesson.

MAKING A FLIGHT LOG

Read the following information. Then complete the flight log in the same brief style as that provided below.

Suppose that you are Captain Armitage recording the flight log for that charter flight to the Channel Islands. Since you don't know the specific date and time period of the flight, you will have to make up that information. Use actual facts of the flight from information found in the story. That information as well as your own ideas will help you finish the flight log. You might begin like this:

December 15, 19____. 8 a.m. (0800 hours): Cleared for take-off to Channel Islands. Fog developing over the Channel.

(1000 hours): Advised by Channel Island control tower that weather conditions too poor to land. Returning to base.

_____
_____
_____
_____
_____
_____
_____
_____
_____
_____

(See Workbook pages 32–33.)

FIGURE 5.5

DRA Lesson Plan (continued)

Objective 2: Research and Study Skills: To locate information in encyclopedias and other references.

Activity.   Introduce the lesson by reminding the students that in the story "Slipstream," Chris David, Captain Armitage's co-pilot, heard jazz music playing as he tried to land the plane. You might also point out to the students that after that happening, Chris did some research and found out that an American jazz musician, Glenn Miller, had died in an airplane crash over the English Channel in 1944.

Ask the students if they know what jazz is. Accept any reasonable answers. Then tell students that they are going to find out a little about the history of jazz.

Divide the students into several groups, and appoint a group leader for each. Assign each group a few questions chosen from those given below. Tell each group leader to assign one or more questions to each student in his or her group. Tell the students that they may use encyclopedias or other references to answer the questions. After each group has completed the assignment, allow time for sharing information. Answers will vary. Brief answers are given in parentheses.

1. When, where, and how did jazz begin? (late 1800's; New Orleans; combined religious and folk music)

2. What is ragtime? Who made it famous? (energetic piano music; Scott Joplin)

3. Who was W.C. Handy? What famous song did he write? (a jazz composer, known for his "Blues" music; "Saint Louis Blues")

4. What is improvisation in jazz? (music that is composed as it is played)

5. What is syncopation in jazz? (shifting the beat of the music)

6. When and where was the Golden Age of Jazz? (during the 1920's in the United States)

7. Who was Bessie Smith? (black blues singer of the 1920's and 1930's)

8. Who was "Fats" Waller? (a black jazz composer and piano player who composed "Honeysuckle Rose")

9. Why is Louis Armstrong famous? What was his nickname? (He was an accomplished black trumpet player and singer. His nickname was Satchmo.)

10. What was the "swing era"? (when bands played happy, relaxed jazz music for vocalists during the 1930's and mid 1940's)

11. Who started the "swing era"? (Duke Ellington)

12. Who was the "King of Swing"? (Benny Goodman)

13. When was boogie-woogie played? Name a song of this type. (during the late 1930's to 1940's; "Boogie Woogie Bugle Boy")

14. What was "bop" or "bebop"? (complicated jazz of the 1940's)

15. What is a combo? (a small group of jazz musicians)

16. What is a synthesizer? (electronic musical instrument of the 1970's)

17. Why do you think some jazz musicians had such names as "Fats", "Count", "King", and "Duke"? (titles given by their fans; sometimes related to physical characteristics)

Objective 3: Creativity: To demonstrate fluency in the invention of solutions to an open-ended story.

Activity.   Have students discuss some of the strange things that happened on Captain Armitage's flight from London to the Channel Islands. Ask students to propose different explanations as to why Armitage and David saw a plane blocking different runways and why they heard jazz music in mid-flight. Encourage students to come up with as many explanations as possible. Their ideas can

FIGURE 5.5

DRA Lesson Plan (continued)

be realistic or in the realm of fantasy and the supernatural.

Although the story doesn't really provide any concrete explanations to the strange phenomena that take place, there are several clues in the story that could be used in the students' proposed solutions: For example, Clue 1. The plane that Armitage and David saw was an obsolete World War II American plane. Clue 2. An American musician disappeared over the English Channel during World War II.

Once students have proposed several explanations, ask each one to write his or her own ideas in paragraph form. Later, let students share their ideas with the rest of the group.

SLIPSTREAM (107–112)

EXTENDED READING FOR STUDENTS

COBALT, MARTIN, *Pool of Swallows* (Nelson, 1974). Mystery in which pools that rise suddenly into swirling floods turn out to have a logical explanation. ● ● ●

GARFIELD, LEON, *Black Jack* (Pantheon, 1968). A sequence of absolutely unbelievable events told in such a way that they seem possible. ● ●

MAYNE, WILLIAM, *The Battlefield* (Dutton, 1967). Set in Yorkshire, England, the mystery in this story has to do with some unusual carved stone which appears to be very old. ●

TOWNSEND, JOHN ROWE, *The Intruder* (Lippincott, 1970). A story by a well-known author, set in England, with a compelling sense of mystery. ● ●

95

FIGURE 5.6

"Slipstream" Story from a Basal Reader

Slipstream

by Sheila Hodgson

He had not liked the job. He was a man in his late forties, a charter pilot accustomed to strain and indifferent to people. Half the shares in the company belonged to him. He was a director of Sonic Flights. He worked long hours in his own interest and took whatever came in the name of profit.

He did not like the job.

It was perhaps the time of year, misty December running up to Christmas. It could have been the passengers, a noisy mob on their way from London to a jazz festival in the Channel Islands. Captain Armitage disliked jazz and ignored the swinging scene. He saw to it that the tour manager paid heavily in advance. He got his clearance from ground control and the aircraft swung lazily into the gray sky.

They were over the Channel when the fog dropped down, lapping round them in thick billows. Armitage sighed. He was not afraid of the calculated risk. But he knew that a quick turnaround, a rigid time schedule, made all the difference between profit and loss. Captain Armitage had no intention of showing a loss.

"Ladies and gentlemen. This is your captain speaking." It always paid to make soothing noises to the customers. "Owing to adverse weather conditions we shall be approximately ten minutes late in arriving. Sonic Flights apologizes for any inconvenience." The loudspeaker crackled regretfully and fell silent.

"Late?" said the copilot, a young man with bleak eyes. "You're not going to try and land in this?"

Armitage grunted. He disliked Chris David, a grammar school type who knew too much technology. A creep who flew by mathematics. Armitage flew on a wing and a prayer.

"We have a bad report."

He would never have employed Chris David, but staff were hard to get at the money Armitage was prepared to pay.

The fog curdled, clots of acid vapor clinging to the tail. They seemed to be the last thing left alive.

"Don't want to disappoint the kids," said Captain Armitage heartily. The aircraft shook and muttered; it seemed to hang without movement among the yellowing clouds. The air parted and lightened, then darkened and closed in on them again. Nine hundred meters below, the ground control for the Channel Islands spoke. The voice sliced upward through the fog and ordered the pilot to return to England.

"Ladies and gentlemen. This is your captain speaking." The loudspeaker gave no hint of Armitage's sour anger. "I am sorry to tell you that weather conditions make it impossible to land. We are therefore flying back to base. Another attempt will be made later in the day."

"Next time I'll walk," said one of the passengers. Jeering applause greeted the remark. A laugh ran through the cabin.

Over the coast the fog thinned to a dirty mist. By the time they approached the airfield the visibility was fair to good. The controller cleared him to land. Armitage swept down the glide path—and stared.

Parked straight across the runway was a light aircraft.

He jerked the nose up, lifted sharply, and circled the gray sky. Armitage had seen some crazy things in the past, had done some himself—but this was not funny.

107 | 108

FIGURE 5.6

"Slipstream" Story from a Basal Reader *(continued)*

This was going to lead to a full inquiry. He felt himself shaking. It was a full minute before he even heard the controller's voice.

"Ariel five seven, why are you overshooting?"

Armitage replied with some violence. Beside him he could hear Chris David gasp.

"Did you see that?" cried Armitage. "Did you see that? Ground control must be crazy. What are they playing at down there?" He repeated the question into the mike. There was a crackling, and then:

"Ariel five seven, why are you overshooting?" The voice sounded puzzled.

It occurred to Armitage that his sight was playing tricks. He was forty-eight and had never felt better. But he treated his body as he did the plane, pushing his demands to the limit. He made a mental note to have his eyes tested after Christmas. He gave instructions to switch over to the instrument-landing system and approach the glide path a second time. As they dropped through the clouds the runway rose smoothly in front of them. And there it was again.

A light aircraft slap across their route.

Armitage yelled. He swung the machine up and away. The control tower cried harshly from below.

"Ariel five seven, Ariel five seven! Do you read? Why are you overshooting. Ariel five seven?"

He became aware of Chris David's flat, astonished eyes.

"We're diverting to Keston."

"Why?"

"Because," said Armitage grimly, "whatever is going on down there, I want no part of it." He ignored the copilot's protests. The engines droned on and the cabin shuddered. Then another sound split the thin air. After a while—

109

"For pity's sake!" It was too much. "Who's playing music? I've got enough on my mind. Tell those clowns back there to shut up."

"Nobody's playing music."

Yet he could hear it. A jazz beat, now loud, now soft. Fear sucked at his throat. He was overworked. He was under pressure.

"When we get to Keston," said Armitage in a tight voice, "you'd better bring her down."

The control tower at Keston was expecting them. The controller sounded tense and authoritative. There was no fog here. At less than three hundred meters David gasped, seized the controls—and flung the aircraft skywards.

"What did you see?" asked Armitage. But he knew the answer.

They flew on to three more airfields. At each, the pattern was the same. Unrest began to spread through the cabin. David went back to reassure the passengers. It was not easy. It was not easy to explain that they were not landing because he and the captain saw—thought they saw—

A kind of syncopated throbbing shook the air, the wail of some jazz instrument. Armitage glanced over his shoulder. All the passengers were strapped in.

110

"About that music—" said Chris David.

Armitage nodded.

They began to analyze it, drawn together by the fellowship of fear.

After the last attempt at landing Armitage exclaimed, "It's the same aircraft! You realize that?"

David looked at him.

"Whatever airfield we try, we're blocked by the same aircraft! It's not possible." Armitage loosened his collar. It was very hot. "That plane down there dates from the Second World War. It's obsolete. It's American, too."

"We are," said Chris David carefully, "having some kind of hallucination." He gave a dry cough.

Armitage dried his hands. Sweat was trickling down his palms. "All the same, we've got to do something, and fast. We're running out of fuel."

Down below, a full-scale alert had been sounded. Four airfields reported the incident. The flight had been checked. The passengers had been identified.

High above, Armitage cruised on through space. When the fuel was gone, he came to a decision. He spoke to Chris David. Then he crash-landed in the English Channel.

They were picked up within the hour, unhurt. For one brief moment David saw Armitage standing on the deck of the rescue ship. His eyes were fixed on the sky. His head was tilted as if he were straining to hear a fading voice.

"All right?" cried David.

Captain Armitage nodded. He tried to hum, but the music had gone.

Weeks later, both men were summoned to appear before an investigatory committee. There was a report in from the salvage party. The chairperson held it up.

"You gentlemen were luckier than you knew." He

tossed the report on the table. "There was a serious fault in your undercarriage."

"Oh?"

"It is not," said the chairperson, "the purpose of my committee to pass judgment on your maintenance. But I have to tell you this. If you had come down on dry land, you would have blown apart."

What had saved them? Luck? Fate?

"Instinct," Captain Armitage said as they were leaving the building. "A trained pilot develops a kind of extra sense. He can tell."

"I don't know," Chris David frowned. "I did a bit of research—out of curiosity. You see, I remembered the name of the tune."

"What tune?"

"The tune we both heard!"

"I didn't hear any tune," said Armitage. And he really believed it.

Chris David clutched his arm. "There was an American musician who disappeared over the Channel. It was during the war at Christmastime. You know the man?"

"No," said the Captain. He hailed a taxi. He did not believe in ghosts, and he was not interested in jazz musicians.

1. Describe the first two landing approaches Armitage tried to make when he was ordered to return to England.

2. Why do you think Captain Armitage and Chris David saw the same plane blocking their way on the different landing strips?

3. Get together with two other students, one playing the part of Armitage and the other playing Chris David. You be the investigator. Role play the investigation.

112

The Directed Reading-Thinking Activity (DR-TA)

The **DR-TA (Directed Reading-Thinking Activity)** approach, developed by Stauffer (1969, 1976), is designed for group-comprehension instruction. Teachers use this approach because of its emphasis on developing higher-level thinking and its ease of use with students' stories and text. The approach involves active comprehension and interchange of children's ideas stimulated by higher-level thinking questions. The value of developing this active comprehension has been connected with higher achievement levels (Gaskins et al., 1993; Taylor, Pressley, & Pearson, 2002). The goals of the DR-TA are to help students set a reading purpose, make predictions using personal background and text-based knowledge, synthesize information directed by reading purpose, verify and revise predictions, and reach story conclusions.

> **DR-TA (Directed Reading-Thinking Activity)** a group reading predictive approach to develop higher-level thinking

The DR-TA involves two key phases. The first is directing and guiding students' thinking processes throughout the story; the second is extension, follow-up activities, and skills development based on student needs identified in the first phase. The DR-TA requires a classroom atmosphere that encourages and values thinking and risk-taking as students form hypotheses and make predictions about story content. The group dynamic should encourage diverse predictions and connections between predictions and story content. You may find that even students who are shy or withdrawn will become engaged in active learning.

First Phase of the DR-TA

The first phase of the DR-TA involves the following three-step cycle:

1. Making predictions using text information and personal background knowledge
2. Reading to verify or alter predictions based on new text information and background knowledge
3. Providing support and proof of predictions based on text and background knowledge

> ▶ *Two Phases of the DR-TA*

A small-group discussion with eight students in a sixth-grade classroom will be used to illustrate these steps. The teacher has read the story "Slipstream" (Figure 5.6 for story text; the page numbers that follow refer to those in Figure 5.6) in advance and identified several predetermined stop-points where students will be asked to make predictions, verify predictions, develop new predictions, and provide support and proof for their predictions. The teacher's stop-points occur after the title (p. 107), after the second paragraph (p. 107), at the bottom of the first page (p. 107), at a high-interest point midway through the story (bottom, p. 109), and immediately preceding the story's conclusion (bottom, p. 111).

Before proceeding with the following discussion, refer to Figure 5.6 and read the story text of "Slipstream" noting the suggested stop-points. This will greatly facilitate your understanding of the DR-TA class discussion.

The students are familiar with the DR-TA approach. Each student has a single, folded piece of paper with which to cover the text below the stop-point, as directed by the teacher. The teacher asks the students to open their books to the story titled "Slipstream," by Sheila Hodgson, in their literature anthology *Wingspan* (Ruddell, Monson, & Sebesta, 1981). This story is about a seemingly indifferent, but money-driven, charter pilot and his copilot, who are flying a tour group from England to a jazz festival in the Channel Islands when they encounter dense fog. (If you have not done so already, please read the story, shown in Figure 5.6, before continuing with the following DR-TA discussion.)

T: With a title like "Slipstream," what do you think this story will be about? [stop-point #1, p.107] [This focusing question at the interpretive level of thinking is designed to encourage predicting outcomes by activating personal background knowledge and to stimulate story predictions among students in the group.]

S1: I think it will be about an airplane flight, because a slipstream has to do with airplanes, and our book is called *Wingspan*.

S2: Your mind is floating in a slipstream of air.

S3: I think the story will be about two people and one who moves very fast in a dangerous direction and the other one gets sucked into this.

T: Those are interesting predictions. Now let's read the first two paragraphs of the story to find out what happens. [A receiving strategy is used with these divergent responses, followed by refocusing on the reading purpose.]

What question-
ing strategy does
the teacher use
in this part of
the discussion?
What level of
thinking must
students use to
answer? What
comprehension
skill is being
developed?

The students place their line markers after the second paragraph of the selection and proceed to read. The teacher observes the students reading, noting their progress.

T: What do you think now? [stop-point #2, p.107]
S1: The story is about this pilot, and he's going on one last flight and quit his job.
T: Why do you think that?
S1: He doesn't like his job.
S2: I think something will happen to put him on the line and it will be dangerous.
S3: It'll have to do with money because he's a part of Sonic Flights.
T: Let's read to the bottom of the page to find out.

The students read the text to the bottom of the page. [stop-point #3, p.107]

T: Now what will happen, and why? [Extending, interpretive level, predicting outcomes.]
S1: Something bad.
S2: I don't think he'll land. Something will happen so that he'll change his mind.
S3: He's a money-making machine, and he'll try to land. He cares more about making money than his passengers.
S5: But if the passengers all die, the pilot will die, too.
S4: Well, I think there's a problem between the captain and the copilot. The copilot will stop him from landing.
T: How many of you think he will land? [Three students raise their hands.] How many of you think he won't try to land? [Five students raise their hands.] [Clarifying strategy encourages all students to synthesize information and reach a tentative conclusion.]
T: Let's read the next two pages, to the bottom of page 109, to find out what happens. [stop-point #4, p.109] [Refocusing on comprehension purpose; reading to verify, reject, or form new hypotheses about story plot.]

The teacher continues the same pattern of interaction at the stop-point at the bottom of page 109, using discussion, verification, and proof. The students are then asked to read to the bottom of page 111, which immediately precedes the conclusion. [stop-point #5, p.111]

In this part of the text, the phantom World War II aircraft continues to block their landing; syncopated jazz music is heard by Armitage, the pilot, and his copilot; their plane's fuel is finally consumed; and they crash-land in the English Channel and are rescued. This section ends with the following text:

Weeks later, both men were summoned to appear before an investigatory committee. There was a report in from the salvage party. The chairperson held it up.

"You gentlemen were luckier than you know."

The following discussion ensues:

T: OK, now how do you think the story will end? [Raising, applicative level, predicting outcomes.]
S1: I think they were saved from a big crash.
T: Why do you say that? [Clarifying, interpretive level, predicting outcomes.]
S1: It says "You gentlemen were luckier than you knew" where we stopped. So, there must have been something wrong with the plane.
S4: Yeah, and the World War II plane was always ahead of them to keep them from landing.
S3: The phantom plane saved them from a big crash.
T: Good. What other ideas do you have? [Extending.]
S2: It's sort of like the opposite of the movie I saw called *Back to the Future*, where they go back in time.
S5: Maybe someone from another time came back to rescue them, like in *Star Trek*.
T: Those are all very good ideas. Now finish the story. [Receiving.]

The students finish reading the story and discuss its conclusion, verifying their conclusions.

How would you
describe the
social dynamic
of this DR-TA
session?

An Example of Cognitive Commerce

Note that the DR-TA approach relies on interpretive, applicative, and transactive levels of thinking, with the major emphasis being on the predicting outcomes comprehension skill. In the "Slip-stream" example, the factual level was used only to guide rereading to verify a specific idea. The discussion began with a wide range of divergent predictions, but as the story progressed, predic-

How To Do . . .

A DR-TA

1. Select the story or text to be read.
2. Determine the stop-points. Stop after the title, after the first or second paragraph, and at points of high suspense or interest. Stop once more just before the end of the story. Use no more than five or six stop-points in any story.
3. Prepare broad, open-ended questions, such as the following, to be asked at stop-points.
   - After the title: "With a title like that, what do you think this story will be about? Why do you think so?"

   ■ **For delayed readers, following the title-prediction question, introduce three words from the story that might be challenging for them. After activities to identify the words, use the words as a focus for further prediction before they read the selection. "What do you think this word will have to do with the story?"**

   - After each stop-point: "What do you think will happen now? What makes you think so? With which prediction do you agree? Why?"
   - Before the conclusion: "How do you think the story will end? Why?"
   - After the story: "Why did the story end this way? How would you have ended the story?"
4. Obtain or prepare cover sheets for children to conceal text that follows stop-points.

DELAYED READER ADAPTATION

tions and speculations began to narrow, based on text and personal knowledge. Most of the students in the group contributed directly to the discussion, and all students were involved in making decisions about possible predictions. Individual contributions converged toward a group conclusion as the story progressed. This is the dynamic thinking interchange referred to as **cognitive commerce.** The teacher created high motivation by stimulating the students' intellectual curiosity as they read, discussed, and continued to read toward the story's conclusion. The students' reading rate increased progressively as the story moved toward its conclusion.

cognitive commerce
a dynamic thinking interchange between teacher and students or between students

Second Phase of the DR-TA

The second phase of the DR-TA approach is follow-up extension activities, based on the teacher's observations of students during directed reading and discussion. It may involve emphasis on vocabulary development. In "Slipstream," for example, words such as *charter, hallucination, salvage,* and *obsolete* are used in story context. Or observations during the lesson may indicate that an emphasis on word analysis is important for some students.

What other vocabulary and concepts would you identify for follow-up?

Tips for Using the DR-TA

The DR-TA can be used with stories in basal readers and with multiple copies of chapters from children's or adolescent literature selections. It is especially good for introducing the first chapter of a novel. Key points to keep in mind in using the DR-TA include the importance of choosing high-interest quality literature, becoming familiar with the story or chapter you plan to use, and identifying in advance four to six discussion stop-points in the text. Stop-points in the body of the text should be chosen so that they lead to new predictions about the story plot and speculations about story characters, events, and ideas. The questioning pattern at the stop-points is presented in How To Do a DR-TA.

In summary, the DR-TA

■ establishes a clear purpose for reading.
■ involves students in active comprehension by calling on their personal background knowledge and text knowledge.
■ develops higher-level thinking using predictions and speculations, reading to verify, revising predictions or forming new ones, and reaching conclusions.
■ uses the social dynamic of group interaction to propose and discuss options and outcomes.
■ helps students arrive at decisions and conclusions based on text and personal knowledge.

➤ *Choose a story or text to develop as a DR-TA lesson you might teach.*

the ★ Highly Effective Teacher ★

➤ *A Summary of DR-TA*

TABLE 5.2
DRA and DR-TA: A Comparison

	DRA	DR-TA
Activates background knowledge	X	X
Builds interest in the story	X	X
Provides structure in directing reading	X	X
Uses follow-up discussion of the selection and follow-up activities to develop concepts	X	X
Can be used with or adapted for use with most literature and content area reading	X	X
Can be used to build higher-level thinking and comprehension skills	X	X
Can easily be used in conjunction with other comprehension strategies	X	X
Relies on story context to introduce vocabulary and concepts		X
Develops vocabulary and concepts as needed after the story is read		X
Can be easily used with children's trade books		X
Is traditionally used in basal reading programs	X	
Introduces preselected vocabulary before the story is read	X	
Provides preselected purpose-setting questions, comprehension questions, activities, and extensions	X	

What are the key differences between DRA and DR-TA?

Comparing DRA and DR-TA

A comparison of the DRA and the DR-TA, based on the DRA and the DR-TA lesson discussions for the story "Slipstream," reveals a number of similarities and several critical differences. These are shown in Table 5.2.

Strategies That Target Specific Comprehension Processes

The following five instructional strategies—PReP (PreReading Plan), QAR (Question-Answer Relationship), ReQuest (Reciprocal Questioning), reciprocal teaching, and GMA (Group Mapping Activity)—provide additional flexibility and targeted instruction in your teaching program. These strategies are designed to focus on specific comprehension processes and can be used separately or in conjunction with the DRA or DR-TA.

PReP (PreReading Plan)

The activation and use of background knowledge relevant to the reading material is a critical aspect of the reading-comprehension process. Judith Langer (1981, 1982) developed **PReP (PreReading Plan)** to help students activate their knowledge schema and extend their prior knowledge about a topic before reading. PReP is appropriate for students at every elementary grade level. Its value is in refining students' knowledge of a topic through group discussion by building anticipation toward the reading experience.

PReP (PreReading Plan)
a strategy for developing the specific comprehension skill of activating and applying background knowledge

The PReP strategy has the potential to stimulate and involve all levels of thinking—factual, interpretive, applicative, and transactive. In addition, PReP can help you gain information about the knowledge students possess on a given topic in order to determine if further instruction is needed before reading. The strategy is appropriate for narrative as well as expository material. It consists of two parts: the instructional phase and the response-analysis phase.

PReP Instructional Phase

The instructional phase of PReP involves three steps that explore students' understanding of the key topic of the story or expository text:

➤ *Three Steps in the Instructional Phase of PReP*

1. *Initial association with the key topic or concept.* The purpose of this step is to encourage free association and divergent thinking. After first identifying a key topic or story concept to explore, the teacher uses such statements and questions as the following (Langer, 1982):

"Tell me anything that comes to mind when [you hear this word, see this picture, . . .]."
"What do you think of . . . ?"
"What might you see [hear, feel, . . .]?"
"What might be going on . . . ?"

For example, with students who were studying the topic of underwater exploration, PReP was used to explore understanding of problems they might expect to find in deep-water exploration. They were shown a picture depicting deep-sea life and asked, "What comes to mind when you look at this picture?" The students' responses reflected different perspectives and different levels of prior knowledge and experiences; responses ranged from "fish and plants" to "divers might get cold or lost if a flashlight breaks" to "divers are in danger because water isn't like land; there is no air."

As the students develop ideas, the teacher records their responses on the board. The objective is to identify any information the students have about the central concept of the text, along with related knowledge and experiences they may have.

Tierney and Readence (2000) recommend a variation in this step, to provide children with more context for the story or expository text. The variation requires that the teacher have students read the title and a paragraph or two before developing associations with the topic. This variation activates background knowledge that is relevant to the reading material.

2. *Reflections on the initial associations.* This step is intended to give students an opportunity to explain their initial responses and to understand their peers' responses. You simply ask, "What made you think of [the initial response]?" This question also helps students evaluate the way their ideas relate to the text topic.

3. *Reformulation of knowledge.* The question "On the basis of our discussion, do you have any new ideas about [the picture, the word, the topic]?" encourages students to probe their memories, evaluate their ideas, and speculate on the text to be read. The intent is to provide an opportunity for them to revise, integrate, and add ideas before embarking on the reading experience.

> How else might you help children develop story context?

PReP Response-Analysis Phase

The response-analysis phase of PReP provides information about the instructional needs of students. Langer (1982) suggests that teachers use observations from the three steps of the PReP instructional phase to determine whether students have sufficient prior knowledge to succeed in

> How will you determine how much students know about the subject of the text you plan to teach?

How To Do . . .

PReP

1. Decide what key concept you wish to focus students' attention on before reading the story or text.
2. Choose a stimulus word, picture, or event to focus students' attention on the topic. Prepare any materials you need.
3. Prepare your stimulus question—for example, "What do you think of when I say 'friendship'?" or "What comes to mind as you look at this picture?"

■ **To give delayed readers a context directly related to the story, have them read the title and a paragraph or two before soliciting associations. McCormick (1992) found that many delayed readers rely on background information to the *exclusion* of text information.**

DELAYED READER ADAPTATION

4. Record students' responses on the chalkboard as they respond to the stimulus question.
5. After students have responded, point to specific responses recorded on the chalkboard and ask individual students, "What made you think of this when I said [initial stimulus question]?"
6. Extend the original question: "On the basis of our discussion, do you have any new ideas about [concept]?"
7. Guide students into the reading: "Our story is about . . . What do you think we might find in the story?"

the reading experience. Students with little knowledge about a concept tend to respond with words that are not quite relevant and may need direct instruction.

QAR (Question-Answer Relationship) Strategy

QAR (Question-Answer Relationship)
a strategy for developing the specific comprehension skill of using information sources to answer questions

The **QAR (Question-Answer Relationship)** strategy (Raphael, 1982, 1986) is designed to connect reading purpose to text and to the reader's personal information sources. QAR is a way to help children (1) understand the thinking demands of questions and (2) learn how to use information sources in responding to questions. The strategy can be used effectively with children from grades 1 through 6.

The QAR strategy classifies questions into four categories of information sources that incorporate the factual, interpretive, applicative, and transactive levels of thinking discussed earlier in the chapter:

➤ *Four Categories of Information Sources*

1. *Right There.* The information is stated explicitly in the text. This QAR requires recall or location of information at the factual level of thinking.
2. *Think and Search.* The information source is still text-based, but the information must be inferred or concluded from various factual statements in the text. This QAR uses the interpretive level of thinking.
3. *Author and You.* The information source is a combination of information from the text and from students' background knowledge. This QAR requires use of the interpretive, applicative, or transactive level of thinking.
4. *On My Own.* The information source is primarily the reader's background knowledge. This QAR uses the applicative or transactive level of thinking.

➤ *QAR Instructional Principles*

QAR is based on four instructional principles:

1. Providing immediate feedback to students
2. Moving from short text passages to longer, more involved text
3. Starting with factual questions in which answers are explicitly stated in the text and progressing to questions based on longer text passages that require interpretive, applicative, or transactive thinking
4. Providing for supportive group instruction at the outset, followed by activities that require greater student independence

Day One: Introducing QAR

The first step is to develop student awareness of the connection between questions and the mental procedures used in responding to them. To do so, you must introduce students to the following categories of question-answer relationships:

- In *Right There,* the answer is stated directly "in the book."
- In *Think and Search,* the answer is "in the book" but must be "put together" from the text information.
- In *Author and You,* the answer is not in the text but must be formed "in your head" from the information the author provides and from your own background knowledge.
- In *On My Own,* the answer is not in the text and must be created "in your head" from your background knowledge.

➤ *Design a QAR wall chart you could use in your classroom.*

The wall chart shown in Figure 5.7 will help you introduce the four types of QARs.

After introducing the four types of QARs, you will need to illustrate each one, using text and related questions in a group discussion. In the following third-grade lesson, the discussion focuses on applying the Right There and Think and Search QARs (Raphael, 1986, p. 518).

Sample Text
Mom put a large plate of meat on the table. Then she went back into the kitchen. She came out with more food. She had a plate filled with carrots. She also had a plate filled with potatoes.

FIGURE 5.7

QAR Wall Chart

In the Book

Right There
The answer is in one place in the text. Words from the question and words that answer the question are often "right there" in the same sentence.

Think & Search
The answer is in the text. Readers need to "think and search," or put together different parts of the text, to find the answer. The answer can be within a paragraph, across paragraphs, or even across chapters and books.

In My Head

On My Own
The answer is not in the text. Readers need to use their own ideas and experiences to answer the question.

Author & Me
The answer is not in the text. To answer the question, readers need to think about how the text and what they already know fit together.

Figure 2 (adapted) from Raphael, Taffy E. (1986, February). Teaching question answer relationships, revisited. *The Reading Teacher, 39* (6), 516–522. Copyright © 1986 by Taffy E. Raphael and the International Reading Association. All rights reserved.

Question and Discussion
What food did Mom put on the table?
T: What food did Mom put on the table?
S1: Meat.
S2: Potatoes.
T: How do you know that this food was on the table? Can you prove it in any way?
S3: It says so in the story.
S4: What does it say about the food in the story?
S3: It says there was meat, potatoes, and carrots.
T: Can you point to where in the story it tells you? [Student points to words *carrots*, *meat*, and *potatoes*.]
T: Great! That information was in the story you just read. That is one place you can go to find answers to questions—in the stories and books that you read.

Question and Discussion
What meal were they eating?
T: [In response to students' saying the text is about dinner] How do you know? Does the text tell you that it is dinner?
C: [In unison] No!
T: Then how do you know?
S1: You don't eat meat with carrots and potatoes for breakfast!
S2: That's what you eat for dinner.
T: How do you know that? What helped you decide on that?

> Which information sources are emphasized in this dialogue?

S3: Because that's what I eat for dinner sometimes.

T: You used a good source of information for that answer—your own experiences. Many times it is important when we're reading and answering questions to think about information up here [points to her head], in our heads.

Continued Discussion

T: When you found the information in the text to tell what kinds of foods Mom brought in, did you find all the information in the same sentence? Where did you find the answer information?

S1, 2, 3: [Simultaneously] In the first sentence. At the end. In the whole story.

T: Exactly! You are all partially right. The information is in many places. For a complete answer, you had to think of all the different parts to the answer, search through the text, and put it all together! That's why this kind of QAR is called a Think and Search. Sometimes we can find all the information we need to answer a question right there in the same sentence, but many times we think and search for information that we have to put together to give a complete answer.

> *Model a dialogue with which you could teach the Author and You QAR or On My Own QAR.*

Continue to develop the QARs using texts of only a few sentences in a small group discussion. In the discussion, emphasize the source of information for each QAR.

Day Two: Review and Practice

Begin with a review of the four QARs, using the wall chart, an overhead projector, or a chalkboard. Prepare in advance two passages of at least two paragraphs in length and four accompanying questions for each passage (one for each type of QAR). Distribute copies of the passages and questions to the class. A sample passage and questions follow.

Nothing to Do!

"Mother, I'm so bored! What can I do?" wailed Holly.

"Why don't you play with my new computer?" her mother replied. She had to shout because the robot was vacuuming the rug. Robots did all the work in the factories and offices, too.

"I'm tired of playing with the computer," Holly said.

"Sometimes it seems as if everyone has nothing to do except to try to think of something to do," she mumbled to herself. "Maybe I can change all that with a little mischief!" An idea suddenly came to her, and she raced away to gather her friends together.

QAR Questions

1. Why did Holly have to shout to her mother?
   Possible answer: The robot was vacuuming the rug. QAR: Right There (factual level)
2. What did Holly want?
   Possible answer: Something new to do. QAR: Think and Search (interpretive level)
3. What do you think Holly will do next?
   Possible answer: She might unplug all the robots. (Answers will vary.)
   QAR: Author and You (applicative level)
4. What would you do to entertain yourself if you lived with Holly's family? (Answers will vary.)
   QAR: On My Own (transactive level)

> How does the QAR strategy help students become independent readers?

Have the students read the passage and answer the questions in small-group settings. The key to this second step is for students to establish clearly the relationship between each question and the source of information that must be used in constructing the answer (i.e., "in the book" or "in my head").

The second passage, which can be modeled after the above passage, may then be read independently by each student, who answers the questions and identifies the type of QAR for each. Groups then convene for students to share and discuss their independent responses. With grades 1 and 2, you may wish to read both passages orally to the whole class or with groups.

Day Three: Extension to Longer Passages

The purpose of this lesson is to review the QAR strategy and then apply it to a longer text. You will need to select two short stories or science or social studies passages that are several paragraphs long. Divide each passage into two or three brief coherent sections. Prepare two or three questions for each section, for a total of five or six questions for the passage. Questions should represent the four QAR categories.

Use the first passage with students working together in a small group. Have them identify and review the QAR categories and consider their responses to each question.

Strategies in Use

Developing QAR Questions

As you read the following passage, think about QAR questions you could pose to students.

LOST IN THE WOODS

Can you imagine being lost in the woods for six days? That is what happened to Mark Steiner, who was lost when he was only nine years old. His parents, together with hundreds of volunteers, searched and searched for him. When they found Mark, he was very ill and had to remain in the hospital for many weeks. This was a frightening experience for a child. Mark never wanted to go hiking or camping in the woods again.

CRITICAL THINKING

1. The question "How old was Mark when he was lost?" is an example of Right There at a factual level. What QAR and thinking level does each of the following questions represent?

   a. How long do you think Mark was lost in the woods?
   b. What would you do if you were lost in the woods?

2. What question could you ask for an Author and You QAR?

3. Develop QAR questions to use with the following passage.

   Then one day as Mark was walking his dog, the dog broke off the leash and ran into the woods. Without thinking, Mark followed. It wasn't until he found the dog that Mark realized where he was—in the woods. And it wasn't so bad!

   That was just the beginning. Now Mark is an expert camper and Boy Scout. In fact, last year he visited the very same woods in which he had been lost!

The second passage, prepared in a similar way, may then be completed independently by the students. The follow-up discussion should emphasize the connection between each QAR search category and the students' responses.

> ➤ *Prepare a day three QAR lesson for "Slipstream."*

Day Four: Application to Classroom Reading

Most students should now be able to apply the QAR search categories to their classroom reading material. The next step is to integrate the strategy into your daily instruction by designing QAR questions for text and following the QAR procedure.

QAR helps students with classroom reading and equips them with instructional language and search processes that will be valuable in directing their thinking and responding in group discussions and individual work. Students also find QARs helpful as comprehension search clues. For example, a student having difficulty with an interpretive question might be prompted to say, "That's a Think and Search question." Reinforce the use of QARs in any discussion; for example, you can respond, "Good, Devon. That was an Author and You question, wasn't it?" Children soon will use this helpful language on their own as they evaluate their own thinking and assist peers in responding to questions.

ReQuest (Reciprocal Questioning)

The purpose of the **ReQuest (Reciprocal Questioning)** strategy is to develop students' active-reading comprehension by helping them learn to ask questions, set reading purposes, and integrate and synthesize information. The ReQuest strategy, designed by Anthony Manzo (Manzo & Manzo, 1990), is especially valuable for developing students' ability to create questions, build comprehension, and self-monitor responses (Coley et al., 1993).

ReQuest uses reciprocal questioning, in which teacher and students take turns assuming the role of the questioner. The teacher's questions serve as the model of question-asking behavior and guide students toward formulating a purpose for reading the full text. The ReQuest strategy can be used effectively across all grade levels. Start by giving each student a copy of the story or content-area text to be read; then use the following seven steps:

ReQuest (Reciprocal Questioning) a strategy that develops question-asking skills for comprehending text

EVIDENCE-BASED PRACTICE

How To Do . . .

QAR

1. Prepare a QAR chart using an illustration like the one in Figure 5.7.
2. Prepare two short passages with questions that use all four categories in the chart.
3. *Day one:* Introduce the QAR chart, display the illustration, and give lots of examples of each category of QAR.
4. *Day two:* Review and practice using QARs. Have children work in small groups to read, answer the questions, and decide on QAR categories for the first passage. Share group decisions in whole-class discussion.
5. Distribute the second passage, and have students read, answer the questions, and choose QAR categories independently (or work on this passage in small groups). Share responses in small groups and whole class.
6. *Day three:* Prepare longer passages with more questions for students to work on first in small groups and then independently.
7. *Day four:* Gradually introduce the QAR strategy in various discussions throughout the school day.

DELAYED READER ADAPTATION

■ **For delayed readers, follow all steps above, but change the pace. Spend one day on Right There questions. Spend the next day on Think and Search questions. Spend the third day with both types, identifying and distinguishing them. Follow a similar pace for the remaining question types.**

> *Seven Steps of ReQuest*

What schemata for teachers' questions and questioning styles might students possess?

1. *Introduction.* Introduce the procedure using such statements as "Let's see how we can improve our understanding of what we read. We will all read silently the text starting with the word 'Salutations!' on page 35 of *Charlotte's Web* and ending with 'Look, I'm waving!' Then we will take turns asking questions about the paragraph and what it means. When it's your turn to ask questions, try to ask the kind of questions a teacher might ask."
2. *Initial reading and student questioning.* Everyone reads the text silently. After reading, close your book and invite students to ask you any question they wish. You will find that students initially ask factual questions. For example, after reading the excerpt from *Charlotte's Web* presented earlier, students may ask "What did the voice say?" or "How do you spell 'salutations'?" or "What does 'salutations' mean?" Students soon will incorporate higher-level questions, following your model.
3. *Teacher questioning and modeling.* When it is your turn to ask questions, have the students close their books, using a marker. You might ask, "Why do you think Charlotte introduced herself by saying 'Salutations!'?" or "Why do you think Charlotte introduced herself to Wilbur at this point in the story?" You can also ask questions that follow logically from questions students asked earlier. Students need to understand that each question deserves to be answered and that "I don't know" responses are valid. Both you and the students should provide explanations as to why a question cannot be answered.
4. *Continued reciprocal questioning.* Silently read the next paragraph or segment of text and follow the turn-taking pattern in steps two and three. Use your questions to demonstrate how the information in this segment connects to the information in previous segment(s)—for example, "What does the word *they* refer to when Wilbur asks, 'What are they and where are you?'"
5. *Setting a purpose for reading.* Continue reading until students have enough information to get the gist of the story and make outcome predictions. Then ask, "What do you think is going to happen? And why do you think so?" Show students how their prediction statements can be turned into questions. Thus, the prediction "I think that, somehow, Wilbur and Charlotte become friends" becomes the question "How do Wilbur and Charlotte become friends?" You or your students should record prediction questions for later reflection. Do not reshape or change students' questions to fit what you know about the story's outcome. Questions not answered by the story may be just as legitimate as those that are answered.

How To Do . . .

ReQuest

1. Select the story, and decide on the length and number of initial reading segments.
2. Preread the story, and determine the aspects of the story your questioning will develop. List some higher-level questions that you wish to use (remember to give the children an opportunity to ask them first).
3. Identify any follow-up activities for the story, and prepare any materials needed.
4. Introduce the ReQuest procedure to the students, and use it with a story.

■ **Delayed readers often have difficulty formulating higher-level questions. Devoting a number of sessions to the QAR strategy before introducing the ReQuest strategy may lessen the problem. In addition, the teacher should model, and think-aloud, the processes involved.**

DELAYED READER ADAPTATION

6. *Silent reading.* Ask students to read to the end of the text to see if their predictions are correct.
7. *Follow-up discussion.* Initiate discussion by asking the prediction questions recorded earlier. The purpose-setting question is the first one to address after reading. If the story did not answer the purpose-setting question, now is the time to acknowledge that: "Our story didn't really answer this question, did it? What questions did it answer? [Pause.] Okay. Let's talk about that." After children are experienced ReQuest users, you may want to let them practice the procedure on their own.

Why is it important to address the purpose-setting question first?

In ReQuest, your questions provide the model for students' question-asking behavior. By emphasizing interpretive, applicative, and transactive questions, you encourage children to ask higher-level questions. Your responses to students' questions also model thinking processes. For example, in response to a student's question "Why did Charlotte want to save Wilbur?" you might reason, "That question really makes me think. To answer that question, I need to think about Charlotte's character. She's really caring. She knows Wilbur may end up in Zuckerman's smokehouse and has to figure out a way to save him. She wants to save Wilbur because she cares about Wilbur and thinks that's the right thing to do."

the **Highly Effective Teacher**

Reciprocal Teaching

The **reciprocal-teaching** strategy is similar to the ReQuest strategy, in that it uses teacher modeling to shape students' questions and predictions. Reciprocal teaching was developed by Palincsar (1984) to increase students' comprehension and comprehension monitoring at all grade

reciprocal teaching a strategy for teaching comprehension self-monitoring skills, based on modeling

What are some advantages of reciprocal teaching for children? What other comprehension sstrategies do influential teachers use?

levels. Even first-grade students have been found to successfully engage in the reciprocal-teaching strategy (Coley et al., 1993; Marks et al., 1993). The following four skill processes are integral to the strategy (Palincsar & Brown, 1986):

➤ *Four Skill Processes in Reciprocal Teaching*

1. *Predicting*—hypothesizing what the author will discuss next in the text.
2. *Question generation*—forming a question based on information in the text and on background knowledge.
3. *Clarifying*—focusing attention on parts of the text that are not clearly understood, searching for the reason for the difficulty, and taking steps to restore meaning.
4. *Summarizing*—identifying the most important idea in the paragraph or up to a given point in the text.

Reciprocal teaching relies on cognitive "scaffolds," or supports (Bruner, 1990), to develop these four comprehension skill processes. The teacher—or a student acting in the role of teacher—temporarily provides carefully structured supports for learners to build a working understanding of the four skill processes. As students gain independence using the procedures in text comprehension, the teacher's role is gradually decreased—in effect, removing the instructional scaffolding. As with ReQuest, the teacher and students take turns leading the discussion. The procedure for introducing and developing the reciprocal-teaching strategy follows (Palincsar, 1984, p. 254):

EVIDENCE-BASED PRACTICE

➤ *Introducing Reciprocal Teaching*

1. *Introduce the procedure.* Provide a short story or content-based passage several pages in length. Read the title and ask for predictions based on the title. Ask the students to read a brief section of the passage to provide story or subject context. Explain that today you will be the teacher, but later they will take turns being the teacher and directing the discussion.
2. *Model the skill processes.* Introduce each of the four skill processes just described—predicting, question generation, clarifying, and summarizing—using the context of the text just read.
   - *Ask and discuss the predicting questions* that you have prepared for this portion of the reading passage. Design questions at a variety of levels of thinking. Questions also should activate students' background knowledge. (Predicting and question generation)
   - *Model clarification of answers* to help the students become aware of comprehension problems, difficult vocabulary, or new concepts. The clarifying strategy helps students understand how to fix a meaning problem, using information in the text, background knowledge, and/or information from classmates' responses. (Clarifying)
   - *Model a brief summary* for the section read, after discussing and clarifying meaning problems. (Summarizing)
   - *Offer a prediction* about what the next section may be about. Your purposes are to help the students develop the four skill processes through your modeling, to show them how these processes help them comprehend the text, and to model the role of discussion leader. (Predicting and question generation)
3. *Prepare students to assume the teacher's role.* Begin to guide and prepare students to assume the role of teacher. For example, to help students form questions, ask, "What question did you think I might ask?" or "If you were the teacher, what question would you ask?" To help students understand and use summarizing skills, you might observe, "Remember that a summary includes the main idea, not lots of details." To help students encourage participation by all members of the group, you might model extending questions, such as "Who has a thought about this question?" or "Who has another prediction?" At this stage, you are starting to transfer responsibility for the discussion to your students.

➤ *Preparing Students for the Teacher's Role*

4. *Guide students as they assume the teacher's role.* After the students have become comfortable with group discussion, identify a student to assume the role of teacher. Provide praise and feedback to the student leader and to students in the group—for example, "That was an excellent question," "That question really makes us think," "Another way you might have asked that question is . . . ," or "You could also summarize the passage by saying . . ."
5. *Use reciprocal teaching in alternate ways.* An alternate use for the reciprocal-teaching strategy is peer and cross-age tutoring. You may also use the strategy with beginning readers, to whom you present the text orally.

Strategies in Use

Modeling Reciprocal Teaching

The following first-grade classroom discussion illustrates reciprocal teaching using text related to aquanauts and underwater exploration. The teacher has just read the story orally to the students, who were previously introduced to the four skill processes central to the strategy.

C1: My question is, what does the aquanaut need when he goes under water?

C2: A watch.

C3: Flippers.

C4: A belt.

C1: Those are all good answers.

T: Nice job! I have a question too. Why does the aquanaut wear a belt? What is so special about it?

C3: It's a heavy belt and keeps him from floating up to the top again.

T: Good for you.

C1: For my summary now: This paragraph was about what aquanauts need to take when they go under the water.

C5: And also about why they need those things.

C3: I think we need to clarify *gear*.

C6: That's the special things they need.

T: Another word for *gear* in this story might be *equipment*: the equipment that makes it easier for the aquanauts to do their job.

C1: I don't think I have a prediction to make.

T: Well, in the story, they tell us that there are "many strange and wonderful creatures" that the aquanauts see as they do their work. My prediction is that they'll describe some of these creatures. What are some of the strange creatures you already know about that live in the ocean?

C6: Octopuses.

C3: Whales?

C5: Sharks!

T: Let's listen and find out. Who'll be our teacher?

Excerpt from Palincsar, Annemarie Sullivan, & Brown, Ann L. (1986, April). Interactive teaching to promote independent learning from text. *The Reading Teacher*, 39 (8), 771–777. Copyright © 1986 by Annemarie S. Palincsar and the International Reading Association. All rights reserved.

CRITICAL THINKING

1. How did the discussion activate the students' background knowledge?
2. How did the discussion model setting a purpose for reading?
3. What dialogue shows that the learners used each of the four skill processes effectively?
4. What dialogue shows how the teacher used positive receiving and scaffolding?

GMA (Group Mapping Activity)

The **GMA (Group Mapping Activity),** developed by Jane Davidson (1982), is an instructional strategy that can be effectively used for building comprehension, based on visual representation, through the integration and synthesis of story ideas and concepts (Baumann & Bergeron, 1993). Group mapping can be used effectively once students have read a literature selection or content-area text.

The GMA strategy asks students to create a graphic representation illustrating their interpretation of the relationship between story characters and plot or between ideas and concepts in expository material. This representation takes the form of a map or diagram with labels based on students' personal understandings. Students are asked to share and interpret their maps, and story understandings are elaborated and extended. The following two steps explain the development of the GMA strategy:

1. *Creating maps.* After students read a selection, explain and demonstrate GMA using samples like the two maps in Figure 5.8. Include the following points in your explanation (Ruddell & Haggard, 1986):
   - A story map is a diagram of what you think the story is about.
   - There is no right or wrong way to draw a story map. You may use lines, words, circles, squares, or any other shapes for your map.
   - Create your map from the story ideas in your mind. Don't look back at the story.

GMA (Group Mapping Activity) a strategy for building comprehension of relationships in story or text, based on visual representation

EVIDENCE-BASED PRACTICE

➤ *Two Steps of the GMA Strategy*

How To Do . . .

Reciprocal Teaching

1. Select a short story or content-based passage that the children can read comfortably.

- **Improved comprehension usually results from use of the reciprocal-teaching strategy; however, studies indicate that students must have sufficient word recognition–word identification skills to handle the selected passage. For all students—but for delayed readers, in particular—be certain the material is at the student's instructional level, not frustration level.**

2. Prepare introductions for the four skill processes of predicting, question generation, clarifying, and summarizing—that is, develop questions for prompting students' predictions, prepare questions that you might ask about the text, find a section of the text that needs clarification and decide how to clarify, and prepare a summary statement.
3. Introduce the activity and story or passage using predicting prompts much like opening questions of a DR-TA. Alert students that today you will act as the teacher during the activity; later, they will assume the teacher's role.
4. Introduce the skill processes; model each using the introductions you prepared (step 2, above). Discuss each skill process explicitly, and provide numerous models of each.
5. Begin asking students to supply teacher-type questions—for example, "What questions might I ask here?" or "If you were the teacher, what questions would you ask?"
6. Begin asking students to assume the teacher's role. Provide guidance and feedback to them.

FIGURE 5.8

Sample Maps for Introducing GMA

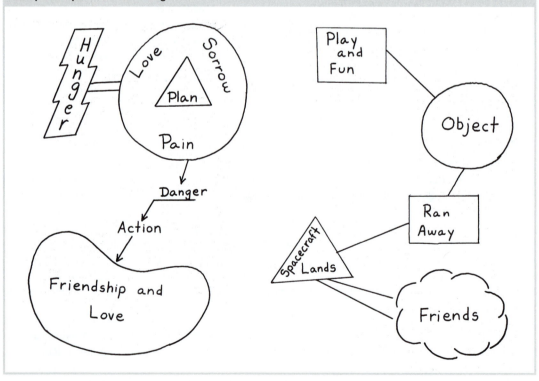

From *Thinking About Reading* (Teachers Edition) by Ruddell & Haggard. Copyright © 1986 by Modern Curriculum Press, Simon & Schuster Education Group. Used by permission.

- There is no right way to map a story. Everyone's map is different. You may find that at first some children experience frustration without a specified structure to follow for their story maps. Reassure them by saying, "You can make your map look any way you want it to look." Encourage reluctant students by asking, "How would you like to start your map?" You will notice that young readers often create maps that are picture-like rather than abstract. After the first mapping experience, the students will understand that they are free to create their own mapping structures. They also will have many new ideas for experimenting with mapping from having seen classmates' maps.

2. *Displaying and sharing maps.* Ask students to hold up their completed maps for the group to see. It helps to say, "Now hold up your maps so that we can see how different they are." Invite a student to share his or her map with the group by saying, "Who would like to share a map with the rest of the group? I would like you to tell about your map and your reasons for mapping the story the way you did." Use prompts that encourage students to explore relationships between the story's characters, events, and plot using the map—for example, "Why did you decide to put an arrow pointing from that character to this other one?" Encourage discussion and interaction between and among students.

Develop and share a map on the information in this section about using GMA. What are some differences between GMAs for literature and GMAs for expository text?

The story map in Figure 5.9 was created by Kris and shared with Carey, both third-grade students, after they read Chapter 9, "Paws on the Snow," from *The Bears on Hemlock Mountain* by Alice Dalgliesh (1952). This story describes the adventures of Jonathan, who is sent over Hemlock Mountain to borrow Aunt Emma's big iron pot to prepare stew for a family celebration. On his way home, he must travel over Hemlock Mountain again. It is just starting to get dark, and he hears the "Crunch! Crunch! Crunch!" of the bears' feet in the snow. The bears are coming closer. Jonathan turns over the big iron pot and crawls under it—just in time. He hears his father's voice calling him from a distance as the story nears the end.

Kris shared her map by explaining that the two long lines showed Jonathan's trip from his home (the bottom left triangle marked "help") over Hemlock Mountain to Aunt Emma's house (at left top with iron pot upside down). She explained that the most exciting part of the story was shown in the box labeled "Danger." This box shows the three bears (triangles) and Jonathan (small triangle), who is safe under the iron pot (small half-circle). Jonathan's father has come from home to search for Jonathan and has scared the three bears off into the woods (three triangles at the bottom right of the page). She felt sure Jonathan would now be rescued.

How To Do . . .

A GMA

1. Prepare "dummy" maps like those in Figure 5.8.
2. After the reading, ask students to construct story maps. Use the following statements to clarify the mapping task:
   a. "A map is a diagram of what you think the story is about. There is no right or wrong way to map. You may use words, shapes, or lines on your map."
   b. Show "dummy" maps, saying, "A map may look like this . . . like this . . . or like this."
   c. "Do not look back at the story while you're mapping. You may look back at it later."
3. Have students display maps "so that we can see how different they are."
4. Ask students to share their maps by telling how they mapped and why they chose to do it that way. Use prompts and questions to clarify and extend their thinking.

- **As an introduction, engage in GMA through whole-group mapping, with the teacher mapping on the chalkboard suggestions offered by class members, followed by small-group mapping (two or three students), before students approach the task independently. Rich discussion during whole-group and small-group mapping can boost text comprehension, as well as task comprehension.**

**DELAYED READER
ADAPTATION**

FIGURE 5.9

Kris's Sample Map Using the GMA Strategy

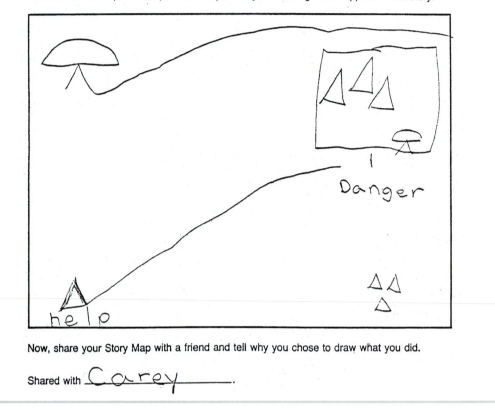

From *Thinking About Reading* (Teachers' Edition) by Ruddell & Haggard. © 1986 by Modern Curriculum Press. Used by permission.

Kris's explanation illustrates excellent integration and synthesis of characters, events, story climax, and the expected resolution. In addition, sharing the map serves as a model for mapping and story interpretation for other students.

Group mapping encourages students to think in new ways about what they have read. Marjorie Siegel (1994) describes **transmediation** as a process in which one sign system (visual representation in mapping) is used as a way of knowing or understanding another sign system (written language). Transmediation occurs when the two sign systems are linked by a meaning. Students who have the opportunity to represent text visually achieve new meanings, insights, and understandings about the text as a result of this experience. Siegel (1994) suggests that allowing students to use visual representation to interpret text invites them to think metaphorically. Davidson (1982) notes that "the act of mapping requires students to make intellectual commitments about their perceptions of the meaning of a passage as they draw relationships, details, or ideas from information in the text" (p. 56). You will find that students' maps provide a window on the mind, revealing important insights into their thinking and comprehension processes.

transmediation
the process of linking different sign systems through shared meanings

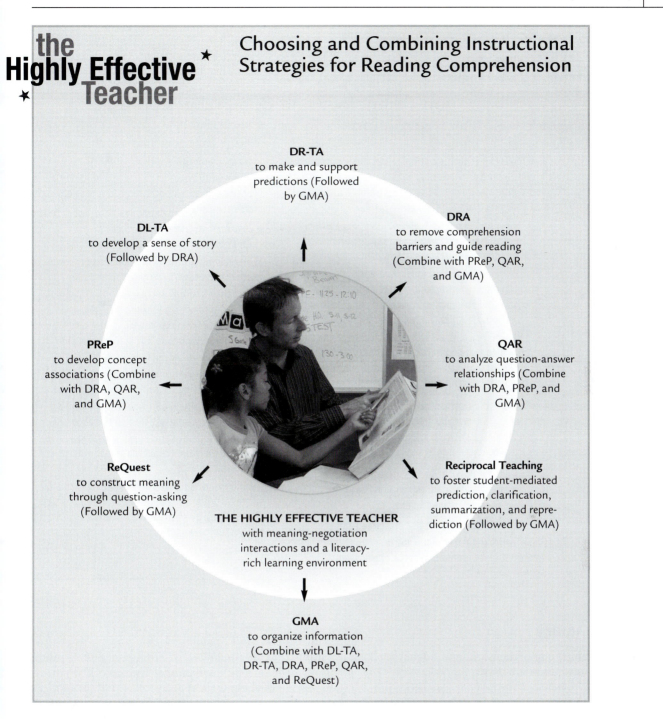

the Highly Effective Teacher ★

Choosing and Combining Instructional Strategies for Reading Comprehension

DR-TA
to make and support predictions (Followed by GMA)

DL-TA
to develop a sense of story (Followed by DRA)

DRA
to remove comprehension barriers and guide reading (Combine with PReP, QAR, and GMA)

PReP
to develop concept associations (Combine with DRA, QAR, and GMA)

QAR
to analyze question-answer relationships (Combine with DRA, PReP, and GMA)

ReQuest
to construct meaning through question-asking (Followed by GMA)

Reciprocal Teaching
to foster student-mediated prediction, clarification, summarization, and repre-diction (Followed by GMA)

THE HIGHLY EFFECTIVE TEACHER
with meaning-negotiation interactions and a literacy-rich learning environment

GMA
to organize information (Combine with DL-TA, DR-TA, DRA, PReP, QAR, and ReQuest)

Summary and Classroom Applications

double entry journal

Reread the introduction to this chapter and review your responses to the Double Entry Journal at the beginning of the chapter. How would you modify your list of comprehension skills? How could Toni use the comprehension strategies described in this chapter?

the Highly Effective Teacher

on Technology and Comprehension Instruction

1. Select a topic for a short report based on the students' interest. To activate background knowledge, ask the students to brainstorm what they already know about a topic and place it on a semantic map. Have the students conduct an Internet search, starting at **www.yahooligans.com,** and spend some time following different links and reading information on the topic. Then have the students return to their semantic maps and add new information they have learned as a result of their Internet search.

2. Visit the Web site for *Sports Illustrated for Kids* at **www.siforkids.com**. Use this site to give the students practice in the four levels of thinking:

   ■ *Factual:* What are the four main sections on this Web site and what do they contain?

   ■ *Interpretive:* Why do you think this Web site was created? Who might be expected to use it? Why?

   ■ *Applicative:* Have the students read about a particular topic and then share their responses with the class. Then ask:

   How do you think you might use the knowledge you gained from reading about different sports-related topics on this Web site?

   ■ *Transactive:* Using this *Sports Illustrated for Kids* Web site, have the students read an online account of an athlete's personal experience. Ask them to imagine that they had this same experience themselves, and write a letter to a friend describing what happened.

3. Have the students use the software, Maxis' SimCity, to develop these levels of thinking. In this simulation game you can build a city by selecting a variety of geographical features, buildings, and scenarios. Various disasters and challenges occur throughout, and users must respond in a variety of ways. A tour of the game may be found at **www.simcity.ea.com**.

4. Use different Web sites to develop QAR strategies. A good site to begin with is **www.pbs.org/wgbh/nova/archive/**. Search this archive for a suitable topic for your students.

Chapter Summary

Developing students' comprehension and higher-level thinking abilities is one of your most important roles as a highly effective teacher. Comprehension instruction must foster active meaning negotiation and comprehension processing, directed by a clear reading purpose and expected use. Instruction must develop text-processing strategies that assist students in comprehending narrative or expository text. Instruction must also activate students' background knowledge and involve their attitudes and values. In addition, teachers must help them learn to monitor their own meaning construction and develop strategies for "fixing up" meanings when comprehension goes awry. These features of active comprehension must operate in concert.

Understanding the factual, interpretive, applicative, and transactive levels of thinking is critical in creating questions and discussions that stimulate rich comprehension of text. The instructional framework for comprehension development presented in this chapter stresses the importance of integrating these four levels of thinking with specific comprehension skills and questioning and discussion strategies.

The group reading instructional approaches—and the Directed Reading Activity (DRA) and the Directed Reading-Thinking Activity (DR-TA)—are two valuable tools designed to integrate the levels of thinking and specific comprehension skills in your classroom. The DRA and DR-TA approaches can effectively guide students' comprehension development and encourage higher-level thinking.

Strategies designed to target specific aspects of the comprehension process include the PreReading Plan (PReP), which activates prior knowledge before reading

Professional Standards and
Reading Comprehension

We again visit *Standards for Reading Professionals—Revised 2003* (International Reading Association, 2004) introduced at the end of Chapter 1. The standards presented in Figure 5.10 provide examples for each of the five standards related to teacher knowledge and instruction and students' comprehension development. These standards gain importance to you as you work toward becoming a highly effective and influential reading teacher. You can see the complete list of Standards for Reading Professionals in Appendix C.

FIGURE 5.10

Professional Standards and the Comprehension Process for Classroom Teacher Candidates

Professional Standard	Example
1. Foundational Knowledge	**Element 1.1** Knows foundational theories related to practices and materials; e.g., understands role of schema theory in developing story comprehension; understands role of background knowledge, attitudes and values, and monitoring strategies in developing students' comprehension.
2. Instructional Strategies and Curriculum Materials	**Element 2.2** Plans for a wide range of instructional practices, approaches, and methods, including technology-based practices; e.g., understands key strategies for the group-comprehension instruction, such as the DRA and DR-TA, and specific targeted comprehension-skills strategies, such as PReP, QAR, ReQuest, reciprocal teaching, and GMA.
3. Assessment, Diagnosis, and Evaluation	**Element 3.2** Recognizes the variability in reading levels across children in the same grade and within a child across different subject areas; e.g., understands how to interpret students' responses and individual student responses that reflect different levels of thinking and comprehension skills; knows how to use questioning and discussion strategies to develop an understanding of a student's thinking and comprehension-skill development.
4. Creating a Literate Environment	**Element 4.1** Collects information about children's interests, reading abilities, and backgrounds, and use this information when planning instruction; e.g., understands how to observe and interpret children's responses in using instructional strategies such as ReQuest, reciprocal teaching, and GMA to obtain information that can be used in instructional planning.
5. Professional Development	**Element 5.3** Actively engages in collaboration and dialogue with other teachers and reading specialists to obtain recommendations and advice on teaching practices and ideas; e.g., can use a key instructional strategy, such as reciprocal teaching with students, make observations of the success and problem areas, share and discuss these ideas with other teachers, and refine the use of the strategy based on that discussion.

Part 2 from IRA. (2004). Professional Standards and Ethics Committee, International Reading Association. *Standards for reading professionals—revised 2003*. Reprinted with permission of the International Reading Association. All rights reserved.

and helps identify students who may need special pre-reading instruction; the Question-Answer Relationships (QAR) strategy, which helps students focus on the thinking demands of questions and use specific information sources in responding; Reciprocal Questioning (ReQuest) and reciprocal teaching, which use teacher modeling to help students understand how to ask questions, set a reading purpose, and integrate information; and the Group Mapping Activity (GMA), which emphasizes the integration and synthesis of information through graphic representations that express students' personal interpretations of text.

Applications: Bridges to the Classroom

1. Audiotape or videotape a DRA or DR-TA lesson in the classroom, and then analyze the lesson to discover how the questioning and discussion strategies described in the chapter are used. As you replay the recording, note the number of times each of the eight strategies is used. What strategies were used most frequently? Why? What strategies do you believe you should have emphasized more? Why?

2. Have a friend videotape or audiotape your teaching. Analyze the questioning strategies you use. To what extent do you emphasize each of the four thinking levels (factual, interpretive, applicative, and transactive)? Which questioning strategies do you rely on most heavily? How can you put more emphasis on higher-level thinking?

3. Observe an experienced or highly effective teacher as she or he guides students' comprehension development. What are some key features of this teacher's approach? What kinds of questions and discussion strategies does he or she use? How might you incorporate some aspects of this teacher's approach in your own teaching?

4. Interview two classroom teachers. Ask them how they define their role in guiding students' reading-comprehension development. What two or three instructional goals do they regard as most important in reading instruction? Why do they consider these goals important? Do you agree?

5. Using a story from a basal text or children's or adolescent literature, develop lesson plans for applying one or more of the instructional strategies described in this chapter: DRA, DR-TA, PReP, QAR, ReQuest, reciprocal teaching, and GMA. Try combining two or more of the strategies in one lesson. Use your plan to teach the lesson to students at the appropriate grade level, or present your lesson plan to classmates. What changes would you make on the basis of students' responses or the critiques of your classmates? Add your plan to your teaching portfolio.

Additional Research and Practice

1. Lenski, S. D., Ehlers-Zavala, F., Daniel, M. C., & Sun-Irminger, X. (2006). Profiles in comprehension. *The Reading Teacher, 60,* 24–34.

   This article provides excellent insight in students' comprehension processes by identifying and describing eight thinking profiles. Instructional interventions are suggested for each profile with emphasis on the importance of matching comprehension instruction to the student's thinking profile. (Practice)

2. Stahl, K. A. D. (2004). Proof, practice, and promise: Comprehension strategy instruction in the primary grades. *The Reading Teacher, 57,* 598–609.

   This discussion emphasizes the importance of comprehension-strategy instruction in the primary grades based on an excel-lent research review of those strategies and concludes with a discussion of instructional implications for teachers. (Practice/Research)

3. Ruddell, R. B. (2004). Researching the influential literacy teacher: Characteristics, beliefs, strategies, and new research directions. In R. B. Ruddell & N. J. Unrau (Eds.), *Theoretical models and processes of reading* (pp. 979–997). Newark, DE: International Reading Association.

   This research synthesis on effective teachers places special emphasis on their instructional characteristics and the ways in which these teachers develop students' comprehension and higher-level thinking through questioning strategies. (Research)

Building Meaning Vocabulary and Comprehension Connections

Wordstruck is exactly what I was—and still am: crazy about the sound of words, the look of words, the taste of words, the feeling for words on the tongue and in the mind.

Robert MacNeil (1931–),
American writer

The investigation of the meaning of words is the beginning of education.

Antisthenes (404–370 B.C.),
Greek philosopher

Vocabulary knowledge is closely connected and critical to your comprehension and understanding of text. Read the opening words in the whimsical poem "Jabberwocky," from Lewis Carroll's (1871/1987) *Through the Looking Glass*, and then respond to the questions that follow.

'Twas brillig, and the slithy toves

Did gyre and gimble in the wabe:

All mimsy were the borogroves,

And the mome raths outgrabe.

What meaning did you derive from this text? What images were created in your mind? Reflect for a moment on the critical role of vocabulary knowledge in your comprehension of these words.

Though little vocabulary meaning is present here, conventional English letter and sound patterns and a familiar grammatical system using word order, connecting words, and inflectional endings are clearly present in the poem. The meaning, however, is somewhat of a mystery and left to individual interpretation. The next stanza begins to shape our understanding, comprehension, and imagery using vocabulary that is more familiar.

Beware the Jabberwock, my son!

The jaws that bite, the claws that catch!

Beware the Jubjub bird, and shun

The frumious Bandersnatch!

Graeme Base's (1987) beautifully illustrated *Jabberwocky* imposes a visual interpretation on Carroll's poem that helps define many of the creative nonsense word labels, such as *slithy toves, borogroves, vorpal sword, Tumtum tree,* and *Jabberwock.* Thus, vocabulary knowledge and reading comprehension are not only interactive but interdependent.

double entry journal

What do you do when you come to an unfamiliar word? What do you do to get new words into your working vocabulary?

Chapter Objectives

After reading and discussing this chapter, you will be able to:

- understand the nature of vocabulary acquisition and key factors that influence this acquisition.
- identify key goals and objectives that will guide your vocabulary instruction using narrative and expository material.
- grasp the importance of creating an active and motivating learning environment for vocabulary instruction.

- understand how to effectively use a variety of strategies to develop vocabulary in three instructional contexts: before, during, and after reading.
- support word learning and build meaning connections to enhance students' vocabulary growth.

the ★
**Highly
Effective
Teacher**
★

Meaning Vocabulary Acquisition

Vocabulary knowledge develops rapidly from preschool years through adulthood. It is estimated that students expand their vocabulary at the rate of 2,700 to 3,000 words per year (Beck & McKeown, 1991; Nagy & Scott, 2004; Shu, Anderson, & Zhang, 1995). This rapid growth is driven by their intellectual curiosity and general maturation (Piaget, 1967) and is fueled by the social use of language with peers and adults (Vygotsky, 1986). Students integrate new word knowledge into their working vocabulary by "trying on" and exploring new words and by using these words with peers and adults at home and school.

Research and
Evidence-Based Practice

Meaning Vocabulary Acquisition and Literacy Development

Did You Know?

- Students acquire new meaning vocabulary knowledge at an amazingly rapid rate, on the average, of about seven words each day (Beck & McKeown, 1991; Blachowicz & Fisher, 2000; Nagy, Anderson, & Herman, 1987; Nagy & Scott, 2004).

- Research suggests, however, that the vocabulary of primary-grade students with higher socioeconomic status is double that of students from families with lower socioeconomic status (Beck & McKeown, 1991; Graves & Slater, 1987; Juel, 1996; Nagy & Scott, 2004; Schwanenflugel & Akin, 1994; Senechal & Cornell, 1993).

- Meaning vocabulary knowledge has long been regarded as critical to students' comprehension development (Anderson & Freebody, 1981; Davis, 1944, 1968; Johnson, Toms-Bronowski, & Pittelman, 1981; Pearson, Hiebert, & Kamil, 2007).

- As students broaden their thinking and become aware of new semantic and conceptual relationships, they increase their reading comprehension ability (Beck & McKeown, 1991; Blachowicz et al., 2006; Blachowicz & Fisher, 2000; Nagy & Scott, 2004; Ruddell & Unrau, 2004a).

- Even though teaching of word meanings has been shown to be of vital importance to the development of reading comprehension, a number of studies report the disturbing finding that vocabulary instruction is a very small part of reading instruction (Graves, 1987); for example, one well-known study has shown that less than 1 percent of instructional time was devoted to vocabulary development (Durkin, 1979).

Goals and Objectives of Vocabulary Instruction

There are three primary goals in vocabulary development. Vocabulary instruction must (1) develop students' background knowledge of concepts and word labels that enable them to comprehend narrative and expository text, (2) teach students how to understand new word meanings independently, and (3) build positive attitudes toward vocabulary learning and encourage independent word learning.

The specific objectives derived from these goals, which guide the development of the vocabulary strategies presented in this chapter, include the following:

➤ Objectives of Vocabulary Instruction

1. To help students develop new vocabulary knowledge in the context of narrative and expository reading material through strategies that involve them in active learning and comprehension
2. To guide students in connecting new vocabulary knowledge to prior background knowledge (Gunning, 2008)
3. To help students understand the importance of checking new vocabulary meaning in the context of the story or exposition
4. To develop and activate vocabulary processing strategies that students will find valuable as they independently determine the meaning of new words
5. To lead students toward positive attitudes, values, and interests related to narrative and expository reading material, thus increasing motivation and independence in vocabulary learning

Graves (1987) describes six vocabulary-learning tasks: (1) learning to read known words, (2) learning new meanings for known words, (3) learning new words representing known concepts, (4) learning new words representing new concepts, (5) clarifying and enriching the meanings of known words, and (6) moving words from receptive to expressive vocabularies. Students need to not only learn new words but also learn *how to* learn words (Graves, 2000; Kibby, 1995; Nagy & Scott, 2004). Table 6.1 (below) presents the vocabulary-learning tasks as learning goals and shows the learner's prior knowledge (student state) for each task.

➤ Six Vocabulary-Learning Tasks

TABLE 6.1

Prior Student State for Learning New Words

Student's State	Learning Goals	Example
1. Knows word meaning aurally	Decoding for reading	Can describe an *elephant* accurately but cannot read the word
2. Knows word meaning but does not express it	Production in writing and speech	Can understand *chaos* but not sufficiently familiar to use it
3. Knows meaning but not word	New label for old concept	Knows the idea of fear and hiding but does not know the word *cringe*
4. Knows partial meaning of word	Extend the attributes for a label	Knows the word *guerrilla* means soldier but does not know the tactics or the type of soldier connoted
5. Knows different meaning for word	New concept for old label	Knows that *force* means strength but does not know the vector meaning
6. Knows neither the concept nor the label	New concept and new label	Knows nothing about atomic structure, including the term *ion*

From "Learning Word Meanings from Written Context," by P. A. Drum and B. C. Konopak, in *The Nature of Vocabulary Acquisition* (p. 76, Table 1), by M. G. McKeown and M. E. Curtis (Eds.), 1987, Hillsdale, NJ: Lawrence Erlbaum Associates, Inc. Copyright © 1987 by Lawrence Erlbaum Associates, Inc. Reprinted with permission of Lawrence Erlbaum Associates and P. A. Drum and B. C. Konopak.

The National Reading Panel, discussed in earlier chapters, scrutinized the research literature to uncover implications for meaning vocabulary instruction. Key findings from this review are summarized in Figure 6.1. (See below.)

Vocabulary researchers (Beck & McKeown, 1991; Blachowicz et al., 2006; Blachowicz & Fisher, 2000; Graves, 2000) recommend that, to address these different tasks in learning new words and learning how to learn words, teachers of vocabulary include rich instruction geared to developing children's independent vocabulary-learning abilities. Four approaches comprise a rich vocabulary program:

EVIDENCE-BASED PRACTICE

➤ *A Program of Rich Instruction*

1. Direct instruction to develop meaning in the immediate context of the material being read
2. Direct teaching of selected words that not only are essential to comprehending the material being read but also have broad utility beyond that context
3. Presentation of word-learning strategies to encourage students to become increasingly independent in identifying meanings of unknown words through meaning context and classroom resources (e.g., using reference aids such as the dictionary)
4. Wide and extensive reading to develop vocabulary learning from context

Active Learning in Vocabulary-Learning Contexts

active learning learning that involves building interest and mental engagement in the construction of meaning

The key to successful vocabulary instruction is getting students actively involved in the vocabulary-learning process (Beck & McKeown, 1991; Blachowicz & Fisher, 2000). **Active learning** ensures mental engagement in the process and also builds high interest in vocabulary study (Kibby, 1995; Nagy & Scott, 2004; Rupley, Logan, & Nichols, 1999). Asking students to memorize fifteen or twenty isolated definitions over the week and take a vocabulary test on Friday does not stimulate children's active participation. Instead, instruction that uses active mental processing encourages students to reason with words and to integrate new information into their background knowledge. Six key principles of vocabulary instruction are presented in Figure 6.2.

Word Reasoning

the **Highly Effective Teacher**

Planning for active involvement should incorporate three types of word reasoning. First, a new word needs to be developed and understood in the meaning context in which it is found (Blachowicz & Lee, 1991; Nagy & Scott, 2004). Texts differ greatly with respect to how reader-friendly they are in presenting new vocabulary. For example, the meaning of *magma* is introduced in a reader-friendly context, through definition and example, in the following paragraph.

> Volcanoes are formed from enormous heat and pressure that build up inside the earth's crust. When the heat and pressure melt and liquify rock, it is known as *magma*. A volcano erupts when the magma is pushed with great force through the top and sides of the volcanic mountain. As the magma reaches the outside of the volcano, it becomes a river of molten rock, and then is called a lava flow.

FIGURE 6.1

National Reading Panel Recommendations on Meaning Vocabulary Instruction

➤ *National Reading Panel Recommendations on Meaning Vocabulary Instruction*

- Attention to teaching and learning of word meanings can lead to gains in comprehension.
- Learning meanings of words before reading a selection is helpful.
- Word meanings should be taught directly through multiple methods (e.g., through many exposures in a variety of rich contexts, through repetition, and through use of high-quality computer programs designed for this purpose).
- Word meanings also can be learned incidentally through copious reading and through oral language experiences.

Adapted from the *Report of the National Reading Panel: An evidence-based assessment of the scientific literature on reading and its implications for reading instruction.* (2000). Washington, DC: U.S. Department of Health and Human Services.

FIGURE 6.2
Key Principles of Vocabulary Instruction

1. Use a variety of approaches for teaching vocabulary to create a program of rich instruction, including direct teaching of vocabulary, use of immediate context to determine meanings, use of classroom vocabulary resources, and extensive reading of a broad range of children's literature and content materials.
2. Use instruction that provides for active learning by teaching your students to "reason with words," using the meaning context in which the words are found.
3. Develop new words by relating them to semantically similar words through contrast and comparison and by creating new contexts and interpretations, which will lead to the integration and connection of word meanings.
4. Remember that vocabulary learning is a social process, and incorporate students' personal motivations to learn new words, including sound and adult-like appeal, immediate usefulness, and peer-group use.
5. Base your selection of new vocabulary for instruction on the importance of the vocabulary to story or content-material comprehension, students' background knowledge, and the friendly or unfriendly nature of the text material.
6. Consider the objectives of your instruction to determine whether to develop vocabulary before, during, or after reading—for example, developing students' vocabulary knowledge, helping them use reading context to construct meaning, connecting new vocabulary meanings to semantically related words, and giving students increased opportunity to identify a personal vocabulary as they learn to reason with words.

EVIDENCE-BASED PRACTICE

However, the word *vibrations* in the following excerpt from *Sharks* (Berger, 1987), a less reader-friendly text, will require further explanation to be fully understood.

> Sharks can quickly pick up the movement of a wounded fish, for example. Suppose someone hooks a fish. The fish flings itself about in the water to get off the hook. A shark can sense the fish's vibrations at great distances. It heads straight for the struggling fish, and often before the catch can be pulled out of the water, the shark has bitten off a mouthful. (p. 12)

The word *vibrations* in this context suggests a rapid, frantic flinging to and fro movement. The text assumes that a child's background knowledge will provide for this understanding. To develop children's understanding of *vibrations*, a teacher might demonstrate through hand actions what a fish's vibrations might look like. The teacher might also guide students in formulating a definition and checking the definition in a glossary or dictionary. In this way, teachers become "context sensitive" to new vocabulary. Many new words developed in reader-friendly text require no teaching, but new vocabulary in unfriendly text needs to be explained and discussed in that context.

Are you "context sensitive" to new vocabulary?

Second, a new word needs to be related to semantically similar words and word groups through comparison and contrast to refine, connect, and integrate meanings (Kibby, 1995). For example, a discussion of the word *magma* might explore how its usefulness in understanding the role of a *magma chamber* as an underground pool of molten rock in a volcanic eruption, or, in another semantic sense—how *magma* is related to *magmatic*—water that rises like magma from deep within the earth through volcanic steam or hot-water springs.

For the word *vibrations*, you might examine how *vibrate*, the base word, is similar to and different from the words *quiver*, *shake*, and *shiver*. Because these words have strong visual properties, students could act out their understanding of each word and use it in the context of the original sentence as they "try on" the meaning. In this manner, they begin to refine the special meaning of *vibrations* as used in the context of the way sharks locate food.

Third, the meaning of new words can be enhanced and connected to that of other semantically related words by creating new and varied contexts and interpretations. Meaning clues and connections between the new words *miser*, *Spartan*, and *frugal* are evident in the following friendly text.

How are these new words semantically related?

> The miser led a Spartan existence. His tiny room contained only a single bed and a rough board desk. He was a frugal person, spending very little for clothing or food. A shaggy grey beard framed his long face, and his ragged clothes hung on his thin long frame.

After discussing the meanings of these new words based on the context, you might engage students in developing meaning connections between these words and their prior knowledge by asking, "How are the words *Spartan* and *frugal* related in describing a miser?" and "Why does the word *Spartan* begin with a capital *S*?" and "What are all the characteristics you think a miser might have, and why?" The value of this type of active involvement in vocabulary learning resides in refining and building semantic connections between the new vocabulary information and children's prior vocabulary knowledge (Kibby, 1995).

Motivation for Word Learning

Your awareness of children's personal motivation and growing independence in learning new vocabulary can be valuable in stimulating vocabulary development (Cudd & Roberts, 1993/1994). A brief review of our discussion from Chapter 2 reveals four motivations for elementary-grade students' word learning (Haggard, 1980):

> *Four Motivations for Word Learning*

1. The word has an appealing, interesting sound and is adult-like in usage (e.g., *fickle, delicious, Internet*).
2. The word involves strong emotion, or mispronunciation could create embarrassment (e.g., *fatigue, centrifugal, dinosaur*).
3. The word has immediate usefulness (e.g., *monitor, perturbed, equation*).
4. The word is common in peer-group usage (e.g., *superhero, spacecraft, wretched*, as in "Wretched Richie").

| What words from students' popular culture and media might you include in vocabulary instruction?

Central to these motivations is the social nature of vocabulary learning and authentic learning experiences that relate to children's multiple worlds of thinking. These motivations explain in part why children have such a strong interest in those *Mesozoic* reptiles with the wonderfully intriguing names such as brontosaurus (thunderlike lizard), stegosaurus (rooflike lizard), tyrannosaurus (tyrantlike lizard), and ichthyosaurus (fishlike lizard). Students have absolutely no trouble learning these words. Many kindergarten and first-grade students possess an amazing knowledge of sharks, from the great white to the hammerhead. You also may be surprised at their abilities to identify and discuss Pokemon characters—Pikachu, Blastoise, Charmander, and Psyduck. These words not only have a fascinating sound and adult-like appeal for students but can be used immediately in authentic conversations with peers and adults.

the ★ **Highly Effective Teacher** ★

| When will you introduce and develop new words?

Criteria for Word Selection

Selecting vocabulary words to teach is an important part of reading instruction, because there usually are more words than there is time for you to teach or cognitive capacity for students to learn. In addition, no two children know or need to know exactly the same list of words. So, you have a responsibility to select words carefully to make the most of the learning episode (Pearson et al., 2007). The following questions are useful in making vocabulary-selection decisions:

- Is the new vocabulary central to the meaning of the story or expository material?
- Which new words, in the context of the reading selection, will present problems for students with limited background knowledge?
- Which vocabulary words are developed in such a reader-friendly context that they do not need to be taught?
- Which vocabulary words are used in reader-unfriendly text, in a context that does not convey meaning, and therefore require introduction or explanation?

> *Base your selection of new vocabulary on your students' background knowledge.*

After reading and examining the text material and identifying potential vocabulary based on these criteria, you will need to decide at what point the new words will be introduced and developed. The three main options—before, during, and after reading—and the conditions for each are presented in Table 6.2.

Before-reading vocabulary instruction is short and to the point. Its purpose is to make sure students have some understanding of words they are going to encounter in text. Before-reading instruction is directed at immediate recall of word meanings while reading; it is not sufficiently

TABLE 6.2
When to Introduce and Develop New Words

Context Conditions	Before Reading	During Reading	After Reading
The words are essential for students' comprehension of the selection.	X		
Student background knowledge is not sufficient for independent understanding.	X		
The words are potential barriers to comprehension.	X		
The words appear in reader-unfriendly text.	X	X	
The students do not already know the words.	X	X	
A goal of instruction is to develop abilities to understand new words independently.		X	
A goal of instruction is to develop abilities to use reference resources in the classroom.		X	
Students will understand the words on the basis of personal prior knowledge or reader-friendly text.		X	
Students can determine meaning from context.		X	X
Small-group discussion is needed to connect new meanings to prior learning.			X
A goal of instruction is to deepen and enrich vocabulary learning.			X
Elaborated discussion is needed for long-term acquisition of vocabulary.			X

extended to "set" the words in memory. Additional practice and follow-up activities are necessary for long-term retention of new words.

Much of during-reading vocabulary instruction is primed before reading by discussing with students strategies for figuring out the meaning of unknown words independently. Students then apply those strategies while reading. Other during-reading instruction occurs when someone asks what a word means and others attempt to define it.

After-reading vocabulary instruction focuses on long-term retention of newly learned words. It requires time for exploring and discussing words and word meanings and for practicing using new words.

If you use a basal reader program, its teacher's guide probably will emphasize teaching words before reading. The identification of new words to be taught will be based mainly on the judgment of the writers of the guide, who will apply their own standards when choosing words. However, it is impossible for even the most experienced guide writer to know your students and their needs. For these reasons, you must make the final decision about which words will be taught and when.

How will you decide whether to introduce vocabulary before, during, or after reading?

the Highly Effective Teacher

Before-Reading Vocabulary Instruction: Teaching Vocabulary in Context (TVC)

Teaching Vocabulary in Context (TVC) is most often used to introduce vocabulary before reading a story but also may be used in follow-up vocabulary reinforcement. The first step is to identify the new vocabulary words to be taught. Apply the criteria discussed earlier, taking into consideration the background knowledge of your students, concepts central to the text, and the reader-friendly or -unfriendly nature of the reading context.

Teaching Vocabulary in Context (TVC) a strategy for before-reading vocabulary instruction

Which four words would you teach to introduce "Slipstream"?

Introducing vocabulary before reading consumes discussion time. For this reason, it is important to select only the four or five words most central to the story or content material that the students do not know. Keep the discussion short; you'll have an opportunity to talk more about words after reading.

The second step in using the TVC strategy is to establish a meaningful story context for introducing the vocabulary items. Provide a brief introduction to establish a story schema and connect the new vocabulary to students' background knowledge. The introduction should include the title and a few ideas related to the central story theme. The point is to provide sufficient information to enable the students to form a general story schema that will help link the new vocabulary to their background knowledge.

> *Present new words in context.*

The third step is to introduce and discuss the new words you believe are essential to understand the story. The rule here is that new words should be presented embedded in the text in which children will encounter them. Write the words you have selected on the chalkboard or on chart paper in the sentences (or sentence fragments) in which they first appear in the story. Read each sentence aloud, and then ask students to speculate about the meaning of the vocabulary words. Write their ideas quickly on the chalkboard, and record other ideas that surface in the discussion. After some discussion of each word, arrive at a definition that the class or group accepts.

Should you teach words that students already know?

The fourth step is to evaluate your students' vocabulary knowledge and determine possible need for follow-up instruction. This step of the TVC strategy provides an excellent opportunity to assess your students' background knowledge.

Strategies in Use — Using TVC with "Slipstream"

Reread "Slipstream" in Figure 5.6, pages 137–138. In this story, charter pilot Captain Armitage is flying a tour group from England to the Channel Islands. Bad weather forces the return of the flight to a succession of airfields in England. Armitage finds each landing strip blocked by the same "phantom aircraft." The investigation following the crash landing reveals a structural defect in the plane that could have been fatal to all on board if they had landed at an airfield. The vocabulary identified in the teacher's guide includes the following words:

adverse	hallucination	light aircraft
calculated risk	indifferent	obsolete
charter	overshooting	syncopated
diverting	salvage	technology
grammar school	slap	

CRITICAL THINKING

STEP ONE: IDENTIFYING NEW VOCABULARY

1. Which of the recommended words would you select for introduction? Why? What other words would you select from the story for introduction?

STEP TWO: ESTABLISH MEANINGFUL STORY CONTEXT

2. What story context would you provide to enable students to build a connection to the new vocabulary? Why?

STEP THREE: INTRODUCING NEW WORDS

3. How would you present the meanings of the new words you have selected for introduction to your students?

4. At what point would you move on to having students read the story?

STEP FOUR: EVALUATING VOCABULARY KNOWLEDGE

5. What would you do if you found that most students already knew several of the words you had selected?

6. How would you evaluate students' background vocabulary knowledge when introducing vocabulary?

How To Do . . .

Teaching Vocabulary in Content (TVC)

1. Preview the story or material to be read, and select four or five words to be taught.
2. Write the words in text sentences on the chalkboard or a chart (or list the words on the board with locational information).
3. Read the sentences aloud, and ask students to speculate on the word meanings.

■ **Underline the targeted word in each sentence. After reading the sentence, focus on the word's identification and pronunciation before speculating on its meaning.**

DELAYED READER ADAPTATION

4. Record the students' ideas about meanings on the board.
5. Arrive at an agreed-on class definition of each word (check a dictionary or glossary if necessary).

During-Reading Vocabulary Instruction:
The Context-Structure-Sound-Resource (CSSR) System

A main objective in vocabulary development is to help students acquire strategies that will lead to independence in constructing meaning for new words in both stories and informational material (Carlisle & Stone, 2005; Dana & Rodriquez, 1992; Kibby, 1995). **Context-Structure-Sound-Resource (CSSR)** is a good strategy to achieve this objective.

Students sometimes are reading independently and encounter a word that is unknown to them. In teacher-guided instruction, a *teacher explanation and brief discussion* may be all that is needed to help students understand a given word. In some cases, however, the word may be important enough or complex enough that additional follow-up discussion or activity targeting this word is warranted even after reading of the selection is completed.

Other times, no available resource (teacher, tutor, parent) may be present when the student comes to a word whose meaning is unknown. For times such as these, the CSSR strategy will prove useful. Developed by William S. Gray in 1946 as an independent-learning tool to assist *word identification*, it can also be used to promote understanding of *word meaning*.

Context-Structure-Sound-Resource (CSSR) system
a four-step strategy for during-reading vocabulary instruction

How To Do . . .

Context-Structure-Sound-Resource (CSSR) System

1. Prepare a chart showing the parts of the CSSR system.
2. Walk students through the system, elaborating on and discussing each part.
3. Using a short passage and four vocabulary words, demonstrate how to use the system. Make sure each of the four words illustrates at least one part of the system.

■ **Natural texts—those not purposely devised to provide a supportive context—may not readily convey word meanings. To compound this problem that all readers must face, delayed readers often are less facile than others at gaining meanings from any context. Delayed readers should *explicitly* be shown *how to* derive word meanings from context, using teacher modeling and specific practice activities and games.**

DELAYED READER ADAPTATION

4. Find opportunities in other learning events to teach or reinforce students' understanding of the system parts. Remind students frequently of the CSSR system.
5. Direct students to apply the CSSR system as they read independently.
6. Debrief children after reading as to how the CSSR system worked.

FIGURE 6.3
Wall Chart for the CSSR Strategy

HOW TO FIGURE OUT A WORD YOU DON'T KNOW

1. **CONTEXT:** Read the entire sentence where you find the word. Do you find any helpful meaning clues? Are there any meaning clues in other parts of the paragraph or story up to this point? Use the clues to help. Can you figure out the meaning? If so, continue your reading.

   If you can't figure out the meaning yet, then check . . .

2. **STRUCTURE:** Look at the word and see if there any parts that you recognize. Roots? Prefixes? Do the word endings help? Use this information with the context clues. Can you figure out the word? If so, continue to read.

   If you are still searching for the meaning, then check . . .

3. **SOUND:** Try to pronounce the word and see if you recognize it. Sometimes you can recognize the meaning of the word when you hear it. Do you know the word? Use this information with the sentence and story context. Now, can you figure out the word? If so, continue your reading.

   If it still doesn't make sense, then check . . .

4. **RESOURCE:** Use the resources available to you. Is there a note in the margin? a glossary? Look up the word in a dictionary or check the Internet. Combine that information with the story context to this point.

   Can you figure out the meaning? Continue reading.

The four steps of CSSR are displayed in the wall chart shown in Figure 6.3. An interesting and important part of making the CSSR system work is understanding that the goal is to exit the system as soon as possible. For example, if students construct useful, sensible meaning from context (Step 1), they do not need to complete more steps. If Step 1 does not work, however, then the student should move on to Step 2. If that step is successful, it is unnecessary to continue; if not, the next succeeding step is tried to derive the unknown meaning.

After-Reading Vocabulary Instruction: Semantic Development and Enrichment Instruction (SDEI) Strategy

Semantic Development and Enrichment Instruction (SDEI)
a strategy for after-reading vocabulary instruction that fosters active learning and deep understanding of words.

EVIDENCE-BASED PRACTICE

The **Semantic Development and Enrichment Instruction (SDEI)** strategy is intended to foster long-term acquisition and development of vocabulary. SDEI is based on the work of McKeown and Beck (1988) and McKeown et al. (1985). Specifically, the strategy (1) focuses on words that are of high interest to students; (2) involves active processing of meaning; (3) requires manipulation and transformation of meaning in new contexts to deepen and broaden word meanings; and (4) encourages students to apply the new words to their own lives and thus guides them in becoming independent word learners.

Research has shown that active processing and substantial and varied practice with words promote solid recall of meaning vocabulary and that this, in turn, results in improved comprehension. For example, McKeown et al. (1985) reported on a series of studies using these principles. The findings clearly demonstrated the effectiveness of the procedure.

In these studies, sets of eight to ten words, based on a common theme such as "moods," "types of people," and others, were targeted for one week per set. Each day of the week, an activity—always using the same words (i.e., that week's set)—required successively deeper processing. For example, on one day students read a full paragraph about each word and had to decide which target word matched the description provided. On a succeeding day, the teacher posed interesting questions about the words to raise thinking to a level above working with simple definitions; for instance, when one of the target words was *hermit*, the teacher asked, "What might a *hermit* have a nightmare about?" (1988, p. 3). After teacher modeling to demonstrate how one could logically think through answers to these types of questions, students responded by generating their own paragraphs about the target words. Other thought-provoking activities are reported in these studies, all of which provided much practice and active learning.

Also, in these studies the rich in-class activities were complemented by what McKeown, Beck, and their colleagues call "out-of-class extensions." For those activities, students were designated "word wizards" when they recorded and reported target words they found in their home settings (in the newspaper, on the Internet, on TV, etc.) or when they purposely used one or more of the week's targeted words in a homework assignment (e.g., in a social studies essay, geography report, etc.).

As noted earlier, the SDEI strategy is an adaptation of the program investigated by McKeown et al. (1985, 1988). This adaptation allows teachers to capitalize on rich vocabulary exercises as well as to use other activities that require deep processing—but to do so in direct relation to the regular daily reading lesson.

To illustrate the SDEI strategy we will return to the story *Slipstream* (see Figure 5.6 on pages 137–138). (Please take a few minutes to quickly reread that story.)

First, *preread* the story that will be the focus of the day's lesson before it is assigned to students. Based on this reading, select five to eight specific words for study of in-depth meaning development after the students have read the story. This word selection should be based on your knowledge of the students and your judgment about words whose meanings will be of interest and new to them. If you are using a basal reader story, as is the case with *Slipstream,* you may rely, wholly or in part, on the key words that are listed in the teacher's manual for the story being taught. Usually, quite a few words are provided in this list; for *Slipstream* you will note there are fourteen words identified. At this point, take a few minutes and review these words in the lesson plan from the teacher's manual (see Figure 5.5 on pages 133–137). When you are using the DRA, as discussed in Chapter 5, you will recall that the teacher will briefly introduce the words by calling the students' attention to each, being certain that all of the words can be pronounced, and talking briefly about the word meanings as used in the story. The specially selected five to eight focus words, however, will receive more intensive attention.

Ask students to read the story silently or orally, and then present these focus words again—by displaying them on chart paper, the chalkboard, or an overhead transparency. It is good practice to initially present the words in the context in which they are found in the story to connect them to their meanings in the text. Using our *Slipstream* story, these words and phrases might be:

"*adverse* weather conditions"
"*unrest* began to spread"
"*syncopated* throbbing shook the air"
"*wail* of some jazz instrument"
"some kind of *hallucination*"
"from the *salvage* party"

Discuss the words briefly with the class and help the students derive the meaning of each word from the story context; for very difficult words, use a dictionary.

After reviewing the story-related meanings of these words, deepen and broaden students' understanding of the meanings of the focus words by using enriching, high-interest practice activities. These activities should be varied to maintain high student interest. Following are three very productive SDEI activities:

1. *Meaning manipulation—questions and sentences.* Encourage students to manipulate meanings and generate thinking about words different from their specific use in the story. Focus attention on connecting the use and meanings of *two* of the target words. For example, ask "Could a *hallucination* ever cause an *adverse* effect? How? Could you give an example?" or "Can you think of a way in which a *wail* might cause *unrest?*" First, students are asked to give a response different from the way the words are used in *Slipstream* but still connected in some way to the story ideas. Next, they are asked to offer responses that are *not* connected to the story. For example, "A *hallucination* could produce an *adverse* effect if the sound of the jazz had caused the plane to crash" (story-related) or "A *hallucination* could produce an *adverse* effect if you thought you saw a werewolf and became very frightened" (unrelated to the story). Have each student record the questions and sentences as well as the meanings for each word in his or her vocabulary journal.

2. *Novel situations and questions.* Pose novel situations and questions about targeted words. Create small groups of three students each and have them discuss the situations or novel questions. For example, "Could a ghost have a *hallucination?*" Students' conversations will frequently range across other meanings so that one student can learn from another's background knowledge. Meanings offered from other contexts also serve as useful comparisons with the story-specific meaning of the word as initially discussed. Provide time for this debriefing for each group. Each student should record the novel situations and questions as well as the word meaning in his or her journal.

3. *Group Design of Questions, Sentences, and Novel Situations.* Instruct the groups to devise questions, sentences, and novel situations similar to those presented in Activities 1 and 2. After intriguing responses centering on the target words have been proposed and developed, pair groups to challenge each other with thought-provoking questions and responses.

How To Do . . .

The Semantic Development and Enrichment Instruction (SDEI) Strategy

1. Preread the story and identify five to eight target words for detailed study. Select these words to account for the following:
   a. the vocabulary needs of your students
   b. high interest
   c. a brief meaningful context for each word
   d. some semantic connection that can be established between word pairs
2. Have students read the story silently or aloud.

DELAYED READER ADAPTATION

■ **At times, when vocabulary load in a story is heavy, for delayed readers it may be best to choose to have students engage in oral reading of the selection (rather than silent). Because word confusions are more immediately apparent during oral reading, the teacher can more easily monitor and assist.**

3. Place each target word in a brief context (such as a phrase from the story) on chart paper, chalkboard, or overhead transparency—e.g., "*syncopated* throbbing shook the air"—and involve your students in active discussion of each word's meaning in the story.
4. Broaden and deepen word meaning using a high-interest semantic development and enrichment activity. Use *two* of the target words in a sentence to model the way in which interrelated meanings can be developed through a question such as, "Could a *hallucination* ever cause an *adverse* effect? How? Could you give an example?" Model an answer and explain the logic of a meaningful connection. Use the two words in a model sentence that is story related; e.g., "A *hallucination* could have produced an *adverse* effect if the sound of the jazz had caused the plane to crash." Then use the words in a sentence that is *not* story related; e.g., "A *hallucination* could produce an *adverse* effect if you thought you saw a werewolf and became very frightened." Explain how the model sentence connects the meanings. (See text discussion for other options that can be used in this step.)
5. Create small groups of students and have them select two additional words from the list, design an engaging question (or a connecting sentence or a novel situation or question), and discuss and connect the word relationships. Provide a specific limited time for this part of the strategy.
6. Debrief each student group by having the students read the connected meanings and give a brief summary of the group's discussion about the connected meanings *or* have each group present their engaging question to another group for discussion. Have the students record their connecting sentence and question and the meaning(s) of each word in their vocabulary journals.
7. Extend the discussion to out-of-school word application by asking your students to become "word wizards" and search for the target words in newspapers, magazines, advertisements, the Internet, or any outside-of-school use. Ask your students to bring in and be ready to share their "find" with their small group and the class.

Throughout this chapter, many activities are suggested that expand students' thinking about vocabulary. Select from those activities as well, to create the variety that instills motivation. Criteria for selecting an activity are (1) the exercise must develop understanding beyond a literal definition and (2) the exercise must broaden understanding beyond a single meaning for the word.

Which strategy for vocabulary building does this activity represent? What follow-up activities might you use with these words?

The final step in the SDEI strategy involves out-of-class extension and application of the words. Ask students to use the target words and become a "word wizard" (McKeown & Beck, 1988) by searching for any of the words in some "out of school" context and to bring in and be ready to share this find in their small groups and with the class. The out-of-school context could be found in a newspaper, a magazine, an advertisement, or any other outside-of-school use.

The SDEI strategy is easily implemented and makes word learning the central focus of classroom life. Students enjoy talking about and playing with words. These types of vocabulary practice have high potential for each student's semantic development and enrichment. The active involvement and manipulation of words and their meanings can lead to expanded meaning acquisition and increased reading comprehension for your "word wizards." The SDEI strategy can also be used as a follow-up strategy for the DRA, the DR-TA, and the DL-TA strategies.

How might SDEI be combined with spelling instruction?

Instruction to Support Word Learning and Build Meaning Connections

Sound vocabulary instruction leads to students' understanding of word-meaning connections and thus increased comprehension of what they read. The following sections present strategies designed to help accomplish this goal. These strategies may be used before or after reading and make excellent follow-up activities for use with CSSR and SDEI. These activities involve information in text and the use of graphic representations to extend meanings. Their purpose is to develop depth of meaning for vocabulary and concepts and to build meaning connections to known words.

Teachers need to develop students' awareness of contextual-meaning clues that they can use in constructing meaning of unfamiliar vocabulary. They must be taught how to use context through direct instruction. As mentioned earlier, evidence shows that many students do not know how to use context effectively to construct meaning (Stanovich, 1991); however, teaching children how to use context increases their ability to do so (Jenkins, Matlock, & Slocum, 1989).

the *Highly Effective Teacher*

➤ *Students must be taught how to use context clues.*

EVIDENCE-BASED PRACTICE

Interactive Cloze

One of the easiest and most productive ways to develop students' ability to use context is through the **Interactive Cloze** activity (Meeks & Morgan, 1978). Interactive Cloze is based on the notion of closure—the ability of the human mind to complete incomplete stimuli. A cloze activity involves a short passage with selected words deleted; the purpose of the activity is for students to use information from the incomplete passage to replace the deleted words. Students work together to accomplish this task.

The Interactive Cloze begins with a short passage in which a few carefully selected words are

Interactive Cloze a fill-in-the-blank procedure for developing in children the ability to use context to derive word meaning

deleted; the first and last sentences of the passage are left intact. For very young students, no more than three to five words should be deleted. For older students, as many as eight to ten deletions are fine. Choose the words to be deleted with the goal of stimulating lots of talk and interaction.

Allow students to work individually or in pairs to replace the deleted words. When everyone has finished, organize the students into groups of four or five and ask them to compare their responses. They must tell why they chose the replacements they did. Each group needs to agree on each replacement. After all groups have finished, read the passage and have the groups compare their replacements for deleted words; conclude by reading the original passage.

This simple activity provides a great deal of instruction and practice using context. To determine replacement words, children must look at the context to see what possible words make sense. Individual replacements are made from the meaning each student constructs for the text, based, in part, on prior knowledge about the text and the topic. Reasons for replacements are shared as students compare and debate individual choices and arrive at group consensus prior to class discussion. Later, these group choices are shared with the whole class.

How could you use Interactive Cloze with CSSR?

Synonyms and Antonyms

synonyms
words with the same or similar meaning

How might you use Interactive Cloze to develop synonyms?

Synonyms are words that have almost the same meaning as one or more other words. Clues for linking synonyms are provided by the surrounding sentence context and students' background knowledge. The development of synonym meaning is illustrated in the following examples:

- After reading the story "The Little Wee Woman and the Great Big Cow," a Scottish folktale adapted by Gay Seltzer, a second-grade teacher made the following observation: "*Little* and *wee* are synonyms because they mean almost the same thing. Let's think of as many words as we can that are synonyms for *little* and *wee*." The words *little* and *wee* were placed on the chalkboard, and the class generated and discussed additional words with similar meaning. These words included *tiny, small, short, miniature, toy,* and *itty-bitty*. The students then "played" with the synonyms—putting various combinations together to create new titles for "The Little Wee Woman . . ." (Ruddell & Haggard, 1986, p. 13).
- In the story "Why Wasn't I Asked to the Party?" by Elizabeth Starr Hill, when the central character, Jan, figures out a way to get invited to the party, the text reads "A buoyant feeling rose in her. Things might be made to work out right after all." The class discussion of

Strategies in Use — Teaching the Use of Context Clues through Modified Cloze Procedure

Susan Wilson prepared the following section of the story "Flibbety Jibbet and the Key Keeper" as an Interactive Cloze passage for her second-grade class.

The Key Keeper was lonesome. Even though he lived in the King's castle, and was liked by everyone, he was still _____. All day he would go about the _____ with his big keys, up and down the long _____. He would go _____ through the crooked halls, locking and unlocking the heavy doors for the King and the King's helpers. After everyone had gone to their room and the doors were _____ for the night, the Key Keeper would go alone to his room to eat his supper. He was lonesome.

CRITICAL THINKING

1. Why did Susan leave the first and last sentences of the passage intact? Why did she choose to delete the words *lonesome, castle, hallways, quickly,* and *locked* from the passage? What words would you have deleted?
2. Explain how you would use this passage with a group of second- or third-grade students.
3. How does the Interactive Cloze activity build vocabulary knowledge?
4. Explain how you would use this activity in combination with the CSSR strategy.

buoyant feeling, using the context of the two sentences, led to the conclusion that such a feeling makes you "feel cheerful" and "like you are floating on air." The students were asked to identify and discuss experiences that gave them a buoyant feeling. They then used the term in a sentence that began "I had a buoyant feeling when . . ." They were asked to follow up with another sentence that began "Other words that mean almost the same thing are . . ." (Ruddell & Haggard, 1987, p. 52).

Antonyms are words with opposite or nearly opposite meanings. As with synonyms, the surrounding context provides important clues to the meaning of antonyms. The following example illustrates the development of antonyms at a fifth- or sixth-grade level. The context for this activity is found in Margaret Roberts's short story "The Promise," which describes a pioneer family moving westward by wagon train across Death Valley in the mid-nineteenth century.

antonyms
words with opposite or near opposite meanings

Death Valley is described in the story as *dreadful, desolate,* and *eerie.* On the basis of the story's context or with the help of a dictionary, decide on the definition of each word. Then decide what word would be the *antonym,* or opposite, of each. Write the antonym and its meaning in the space provided.

	Antonym	Definition
dreadful	_____	_____
desolate	_____	_____
eerie	_____	_____

How do the antonyms and definitions you found help you understand the words from "The Promise"?

Similes and Metaphors

Similes are figures of speech that create mental images by comparing two unlike things (e.g., "The little girl is like a rose"). Similes use the words *like* and *as.* Again, the context of the text is critical to meaning construction, as illustrated in the following examples (Ruddell & Haggard, 1986, p. 74):

similes
figures of speech that use *like* or *as* to compare two unlike things

- After reading the story "Laurie and the Cowardly Lion" by Betty Broadbent Carter, a second-grade teacher reread the following sentences from the story and wrote them on the board.

  Her stomach was flip-flopping like a fish out of water.
  Arthur tore out of his house like a tornado.

  She then explained that authors use comparisons to help us picture the events in our minds. Students discussed the comparisons and then created new ones to complete the sentence stems.

  Her stomach was flip-flopping like _____.
  Arthur tore out of his house like _____.

- The following activity was developed by a sixth-grade teacher after students had completed reading a chapter in John Fitzgerald's "Tom Spots a Card Shark." The teacher explained the simile as a figure of speech and read two examples from the story.

  When it came to money he was like a bloodhound on the trail of a fugitive. Mr. Walters looked as surprised as a man who opens a can of beans and finds peas inside instead.

  After discussing the examples, the students completed the following sentences, creating their own comparisons and images:

  My dog has a nose as _____.
  My friend runs like _____.
  My bike sounds like _____.
  My cat has fur as _____.

The students then shared their similes by discussing them in partner teams.

metaphors
figures of speech that directly compare unlike things

Metaphors also develop comparisons to suggest a close resemblance, but the comparisons are direct and do not use the word *like* or *as* (e.g., "She is a gem"). Encourage students to recall metaphorical comparisons that they use in daily life. The following examples illustrate direct and implied comparisons of this type: "The chorus swooped and soared" and "The bathers were beached seals rolling in the sun."

Concept Webs

concept web
a simple diagram used to connect a concept to prior knowledge and to text

A **concept web** is a simple diagram or map used to develop and connect a key concept to students' prior knowledge and understandings and to connect the concept to information presented in the reading text. This strategy can be used from kindergarten through the upper grades. The concept should have central importance to the narrative or expository material being read. Write the concept on the board and circle it. Then elicit information about the concept from students' background knowledge. Build the web by drawing lines to connect semantically related concepts and ideas around the central concept.

➤ *Concept webbing gives students an important strategy for integrating knowledge in a reading experience.*

Concept webs provide students with an important strategy for developing and integrating knowledge in a literary or content area reading experience. The concept web shown in Figure 6.4 was developed by a fourth-grade class after reading *Sharks* (Berger, 1987). This web summarizes key features of a variety of sharks. After the discussion, the students created drawings of sharks based on the summary information from their web and details from the book. The teacher displayed their work on the bulletin board under the caption "Sharks I Know."

Semantic Maps

semantic maps
diagrams that show complex relationships among concepts

Semantic maps are similar to concept webs but are used to develop more complex relationships. These maps are graphic representations that can be used to help students understand the relationships among concepts, story characters, plot development, and key ideas in the reading text. Semantic maps can be used across the grades but vary in complexity depending on the grade level. Semantic maps can be used before reading—to activate students' background knowledge about a concept or topic and to introduce new concepts—or after reading—to summarize and integrate ideas.

Semantic mapping begins when the teacher writes the central concept on the board. The children then brainstorm ideas about the concept, which the teacher records in random order on the board, probing and extending students' responses. When no new ideas are forthcoming, the teacher guides the class in organizing the ideas by classifying or categorizing them. Then he or she asks the students to construct individual maps (or a group map) showing the classifications and connections.

How is semantic mapping similar to the Group Mapping Activity (GMA)? How is it different?

The map-creation phase involves active discussion and comprehension, as students are encouraged to connect and integrate ideas using the scaffolding of the map categories. The last

FIGURE 6.4

Fourth-Grade Concept Web for *Sharks*

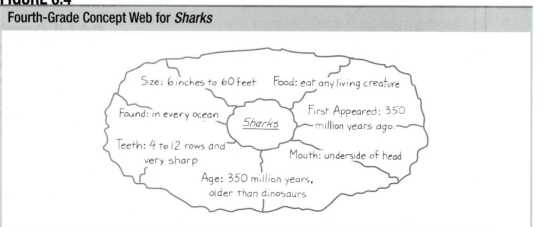

Strategies in Use

Concept Webbing with *Mufaro's Beautiful Daughters*

Mrs. Wong used concept webbing with her third-grade students after the class read *Mufaro's Beautiful Daughters* (Steptoe, 1987). This sensitively illustrated West African tale is about Mufaro, a villager, who has two beautiful but very different daughters. Nyasha is considerate and helpful, whereas Manyara is greedy and ambitious. When the great king decides to choose a wife, Mufaro sends his daughters. On the journey, their true nature is revealed. This knowledge strongly influences the king's decision and the story outcome. The concept webs from the class's discussion are shown here.

CRITICAL THINKING

1. Why do you think that Mrs. Wong selected the two words *kind* and *selfish* as the central concepts for the webs?
2. How do the webs connect each concept to the story and to students' background knowledge?
3. How could you connect this discussion on concept webs to the previous discussion on synonyms and antonyms?
4. What levels of comprehension (see Chapter 5) do concept webs emphasize?

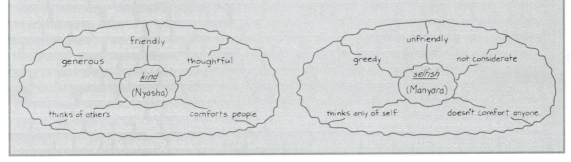

phase of mapping involves the students in rereading text and verifying understandings, leading to map revisions and extensions. The process is highly effective in helping children organize and integrate new concepts with their background knowledge.

A First-Grade Semantic Map for "Kate and the Zoo"

The semantic map in Figure 6.5 (page 176) was created in a first-grade classroom after students read the basal reader story "Kate and the Zoo" (Heimlich & Pittelman, 1986). The DRA was used to develop the story through vocabulary introduction and story discussion. After story discussion, the following steps were used to create the semantic map:

1. The teacher printed the title "Kate and the Zoo" (main idea) on the chalkboard and drew a circle around it.
2. The five topic headings (secondary categories) were printed on lines drawn from the main idea (e.g., "Things Kate sees at the zoo" [factual], "How Kate feels" [interpretive]).
3. The students were involved in a discussion of ideas remembered from the story (supporting details). After each student responded, he or she was asked under which category that information would be written. The teacher added that information to the map and encouraged other students to add new information under the same heading.
4. The following day, the class reviewed the map and reread the story for the purpose of adding new information.
5. The completed map was photocopied and given to each student to take home and use to retell the story to her or his parents.

> ➤ *Steps in Creating a Semantic Map*

This semantic-mapping lesson took place early in the school year and was one of the students' first experiences in creating semantic maps. For this reason, the teacher assumed an active role in structuring the lesson by identifying topic headings and developing supporting details related to each. A less-structured approach can be used after students have experience creating semantic maps: The teacher writes the main topic on the chalkboard, leads a brainstorming discussion, lists students' ideas, and has the students decide the category headings.

FIGURE 6.5

First-Grade Semantic Map for "Kate and the Zoo"

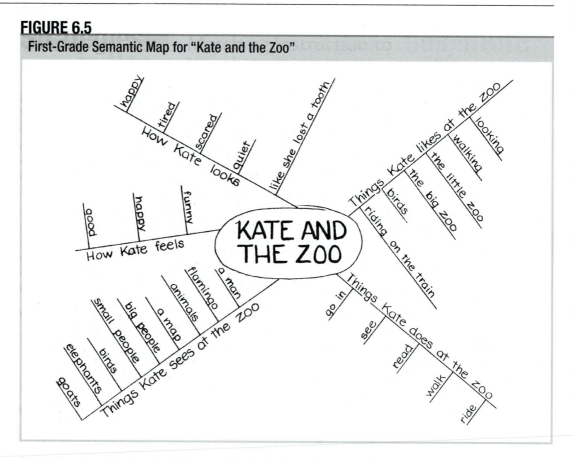

Source: Figure from Heimlich, J. E., & Pittelman, S. D. (1986). *Semantic mapping: Classroom applications.* Newark, DE: International Reading Association. Reprinted with permission.

A Fourth- and Fifth-Grade Map for *Sharks*

Semantic mapping can be used effectively as a before-reading and after-reading vocabulary-development strategy. The semantic map in Figure 6.6 illustrates a before-reading map, and Figure 6.7 (page 178) shows extended work on the same map after reading and research (Heimlich & Pittelman, 1986). These maps were created by students in grades 4 and 5 over a three-day period, using the central theme of sharks.

During the first day of instruction, students brainstormed ideas about the main idea and central concept (sharks), which was written on a transparency and projected overhead. The teacher recorded details as students activated their background knowledge (supporting ideas) about sharks. Students and teacher then generated secondary categories, such as characteristics and habitat, and organized supporting ideas under the main categories.

After reading the story, students added new information about sharks to the map, using a different color marker. On the second day of instruction, students reviewed the semantic map in Figure 6.6 and identified vocabulary and ideas that they wanted to investigate. This recorded information served as the basis for research. Research questions included "What are sharks' natural enemies?" and "Are all sharks dangerous?"

On the third day of instruction, students shared their independent research and added this new information to the map, using a different color marker. Using various colors helps students differentiate information on the basis of their prior background knowledge (day one, introduction), their reading (day one, discussion), and their research (days two and three). The added text in Figure 6.7 (page 178) represents information from research and the third day of discussion.

| How could semantic mapping be used with SDEI?

Semantic Feature Analysis (SFA) an instructional strategy to build vocabulary, based on shared features of meaning among words

Semantic Feature Analysis (SFA)

Semantic Feature Analysis (SFA) is an instructional strategy used to develop vocabulary knowledge by establishing shared meaning relationships among words. Words that share seman-

FIGURE 6.6

Semantic Map on Sharks—Day One

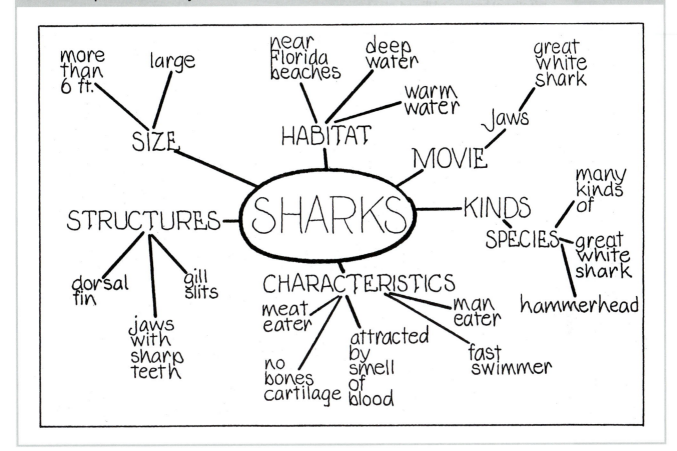

Source: Figure from Heimlich, J. E., & Pittelman, S. D. (1986). *Semantic mapping: Classroom applications.* Newark, DE: International Reading Association. Reprinted with permission.

tic features define a central concept or semantic category. For example, a kitten and a goldfish are both in the same semantic category of "pets" because they both are special animals that live with us, must be fed and cared for daily, receive love, and give us enjoyment and comfort. But kittens and goldfish obviously differ in appearance, in what they eat, and in the way they breathe. Further, kittens and goldfish are very different from their genetic relatives the tiger and the shark. Our understanding of the semantic features for the category "pets" serves as the basis for understanding and differentiating the concept labels *kitten, goldfish, tiger,* and *shark.*

SFA begins with a grid constructed for a concept (e.g., "pets"), in which elements or exemplars of the concept are listed vertically (e.g., kitten, goldfish, dog, bird, snake, rat) and features of one or more exemplars are listed horizontally (e.g., has four legs, swims, learns tricks, is cute, is found in wild). Distribute copies of the grid to the students and ask them to decide individually which feature matches each word; they are to put a plus (+) for features that do match and a minus (–) for those that do not (Figure 6.8 page 179). After students have completed the grid, have them compare their responses in pairs or small groups and then share the responses with the whole class. Students may then add more exemplars of the concept and more features to continue the analysis.

You can expect differences of opinion in the students' discussion of SFA grids. One way to handle these differences is to have students change the coding system by adding an asterisk (*) for "sometimes matches." Alert students before the discussion that they can expect to disagree and should listen to one another's explanations.

SFA is useful for building understanding of central characters in children's literature, as well as central concepts in the content areas. The SFA shown in Figure 6.9 (page 179) is based on a

Which feature matches which word?

➤ *Semantic Feature Analysis is also used to compare story characters.*

FIGURE 6.7

Semantic Map on Sharks—Day Three

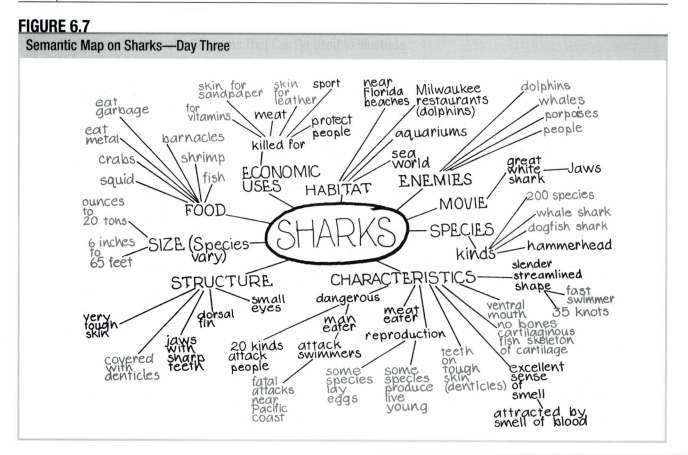

Source: Figure from Heimlich, J. E., & Pittelman, S. D. (1986). *Semantic mapping: Classroom applications.* Newark, DE: International Reading Association. Reprinted with permission.

How To Do . . .

Concept Webbing and Semantic Mapping

1. Determine a major concept or topic central to the reading or area of study (e.g., spring, friendship, electricity).
2. Write the name of the concept or topic in the center of the chalkboard, overhead transparency, or easel chart page.
3. Ask students to brainstorm their knowledge and ideas about the topic.
4. Record their ideas on the board. If you are doing webbing, draw lines to show connections and relationships.
5. Invite students to develop categories or classifications for the ideas and to create their own semantic maps from their classification scheme, or guide the class in developing categories for organizing the ideas and lead the group in developing a semantic map from the information on the board.

■ **Don't do assumptive teaching; that is, don't assume that all students in a group understand concepts and recognize words when some may not. If in doubt, discuss. As one example, when the secondary category "habitat" is generated in the *sharks* discussion illustrated here, the sensitive teacher will be certain that delayed readers in the group *can* pronounce the word "habitat" and *do* know its meaning.**

DELAYED READER ADAPTATION

FIGURE 6.8

Semantic Feature Analysis for "Pets"

	has four legs	can swim	learns tricks	is cute	is found in wild
kitten	+	+	+	+	—
goldfish	—	+	—	+	—
dog	+	+	+	+	—
bird	—	—	+	+	+
snake	—	+	—	—	+
rat	+	+	+	—	—

sixth-grade classroom analysis of the feelings and emotions of the four main characters in Patricia MacLachlan's (1985) Newbery Award–winning book *Sarah, Plain and Tall,* as expressed in the first two chapters. This book tells the story of Sarah, who answers an ad for a mail-order bride. She leaves her home in Maine and travels to the Great Plains to marry Papa, a widower with two children, Anna and little Caleb.

FIGURE 6.9

Semantic Feature Analysis of Central Characters after Reading Chapters 1 and 2 of *Sarah, Plain and Tall*

Feelings / Characters	Anna	Caleb	Papa	Sarah
sad	+	+	+	?
lonesome	+	+	+	?
anxious	+	+	+	+
anticipating	+	+	+	+
curious	+	+	+	+
worried	+	+	—	–
happy	+	+	+	?

Source: Figure from Pittelman, S. D., Heimlich, J. E., Berglund, R. L., & French, M. P. (1991). *Semantic feature analysis: Classroom applications.*

Vocabulary Logs or Journals

vocabulary logs
a system for
recording new
words to learn

Vocabulary logs or journals provide a systematic way for students from kindergarten through the upper grades to record and learn new words and concepts. Words entered into the students' logs may be based on the SDEI, words of high personal interest discovered in content areas such as science and social studies, or words from newspapers, magazines, television, and the Internet. The logs or journals also may include individual or class definitions, words in sentence contexts, drawings, pasted and labeled magazine and newspaper clippings with new vocabulary words, content area vocabulary, and terms researched in the dictionary or encyclopedia. Concept webs, semantic maps, and SFAs may also be included.

Vocabulary logs provide a natural reservoir of new words. As you become comfortable using SDEI and apply the strategy to vocabulary study in literature, science, social studies, and other areas, the students' vocabulary logs will become especially useful. By recording vocabulary and definitions and by using these words in context, students will begin to form their own dictionary reference resource for spelling and writing.

Consider the following options for organizing the vocabulary logs or journals.

➤ *Vocabulary logs provide a natural reservoir of new words.*

1. *Alphabetical organization.* Words are added in a dictionary-like fashion on a daily basis. The value of this approach is ease in locating words to use. The disadvantage is that semantically related words lose their meaning connection when alphabetized.
2. *Chronological organization.* Words are recorded as they are given or encountered. Semantic word groupings are preserved, but students will have more difficulty quickly locating a word.
3. *Subject-matter organization.* Specific sections of the log are devoted to reading, science, social studies, mathematics, and so on. Quick location of words and continuity in collecting content area vocabulary are benefits. The disadvantage is dividing vocabulary into subject-matter domains, which inhibits the integration of knowledge.

➤ *Options for Organizing Vocabulary Logs*

A combination of approaches might provide the greatest flexibility. Whatever system of organization you or your students elect to use for vocabulary logs, the main point to keep in mind is that the organization of log and journal entries should support your teaching style, your students' motivation to acquire vocabulary, and ease of word location. Your periodic responses to journal entries, written in the margin of the students' logs, will provide feedback for the students and insight into their vocabulary growth.

Word-Sleuthing Strategies

| How will you inspire your students to become word sleuths?

Encourage students' interest in the study and collection of words in school and at home by including word sleuthing in SDEI activities. The goal is to build high interest and motivation in word sleuthing and a positive attitude toward investigating new vocabulary and concepts (Fry, 2004; Fry, 2006; Kibby, 1995). For example, discuss important contributions to English from other languages to encourage children to explore the source of "borrowed" words. This type of discussion will develop positive interest not only in word sleuthing but also in the study of different cultures. As you examine these borrowings, note how they may be grouped into categories such as animals, foods, clothing, household objects, customs, and the environment. Students can develop this new vocabulary through concept webs, semantic maps, or SFA. Some examples of word borrowings are shown in Table 6.3.

➤ *Sleuthing for Borrowed Words*

Developing interest in the source and origin of words can lead to a long-term interest in vocabulary building. Borrowed words should be the topic of frequent vocabulary self-collections. High motivation to use classroom resources such as the dictionary, thesaurus, and encyclopedia may develop from the study of borrowed words.

➤ *Making Sense of Newly Coined Words*

Students' word study can be extended easily to new coinings and combinations and to new meanings attached to familiar words to label discoveries and inventions. For example, *astronaut*, derived from the Greek, literally means "star [*astro*] sailor [*naut*]." The language of computers would make an interesting vocabulary study. Students also might consider the reasoning behind trade names of commercial products.

Another interesting point for young word sleuths is how many common words began as product names—for example, *Kleenex, Xerox, Ping-Pong*. By sensitizing students to vocabulary found in their daily environment, you will encourage word sleuthing and contribute to students' spontaneous and continued vocabulary learning.

TABLE 6.3

Examples of Word Borrowings from Other Languages

Language or Culture	Vocabulary Examples
African	*banjo, goober* (peanut), *chigger, hoodoo, voodoo*
Chinese	*dim sum, wonton, foo yung*
Dutch	*coleslaw, cookie, boss, sleigh, waffle, Santa Claus*
French	*prairie, chowder, buccaneer, levee*
German	*fat-cakes* (doughnuts), *smearcase* (cottage cheese), *dunk, hex*
Greek	*acrobat, magic, barometer, elastic, tactics*
Italian	*balcony, opera, piano, umbrella, volcano*
Japanese	*haiku, aikido, origami, sumo*
Mexican	*burro, chili, pronto, patio, tornado, cafeteria*
Native American	*opossum, moose, skunk, woodchuck, hickory, pecan, persimmon, powwow, caucus*
Middle Eastern	*caravan, khaki, shawl, sherbet, chess, lemon, turban, borax*
Russian	*steppe, vodka*
Spanish	*mosquito, armada, alligator*

Adapted from Baugh, 1957, and Pyles, 1964.

the Highly Effective Teacher*

on Technology and Meaning Vocabulary Development

1. Introduce five new vocabulary words to the class. Have the students work in pairs and ask them to write a brief paragraph using a word-processing program. Show the students how to use the thesaurus tool in the program, and have them substitute synonyms for their vocabulary words in the paragraph. Compare the two paragraphs and critique them by noticing the differences in their effectiveness and clarity.

2. Have the students use words from their vocabulary logs and include them in a letter to an e-mail pen pal. A good site to find pen pals is **www.epals.com/.**

3. Have the students research a topic of interest and select vocabulary words that are new to them. Then introduce five new vocabulary words to the class. Have the students work in pairs and ask them to write a brief paragraph using these new words. Teach the students to insert links into their paragraphs using a word-processing program. For example, in writing about marine plants they would include a link for the words *photosynthesis* and *algae.* The links should contain definitions of these key words.

4. Create a class semantic map on a particular topic. Instead of words describing the topic, make a semantic map that consists of Web sites that focus on different aspects of the topic. For example, if the topic were antelopes, the map would include Web sites that describe the animals' physical characteristics, habitat, and diet.

5. Use the Internet to search for graphics that represent vocabulary words. Print the graphics, and use them to create a thematic-based collage on a selected topic. Some good sites for clip art include **www.kidsdomain.com/clip/** and **www.nzwwa.com/mirror/clipart/.**

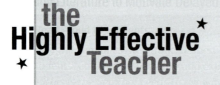

the Highly Effective Teacher

Instructional Strategies for Meaning Vocabulary Development

TVC
to preteach vocabulary
(Combine with DRA,
QAR, and GMA)
(Before reading)

CSSR
to develop a functional system for learning new words
(Combine with DR-TA,
DRA, and ReQuest)
(During reading)

SDEI
to acquire and develop
reading vocabulary
(Combine with DL-TA,
DR-TA and DRA)
(After reading)

**Synonyms and Antonyms;
Similes and Metaphors**
to teach the use of comparisons as meaning clues
(Combine with vocabulary
log or journal)
(Before or after)

Interactive Cloze
to acquire and develop
vocabulary in meaning
context (Combine with
vocabulary log or journal)
(During or after)

**Vocabulary Log or Journal;
Word Sleuthing**
to record and learn
new words
(Combine with SDEI)
(Before or after)

**THE HIGHLY
EFFECTIVE TEACHER**
with meaning-negotiation
interactions, a literacy-rich
learning environment, and
instructional strategies for
reading comprehension

**Concept Web/
Semantic Map**
to develop word and concept associations through
graphic organizers
(Combine with DL-TA,
DR-TA, DRA, PReP,
ReQuest, and SDEI)
(Before or after)

SFA
to develop concept relationships
through feature analysis (Combine
with DL-TA, DR-TA, DRA,
QAR, and SDEI) (Before or after)

Summary and Classroom Applications

double entry journal

Review the list of things you do when you come to an unfamiliar word. How closely does your system match strategies discussed in this chapter? How well do your strategies support your acquisition of new working vocabulary? Which strategies do you especially want to try in your classroom?

Chapter Summary

Vocabulary knowledge is a critical part of the comprehension process. This chapter presented three goals for vocabulary learning: (1) developing and connecting new vocabulary to students' background knowledge, (2) developing students' strategies for constructing meaning for unknown words, and (3) building positive attitudes toward, and increasing independence in, vocabulary learning. Specific objectives for any instructional program grow directly from these goals.

Principles of vocabulary instruction stress the importance of active learning and rich instruction as students are encouraged to construct meaning by "reasoning with words." Students' personal motivation is critical to vocabulary development if teachers are to instill in students the desire to develop concepts over their lifetime and become increasingly independent word learners.

Careful consideration must be given to the selection of new vocabulary for direct teaching as well as for systematic instruction in how to construct meaning for unknown words. The strategies developed in this chapter provide important options in teaching vocabulary before reading (TVC), during reading (CSSR), and after reading (SDEI). Follow-up activities provide practice and opportunities for students to gain in-depth, complex understanding of words and concepts.

FIGURE 6.10

Professional Standards and Meaning Vocabulary Development for the Classroom Teacher

Professional Standard	Example
1. Foundational Knowledge	**Element 1.4** Demonstrates knowledge of the major components of reading, such as vocabulary and background-knowledge development; e.g., explains the influence of various factors such as home environment on vocabulary development; explains how vocabulary development is connected to and central to reading comprehension.
2. Instructional Strategies and Curriculum Materials	**Element 2.2** Uses a wide range of instructional practices and methods for students at different stages of development; e.g., uses a variety of vocabulary strategies, such as TVC, CSSR, and SDEI, to teach students who are at various developmental levels; explains the evidence rationale that supports a given strategy selection.
3. Assessment, Diagnosis and Evaluation	**Element 3.3** Uses assessment information to plan, evaluate, and revise effective instruction for students at different developmental stages; e.g., uses observational information from strategy instruction, such as TVC, CSSR, SFA, and SDEI, to evaluate student progress and plan further instruction.
4. Creating a Literate Environment	**Element 4.1** Uses students' interests, reading abilities, and backgrounds as foundations for the reading program; e.g., knows how to collect information on students' interests and background knowledge and interprets and uses this information to select instructional activities and strategies such as concept webs, semantic maps, and SFA.
5. Professional Development	**Element 5.2** Continues to pursue the development of professional knowledge; e.g., identifies specific instructional questions related to the improvement of teaching of vocabulary; participates in local school workshops and subscribes to a professional journal to continue to increase knowledge and understanding of vocabulary instruction.

Part 2 from IRA. (2004). Professional Standards and Ethics Committee, International Reading Association. *Standards for reading professionals—revised 2003*. Reprinted with permission of the International Reading Association. All rights reserved.

Professional Standards and
Meaning Vocabulary Development and Comprehension Connections

The standards presented in Figure 6.10 provide examples of vocabulary development and comprehension connections instruction for each of the five areas of professional standards (International Reading Association, 2004). You can see the complete list of Standards for Reading Professionals in Appendix C.

Applications: Bridges to the Classroom

1. Arrange to visit a classroom and observe the teacher and students as they read and discuss a story or other text. What strategy or strategies do they use if they encounter an unfamiliar word or have trouble understanding a word? What do you notice about meaning-construction strategies used by the very best readers? And the strategies used by struggling readers? How do their strategies differ? Discuss your findings with a classmate.

2. During a classroom observation, examine how the teacher develops new vocabulary. How are new words introduced and developed? In what ways and to what extent are semantic connections made between new vocabulary and students' prior vocabulary knowledge? What changes might you make if you were teaching the lesson?

3. Obtain a teacher's guide for a basal reading program at the grade level of greatest interest to you. Locate an interesting story and read it. Review the strategies described in this chapter, and develop one or more of them to use with vocabulary instruction for this story. Add these lesson plans to your teaching portfolio.

4. From a newspaper, identify two vocabulary items you believe would be appropriate for students at the grade level you plan to teach. Briefly describe how you would introduce these words, accounting for use of context, prior background knowledge, and high interest.

Additional Research and Practice

1. Pearson, P. D., Heibert, E. H., & Kamil, M. L. (2007). **Vocabulary assessment: What we know and what we need to know.** *Reading Research Quarterly, 42,* 282–296.

   This excellent discussion explores the definition of vocabulary, what vocabulary assessments actually measure, and what they could measure—and proposes a specific research agenda that is needed. This article provides excellent insight into the nature of vocabulary learning and how it is and should be measured. (Practice/Research)

2. Palmer, B. C., & Brooks, M. A. (2004). **Reading until the cows come home: Figurative language and reading comprehension.** *Journal of Adolescent and Adult Literacy, 47* (5), 370–378.

   This discussion provides excellent teaching ideas for helping at-risk students of English as a second language (ESL) and specific learning disabilities (SDL) students learn how to interpret various forms of figurative language, leading to increased reading comprehension. (Practice)

3. Blachowicz, C. L. Z., & Fisher, P. (2000). **Vocabulary instruction.** In M. L. Kamil, P. B. Mosenthal, P. D. Pearson, & R. Barr (Eds.), *Handbook of reading research: Volume III* (pp. 503–523). Mahwah, NJ: Lawrence Erlbaum Associates.

   This extensive summary and synthesis of vocabulary-development research identifies four central vocabulary principles, develops applications of research to practice, and examines various ways to adapt instruction to specific student and classroom needs. (Research)

CHAPTER 7

Using Literature, Reader Response, and Engagement to Enhance Motivation and Comprehension

When we read a story, we inhabit it.

John Berger (1918–),
American author

All I cared about was that she had made tea cookies for me and read to me from her favorite book. It was enough to prove that she liked me.

Maya Angelou (1929–),
American poet and writer

Dale Shogren decided to explore the theme of gateways with the beginning readers in her class. She knew that literature experiences could provide gateways for readers—gateways leading to new encounters, people, places, ideas, times, and, sometimes, rich, enchanted lands.

As she developed the gateways theme, she reflected on her own experiences. In the primary grades, literary gateways had led her to participate in imaginative travels with Max in *Where the Wild Things Are* (Sendak, 1963) and feel empathy with Charlotte and Wilbur in *Charlotte's Web* (White, 1952). Later, in the intermediate grades, Dale had experienced love and adventure with Billy, Old Dan, and Little Ann in *Where the Red Fern Grows* (Rawls, 1961) and the awakening of friendship and a sense of belonging with Mary and Colin in *The Secret Garden* (Burnett, 1911).

For Dale, and her students, learning to read means more than learning the "how to" part; it means building the satisfaction of reading and the desire to read—the "want to" part. As Grande (1965) so aptly noted, "Literature, as expression of human strife, conflict, feelings, and ideas, must engage the student's active response, evoking his fund of intellectual and emotional experience. . . . It would be unfortunate not to relate the individual student's personal experience to his (or her) interpretation of literature" (p. 12).

Dale's colleague, Pat Derkum, has posted in her classroom an essay that she wrote as an education student about favorite books she read as a child. This essay inspires Pat as she develops her literature program for students each year. In it, she remembers reading with her mother the *Little House* series by Laura Ingalls Wilder (1934).

I received the full set of the *Little House on the Prairie* books at the end of first grade. They came in a nice yellow box and were the first "grown-up" books I had ever owned ("grown-up" meaning they were not picture books but chapter books). While I could not really read them at this point in my life, I consider this time as the time I was truly hooked on books for life. I was so proud of these books and the way they smelled in their new box. The gift of these books made me realize that I was a reader of books. Not only was I a reader, but an owner of books, and that was almost as exciting. I have many good memories of sitting next to my mom on the couch while she read these books aloud. Together we lived with Laura in the Big Woods, on the prairie, etc. I remember picturing the invasion of the locusts, and the one-room school houses. While I listened to, and later read, these books aesthetically, I believe efferent knowledge "snuck around" the corners. How else but through these books could I have understood what it was like in the pioneer times?

Later on, of course, I read these books for myself many times. The covers are shabby now, but the box still holds them all. Over the years, I developed a real identification with Laura. I wore my hair in pigtails like she did, and my favorite dress was a prairie-type dress with an apron attached. Being a timid person, I empathized with Laura when she could not control the big boys in her classroom, as big boys intimidated me, too.

In conclusion, this set of books has not had an earth-shattering effect on me as a person and hasn't changed my life in any major way. Yet the *Little House* books enriched my life more than any other books, because I identified with Laura so much. Also, since they were my first "real" books, and I was so proud of the fact that they were mine, I think that they helped start my love for books in general.

These ideas clearly reveal Pat's close identification with the central story character, Laura, and her excitement about and awareness of becoming an "owner" and a reader of books—even the smell of the new books evokes positive associations with reading and literature. Like Pat and Dale, you want to build a literature program that includes strategies for fostering students' emotional responses, positive associations, and positive attitudes toward literature and reading through the experiences you provide in your classroom.

Reprinted by permission of P. Derkum

double entry journal

What was the power of personal involvement with literature in your own childhood experiences? Think of one book you encountered between kindergarten and grade 6 that has special memories for you. What was the title of the book, and who was the author? What do you remember about the story? How did you respond to it? Do your memories reveal close identification with the central story character? What impact did the book have on you?

Chapter Objectives

After reading and discussing this chapter, you will be able to:

- understand the seven goals and seven objectives of a high-quality literature program.
- explain the three key steps in the reader motivation and response process and the role of the two instructional stances in developing reader response and engagement.
- grasp the importance of the six internal reader motivations and that of external motivation in influencing a student's commitment and intention to read.
- identify the types of literature, both fiction and nonfiction; select high-quality literature for stu-

dents; help students choose books independently; and develop a high response and engagement classroom reading center.
- understand how to use a wide variety of instructional strategies for teaching literature, ranging from reading aloud, storytelling, and literature-response journals to book clubs, literature circles, and the investigative questioning procedure in achieving your goals and objectives.
- evaluate your students' progress in responding to and engaging literature both in and out of school.

Goals of a Literature Program

As you actively involve and immerse students in children's and adolescent literature, remember the following seven goals:

➤ *Seven Goals of Literature Programs*

1. To provide students with a range of literature experiences that build on and extend their knowledge base, including an awareness of people and other living things, of events, and of ideas not present in their own life experiences
2. To bring students' prior knowledge, life experiences, and values into sharper focus by examining and contrasting the many aspects of life represented through literature

3. To provide students with aesthetic pleasure through the joy of language and to encourage the appreciation of life experiences by isolating, magnifying, or contrasting "slices of life" for aesthetic observation

4. To develop students' self-understanding through insight into their own behavior as they encounter a broad range of human behavior

5. To develop students' awareness of language as a powerful means of human expression as they experience the skillful use of imagery, drama, humor, and pathos

6. To provide opportunity for wide reading that can serve to broaden conceptual knowledge, increase reading fluency, and develop higher-level thinking

7. To create authentic learning conditions that provide you and your students the opportunity to assess learning progress and design appropriate literature-based instruction.

These goals assume that teachers are, themselves, eager consumers of children's and adolescent literature—knowledgeable from first-hand experience about a wide range of poetry, books, stories, biographies, and informational texts appropriate for the students they teach and committed to the principles and values on which literature programs rest. Effective literature programs require that teachers read from the libraries their students use and demonstrate daily their own love of reading and responding to literature (Brozo & Simpson, 2007; Moss & Fenster, 2002; Olness, 2007). Ellen Jackson, a kindergarten teacher, is this kind of teacher. In her classroom, poetry infuses the classroom day: Ellen recites poetry, the students chant and recite poetry, poems are sent home in the daily take-home packets, and they commit poems to memory. At the end of the year, students bind all the poems they learned into a "Poetry Book," which they take home to save.

Ellen just completed a study of the effects of her approach. She interviewed students and parents and found that her kindergarten students, now well into fourth, fifth, and sixth grades, remember vividly their poetry-learning experiences in her classroom and still return to their Poetry Books with pleasure. First-, second-, and third-grade students continue to read their Poetry Books at home.

A well-designed literature program should address specific objectives that closely parallel the literature goals just identified. These objectives include the following:

1. Fostering high motivation to read by exploring new characters and people, living things, and events and ideas that connect to—and go beyond—students' own life experiences

2. Developing new concepts, background knowledge, and active comprehension, using a broad range of literature selections and sharing these through classroom discussions

3. Enjoying the aesthetic pleasure derived from experiencing literature that uses language and illustrations to portray life and bring slices of life into sharper focus

4. Developing understanding of self through identification with central story characters and their experiences

5. Understanding the power of language to convey human experiences and emotions (ranging from happiness to sadness and from love to anger) through narration, exposition, and poetry

6. Increasing reading fluency and higher-level thinking through many experiences with literature

7. Providing authentic learning opportunities for assessment of learning progress by you and your students that can provide the basis for developing appropriate instruction

Although literature holds the potential to develop these objectives, you, as the teacher, play the critical role in creating the classroom environment necessary to reach them. Your success also depends on your ability to (1) understand reader motivation, (2) understand the role of instructional stance in developing reader motivation, (3) select and use literature in your classroom, (4) select and use effective approaches and strategies for teaching literature, and (5) evaluate students' responses to literature.

Three Steps in the Reader-Motivation and Reader-Response Process

Central to reader motivation is the development of each student's positive self-concept as a reader and as a person (Olness, 2007). As Carl Rogers, the noted psychologist (1961), observed, a student's **self-concept** is not developed independently but develops as a product of her or his

the **Highly Effective Teacher**

What experiences have you had with effective literacy teachers like Ellen?

➤ *Specific Objectives for Literature Programs*

➤ *Teachers' Roles in Literature Programs*

What role do literature experiences play in self-concept and reader motivation?

self-concept an individual's way of seeing and thinking about himself or herself, based on interaction with others

interaction and integration with other people, including parents, siblings, friends, and teachers. A positive self-concept enhances the reader's ability to identify with story characters; in turn, literature can help build a positive concept of self.

Reader Identification

Literature experiences expand a student's familiarity with "other selves," aspirations of others, and activities of others. Contrasting the self with others, including fictional others, can enhance self-understanding (Barone et al., 1995).

The first step in building high motivation and self-concept is **reader identification** (Ruddell, 1991; Ruddell & Unrau, 2004b; Russell, 1970), in which the student is able to "live through" a literary character. The reader responds to the story by entering into the plot with a story character, as you may have done with Charlotte, Wilbur, or Templeton in *Charlotte's Web* (White, 1952). To what extent does each character represent you and cause you to reflect on your own perception of self as you enter into the story?

A strong theory base supports the idea that reader identification is a real psychological event (Mathewson, 2004; Rosenblatt, 2004; Ruddell, 1991; Ruddell & Unrau, 2004b; Russell, 1970). Through reader identification, students (and adults) experience what the character experiences in his or her adventures. As the plot develops and the character is acted on by external forces and circumstances and responds to them, readers imagine themselves experiencing similar responses and actions. Identification may involve encountering major difficulties and disappointments or solving problems.

Catharsis

As the story plot unfolds and the character achieves significance, the reader may experience similar emotional responses and reactions. This second step in the reading-motivation process is known as **catharsis.** Catharsis produces a response of relief, a reduction of the reader's feeling of tension, and, in effect, a venting of emotions. How did you feel, for example, when Charlotte saved Wilbur from the smokehouse by weaving "SOME PIG!" in her web? How did you feel when Charlotte died?

Insight

Through identification and catharsis, the reader begins to achieve a deeper understanding and improved perception of self (Barone et al., 1995). This third step in the reader's response is **insight.** The congruence, or "fit," of a student's life experiences with those of a central story character leads not only to rediscovering himself or herself in a literary work but also to developing positive attitudes toward literature. A reader will choose favorite books on the basis of insights they provide.

Influence of Instructional Stances on Reader Response

The development of reader motivation and response through identification, catharsis, and insight is strongly influenced by the teacher's **instructional stance,** or basic attitude toward literature. Rosenblatt (2004) has identified two stances from which readers engage text. These stances have different purposes and influence the way readers respond to text. An efferent stance shifts the reader's thinking to content and the analytical search for information to be retained. An aesthetic stance draws the reader into the text. A critical aspect of teaching literature is to recognize the relationship between the predominant instructional stance a teacher assumes and the outcomes of the literary event.

The Efferent Stance

An **efferent stance** focuses attention on reading for content and information to be taken away from the text. Teachers frequently rely on the efferent stance when teaching subject-matter con-

---

reader identification
an individual's ability to associate himself or herself with, and have vicarious experiences through, a literary character

catharsis
an individual's emotional response to vicarious experience through identification with a literary character

insight
an individual's change in understanding or self-perception through identification and catharsis

What insights do you have into Charlotte's role as a mother figure and Templeton's frustrations?

instructional stance
basic attitude, aesthetic or efferent, toward a piece of literature

efferent stance
an instructional perspective based on the belief that the literature under consideration is being read for the purpose of retaining information

Strategies in Use

Choosing an Instructional Stance

Examples of Question Prompts for the Aesthetic Instructional Stance

1. *Evoking past experience.* What do you think the story (or chapter) will be about (after reading title)? What do you think is happening in this illustration (cover or early illustration)? What do you think about this situation and why?

2. *Relating student's experience to the story.* Has anything happened to you that was like (incident in the story)? Tell me about it. If you were (central character in the story), what do you think could happen to you? Have you ever done anything like what (central character) did in the story? Tell me about it.

3. *Story discussion.* If you had been (central character) when (critical story event) happened, how would you have felt and reacted? How do you think (central character) felt when (critical event) happened? Why do you think (central character) did (critical event) at that point in the story?

4. *Story identification, catharsis, insight.* Was there someone in the story who did something that you would like to do? Who was it? Why would you like to do that? Which character would you choose to be from all those in the story? Why? What do you think happens to (central character) after the story ends?

5. *Author discussion.* Imagine for a moment that you are talking to the author of this book. What questions would you ask? What do you think was the author's reason for having the story end the way it did? Do you know of any other books written by this author?

Examples of Question Prompts for the Efferent Instructional Stance

1. *Evoking past experience.* What do you know about (central character)? What does this picture tell us about (central character)?

2. *Relating student's experience to the text.* Have you ever seen (or touched) a (central topic or concept)? What reaction did you have when this happened?

3. *Information discussion.* How would you describe (central character, topic, or concept)? What idea did you find that was most interesting to you in the book?

4. *Information insight.* What new ideas did you learn from this book? What idea would you like to know more about? How could you find out more about this idea?

5. *Author discussion.* If you could talk to the author, what would you like to ask? Do you know of any other books written by this author?

CRITICAL THINKING

1. For which instructional literature goals would you choose the aesthetic stance? For which instructional goals might you choose the efferent stance?

2. Which stance seems better overall for the goal of encouraging active reader response and positive attitudes toward literature and reading? Why?

3. If you were adopting an instructional stance that was predominantly aesthetic, what other questions could you ask in addition to those just listed?

4. Why is the word *predominantly* used to qualify *aesthetic* and *efferent,* as in *predominantly aesthetic* and *predominantly efferent*?

tent for the purpose of increasing students' knowledge and assisting them in remembering information after reading. However, informational text does not require an efferent stance; it may be read from an aesthetic stance (Rosenblatt, 2004).

Unfortunately, many classroom teachers and publisher-produced reading programs also use the efferent stance in developing children's literature experiences. Teachers' questions may focus almost solely on factual and content knowledge and require students to recall specific bits of literal information. In teaching subject knowledge, in science or social studies, for example, the value of literal questioning is dubious. In teaching literature, it is counter to the goal of appreciation and deep understanding, which requires higher-level questioning at the interpretive, applicative, and transactive levels.

The Aesthetic Stance

aesthetic stance an instructional perspective based on the belief that the literature under consideration is being read for the purpose of understanding, enjoyment, and appreciation

The **aesthetic stance** implies a transaction between the reader and the text as the reader crosses over and enters into "the journey" of the work to experience the story, the event, or the ambiance created by the text (Rosenblatt, 1985, 1988, 2004). This transaction involves a shared, or reciprocal, process between the reader and the text. The reader synthesizes "ideas, sensations, feelings, and images from his or her past linguistic, literary, and life experiences" to form a new experience. This process and the new experience are referred to as the evocation (Rosenblatt, 1985, p. 40).

The aesthetic stance and the efferent stance are both legitimate and useful instructional approaches that teachers can adopt appropriately, depending on their instructional goals and objectives (Lehman & Scharer, 1996). In most reading experiences, both stances are used to some extent. If your goal is to encourage active reader response in a literature program and to develop students' positive attitudes toward reading, it is important that you use the aesthetic stance. Instead of asking who was in a story and what the main character did to solve his or her problem, ask questions that encourage students to identify and empathize with the character and to enter the story and reading experience fully. For example, ask, "How did you feel when that happened?" "Why do you think Max did that?" "What would you have done when Sarah came?" and "How do you think Karana got the courage to go on?" as students read *Where the Wild Things Are* (Sendak, 1963), *Sarah, Plain and Tall* (MacLachlan, 1985), and *Island of the Blue Dolphins* (O'Dell, 1960). The main objective of these aesthetic-stance questions is to evoke an understanding of family, love, loss, courage, loneliness, and friendship. As students identify and transact with characters and events, they gain understanding of "other selves," both imaginary and realistic, and deeper insight into themselves.

What aesthetic-stance questions might you ask about *Charlotte's Web?*

You can encourage a predominately aesthetic stance by helping students transact with text through close identification with central story characters and text topics. Your ability to do this will depend not only on your knowledge of your students and their motivations and interests but also on your knowledge of children's and adolescent literature. Your goal should be to connect students with the literary work through discussions that link students' background knowledge, personal interests, and responses to the story characters, plot, language, format, and illustrations (Mathewson, 2004; Morrow & Gambrell, 2000).

Sources of Reader Motivation

➤ *Reader's Intention and Commitment*

The desire to read is strongly influenced by the reader's intention (Ruddell & Unrau, 2004b). Intention to read is a "commitment to a plan for achieving one or more reading purposes at a more or less specified time in the future" (Mathewson, 2004, p. 143). Commitment, in turn, is strongly influenced by the reader's internal and external motivations (Ruddell & Unrau, 2004b). It thus becomes important to understand the internal and external motivations that influence a student's commitment and intention to read.

Internal Reader Motivations

A look at six types of internal reader motivations provides insight into students' desire to read. Your awareness of these motivations is important in determining the aesthetic instructional stance you wish to adopt to guide students' approach to text (Mathewson, 2004; Ruddell, 1991, Ruddell & Unrau, 2004b; Russell, 1970). Most quality children's literature holds potential for activating one or more of the following internal reader motivations:

1. *Problem resolution.* Some texts allow the student to see himself or herself as successful in problem solving or problem resolution. Books with high potential for problem-resolution identification include the following: *The Gingerbread Boy* (Egielski, 1998), *Alexander and the Wind-Up Mouse* (Lionni, 1969), *The Bears on Hemlock Mountain* (Dalgliesh, 1952), *It's Not the End of the World* (Blume, 1972a), *Mufaro's Beautiful Daughters* (Steptoe, 1987), *Island of the Blue Dolphins* (O'Dell, 1960), *Harry Potter and the Sorcerer's Stone* (Rowling, 1998), *Under the Quilt of Night* (Hopkinson, 2002), and *Treasure Island* (Stevenson, 1883/2006).

> *Six Types of Internal Reader Motivations*

2. *Prestige.* In many books, entering the story enables the student to become a person of significance, and no longer a boy or girl in an adult world. The reader becomes an individual with adult-like status who exerts control over his or her surroundings. Books such as the following stimulate this type of motivation: *Engelbert Joins the Circus* (Paxton, 1997), *Henry the Explorer* (Taylor, 1966), *Tico and the Golden Wings* (Lionni, 1964), *Where the Wild Things Are* (Sendak, 1963), *The Man from Snowy River* (Paterson & Macarthur-Onslow, 1981), *Return to Hawk's Hill* (Eckert, 1998), *Becoming Joe DiMaggio* (Teta, 2002), and *Ruby Lou, Brave and True* (Look, 2004).

3. *Aesthetic appreciation.* Reading often involves the elevation of an aesthetic sense, ranging from appreciation of the beauty of nature to the enjoyment of family interaction and harmony. This motivation is addressed in books such as the following: *On the Banks of Plum Creek* (Wilder, 1937), *When I Was Young in the Mountains* (Rylant, 1982), *My Place* (Wheatley & Rawlins, 1987), *Sarah, Plain and Tall* (MacLachlan, 1985), *Thank You, Mr. Falker* (Polacco, 1998), *Classical Poetry: An Illustrated Collection* (Rosen, 1998), *Swimming Upstream: Middle School Poems* (George. Ill. Tilley, 2002), and *Sarah Special* (Codel, 2003).

Which sources of internal reader motivation might *Charlotte's Web* stimulate?

4. *Escape.* Involvement with text can enable the reader to leave the realities of daily existence. This involvement may take the form of identification with a character of similar age and experience or with an explorer or traveler, as the student's "self" travels to faraway places doing unfamiliar and exotic things. Books such as the following provide wonderful escapes: *Now We Are Six* (Milne, 1927), *Where the Wild Things Are* (Sendak, 1963), *Ramona Forever* (Cleary, 1984), *Matilda* (Dahl, 1988), *The Lion, the Witch, and the Wardrobe* (Lewis, 1950), *The Adventures of Captain Underpants: An Epic Novel* (Pilkey, 1997), *The Secret of the Eagle Feathers* (McKinley, 1997), *The Waterstone* (Rupp, 2002), and *Satch and Me* (Gutman, 2006).

5. *Intellectual curiosity.* The desire to discover is an important motivation, as the curious mind works to untangle mysteries and explore our present world and other worlds. Books such as the following lead the reader into discovery and exploration: *The Eleventh Hour: A Curious Mystery* (Base, 1988), *The Great Valentine's Day Balloon Race* (Adams, 1980), *Navajo Coyote Tales* (Morgan, 1988), *The Tram to Bondi Beach* (Hathorn, 1981), *Soaring with the Wind: The Bald Eagle* (Gibbons, 1999), *The Kid Who Invented the Popsicle* (Wulffson, 1997), *Mammoths: Ice-Age Giants* (Agenbroad & Nelson, 2002), and *Al Capone Does My Shirts* (Choldenko, 2004).

6. *Understanding self.* Books help us to delve into the self, to understand our personal drives, hopes, and aspirations and those of the people in our life. Books of this type include *Dear Phoebe* (Alexander, 1984), *Alexander and the Terrible, Horrible, No Good, Very Bad Day* (Viorst, 1972), *Millicent and the Wind* (Munsch, 1984), *Tales of a Fourth Grade Nothing* (Blume, 1972b), *Everybody Needs a Rock* (Baylor, 1974), *The Secret Garden* (Burnett, 1911), *The Summer My Father Was Ten* (Brisson, 1998), *Riding Freedom* (Ryan, 1998), *Simply Alice* (Naylor, 2002), and *Kira-Kira* (Kaduhata, 2004).

Capitalizing on these internal reader motivations requires adoption of an aesthetic instructional stance, which leads to identification with story characters and story content. Your awareness and use of these internal motivations will encourage students to "step into the story" experience and live through the story characters (Barone, Eeds, & Mason, 1995).

the ★ Highly Effective Teacher ★

What books have you read lately that were recommended by friends?

External Reader Motivations

External reader motivations are also present in literature experiences; they include teacher expectations and peer recommendations and influence. The expectations you hold for students have a powerful effect on their behavior and achievement in school. Your expectations for literacy experiences direct and guide students' responses to text and their continuing relationships with books and reading. Peer influence on literature selections is likewise important. Students can and do spontaneously share favorite authors and high-interest books such as Judy Blume's *It's Not the End of the World* (1972) and *Then Again, Maybe I Won't* (1971), but they tend to do so more frequently in a classroom or other environment that encourages sharing. Our observations of effective teachers as they introduce literature reveal that they effectively use both internal and external reader motivations and place major emphasis on an aesthetic instructional stance (Ruddell, 1991, 1995).

Research and Evidence-Based Practice

The Effect of Reader Response and Engagement on Motivation and Comprehension Development

Did You Know?

- Research shows that a surprisingly small number of teachers, between 1 and 30 percent, engage students in active thinking. That is using authentic questions with no predetermined answers that require higher-level comprehension beyond the factual recall of information. This was found to be especially true for teachers working with lower-achieving students (Goodlad, 1983; Guszak, 1967; Nystrand, 1999; Ruddell, 2004).

- Teacher modeling in small- and large-group instructional discussions can demonstrate the use of language and strategies that students can use in interpreting, clarifying, and engaging in literature-based discussions (Brown, Palincsar, & Armbruster, 2004; McGee, Courtney, & Lomax, 1994; Wells, 1999).

- The instructional stance taken by the teacher—that is, aesthetic or efferent—will strongly influence the students' reading stance, purpose, and level of understanding. The aesthetic stance opens discussions, provides time to respond, gives opportunity to talk, and encourages personal and intertextual connections. Research shows that this stance leads to significantly higher levels of personal understanding and achievement (Cullinan, Harwood, & Galda, 1983; Many, 2004; Ruddell, 2004; Wang & Guthrie, 2004).

- Encouraging students to actively participate in small-group discussions that are highly interactive and trans-

actional will assist them in acquiring special language and strategies. This language and these strategies have been shown to be of value to students by increasing their level of participation, clarifying confusions that resolve their cognitive conflicts, and increasing their personal understanding and achievement (Almasi, 1995; Brown et al., 2004; McMahon et al., 1997; Ruddell, 2004; Vinz et al., 2000).

- Highly effective teachers frequently tap internal student motivations. Using these motivations has been shown to help stimulate intellectual curiosity, explore self-understanding, use aesthetic imagery and expression, and motivate the desire to solve problems (Cullinan, Harwood, & Galda, 1983; Many, 2004; Ruddell, 2004).

- Readers use the books they read, in effect their "text worlds," to better understand socialization for participating in their own lived-in worlds (Christian-Smith, 1993; Galda & Beach, 2004; McGinley & Kamberelis, 1996).

- A student's image of self as a reader (self-schemata) and belief of what he or she is capable of doing and learning (self-efficacy) strongly influences the reader's motivation for engaging in reading (Garcia & Pintrich, 1994; Guthrie, Wigfield, Metsala, & Cox, 2004; Schunk, 1991, 1994).

- A student's motivation to read directly increases the amount read. This in turn increases reading comprehension and reading achievement (Baker & Wigfield, 1999).

Types of Children's and Adolescent Literature

Various classification systems have been used for children's and adolescent literature, based on instructional need or focus, reading-ability level, subject area, and social theme. The organizational system used in most school libraries is shown in Table 7.1; its broad categories are the three general **literary genres** of fiction, nonfiction, and poetry.

Fiction

The genre of **fiction** includes literature in the form of imaginary narration. Realistic fiction is designed to mirror children's reality, whereas fantasy frees the reader from the constraints of everyday life. Fiction uses five structural elements that work together to create a story: plot, characterization, setting, point of view, and theme (Lukens, 1995). Your awareness of these elements will help you plan instruction and encourage children to construct meaning and to create their own stories using these elements.

Plot

The story plot develops the relationship between the characters and setting through a sequence of events that develops a central goal and leads to the story climax and conclusion. Plot development involves a major problem or conflict that must be resolved to reach the story goal and represents the "how" of the narrative. In a work of fiction, the story beginning places characters in the story setting and develops the central conflicting problem through story events. The middle of the story develops the plot through key events involving the reader, extends the story goal, and builds to a story climax. The end of the story resolves the problem, as the central characters come to terms with the conflict and the goal is achieved.

literary genres
broad categories of literature or literary tradition, such as fiction, nonfiction, and poetry

fiction
a literary genre for narratives portraying imaginary characters and events

> *The elements of fiction include plot, characterization, setting, point of view, and theme.*

TABLE 7.1

Classifying Children's Books for Easy Reference

Fiction	**Realism: Mirrors Reality**
	Modern, e.g., *The Boy Who Wouldn't Say His Name; When I Was Young in the Mountains; Millicent and the Wind; Ramona Quimby, Age 8; A Pair of Red Clogs; Good-Bye to Budapest; Where the Red Fern Grows; Return to Hawk's Hill; Judy Moody Saves the World.*
	Historical, e.g., *Sarah, Plain and Tall; Little House on the Prairie; Johnny Tremain; Ishi, Last of His Tribe; Island of the Blue Dolphins; Drummer Boy: Marching to the Civil War; Joining the Boston Tea Party.*
	Fantasy: Frees Reader from Bonds Imposed by Existence
	Modern, e.g., *Where the Wild Things Are; Danny and the Dinosaur; Flossie & the Fox; Charlotte's Web; The Little Prince; Charlie and the Chocolate Factory; The Lion, the Witch, and the Wardrobe; Harry Potter and the Sorcerer's Stone; The Witch Who Wanted to be a Princess.*
	Traditional, e.g., *Mufaro's Beautiful Daughters; Stories to Solve: Folktales from Around the World; The People Could Fly* (folktale); *Cinderella; Puss in Boots* (fairy tale); *Once a Mouse; North Wind and the Sun* (fable); *The White Archer: An Eskimo Legend; Myths of the World* (myths); *Stone Soup; Legend of the Milky Way* (legend); *The Gingerbread Boy; Cinderella.*
Nonfiction	Biography/Autobiography: detailed account of a specific life, e.g., *And Then What Happened, Paul Revere?; Anne Frank: The Diary of a Young Girl; Black Cowboy, Wild Horses: A True Story; Will Rogers: An American Legend.*
	Exposition: exploration of new and interesting concepts and ideas, e.g., *I Like Caterpillars; The Sense of Wonder; Sharks; Why Do Volcanoes Erupt?; This Is the Sea that Feeds Us; Under the Ice.*
Poetry	Anthologies/single-author books of rhymes, verse, and songs, e.g., *The Real Mother Goose; Where the Sidewalk Ends; A Child's Garden of Verse; Classic Poetry: An Illustrated Collection; I Invited a Dragon to Dinner: And Other Poems to Make You Laugh Out Loud.*

For example, at the outset of *Alexander and the Wind-Up Mouse*, Lionni (1969) develops two central characters: Alexander, the real mouse, and Willy, the toy mouse. The central conflict is introduced as Willy is set aside to be thrown away after Annie receives new toys for her birthday. The climax of the story focuses on Alexander's rescue of Willy as he follows the magic lizard's advice and searches for the special purple pebble. Story resolution is reached as Alexander finds the pebble and the lizard changes Willy into a real mouse. The story concludes as Alexander and Willy rejoice and dance in the garden until dawn.

Characterization

Story characters are critical to the development of the narrative. The characters may take the form of real people or personified animals or plants. Characterization accounts for the "who" of the story. The characters come alive for the reader through the author's use of description, action, conversation, and illustration. Through these literary devices in Lionni's story, the reader is able to identify with the fear, anxiety, and joy that Alexander and Willy experience.

Setting

Story setting invites the reader to project self into the environment and surroundings through visualization. Simple settings for some stories are established through a brief verbal description or illustration; more complex settings may involve historical time periods and the development of events in different places over time. The story setting represents the "where" and the "when" of the story. The setting for Alexander and Willy is established largely through Lionni's illustrations depicting locations in or around Annie's home.

Point of View

Point of view refers to the perspective of the narrator or storyteller. A story may be told in the first person through the eyes of the main character or by a narrator who is omniscient and sees and knows all. An objective point of view creates the sense that the reader is an eyewitness to the story events.

Alexander and the Wind-Up Mouse is told from an objective point of view; the reader observes Alexander and Willy firsthand as the story develops. An interesting contrast of viewpoints occurs when the same story is told from different characters' points of view. For example, Galdone (1970) presents the traditional story of *The Three Little Pigs* from the objective eyewitness perspective, whereas Scieszka (1989) tells *The True Story of the Three Little Pigs!* from the self-serving, first-person point of view of the wolf.

Theme

The story theme communicates the underlying story meaning, usually emphasizing human values the author wishes to impart. The theme may be stated directly, as in the conclusion of most fables, or developed indirectly, as in *Alexander and the Wind-Up Mouse*, where the values of love and caring develop a friendship theme. Themes are carefully woven into the story as characters interact through events and settings and the plot unfolds. Discussions of story theme provide wonderful opportunities for students to explore values and beliefs as they interact and problem-solve together.

> What are the plot, characterization, setting, point of view, and theme of a work of fiction you have read recently or are reading now?

Nonfiction

nonfiction
a literary genre for expository writing about actual people, events, and subjects

The genre of **nonfiction** includes explanations or descriptions of people, events, and subjects through biography, autobiography, and exposition. Biographical and autobiographical selections such as *And Then What Happened, Paul Revere?* (Fritz, 1973) and *Anne Frank: The Diary of a Young Girl* (Frank, 1967) also may contain some structural elements of fiction.

Nonfiction has clearly defined text patterns: description, sequence of events, cause and effect, comparison and contrast, and problem solution (Kane, 1998; Meyer & Freedle, 1979; Pearson & Camperell, 1994). Expository books and essays often use a combination of these text-structure patterns:

■ *Description*, or listing, develops an explanation by providing key characteristics and examples. *Sharks* (Berger, 1987), for example, describes a wide range of sharks, from the thresher to the great white, and provides detailed examples and illustrations.

- *Sequence of events* relies heavily on order or time sequence in explanation. Many science and social studies books trace development and change over time. This pattern is evident in *Dinosaurs All Around: An Artist's View of the Prehistoric World* (Arnold, 1993), which explains the process of developing a museum display.
- *Cause and effect* provides a logical connection between antecedents and consequences or outcomes. Again, this pattern of exposition frequently is used in science books (e.g., the process of desert formation) and social studies books (e.g., the Revolutionary War).
- *Comparison and contrast* builds understanding of similarities and differences between ideas or events. Books with a strong informational content often develop concepts through comparison and contrast, such as the differences and similarities in active and dormant volcanoes in *Why Do Volcanoes Erupt?* (Whitfield, 1990).
- *Problem solution* uses reasoning to think through a problem and provide possible solutions. For example, *Rachel Carson: A Woman Who Changed Our World* (Adams, 1978) analyzes the problem of pollution caused by DDT, the disastrous environmental effects, and the solution of controlling pesticides.

> How are description, sequence of events, cause and effect, comparison and contrast, and problem solution used in a work of nonfiction you are reading now?

The discussion in Chapter 8 will focus on instructional strategies designed to help students construct meaning and develop fluency in reading nonfiction or expository text in content areas.

Poetry, Rhymes, and Jingles

The literary genre of **poetry** includes rhythmical compositions that stimulate the imagination and magnify key thoughts and ideas. As you familiarize yourself with children's and adolescent books, be sure to include books of poetry. While fantasy throws off the constraints of realism, poetry allows ideas just to be. Thoughts, images, and feelings can be presented as elaborately, briefly, simply, or abstractly as desired. Through content, poetry reaches out to young children as they enjoy humor and animal adventures, as well as their most vital interest—themselves. Ciardi's (1964) "And Off He Went Just as Proud as You Please" captures people's preference for their own name. Aldis's (1955) "Everybody Says" suggests a way that people can look at themselves as individuals. For the older student, identification with strong character traits can be an important avenue to growth and understanding of self, as illustrated in Clark's (1985) "Charles."

> **poetry**
> a literary genre for brief, intense, rhythmical compositions of lines that may or may not rhyme

Imagery is a gift of poetry. Although prose can create imagery for the reader, poetry often does so more powerfully. A classic example is Sandburg's "Fog." Children's imaginations can be easily aroused with a question such as "What color do you think of when you think of Mondays?" or "What color do you think of when you picture a fierce wind blowing?" O'Neill (1961) evokes these and other images in *Hailstones and Halibut Bones*.

Rhythm also plays an important role in poetry (Bownas, McClure, & Oxley, 1998). Milne captures a special rhythm for very young children in "Happiness." In Milne's "Disobedience," a satisfying rhythm lets the young student exert a certain amount of control over Mother. Older students respond to the rhythm and humor in his poem "The King's Breakfast."

> What poems did you enjoy most in your childhood?

Forms of poetry include narrative poetry, which tells a story; lyric poetry, written like a song; and free verse, ungoverned by rules of rhyme or rhythm. Students also enjoy highly structured poetic forms, such as haiku and limericks, as well as nonsense humor (most students delight in the works of Edward Lear). Examples of poetry anthologies are presented in Figure 7.1.

Rhymes and jingles are not poetry in the formal literary sense but are from folklore. They range from Mother Goose rhymes to Burgess's (1929) "Purple Cow." Older readers will be challenged by the tongue-twisters in Strong's (1955) "The Modern Hiawatha." Like folktales, many rhymes and jingles reflect the culture from which they come. A wonderful multicultural collection of these is *Skipping Around the World* (Butler, 1989). Helping students record their jump-rope and clapping-game rhymes legitimizes and gives recognition to a kind of poetry students already know.

> How might you use poems, rhymes, and jingles to develop students' expressive writing?

Selecting Literature

The selection of literature to implement your classroom literature program deserves careful consideration. The fiction and nonfiction books you select must reflect the broad range of interests and ability levels of your students. Your resources need to include a collection of full-length

FIGURE 7.1

Bookshelf: Poetry Anthologies for the Classroom

Dunning, S., Luders, E., and Smith, H. (Eds.). (1967). *Reflections on a Gift of Watermelon Pickle*. New York: Lothrop, Lee & Shepard.

Gilooly, E. (Ed.). (2001). *Poetry for Young People: Robert Browning*. (J. Spector, Illus.). New York: Sterling.

Hoberman, M. (1994). *My Song Is Beautiful: Poems and Pictures in Many Voices*. Boston: Little, Brown.

Hopkins, L. B. (1987). *Pass the Poetry Please*. New York: Harper.

Hughes, L. (1993). *The Dream Keeper and Other Poems*. New York: Knopf.

Katz, B. (Ed.). (2004). *Pocket Poems*. (M. Hafner, Illus.). New York: Dutton.

Kennedy, C. (2005). *A Family of Poems, My Favorite Poetry for Children*. New York: Hyperion.

Mendelson, E. (Ed.). (2001). *Poetry for Young People: Edward Lear*. (L. Huliska-Beith, Illus.). New York: Sterling.

Rosen, M. (1998). *Classical Poetry: An Illustrated Collection*. Cambridge, MA: Candlewick Press.

children's and adolescent trade books (nontextbooks) for your classroom and school library. The questions in Figure 7.2 provide a checklist for choosing quality trade books for your classroom.

> ➤ *Develop a wish list of new books you want for your classroom literature collection.*

A classroom literature collection is developed over time, as you collect favorite books for classroom use. You should have multiple copies (six to ten) of a number of paperback titles available for group reading and response. As you encounter new books in the school library, the public library, bookstores, and book displays at professional conferences, update the list of books that you want to add to the collection. Keep this list current and complete—author, title, publisher, ISBN (International Standard Book Number used for ordering a book), and price—and ready to submit on a purchase order on short notice. When school funds suddenly become available at the end of the school year or during the summer, the teachers whose completed purchase orders are on the principal's desk are the ones who get the books.

General references that provide brief descriptions of children's and adolescent books are listed in Figure 7.3. Such easy-to-use resources identify general categories of literature, as well as themes and topics for matching books to children's interests.

Reading Interests in the Primary Grades

Students' reading interests at different age and grade levels remain relatively stable. As noted in Chapter 2, in kindergarten and grades 1 and 2, children like to read picture books, picture storybooks, predictable books, fairy tales, folktales, modern fantasy, and humor. These books frequently center on animals, nature, family, and child characters of the children's ages (Galda, Ash,

FIGURE 7.2

Key Questions to Help You Choose Quality Literature for Your Classroom

1. Will the story or information appeal to readers with the interests and maturity of the students in my classroom?

2. Is the book written at a level that my students can read with ease?

3. If fiction, does the book include such features as vivid characterization, compelling illustrations, and a high-interest plot, using language and style that will encourage children's identification with the characters and draw them into the story?

4. If nonfiction, does the book develop opportunities to discover new worlds and people, other living things, events, and ideas, thereby expanding the background knowledge and experiences of the children?

5. Do I personally enjoy the selection, and can I "place" the book with one or more of my students, using the internal reader motivations discussed earlier?

6. Is the selection appropriate for my instructional goals—for example, reading for pleasure or reading to develop important information or content as a part of a unit or theme development?

7. Does the book have potential for a variety of uses in my classroom, such as pure enjoyment, independent reading, and reading aloud?

FIGURE 7.3

Bookshelf: Reference Works for Choosing Children's and Adolescent Literature

Buss, K. & Karnowski, L. (2000). *Reading and Writing: Literary Genres.* Newark, DE: International Reading Association.

Freeman, E. B., Martinez, M., Yokota, J., & Temple, C. A. (2006). *Children's Books in Children's Hands: An Introduction to Their Literature.* Boston: Allyn & Bacon.

Gambrell, L. B., and Almsi, J. F. (1996). *Lively Discussions! Fostering Engaged Reading.* Newark, DE: International Reading Association.

Hearne, B. (1990). *Choosing Books for Children.* New York: Dell.

Hillman, J. (1999). *Discovering Children's Literature.* Upper Saddle River, NJ: Prentice Hall.

Huck, C., Hepler, S., Hickman, J., & Kiefer, B. (2001). *Children's Literature in the Elementary School.* Boston, MA: McGraw-Hill.

International Reading Association. (1992). *Kids' Favorite Books.* Newark, DE: Author.

Lima, C. W. (2006). *A to Zoo: Subject Access to Children's Picture Books* (7th ed.). Westport, CT: Libraries Unlimited.

Moss, J. F. (1996). *Teaching Literature in the Elementary School: A Thematic Approach.* Norwood, MA: Christopher-Gordon.

Norton, D. E. (2003). *Through the Eyes of a Child: An Introduction to Children's Literature,* 6th ed. Upper Saddle River, NJ: Prentice Hall.

Trelease, J. (2005). *The New Read-Aloud Handbook,* 6th ed. New York: Penguin.

Young, T. A. (Ed.). (2006). *Happily Ever After: Sharing Folk Literature with Elementary and Middle School Students.* Newark, DE: International Reading Association.

& Cullinan, 2000; International Reading Association, 1999b; Monson & Sebesta, 1991). At this level, students are also interested in general information books, including those in history and science. In grades 3 and 4, their interest in nature and animals continues, and strong interest develops in adventure stories that include personal experiences familiar to the students.

Students respond to literature in the primary grades by focusing on the story action as a pattern of events, rather than on features such as point of view or the story theme. First-grade and some second-grade students favor retelling and brief story synopses with global evaluation responses, such as "It's good." When asked to explain why they like or dislike a story, their responses usually involve a single incident, such as "I liked it because the troll fell in the water" (Applebee, 1978). Third graders tend to use special categories for evaluating a story, such as "dreary" or "interesting" (Martinez & Roser, 1991).

Reading Interests in the Intermediate and Middle School Grades

In grades 4 through 8, students develop a strong interest in narrative adventure and fantasy. Informational reading interests range from ocean and space topics to computers and sports. You will find that reading preferences for boys and girls start to diverge somewhat during these grades. Boys show a stronger preference for topics related to mystery and nonfiction, while girls prefer animal stories, westerns, fairy tales, and realistic fiction (Galda, Ash, & Cullinan, 2000). At these grade levels, interest in specific books is strongly influenced by peer sharing and peer recommendations.

In the intermediate grades, students' responses to stories become more elaborated and complex. They tend to use a more detailed synopsis and retelling in a story-response discussion than do students in the primary grades. They have a more advanced sense of narrative, which includes expectations of characters, story setting, and story goals. They also demonstrate growing concern for analyzing the structures of stories and creating generalizations about story meaning. By grade 6, students begin to provide tentative explanations of symbolic and thematic features of stories.

Research on students' interests across the grades reveals that at all levels they prefer books that have well-developed characters who confront problems and seek solutions and plots that focus on characters with different points of view. Students also prefer books that provide for predictability, security, and, not surprisingly, a happy ending (Galda, Ash, & Cullinan, 2000).

> *Students of all ages prefer books with strong characterization, active problem solving, different points of view, predictability, messages of security, and happy endings.*

Working with Librarians

Your school library and librarian are important resources for your students and for you, as you seek to expand your classroom book collection. Arrange a tour of the library early in the school year to introduce your students to the library and familiarize them with book location and checkout procedures. A collaborative relationship with the librarian becomes very important as you "become attuned to student voices while generating student-centered curricula" (Giorgis & Peterson, 1996, p. 482). The librarian can help identify books for developing thematic units on topics ranging from families and friendship in the primary grades to Western expansion or space exploration at the intermediate levels. Many school librarians are skilled in the art of storytelling or know storytellers who will visit your classroom. After a storytelling experience, ask the librarian to make follow-up literature available for checkout or for use in your classroom. You will also want to arrange to check out thirty to forty books for the classroom literature center; every two to four weeks, you should exchange them for new titles. The public library in your area can be used for the same purposes.

Helping Students Choose Books Independently

How do you choose books to read?

Considerations for creating the K–1 classroom reading center are discussed in Chapter 3.

Students' interest in books is a major factor in book selection. However, students sometimes experience difficulty in choosing books within their comfortable reading range and are averse to reading books the teacher recommends. Veatch (1968) recommends a simple technique to help students identify books they can read successfully. You can easily teach your students this "five-finger test," described in the How To Do. This simple technique gives students a general idea of the difficulty and readability of a book, helping them choose appropriate books independently.

Developing the Classroom Reading Center

The literacy environment you create will contribute to your goals and objectives for literature instruction, especially by providing a variety of high-interest books in an attractive physical environment that promotes individual and small-group reading and response (Olness, 2007). The reading center that houses the classroom literature collection should be highly functional and physically inviting to students. Figure 7.4 presents a specific plan you may wish to follow for creating a classroom center.

How to Do . . .

Veatch's (1968) Five-Finger Test for Choosing Books to Read

1. Choose a book you think will interest you.
2. Open the book to a page that is mostly print.
3. Start reading from the top of the page, and each time you run into a word you don't know, put up a finger. A word you don't know is a word you can't say or a word for which you don't know the meaning. If the word is the name of a person or place, you don't have to count it.
4. Read to the end of the page and see how many fingers you have up.
5. Decide how hard the book will be for you. If you have zero to one fingers up, the book will be easy for you to read; two to five fingers up, the book will be of medium difficulty; six or more fingers up, the book will be a challenge to read.

■ **Books read independently should be easier than those read under teacher guidance. Be certain that you have a wide range of books available on your library shelves for independent reading—including plenty that will be easy enough for delayed readers to enjoy without your help.**

FIGURE 7.4

Developing a Classroom Reading Center

1. Select an easily accessible area that can be sectioned off by using portable partitions. The area should be large enough to be used comfortably by five or six students. A corner of the classroom will provide two walls for visual displays.

2. Place colorful posters relating to books and reading on one wall of the center. Attractive posters can be obtained from the Children's Book Council (67 Irving Place, New York, NY 10003) and the American Library Association (50 East Huron Street, Chicago, IL 60611).

3. Use the center's bulletin board to display children's and adolescent literature-related art and written responses. These may take the form of drawings of a favorite story character or a key story event, individually designed book advertisements, or letters to book authors.

4. Provide a cassette player or recorder, headphones, and recorded stories together with the associated books for listening and reading.

5. Develop a collection of children's and adolescent books representing a wide range of literary experiences at different reading levels, using the classification categories presented in Table 7.1. Call on your school library and the public library to help in this effort. Set a goal of from five to eight books per child for the book collection (Huck, 1976).

6. Add magazines, newspapers, television guides, and other reading materials that you and your students use and read daily. Also, add to the center books that children have written, illustrated, and published.

As you develop the reading center, the most critical element will be identifying a wide range of fiction, nonfiction, and poetry that fit the reading interests, reading levels, and motivations of your students. You can expand this collection by getting contributions from parents, sponsoring (or persuading parents to sponsor) fundraisers for book purchases, and, if you are fortunate, drawing on school monies designated for the purchase of children's and adolescent literature. Many excellent books are available as inexpensive paperbacks. Students also can enroll in a paperback book club to start a personal book collection, to be shared with other children in the class during the year.

The list of children's and adolescent books in Table 7.2 (page 200) is based on a recent literature survey of favorite books used by teachers and their students. This list identifies the most frequently selected books at each grade and suggests a range of titles to include in your classroom literature collection.

To encourage students' independent reading at home, devise a simple book checkout system for the literature and reading center. In the primary grades, students may bring a self-selected

> *The reading center is important in helping students develop positive attitudes toward literature, new background knowledge, and reading enjoyment.*

What is the most important thing to remember when choosing books for your classroom reading center? Do you have favorite books that you would want your students to read?

TABLE 7.2

Teachers' and Students' Favorite Books for the Classroom Reading Center

Grade Level	Book Titles
Kindergarten	*Alligators All Around: An Alphabet* (Sendak); *Bringing the Rain to Kapiti Plain: A Nandi Tale* (Aardema); *Can You Make a Pig Giggle?* (Ashman); *Cinderella* (Perrault); *Counting Crocodiles* (Sierra); *Mother Goose: A Treasury of Best-Loved Rhymes* (Piper); *Peter and the North Wind* (Littledale); *The Very Hungry Caterpillar* (Carle); *Why Mosquitoes Buzz in People's Ears* (Aardema)
Grade 1	*Anansi the Spider: A Tale from the Ashanti* (McDermott); *Engelbert Joins the Circus* (Wilson); *Frog and Toad* (Lobel); *Little Bear* (Minarik); *Mr. Rabbit and the Lovely Present* (Zolotow); *Rosie's Walk* (Hutchins); *Snow Ponies* (Cotten); *The Three Little Pigs* (Galdone); *The Very Busy Spider* (Carle)
Grade 2	*Franklin and Harriet* (Bourgeois); *I Wish My Brother Was a Dog* (Meisel); *The House on East 88th Street* (Waber); *Miss Nelson Is Missing!* (Allard & Marshall); *Miss Rumphius* (Clooney); *Owl Moon* (Yolen); *The Story of Ferdinand* (Leah); *A Taste of Blackberries* (Smith); *Where the Wild Things Are* (Sendak)
Grade 3	*The Case of the Elevator Duck* (Berends); *Charlie and the Chocolate Factory* (Dahl); *The Dinosaurs of Waterhouse Hawkins* (Kerley); *Look to the North: A Wolf Pup Diary* (George); *The Hundred Dresses* (Estes); *Mufaro's Beautiful Daughters* (Steptoe); *Ramona Quimby, Age 8* (Cleary); *The Story of Jumping Mouse* (Steptoe); *Superfudge* (Blume)
Grade 4	*Bridge to Terabithia* (Paterson); *Dear Mr. Henshaw* (Cleary); *In the Year of the Boar and Jackie Robinson* (Lord); *Island of the Blue Dolphins* (O'Dell); *Mrs. Frisby and the Rats of NIMH* (O'Brien); *Ms. Frizzle's Adventures: Ancient Egypt* (Cole & Degen); *Sarah, Plain and Tall* (MacLachlan); *The Adventures of Captain Underpants: An Epic Novel* (Pilkey); *The Velveteen Rabbit* (Williams)
Grade 5	*The Dark Is Rising* (Cooper); *The Indian in the Cupboard* (Banks); *Johnny Tremain* (Forbes); *Martin's Big Words: The Life of Dr. Martin Luther King, Jr.* (Rappaport); *My Side of the Mountain* (George); *Robin Hood—Prince of Outlaws* (Miles); *The Secret of the Eagle Feather* (McKinley); *The White Mountains* (Christopher); *Witch of Blackbird Pond* (Speare)
Grade 6	*Anne Frank and Me* (Bennett & Gottesfeld); *Are You There, God? It's Me, Margaret* (Blume); *Hatchet* (Paulsen); *Jackie Robinson: Baseball's Civil Rights Legend* (Coombs); *James and the Giant Peach* (Dahl); *The Lion, the Witch, and the Wardrobe* (Lewis); *Mrs. Frisby and the Rats of NIMH* (O'Brien); *The Secret Garden* (Burnett); *Where the Red Fern Grows* (Rawls)
Grades 7 and 8	*Baseball in April and Other Stories* (Soto); *Chinese Handcuffs* (Crutcher); *Emily in Love* (Rubin); *From the Mixed-Up Files of Mrs. Basil E. Frankweiler* (Konigsburg); *One Night* (Qualey); *The Sign of the Beaver* (Speare); *To Kill a Mockingbird* (Lee)

book to you at a specified daily checkout time. On a 3-by-5-inch card, note the date, the child's name, and the book title, and then file the card under the student's name or, for older students, under the author's name. Once this procedure is established (over a three- to four-week period), most students will be able to make and file checkout cards on their own.

Instructional Strategies for Teaching Literature

To implement your literature goals and objectives, you need to understand a variety of instructional strategies that can be used to enhance students' positive attitudes and active comprehension. These strategies are designed to create high interest, motivation, and active comprehension.

Each strategy assumes the importance of the reader-response process (identification, catharsis, and insight), the instructional stance (aesthetic or efferent), and students' internal reader motivations (problem resolution, prestige, aesthetic appreciation, escape, intellectual curiosity, and understanding self). To use the reader-response process, stance, and motivations in your teaching, you will need to ask yourself four basic questions:

1. What can I conclude about the key interests and motivations of my students on the basis of what I know about them and have observed in my classroom?
2. Given these interests and motivations, what literature selections would hold high appeal for them?
3. What internal reader motivations play a role in building reader identification and interest in a particular literature selection?
4. What instructional strategy or strategies will be most effective in developing the literature experience?

> ➤ *Four Basic Questions for Literature Instruction*

Reading Aloud: Sharing Stories and Poems

Reading literature and poetry aloud to students is an important way to increase their enjoyment of literature and to provide an opportunity for active comprehension and reader response (Temple et al., 2008). **Reading aloud** is a traditional classroom practice appropriate for all grades. It allows you to model fluent oral reading and your own active involvement in and enjoyment of reading. Reading aloud is flexible, serving a variety of instructional purposes, from appreciating the beauty of language to making story predictions (Trelease, 1995).

> **reading aloud**
> a traditional classroom practice of reading literature orally to children

Reading aloud works best if you schedule regular times each day—five to fifteen minutes, depending on your purpose (Hoffman, Roser, & Battle, 1993). Some teachers schedule reading aloud at the beginning of the school day and at selected reentry points during the day (after recess and lunch, for example) to establish a mood and create a sense of classroom unity while sharing quality literature (Barrentine, 1996). Other teachers use the reading-aloud experience as a regular part of initiating and developing a literature, social studies, or science unit. Highly effective teachers read aloud to students as often as they can every day, in both planned and spontaneous experiences.

The reading-aloud experience may be self-contained, such as sharing a poem or story or reading the beginning paragraphs to introduce a new book, or it may be extended and ongoing, as you present serial installments of a book over several weeks. Good candidates for extended reading aloud are *Ramona Quimby, Age 8* (Cleary, 1981) and *Charlotte's Web* (White, 1952) in the primary grades and *From the Mixed-Up Files of Mrs. Basil E. Frankweiler* (Konigsburg, 1967) and *The Lion, the Witch, and the Wardrobe* (Lewis, 1950) in the intermediate grades. Trelease's anthologies *Hey! Listen to This: Stories to Read Aloud* (1992) for the early grades and *Read All About It* (1993) for grades 4 through 8 are excellent resources for your classroom. Figure 7.5 lists examples of literature suitable for reading aloud.

Expect minor distractions when reading to the whole class or to small groups. Some students will enter into the story with total concentration, but others like to doodle and draw or may comment on story events and whisper to other students. Note that choral response to the spoken word is part of some cultural traditions. The How To Do on page 203 lists six steps for reading aloud.

Storytelling

The most natural and intimate way to communicate a story is simply to tell it. **Storytelling** can be used effectively at all elementary and middle school grade levels. It provides a way that you can give of yourself and share a personal appreciation for literature using stories you especially like. A good storyteller enters into the story, lives in it, and in effect loses self in the story. You probably have been held spellbound by stories told by grandparents, aunts or uncles, a family friend, a former teacher, or a storyteller around a campfire.

> **storytelling**
> a traditional practice of presenting literature-based narrative and oral traditions without the use of text

As in reading aloud, the storyteller must carefully prepare for the story presentation. Begin by identifying the story you want to tell and the purpose of the storytelling experience. Choose a

FIGURE 7.5

Bookshelf: Examples of Literature to Read Aloud

Badoe, A. (2001). *The Pot of Wisdom: Ananse Stories*. Toronto: Groundwood Books.

Blake, R. J. (1997). *Akiak: A Tale from the Iditarod*. New York: Philomel.

Canon, J. (1993). *Stellaluna*. San Diego: Harcourt.

Cleary, B. (1968). *Ramona the Pest*. New York: Morrow.

Cowley, J. (2005). *Chameleon, Chameleon*. New York: Scholastic.

Dalgliesh, A. (1982). *The Courage of Sarah Noble*. New York: Charles Scribner's Sons.

Dorros, A. (1991). *Abuela*. New York: Dutton.

Fletcher, R. (1997). *Spider Boy*. New York: Clarion.

George, J. C. (1997). *Julie's Wolf Pack*. Scranton: HarperCollins.

Konigsburg, E. L. (1967). *From the Mixed-Up Files of Mrs. Basil E. Frankweiler*. New York: Dell.

Lasky, K. (1998). *Alice, Rose, and Sam*. New York. Hyperion.

Lee, H. (1960). *To Kill a Mockingbird*. New York: HarperCollins.

Lester, J. (1987). *The Tales of Uncle Remus: The Adventures of Brer Rabbit*. New York: Penguin Books.

———. (1994). *John Henry*. New York: Dial.

Lewis, C. S. (1950). *The Lion, the Witch, and the Wardrobe*. New York: Macmillan.

McCloskey, R. (1941). *Make Way for Ducklings*. New York: Viking Penguin.

———. (1971). *Homer Price*. New York: Viking Penguin.

O'Dell, S. (1960). *Island of the Blue Dolphins*. New York: Dell.

Pinkney, J. (2000). *Aesop's Fables*. New York: Sea Star/North-South.

Reiser, L. (2006). *Hardworking Puppies*. Orlando, FL: Harcourt.

Roberts, W. D. (1998). *Secrets at Hidden Valley*. New York: Simon & Schuster Children's Books.

Schanzer, R. (2001). *Davy Crockett Saves the World*. New York: HarperCollins.

Sendak, M. (1963). *Where the Wild Things Are*. New York: HarperCollins.

Soto, G. (1990). *Baseball in April and Other Stories*. New York: Harcourt Brace Jovanovich.

Speare, E. (1983). *The Sign of the Beaver*. Boston: Houghton Mifflin.

Stevens, J. (2005). *The Great Fuzz Frenzy*. San Diego, CA: Harcourt.

What narrative elements and patterns enable storytellers to rivet the attention of listeners?

story that you like and that you think your students will also like. The story should have a plot that is compact and that establishes the central story problem early. The setting should be sufficiently detailed to enable the listener to create clear mental images. The characters should be limited to only a few, and their features and behavior should be established early to provide easy identification and to help children enter into the story. The story resolution should hold the listeners' attention until the very end.

Folktales such as *The Three Little Pigs* and *Three Billy Goats Gruff* have these characteristics. There is also a sense of predictability and story rhythm, which allows the listener to participate in the telling ("He huffed, and he puffed, and . . ."). Other appropriate story forms include cumulative tales such as *Henny-Penny* (Galdone, 1968) and *One Fine Day* (Hogrogian, 1971). An excellent collection of African-American folktales can be found in *The People Could Fly* (Hamilton, 1985). Fairy tales, myths, and legends also provide a wide array of stories for classroom telling, as do classic children's books, such as *Make Way for Ducklings* (McCloskey, 1941) and *Little Toot* (Gramatky, 1939).

Prepare to tell your story by reading it carefully and visualizing its pattern. How will you develop the setting and the characters? How does the beginning of the story develop, and how does the plot unfold? How will you end the story? Next, decide whether you will commit the story to memory or tell it in your own words using key phrases, rhymes, or appealing language descriptions used by the author. Finally, you will need to decide how you will introduce the story. The introduction may be as simple as "This is a story about . . . ," or more detail may be required to establish the source of the story and how it came to be written. Finally, decide on what type of reader response you want at the conclusion of the story.

How To Do . . .

Reading Aloud

1. Identify the literature selection or poem you want to read aloud and familiarize yourself thoroughly with the work. Decide what reader response you desire from students at the conclusion of your reading.

2. Read silently, and then practice reading orally to capture the sounds of words, rhymes and rhythms or timing, and the mood and feeling you wish to create.

3. Prepare students for the reading with background information on your reason for selecting the piece, information about the author and subject, or a reminder of where the previous reading ended.

4. Make sure students are comfortable for listening, remind them of any ground rules you and they have established for reading-aloud time, establish an atmosphere, and signal the start of reading.

5. Use appropriate voice and intonation variation to establish characters, setting, plot, and emotional response. Use a reading pace that matches your own visualization of the story. Let your enthusiasm for the story show in your reading.

6. Adapt your reading according to students' expressions of interest and response. Signal the conclusion, and invite reader response and sharing. If the reading is an installment of a longer work, encourage summarizing and prediction.

- **Because delayed readers' listening-comprehension levels almost invariably are higher than their reading levels, seldom are adaptations needed when you are reading *to* them. These students can enjoy and understand the same selections you read to the rest of the class.**

DELAYED READER ADAPTATION

How To Do . . .

Storytelling

1. Select the story you wish to tell; check for strong plot lines and a manageable number of characters.

- **A good rule of thumb is to base stories to be told on selections a little above the reading levels of the students. This practice exposes students to meaning vocabulary they will have to contend with on their own in the near future. Helpful to all students, this procedure is especially useful for delayed readers, who read less and thus have fewer opportunities to enrich their knowledge of word meanings.**

DELAYED READER ADAPTATION

2. Read the story over a number of times, visualizing its pattern.
3. Look for repeated language patterns and rhythms.
4. Block the story into parts for learning. Decide what, if any, language from the story you wish to include in your presentation.
5. Decide how you will introduce the story, including any environmental arrangements.
6. Decide what, if any, response you want from the students after the storytelling event.
7. Continue rereading the story, and begin practicing your own presentation.
8. Practice telling the story aloud until you feel comfortable and confident.
9. Tell the story to your students.

> ➤ *Storytelling
Workshops*

Storytelling workshops sponsored by community groups can help you develop this special ability. A number of storytelling organizations, classes, and conferences are available; at literacy conferences sponsored by professional organizations (the International Reading Association, state reading councils and conferences, and the National Council of Teachers of English) and their affiliates, storytelling sessions are common. Also keep in mind community storytellers who may be available to visit your classroom, and consult resources such as *Using Literature with Young Children* (Jacobs, 1965) and *The Family Storytelling Handbook: How to Use Stories, Anecdotes, Rhymes, Handkerchiefs, Paper, and Other Objects to Enrich Your Family Traditions* (Pellowski, 1987).

Literature-Response Journals

**Literature-
Response Journal**
a place where written individual reader responses are recorded

Opportunities for literature response and engagement can be provided through journal writing as well as through discussion (Meehan, 1997/1998; Spiegel, 1998). A **Literature-Response Journal** gives students a place to record their responses to what they read, providing an opportunity for the teacher to write back to them. Literature-Response Journals can be used effectively in the primary grades, as students begin to record ideas in picture and written form, and in the intermediate grades. These journals enable students not only to share and record ideas but also to revisit responses periodically to reflect on, extend, and refine their ideas and thinking.

The Literature-Response Journal has been described as "a sourcebook, a repository for wanderings and wonderings, speculations, questionings . . . a place to explore thoughts, discover reactions, let the mind ramble—in effect, a place to make room for the unexpected" (Flitterman-King, 1988). It is also, simultaneously, a way for teachers to gain insight into students' meaning-construction process and the way they actively engage in responding to literature.

To initiate Literature-Response Journals, you will need to purchase or have students bring in folders or spiral-bound or three-ring notebooks to serve as journals. Introduce the journals by establishing the purpose and response atmosphere for journal writing. Atwell (1984) aptly describes this initiation process:

> What is the teacher's role in the Literature-Response Journal instructional strategy? What are five patterns of literature response among older students?

This folder [or response journal] is a place for you and me to talk about books, reading, authors, and writing. You're to write letters to me, and I'll write letters back to you. In your letters to me, talk with me about what you've read. Tell me what you thought and felt and why. Tell me what you liked and didn't like and why. Tell me what these books meant to you and said to you. Ask me questions or for help, and write back to me about my ideas, feelings, and questions. (p. 241)

This introduction assumes an aesthetic instructional stance and establishes the view that students' personal feelings and ideas will be valued. In addition, it clearly indicates that the teacher and student will be reacting to each other's responses and exchanging ideas.

Question prompts help students write journal responses. These prompts should be open-ended and rely on higher levels of thinking. Figure 7.6 (page 205) lists twelve prompts for use with fiction (Farnan, 1992). Note that these prompts encourage the reader to respond by constructing meanings based on personal interaction and transaction with the text. Each student should be able to select any one or more of the prompts to develop literature-response writing.

FIGURE 7.6

Wall Chart with Question Prompts for Literature-Response Journals

1. Who was your favorite character? Why?
2. Which character did you dislike most? Why?
3. Are you like any character in the story? Explain.
4. If you could be any character, who would you be? Explain.
5. What does this story remind you of in your life?
6. What kind of person do you think the author of this story is?
7. How do you respond to this story so far?
8. Do you share any of the characters' feelings in the story? Explain.
9. Tell about a time when you had an experience or problem like _____'s. How did you solve your problem?
10. How would you interpret _____'s situation at this point in the story? What advice would you give at this point?
11. What is the most important word, phrase, or paragraph in the story? Explain.
12. If you were a teacher, would you want your students to read this story? Tell why.

> *Develop a list of prompts similar to those in Figure 7.6 for use with nonfiction.*

Respond to your students' journal writing on a regular basis for the purpose of exchanging ideas and thoughts with children about the literature, not to correct spelling and grammar. It is important that you search for positive features in children's responses but also that you be honest when ideas are not understood. Graves (1990) comments that early in this process students may write neutral accounts and summaries of what they read and only later begin to write true responses, in which they talk about the effect of the literature on their lives or connect ideas from the text to their insights or ideas. True responses can sustain dialogue between teacher and students on a topic for weeks.

> *Five Patterns Noted in Literature-Response Journals*

Hancock (1992) has identified five patterns in students' Literature-Response Journals at the sixth-grade level: (1) character interaction (student talks to or offers advice to characters), (2) character empathy (student reacts to emotions expressed by characters), (3) prediction and validation (student expresses belief about what will happen and confirms or denies original thinking), (4) personal experiences (student connects own life experiences to those of main characters or to story events), and (5) philosophical reflections (student reveals personal values and convictions). You may wish to comment on patterns you observe in students' writing and prompt them to try other patterns of response. You might ask, for example, "In what other ways could you respond to the main character?" and "How do you connect your personal experiences to the story?"

As students become experienced at gaining insight from Literature-Response Journals, encourage them to share selected responses with a partner on a voluntary basis. Discuss the concepts of privacy and confidentiality before students do peer-journaling. You will find that students respond positively to both peer and individual Literature-Response Journals.

Literature-Response Groups

Literature-response groups provide an opportunity for students to share their ideas and viewpoints about a piece of literature (Lehr & Thompson, 2000). Discussion involves specific question and statement prompts, based on your instructional objectives. Some examples follow:

literature-response groups
structured discussion groups in which students share ideas about a literature selection

1. Tell about a time when you had an experience or a problem like Ira's in *Ira Sleeps Over* (Waber, 1972). How did you solve your problem?
2. How do you interpret Dicey's situation in *Dicey's Song* (Voight, 1983)? What advice would you give her at this point?
3. If you were going to interpret this part of *Farewell to Manzanar* (Houston & Houston, 1973) as art, music, or dance, what would it look, feel, or sound like? What would be the most effective way to present your interpretation?

> *Discussion Prompts for Literature-Response Groups*

After working through the prompts individually, students enter into small-group discussion (four or five students in each group) and then share their results in a large group. Response groups should have clear instructions on what they are expected to achieve during their discussion time and to contribute to the whole-class discussion. Reading-response groups may be used occasionally on a small scale or they can be brought together for an entire literature unit in which children propose, design, and develop a group project.

Because reading-response-group instruction is less structured than teacher-led discussions, groups occasionally have difficulty being successful. Students get off the subject or off task. When reading-response groups do work well, the key to success appears to be well-constructed and well-communicated task goals that clearly define what students are to do. Students are more successful when they have an interest in the literature-response topic and experience with cooperative learning or collaborative group work.

> *Literature-Response Groups with Nonfiction*

The literature-response-group strategy can also be used to respond to expository writing in content areas such as science and social studies. The main difference is that the prompts to guide discussion focus more explicitly and narrowly on the text content than do literature prompts. O'Flahavan (1989) recommended that teachers use three questions with subject-area response groups, focusing on the following areas: (1) background knowledge—what the children already know about the text topic, (2) ideas derived from the text—what meaning students construct, and (3) ideas that go beyond the text—how students interpret or react to the text. In a social studies unit on community, for example, the following three reading-response prompts might be used:

What is the purpose of each question prompt in this example?

1. In your own words, describe our neighborhood community. What do you think are the most important parts of a community?
2. Based on what you read, what new ideas would you add to your definition of "community"? Why are you adding those ideas?
3. What would you like to add to or change about our community? What would you do first? Why?

You can make subject-area reading-response groups more effective by taking time to refine the discussion prompts you develop. Prompts should focus on important ideas rather than niggling details; they should invite students to "think big," beyond the limits of the text; and they should make them curious and eager to learn more.

How To Do . . .

Literature-Response Groups

1. Determine your discussion objectives for the lesson or unit (literature or content area).
2. Establish literature-response groups (four to five students in each group).
3. Ensure that students know how to work in literature-response groups; develop and communicate expectations for group work.
4. Focus attention on the response prompts; these may be identified by number from your wall chart of prompts, written on the board, or prepared as a handout for each group.
5. Observe students working in their literature-response groups, and monitor group progress.
6. Lead whole-class discussion of groups' responses to prompts; encourage students to reflect on the response-group process.

- Because all classrooms have students reading at a wide range of levels, to be a highly effective teacher you will use several different books for literature-response groups. For example, one group of advanced readers may read and discuss a piece of children's or adolescent literature that might be somewhat difficult for the average student in that grade. Several small groups may be comprised of average readers enjoying and sharing ideas about a different book of good literature. Another group can be delayed readers, who, like their peers, are reading a high-quality book, but one commensurate with their reading level.

DELAYED READER
ADAPTATION

The Book Club

The **book club** strategy shares many of the procedures used in developing literature-response groups. The central philosophy behind the book club strategy is to provide a learning context and an opportunity for students to become fully engaged in authentic and "grand conversations" (Eeds & Wells, 1989) that provide for exploration and interpretation of their ideas based on a literature selection (Frank, Dixon, & Brants, 2001; Kong & Fitch, 2003; Kooy, 2003; Tierney & Readence, 2000, pp. 93–98).

The instructional process for the book club uses the following features in literature exploration:

1. *Literature selection.* The teacher and students select the literature text. The same text may be used by the entire class or several books may be identified that connect to a common theme. High-interest text and appropriate difficulty level are critical to the success of the book club.
2. *Community share.* The teacher involves the whole class in developing "mini-lessons" necessary for conducting discussions, reading, writing, and vocabulary development. This "share" is used at the beginning of an individual lesson or a unit and may involve direct instruction by the teacher, scaffolding of student discussion, identification of key discussion issues, and purpose-setting discussion.
3. *Discussion groups.* May be teacher- or student-led and extend over fifteen to twenty minutes. Discussions are designed to actively engage a small group of students around a high-interest question or idea related to a specific section of a trade book. For example, after reading Chapter 11 of *Charlotte's Web,* "How do you think Charlotte felt after weaving the words "SOME PIG!" in her web? How would you have felt? Why?" These discussions may also range from supportive exploration of students' ideas to mini-lessons on such areas as word recognition and comprehension.
4. *Sustained reading.* Actively involves students for at least seventy-five minutes each week. This time may be distributed across activities such as high-interest reading, reading logs, or mapping. Teacher observations of student participation in these activities become important to guide and assist in instructional planning.
5. *Writing activities.* Viewed as critical to encourage students' active engagement and personal response to literature. These may take a variety of forms, including summary and synthesis writing, semantic mapping, and literature-response journal writing.

Literature Circle

The **literature circle,** while possessing similar instructional objectives, is somewhat more structured than the Book Club. Role assignments and principles of cooperative learning are used to help students work together and share discussions based on personal response to literature (Long & Gove, 2003).

The literature-circle strategy is initiated as the teacher presents an overview of four or five high-interest literature selections of varying difficulty levels. Ideally there will be a theme or themes that can be used to connect these texts. Each selection must be available in multiple copies. Individual students are encouraged to explore each text briefly to identify the text of greatest interest.

The teacher then forms several literature circles, consisting of five or six students each, based on student interest and reading level. After each circle has been formed, specific student roles are identified by each group. The roles represent various jobs needed to facilitate the discussion of the literature selection. These include the *discussion leader,* who develops questions and keeps the discussion on track; the *summarizer,* who provides a final summary of the selection; the *illustrator,* who provides a graphic summary of the piece; the *literary reporter,* who identifies key words or short passages that create outstanding imagery; and the *connector,* who connects the text world to the students' real world. These student roles should change periodically to enable each student to serve in a different role. The above roles, definitions, and student identifications should be placed on chart paper for easy student reference.

The literature circles will normally continue over several weeks, depending on the length of the book selected by each circle. You will need to visit each circle on a weekly basis to note progress, to help students follow their assigned roles, and to encourage discussion.

book club
an instructional strategy designed to engage students fully in conversations about literature

➤ *Five Book Club Features*

literature circle
a literature discussion group that uses cooperative-learning principles and role assignments to explore literature

➤ *Literature-Circle Roles*

Upon completion of the literature selections, you may elect to have the students who represent the same roles in each circle meet and share their ideas on their book. For example, the discussion leaders would all meet together and the same would hold true for all of the summarizers, and all of the illustrators. This provides the opportunity for each student to learn about the books read in other groups.

To conclude the literature-circle experience, students in each group should decide on how best to present its book to the class. This may take a variety of forms such as a book advertisement, a book-review panel, a mystery book jacket, or other book-sharing presentations such as those developed in the following discussion.

Book-Sharing Strategies

Book reports have been used by teachers over the years as a way of ensuring that students read books. This is still the case in many classrooms. In your elementary school years, you probably experienced the dreaded "Book Report Due Day." The night before Due Day, you finished reading or skimming the book in order to do the report. This often involved writing the name of the author, the book title, and, in the intermediate grades, the publisher and copyright date at the top of the page, followed by a detailed summary of the book. Enterprising students learned how to mine book-jacket text to create summaries; some students simply plagiarized. Teachers returned book reports with red-lined corrections and little if any comment on students' ideas about the book.

Most children abhor book reports, and rightly so. Book reports are the epitome of teaching as inquisition—in which children must "prove" they have consumed text—and the antithesis of what we should be doing with books in school. What we should be doing is engaging in "grand conversations" (Eeds & Wells, 1989) about books children have read and enjoyed.

Consider other ways for students to share their reading interests and responses. Start by making sure that students are reading books they like and can read comfortably. Clarify that the purpose of book sharing is to share with others ideas and responses about books. Then design book-sharing options that actively involve students in oral and written discussions and artistic expression. Nine suggestions for book-sharing activities follow:

> *Nine Book-
> Sharing Ideas*

1. *Partner book sharing.* Students share responses through their Literature-Response Journals. In targeted sharing, they might, for example, share responses to only the first chapter of the book to pique reader interest.
2. *Small-group book sharing.* Students are divided into groups of three or four individuals; each student brings a favorite book and describes a favorite character or part of the book.
3. *Individual or partner letters to the book's author or illustrator.* Students write letters for the purpose of sharing enjoyment of a book or character or asking a question about a character or about the way the book was written and illustrated.
4. *Individual or partner illustrations of a favorite character from a favorite book.* Illustrations might be used for a bulletin board display titled "My Favorite Book Character."
5. *Individual, partner, or small-group book advertisement.* Using book characters and a key story event, students prepare billboard advertisements to "sell" the book to other students. Advertisements might be used for a bulletin board display titled "Will You Buy It?"
6. *A partner or small-group "Television or Internet Book Review Panel."* Students present the pros and cons of their most and least favorite books, either in a talk-show format or on the computer. Students might produce the show on videotape or publish the reviews on the Web.
7. *An individual- or partner-designed "Mystery Book Jacket."* On the front of the jacket, students give clues to the story in artwork or written form; the book's author and title are hidden on the inside of the jacket. The book jackets might be displayed on a bulletin board with the title "Do You Know This Book?"
8. *Self-stick note responses.* Students respond to passages they select in a story by writing their response on a self-stick note and attaching the note to the page beside the passage. Later, they select several of their responses to share with a partner or small group. Self-stick notes may be used when they are reading different books or the same book.
9. *Bookmark response and sharing.* Prepared bookmarks invite students to respond to their reading (e.g., "If you were to create a dance from this story, what would it be like?" "If you

wanted to interview a character from this book, which one would it be and why?" "What song does this book remind you of?"). Students develop their responses and share them with a partner or group.

Sustained Silent Reading (SSR)

Sustained Silent Reading (SSR) is an instructional strategy that involves everyone reading every day in the classroom, including the teacher. This strategy, which has been used effectively in schools over the past several decades, is appropriate for all grade levels (Gambrell, 1996; McCracken & McCracken, 1978). SSR is designed to build positive attitudes toward reading and to give students a daily opportunity to read material of their choice. In SSR, students choose their own reading material, which may be books, magazines, and other materials. The time period for SSR ranges from five to fifteen minutes, depending on grade level.

Prepare students for SSR one or two days beforehand. Emphasize that a special reading time will be set aside for everyone in the classroom to read a favorite book or other reading material. At the kindergarten and primary grade levels, designate five to ten minutes, and for the intermediate grades, ten to fifteen minutes. Each student should select reading matter from the classroom literature collection, school library, or home. Be sure that you select your favorite book for SSR also. To make simple markers with which to indicate stopping and starting points, you or the students can cut strips of construction paper and write each reader's name on one. Establish the following rules for SSR, and review them before you initiate the strategy (Tierney, Readence, & Dishner, 1990):

1. Everyone in the room reads during SSR.
2. No interruptions are allowed during SSR. If you have questions or comments, you will need to wait until everyone is finished reading. SSR is silent reading. Talking and whispering do not count as SSR.
3. You will not be asked to report on what you have read.
4. SSR reading time will be for _____ minutes, every day starting at _____ and ending at _____ .

A simple wall chart with these four rules will remind students about SSR. Have substitute books on hand for students who forget their books.

Some teachers and students find the "no talking or whispering" rule of SSR too restrictive given students' natural inclination to read and talk about books together. You can adjust this rule according to your instructional goals and the needs of your students. Using SSR daily with students and modeling reading enjoyment builds positive attitudes toward reading and self-selected reading material.

Reader's Theatre

Teachers use Reader's Theatre to create interest in and enthusiasm about literature (Black & Stave, 2007; Martinez, Roser, & Strecker, 1998/1999). In **Reader's Theatre,** students do not dramatize stories; rather, story characters come to life through students' voices as they read character parts in dramatic play form and use gestures to accompany their reading. This strategy develops students' understanding of characterization, setting, plot, and problem resolution. The script is formed using a narrator, who relates descriptive passages, and reader-actors, who speak characters' dialogue. Students have the opportunity to enter and become part of the work as they interpret the script. Reader's Theatre can be used with students across the elementary grades but is most effective after students have gained some fluency.

Introduce Reader's Theatre by telling your students that actors work together to read a play script without costumes or actions. Discuss the similarities and differences between television or movie scripts and characters' dialogue in narrative text. Consider possible stories you might use—favorite stories that contain interesting characters, plenty of dialogue, a story plot with high suspense, and a special ending. Some examples for the primary grades are storybooks such as *Miss Nelson Is Missing!* (Allard & Marshall, 1977) and *Hi, Cat!* (Keats, 1970). At the upper primary, intermediate, and middle grades, chapter selections might include Chapter 11 ("The

---

Sustained Silent Reading (SSR) an instructional strategy in which students and teacher read silently in class every day

➤ *Classroom Rules for SSR*

the Highly Effective Teacher

Reader's Theatre a group strategy in which students take roles to read aloud a script they create from a literature selection

Strategies in Use — Using Sustained Silent Reading (SSR)

Ms. Koffman decided to try SSR with her fifth graders. On the first day, she reminded students of the four SSR rules and indicated that they would read for fifteen minutes. Each student had selected a book to read and had prepared a personal bookmark. Ms. Koffman reminded students that they would not be asked to report on what they were reading. She then asked students to open their books and begin reading. She set a kitchen timer for fifteen minutes to keep track. Ms. Koffman then joined her students in SSR, reading one of her own favorite books.

After about ten minutes, Ms. Koffman heard talking and observed Mark, José, and Kevin discussing their soccer game at recess. She made the decision to stop SSR at this point. She asked all the students to insert bookmarks and close their books. She walked over to where Mark, José, and Kevin were sitting and briefly reviewed the SSR rules with the class. She then reset the kitchen timer for ten minutes and asked the students to resume SSR.

When the alarm sounded to conclude SSR, Ms. Koffman asked the students to insert book-marks, close their books, and place them in their desks. She briefly reviewed the SSR rules again and indicated that they would continue SSR the next day.

Ms. Koffman used SSR for five days and successfully established the routine with her students. At the beginning of the next week, she decided to conclude the SSR experience with a shared response and asked students to record their ideas in their Literature-Response Journals, using a prompt of their choice.

CRITICAL THINKING

1. Do you agree with the way Ms. Koffman handled the interruption by Mark, José, and Kevin on the first day of SSR? Why or why not?
2. Why is a timing device such as a kitchen timer useful in implementing SSR?
3. Why was it important that Ms. Koffman participate in the SSR experience with her students?
4. What other literature activities or strategies would you use to follow the SSR experience?

Miracle") in *Charlotte's Web* (White, 1952) and Chapter 2 ("What Lucy Found There") in *The Lion, the Witch, and the Wardrobe* (Lewis, 1950).

Distribute a photocopy of the selection to each student. Have the students work in small groups to decide what parts of the selection should be narrated; students may wish to make some deletions or minor revisions for this purpose. Also, have students decide who will act as narrator and key characters, what their reading parts will be, and what simple props (e.g., hats) and sound effects would help carry the story. Record all the students' decisions and roles.

How might you use Literature-Response Journals with Reader's Theatre?

Prepare for the production by gathering props at the place where the Reader's Theatre will take place and having each student read his or her part silently. Let students use colored highlighter pens to mark their speaking parts. Then have the narrator and actors practice reading the story aloud. Encourage students to use voice intonation and expression to convey the feelings, emotions, and moods intended in the story. Students who are not in the production can be the audience. Coach audience members to use their imaginations as they listen to help create the characters and story setting in their minds. After the performance, explore how different roles were portrayed, how the production might be revised and refined, and how the audience reacted.

Investigative Questioning Procedure (InQuest)

Investigative Questioning Procedure (InQuest)
an instructional strategy in which children respond to literature by taking different points of view

Investigative Questioning Procedure (InQuest) (Shoop, 1986) is an instructional strategy designed to encourage children to enter a story by role playing. Students respond to the story by taking the point of view of either the central character or an investigative reporter who interviews the central character about story events. The teacher identifies a stop-point in the story at which an important story event occurs. The students then imagine a news conference at the scene of the event. One student assumes the role of the major character and is interviewed by student

How To Do . . .

Reader's Theatre

1. Introduce, explain, and discuss the concept of Reader's Theatre with your students. Be sure to distinguish Reader's Theatre from dramatization.
2. Consider stories for adaption to a Reader's Theatre production. Select several from which your students may choose.
3. Reproduce copies of the selected story so that each member of the group has his or her own copy.
4. Guide students as they mark the story to create the narrator part; assist them in deciding how much of the descriptive content of the story should be part of the narrator's role.
5. Guide the group's determination of any minimal props or sound effects needed. Record these on the chalkboard.
6. Have students choose roles and go through the story as a group, each marking his or her speaking parts with a highlighter pen.
7. Give the members of the group an opportunity to practice reading, both within the group and independently, working on their own parts.
8. Do the performance. Lead a follow-up discussion with the group and the audience.

- **Reader's Theatre is a particularly beneficial strategy for delayed readers because of opportunities to repeatedly read a selection—doing so for authentic reasons (an original reading when the story is selected, rereading to determine the parts the narrator should take, and so on). You can add additional meaningful practice for delayed readers in a number of ways—for example, practicing your own part orally with a partner; after the original performance, reading it as a group presentation to a lower grade. Do be certain that the text selected is at the student's instructional level, not frustration level. Grouping students in your class by reading level for this activity is a solution to the latter concern.**

DELAYED READER ADAPTATION

reporters. The goal is to explore how character traits, story setting, story events, and story plot fit together to form a story. InQuest has been used effectively with students from grades 3 through 6.

Introduce InQuest by leading a discussion about reporters and the questions they ask. The objective is to help students understand how to form questions that will reveal information about character traits and motivation, story setting, events, and how these are connected to the plot. Shoop (1986) suggests that students view examples of investigative reporting in the media to discover the types of questions asked. Explain the following questioning principles:

- Questions that get longer responses are most desirable.
- Questions that receive yes/no answers can be followed by "Why?" to obtain more information.
- Interview questions often elicit information, a reflection, an evaluation, or a prediction.
- A good interview has a variety of question types.

➤ *Principles for Investigative Questioning*

Next, identify a literature selection from your basal reader or a story that contains an interesting central character and clear plot development, and distribute copies.

Ask students to read the story and stop at the place you designate, a stop-point that represents a point of critical action in the story. For example, in *Charlotte's Web* (White, 1952), a good InQuest stop-point occurs on page 77 when Lurvy takes Wilbur's breakfast to the barnyard early one morning and discovers the words "SOME PIG!" in a spider's web. Ask students to keep in mind the questions they would like to ask the character (in this case, Lurvy) at this point. Students role-play a news conference as investigative reporters representing the school paper.

The student being interviewed takes the point of view of the character and answers the reporters' questions using the information revealed up to that point in the story. The reporters

the Highly Effective Teacher

on Technology and the Use of Literature

1. Visit the Web site for Aaron Shepard's Reader's Theatre: **www.aaronshep. com/rt.** Choose a script for your class to use in a Reader's Theatre performance.
2. Divide the class into small groups. Have the students in each group choose a category to read from the Online Children's Stories Web site: **www.acs.ucalgary.ca/ ~dkbrown/stories.html.** Have the students record their impressions in their Literature-Response Journals.
3. Select a story from the Web site Myths and Fables from around the world, located at **www.afro.com/children/myths/**

    myths.html. Construct questions for students based on instructional objectives. Divide the class into reading-response groups where students can share their views and ideas.
4. Have students write poetry and post it at **www.poetryzone.ndirect.co.uk/index2. htm.**
5. Use the resources found at the Children's Literature Associations Web site: **www.acs. ucalgary.ca/~dkbrown/assoc.html,** or at the SuperKids Educational Software Review Web site: **www.superkids.com.** Have students share their favorites with the class.

use questions designed to elicit information about previous story events leading up to and explaining the event. For example, how did Lurvy discover the words in the web, how does he think the words got there, what does he think "SOME PIG!" means, and what will he do next? You may wish to model the role of the central character or reporter.

Use a follow-up discussion to identify some examples of good interview questions and responses students used. This discussion should reinforce the idea that evaluating information and forming predictions while reading can be of value in understanding character motivation, story events, and plot.

Evaluating Students' Progress in Responding to Literature

Evaluating students' responses to literature is an ongoing process over the school year. Evidence of growth can be found in observations of the students as they engage in, transact with, and respond to literature experiences (Lehr & Thompson, 2000). These observations will provide information that will enable you to adjust your instruction. The questions in Table 7.3 provide a checklist for informal evaluations. Your observations based on these questions will also provide important clues about the success of your literature program.

Summary and Classroom Applications

double entry journal

Go back to your notes in the Double Entry Journal at the beginning of the chapter that describe a book with special memories for you from your K–6 years. What predominant stance did you use when reading this book? What were your internal reader motivations when responding to the book? Which strategies presented in this chapter would you use to share this book with students?

TABLE 7.3

Evaluating Students' Progress in Literature Response and Engagement

	Often	Sometimes	Never
1. Do my students enjoy listening to stories read aloud and told in the classroom? Do they ask for certain books to be read over and over?	_____	_____	_____
2. Do they exhibit strong interest and enthusiasm in reading and exploring and checking out new literature from the classroom reading center and from the school library?	_____	_____	_____
3. Do they enjoy identifying and exploring informational books from the classroom reading center and the library?	_____	_____	_____
4. Do my students look forward to entering their ideas in their Literature-Response Journals and to participating in discussions of stories in class? Do they respond to my written responses and observations in their journals?	_____	_____	_____
5. Do they informally exchange information about story characters and story plots? Do they share ideas about content from informational books?	_____	_____	_____
6. Do they enter into response discussions eagerly and enthusiastically?	_____	_____	_____
7. Do they exhibit an understanding of and empathy with story characters in reading-response discussions and journals? In their discussions and journals, do they show growth in their ability to apply story-based insights to their own lives?	_____	_____	_____
8. Are the students becoming more fluent readers? Are they growing more independent in choosing books to read?	_____	_____	_____
9. Do they ask to take books home to read and share with a parent or sibling?	_____	_____	_____
10. Do they exhibit a sense of pride in literature-related projects, such as creating book posters, mystery book jackets, or other literature-related writing for display in the classroom?	_____	_____	_____

Chapter Summary

This chapter focused on the use of children's and adolescent literature and reader-response experiences to enhance students' positive attitudes and motivation toward reading and active comprehension. The use of high-interest literature and the opportunity for response to it are critical in achieving this end. The reader-response process involves reader identification, catharsis, and insight. Awareness of the six internal reader motivations, ranging from problem resolution to understanding self, also helps teachers connect students to literature.

Choosing a suitable instructional stance is basic to successful literature instruction. The aesthetic instructional stance helps students identify with story characters and enter into and transact with the story; it also provides an opportunity for story response and idea sharing. The efferent instructional stance is appropriate for idea and concept development.

The selection of appropriate literature and expository text for your classroom reading center is central to highly effective literature instruction. Highly effective teachers are familiar with quality children's and adolescent literature and connect these books with students' reading interests. Fiction, nonfiction, and poetry are three broad categories of literature, or literary genres. The school library, librarian, public library, and parents are important resources for literature instruction.

Instructional approaches and teaching strategies designed to encourage reader motivation, reader response, and active comprehension include reading aloud, storytelling, Literature-Response Journals, literature-response groups, Book Clubs, literature circles, book sharing, Sustained Silent Reading, Reader's Theatre, and InQuest.

Evaluation of students' progress in the classroom literature program through informal observation is an ongoing process with the goal of building positive attitudes and active comprehension through reader response to literature.

the Highly Effective Teacher

Strategies for Teaching Literature Response and Engagement

Reading Aloud
for enjoyment and motivation (combine with DL-TA)

Storytelling
for enjoyment and motivation (combine with GMA and concept webs or semantic maps)

Book Sharing
for enjoyment and motivation (combine with synonyms and antonyms, similes and metaphors, and SFA)

Literature-Response Groups
to develop skills in reading, writing, and sharing ideas through discussions (combine with DR-TA, DRA, GMA, and SDEI)

Literature-Response Journals
to record responses to literature (combine with DL-TA, DR-TA, ReQuest, reading aloud, storytelling, and vocabulary log or journal)

Book Club
to become fully engaged in exploring and interpreting literature (combine with literature-response groups, Literature-Response Journals, and SSR)

Literature Circle
to help students to work together and share personal responses to literature (combine book sharing, reading aloud, and Literature-Response Journals)

Reader's Theatre
to interpret and express stories (combine with DR-TA, DRA, and reading aloud)

THE HIGHLY EFFECTIVE TEACHER
with meaning-negotiation interactions, a literacy-rich learning environment, and instructional strategies for reading comprehension, vocabulary development, and word recognition and identification skills

SSR
to practice reading (combine with Literature-Response Journals)

InQuest
to analyze stories (combine with DR-TA, DRA, and ReQuest)

Applications: Bridges to the Classroom

1. Review the strategies discussed in this chapter and select one that has strong appeal for you. Describe how you would use this strategy to introduce a favorite literature selection to a small group of students at the grade level of your choice. If possible, implement your plan in practice teaching. Do students respond as you expect? What changes would you make to improve your literature instruction using this strategy?

2. Design a checklist you could use to identify a predominantly aesthetic stance and a predominantly efferent stance. Arrange a classroom observation, and use your checklist as you observe the teacher and students. What do you find regarding the teacher's instructional stance? How do students' responses reflect the teacher's stance? Share your ideas with a peer partner.

Professional Standards and Literature Instruction Using Response and Engagement Strategies

The standards identified in Figure 7.7 provide examples from literature instruction using response and engagement strategies for each of the five major standards found in the International Reading Association's *Standards for Reading Professionals—Revised 2003* (2003). These standards describe a number of teaching competencies critical to becoming an effective literacy teacher. You can see the complete list of Standards for Reading Professionals in Appendix C.

FIGURE 7.7

Professional Standards: Using Literature to Enhance Reading Motivation and Comprehension

Professional Standard	Example
1. Foundational Knowledge	**Element 1.4** Demonstrates knowledge of components of reading related to children's literature, including reader motivation and response, the influence of instructional stance on reader response, developmental reader interest, and types of children's literature; e.g., explains the steps in reader motivation and response, the role of instructional stance on reader response, and key sources of internal and external reader motivation.
2. Instructional Strategies and Curriculum Materials	**Element 2.2** Uses a wide range of instructional practices and materials for students at different stages of reading development; e.g., understands various types of literature and the connection to reader interest and motivation, uses a variety of instructional strategies such as Literature-Response Journals and groups, Book Clubs, literature circles, SSR, and InQuest to engage readers and develop increased comprehension and fluency.
3. Assessment, Diagnosis, and Evaluation	**Element 3.3** Uses assessment information to plan, evaluate, and revise instruction for students by using different types of literature at appropriate difficulty levels; e.g., uses observational information from reader-interest inventories, reader-response to various types of literature, and student responses to the literature-response and engagement inventory to evaluate student progress and adjust and plan further instruction.
4. Creating a Literate Environment	**Element 4.2** Uses a large supply of books, representing multiple levels, broad interests, and cultural and linguistic backgrounds; e.g., is knowledgeable about a wide range of literature, representing various levels of difficulty, interests, and cultural and linguistic backgrounds; organizes a classroom reading center that provides a range of literature at various difficulty levels with high interest; creates an attractive literacy environment that promotes a high level of individual and group-reading engagement and response.
5. Professional Development	**Element 5.1** Displays positive disposition related to reading and the teaching of reading; e.g., ensures that students project caring attitudes related to reading and to each other in the classroom, provides individual attention to each student to encourage positive and engaging experiences with literature at appropriate interest and difficulty levels, encourages individual response and engagement in small-group settings, and shares personal reading interests to provide positive disposition and role models for students.

Part 2 from IRA. (2004). Professional Standards and Ethics Committee, International Reading Association. *Standards for reading professionals—revised 2003*.

3. How was the process of identification, catharsis, and insight involved in your response to a book that profoundly influenced you? How did this process influence your motivation to read? How were your prior knowledge and experience connected to the identification and motivation process?

4. Review the literature-instruction goals and objectives discussed at the beginning of this chapter. Select one goal and corresponding objective, and note several specific questions or observations that would enable you to assess how well this goal and objective were being met. Arrange to observe a classroom teacher at the appropriate grade level, and use your evaluation checklist. What evidence do you find that the goal and objective are being addressed? How can you improve your checklist on the basis of your observations?

5. Develop an annotated list of children's and adolescent literature you wish to collect for your classroom reading center. Include a variety of literary genres in your selections and consult lists of award-winning children's literature. Read your selections on an ongoing basis and note ideas for using various teaching strategies in your literature instruction. Keep the list in your teaching portfolio.

Additional Research and Practice

1. **Ambe, E. B. (2007). Inviting reluctant adolescent readers into the literacy club: Some comprehension strategies to tutor individuals or small groups of reluctant readers.** *Journal of Adolescent & Adult Literacy, 50,* 632–638.

   This article explains how specific content area strategies and materials can be used to appeal to middle school students' interests. Emphasis is placed on the importance of increasing student motivation, developing prior knowledge, teaching specialized vocabulary, and utilizing the DR-TA comprehension strategy. (Practice)

2. **Long, T. W., & Gove, M. K. (2003/2004). How engagement strategies and literature circles promote critical response in a fourth-grade, urban classroom.** *The Reading Teacher, 57* (4), 350–361.

   This interesting, well-documented article provides a rational and detailed description of three engagement strategies— (1) ask, listen, honor, respond, and encourage; (2) investigate and find out; and (3) pose and solve problems—to promote a critical response comprehension approach teaching fourth-grade African American students. (Practice)

3. **Kong, A., & Fitch, E. (2002/2003). Using book club to engage culturally and linguistically diverse learners in reading, writing, and talking about books.** *The Reading Teacher, 56* (5), 352–362.

   This action research project provides an excellent description of the use of Book Club as a highly motivating way to increase readers' engagement with literature, leading to improved comprehension for fourth- and fifth-grade students. (Research/Practice)

CHAPTER 8

Developing Reading and Writing in Content Areas

Books are the carriers of civilization. Without books, history is silent, literature dumb, science crippled, thought and speculation at a standstill.

Barbara W. Tuchman (1912–1989),
American historian and author

Reading furnishes the mind only with materials of knowledge; it is thinking that makes what we read ours.

John Locke (1632–1704),
European philosopher

The following story, shared by Nancie Atwell (1990), captures the essence of sixth-grade reading and writing in the content areas (in this case, social studies) as many of us experienced it.

I think the assignment was typical: Pick a country and write a report about it. Describe its history, system of government, geography, population, major occupations, and natural resources. Include a topographical map, a bibliography, and an illustrated cover. At least twelve pages long. Due in one month, as homework.

Full of Anglophilia and sixth-grade arrogance I put in a bid for Great Britain, which the teacher okayed. This meant I would have to come up with four versions of all the above, one each for England, Ireland, Scotland, and Wales. Never mind that to do even one of the subtopics justice would require at least a book. . . .

The weekend before the report was due I finally adjourned to my bedroom and began. By Sunday afternoon I knew I was in deep trouble. I stayed up as late as my mother would allow that night, hardly slept, and went to school empty-handed the next morning. While my classmates bustled around me putting the finishing touches on their illustrated covers, I pretended to be fascinated with the inside of my desk. When the reports were passed up the rows to the front of the room, I held my breath. And the teacher . . .

Never mentioned the missing report. Not that day, not ever. For the remaining three months of the school year I lived, alternately, in dread and anticipation of the moment when she would take me aside and end the torture, a word I don't use lightly. I thought about the report all the time but had no idea what to do about it now that the deadline was past.

On the last day of sixth grade, in the flurry of cleaning up the room and saying our good-byes, my teacher handed back the social studies reports. I escaped to the girls' room when I saw her come around from behind her desk with a stack of illustrated covers in her arms, and that was that—except for the gnawing at my conscience that has never eased in all these years. What I realized in writing about this memory is that my sixth-grade teacher did not discover until the last day of school that I hadn't submitted the report. For the same reason that I had postponed writing it she had postponed grading it: sheer boredom. The reports, as tedious to read as they were to write, informed and entertained no one. I can't blame the teacher. The sixth-grade curriculum required a report on a country, and she had obliged. (pp. xi–xii)

Nancie Atwell's story is a vivid example of how well-intended, but not well-thought-out, instructional practices can cause learning events to go awry.

double entry journal

Describe an experience you have had that Nancie Atwell's story brings to mind. Then reflect on your favorite content area—science, social studies, English, art, or music—as a student. What kinds of reading and writing activities or experiences did your teachers use in that content area?

Chapter Objectives

After reading and discussing this chapter, you will be able to:

- understand the close relationships among reading, writing, and learning.
- visualize what students and teachers need to do to effectively read and comprehend content area text.
- guide students' successful reading and understanding of content area text by using a variety of instructional strategies, ranging from the content DR-TA and GMA to the SDEI and K-W-L Plus.

- help students gain skill and power as writers by using instructional strategies, ranging from the writing workshop and guided writing to content area journals and the beginning-research strategy.
- integrate reading and writing across the curriculum by using the authoring cycle, content area theme cycles, and thematic literature-based units.

Relationships among Reading, Writing, and Learning

> *Reading and writing are integral parts of the learning process.*

> *Study-skills instruction should be embedded in content area learning.*

In the field of reading and language development, the phrases *reading and writing across the curriculum* and *content area reading and writing* emphasize the fundamental importance of reading and writing in subject area learning. Where once educators viewed reading and writing as important but essentially technical adjuncts to learning—that is, as learning tools or study skills, which learners use in the course of acquiring knowledge—they now understand that reading and writing are integral parts of the learning process itself. The study-skills perspective was based on the belief that certain reading behaviors—for example, identifying main ideas, separating main ideas from significant details, and using graphs and charts—contribute to reading ability and thus to learning from subject-area texts. The greater the reading and study skills, the more students could learn from text. Study skills such as those listed in Figure 8.1 are critical for students to learn but should be taught in the context of literacy and content area learning rather than in isolation. Study-skills instruction is ideally embedded, contextual, authentic, and incidental to reading and writing purposes (Bean, 2000).

Today, reading and writing connections to learning are viewed from a new vantage point. Readers construct (or create) meaning *in the very act of reading,* as they extend their prior knowledge base, arrive at new insights, integrate new information, and construct new subject-area knowledge. These constructions of meaning during and after reading are influenced not only by application of reading and study skills but, more important, by the myriad interactions and transactions that occur in reading events—transactions involving readers' prior knowledge base, reader intent or stance, social interactions, reading and learning goals, and instructional decisions (Brozo & Simpson, 2007; Cote & Goldman, 2004; Moss, 2004; Ruddell & Unrau, 2004a).

FIGURE 8.1

Key Embedded Study Skills

1. Understanding and using book parts (tables of contents, indexes, marginalia, glossaries, etc.)
2. Alphabetizing, using headings and pronunciation guides, understanding abbreviations in reference sources (dictionaries, encyclopedias, atlases, etc.)
3. Using other references (telephone directories, newspapers, etc.)
4. Using the library (card files, data bases, Dewey Decimal System, etc.)
5. Adjusting reading to purpose (skimming, scanning, intensive reading)
6. Reading graphs, charts, maps, globes, and other pictorial information
7. Notetaking
8. Finding main ideas, separating main ideas from important details
9. Outlining
10. Summarizing
11. Report writing

Similarly, writers achieve insight *in the act of writing*. They develop new ideas as they write and from what they write (Heffernan, 2004). You probably have had the experience of writing something and realizing that you didn't know what you'd written until it came off the end of your pencil (or appeared on your monitor screen). Such experiences illustrate how writers achieve insight and create new thoughts as they write. Writing thus becomes a means for working through new ideas and constructing new knowledge rather than being simply a tool for recording what was previously learned.

The goal of content area reading and writing instruction is to create thoughtful readers and writers in mathematics, science, and social studies and to give children the deeply satisfying experience of really learning in school (Olness, 2007). Think about a time in your life when you *really* learned—a moment, an entire year, or an even longer period in or out of school. Remember how you felt and what you did during that learning time. Your memories might include visceral responses to learning (excitement, exhilaration, a sense of "having fun"); the realization that learning was easy and self-propelled or self-perpetuating; lots of talking about learning topics with interested others; solid, clear connections between what you were learning and what you already knew; avid reading and writing that became natural, integral parts of the learning process; curiosity and intense interest; a feeling that time was flying by during learning events.

> ➤ *Learning is doing.*

> ➤ *Learning is a source of personal satisfaction.*

This kind of eager learning response is the hallmark of real learning. If you are to create a learning environment that encourages such a response, you must be willing to look honestly at traditional instructional practices and eliminate those that are not rich, complex, and complete. Further, you must guide students' reading and writing in subject areas so that avid reading and writing become a natural part of all learning.

Table 8.1 (page 220) identifies the student's task and the teacher's role requirements necessary for effective reading and comprehension of content area text. These requirements closely parallel those found in the comprehension discussion in Chapter 5 (see Figure 5.2, page 124) and provide the basis for developing instructional strategies to help students achieve subject-area literacy.

the ★
**Highly
Effective
Teacher**
★

What is involved in learning from text?

Content Area Literacy in Perspective

The central role of reading and writing in content area learning compels teachers to reexamine how they view subject-area literacy and what they do in classrooms under the aegis of "teaching reading and writing in the content areas." Students' general reading and writing abilities will not transfer automatically to subject-area learning (Gunning, 2008; Yopp & Yopp, 2000b). Subject-area instruction must guide students' reading and writing to produce the kind of literacy interactions and transactions that yield rich, full learning opportunities. Such instruction not only assists students in learning the content but also teaches them how to become increasingly independent, fluent readers and writers in subject areas (Pappas, 2006).

TABLE 8.1

Student and Teacher Requirements for Effective Reading and Comprehension of Content Area Text

The Student's Task Is To	The Teacher's Role Is To
1. *Establish* a clear reading purpose and expected use of the reading experience.	1. *Discuss and negotiate* a clear understanding of purpose and expected use.
2. *Activate* background knowledge and content related to the text.	2. *Help* students *activate* background knowledge and *connect* to the content of the content area text.
3. *Recognize and acknowledge* attitudes and values related to the text content and use of the constructed meaning.	3. *Discuss and help connect* prior attitudes and values to the text content and reading experience.
4. *Use* key reading strategies to help comprehend text *during* reading and *after* reading as guided by the purpose and expected use.	4. *Develop* content area text processing strategies and the understanding of *how* and *when* to use these strategies, depending on the reading purpose and use.
5. *Activate* monitoring strategies to *check meaning construction* related to purpose based on background knowledge, text-based information, and discussion.	5. *Teach* students to be *aware of* the need to check meaning and *how to* check meaning using prior knowledge, text-based information, and classroom and community resources.
6. *Actively use* this process to acquire new concepts, knowledge, and understandings, and to integrate this learning with prior knowledge.	6. *Provide opportunity* to acquire and integrate new knowledge with prior knowledge through discussions, negotiated meaning, and active learning.

The strategies presented in this chapter will do three things:

1. Provide maximum opportunity for students to interact and transact with text, with their own prior knowledge base, and with each other for the purpose of learning.
2. Guide students' reading and writing in subject-area learning so that they become increasingly fluent subject-area readers and writers.
3. Integrate general reading and writing instruction with subject-area learning.

Teachers have a major responsibility for developing students' literacy abilities in subject areas. The instruction and the guidance they receive in their elementary and middle school years become the foundation for their growth and independence in subject-area reading and writing in later years.

Reading in the Content Areas

> *Strategies of Expert Readers*

The research conducted during the past three decades provides an excellent profile of the text-comprehension strategies that highly effective readers use. These strategies are summarized in the Research and Evidence-Based Practice: How Expert and Strategic Readers Comprehend Text feature on page 221.

Developing these expert-reader strategies should be the objective of content reading instruction in science, mathematics, and social studies. Students' strategic reading abilities with subject-area text must be developed without relying on the study-skills approach—rather, instruction must emphasize building connections, monitoring reading progress, repairing faulty comprehension, synthesizing information within and across texts, and using other reading strategies of expert readers.

Writing in the Content Areas

> *Writing should influence the learning process.*

Over the past decade, educators' understanding of the relationships between writing and learning has changed and broadened. The traditional role of writing in subject-area learning has been to record and document learning rather than to influence the learning process itself. This has led to an emphasis on written book and research reports and term papers.

Beginning with the first informational report they copied from an encyclopedia, students long perceived that the purpose of writing in subject-area learning was to "show what you know," even when using others' words rather than their own. Until the early 1980s, virtually all discussion of writing in subject areas focused on some form of report writing and the skills necessary for report writing, with an emphasis on mechanics like punctuation and outlining (Beach, 1983).

As with reading, writing instruction in the content areas must emphasize instructional practices and strategies that build connections between students' past knowledge and new information; enable them to monitor their meaning construction and to develop creative and meaningful syntheses of new information; and facilitate asking questions of themselves, the authors they encounter, and the text they compose (Heffernan, 2004).

the
**Highly
Effective
Teacher**

Guiding Students' Reading in Content Area Instruction

Teachers can guide students' reading of content area text by adapting, combining, and applying the instructional strategies discussed in Chapters 3 through 7 of this text. Strategies that are particularly effective in combination are the content Directed Reading-Thinking Activity (DR-TA), Group Mapping Activity (GMA), and Semantic Development and Enrichment Instruction (SDEI).

Content DR-TA

The content DR-TA adapts the DR-TA to subject-area texts (Haggard, 1989; M. R. Ruddell, 1988). This strategy begins with students gathered in two- or three-person teams. Each team has paper, pencil, and the text to be read. Student teams are first asked to write down everything they know about a general topic within which the lesson topic fits. For example, you might say, "Jot down everything you know about sharks," "Jot down everything you know about addition," or "Jot down everything you know about the Mississippi River." The students work together in their teams to compile a list, with one member of the team recording ideas. In general, give teams seven to eight minutes to work so that students have time to do some memory

> The DR-TA was introduced in Chapter 5. How is the content DR-TA different?

Research and Evidence-Based Practice

How Expert and Strategic Readers Comprehend Text

Did You Know?

- They constantly search for connections between what they know and the new information they encounter in the text as they read.

- They learn very early to distinguish important from less important ideas in the text they read.

- They take steps to repair faulty comprehension once they realize that they have failed to understand something.

- They sometimes consciously, and almost always subconsciously, ask questions of themselves, the authors they encounter, and the text they read.

- They continually monitor the adequacy of the summaries of text meanings they create, and they revise

these as the text progresses, with both expository and narrative material.

- They are especially adept at synthesizing information within and across texts and reading experiences.

- They make inferences during and after reading to achieve a full, integrated understanding of what they read.

These key conclusions regarding expert and strategic readers are derived from the following research and research reviews: Block & Pressley (2001); Cote & Goldman (2004); Duke et al. (2007); Guthrie & McCann (1997); Pearson et al. (1992); Pressley (2000); Pressley & Afflerbach (1995).

searching. With very young students and certain topics, reduce the working time to five or six minutes. As the students work, circulate around the room to hear what information is being exchanged, to find out what students already know, and to assist if teams are having trouble getting or staying on task.

After students have jotted down ideas, announce the specific topic of the lesson and give directions that focus the students' attention on that topic: "Today we're going to read a section in our text called 'Meet the Sharks.' On your list, put a check mark beside information you think you'll find in your reading. Add any new ideas that occur to you." After two or three minutes, have students read the text, circling or asterisking any listed ideas they find in their reading.

The students read the assignment individually; however, you can expect a considerable "buzz" of working discussion while they read. Because the student teams have generated their lists cooperatively, there's a tendency for them to notify each other when something on their list appears in the text; there is also a certain amount of claiming of ideas that individuals contributed to the list. Students will read to each other, chat about information found in the text, and discuss what items on their list should or should not be circled or asterisked.

After the reading, lead a short discussion on what information the students already knew and what information they learned in reading. This discussion might be directed by the question "What are some things you already knew about varieties of sharks?" followed by "What are some new things you learned about sharks?" The goal is to give the students an opportunity to begin the process of organizing the knowledge they've constructed during the learning event.

Group Mapping Activity (Content GMA Study Maps)

> ➤ *GMA was introduced in Chapter 5. How are content GMA Study Maps different?*

The GMA (Davidson, 1982), as it is used in content area instruction, focuses on Study Maps. The GMA is designed to help students integrate and synthesize information from text. As a study aid, maps are particularly useful in guiding students' learning and developing their ability to understand and remember information. Maps give students the "big picture" of topics that are taught over a period of days or weeks; they also capture and hold important details.

Content area Study Maps focus explicitly on the topic of study (e.g., varieties of sharks, adding three-place numerals, the flooding of the Mississippi) and function as a way to record and

How to Do . . .

A Content DR-TA

1. Ask student teams to list everything they know about a *general topic* (e.g., sharks, addition, the Mississippi River).
2. Announce the *specific topic* (e.g., varieties of sharks, adding three-place numerals, lessons of the Mississippi).
3. Ask students to predict what information on their lists will appear in the text, using a check mark (✓) to denote the information; have them add any new ideas to their lists.
4. Have students read the assignment and note how well they predicted by circling or putting an asterisk by any predicted ideas they find.

■ **Content area texts are frequently quite challenging for delayed readers. Partner reading is often a solution. Dyads (i.e., groups of two) read quietly together, helping each other with problem words. For content DR-TA, they would then work cooperatively to confirm the predictions.**

5. Lead a short discussion about what students knew before they read and what new information they found ("How well did you predict?" or "What were some of the things you knew before we read? What are some new things you found?").

keep information during a period of time or unit of study. An example of instructions for developing Study Maps follows (M. R. Ruddell, 1993):

> Without looking back at the book or talking to anyone, map your understanding of the important ideas in the reading we just did on varieties of sharks. You are going to use this map to record information as we go through our unit on sharks. Later, the map will help you as you develop your own shark project. Be sure to include on your map all the information you think is important. (p. 135)

As the students create their maps, you should observe, offering help to those who need it. Assure them that they can review the text later; avoid letting them get bogged down with the text in an attempt to get every detail on the map.

Working within their teams, students share their completed maps with one another. Direct students to identify for their team what they considered important in the reading, how they chose to organize their map, and why they organized it as they did. The other team members respond by asking questions to draw out more information (e.g., "Why did you organize your map that way?"). After sharing, teams make sure that everyone's map has all the important information on it. This is the time to encourage the students to check the text so that their maps are as complete as possible.

Study Maps reflect students' individual prior knowledge and thus will naturally vary considerably in appearance and emphasis (Walpole, 1998/1999). If your instructional purpose for using the maps is to prepare students for a test and you have specific information or knowledge goals that the test will cover, make sure students have every opportunity to know what those goals are. If you see maps that suggest confusion or misunderstanding, work individually with students to clarify meanings and eliminate any misunderstandings. Study Maps often change and grow when used throughout a unit; invite students to make changes or to start over, as they wish.

How does cooperative learning in DR-TA and GMA support content area comprehension?

Content Semantic Development and Enrichment Instruction (SDEI) Strategy

The content SDEI strategy can be used in content area learning in the same way SDEI is described in Chapter 6, pages 168–171. In this case, *focus words* are selected from the subject-matter textbook.

Because content area texts—that is, expository or information texts—are designed to teach new information, it logically follows that there often is much new vocabulary in these materials. This vocabulary is not commonly used in students' everyday language (Pappas, 2006). It would be quite surprising if you found that your elementary or middle school students' daily, informal

How might SDEI help students learn technical vocabulary in the content areas?

How to Do . . .

A Content GMA Study Map

1. Ask students to map what they believe to be the important information from the text without talking to anybody or looking back at the text. Remind the children that the maps will be used throughout the unit and should include all the information they consider to be important.
2. Have students share their maps with their partner or team. Remind them to tell each other *what* they chose to include, *how* they chose to map, and *why* they made choices they did.
3. Have partners or teams work collaboratively to finish the maps. Encourage students to refer to the text at this time.

- ■ **Delayed readers usually respond quite well to activities that help them organize information through a schematic drawing (such as a Study Map). In addition to focusing on selection of content, it is important to give preliminary instruction on how to prepare such a drawing and to describe various options for schematics. To review helpful suggestions for doing this, see the How To Do in Chapter 5 that discusses GMA for use with stories (page 154).**

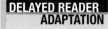
DELAYED READER ADAPTATION

interactions with their friends and parents were peppered with words and phrases such as "latitude," "minuend," "constitutional reform," "photosynthesis," and "cerebellum"! In fact, one reason students frequently have more difficulty with expository text (i.e., information material) than they do with narrative text (i.e., story-type material) is because of the heavy vocabulary load—unfamiliar words and lots of them. Understanding the meaning of this specialized vocabulary is often necessary for understanding the passage. What is more, this new vocabulary is not introduced at a moderate pace found in basic story-type material commonly used in reading instruction.

For these reasons, new content words are especially good candidates for the rich development activities and deep processing inherent in the SDEI strategy.

Other Vocabulary Development Strategies

Concept webs (see Figure 6.4, page 174), semantic maps (see Figures 6.5, 6.6, and 6.7 on pages 176, 177, and 178), and Semantic Feature Analysis (SFA) are also useful in vocabulary-development strategies for content area reading. An example of SFA applied to the study of planets is found in Figure 8.2. (See below.)

K-W-L Plus

K-W-L Plus
a reading comprehension strategy based on students' analysis of their prior knowledge, learning goals, and new learning; supplemented by mapping

K-W-L Plus (Carr & Ogle, 1987; Ogle, 2004; Tierney & Readence, 2000) resembles a combination of the content DR-TA and the GMA. *K* stands for what students already know, *W* represents what they want to know, and *L* is what they learned. *Plus* refers to mapping. K-W-L Plus begins with students listing everything they know about a topic under the *K* on a K-W-L worksheet (Figure 8.3, page 227). The students then brainstorm what they want to know about the topic and list those items under *W* on the worksheet. They then read the passage and summarize what they've learned under the *L* on the worksheet. Note in Figure 8.3 that information in column *L*

FIGURE 8.2

A Student's Semantic Feature Analysis of Planets in Earth's Solar System

Planets in the Earth's Solar System						
	Closer to the Sun Than the Earth	Larger Than Earth	Has Moon	Has Rings	Inner Planet	Orbits the Sun
Earth	−	−	+	−	+	+
Jupiter	−	+	+	−		−
Mars	+	−	+	−	+	+
Mercury	+	−		−	+	+
Neptune	−	+		−		−
Pluto	−	+		−		−
Saturn	−	+		+		−
Uranus	−			−		−
Venus	+	−	+	−	+	

+ = Student believes feature is true of that planet
− = Student believes planet lacks that feature
Matrix items will later be checked against reading material.

Figure from Cunningham, Patricia M., & Cunningham, James W. (1987, February). Content area reading-writing lessons. *The Reading Teacher, 40* (6), 506–512. Copyright © 1987 by Patricia M. Cunningham and the International Reading Association. All rights reserved.

How to Do . . .

Content SDEI

1. From your geography, history, science, or health book, select five focus words for your content area lesson to be used for detailed study. Choose the words that are most critical for understanding the topic being studied and that will be very useful to know in future lessons on the topic.
2. Provide an overview of these and other possible problem words, briefly attending to pronunciation and meaning.
3. Have students read the selection.

■ **If all students in the class are working from the same content area selection (book, article, etc.) and if the selection is to be read silently, be particularly sensitive to the needs of delayed readers. The heavy vocabulary load in content area texts can be challenging for average students and is especially so for delayed readers. Remain in the vicinity and help with word identification as needed.**

DELAYED READER ADAPTATION

4. After discussing important information from the selection, use the chalkboard to place each focus word in a brief context taken directly from the material just read. Involve your students in active review of each word's meaning in the content area lesson.
5. Broaden and deepen understanding of word meanings through a high-interest semantic development and enrichment lesson. For example, you might choose from one of the following (or from other activities suggested in this book that take word study beyond the simple stating of definitions): (a) Pose intriguing questions about one or two of the words, such as "If a chair is made of wood and wood comes from trees, could *photosynthesis* occur in a chair? What part of this word's meaning gives you the answer to the question?" (b) Place students in groups of three. Ask them to write similar questions for the other target words. Have groups challenge each other with their questions. (c) As a whole group, rewrite definitions of target words so that they could be understood by students in a lower grade (e.g., fourth-graders are asked to rewrite the definition of *cerebellum* so that first-graders would understand it). The teacher writes students' ideas on the board, making changes as they are offered until the rewriting is accomplished successfully to meet the goal.
6. Students look for target words in out-of-school settings. Examples are brought to class, discussed, and placed in individual context area vocabulary notebooks.

is categorized and given category designations. These designations become the starting point for developing maps based on K-W-L (Figure 8.4, page 227).

K-W-L Plus is also suited to partnership and student teamwork. Keep copies of K-W-L worksheets readily available to assist you in directing learning in class and for students pursuing independent research and study. K-W-L worksheets and maps also are useful for evaluating student progress.

Directed Inquiry Activity (DIA)

The **Directed Inquiry Activity (DIA)** is an instructional strategy developed to apply the DR-TA to subject-area instruction (Thomas, 1986). The DIA, while similar to the content DR-TA, is more structured. This strategy has students predict the content of text, uses students' prior knowledge, and relies heavily on follow-up response probes.

In preparation for the DIA, develop—at different thinking levels—five or six inquiry questions from the material to be read. These questions, which should focus on important ideas and issues raised by the lesson text, will be used initially to get children to make some predictions about what the text will contain (e.g., "What significance do the symbols on the map have for a specific country? How do you think this information will help in understanding the text?" or

Directed Inquiry Activity (DIA) an instructional strategy that applies DR-TA to content area instruction, using predictions and question probes

Strategies in Use

Combining DR-TA, GMA Study Maps, and SDEI

Mary Hervey's fifth graders were excited about the comet Hale-Bopp they had watched during the months of March and April. She photocopied a news article titled "The Mystery of the Great Comet" for each member of her class. In preparing to use this scientific article, she reviewed the How To Do steps for the content DR-TA, GMA Study Maps, and SDEI, which she planned to use in combination.

Mary divided the class into three-person teams and initiated the content DR-TA by asking each team to list everything they knew about the general topic of comets in five or six minutes. One member of each of the nine teams was elected to record the ideas. The noise level in the room increased as students searched their memories and shared ideas about comets. Next, Mary announced the specific topic—the article "The Mystery of the Great Comet," about the Hale-Bopp comet the students had watched in the sky. She then asked students to review their lists, take two or three minutes to put a check mark beside any information they thought they would find in the article, and add any new ideas.

Mary passed out the article for students to read; she instructed them to circle or underline any ideas from their list that they found in the article. Afterward, they compared their prior knowledge about comets with the new information they learned from the news article.

Mary then moved her students to a Content GMA, during which they included on their maps all of the information they thought was important about the comet Hale-Bopp. After mapping "The Mystery of the Great Comet," members of each student team shared their maps with each other and explained *what* they believed was important in the article, *how* they chose to organize their map, and *why* they organized it as they did.

After the GMA activity, with twenty minutes remaining in the period, Mary used the SDEI strategy to broaden and deepen her students' understanding of several word meanings. From the Hale-Bopp article, she had identified three focus words—*comet, asteroid,* and *orbit*. She had listed the words on the chalkboard in the context in which they were found in the article. First, she asked *what* the word seemed to mean in the article and *why* the word was important to the article. She then posed several questions not answered in the article to extend her students' thinking. For example, "Based on the meanings we just discussed and on the information you read in the article, could an asteroid become a comet? Tell why you think your answer is correct." She allowed the students to debate their points, realizing that this discussion would promote deeper understanding. After checking the definition of each word, the students entered the words on their GMA Study Maps where they seemed to make the most sense.

To prepare for an assignment to use the words in an out-of-school setting, she returned to the vocabulary item *orbit* and asked the students to research the orbit of Hale-Bopp in relation to Earth and our sun. She encouraged her students to use the Web and, if possible, to involve their parents. The next day, after sharing their findings on the orbit of Hale-Bopp, the definition of each word was briefly discussed and added to each individual's content area vocabulary notebooks.

CRITICAL THINKING

1. What is the value in using this combination of instructional strategies (content DR-TA, GMA Study Maps, and SDEI)?
2. What role did reading and writing play in meaning construction as these strategies were used?
3. What opportunities were present for negotiating meaning collaboratively among the students?
4. What follow-up lesson would you develop based on Mary's lesson?

FIGURE 8.3

K-W-L Worksheet on Killer Whales

K (Know)	W (Want to Know)	L (Learned)
They live in oceans.	Why do they attack people?	D—They are the biggest member of the dolphin family.
They are vicious.	How fast can they swim?	D—They weigh 10,000 pounds and get 30 feet long.
They eat each other.	What kind of fish do they eat?	F—They eat squids, seals, and other dolphins.
They are mammals.	What is their description?	A—They have good vision underwater.
	How long do they live?	F—They are carnivorous (meat eaters).
	How do they breathe?	A—They are the second-smartest animal on earth.
		D—They breathe through blow holes.
		A—They do not attack unless they are hungry.
		D—They are warm-blooded.
		A—They have echo-location (sonar).
		L—They are found in the oceans.

Final category designations developed for column L, information learned about killer whales: A = abilities, D = description, F = food, L = location.

Figure from Carr, Eileen M., & Ogle, Donna M. (1987, April). K-W-L Plus: A strategy for comprehension and summarization. *Journal of Reading, 30* (7), 626–631. Copyright © 1987 by Eileen M. Carr and the International Reading Association. All rights reserved.

"Why do you think the purchasing power of the dollar has shrunk over the years? What factors might have produced this?") Questions may be written on the chalkboard or on individual worksheets for the students to use.

> *What thinking levels should inquiry questions represent?*

Ask students to preview the reading assignment, and show them how to page through the text, glancing at chapter and topic headings, reading bits and pieces of text, and looking at charts and graphs. After previewing, students use their background knowledge and the information they obtained from previewing to predict responses to the inquiry questions. Their predictions are recorded on the board or on the worksheets. Probe students' responses to find out how they arrived at their predictions (e.g., "What makes you say that?"). Following the discussion of their

FIGURE 8.4

Map Generated from a K-W-L Worksheet

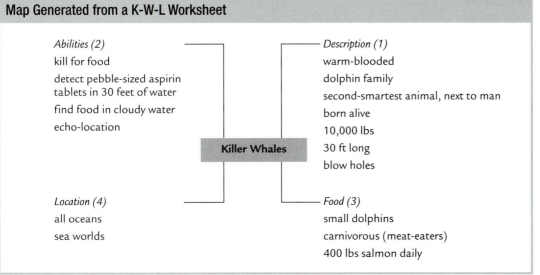

(1) through (4) indicate the order of categories the student chose later for writing a summary.

Figure from Carr, Eileen M., & Ogle, Donna M. (1987, April). K-W-L Plus: A strategy for comprehension and summarization. *Journal of Reading, 30* (7), 626–631. Copyright © 1987 by Eileen M. Carr and the International Reading Association. All rights reserved.

How to Do . . .

K-W-L Plus

1. Have students brainstorm what they know about the lesson topic (you may want to use partnerships or teams).
2. Direct them to organize what they know and make a list of their knowledge in the *K* column of the K-W-L worksheet.
3. Have students then list what they want to know about the topic in question under the *W* column; they should anticipate what they are going to read as much as they can.
4. Direct students to read the assignment; they may add questions to their *W* list as they read, if they wish.

DELAYED READER ADAPTATION

- **Because content area text often is more difficult to read than narrative, story-type material, post a chart of strategies to use when the going gets rough. McCormick (2007, p. 412) suggests these: (a) slow down and reread the hard part; (b) look back in the text and reread (text reinspection); (c) quickly skim the text ahead to see if the difficult parts are explained; (d) talk through your confusion with a partner; and (e) underline the hard parts and ask the teacher for help.**

5. Have students list what they learned under the *L* column and then categorize learned information and label the categories.
6. Ask students to develop their own maps, using the categories and information learned.
7. Lead a discussion as students display and explain their maps.
8. Develop appropriate follow-up activities.

---

predictions, the children read the passage to confirm or adjust the predictions, and then they generate additional responses to the inquiry questions.

> **How could the DIA be combined with reading-response groups (see Chapter 7) for content area (rather than literature) instruction?**

The DIA can be adapted for cooperative learning. Students work with partners or in teams to preview text and predict. Partners/teams then share their predictions and answer your questions probing their reasoning. After reading, the partners/teams develop collaborative responses to the inquiry questions and share these responses in whole-class discussion.

The DIA is particularly useful for focusing student attention on specific learning objectives. Inquiry questions should be broad-based and focus on important issues, and they should lead to further inquiry and investigation.

Guiding Students' Writing in Content Area Instruction

> **Impact of the National Writing Project**

Teaching practices to guide students' writing have been revolutionized as a result of teachers' participation in National Writing Project programs, which have turned teachers into writers. Teachers' growing awareness of their own power as writers and more fully integrated views of the reading and writing processes have led them to implement Writing Project practices, especially writing workshop.

Writing Workshop

writing workshop
writing instruction that involves daily immersion in the writing process

In **writing workshop,** a period of classroom time is set aside each day for students to be immersed in writing (Atwell, 1998; Calkins, 1991; Chihank, 1999). Ideally, writing workshop begins with children's entry into school and extends throughout the elementary grades and into middle and secondary schools.

Writing workshop focuses on process—engaging students in productive writing behaviors and events that lead to ever-increasing writing fluency and sophistication—rather than on product, although many examples of polished writing emerge from workshop activities. Priority is

How to Do . . .

A DIA

1. Determine lesson objectives, and write five or six inquiry questions that reflect these objectives.
2. Decide what portion of the text the students are to preview and note specific text features they should consult (e.g., chapter headings, marginal notes, charts and graphs, etc.).
3. Write the inquiry questions on the chalkboard or on a worksheet to be reproduced and distributed to students. Leave room for predictions and other responses.
4. Ask the students to preview the reading assignment and make predictions about the inquiry-question responses.
5. Lead a discussion in which they share their predictions; be sure to probe responses for logic and reasoning.
6. Have students read the assignment.
7. Lead a discussion to reexamine inquiry-question responses and refine knowledge in the light of new information. As a group, develop ideas and questions for further inquiry.
8. Lead or assign any follow-up activities (GMA and SDEI would both be appropriate).

■ **For delayed readers whose difficulties lie with comprehension, devoting time to thoroughly discussing a few higher-level questions may be instructionally more beneficial than answering numerous quick and easy ones. This is why DIA and other strategies described in this chapter are superior to conventional comprehension instruction for delayed readers.**

DELAYED READER ADAPTATION

given to providing students with the autonomy to decide on their writing topics and styles and to make critical decisions about editing, the final form a piece of writing takes, how and whether to submit a piece for grading, and other aspects of writing production. In implementing these writing workshop principles, you will need to consider instructional time, classroom environment, workshop structure, student writing time and conferences, sharing time, and record keeping and evaluation.

Writing-Workshop Time

Class time is essential for writing workshop, which works best when it happens every day and when it covers a good portion of the morning or afternoon. At minimum, writing workshop needs to occur three days a week (Graves, 1983), preferably the same three days. A regular and dependable schedule stimulates children to anticipate writing—to gather information, to consider alternate ways of saying things, and to revise and rethink their writing and ideas even when they are not in school. This anticipation and rehearsal for writing are part of how professional writers work, and how they polish their writing and their thinking.

Why are anticipation and rehearsal important in writing instruction?

To find time for writing workshop, you may want to reconsider the amount of time you have allocated for reading, spelling, and language arts. You might integrate all or most of this time and instruction into a reading-writing workshop. Or you may prefer to combine writing workshop with project- or theme-based instruction that integrates other subject areas. Also, careful analysis of your weekly schedule might reveal slack time that you can creatively combine with other "found" time for a writing-workshop schedule.

Writing-Workshop Environment and Organization

Writing workshop requires writing equipment and supplies, including generous amounts of lined and unlined paper of different sizes and shapes and all manner of writing utensils. Students of all ages like to experiment with various writing media. In classrooms where computers are available, students may wish to occasionally bypass pencil and paper altogether. You will also need folders and portfolios in which to file drafts, works in progress, and lists of writing ideas and to display finished pieces. Writing-workshop classrooms require places and systems for the storage of children's writing. Journals and notebooks abound in such classrooms.

The classroom arrangement for writing workshop must be flexible and conducive to workshop activities. Ideas for creating a classroom writing center were discussed in Chapter 3 of this text. For writing workshop, Galda, Cullinan, and Strickland (1993) also recommend a separate "Do Not Disturb" table where talking is not allowed, for children who want to write uninterrupted. A "Do Not Disturb" sign at a student's desk signals the same intent. Writing-workshop classrooms need to be flexible enough that furniture can be rearranged at the end of each workshop session for whole-class sharing. The focal point becomes the **Author's Chair,** where a student sits when he or she is sharing work with the class. It can be special or different in some way from the other chairs in the classroom.

Writing-Workshop Instruction

Writing workshop comprises three major events: (1) mini-lessons, (2) writing time and conferences, and (3) sharing time. Each event involves a number of activities, so writing workshop classrooms appear very busy. You are establishing a community of writers, and individuals in this community will interact with one another in the process of creating text.

Mini-Lessons

Mini-lessons are short, to-the-point instructional episodes in which one topic or skill is taught (Lunsford, 1997). Each writing-workshop session begins with a mini-lesson, which rarely exceeds ten minutes. Mini-lessons end with a status report in which each student identifies his or her working goal for that day. Early in the year, when you are introducing students to writing workshop, mini-lessons may focus more on workshop procedures and protocols than on writing issues. Nancie Atwell (1998) uses her first mini-lesson as follows: (1) to model her own thinking process as she considers topics she'd like to write about and the thinking and rehearsal she does before actually beginning to write (e.g., "When I am writing a research report, I usually begin by . . ."); (2) to guide students in selecting their first writing topic for the year (e.g., "Think about possible topics you would like to write about right now. Think about experiences, events, and feelings you might write about. Jot your ideas down, and we'll talk about them."); and (3) to establish workshop guidelines (pp. 83–84). (Figure 8.5, page 231, provides a list of writing-workshop guidelines.) These three elements of Atwell's first mini-lesson are designed to move students immediately into writing-workshop behaviors and to set the tone for how the workshop will proceed throughout the year.

Writing Time

Writing time, which comprises the bulk of the writing workshop, should be at least thirty minutes each day. Mini-lessons end and writing time begins with the status-of-the-class roll-call report, in which students answer the question "What are you doing today?" Atwell (1998) calls this the "status-of-the-class conference" and explains that taking three minutes to poll students

Author's Chair
a special chair from which a student reads his or her work to the class

What possibilities can you visualize for using the Author's Chair?

mini-lessons
brief, concentrated, instructional episodes

➤ *Mini-Lessons for Writing Workshop*

How would you design a mini-lesson for a writing workshop? How might a mini-lesson early in the year differ from one conducted later when students have more experience?

FIGURE 8.5
Rules for Writing Workshop

1. Save everything: it's all a part of the history of the piece of writing, and you never know when or where you might want to use it.
2. Date and label everything you write to help you keep track of what you've done (e.g., *notes, draft #1, brainstorming*).
3. When a piece of writing is finished, clip everything together, including the drafts, notes, lists, editing checksheet, and peer-conference form, and file it in your permanent writing folder.
4. Record every piece of writing you finish on the form in your permanent writing folder. Collect data about yourself as a writer, look for patterns, and take satisfaction in your accomplishments over time.
5. Write on one side of the paper only and always skip lines or type double-spaced. Both will make revision, polishing, and editing easier and more productive for you.
6. Draft your prose writing in sentences and paragraphs. Draft your poems in lines and stanzas. Don't go back into a mess of text and try to create order. Format as you go.
7. Get into the habit of punctuating and spelling as conventionally as you can *while* you're composing: this is what writers do.
8. When composing on the word processor, print at least every two days. Then read the text with a pen in your hand, away from the computer, and see and work with the whole, rather than a part at a time on the screen.
9. Get into the habit of beginning each workshop by reading what you've already written. Establish where you are in the piece and pick up the momentum.
10. Understand that writing is thinking. Do nothing to distract me or other writers. Don't put your words into our brains as we're struggling to find our own.
11. When you confer with me, use as soft a voice as I use when I talk to you: *whisper*.
12. When you need to confer with peers, use a conference area and record responses on a peer-conference form so that the writer has a reminder of what happened.
13. Maintain your proofreading list and refer to it when you self-edit.
14. Self-edit in a color different from the print of your text and complete an editing checksheet to show what you know about conventions of writing.
15. Write as well and as much as you can.

about what each is doing that day creates immediate focus for the student's writing and is time well spent (p. 89). She also recommends teaching students "writer language" (*draft, revise, abandon, conference, edit*) so that they can be precise about their actions. Each student's progress should be recorded frequently on a form like the one in Figure 8.6. See page 232.

Writing time is for the business of writing. In kindergarten and first grade, young students are invited to draw and to write "as best they can" (Calkins, 1986). In the primary-grade writing workshop, you can expect students to be drawing, drawing and writing, writing and illustrating, and using unconventional written forms. In upper grades, the issues are different; instead of children who are not yet writing conventionally, you will have students who are writing the same cartoon-character story over and over. In all classrooms, students learning English as a second language (ESL) may create combination first-language-and-English text or may use many graphics and drawings to support or replace written text. ESL students and other students with language or learning differences may be reluctant to produce written text at all.

It is important that they begin putting their thoughts on paper, whatever the form. Your role is to honor what students are doing (even if their stories and accounts are repetitive or mundane), give them many opportunities to write and to read their work, surround them with written language, and encourage risk-taking and experimentation. Your response should support the conditions for literacy learning developed by Cambourne and Turbill (1987; see Chapter 3).

What other challenges might you or your students face during writing time?

the Highly Effective Teacher

What are the conditions for literacy learning?

FIGURE 8.6

Writing Discussion Record Form

Student Name	Writing Discussion Topic or Problem	Comments (Self, Peer, Teacher)	Date

Writing Conferences

Conferences occur throughout the writing workshop to satisfy the principles that "writers need response" and "writers learn mechanics in context." The most frequent conference is between teacher and student, as you circulate around the room, pausing to talk with individual students as they write. Your goal is to stop frequently at students' desks or writing areas and conduct short, to-the-point conversations that assist and guide them in their writing. The following opening questions may be used in a conference: "How are you doing?" or "Where are you in your writing now?" Table 8.2 (page 233) presents key questions that can help students solve their writing problems.

➤ *Peer Conferences*

Writing workshop also involves peer conferences. Partners or small groups of students share their writing with one another and receive assistance and ideas for moving their writing forward through peer editing. Students require some preparation for and practice in peer conferencing and editing. They need many opportunities to observe as you guide individual conferences and editing sessions (Kucera, 1995). In addition, you need to conduct mini-lessons and simulations to demonstrate peer conferencing and editing procedures. Simple guidelines for peer conferees follow:

1. When listening to or editing someone else's writing, first say or write what you found interesting about the piece.
2. Ask questions that allow the writer to solve problems and improve the work. Questions should begin "How could you . . . ?", "How might you . . . ?", or perhaps "What do you want . . . ?"

The mechanics of editing practices and procedures also need to be taught—for example, how to identify and signal spelling and punctuation errors, how to suggest sentence or paragraph reconstruction, and how to discuss editing recommendations with authors. A great simple source for young writers' checklists on editing (for primary, intermediate, and middle school grades) is *Writing Yellow Pages: For Students and Teachers* (1988).

➤ *Self-Conferences*

Self-conferences also are an important part of writing-workshop procedures. Self-conferences occur when students spend time thinking about their writing metacognitively. They step outside their personal attachment to their writing, look at their work objectively, and begin to ask questions to guide their writing development. Calkins (1986, p. 19) suggests the following questions for structuring self-conferences, which you may wish to post in your classroom writing center:

➤ *Questions for Structuring Self-Conferences*

- What have I said so far? What am I trying to say here?
- How do I like what I've written so far? What's good here that I can build on?
- What's not so good that I can fix?
- How does it sound? How does it look?
- How else could I have written this?
- What will my reader think as he or she reads this?
- What questions will readers ask? What will they notice? Feel? Think?
- What am I going to do next?

TABLE 8.2

Discussion Questions That Can Help Students Identify and Solve Writing Problems

Writing Problem	Teacher or Peer Question
Piece lacks focus.	What is the most important idea in this paragraph? section? story?
Main idea fails to develop clearly.	What is your "big idea"? How can you start with that? What will you do next?
Lack of development of critical information needed to understand discussion.	Tell me more about your idea here. What will a reader need to know from your discussion to understand what you are trying to say?
Too much information packed into a brief discussion.	Is all of this information needed? What part could be omitted?
Organization and writing lacks cohesion.	What is the key idea in your writing? How can you build on this idea to develop and explain it to your audience? What more do we need to know to clearly understand your discussion? story?
Writing style is too informal? formal?	Who is your audience? What do you think their expectations will be for your writing?
Lack of attention to mechanical detail: spelling? handwriting? punctuation?	Have you proofread your paper for spelling? handwriting? punctuation? Has your peer partner proofread your paper?
Conclusion does not end well.	What do you want your reader to understand or feel about your discussion at the end? Does your conclusion do this?
Closing the discussion.	What are your next steps in revising this piece?

Sharing Time

Writing workshop is brought to an end each day in a sharing-time meeting. One to three students elect to take turns sitting in the Author's Chair and read a finished piece or work in progress to the entire class. The point of sharing time is to make real to young writers the concepts of audience and audience response and to encourage and celebrate the natural human desire to share creative products.

Provide mini-lessons on sharing-time meeting procedures. Determine boundaries of peer response to Author's Chair readers that seem appropriate to you, and communicate these expectations to students. For example, one sharing-time meeting procedure might specify that, when seeking assistance, the author should tell the class what he or she wants before reading. Another guideline might suggest that students respond to finished work by calling attention to interesting ideas and uses of language.

Record Keeping and Evaluation

Procedures for keeping records of and evaluating writing-workshop activities need to be carried out accurately and consistently. Documentation is important, because the writing workshop is unlike traditional instruction, where everyone is doing essentially the same thing in the same way. It is also important to monitor each student's writing progress, including progress in specific writing skills, as you will want to provide productive feedback to students and parents.

The writing discussion record form (shown in Figure 8.6, page 232) provides an easy and convenient way to monitor what students are doing during writing workshop. You can keep each week's completed forms in a permanent record book. In addition, you should maintain a conference log, with a number of pages allotted for each student. Each time you confer with a student, assist a student in editing, or read a finished piece, write a dated entry in your conference log. Focus on how a student's work is demonstrating what he or she knows and can do.

Why is the concept of audience important to writers?

What rules do you think students should observe when responding during sharing time?

How can the record form be used both before and after writing?

➤ *Conference Log*

> *Students'*
> *Writing Portfolios*

At regular intervals during the school year (report card time), you will need to formally evaluate your students' writing development. Portfolio assessment is appropriate for evaluating students' writing-workshop work. Teacher Linda Rief (1990) decided, for example, that portfolio assessments would include "each student's two best [written] pieces chosen during a six-week period from his or her working folder, trimester self-evaluations of process and product, and, at year's end, a reading/writing project" (p. 24).

Here are the questions Rief used to guide students' self-evaluations (p. 28):

- What makes this your best piece?
- How did you go about writing it?
- What problems did you encounter?
- How did you solve them?
- What makes your most effective piece different from your least effective piece?
- What goals did you set for yourself?
- How well did you accomplish them?
- What are your goals for the next twelve weeks?

Why is it important that students develop their own portfolios?

These questions can be readily adapted for younger students. Rief also suggests that they evaluate their own work by arranging their finished pieces from the grading period in order from most effective to least effective and writing a rationale for their choices. Following submission of writing portfolios and self-evaluations, you will need to write your response to each student. Your responses should become personal, substantive discourses with students about their accomplishments in your classroom.

How to Do . . .

Writing Workshop

1. Establish the writing-workshop schedule—days and times.
2. Gather and store paper, pens, pencils, folders, journal notebooks, and other writing-workshop materials.
3. Decide how materials, supplies, and equipment will be dispensed or used.
4. Arrange the room to accommodate writing areas, centers, meeting areas, and so forth.
5. Make any signs you wish to post (e.g., self-conferencing questions, procedural guidelines, or work-area labels).
6. Develop and prepare all record keeping and evaluation forms and materials. Write the evaluation procedures.
7. Decide what signals you want to use—how you'll get everyone's attention during writing time, how you'll signal end of writing time, etc.
8. Prepare your first mini-lesson. Reflect on how you choose topics for writing, choose two or three examples of very different kinds of writing you have done, and be prepared to explain to your students how you arrived at those topics.
9. Plan your next two mini-lessons.
10. Set up the permanent record book and/or conference and skills log. Fill in children's names on log pages and status-of-the-class record forms.
11. Initiate the workshop.

- **Delayed readers may have difficulty with the mechanics of writing, particularly with spelling. Spelling, like reading, develops in phases. If intermediate grade, and older, students have not yet progressed to a phase of conventional spelling, teachers must *preplan* for ways to handle this. Some questions to consider: (a) At the draft stages, is unconventional spelling acceptable? (b) Does the student have dictionary skills that can help? (c) Are the dictionaries in your room at an easy enough level for your delayed readers to use? (d) Would an individual file box of problem words at the student's desk, filed alphabetically, be helpful? (e) How do highly effective teachers in your building handle this problem?**

DELAYED READER
ADAPTATION

In her most recent reflections on the writing workshop, Calkins (1991) suggests a variation on the workshop, in which participants (students and teacher) keep notebooks with them at school and at home in which they record moments of their lives, reflections, words and phrases that have a special sound, family stories, and ideas. The content of these notebooks then becomes the focus of much of writing workshop. In mini-lessons and conferences, teachers invite students to read and reflect on notebook entries so that early in the workshop attention is concentrated on writing in the notebook itself. Students continue to add phrases, words, and drafts of ideas to their notebooks, with little pressure to redraft, revise, edit, and publish. After gathering this mosaic of many different kinds of writing, students then develop their own substantive writing projects. In time, whole classes launch research projects that serve as the nucleus for writing workshop activities.

➤ *Writing Workshop Notebook Mosaics*

New visions of writing workshop continue to evolve. Your approach probably will not be the same as Atwell's or Calkins's, nor will it be the same each year.

Six Steps of the Writing Process

The six steps in the writing process have been identified as prewriting, drafting, revising, editing, sharing, and publishing. These steps reflect what writers do in their continuing development as writers and thus describe much of the daily activity that sustains writing workshop.

1. In *prewriting,* writers select a topic, consider content, decide what form or design their writing might take, and anticipate and mentally rehearse what they will write. Students' working folders for writing workshop might contain lists of topic possibilities, notes, random ideas, story starters, schematics, abandoned works in progress, and other written artifacts that students may review periodically as they consider writing topics. During prewriting, students may brainstorm, diagram, or create maps and outlines to guide them in their writing. Rehearsal occurs when children try out the opening words of a poem or story, consider various ways to order events or ideas, and envision alternate endings.

   > What instructional strategies could be used with the prewriting step of the writing process?

2. In *drafting,* writers get words on paper. Be sure your students understand that drafts are not finished pieces. Drafts are messy with mark-outs, margin notes, arrows, and cut-and-paste sections. Drafting issues include idea development, design or genre options (e.g., poetry, fiction, nonfiction), language precision, and idea elaboration. Rehearsal is part of drafting, as authors continue to anticipate the content and design of their work.

3. *Revising* is difficult to separate from drafting because many writers revise as they draft and redraft after first writing. A goal of writing workshop is to improve idea development and clarity and to make revision a natural and reasonable part of the writing process. All work is not revised, however; some texts are abandoned when they fail to develop or satisfy, and other drafts may require only minor edits.

4. *Editing* is the final revision stage in which pieces are prepared for publication. Editing includes content changes (wording and idea elaboration) and attention to mechanics (spelling and punctuation). At this point in the writing process, students may rely on dictionaries, thesauruses, grammar books, and other reference texts. Mini-lessons on editing frequently teach a specific mechanical skill in the context of real writing, such as the use of quotation marks in dialogue, capitalization, spelling demons, and uses for italics and semicolons.

   > What steps of the writing process offer the best opportunities for embedded-skill instruction?

5. *Sharing* includes students calling out their writing topics in status-of-the-class conferences, conferring with teachers and peers during writing time, reading their work to a friend, pinning work on the bulletin board, sharing from the Author's Chair, and taking work home to show family and friends. Sharing is the only way writers have of knowing what's getting through to their audience—what the audience understands and remembers about their work (Graves, 1990).

6. *Publishing* is a formal way of sharing. A published work may take the form of stapled pages, a cloth-bound book written and illustrated by the students, comb-bound books finished at a local print or duplicating shop, a multimedia presentation, or a posting on the school's Web site. Computers offer desktop and multimedia publishing programs that students can use for all six steps of the writing process. Most often, students publish carefully copied, polished written pieces by displaying them in the classroom, including them in class-assembled books, and adding them to their portfolios (Chihank, 1999).

   > How does each step of the writing process offer opportunities for integrating technology with content area instruction?

Guided Writing

guided writing
an instructional
strategy for devel-
oping expressive
writing, using
prompts that stim-
ulate visualization,
identification, and
vicarious experience

Guided writing (Prenn & Honeychurch, 1990; Tierney & Readence, 2000) is intended to develop students' ability to think about subject-area topics through expressive writing. Expressive writing is "thinking aloud on paper"—writing in which personal thoughts and feelings about topics and ideas are explored. The goal of expressive writing in subject-area learning is to give students the opportunity to connect with learning topics by voicing their own thoughts, experiences, and opinions. Expressive writing also provides a foundation for subsequent study and more formal writing.

Guided writing is particularly useful at the beginning of a unit of study but may be used periodically throughout a unit. You read a series of writing prompts that ask students to assume roles and imagine scenes in a topic-related mini-drama. The prompts can be invented or adapted from written accounts of historical events or adventures of discovery. The prompts guide them in exploring their knowledge base, experiences, feelings, beliefs, and view of themselves in relationship to the topic. The students then do the actual writing in writing journals or learning logs.

➤ *Guidelines for
Guided-Writing
Lessons*

Prenn and Honeychurch (1990) recommend three guidelines for guided-writing lessons:

1. Tell the students that the writing they do during the lesson is not going to be graded.
2. Instruct them to write immediately after the prompt is read. Reread the prompt questions a few times as the children write. Keep the pace moving, and let the students know you're going to move to the next prompt when approximately two-thirds of the class have finished writing.
3. Have students share their writing with the class.

Content Area Journals

Journal writing has become an accepted component of subject-area learning at all educational levels (Duke & Bennett-Armistead, 2003) and is especially popular in elementary classrooms. Entries in journals used for guiding children's subject-area writing can be structured through prompts such as the following:

➤ *Journal-
Writing Prompts*

- Write everything you can remember about what you learned about long division today.
- On the basis of our observations and records from the past week, what conclusions can you draw about our current weather pattern?
- What was the hardest thing about completing last night's language-arts homework? What was the easiest?

What other
ideas might you
try in your class-
room for daily
journal writing
that includes
writing in the
content areas?

Many teachers use a "letter to the teacher" format for writing, which allows the conversation between teacher and student to be personal (Thompson, 1990). Another popular journal-writing format is the Quick Write, in which students at various times during the day or during a lesson respond to their learning by writing for three or four minutes. All journal entries are dated.

Because journal writing involves written conversations, you must read what your students write and respond in writing to them. Journal reading and response should be done overnight or over the weekend so that journals are back in students' hands the following school day. A reasonable schedule, if children are writing in their journals every day, is to read and respond to each student's journal about once a week.

To use journals as part of subject-area instruction, you need to answer the following key questions:

1. What is your purpose for instituting journal writing with subject area instruction?
2. How often and when do you want students to write? In what subject area(s)?
3. Will you let them write anything they want, or do you want to use prompts? If you want to use prompts, what prompts will you use?
4. Where will journals be kept? Will you let students take them home overnight? What will you do if a journal is lost?
5. What other rules or standards will you apply to journal writing?

Journal writing lets students wonder, ruminate, work through difficult ideas, record their thinking, and confide in you their important thoughts and big ideas. Journals are private and personal and therefore highly confidential; no one should share journal excerpts without express permission from the person or persons involved in the journal entry.

Double Entry Journals

Examples of the kinds of prompts used for a **Double Entry Journal (DEJ)** (Vaughn, 1990) appear at the beginning and end of each chapter in this text. Generally, the related prompts are on facing pages. Students initially respond to a writing prompt on the left-hand page (e.g., "List or draw everything you know about trees"). Then, after instruction, students use the facing right-hand page to elaborate on the ideas and information written or drawn on the left-hand page. The goal is to develop new insights and ideas. Between left-hand-page brainstorming and right-hand-page consolidation of knowledge, a learning event of some sort—reading, demonstration, simulation, discussion—takes place that encourages construction of new knowledge by combining prior knowledge and the learning event. Writing prompts for left-hand-page and right-hand-page writing may be both content specific and procedural.

DEJs are useful to guide subject-area reading and content review. Prompts should be based on what you want students to know or be able to do after the reading. DEJs also are a means for teaching students how to develop and organize their thinking and learning.

Learning Logs

A **learning log** is another special kind of journal (Blake, 1990) that focuses specifically on subject-area learning. Students can use learning logs to record the brainstorming they do for content DR-TAs or K-W-L Plus and to keep maps. Much learning-log writing comes from prompts that teachers provide before, during, and after learning events. Prompts may be both content specific ("What is a habitat?") and procedural ("What was the hardest part of the experiment?"). Each learning-log entry is dated.

A key to successful use of learning logs is that teachers' writing prompts must be generative and contribute to rich learning experiences. Learning-log prompts might ask students to think about what they already know about a topic and serve as the starting point for discussion and reading: "List everything you know about fractions" or "Describe why you think it's warmer in the summer and cooler in the winter." Other prompts might focus on learning goals: "What would you like to learn about Native Americans?" or "What do you want to know about electricity?" Some prompts are expressive: "Pretend you are a delegate to the Constitutional Convention of 1787. Write a letter home describing your experiences and participation at the convention." Learning-log prompts are limited only by topic scope and your imagination.

Beginning Researchers and Embedded Study Skills

Donna Maxim (1990) describes a project she launched to move her third-grade students away from the traditional informational report-writing mode (plagiarism, tracing, and tedium) and to teach them how to become real researchers. First, Maxim taught students how to take notes and develop research ideas from listening; second, she developed their ability to take notes after reading; and third, she taught students how to actually implement a research plan.

Phase One: Taking Notes and Developing Research Ideas from Listening

The program begins with teaching students how to take notes without copying ("reading and writing at the same time," as Maxim calls it) through the simple expedient of reading to students rather than having them do the reading themselves. You read a book or book section to the class, and students take notes on what they hear. (Some books suitable for teaching notetaking are identified in Figure 8.7, page 239.) After the reading, students record in their logs (1) facts and information they recall from listening to the reading and (2) questions and speculations generated by these facts and this information. Demonstrate this process for students at first. After each listening-notetaking experience, they share their notes and questions with the class. You then lead a discussion in which the students speculate on research projects that might grow out of the information and questions they've collected.

Double Entry Journal (DEJ) a form of journal in which the writer responds to related prompts before and after learning

➤ *Uses of DEJs*

learning log a form of journal in which the writer chronologically records content-specific and procedural information before, during, and after instruction

➤ *Learning-Log Prompts*

How is this phase of beginning research similar to that of the DL-TA?

Strategies in Use

Using Prompts in Guided Content Area Writing

The following guided-writing prompts for writing sessions are based on the work of Patricia Collins (1990) and used with fifth graders as part of a unit on space.

Prompt 1: You have decided to apply for the U.S. astronaut training program. A college graduate and scientist, you've decided that becoming an astronaut is perfect for you. What are your reasons for making this decision? What do you expect to get from participating in the program? What do you want to achieve as an astronaut?

Prompt 2: You have recently completed your astronaut training and are ready for your first extended trip into space. Your scientific mission is the maintenance and repair of the Hubble space telescope. What do you expect this mission will be like? How will your space walk to repair the telescope proceed? What will you say to your family and friends before leaving on this trip?

Prompt 3: You have now been in space for several days. During your space walk earlier today, you found that a small meteorite had dented one side of the telescope's shield. What will you do to repair this dent? What did you see and feel on your space walk? Describe the Earth as you see it now.

Prompt 4: You have returned from your mission and are being debriefed at the space study center in Huntsville, Alabama. What will you tell the other scientists and officials about your experiences? Were you successful in repairing the Hubble telescope? What did you learn on your space walk?

Prompt 5: You, the astronaut, are standing in your backyard. It is a clear, starry night. What do you see and feel? What do you know about the great space above you? How do you describe it now? What are your hopes and plans for your next mission?

Prompt 6: With a friend, plan a visit to NASA's Challenger Space Center on the Web. What information can you find on the Hubble telescope and the role of astronauts in maintaining it? What information can you find that explains why scientists want to make observations and conduct experiments in the weightlessness of space?

The students let their imaginations fly. Most produced several pages in each session. Their teacher always marvels at their inventive imagery and powers of description—and the risks her students take with their writing. It helps that they know their work will not be graded. At the same time, they know their writing will get lots of reader and listener response from their teacher and their classmates.

CRITICAL THINKING

1. In what specific ways might these prompts support a thematic unit on space?
2. What aspects of guided writing encourage writing productivity and increase the fluency and volume of student writing?
3. Create new prompts to continue this guided-writing activity for another two days. Create a set of prompts for a content area you plan to teach.
4. Could guided writing be used for purposes other than expressive writing? Explain.
5. How might you combine writing workshop with extended guided writing, and for what purposes could you do so?

Phase Two: Reading and Taking Notes

> *Develop guidelines you would use with your students for taking notes from reading.*

After students gain experience in listening and taking notes, they're ready to learn reading and notetaking skills. Begin by distributing informational magazines to them. (Maxim used back issues of *Zoobooks,* published by Wildlife Education Ltd.) Have students look at the cover and generate questions they think they will find answers to inside and record these questions in their logs. Then they leave their desks and sit elsewhere in the room to read the magazine. After ten minutes, they leave their magazines, return to their desks, and write any answers they found to their questions.

FIGURE 8.7
Bookshelf: Examples of Books Appropriate for Developing Notetaking

Nonfiction

Bateman, R., and Archbold, R. (1998). *Safari*. Boston: Little, Brown.

Deedy, C. A. (2000). *The Yellow Star: The Legend of King Christian X of Denmark*. (H. Sorenson, Illus.). Atlanta, GA: Peachtree Publishers.

Frank, A. (1967). *Anne Frank: The Diary of a Young Girl*. New York: Doubleday.

Gibbons, G. (1998). *Soaring with the Wind: The Bald Eagle*. New York: Morrow.

Rappoport, K. (2005). *Ladies First, Women Athletes Who Made A Difference*. Atlanta: Peachtree.

Tompert, A. (2000). *Saint Nicholas*. (M. Garland, Illus.). Honesdale, PA: Boyds Mills Press.

Fiction

Armstrong, A. (2005). *Whittington*. New York: Random House.

Fisher, L. E. (2001). *God and Goddesses of the Ancient Norse*. New York: Holiday House.

George, J. C. (1972). *Julie of the Wolves*. New York: Harper/Collins.

Williams, C. L. (1998). *If I Forget, You Remember*. New York: Random House.

Winter, J. (1988). *Follow the Drinking Gourd*. New York: Knopf.

Yolen, J. (1998). *Raising Yoder's Barn*. Boston: Little, Brown.

Maxim reports that students found this exercise difficult; they wanted to look back at their reading and do the kind of copy-notetaking they had become used to. If you persist, however, they will come to realize that they can indeed take notes without copying. Keep the source material within a range of reasonable difficulty and repeat the activity frequently.

Phase Three: Initiating and Carrying Out Research

Students now see how their newly learned notetaking skills can help them conduct research. For their research, make available to students as many school and community resources as possible (print and nonprint). As they become acquainted with various study materials and resources, they record in their logs ideas and questions they deem worthy of further investigation. Through class discussion and individual conferences, each student frames a specific research question, identifies resources, and decides on a research plan. Students then launch their projects and carry them out. The beginning researcher strategy thus provides guided, sheltered simulation of a productive research process in conjunction with a unit of study for which students will do research.

> What other study skills could you teach in the context of doing a research project?

> How could you continue beginning research using writing workshop?

Developing Students' Handwriting

Handwriting instruction is still very much a part of the elementary classroom. In most schools, students use manuscript form (circles and sticks) through second grade, making a transition from manuscript to *cursive* form in late second or early third grade. They need to practice writing to arrive at their own handwriting style. The goals of handwriting instruction and practice are *legibility* and *consistency;* that is, students' handwriting needs to be readable by others and to have a certain consistency—tall letters about the same height, short letters about the same height and width, letters and words evenly slanted, *l*'s consistently loopy, *t*'s consistently unloopy, etc. The way to reach these goals is first to provide instruction and very short doses of rote practice. Then give children lots of real writing time. As in the writing workshop, discuss and model handwriting during conferences and mini-lessons that focus on publishing finished pieces. Encourage their experimentation with handwriting just as you encourage their experimentation with other language forms. Be sure to notice and comment when their handwriting improves. Work on and improve your *own* handwriting—and let students know you're doing so. Guide your students in self-analyzing their handwriting—for example, teach them to use the rating scale found in Figure 8.8 (page 241).

> How could you embed handwriting instruction and practice in writing instruction?

How to Do . . .

Beginning Researcher

1. Decide on the unit of study topic and learning objectives.
2. Collect many and diverse resources for the unit. Make arrangements for visiting speakers, taking field trips, and so forth.
3. Collect many books, both nonfiction and fiction, that relate to the unit.
4. Mark reading passages in the books and determine the order in which you wish to read at least the first few books.
5. Arrange for all students to be supplied with learning logs.

Phase I: Listening and Notetaking

6. Begin the listening and notetaking phase. You may want to first demonstrate the process by having students contribute ideas aloud, record them on chart paper, and then generate questions as a group. Remember:
   a. All learning-log entries are dated.
   b. Students take notes on facts and information they got from the reading *after* the reading is finished. All notes are recorded in learning logs.
   c. Notes are followed by questions and ideas for further research.
7. Continue reading to them each day from a variety of the books you've collected. Have them listen, take notes, and generate questions each day.

Phase II: Reading and Notetaking

8. Find sufficient copies of an informational magazine so that each student may have a copy.

■ **Phase I is suitable for whole-class learning, even with delayed readers in the group, because the teacher provides precise explanations, models, and think-alouds; provides guided practice, and reads to the students. Phase II is more suitable for small-group instruction so that the needs of a range of students may be met. Select informational magazines at two or three reading levels. An excellent source for these selections is *Magazine for Kids and Teens* (Stoll, 1997).**

9. Distribute magazines, but ask students *not* to open them.
10. Have them look at the front of their magazines and generate questions that they think will be answered by an article inside. The questions are recorded in learning logs.
11. Have students leave their desks, logs, and pencils and find another place in the room to read their magazines. Let them read for ten minutes.
12. Have students *leave their magazines where they read,* return to their desks, and take notes from memory about the answers they got to the questions they had generated.
13. Lead a discussion in which they share the notes they took.
14. Repeat the exercise using other magazines and moving to textbook text when it seems appropriate.

Phase III: Initiating and Carrying Out Research

15. Concurrent with Phases I and II, involve students in a number of experiences and events related to the unit of study. Tell them that they will be doing research later in the unit.
16. Introduce students to resources in school and community libraries.
17. Toward the end of Phase II, when students have become confident of their ability to take notes without copying and are well acquainted with materials and unit research possibilities, work with them in developing individual research projects.

FIGURE 8.8
Rating Scale for Handwriting

I. Rate the Quality of Your Handwriting
Excellent (1), Good (2), Average (3), Fair (4), Poor (5)

_____ Neatness

_____ Arrangement (margins, indentations)

_____ Legibility

II. Locate the Trouble Spots in Your Handwriting
Check (✓) one or two areas in which you need special practice:

_____ Slant (Do all your letters lean the same way? Are your down strokes really straight?)

_____ Space (Are the spaces between letters and words even?)

_____ Size (Are your tall letters, i.e., *l, h, k, b,* and *f,* about three times as tall as the small letters; the middle-sized letters, i.e., *t, d,* and *p,* twice the height of small letters; and the lower loop letters one-half space below the writing line?)

_____ Alignment (Are all tall letters evenly tall and all small letters evenly small? Are all letters resting on the line?)

_____ Line Quality (Is the thickness of letters about the same throughout the page?)

_____ Ending Strokes (Are the endings without fancy swinging strokes, and are they long enough to guide the spacing between words?)

_____ Letter Formation (Are the loops open and equal in size? Are the hump letters *m, n, h,* and *u* rounded? Are the letters *o, d, a, g, p,* and *q* closed? Have you made long retraces in *t, d,* and *p?* Are your capital letters well formed?)

_____ Number Formation (Do you use the correct form? Do you use the correct slant? Are the symbols well aligned?)

From Cathy Collins Block, *Teaching the Language Arts* (2nd ed.). Published by Allyn & Bacon, Boston, MA. Copyright © 1995 by Pearson Education. Reprinted by permission of the publisher.

Integrating Reading and Writing across the Curriculum

The integration of reading and writing experiences across the curriculum increases the content students learn, as well as the development of literacy abilities in content areas (Gavelek et al., 2000). The integrated curriculum is not merely a process of combining different subject areas so that one subject is taught in the presence of others; rather, the truly **integrated curriculum** involves students in identifying high-priority topics and areas of interest, guides them as they plan their own learning, and guides literacy events and processes along the way. When this happens, you provide the opportunity for students to *really learn*—to be engaged, eager, active learners determined to find the answers to questions they raise (Ciardiello, 2003).

Regie Routman (1991) recommends that when planning for integrated learning experiences, teachers answer the following questions about the project they're hoping to launch:

- What important concepts do I want students to learn?
- Why should students learn these concepts? Are they intellectually rich and important?
- What learning experiences will help develop these conceptual understandings?
- What skills and strategies am I helping my students develop?
- Am I setting up a climate that encourages inquiry and choice?
- Am I putting in place alternate evaluation procedures?
- What student attitudes am I fostering?

Answering Routman's questions will help you sort out and specify what you are doing and why. Clarity of purpose is important in planning complex learning experiences.

integrated curriculum problem- or question-based, student-directed plan for learning that transcends content area boundaries

➤ *Guidelines for Integrated Learning Experiences*

Project-Based Reading and Writing: The Authoring Cycle

As the phrase itself suggests, project-based reading and writing centers around a major class project that you decide to undertake. The project may be ongoing throughout an entire school year—publishing a newspaper or magazine, for example—or it may be short term—cleaning up a local park or developing an extended genealogy of the class "family."

➤ *Curriculum as Project-Based Inquiry*

Harste (1994) emphasizes the importance of inquiry—a deeply felt, inner need to know—as the foundation for project-based writing: "Viewing curriculum as inquiry means that I envision classrooms as sites of inquiry, or as communities of learners. Inquiry is not a technical skill to be applied at will, but rather a philosophical stance that permeates the kinds of lives we choose to live" (pp. 1230–1231). Inquiry is the driving force behind project-based reading and writing.

➤ *The Authoring Cycle*

Harste and Short (1988) use the "authoring cycle" to describe project-based writing (see Figure 8.9 below). Their discussion of the authoring cycle captures the essence of the writing process.

In inquiry learning, students and teachers examine what they already know, look around their world, and decide what it is they want to learn more about (Schmidt et al., 2002). All writing and learning then grows from exploring questions generated by what the group wants to know. Intensely focused reading and writing stemming from the inquiry topic is more authentic than traditional formal instruction. Consider how much more engaging it is for a classroom of students to write logs, analyses, newspaper accounts, poems, and scientific essays based on experiments they conducted during a visit to an amusement park (e.g., wind resistance during roller coaster rides, heart rate and pulse studies on various rides) than to practice these kinds of writing by studying texts and doing exercises.

Begin project-based writing by leading a class discussion about "Things We Know." Let students work in pairs or groups to list what they know, and give them plenty of time before sharing ideas in whole-class discussion. Repeat this process with "Things We Don't Know" and "Things We Want to Know." This phase may take several days. Then work on shaping the project idea with the class.

FIGURE 8.9

The Authoring Cycle

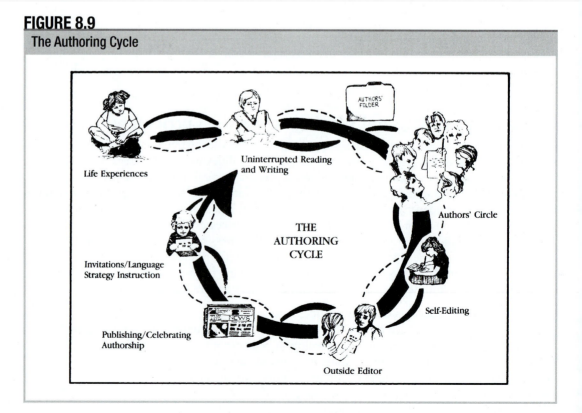

Sinatra et al. (1990) describe a project they developed with urban middle school students in which the students worked in pairs to explore various aspects of their neighborhood. The students began the project by planning and taking snapshots of parts of the neighborhood they wished to investigate. The partners then used the photos to produce a storyboard to tell their story about the neighborhood. The storyboard served as the outline for a written essay. Sinatra and associates call this a "visual literacy" approach because the visual aspect of the project supports literacy (p. 613).

> ➤ *An Example of Project-Based Learning*

Content Area Theme Cycles

Theme cycles are described by Altwerger and Flores (1991) as cycles of study in which students negotiate the theme for instruction through class discussion and deliberation. In theme cycles (as in inquiry projects), students do most of the planning and carrying out of theme activities, including practical writing (e.g., of letters inviting guest speakers) and other writing.

Lois Bird (personal communication, 1991) tells of a theme project carried out by an intermediate grade class in a low-income neighborhood. In a class discussion one day, the students began talking about the many ways their neighborhood was blighted: unkempt yards and streets; lack of physical safety on sidewalks and streets; lack of police presence; a run-down, weed- and vermin-infested park where children could no longer play; and on and on. The students grew convinced that they should clean up the neighborhood, and this became their class theme. To carry out their work, they wrote letters to the mayor and other city officials, informing them of the many neighborhood problems; invited the chief of police to visit the class to talk about ways the community and local police could work together to improve the area; and instituted a community coalition of adults, children, businesses, police, and school staff to address neighborhood problems. Writing was integral to this theme project, not only because of the practical communication that needed to be done but also because of the many opportunities the project provided for students to write about the work they were doing on behalf of their neighborhood.

A theme may grow naturally from a class discussion, an experience students have, a local or world event, or a "teachable moment" you encounter. Whatever its source or impetus, help students develop the theme through the writing process.

theme cycle
cyclical instruction in which students negotiate the topical or conceptual theme and plan and carry out theme activities

How would both reading and writing become an integral part of this theme cycle?

How could you integrate literature with content areas using theme cycles?

Thematic Units: Integrating Literature

Developing thematic literature-based units offers many opportunities to integrate literature with other content areas of the curriculum. A **thematic unit** is a cross-disciplinary instructional plan based on key unifying topics or concepts. To develop a thematic unit, begin by identifying the specific objectives that you wish to accomplish. These may include building reading motivation and response through identification with main story characters, providing experience with the writing process, and learning about a specific concept related to, for example, ecosystems or endangered species (science) or historical events or cultural differences (social studies). Choose a unifying theme that will enable you to integrate specific literature with your content objectives. Themes may be topical or conceptual. For example, in the primary grades, you might have a thematic unit on the topic of "my family" or "foxes." A conceptual theme might be the importance of friendship.

Gather literature and text that relate to the theme and brainstorm ideas for using the theme to integrate the literature selections with content-area materials (Roser & Keehn, 2002). If possible, share your ideas with another teacher who has similar interests or who might consider co-teaching a thematic unit with you.

Combining literature and content area subjects adds interest and depth to study (Moss, 2004; Schmidt et al., 2002). For example, historical fiction and biography can provide motivation and insight in the study of the American Revolution. A book such as *Early Thunder* (Fritz, 1987) can help build an understanding of the conflict that early colonists experienced between loyalty to the king and rebellion (Johnson & Ebert, 1992).

The topical thematic unit on foxes developed for a group of inner-city second-grade students by Julie Stevenson (1990) illustrates the integration into a unit of various areas of the curriculum

thematic unit
an instructional plan involving a number of content areas and based on a unifying topic or concept

How might thematic units encourage professional collaboration in your school?

How to Do . . .

Thematic Units

1. Identify the instructional objectives for the unit (i.e., "What do I want my students to know or to be able to do when the unit is finished?").
2. Choose a unifying theme. The theme may be topical or conceptual.
3. Select literature and informational books for use in developing the theme.

■ **Using thematic units presents opportunities to include delayed readers in class projects and makes learning easily accessible to them. Ask your librarian for help. If a social studies theme involves, for example, women in American history, ask for biographies and historical fiction written at several reading levels, from very easy to easy to mid-level to challenging. For any content area topic, books are available across a wide range of reading levels.**

4. Determine activities, events, and projects useful in achieving unit objectives. Guide the class in carrying out the activities, events, and projects.
5. Evaluate the effectiveness of the unit as a whole.

DELAYED READER ADAPTATION

➤ *Example of a Topical Thematic Unit*

(Figure 8.10, page 245). This topical unit was designed to build students' motivation and interest in reading and simultaneously to develop meaning-construction strategies and new content information. The unit was also intended to expand concepts developed in a basal reading story on foxes that was used in Stevenson's classroom.

The unit relied on three literature selections: *Flossie and the Fox* (McKissack, 1986), *Rosie's Walk* (Hutchins, 1968), and *One Fine Day* (Hogrogian, 1971). The instructional strategies used in developing the unit included read-aloud story sharing, Literature-Response Journals, Reader's Theatre, DR-TA, and GMA. The culminating event was the creation of a big book about foxes, dictated to Stevenson by the children and illustrated by the students.

➤ *Example of a Conceptual Thematic Unit*

Gross (1989) designed a conceptual thematic unit for intermediate and middle school students based on the novel *Julie of the Wolves* (George, 1972), about the experiences of a lonely Eskimo girl. Supporting materials for the unit included *The Call of the Wolves* (Murphy, 1989), *Alaska Wildlife: A Coloring Book* (Holen, 1988), *Zoobooks: Wolves* (Wildlife Education, 1989), and nonfiction books on the wilderness, necessary survival skills, and life in the arctic. The three basic concepts developed in this unit were as follows:

1. Young people from different cultures have similar feelings and the need to be loved and cared for within a family environment, as well as the desire to be independent and competent.
2. Society changes, and old ways sometimes clash with new ways.
3. Respect for all living things is important if people are to maintain a balance of nature in the environment.

The teacher used a variety of instructional strategies to develop this unit. The unit integrated the following areas of the curriculum:

■ *Social Studies:* study of the geography of Alaska, Eskimo customs and culture, and the history of Alaska (including statehood)
■ *Science:* study of the habits and culture of wolves, endangered species, and ecosystems
■ *Math:* construction of graphs of past and present wolf populations in Alaska; charting of variations in snowfall in different seasons; and the use of wilderness supply catalogs to plan for and order expedition supplies
■ *Art:* construction of posters to create awareness of endangered wildlife; design of wildlife stamps; construction of models of huts, igloos, and totem poles; and drawing of Eskimo clothing

FIGURE 8.10

A Second-Grade Topical Thematic Literature Unit on Foxes

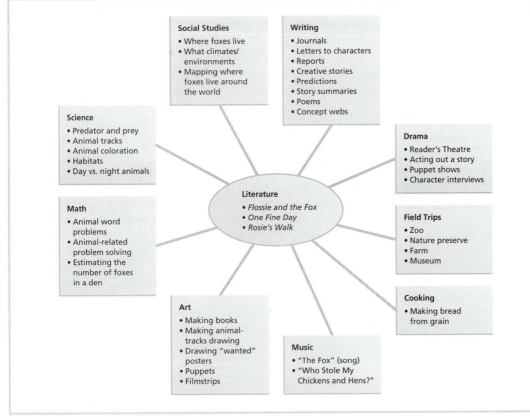

Reprinted with permission of J. Stevenson.

In addition, the students planned a school assembly on endangered species and read stories featuring wolves to kindergarten and first-grade children. Activities included field trips to the zoo and the science museum to study wolves and visits from guest speakers, who discussed endangered wildlife, and storytellers, who presented Eskimo folktales and legends.

The development of thematic units that integrate literature and the content areas requires planning and creative effort on your part. You will find, however, that the motivation, interest, and conceptual development of your students will be greatly enhanced by an integrated thematic approach (Bruning & Schweiger, 1997).

Summary and Classroom Applications

double entry journal

Reflect on your early experiences in content area learning described in the Double Entry Journal at the beginning of this chapter. Which strategies seem best suited to your teaching style and beliefs about literacy development? To what extent are the strategies presented in this chapter represented in those experiences?

the Highly Effective Teacher
on Technology and Content Area Instruction

1. Divide the class into small groups. Have half the groups visit the Web site **www.yahooligans.com** to conduct Internet research on a particular topic. Have the other groups collect research information from non-Internet sources. Construct a class map based on all the information gathered by the groups. Compare the differences in the kinds of information collected.

2. Use The Learning Company's *American Girl Premiere* software, which allows students to write their own American Girl stories (from the popular dolls and books based on American history). This software provides opportunities to use historically accurate sets and accessories to write plays and to record audio.

3. Use the K-W-L Plus strategy to research a well-known woman who has made an important contribution to our culture, by visiting the Web site **www.distinguishedwomen.com.**

4. Visit the Web site **http://rs6.loc.gov/amhome.html,** which is the American Memory Historical Collections site for the National Digital Library and contains original source material for seven million digital items. Have the students work in pairs to prepare a class presentation based on what they have learned.

5. Conduct a DIA to support your instructional goals for a social studies project on Egypt. Use the **www.virtual-egypt.com** Web site, which offers a virtual tour of Ancient Egypt, as well as other resources such as maps, photographs, and favorite books in this project.

Chapter Summary

Because students construct meaning in the act of reading and writing, instruction must promote rich reading and writing experiences. The content DR-TA, GMA, and SDEI combination; K-W-L Plus; and the Directed Inquiry Activity (DIA) are useful strategies for guiding students' subject-area reading. All of these strategies help children connect their prior knowledge, information in text, and information they gain from one another and through experience.

The writing workshop and related strategies such as guided writing, content area journals, and beginning research are recommended for developing students' writing in subject areas. They are good alternatives to the traditional informational report, which has dominated subject-area instruction in elementary classrooms. Students learn by writing. Therefore, writing needs to permeate subject-area instruction.

Project-based learning, content area theme cycles, and literature-based thematic units are all ways to bring reading, writing, and subject-area learning into an integrated whole. These approaches assume that students should be involved in making important decisions about what is to be learned and that real learning arises from the complex events of research and project planning and implementation.

Professional Standards and
Teacher Knowledge for Reading and Writing in the Content Areas

Figure 8.11 presents the major standards for reading professionals (*International Reading Association, 2004*), specific elements for classroom teacher candidates, and examples for each of these. You should be well on the way to understanding how your professional knowledge and practice equip you to meet these standards. You can see the complete list of Standards for Reading Professionals in Appendix C.

FIGURE 8.11

Professional Standards and Content Area Reading and Writing for Classroom Teacher Candidates

Professional Standard	Example
1. Foundational Knowledge	**Element 1.1** Knows foundational theories related to practices and materials for classroom use; e.g., understands the role of schema theory in developing expository-text comprehension; understands research findings that identify characteristics of effective readers and the connection of these findings to content area literacy instruction.
2. Instructional Strategies and Curriculum Materials	**Element 2.2** Plans for use of a wide range of instructional practices, approaches, and methods, including technology-based practices; e.g., understands use of key strategies for content area reading comprehension development such as content DR-TA, GMA, SDEI, and K-W-L Plus, and writing instruction, including writing workshop, journal writing, and beginning researcher.
3. Assessment, Diagnosis, and Evaluation	**Element 3.3** Uses assessment information to plan, evaluate, and revise effective instruction to meet the needs of all students; e.g., understands how to use observations from the GMA and K-W-L Plus to understand students' background knowledge and ability to integrate information during content area reading and how to adjust instruction based on this information; understands the seven principles of writing workshop and can implement these; uses writing conferences to provide for individual content area writing needs.
4. Creating a Literate Environment	**Element 4.1** Uses students' interests, reading abilities, and backgrounds as foundations for the reading and writing program; e.g., uses strategies such as DR-TA and K-W-L Plus to identify student background knowledge and interests and then incorporates this information into such strategies as thematic units and theme cycles.
5. Professional Development	**Element 5.3** Actively engages in collaboration and dialogue with other teachers and reading specialists to obtain advice on teaching practices and ideas; e.g., uses and shares key instructional strategies such as K-W-L Plus and SDEI or writing workshop and guided writing with fellow professionals and obtains feedback on adapting and increasing the effective use of these strategies.

Part 2 from IRA. (2004). Professional Standards and Ethics Committee, International Reading Association. *Standards for reading professionals—revised 2003*. Reprinted with permission of the International Reading Association. All rights reserved.

Applications: Bridges to the Classroom

1. Locate a high-interest content article or a chapter from a social studies, science, or mathematics text on a topic appropriate for the grade level you plan to teach. Develop an instructional plan to use integrated content DR-TA, GMA Study Maps, and SDEI to teach this content area material. What value do you see in combining these strategies in instruction? What are the limitations in doing so? Share your plan and ideas with a class partner.

2. You have become familiar with the use of the Double Entry Journal (DEJ) from your experience with this text. Obtain a copy of a social studies or science textbook at a grade level that interests you, and read the first two chapters to identify what you would want your students to know and be able to do after reading. Now design DEJs, using your objectives as the basis for before-reading and after-reading prompts to focus the readers' purpose. If

the Highly Effective Teacher

Strategies for Integrating Reading and Writing in the Content Areas

Content DR-TA, GMA, SDEI, and K-W-L Plus to guide reading of text (combine with thematic units, writing workshop, project-based units, and theme cycles)

Writing Workshop to develop writing fluency and skill (combine with theme-based and literature instruction strategies)

Beginning Researcher to develop research knowledge and skills (combine with thematic units, project-based units, and theme cycles)

Learning Logs to record brainstorming and keep maps (combine with DR-TA, K-W-L Plus, concept webs, and semantic maps)

DIA to apply DR-TA to content area reading and to predict content on the basis of prior knowledge (combine with thematic units and writing workshop)

Thematic Units to connect concepts and literature and content area instruction (combine with DR-TA, DRA, PreP, SDEI, concept webs, semantic maps, synonyms and antonyms, similes and metaphors, SFA, Literature-Response Journals, SSR, Reader's Theatre, and reading-response groups)

Journal Writing and Double Entry Journals to respond to text and to connect concepts and content (combine with DR-TA, DRA, GMA, SDEI, InQuest, thematic units, K-W-L Plus, and theme cycles)

THE HIGHLY EFFECTIVE TEACHER with meaning-negotiation interactions, a literacy-rich learning environment, and instructional strategies for teaching reading comprehension, vocabulary development, word recognition, word identification skills, and children's and adolescent literature

Guided Writing to develop expressive writing (combine with synonyms and antonyms, similes and metaphors, PReP, and storytelling)

Project-Based Reading and Writing to inquire about and explore topics in depth (combine with GMA, SDEI, concept webs, semantic maps, SFA, reading aloud, storytelling, reading-response groups, Literature-Response Journals, Reader's Theatre, and writing workshop)

Theme Cycles to develop self-selected topics for study and action (combine with GMA, SDEI, concept webs, semantic maps, SFA, reading aloud, storytelling, reading-response groups, Literature-Response Journals, Reader's Theatre, and writing workshop)

---

possible, test the effectiveness of your DEJs with actual students.

3. Develop a personal teaching script for introducing and demonstrating writing workshop to students over a five-day period. How will you integrate computer-based technologies in your writing-workshop program?

4. Reflect on your specialized content knowledge to identify topics in which you have both expertise and interest. Your knowledge and interest may come from travel, special skills or talents, or your academic preparation. Develop one topic or theme in terms of theme cycles and project-based instruction. For example, sketch out a possible unit of instruction using the project launch questions proposed by Regie Routman (see page 241). Share your ideas with a class partner and refine your thematic unit. What materials will you use?

Additional Research and Practice

1. Duke, N. K., Purcell-Gates, V., Hall, L. A., & Tower, C. (2007). Authentic literacy activities for developing comprehension and writing. *The Reading Teacher, 60,* 344–355.

   This article includes highly practical, sound teaching suggestions for combining reading comprehension and writing instruction, with an emphasis on content area text. (Practice)

2. Moss, B. (2004). Teaching expository text structures through information trade book retellings. *The Reading Teacher, 57* (8), 710–718.

   This well-written article is rich with illustrations and examples for developing a clear understanding of description, sequence, comparison and contrast, cause and effect, and problem and solution expository structures, and it provides a "richness of retelling scale" to assist in student assessment and further instruction. (Practice)

3. Morrow, L. M., Pressley, M., Smith, J. K., & Smith, M. (1997). The effect of a literature-based program integrated into literacy and science instruction with children from diverse backgrounds. *Reading Research Quarterly, 32* (1), 54–76.

   This innovative study examines the impact of an integrated literature-based program for literacy and science instruction on achievement, literature use, and attitudes toward the literacy and science program. (Research)

Assessing Students' Progress in Literacy Development

*Reading performance assessment must look at the reading act in process
or judge comprehension of a text as it is applied in some realistic way.*

Roger Farr,
Literacy Assessment and Test Development Expert, Indiana University

*Yes, end-of-year tests can be used to evaluate instruction and
even tell us something about individual students, but such exams are
like shopping mall medical screenings compared to the in-depth and
ongoing assessment needed to genuinely increase learning.*

Lorrie A. Shepard,
Literacy Educator and Assessment Authority, University of Colorado at Boulder

On a Wednesday morning early in February, Bob Irish continued his reading from Wilson Rawls's (1961) *Where the Red Fern Grows* with his sixth-grade students. He had been reading a chapter on alternate days, using the Directed Listening-Thinking Activity (DL-TA).

He found Rawls's book had captured the interest of his students as they followed the adventures and heartwarming story of Billy and his two hunting dogs, Old Dan and Little Ann. Bob had prepared the DL-TA by reading Chapter X, which describes a raccoon-hunting expedition by Billy and his dogs. Bob flagged key high-interest stop-points to be followed by the questions "What do you think will happen next? Why?" Toward the end of the chapter, Old Dan disappears but is found by Little Ann—trapped in an old muskrat den and in danger of drowning. At this point, Bob had decided to ask, "How do you think this chapter will end? Why?" He planned to use the group mapping activity (GMA) to conclude the lesson. He used the DL-TA to develop his students' higher-level thinking, with emphasis on predictions, and the GMA to build story integration, plot development, and story-synthesis abilities. Reading motivation and interest were also very important because he wanted his students to become self-motivated readers.

Just after recess, Bob read Chapter X and used the DL-TA strategy. The DL-TA went very well, as did the GMA following the story reading. He noticed that a few of his students—Gina,

Maureen, and José—made excellent predictions and could express the reasons for their ideas. They also mapped the chapter reading in a way that developed the connections between Old Dan's disappearance, his discovery by Little Ann, and his rescue by Billy. In contrast, Bob observed that Paul and Steve seemed reluctant to participate in story predictions and discussion. Their comments were only remotely related to the story context, and their maps did not connect concepts to reveal the story development and plot.

Bob had noted a similar problem in the responses and maps created by Paul and Steve for the previous chapter reading. He made a quick observation on a self-stick note: "2/7—Paul—Chap. X predict. & map. prob." After making a similar note for Steve, he stuck the notes in the boys' portfolio folders. He would meet with the two boys later in the day to briefly review the story line and plot development in Chapter X and work with them on how the concepts in their maps might be connected and integrated to reflect the story plot development. He would then continue his assessment, carefully observing responses as they read Chapter XI on Friday.

double entry journal

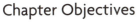

Are you aware of ever having been assessed the way Bob assessed his students? What do you remember about the ways your reading and writing were assessed in school? How did these assessments influence your motivation to read and write? How did they influence your self-concept as a reader and a writer?

Chapter Objectives

After reading and discussing this chapter, you will be able to:

- identify the seven key principles that are critical to good instructional assessment and will lead to an understanding of student progress and instructional planning.

- develop familiarity with and effectiveness in using a variety of literacy-assessment strategies, ranging from quick notes and interest inventories to miscue analysis and running records to identify student needs and plan instruction.

- grasp an understanding of portfolio assessment and how it can be effectively applied to literacy learning in the classroom.

- understand the strengths and weaknesses of formal literacy assessment and how to interpret results using key testing concepts.

- effectively communicate student literacy progress to parents.

Understanding the Role of Assessment in Instruction

The first eight chapters of this book have introduced and developed many instructional concepts that are critical to your literacy-teaching success. These concepts are basic to understanding the content of this chapter. The information in this chapter is also of critical importance to your teaching success, and it will help you develop a detailed understanding of the assessment of student literacy progress.

Assessment of students' progress involves gathering information on student achievement from a wide range of sources and is an important part of teaching. Opportunities abound throughout the school day to observe students as they learn and apply meaning-construction processes. For example, you can note students' use of predictions and higher-level thinking as you use a DL-TA or a DR-TA with high-interest fiction, and you might observe their selection of literature for free-reading time, which reveals their growing and expanding reading interests. These observations provide insights that help you understand your students' literacy growth and plan instruction both for individual students and for small and large groups.

Assessment also is likely to be necessary to satisfy the information demands of your school, school district, state department of education, and federally supported programs (McCormick, 2007; Valencia & Wixon, 2004). Mandatory state testing is becoming more frequent. Forty-eight states have enacted policies on statewide testing and use a combination of multiple-choice and performance-based assessments (*Education Week*, 2000; Valencia and Wixon, 2004). Because of these various demands, you probably will be involved in administering standardized achievement tests. When you receive test-score information from such testing, you will need to be able to interpret the results. Both formal assessment and your informal classroom observations can be critical to students' literacy development and your literacy instruction.

➤ *Both formal and informal assessments are critical to students' literacy development.*

Principles of Assessment

Over the past few decades, educators' beliefs about and understanding of assessment have changed dramatically (Shepard, 2004). Moving from the behavioral objectives and accountability of the 1970s and early 1980s, most educators now advocate assessment that is situated in real, or authentic, classroom learning. The present view holds that classroom-based assessment must favor observations of students as they are engaged in real classroom literacy activities (Shepard, 2004). Although confirming information may be derived from multiple-choice test items, this type of assessment provides only limited insight into students' meaning-construction processing and is far removed from authentic literacy tasks. Important contemporary views and practices related to reading assessment are summarized in Table 9.1 (page 252).

.TABLE 9.1

Some Contemporary Views and Practices in Reading Assessment

Views	Classroom Practice
Reading comprehension is based on prior knowledge.	Do not mask this relationship by using short passages on many different topics.
A complete story or text has structural and topical integrity.	Use longer passages that have the integrity of authentic text.
Inference is essential to comprehend even small units of text.	Do not rely on performances or test items based entirely on literal comprehension.
Student diversity means that many possible inferences can fit a question or text.	Use objective test items with only one correct answer with caution.
The ability to vary reading strategies as needed is a hallmark of expert readers.	Assess how and when students vary their reading strategies for different conditions and purposes.
The ability to synthesize information within and between texts is a hallmark of expert readers.	Include but go beyond finding the main idea of a paragraph or passage to emphasize higher-level thinking.
The ability to ask and answer questions of text is a hallmark of expert readers.	Frequently ask students to create or select questions about text they have read.
All aspects of a reader's experience influence reading comprehension.	Emphasize good reading habits and attitudes as a condition of performance.
Fluency, automaticity, and metacognitive ability are hallmarks of expert readers.	Use tests that embed rather than isolate skills and recognize fluency.
Learning from text involves application in meaningful contexts.	Provide authentic contexts in which students can demonstrate their knowledge through application and transfer tasks.

Adapted from Valencia, Sheila W., & Pearson, P. David. (1987, April). Reading assessment: Time for a change. *The Reading Teacher, 40* (8), 726–732. Copyright © 1987 by Sheila W. Valencia and the International Reading Association. All rights reserved.

authentic assessment evaluation of progress based on observations of students as they are engaged in real and meaningful classroom literacy activities

The following seven principles derive from an **authentic assessment** perspective, which requires that assessment information be based on teachers' observations of their students as they are engaged in real and meaningful classroom literacy events.

1. Assessment should be based primarily on observations of students engaged in authentic classroom reading and writing tasks. Instructional goals—such as developing higher-level thinking at the interpretive, applicative, and transactive levels as well as children's self-selection of high-quality literature and their proficiency in a variety of writing tasks—can be best assessed through observations of students in real learning settings. The use of standardized achievement tests may serve to confirm general achievement levels but holds limited instructional value.

Why is approximation a positive event in literacy learning?

2. Assessment should focus on students' learning and the instructional goals of your curriculum. This focus enables you to observe meaning-construction processes and to identify students' strengths and instructional needs. It is important to remember that students' approximation of a new skill or concept is a positive event in the learning process. Your support and encouragement of students as they strive to reach the instructional goals you set is critical in the recursive cycle of teaching and learning.

3. Assessment should be continuous, based on observations over a substantial period of time. The acquisition of new concepts and literacy strategies requires a supportive classroom environment and time and opportunity to use the new concepts and strategies. It is important to note individual students' progress and growth in various aspects of reading and writing, ranging from story and character interpretation to the use of imaginative language and imagery in story writing.

What is an example of cultural bias in assessment? Of gender bias?

4. Assessment should take into account the diversity of students' culture, language, and special needs. In short, your assessment must be equitable and avoid systematically biased evalua-

tions of individuals or groups of students because of language; culture; gender; or physical, cognitive, or social characteristics. Equity requires sensitivity to student characteristics and needs and, in some cases, the use of special services for students' assessment.

5. Assessment should be collaborative and include the active participation of students. Ongoing authentic assessment provides many opportunities for students' participation, such as their use of Literature-Response Journals to which you respond, or self-evaluation checklists that they collaboratively create for their own writing. Students need a clear understanding of your instructional goals, standards, and values. You, in turn, need to understand clearly their perceptions of these goals and values and what is important to them. A central goal of assessment is to encourage students to assume greater responsibility for their own assessment and learning. Information derived from collaborative assessment will help you communicate to parents the reading and writing progress of their students and enlist their support.

6. Assessment should be based on a variety of observations rather than on one assessment approach; that is, your interpretive evaluation of student growth should be based on observations from many sources. For example, students' interactions during writing conferences and during literature discussions using the DR-TA and GMA provide rich information about their thinking processes. By contrast, standardized achievement test scores may provide quantitative information on reading comprehension and writing proficiency (how much) but little indication of the "why" of student progress.

Why should you base assessment on a variety of observations?

7. Assessment must be knowledge-based and reflect the most current understanding of reading and writing processes (see Table 9.1). Your knowledge and beliefs about reading and writing processing will strongly influence your assessment of your students' progress and the way you provide for their instructional needs. For example, you might decide to use higher-level thinking strategies (such as the DR-TA, GMA, and reciprocal teaching) or wait time during discussions or to provide certain mini-lessons during writing workshop.

Research and Evidence-Based Practice

Teacher Assessment and Classroom Instruction

Did You Know?

- Teachers are the most critical and important assessment tool, as they carry out ongoing classroom assessment and use these results in their instructional decision-making (Valencia, 2000; Valencia & Au, 1997; Wolf & Reardon, 1996).

- When teachers use ongoing assessment, student achievement has been shown to improve (Black & William, 1998; Falk & Ort, 1998; Valencia, 2000).

- Students who are actively engaged in their own self-assessment become more directed, more focused, and more likely to grow and learn (Andrade, 2000; Underwood, 1998).

- Teacher assessment of student progress is essential in order to plan for differential instruction in literacy areas ranging from word identification and recognition to comprehension development, which, in turn, leads to higher

student achievement (Ruddell, 2004; Ruddell & Unrau, 2004a; Juel and Minden-Cupp, 2004).

- Teachers believe that assessment of individual students is the most important tool in instructional planning, while administrators and legislators rely most heavily on achievement test results to interpret student progress (Ruddell & Kinzer, 1982).

- Standardized achievement testing is designed to provide some measure of how much your students have learned while informal assessment and observations provide important clues to why and how your students use word identification and comprehension skills to construct meaning and to plan the next steps for instruction (Denton, Ciancio, & Fletcher, 2006; Farr & Beck, 1991; Hiebert & Hutchison, 1991; and Valencia & Wixon, 2000).

Assessment and Classroom Observations

> *All instructional strategies described in this book provide opportunities for classroom observations.*

A wide variety of instructional strategies for reading and writing development have been discussed in Chapters 3 through 8. Each of these strategies provides an opportunity to observe and assess students' growth. For example, observation and assessment of their writing progress is a critical part of the writing workshop, discussed in Chapter 8. You will recall that this assessment involves documentation, monitoring of progress with specific writing skills, and evaluation and interpretation that give productive feedback to individual students. The common denominator for all strategies is the opportunity to observe students as they construct meaning using their background knowledge, thinking strategies, and interactions during discussion with you and with peers (Brozo & Simpson, 2007; Ruddell & Unrau, 2004a).

Sources of Information for Assessment

EVIDENCE-BASED PRACTICE

Assessment observations of your students should be made over time—weeks or months, depending on your instructional objectives and goals (Shepard, 2004). You will need to develop a systematic way of recording and analyzing students' learning processes and products. You also will need to decide what observations and samples of their work to collect at the beginning of the school year as a baseline for noting growth. Your baseline collection for each student may include the following types of information:

> *Baseline Information for Assessment Purposes*

- Brief notes reflecting immediate learning observations
- Developmental observations over a longer time period
- Interest inventory observations
- Literature Response Journal entries
- Students' drawings, illustrations, and related writing
- Selected writing samples and reports
- Student self-assessment information
- Letters and notes to and from other teachers and parents
- Informal Reading Inventory information

At the start of the school year, decide on the time intervals at which you will record observations and collect samples of students' work. This schedule may or may not coincide with the report card period in your school district. Your evaluation plan should involve your students in deciding what work they would like to have included in the collection. You may wish to use the Early Reading and Writing Assessment Checklist in Figure 3.20 (in chapter 3) to assess the five critical areas of early literacy development for students in kindergarten and first grade.

Quick Notes for Recording Observations

Insights about students' learning will occur to you during instruction, when you have little time to record your ideas. A simple procedure is to use self-stick notes for quick observations. Include on each note the date, the student's name, and one or two words quickly jotted down—enough information to remind you of the observation or insight. Simply stick several notes on a clipboard for ready access. Then, for example, as you interact with students during a DR-TA and observe that Kareem has difficulty forming story predictions, you might note "9/15—Kareem—story predict. prob." Remember to include observations of their successes as well, such as "9/22—Kareem—great story insight."

> How could you use self-stick-note observations in planning instruction?

Using an Interest Inventory

Information about students' interests becomes important as you plan instruction to activate their personal motivations. Ways of determining their special interests include observing their selections of literature and their choices of individual activities during free time. Your interactions with students during classroom instruction and conversations with them on the playground and during lunchtime will often reveal interests and motivations that otherwise would be unknown to you.

Strategies in Use

Using Different Sources of Information to Determine Literacy Progress

Marlene, one of Carol Avery's first-grade students, has just completed a special story. As you read Carol's description of the writing conference she had with Marlene, refer to Marlene's story, shown below.

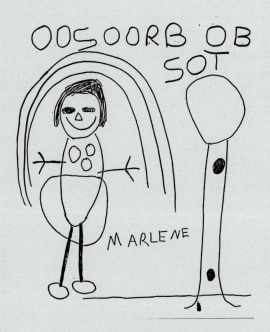

I asked Marlene to read her writing to me. "I am outside, under a rainbow and beside a tree," she read as she moved her finger under the letters in a very precise, deliberate fashion.

"Tell me about these O's," I responded. Marlene looked at me and giggled that I didn't see what was so obvious.

"Those aren't O's," she said. "They're circles."

"Circles?" Now I was puzzled. "Well, why did you decide to put circles in the middle of your writing?"

"Because. See, I couldn't tell what letters make those sounds so I just put circles for what goes there because something

goes there only I don't know what. I can't tell what letter makes that sound, so I just put circles."

Marlene read and pointed her way through the line again. "I am—oops, I forget to write *I*." Her finger lands under the first circle as she says *am*. She continues on, and I can see that Marlene has correctly written *S* for *side*, *RB* for *rainbow*, *BS* for *beside*, and *T* for *tree*. The sounds she was unable to identify are vowel sounds, but Marlene was able to develop a strategy to deal with this.

When I looked again at Marlene's writing and listened to her explanation, I understood that she could distinguish vowel sounds in words but could not identify them with a corresponding letter.

CRITICAL THINKING

1. What observations can you make that will provide some clues to Marlene's literacy progress? You may wish to briefly reexamine the Early Reading and Writing Assessment Checklist, found in Figure 3.18, to assist you in your interpretations.
2. Do you think Marlene has a positive attitude toward literacy events? Why or why not?
3. What authentic assessment strategies did Carol use to explore Marlene's literacy progress?
4. How should Carol use her assessment of Marlene's literacy progress to plan instruction?
5. What should Carol look for as a measure of growth in Marlene's literacy development?

Excerpt from "Are We Listening?" by Carol Avery, reprinted with permission from *Organizing for Whole Language* edited by Yetta M. Goodman, Kenneth S. Goodman, and Wendy J. Hood. Copyright © 1991 by Yetta M. Goodman. Published by Heinemann, a division of Reed Elsevier Inc., Portsmouth, NH.

An **interest inventory** such as the one in Figure 9.1 (page 256) provides another excellent way to identify students' school and out-of-school interests and motivations. You will need to administer the inventory individually in the early primary grades because of their limited writing abilities. Upper primary- and intermediate-grade students can complete the inventory independently, but you will obtain more direct and rich information if you administer the inventory orally

interest inventory
a rating form for identifying students' personal interests in and out of school

FIGURE 9.1

Interest Inventory

Name: _____ Age: _____

Grade: _____ Date: _____

1. What do you like to do at school when you can do anything you want to?

   _____

   _____

2. Do you like to read? _____ If so, what are your favorite books?

   _____

   _____

3. Do you have any books of your own? _____ If so, what is your favorite one?

   _____

   _____

4. What do you like most about reading? _____

5. How do you know if someone is a good reader?

   _____

6. Check the activities that you like best.

   a. Reading books _____

   b. Listening to stories _____

   c. Going to the library _____

   d. Watching TV _____

   e. Going to the movies _____

   f. Going to the zoo _____

   g. Using my computer _____

   h. Playing with my friends _____

   i. Playing with my brother or sister _____

   j. Helping my mother or father at home _____

7. What do you like to do when you go home from school? _____

   _____

8. Of all your toys and other things at home, what do you like best? _____

   _____

   Why? _____

9. What are your special interests outside of school? _____

   _____

10. If you could have three wishes, what would they be?

    a. _____

    b. _____

    c. _____

This inventory may be reproduced for classroom use.

to individual students. Items 6 and 8 will need to be adjusted to account for upper elementary and middle-school student interests and activities.

Using the Reading Achievement Inventory

The **Reading Achievement Inventory (RAI)** provides a systematic way to record your observations of an individual student's reading progress using routine classroom literacy activities and interactions. It is easily employed during instruction involving the strategies discussed in this book, such as the DL-TA, content DR-TA, SDEI, and GMA. The RAI will help in your assessment of individual student progress, act as a map to guide instruction, and assist in discussions with students and parents.

The RAI requires observing and evaluating the reading achievement skills and motivations identified in Figure 9.2 (page 258). The three areas of the RAI consist of (1) word identification, (2) comprehension and vocabulary, and (3) motivation. The How To Do will assist you in using this inventory with your students.

Word Recognition and Identification

This first category is designed to reflect a student's progress toward word recognition and independent word identification skills. These skills extend along a continuum and range from print awareness and phonemic awareness and segmentation at the beginning stages to context-clue strategies and reading fluency at more advanced stages. Each of these seven skills is critical to the development of the skilled and fluent reader. You will recall that instructional strategies useful for developing these skills are discussed in Chapter 4.

Comprehension and Vocabulary

This second category provides insight into each student's progress in constructing meaning from narrative and expository text. The importance of reading purpose and expected use directs the reader's search for meaning. Your observations of the reading strategies used by

> How could you use an interest inventory in planning instruction?

> **Reading Achievement Inventory (RAI)**
> a rating form for recording observations of students' routine literacy activities and interactions

> Which strategies in this book offer opportunities to see how students are progressing in word recognition and identification?

> Which strategies in this book offer opportunities to see how students are progressing in comprehension and vocabulary development?

How to Do . . .

The Reading Achievement Inventory

1. Make copies of the inventory, one for each student, and keep them on your desk or in a convenient place in the room.
2. Organize your thinking and observations around the three areas of the inventory because the items under each area serve to define that area in an easily understood way.
3. Start slowly, selecting three or four students for observation over several days' time, with the goal of completing a set of observations for all of your students during the first four to six weeks of school and, thereafter, every six weeks.

- **At the beginning of the school year, if you suspect that certain students are delayed readers, you might wish to begin your observations with *them*—thus allowing you to start instruction to assist them as soon as possible. Teachers should study their students' records prior to the school year. Among other valuable insights about the students, this will provide indications of who might be experiencing delays in reading development.**

4. Note each student's progress by circling the appropriate number on the checklist. First, note success areas; then, identify areas that require special attention.
5. Sensitize yourself to the importance of making regular observations to identify the student's progress and using this information in designing and shaping your instructional program.
6. Use the RAI not only in instructional planning but also in conferences with your students and with their parents.

DELAYED READER ADAPTATION

FIGURE 9.2
Reading Achievement Inventory

Reading Achievement Inventory (RAI)

Student Name _____ Grade _____ Date _____

Note to Teacher: Draw a circle around the number key that best describes your assessment of the student's reading performance.

Key: 1 = Often 2 = Sometimes 3 = Seldom

1. Word Recognition and Identification

1. Demonstrates use of print awareness (letter names, letter recognition)	1	2	3
2. Understands use of phonemic awareness and phonemic segmentation	1	2	3
3. Demonstrates understanding of letter-sound relationships (consonants, vowels)	1	2	3
4. Uses letter patterns and rhyme in identifying new words	1	2	3
5. Applies syllable identification (prefixes, suffixes, roots, compound words)	1	2	3
6. Uses context-clue strategies (sentence, definition, contrast-comparison, example-illustration)	1	2	3
7. Possesses rapid-recognition vocabulary and reading fluency	1	2	3

2. Comprehension and Vocabulary

1. Establishes clear reading purpose and expected use of content	1	2	3
2. Demonstrates excellent background knowledge on wide range of topics	1	2	3
3. Uses varied reading strategies that fit purpose and text	1	2	3
4. Comprehends material at factual level	1	2	3
5. Comprehends material at interpretive, applicative, and transactive levels	1	2	3
6. Connects new vocabulary knowledge to prior background knowledge	1	2	3
7. Holds positive attitude toward new word exploration and meaning construction	1	2	3

3. Motivation

1. Enjoys exploring new characters, people, and places through books	1	2	3
2. Actively seeks new concepts through narrative and expository text	1	2	3
3. Derives aesthetic pleasure from language and illustrations in literature	1	2	3
4. Engages in discussions of ideas developed in both fact and fiction text	1	2	3
5. Uses internally driven motivations such as problem resolution, prestige, escape, and understanding self	1	2	3
6. Utilizes discussion strategies useful in probing and sharing text-based ideas	1	2	3
7. Demonstrates high level of fluency and wide reading interest	1	2	3

each student will provide insight into the student's meaning-construction process and the levels of thinking used. The student's ability to integrate new vocabulary into background knowledge and use this vocabulary in the comprehension process is of critical importance in developing meaning. Finally, the student's positive attitude toward new word exploration will lead to increased acquisition of background knowledge and in turn comprehension achievement. You will find a quick review of Chapters 5 and 6 helpful in designing instruction based on your observations.

Motivation

Which strategies in this book offer opportunities to see how students are progressing in motivation to read?

This third category sheds insight into the student's desire and motivation to read. The enjoyment of exploring "new worlds" through books and the active search for new concepts reflect the student's "want to" of the reading process. The use of internal reader motivations and discussion strategies provides strong clues to the development of reader interest and high-level fluency. You will find the discussion and ideas in Chapter 7 helpful in planning instruction designed to meet the student needs identified through your student observations based on items in this category.

Using Informal Reading Inventories

The **Informal Reading Inventory (IRI)** provides for observational evaluation of students' unrehearsed oral reading. The IRI can serve at least three purposes:

1. It helps you understand how a student constructs meaning and applies word identification strategies. This is especially useful for a student you believe is encountering special reading problems.
2. It provides a rough indication of reading placement level for a student.
3. It offers insight into a student's comprehension and use of word identification strategies as he or she reads aloud and interacts during small-group instruction.

The IRI is administered to students individually, using prepared reading passages that have approximate grade-level indications. If you are using a basal reader or have one available, you may wish to construct your own IRI using reading passages representing various grade levels. Commercially available IRIs include reading passages, graded word lists, observation forms, and specific scoring instructions. Examples of such IRIs include the *Basic Reading Inventory* (Johns, 2005) and the *Analytical Reading Inventory* (Woods & Moe, 2007). Some publisher-produced inventories, such as the *Classroom Reading Inventory* (Silvaroli & Wheelock, 2004), include a literature-type format for evaluating students' ability to make predictions, analyze characters, perceive problems, and anticipate outcomes. Many basal reading programs provide an IRI in the teacher's guide, based on selected passages and related questions representing different grade levels in the program.

To effectively use the IRI with students, you need to do the following:

- Understand the concept of reading miscues and the types of reading miscues that arise as children attempt to construct meaning.
- Become familiar with the administration of the IRI and the notational system used to record students' responses.
- Consider how to interpret reading miscues and other student responses as clues to the word identification and comprehension strategies used by the children.
- Determine how to use the IRI to identify students' reading strengths and instructional needs, for use as an aid in planning instruction.

Oral Reading Miscue Analysis

In the context of oral reading, the term *miscue* was introduced by Yetta and Kenneth Goodman to describe a student's response when that response differs from the printed text (Goodman, 1972; Goodman, 1991b; Goodman & Goodman, 2004). *Miscue* was introduced to replace the label *error*, which reflected the attitude that any deviation from written text during oral reading was an error made by the reader. Through their observations of many oral reading episodes, the Goodmans and their colleagues noted that not all deviations from text were wrong, in that they did not deny or distort text meaning and often served as a means for self-correction. Further, they realized that an analysis of deviations could provide information about readers' expectations for print, their background knowledge, how they approach new words in text, how they process text, and more. *Miscue* thus was intended to remove the stigma of *error* and the accompanying assumptions of pathology (something is "wrong") when readers deviate from written text in oral reading.

Oral reading miscues are important indications of a reader's thinking processes and the comprehension and word identification strategies he or she uses. **Miscue analysis** allows you to examine the qualitative aspects of a student's reading—you search for explanations based on the quality of responses. A quantitative approach, such as counting the number of deviations, might indicate that a student is experiencing difficulty but would shed little light on the nature of the difficulty.

Questions for Identifying Miscues

Yetta Goodman (1972) suggests three questions that you might ask yourself about a child's oral reading:

1. Why do readers make miscues?
2. What categories or patterns do the miscues make?
3. What is the significance of the miscue pattern?

Informal Reading Inventory (IRI) an individually administered test of children's unrehearsed oral reading abilities

➤ *How to Use an IRI*

| What is a miscue?

EVIDENCE-BASED PRACTICE

miscue analysis a system for evaluating the quality of students' oral reading and identifying strengths and specific areas of difficulty

Table 9.2 (see below) presents seven questions (Goodman, Watson, & Burke, 1987) that are helpful in searching for and interpreting miscue patterns.

➤ *Criteria for Miscue Significance*

Miscues are closely connected to the oral language, background knowledge, word identification strategies, and comprehension strategies of the student. As Table 9.2 suggests, miscues are significant when they

1. alter the meaning and interpretation of the text.
2. reflect consistent word identification patterns that over-rely on one cuing system (e.g., graphic, phonemic).
3. interfere with comprehension and construction of meaningful relationships in text.
4. affect reading fluency, which may or may not influence comprehension and meaning construction.

Miscues are less significant when they

1. are self-corrected by the child during reading.
2. do not alter the interpretation of the text.
3. are dialect-related and do not change the meaning of the text.

System for Recording Miscues

As you administer the IRI or an oral reading miscue analysis, you will need a quick and efficient system for recording a student's miscues. You will require a photocopy of the text to be read, and a tape recorder is helpful to capture the student's oral reading, especially while you learn to use the notational system. Then you can replay parts of the student's reading to check the accuracy of your miscue-analysis notations.

TABLE 9.2

Evaluating the Significance of Miscues

Question	Significance
1. Is a dialect variation involved in the miscue?	A *yes* answer indicates that the student is constructing meaning using the language that sounds right to him or her. Dialect miscues that do not change meaning *according to the rules of that dialect* are not considered significant.
2. How much does the miscue look like what was expected?	A high degree of similarity indicates that the student was attending to graphic features as well as context to construct meaning.
3. How much does the miscue sound like what was expected?	A high degree of similarity may indicate dialect involvement that the student was attending to phonological cues more than to context or meaning cues.
4. Is the grammatical function of the miscued word the same as that of the word in the text (e.g., is a noun substituted for a noun)?	A *yes* answer suggests that the student understands the syntax of English and expects to find appropriate parts of speech in their appropriate places in text.
5. Is the miscue corrected?	Self-corrections indicate that the student has realized his or her miscue and is correcting to achieve consistency in meaning construction. Self-corrections are not considered significant.
6. Does the miscue occur in a context that is semantically acceptable?	A *yes* indicates that the student understands meaning relationships and is constructing meaningful text. Semantic miscues may substitute word meanings without changing the meaning of the text (e.g., *blanket* and *cover*).
7. Does the miscue result in a change of meaning?	A *yes* indicates that the meaning the student constructed is different from the expected meaning.

Questions from Goodman, Y. M., Watson, D. J., & Burke, C. L. (1987). *Reading Miscue Inventory.* Richard C. Owen Publishers. Reprinted with permission.

The following notational system identifies four types of *meaning-influence miscues*—miscues that influence comprehension—and three types of *fluency-influence miscues*—miscues that influence mainly reading rate. The four meaning-influence miscues are as follows:

➤ *Notations for Meaning-Influence Miscues*

1. *Omission of a word, part of a word, or punctuation,* as reflected in oral reading intonation. Circle the word, word ending, or punctuation. Omissions may be more or less significant, depending on whether they interfere with meaning. Omission of word endings may be dialect related. Frequent omissions usually interfere with meaning.

   Example: She (had) wanted to take a ride . . .

   Example: They mov(ed) like water.

2. *Substitution of a word.* Draw a line through the word, and write the substituted word above it. This miscue is significant if it interferes with meaning.

   Example: Angela ~~was~~ seven. (is)

   Example: The women all ~~wore~~ beautiful white dresses. (were)

3. *Insertion of a word, word ending, or words.* Place a caret (^) at the point of insertion, and write the inserted word, word ending, or words above the line. This miscue frequently occurs when a student relies on his or her normal oral language pattern and expectations regarding the text. This is not significant unless the meaning is significantly changed.

   Example: She wanted to take ^some dancing lessons.

4. *Word provided by the teacher,* after a five-second pause or upon recognition that assistance is needed. Place a *T* (for *teacher*) over the word supplied. This miscue is usually significant: Frequent need for the teacher to pronounce words suggests that the reading material is too difficult or the student needs to develop more background knowledge and word identification skills.

   Example: The women all wore beautiful [T] white dresses.

The three fluency-influence miscues are as follows:

➤ *Notations for Fluency-Influence Miscues*

1. *Self-correction of miscue.* Record the initial miscue as it is made. After the self-correction, circle the word and place a *C* above the circle. This miscue indicates that the student is actively monitoring the meaning-construction process and applying "fix-up" strategies to derive meaning.

   Example: He saw some dancers (on)[C/in] TV.

2. *Repetition of a word.* Underscore the word or words repeated, using a reverse arrow. Word repetition is often used by students to mark time to apply word identification skills to the next word or group of words. This may indicate the need for reading material that is at a lower level of difficulty.

   Example: Angela was seven years old.

   Example: She wanted to take dancing lessons.

3. *Word-by-word reading and hesitation between words.* Place a check mark between the words where hesitation occurs. Hesitation suggests a fluency problem, especially if the words are those that occur with high frequency. This may indicate the need to encourage practice with high-interest material at a lower level of difficulty.

   Example: Angela ✓ is ✓ seven ✓ years ✓ old.

Using a Running Record

Marie Clay (1985) developed the **running record** to provide an easy and convenient way to observe and analyze students' reading progress. The running record differs from miscue analysis in several important ways. You do not need a copy of the text the student is reading because your

running record
a simplified notational system for recording students' reading performance

Strategies in Use

Applying Miscue Analysis

Rebecca is an outgoing and popular second-grade student. Her teacher, Judy Barnes, notes that Rebecca appears to have difficulty applying word identification skills but has average or above-average comprehension ability. In spelling during writing activities, Rebecca relies heavily on letter-name spelling—she uses letters to stand for sounds, with few vowels and silent letters represented. Judy also indicates that Rebecca's reading interests are very limited, although she is very verbal and expresses great interest in illustrating her own stories.

Judy picks out a passage that she believes is appropriate for Rebecca's reading level. Following is Judy's miscue transcript (using the same miscue recording system described in the text) for Rebecca's reading of the passage.

A Trip to the Store

Bill and Jimmy were on their way to the store.
They walked down the street.
Jimmy said, "That dog is looking out the window."
"Yes," said Bill. "He is the worst one in town. I am glad he is inside today."
The boys came to the store. They went to the IN door.
Swoosh!
The door opened all by itself!
"Wow," said Jimmy. "Look at that! A magic door!"
"You are silly!" said Bill. "The new doors work by electricity."
"What's electricity?" asked Jimmy.
"I'll tell you later," said Bill. "Come let's get the bread."
The boy's mother needed bread for sandwiches.
Bill looked for a long time. The bread had been moved to a new place in the store.
Then he spotted it.
But where was Jimmy?

After Rebecca reads the passage, Judy asks her the following questions. Her responses are noted after each question.

1. What did the boy's mother need from the store? (factual) — *some bread*

2. What made the door work? (factual) — *electric*

3. Why did Bill have trouble finding the bread? (factual) — *'cause it moved to a new place*

4. Why did Bill think the dog was the worst one in town? — *'cause he might bite everybody that comes next to him younger*

5. Do you think Bill was older or younger than Jimmy? (interpretive)

6. Why do you think so? (interpretive) — *I just think he's younger*

7. Where would you have looked for Jimmy? applicative) — *Look all over the store and in the cereal toy place*

8. What would you do if you did not find him there? (applicative) — *I'd call the police and tell them all about the thing that happened, and tell them what he looks like and describe him. Then I'd drive in the police car and point out if I see him.*

CRITICAL THINKING

1. Examine Rebecca's miscues. What is your reaction to the total number of miscues? To the meaning-influence miscues? To the fluency-influence miscues?

2. What miscue patterns can you identify? What do these miscues suggest to you about Rebecca's reading fluency? Her meaning-construction ability?

3. What do Rebecca's responses to the comprehension questions suggest to you about her meaning-construction process? Levels of thinking? Were you surprised at Rebecca's comparatively high level of comprehension? If so, why?

4. Based on the miscue analysis and comprehension responses, what instructional recommendations would you make to Judy to help Rebecca in word analysis and fluency? in comprehension? in reading motivation and interest?

How to Do . . .

Your Own IRI

1. From your basal reader or from literature selections, select reading passages that are approximately one hundred to two hundred words long.
   - Try to find passages that represent a self-contained part of a story, such as an introductory episode or one complete story event.
   - Identify six to eight selections that represent different levels of difficulty from grades 1 through 6 (e.g., sample different grade-level stories from a basal reader).
   - Use your own judgment about difficulty level, because stories within a given grade level of a basal reader can vary by one or even two grade levels in difficulty.
   - Check your judgment on approximate grade level, using the Fry Readability Graph, shown in Figure 9.4.
   - Make up a title for each of your selections.
2. Photocopy the selected pages, some of which will contain illustrations; type the title on each; mount them on tagboard; and place your sample passages in a three-ring binder for easy use.
3. Develop six to eight comprehension questions for each passage, including factual (two or three), interpretive (two), applicative (two), and transactive (one or two) questions (see Chapter 5).
4. Retype the passages in double-spaced format for your binder, to facilitate miscue coding during the student's oral reading.
   - Write the number of words at the end of the passage to help you estimate the percentage of miscues.
   - Make several photocopies of the passages and your accompanying comprehension questions for future use. (One complete set of passages and comprehension questions will be needed for each administration of the IRI, so you will want to save your originals, too.)

- **If the students in your class comprise a very wide range of reading levels, you may wish to purchase one of the commercially available IRIs instead. While some teachers want to have an IRI based specifically on their basal reader, preparing versions to accommodate all levels can be time consuming. Many commercially prepared IRIs today have been carefully developed and have the advantage of multiple passages at each reading level so that retesting at a later time, usually necessary with delayed readers, can be accomplished with a different passage. Many also have longer passages to more closely approximate authentic reading.**

DELAYED READER ADAPTATION

5. Before you administer the IRI, determine a reading-level starting point (passage difficulty) for the student, based on your instructional observations.
6. As the first passage, use the passage at the level just below the starting level, to ensure reading ease. Use a tape recorder, especially at first, to assist you in checking and refining your coding.
7. Create a comfortable and informal setting for the administration of the IRI, and explain to the student that you are interested in learning more about his or her reading.
8. Begin by asking the student to read the title of the selection and tell what he or she thinks this selection might be about. As each passage is read, use the miscue notational system discussed earlier and ask the questions you have prepared. Or you may wish to use the running record procedure.
9. During the reading, carefully observe the student's interest and persistence in reading the passage.
   - Continue to administer the IRI passages until comprehension drops to approximately the 75 percent level or you note about fifteen significant miscues per hundred words (15 percent). At this point, you have reached the student's frustration level (see Table 9.3, page 265).
   - Use the information in the table to determine the student's approximate instructional- and independent-reading placement levels.
10. Complete your analysis and interpretation of the IRI information, and incorporate your insights into your instructional planning and selection of reading experiences for the student.

the Highly Effective Teacher

➤ *Notations for Running Record*

EVIDENCE-BASED PRACTICE

How do running records help you identify students' strengths and weaknesses as readers?

notations can be made on a blank sheet of paper. A running record thus can be completed in an authentic context on any text the student is reading, including self-selected text. To take a running record, you make a check mark for each word read correctly (see next page, Figure 9.3). When a miscue occurs, you record the text word and write above it the word the student said. If the student self-corrects, record the original pronunciation and write *SC* beside it. When you must pronounce a word for a student, indicate the word he or she said and write *T* (told) below the word, indicating that you provided support. Other helpful notations include the following:

R, along with an arrow below the word, word group, or sentence, indicates repetition.
A indicates student appeal for help.
A hyphen *below* the line indicates insertion of a word.
A hyphen *above* the line indicates omission of a word.
W indicates wait time or hesitation.

When a proper name is missed repeatedly, count one miscue. When a sentence is omitted, count each word as an error; however, do not count self-corrections as errors (Clay, 1993, pp. 27–29). Figure 9.3 (page 264) shows a full sample of a running record.

Clay (1993) recommends analyzing student responses for three aspects of the reading process: the use of meaning (M), reflecting the child's world knowledge; structure (S), suggesting language-based knowledge; and visual cues (V), indicating the part of the word to which the student is attending. This aspect of the analysis is carried out in Figure 9.3 in the right-hand column "Cues Used" for error-based words (E) or self-corrected words (SC).

If you are to use the running record in planning instruction, your interpretation needs to take into account the difficulty of the text, indicated by the accuracy of words read. In the analysis in Figure 9.3, the accuracy rate (ACC) is 66 percent, indicating that Cory is struggling with the text (below 90 percent) but appears to understand what he is reading. Clay (1993) recommends that, ideally, challenging material should be read at approximately the 90-percent level of accuracy, while independent reading should be at the 95- to 100-percent level. Your interpretation of the running record will lead to identification of areas of strengths and limitations, which will enable you to effectively plan instruction for the student.

Estimating Approximate Reading Levels

reading levels degrees of reading proficiency—independent, instructional, or frustration—based on graded text

Independent, instructional, and frustration **reading levels** are descriptors frequently used to identify three distinct degrees of reading proficiency. These levels, based on the estimated grade-level difficulty of texts, are useful as reminders that reading ability is multidimensional. That is, no student reads only at, say, the first- or fifth-grade level; rather, students read differentially at various levels. The independent reading level is the highest level at which a student can read with ease. Reading at this level is characterized by fluency, normal intonation, few miscues, and no physical signs of stress or tension. The instructional reading level is the level at which a student can read comfortably with teacher guidance. Reading at this level is generally proficient, with some miscues and some need for assistance. The instructional level is an approximation or estimate based on teacher judgment. The frustration reading level is the lowest level, at which reading and learning break down. Reading is halting, often in an unnatural intonation or monotone, and is accompanied by physical signs of stress. Guidelines for estimating students' reading levels, based on placement-level studies (Betts, 1946; Johnson, Kress, & Pikulski, 1987; Leu & Kinzer, 1999; Powell, 1970; Ruddell & Williams, 1972), are presented in Table 9.3 (page 266).

readability scales system for estimating the degree of difficulty of text for readers

A variety of scales are used to estimate the readability levels of textual materials. Three widely used **readability scales** are the Spache (1953), appropriate for primary grades; the Dale-Chall (1948), used for grades 4 and up; and the Fry (1977b), appropriate for grade 1 through university levels. The Fry Readability Graph and directions for its application are found in Figure 9.4 (page 267).

You may wish to spend time exploring the online Readability Statistical Tool at www.interventioncentral.org/htmdocs/tools/okapi/okapi.shtml. Cut and paste a section of text into the form provided, and the tool estimates readability using the Space formula, grades 1 through 3, or the Dale-Chall formula, grades 4 and higher.

FIGURE 9.3

Cory's Running Record

CORY'S RUNNING RECORD

Text: On a Cold Cold Day   Text Level [3]

Scores: Running Words / Error 33/10   Error Rate [1:3]   ACC. [66%]   SC Rate [1:4]

Page	Title and level: On a cold cold day	E	SC	Cues used E	Cues used SC
2	✓ On ✓ a ✓ cold ✓ cold ✓ day ✓/A rat|R ✓/wears ✓/a ✓/hat				
3	√On|sc a|sc cold|sc cold|sc|R A fox wears socks		4	M ⑤ V M ⑤ V M ⑤ V M ⑤ V	Ⓜ s Ⓥ Ⓜ⑤ V Ⓜ⑤ V Ⓜ⑤ V
4	✓/A ✓/giraffe ✓/wears ✓/a Coat/scarf	1		M ⑤ V	
5	A/– goat/goats ✓/wear ✓/coats	2		M ⑤ V Ⓜ⑤Ⓥ	
6	Kangaroo/Kangaroos ✓/wear ✓/shoes	1		Ⓜ⑤Ⓥ	
7	A/– Cat/Kittens ✓/wear ✓/mittens	2		M ⑤ V Ⓜ⑤Ⓥ	
8	√✓/And –/Paul ✓/wears all/them of/all them/ñ Ⓦ|R	4		M ⑤ V M ⑤ V M ⑤ V M ⑤ V	

Analysis:
Cory's dominant cuing system is structure. Those neglected are meaning and visual.
Meaning is cross-checked against structure, resulting in self-correction. (Cold/SC / Socks)

You may wish to make your own Informal Reading Inventory to assist you in assessing individual students' literacy progress or in estimating their reading placement. Use your own IRI with students who seem to be having a reading problem.

Portfolio Assessment

As you will recall, a portfolio is a representative collection of a student's work during the school year, in progress or completed, and it can serve as the basis for evaluation. The portfolio approach to literacy assessment has strong appeal for three reasons (Valencia, 1990):

1. Portfolios allow you to capture and capitalize on the best work that each student has to offer.

> *Benefits of Portfolio Assessment*

TABLE 9.3

Determining Approximate Reading Levels

Reading Level	Observations	Miscue Accuracy		Comprehension Accuracy
Independent	Reads fluently; few miscues; self-corrects; self-monitors; comprehends easily; shows high interest	95% + (5 miscues per 100 words)	with	90% +
Instructional	Reads with fluency; some miscues; some word-by-word reading to provide processing time; comprehends less easily; expresses reading interest	90% + (10 miscues per 100 words)	with	75% +
Frustration	Reads with hesitation; limited fluency; large number of miscues; frequent word-by-word reading; limited comprehension; shows little interest; avoids reading	85% + (15 miscues per 100 words)	with	75% −

the Highly Effective Teacher

What samples resulting from the use of other strategies in this book could you and your students collect for portfolios?

the Highly Effective Teacher

➤ *Purposes for Portfolio Assessment*

2. Portfolios encourage you to use many different ways to evaluate learning and literacy growth.
3. Portfolios permit the evaluation of students' authentic literacy tasks, a type of evaluation that cannot be found in formal achievement testing.

The development of the portfolio requires collaborative selection of samples of work based on your instructional purposes and goals (Valencia & Wixon, 2000). For example, after a piece of high-interest fiction has been introduced using a DR-TA, the student's story map (GMA) and an accompanying Literature Response Journal entry may be included to document progress toward your goal of developing story integration and synthesis and fostering personal response to literature. Your evaluation of these samples will not only provide insight into the student's success in achieving this goal but also supply clues enabling you to plan effectively for that student's instructional needs.

A portfolio may take the form of a designated folder (the accordion-type folder works well) used to hold a representative sample of the student's work over the school year. The folder can easily be personalized by including a photograph or a self-drawn portrait along with her or his name. The contents of the folder should reflect a range of instructional goals and purposes and include such items as "show-case" written work that has been polished and selected by the student, self-evaluation checklists, and progress notes from conferencing. The portfolio folder thus demonstrates literacy growth through both process and product over time.

Establishing Instructional Purposes

As you begin to use portfolio assessment, you will need to focus on the purposes of your instruction and how these may be reflected in students' portfolios. The following ten potential purposes, from the California Assessment Portfolio Project (California State Department of Education, 1989), may be helpful in stimulating ideas in this initial step:

1. To examine students' reading and writing progress over a given time period
2. To identify instructional strengths and areas needing special attention
3. To assist students and teachers in setting goals
4. To involve students in a process of self-evaluation
5. To provide student ownership, motivation, sense of accomplishment, and participation
6. To serve as a vehicle for publication
7. To demonstrate to students their own progress and growth
8. To serve as a means for reporting student progress to parents and the public
9. To serve as the basis for parent conferences
10. To supplement or substitute for state-mandated testing

FIGURE 9.4

The Fry Readability Graph

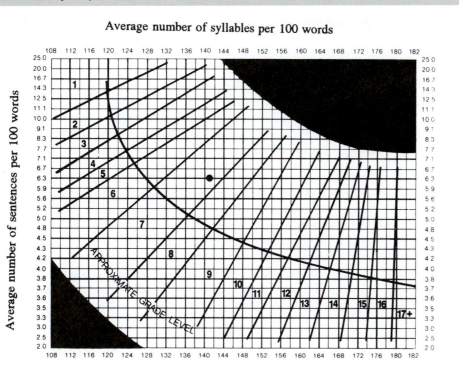

Average number of syllables per 100 words

1. Randomly select three (3) sample passages and count out exactly 100 words each, beginning with the beginning of a sentence. Count proper nouns, initializations, and numerals.
2. Count the number of sentences in the 100 words, estimating length of the fraction of the last sentence to the nearest one-tenth.
3. Count the total number of syllables in the 100-word passage. If you don't have a hand counter available, an easy way is to simply put a mark above every syllable over one in each word; then when you get to the end of the passage, count the number of marks and add 100. Small calculators can also be used as counters by pushing numeral 1, then pushing the plus sign (+) for each word or syllable when counting.
4. Enter graph with *average* sentence length and *average* number of syllables per sentence; plot dot where the two lines intersect. Area where dot is plotted will give you the approximate grade level.
5. If a great deal of variability is found in syllable count or sentence count, putting more samples into the average is desirable.
6. A word is defined as a group of symbols with a space on either side; thus, *Joe, IRA, 1945,* and *&* are each one word.
7. A syllable is defined as a phonetic syllable. Generally, there are as many syllables as vowel sounds. For example, *stopped* is one syllable, and *wanted* is two syllables. When counting syllables for numerals and initializations, count one syllable for each symbol. For example, *1945* is four syllables, *IRA* is three syllables, and *&* is one syllable.

From Edward Fry, Fry's readability graph: Clarification, validity, and extension to level 17. *Journal of Reading, 21.* Reprinted with permission by author.

Note that these purposes incorporate assessment, goal setting, and instructional planning (items 1–3); student-centered purposes (items 3–7); and communication with parents, the public, and other educators (items 8–10). You probably will want to add other purposes as you initiate portfolio assessment in your classroom.

the ★
Highly
Effective
Teacher
★

➤ *What to*
Include in a
Portfolio

Determining What to Include in Students' Portfolios

Your purposes and goals of instruction will determine, in large part, what is included in students' portfolios. Essentially, you need to ask yourself: "What meaning-construction processes and products are my students involved in that can be used to reflect their growth in literacy development?" Your answer to this question will lead to a rich assortment of possibilities for portfolio contents. The following list suggests items that might be included in a portfolio (Ruddell, 2006):

1. Observational assessments you have completed during a given time period, including your informal self-stick notes and more structured observational instruments such as the Early Reading and Writing Assessment Checklist (early primary grades; see Figure 3.18, pages 80–81), the interest inventory (all grades; see Figure 9.1, page 256), and the Reading Achievement Inventory (all grades; see Figure 9.2, page 258).
2. Self-assessment student responses collected over a period of time.
3. Student writing samples demonstrating various stages of writing revision over several weeks.
4. Maps from literature-based Group Mapping Activities and related writing samples.
5. Literature Response Journals.
6. Vocabulary Logs.
7. Book-sharing activities ranging from letters to "Mystery Book Jackets."
8. Showcase selections, identified for inclusion by the student. These selections should have moved through the cycle of prewriting, drafting, revising, editing, sharing, and publishing (see Chapter 8). Again, these selections should reflect work over time.

the ★
Highly
Effective
Teacher
★

What is the
value of includ-
ing in a portfolio
work that
reflects a range
of quality?

Involving Students in Portfolio Development and Evaluation

As you communicate your instructional intent and expectations to students, they will become actively involved in building their portfolios. They need to understand that their portfolios should contain samples of their work that reflect different aspects of their reading and writing growth. Conferring with your students using writing-workshop questions (as discussed in Chapter 8) will greatly assist them in developing self-evaluation processes and will increase their interest in portfolio collection. Questions such as the following lead to personal insights and active involvement in self-assessment:

- What makes this your best piece?
- What makes your most effective piece different from your least effective piece?
- What goals did you set for yourself?
- Did you accomplish these goals?
- What are your goals for the next several weeks?

Encourage students to use these questions to guide their written self-evaluations. Having them write explanations of their showcase pieces can increase interest, involvement, and self-analysis. The student response map in Figure 9.5, "My Portfolio and Me," from a second-grade ACOT (Apple Classroom of Tomorrow) (Denver & Leedham, 1992), can be used to facilitate showcase explanations.

Criteria for Evaluating Student Portfolios

Your evaluation of students' portfolios will take two forms—formative and summative. Formative evaluation consists of using the portfolio during individual student conferencing. For example, you may focus on a student's current piece of writing and examine the student's progress in relation to work previously collected in her or his portfolio. Or you may study a student's collection of work to detect ongoing interest or motivation problems in reading.

FIGURE 9.5
My Portfolio and Me

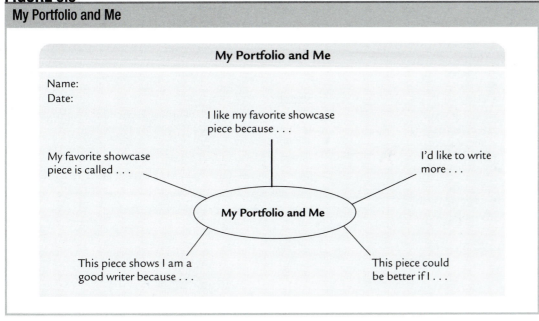

Reproduced with permission of Stevens Creek Elementary School.

Overall, or summative, portfolio evaluation at periodic intervals over the school year is designed to assess each student's reading and writing progress. You may decide to schedule this evaluation to coincide with preparation for report cards and parent conferences. The criteria you use in this evaluation should relate directly to your instructional goals and purposes.

> *Portfolios can be used for both formative and summative assessment.*

Two examples of criteria for portfolio analysis (Tierney, Carter, & Desai, 1991) are presented in Figure 9.6 (page 270), which identifies general evaluation criteria for reading and writing, and in Figure 9.7 (page 271), which offers a rubric for holistic assessment.

Formal Assessment

This chapter has focused on informal assessment and observations that relate directly to your instructional program. In all probability, however, you will be required to administer a standardized achievement test of some type during the school year. Therefore, it is important to understand the use of **formal assessment** and key concepts related to testing.

formal assessment standardized testing

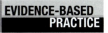

The major purpose of formal (standardized) achievement testing is to obtain some indication of how much your students have learned. This is in contrast to informal assessment and observations, which focus on why and how your students use reading and writing processes to construct meaning (Valencia & Wixon, 2000). It is important to ask and answer the following questions about formal assessment:

1. What is the purpose of the testing?
2. How does the formal assessment relate to my instructional program?
3. What information can I expect to obtain from the test?
4. How will this information be used at the classroom, school, and district levels?

Research (Ruddell & Kinzer, 1982) suggests that most teachers believe that achievement testing, combined with assessment of individual students, is of value in instructional planning. Local school district office personnel use test data to identify achievement trends for the school district and to make comparisons with state and national achievement levels (Valencia & Wixon, 2000). Yet most school personnel express the view that too much time is spent on formal testing. Achievement test results are best used as one piece of information, which is combined with authentic classroom

FIGURE 9.6

Portfolio Analysis

Types of Reading/Writing
- Projects
- Genres
- Selection

Process
- Goal Setting
- Problem Solving
- Engagement
- Use of Resources
- Troubleshooting

Self-Evaluation
- Analysis
- Ongoing Goals

Improvement, Effort, Motivation

Other:

Types of Reading

Process
- Planning
- Comprehension Strategies
- Engagement
- Decoding and Troubleshooting
- Versatility

Reading-Writing Relationship

Reflection and Reconsideration

Self-Evaluation
- Analysis
- Ongoing Goals
- Motivation

Other:

Types of Writing

Process
- Planning
- Problem Solving and Troubleshooting
- Revision
- Use of Resources (Peers, Books)

Reflection and Reconsideration

Self-evaluation
- Analysis
- Ongoing Goals
- Motivation

Other:

Portfolio Analysis   Name: _____

Date: _____

Overall

Well organized—3 pieces of writing: 2 expository; 1 personal narrative. Table of contents for reading and writing sides.

Variety of books read—7 total.

Self-evaluation—brief but specific to each piece.

Sets goals.

Highly interested in developing her portfolio.

Reading Strengths/Needs

Responses—mostly retelling. Includes primary characters and major events. Good supporting details. Reading a lot! Good personal reflection. Interest high. Could take a more personal stance in journal.

Writing Strengths/Needs

3 pieces—all include personal evaluation.

Wants help with paragraphing.

Writing has beginning/middle/end. Strong voice.

Sentence-level errors.

Informational piece—includes use of variety of sources.

Good details.

Material from *Portfolio Assessment in the Reading-Writing Classroom* by Robert J. Tierney, Mark A. Carter, and Laura E. Desai. Copyright © 1991 by Christopher-Gordon Publishers, Inc. Used by permission of the publisher.

observations to assess students' progress and identify their instructional needs (International Reading Association, 1999a).

The assessment needs and viewpoints of the classroom teacher and other school personnel are shown in Figure 9.8 (page 273). These different views require understanding on the part of teachers and other school personnel to remove the wall between them and combine the positive aspects of both viewpoints.

FIGURE 9.7
Portfolio-Analysis Guide

Beginning

Students may appear to be at the beginning stages for a number of different reasons: they may be emerging learners or learners who are only partially engaged with the classroom community in this activity. They have yet to realize their full potential: they may not be aware of or engage with their potential. These portfolios exhibit:

- Some or very little versatility, little risk taking in trying out new forms, a preference for routine tasks over exploration.
- Detachment from the portfolio process.
- Unidimensional self-evaluations: either global statements or focusing on one aspect of the work.
- Individual pieces reflect inexperience with written organization, Standard English conventions, and/or written development of ideas. Their message may be distorted due to surface-feature errors.
- Responses include brief restatement of an incident and little evidence of personal stance or involvement.
- Limited interest in or use of reading and writing beyond classroom requirements.
- Ongoing goals and goal-setting processes are either global or sketchy.
- Improvement: few shifts apparent.
- Problem-solving processes reflect few resources, disengagement, lack of confidence, and/or lack of motivation.
- Limited use of resources such as sharing or peer input.

Intermediate

Developing learner exhibits strengths and independence in selected areas and potential yet to be realized in others. These portfolios exhibit:

- Expanding versatility.
- A reasonable effort to complete the portfolio with some attention to detail, organization, and overall aesthetics.
- Self-evaluations that may be multidimensional but lack specific details and/or breadth.

- Individual pieces that falter on more than one feature. For example, papers may meander from the topic at times or there may be significant spelling or punctuation errors. The pieces in the portfolio falter in development, structure, and/or sophistication of ideas without distorting the central message.
- Responses include comments about important incidents, but their focus is narrow and has little development.
- Some interest in using reading and writing beyond assignments in classroom.
- Goal setting occurs, but is restricted or does not grow or shift across time.
- Depends on repetitive use of strategies for problem solving.
- May use resources and support in a rote fashion.

Advanced

More fully engaged, independent learner. These portfolios exhibit:

- Versatility in the variety of forms chosen.
- Clear organization of contents.
- Multidimensional self-evaluations that include reflections about a wide variety of observed traits: process, text features, surface features, voice, word choice, audience awareness, perspective, and purpose.
- Individual pieces that have a strong voice, stay on topic, are well organized, have well-formed sentences, and demonstrate effective word choice.
- Responses represent strong engagement and understanding of story elements: key issues are discussed.
- Uses reading and writing for many different reasons. Motivated to go beyond class assignments.
- Goal setting is expansive and shifts in relevant ways across time.
- Problem solving involves using various resources in expansive and meaningful ways.
- Flexible use of resources and support.

Material from *Portfolio Assessment in the Reading-Writing Classroom* by Robert J. Tierney, Mark A. Carter, and Laura E. Desai. Copyright © 1991 by Christopher-Gordon Publishers, Inc. Used by permission of the publisher.

Formal Testing Instruments

The development of standardized achievement testing instruments requires enormous investments of time and money. **Norm-referenced tests** are administered to large numbers of students to identify norms. The norms represent the average performance of a large number of students at a specific grade and age level. When you administer an achievement test to your students, you are comparing their achievement to the achievement of the norming group used in developing the test. Thus, you need to know the characteristics, including socioeconomic and cultural diversity, of the norming group. This information is provided in the test's technical manual.

norm-referenced tests
formal assessments based on the scores of a particular group of students

How to Do . . .

Portfolio Assessment

1. Identify specific instructional goals and projects that could be used to develop these goals (e.g., mapping and written story summaries, Literature Response Journals, progressive writing samples based on writing workshop). Then select one or possibly two projects that you and your students find of special interest.
2. Discuss with your students your goals and expectations in building portfolios.
   - Consider what projects you will start with and how each student will select items to go into his or her portfolio.
   - Use the chalkboard or chart paper to record key selection ideas and criteria.
3. Provide folders (preferably accordion-type with rubber bands around them), and have each student personalize the portfolio with her or his name and, if possible, a photograph or self-portrait.
4. Decide on the first portfolio items to be included, and initiate this work through group discussion and individual conferencing.
5. Discuss showcase items, and determine how these are to be developed (e.g., by progressing through the writing-workshop stages of prewriting, drafting, revising, editing, sharing, and publishing).
6. Encourage your students to share their portfolios with peers and with their parents at open house.
7. Review each student's portfolio at regular intervals, and provide an overall evaluation of his or her progress.
   - Use the sample guides shown in Figures 9.6 (page 270) and 9.7 (page 271) to assist you in the design of your own overall evaluation form.
   - Confer with each student on his or her progress, and identify areas of success and those that need work.
   - Establish collaborative goals based on your evaluation and discussion.
8. Update portfolios at regular intervals by encouraging students to decide what work is to be retained and what work might be added to illustrate their progress over the past several weeks.
9. Use the portfolios during parent conferences to demonstrate students' progress and special instructional needs.

- **Maintaining portfolios can be especially useful in documenting progress of delayed readers. Therefore, in addition to the single-focus portfolio with child-selected items described here, you may also wish to compile an ongoing, more generalized type of portfolio folder for these students. Items can include audiotapes of oral readings taken at various times in the year, copies of IRI results (early in the year, midyear, end of year), spelling samples within the context of student writing over the course of the year, teacher observational notes, lists of literature books with dates read, and others. This portfolio is not shared with peers but is used confidentially (a) to plan instruction for the student, (b) to demonstrate progress and set goals with the student, and (c) to share with parents in conferences about the student.**

DELAYED READER ADAPTATION

achievement test
a survey of students' general achievement using norm-referenced formal assessment

A survey test, or an **achievement test,** measures the general achievement of students in reading and literacy development (or in other areas such as mathematics or social studies) relative to the student group on which the test was normed. Such tests usually have several subtests—such as comprehension, vocabulary, and word identification—which are combined to provide a total reading score. Examples of standardized achievement tests include the *Comprehensive Test of Basic Skills*, grades K–12 (CTB/McGraw-Hill); *Educational Development Series*, grades K–12 (Scholastic Testing Service); *Metropolitan Achievement Tests*, preprimer–12 (Psychological Corporation); and the *Stanford Achievement Test*, 1–13 (Harcourt Brace Educational Measurement).

FIGURE 9.8

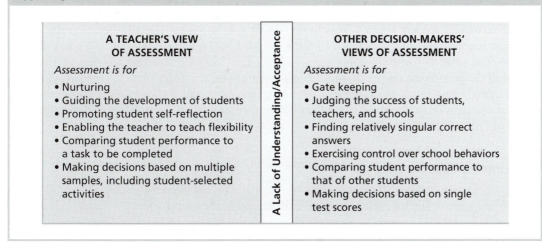

Opposing Views of Assessment

A TEACHER'S VIEW OF ASSESSMENT	A Lack of Understanding/Acceptance	OTHER DECISION-MAKERS' VIEWS OF ASSESSMENT
Assessment is for		*Assessment is for*
• Nurturing		• Gate keeping
• Guiding the development of students		• Judging the success of students, teachers, and schools
• Promoting student self-reflection		• Finding relatively singular correct answers
• Enabling the teacher to teach flexibility		• Exercising control over school behaviors
• Comparing student performance to a task to be completed		• Comparing student performance to that of other students
• Making decisions based on multiple samples, including student-selected activities		• Making decisions based on single test scores

From Farr, R. (1992, September). Putting it all together: Solving the reading assessment puzzle. *The Reading Teacher, 46* (1), 26–37. Reprinted with permission of Roger Farr and the International Reading Association. All rights reserved.

Diagnostic tests identify strengths and weaknesses. These tests differ from the surveys and test batteries in that they measure more specific skills (e.g., reading comprehension, vocabulary, visual and auditory discrimination, structural analysis, phonics). These tests provide group and individual scores as well as a profile of scores. A diagnostic test may be designed for group administration—such as the Stanford Diagnostic Reading Test—or for individual administration, such as the Diagnostic Analysis of Reading Tasks and the Gates-McKillop-Horowitz Reading Diagnostic Test.

diagnostic test
formal assessment of students' specific skills

Criterion-referenced tests indicate whether a student has met specific instructional goals or criteria. These tests are not normed to permit comparison of a student's achievement to that of other students; rather, they compare a student's performance to predetermined criteria. The student is required to reach a minimum level of competency to pass or advance in the curriculum. Outcome-based education relies on criterion-referenced testing. Examples of criterion-referenced tests include the tests in reading-management systems such as Fountain Valley and end-of-unit tests in basal programs.

criterion-referenced tests
formal assessments comparing students' performance to predetermined criteria

Concepts of Validity, Reliability, and Standard Error of Measurement

Three essential concepts that you need to be familiar with as you examine, administer, and interpret achievement tests are validity, reliability, and standard error of measurement. **Validity** refers to the ability of a test to measure what it purports to measure or what it should measure—the skills and knowledge taught in your curriculum. Other kinds of validity apply to the content of test items and the theoretical constructs on which they are based. **Reliability** refers to the stability of test scores over several administrations of the test to different groups of similar students over time. High reliability gives you confidence that your students' scores accurately reflect their performance. Reliability should range from 0.7 or above for a group assessment to 0.9 or above for an individual assessment. Information in a test's technical manual will indicate how its reliability was determined. Valencia (1990) notes several features of informal classroom observations that contribute to their validity and reliability:

validity
the degree to which a test measures what it purports to measure

reliability
the degree to which a test produces similar scores in repeated administration to different groups of similar individuals

1. You establish validity by achieving common understanding with students of your goals and the criteria you will use to evaluate these goals.
2. Assessment is ongoing throughout the school year as you observe, collect, and evaluate, using many indicators related to students' reading and literacy achievement. This ongoing "why" and "how" information contributes to the validity and reliability of measures of assessment.

➤ *Validity and Reliability in Classroom Observations*

**standard error
of measurement
(SEM)**
a numerical esti-
mate of test error,
used when inter-
preting a test score

➤ *Kinds of
Test Scores*

| Why must cau-
tion be used in
interpreting GE
scores?

3. Evaluations are based on observations of students' activities and product development and the use of structured observations, which tend to have both validity and reliability.

In formal testing, the **standard error of measurement (SEM)** is a numerical estimate of the test error in a student's score. This number tells you how sure you can be of interpreting a given test score correctly. For example, if SEM = 4 for Lisa's reading comprehension test score of 34, her true score is somewhere between 30 (−4) and 38 (+4). You can see that as the SEM increases, the greater the test error and the less reliance you can place on a given score. You cannot interpret a test result as demonstrating an achievement gain or loss unless you know how much of the gain or loss may be due to the SEM. Cautions in using standardized tests are presented in Figure 9.9 (see below).

Interpreting Test Results

As you score your students' tests or look at test results received from the testing coordinator, you need to be aware of the following terms and the concepts they represent:

1. *Raw Score.* The raw score is the number of questions answered correctly on the test or, in some cases, the number of correct items minus some percentage of incorrect items, used as a guessing penalty.
2. *Mean Score.* The mean score is the average obtained by totaling all scores and dividing by the number of different scores.
3. *Median Score.* The median is the middle score when results are listed from highest to lowest. Mean (the average) and median (the midpoint) scores are often the same for any one test.
4. *Mode Score.* The mode score is the score with the highest frequency of occurrence, or the score obtained by the largest number of students.
5. *Grade Equivalent (GE) Score.* The grade equivalent score is obtained by converting the raw score to a grade-level estimate. GE scores are derived through statistical interpretation of the norming group's raw scores. A GE score of 2.9 is interpreted as second grade, ninth month. GE scores assume a ten-month school year. These scores are frequently communicated to

FIGURE 9.9

Cautions in Using Standardized Tests

1. Standardized achievement tests are designed to measure highly generalized skills.
2. These tests do not measure specific instructional objectives nor do they account for the "how" and "why" of your students' reading and writing processing.
3. Achievement tests should not be the only basis for planning or evaluating an instructional program, because only a few of the complex literacy skills can be sampled in any one measurement instrument.
4. Standardized achievement tests include tasks closely related to those used to measure intelligence, so they reflect factors other than the effectiveness of classroom instruction.
5. The "objective" scores for standardized literacy achievement tests are based on norming groups, and these tests tell little about student achievement unless the norming groups are completely and accurately defined and the students in these groups have characteristics similar to those of your students. Because of this, boards of education, the community, parents, the media, and even professional educators often misinterpret achievement test results.
6. Pressure for high test scores can corrupt standardized tests, and direct teaching of test-related items ("teaching to the test") can result in test scores that are an invalid measure of student achievement.
7. Reliability measures for group achievement tests, provided they are not corrupted by special preparation, are used to provide some assurance of the comparability of results. However, these measures assume that the tests are administered in the same manner and at the same time in the school year and that your students have the same characteristics as the students in the norming group.
8. Group tests can measure group achievement with some degree of accuracy, but the test score of an individual student is subject to a significant error of measurement and should not be used as the sole basis for grouping and placement of that student.

parents who are anxious about their student's progress. It is important, however, to use caution in interpreting the GE score. First, remember that the GE score is converted from a raw score through statistical interpolation. Second, keep in mind that a GE score of 2.9 doesn't tell you very much about a student in a real sense, relative to other students. A GE score of 2.9 must be interpreted relative to a student's current grade level. For example, a GE score of 5.4 for Amika, who is near the end of second grade, does not indicate that reading material at the fifth-grade level is appropriate for her.

6. *Percentile Rank.* The percentile rank also is a converted score based on a student's raw score. This rank tells the position of the raw score, from the 1st to the 99th percentile, among the norming group's scores. (Recall that the norming group's scores are the test results of the original students used by the test publisher in norming the test.) For example, a 90th percentile rank means that Jaime scored as high as or above 90 percent of the students in the original norming group (and below 9 percent of those students). Percentile ranks are often erroneously confused with percentage of correct responses, but these two measures are not related. Percentile ranks are useful for understanding a student's relative achievement and may be helpful information to use in discussions with students and parents.

7. *Stanine Score.* A stanine score is a statistical interpretation of a percentile score. It is interpreted on a nine-point scale of standard scores ("standard nine"). The stanine score of 5 represents the mean (average) in the scale and is approximately at the 50th percentile. Stanine scores are most useful for comparing student progress from fall to spring, or from one year to the next.

It is important to carefully examine the administration and technical manual of the particular test you will be using in order to understand specific test features. Such knowledge will assist you in making an informed interpretation of students' test scores.

> How would you explain percentile rank to parents?

Communicating Student Progress to Parents

Your communication with parents creates a vital link between home and school. Parents depend on you to provide information on the progress of their student. You, in turn, depend on parents to provide the personal and academic home support that will enable the student to achieve effectively in school. It is important that parents clearly understand the goals and purposes of your

the Highly Effective Teacher ★
on Technology and Assessment

1. Have your students use a word-processing program to create portfolios of their work. This work could include writing samples and pictures. You may want to include their work in a class Web page.

2. Visit the Mid-continent Research for Education and Learning Web site at **www.mcrel.org.** McREL is a private, nonprofit organization conducting research on educational standards.

3. Visit the How to Use Tests in Print Web site at **www.unl.edu/buros/howtotip.html** for critiques of achievement tests that you want to know more about.

4. Have your students send e-mail to their classmates and to you regarding their responses to books they are reading independently. This will provide you with another tool for assessing their progress as readers and writers.

5. Create online reflective journals where both you and your students may share thoughts and ideas about literacy challenges and achievements.

6. For additional information on assessment, visit The National Center for Research on Evaluation, Standards, and Student Testing at **http://cse.ucla.edu.**

What guidelines should you follow for communicating student progress to parents? How will measurement and evaluation influence your instructional planning?

In what ways can you use student evaluation to encourage parental involvement?

instructional program, your expectations for their student, your evaluation procedures, and his or her progress during the school year. It is just as important that you and parents collaboratively determine next-step goals for their student.

Parental involvement in your classroom will vary widely. Some parents will gladly contribute several hours each week under your direction to tutoring or story reading and discussing with small groups. Others will be supportive of their student's growth but be unable to participate because of work schedules or home responsibilities. Still others will need encouragement to demonstrate interest in their student's progress and provide home support. Whatever the level of parental interest and support, your role in communicating to parents is very important.

One way to get parents involved is to send students' work home periodically to highlight their reading and writing progress. For example, you and the students may select portfolio samples and showcase pieces to show parents. You might wish to attach the sample parent response sheet shown in Figure 9.10 to the student's work (Denver & Leedham, 1992).

➤ *Parent-Teacher Conferences*

Open house provides another opportunity to present an overview of your program to parents and to display students' work. The time provided at most evening open-house events, however, is limited. One of the most effective vehicles for interpreting your program and children's progress is the parent-teacher conference—a one-on-one opportunity to show and explain students' work and to engage parents in a reciprocal relationship with the school.

➤ *Developing and Using Report Cards*

The report card is another way in which student progress is communicated to parents. The reporting in some school districts is limited to a narrow view of reading and writing development expressed in the form of letter grades. Particularly at the kindergarten and primary-grade levels, broader descriptions of students' progress are necessary, using more authentic assessment.

the **Highly Effective Teacher**

You can supplement any report by providing descriptive categories and comments, following the pattern of the Reading Achievement Inventory and portfolio assessment. Especially consider the following guidelines when developing and using report cards (Tierney, Carter, & Desai, 1991):

1. Keep report cards as open-ended and descriptive as possible.
2. Focus on the student's achievements and ongoing learning goals rather than on weaknesses or failures.
3. Expand the list of descriptors of possible topics for discussion to include those that follow portfolio use, the Early Reading and Writing Assessment Checklist, and the Reading Achievement Inventory.
4. Involve students and parents in developing a collaborative report that describes and communicates progress and goals.

FIGURE 9.10
Parent Response Sheet

Stevens Creek Portfolio Project
Parent Response Sheet

Student's name _____

Date _____

Which writing sample was your *student's* favorite? _____
_____
_____

Why did he/she select it as the favorite? _____
_____
_____

What was *your* favorite writing sample? _____
_____
_____

Why? _____
_____
_____

Other comments _____
_____

Reproduced with permission of Stevens Creek Elementary School.

Summary and Classroom Applications

double entry journal

What assessment practices described in this chapter do you use now or expect to use in your classroom? How do these practices differ from those you experienced as a student? How do these practices assist you in planning for instruction?

Chapter Summary

Educators' understanding of and viewpoints on reading and literacy evaluation have changed in striking ways over the past decades. The seven assessment principles, presented early in the chapter, focus on your classroom goals and authentic assessment that is based on your observations of students' learning.

Your classroom observations generate vital information on the progress of your students and provide the basis for instructional planning. Observations focus on the "why" and "how" of meaning construction in students' literacy growth. You need a systematic way of recording and analyzing your students' learning processes and their products. Some observations will be quick and "on the spot," as you make a brief comment on a self-stick note, placed in a student's file for later examination. Others, such as the interest inventory and the Reading Achievement Inventory, will provide information over a longer period of time and serve as a map to guide instruction as well as student and parent discussions.

Informal Reading Inventories, oral reading miscue analysis, and the running record will be valuable in assessing a student's reading progress, to identify strengths and areas needing greater instructional support. Portfolio assessment requires developing a collection of a student's work, in progress or completed, throughout the school

How to Do . . .

A Parent Conference

1. Prepare for the conference by reviewing your observation notes on the student's progress during the specified reporting period. Select samples from the student's portfolio that can be used to communicate progress.

2. Send home a letter that specifies the time and location of the conference, explains your expectations for the conference, and encourages parents to think about issues important to your discussion.

3. Your letter should contain a bottom tear-off portion, also showing time and location, to be returned with the student, confirming that the parents can meet with you or asking the parents to suggest an alternative meeting time, if this is necessary.

4. Locate the conference in a comfortable setting in your room where the parents can see displays of students' work. Arrange chairs for a side-by-side discussion designed to open communication as much as possible.

5. If the parents' language is not English, you may need to arrange for an interpreter.

6. Initiate the conference by briefly explaining the nature of your instructional goals and purposes, and connect these to specific samples of the student's work.

7. Describe and interpret the student's successful progress in your program, including such areas as reading comprehension development, writing progress, ability to engage in class discussions, and use of free activity time and your perception of her or his special interests and motivations.

8. Use the conference to clearly communicate instructional needs and special problems that you have identified and to encourage the parents to provide insight into the student's areas of success and need.

9. Summarize the conference, and then set out next-step goals for the student; collaboratively identify ways in which home and school will support the student's progress.

DELAYED READER ADAPTATION

■ **A frequent question of parents whose student is a delayed reader is, "Why?" They want to know what caused their student to progress through the stages of reading development more slowly than other students of the same grade. The parents may have received misinformation through newspapers, magazines, and other nonprofessional sources unfamiliar with current literacy research. This question is so common that it is wise to prepare for it before the conference. Some information on the topic is discussed in Chapter 10 in the section titled Causes of Reading Delays.**

year. This form of assessment—a collaborative effort between you and your students—involves identifying their best work, evaluating their literacy growth using authentic literacy tasks, and developing their sensitivity to their own literacy progress.

Formal assessment, using standardized achievement tests, provides information on how much students have learned relative to other students on whom the various test instruments were standardized. Key concepts that are critical to understanding this form of testing include validity, reliability, and standard error of measurement. Performance measures range from raw score to mean score, median score, mode score, GE score, percentile rank, and stanine score. Keep in mind that standardized tests are designed to measure highly generalized skills and should represent only one of many factors used in planning and evaluating students' instructional progress.

The communication of a student's progress to parents creates a vital link between home and school. Your discussions with parents should convey your instructional goals, your expectations, the way in which you evaluate progress, and their student's literacy growth. One of the most effective ways this communication can be accomplished is through one-on-one discussions in which you use samples of a student's work to demonstrate areas of literacy progress and areas needing continued emphasis. Parental support plays a key role in the success of literacy instruction.

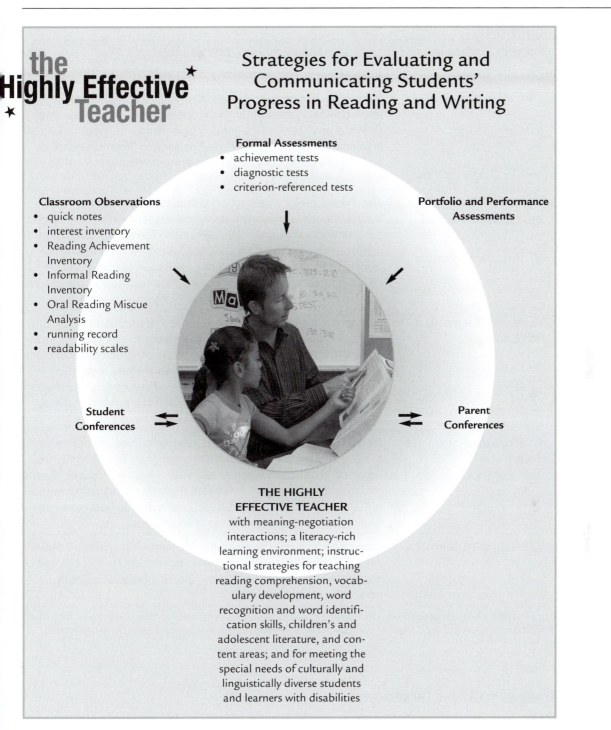

the
Highly Effective Teacher

Strategies for Evaluating and Communicating Students' Progress in Reading and Writing

Formal Assessments
- achievement tests
- diagnostic tests
- criterion-referenced tests

Classroom Observations
- quick notes
- interest inventory
- Reading Achievement Inventory
- Informal Reading Inventory
- Oral Reading Miscue Analysis
- running record
- readability scales

Portfolio and Performance Assessments

Student Conferences

Parent Conferences

THE HIGHLY EFFECTIVE TEACHER
with meaning-negotiation interactions; a literacy-rich learning environment; instructional strategies for teaching reading comprehension, vocabulary development, word recognition and word identification skills, children's and adolescent literature, and content areas; and for meeting the special needs of culturally and linguistically diverse students and learners with disabilities

Professional Standards and
Teacher Knowledge for Literacy Assessment

The classroom teacher standards found in Figure 9.11 (page 280) illustrate the use of instructional assessment for each of the five standards found in the International Reading Association's *Standards for Reading Professionals—Revised 2003* (2004). These standards identify examples of key assessment practices used by the effective literacy teacher. You can see the complete list of Standards for Reading Professionals in Appendix C.

FIGURE 9.11

Professional Standards and Literacy Assessment for the Classroom Teacher

Professional Standard	Example
1. Foundational Knowledge	**Element 1.3** Demonstrates knowledge of reading acquisition and variations related to cultural and linguistic diversity; e.g., understands developmental benchmarks in reading development and the role of assessment in gaining insight into individual student learning; demonstrates understanding of contemporary views and practices in reading and writing assessment.
2. Instructional Strategies and Curriculum Materials	**Element 2.3** Uses a wide range of curriculum materials in effective reading instruction for learners at different stages of reading development; e.g., identifies a student's independent, instructional, and frustration reading levels through observations and assessments and uses appropriate reading materials to meet the student's independent and instructional needs; demonstrates knowledge of reading materials appropriate for various developmental, cultural, and linguistic differences of students.
3. Assessment, Diagnosis, and Evaluation	**Element 3.4** Communicates results of assessments to students, parents, colleagues, and administrators; e.g., interprets a student's reading profile from observations and various assessments ranging from quick notes and interest inventories to running records and achievement tests; effectively communicates these interpretations to parents and administrators; uses portfolio assessment and interprets achievement progress to students, parents, and the school community.
4. Creating a Literate Environment	**Element 4.1** Uses students' interests, reading abilities, and backgrounds as foundations for the reading and writing program; e.g., understands how to collect information about students' interests, reading abilities, and backgrounds using observations and assessment inventories; knows how to use this information to select reading materials that match students' reading interests, reading levels, and backgrounds.
5. Professional Development	**Element 5.2** Continues to pursue the development of professional knowledge; e.g., identifies specific questions related to assessment and reading and writing instruction; demonstrates specific strategies for finding answers to those questions.

Part 2 from IRA. (2004). Professional Standards and Ethics Committee, International Reading Association. *Standards for reading professionals—revised 2003.* Reprinted with permission of the International Reading Association. All rights reserved.

Applications: Bridges to the Classroom

1. Arrange to visit an elementary classroom at a grade level that interests you. With the help of the teacher, identify one student for observation during your visit, and use the Reading Achievement Inventory (Figure 9.2) in observing the student. What insights did you glean regarding the student's literacy development? What recommendations do you have for instruction? Share your observations and insights with the teacher, and obtain her or his ideas on the student's progress.

2. Review the interest inventory (Figure 9.1), and add additional items you believe may be important in assessing students' interests. Arrange to interview a student, and use the interest inventory as an interview guide. Describe your insights into the student's in-school and out-of-school interests. What suggestions for instruction would you recommend on the basis of your interview? Share your ideas with a class partner.

3. Identify a teacher who uses some form of portfolio assessment, and develop a series of questions you would like to ask that teacher about what should be included in the portfolio and what criteria are used for evaluating student portfolios. Interview the teacher, and summarize the information you obtain. Use what you learn to develop a personal plan for implementing a system of portfolio assessment in your classroom.

4. Arrange to administer a published formal Reading Inventory or an IRI you construct yourself (see How To Do Your Own IRI) to a student in the second, third, or fourth grade.

Use the miscue notational system presented in this chapter or the one provided in the manual of the publisher-produced IRI. Analyze the student's reading responses, paying particular attention to meaning influence and fluency influence miscues. On the basis of your interpretation of the student's responses, what instructional recommendations do you have for him or her?

Additional Research and Practice

1. Tierney, R. J. (1998). **Literacy assessment reform: Shifting beliefs, principled possibilities, and emerging practices.** *The Reading Teacher, 51* (5), 374–390.

   This distinguished-educator-series article presents thirteen key principles for literacy assessment developed from personal ideals and practice as well as theory and research. (Practice)

2. International Reading Association. (1999). **High-stakes assessments in reading: A position statement of the International Reading Association.** *The Reading Teacher, 53* (3), 257–263.

   This position statement identifies key questions and problems related to high-stakes testing and offers important recommendations to teachers, researchers, parents, and policymakers. (Practice)

5. From your professor, the library, a classroom teacher, or a school district office, obtain a copy of a widely used standardized reading achievement test and the test manual. Review the test items and the test administration manual, and develop a summary of your impressions about validity, reliability, standard error of measurement, and test interpretation. Discuss your findings with classmates.

3. Denton, C. A., Ciancio, D. J., & Fletcher, J. M. (2006). **Validity, reliability, and utility of the Observation Survey of Early Literacy Achievement.** *Reading Research Quarterly, 41,* 8–34.

   This article about a popular assessment tool portrays well a principle of good testing—namely, there are no perfect assessment instruments and, even with those of higher quality, the highly effective teacher must be aware of the specific strengths and weaknesses of any procedure or test. (Research)

CHAPTER 10

DELAYED READERS

Instructing Delayed Readers in a Regular Classroom Setting

Sandra McCormick, Professor Emeritus
The Ohio State University

> *Teaching at-risk and delayed readers the skills and strategies that are congruent with success in the mainstream must begin early and continue for many years. There are no shortcuts.*
>
> Irene W. Gaskins,
> *Distinguished Educator and Founder and Director of Benchmark School*

> *It will all come down to putting children with expert teachers who have the time and resources necessary to support diverse groups of children.*
>
> Richard L. Allington,
> *Former President of the International Reading Association, University of Florida*

Amy Hernandez, who will start her first year as a teacher in a few days, is working in her new classroom on a hot August morning one week before school is to begin.

Over the last couple of days she has designed two exciting and informative bulletin boards, unboxed a variety of appealing books for her library corner, and organized a writing center. She now turns to examining the records of students who will be in her third-grade classroom.

Some feelings of apprehension emerge when she finds that several of these children are not reading at third-grade level. In this class of twenty-nine students, there are Paul, Rob, and Diane whose standardized test scores and informal assessments all indicate their reading attainment to be similar to that of the average student at about mid-second grade. And then there is David. At the end of the previous school year, although David's teacher had recorded math scores for him showing above-average achievement, she specified the book that he was currently reading as one typically used with students near the end of first grade. Most worrisome is Lucy, whose first- and second-grade teachers both had included many notes of concern in her file. At the end of each school year, Lucy was designated by each teacher as a nonreader, despite her average intelligence and much reading instruction. With twenty-four other students in her class, Ms. Hernandez wonders what she can do to meet the needs of these five students in the upcoming year.

double entry journal

Reflect, for a moment, on the descriptions of the five students in Ms. Hernandez's class. Select one of these students and briefly describe what reading strategies you might use with the student. How might you explain the nature of this student's reading progress?

Chapter Objectives

After reading and discussing this chapter, you will be able to:

- understand which students in your class may be delayed readers, distinguish between their levels of need, and know what may and may not be causes of reading delays.
- follow important principles for working with delayed readers and for managing their instruction.
- distinguish the two critical aspects of assessment for delayed readers: (a) assessment to determine instructional level and (b) assessment to determine strengths and weaknesses.

- select activities for instructing word recognition and word identification strategies to delayed readers, and understand the phases of word learning to which these should be applied.
- consider special needs that delayed readers may have in relation to comprehension of story-type text and content area text.
- consciously avoid benign neglect of delayed readers and know ways to motivate them.

Understanding Delayed Readers

A Definition

Many terms have been used to denote students whose reading levels are below the average for their class; for example, terms such as *struggling reader, disabled reader,* or *dyslexic*.[1] In this book we use a designation that currently is gaining favor: *delayed reader* (Gaskins, 1998; McCormick, 2007). This phrase is becoming the expression of choice because it implies a positive view. It suggests that students whose reading levels are below the norm—no matter to what degree—are simply *delayed* in their development and with appropriate instruction will progress and ultimately attain reading success.

> *Students make the journey from prereader to capable reader at different rates.*

This belief is in contrast to some previously held positions about reading difficulties, which assumed that these students' reading responses were unusual (perhaps even odd), sometimes intractable, and always hard-to-understand aberrations of "normal" reading behaviors.

One good way to understand the distinction between these positions is to think about them in relation to word learning and the phases you read about in Chapter 4. All students progress through these word-learning phases on the route from prereader to accomplished reader. However, different individuals make this journey at different rates: Some students may move through the phases more quickly than the average reader, others may take a little longer than the norm, and still others may take considerably more time. Nevertheless, they all go through the same stages.

Knowing this will help you avoid incorrect interpretations of students' reading behaviors. Let's look at an example. Suppose a second grader, third grader, or fourth grader, for instance, attempts to read words by primarily attending to the gross shape or length of the words, attends only to certain letters in words rather than all of them, does not use any letter sounds in word

---

[1]The term *dyslexia* was coined in the late 1800s. Over time it has been defined in numerous, often opposing, ways (e.g., one definition indicates that *dyslexia* is the designation for reading problems with neurological bases, while another definition states that the term refers to all reading difficulties except those with a neurological base). Although most of the many differing definitions do agree that the terminology relates to reading anomalies linked to word recognition and word identification (rather than comprehension), another negative feature of this word is that it is associated with various myths. One myth frequently spread through the lay press is that letter and word reversals indicate this mysterious "condition," while, in fact, reversals are normal developmental behaviors seen equally as often among young average readers as among those who experience reading delays. Because this has come to be a misunderstood and misrepresented label, educators often shun its use.

recognition, and needs an unusually large number of exposures to a word to remember it. At one time such behaviors might have led to a "diagnosis" of neurological dysfunction, or visual perception difficulties or other similar conclusion about the root of this child's seemingly bizarre approach to word reading. However, there is a simpler explanation. The student is still in the pre-alphabetic phase of word learning (see Chapter 4 and Figure 10.4, page 294). While his or her reading development has been considerably delayed, it is neither peculiar nor deviant. Such an approach to word reading would not surprise us at all if the student were in kindergarten or early first grade where the pre-alphabetic phase of word learning is common (Ehri, 1991).

Current research and authority opinion (e.g., Gaskins et al., 1997a, 1997b) suggest that knowing the phase of word learning is important to instructional efforts with delayed readers whose difficulties lie with word recognition and word identification. If instruction is adjusted to the needs of students within that phase, then reading development can progress.

Although our hypothetical example here dealt with word reading problems, the same principle applies if the student's difficulties lie with comprehension of text. With appropriate instruction, all students can progress in literacy skills.

EVIDENCE-BASED PRACTICE

➤ *As a guide for instruction, knowing a delayed reader's phase of word learning is important.*

Levels of Need

Corrective Reading Programs

➤ *Three Types of Reading Programs, Based on Severity of Delay*

The needs of delayed readers vary. As can be noted from Ms. Hernandez's class, one of the ways these students differ is in the severity of their delays. Paul's, Rob's, and Diane's delays are mild. Students with *mild delays* may show slightly slower progress across all general areas of reading (e.g., word recognition, word identification, comprehension, and knowledge of word meanings). Or they might do quite well in most areas but have difficulties with one or two others.

For Paul, Rob, and Diane a *corrective reading program* carried out in a regular classroom setting under the guidance of the regular classroom teacher would probably meet their needs well (Duffy-Hester, 1999). In fact, that is the most typical way in which the instruction of students with mild delays is handled. In some cases, these students' programs are planned by the teacher, based on careful observation followed by a selection of literacy activities individualized to the students. In other cases, preplanned, successful programs—such as Early Intervention Reading (EIR)—are implemented (Figure 10.1).

FIGURE 10.1

Early Intervention in Reading (EIR)

Early Intervention in Reading (EIR) was developed to provide special instruction for low-achieving first-grade students (Taylor et al., 1995; Taylor, Strait, & Medo, 1994). The program is conducted by the classroom teacher in the regular classroom setting. Characteristics are as follows:

✓ The teacher is trained to develop the program and works with five to seven low-achieving students in the regular classroom.

✓ Students are assigned to this group on the basis of teacher observation and a phonemic awareness test.

✓ In-class instruction consists of fifteen to twenty minutes of supplemental daily reading instruction. Students also are read to individually by an aide or a peer for an additional five minutes each day.

✓ Instruction takes place over three-day cycles, using a picture storybook in Big Book format. To begin, readers follow the teacher as she or he reads and tracks (points to the words while reading) the story.

✓ Instructional emphasis is then on choral rereading of the stories, guided writing to develop phonemic awareness and awareness of sound-symbol correspondences, strategic word identification (including sounding and blending), story retelling, and comprehension.

✓ Structured daily observations are used to assess progress and plan instruction.

✓ Transition to independent reading occurs as the teacher works with pairs of students, instead of the group, and as the students read stories that the teacher has not previously read aloud with them.

Remedial Reading Programs

Many students with *moderate delays,* such as Ms. Hernandez's prospective student, David, receive a portion of their reading instruction as part of a *remedial reading program.* This may be a federally funded Title I program or a special district-sponsored reading class. Remedial reading programs typically have the following features (McCormick, 2003; Ruddell, 2006). Students who are achieving in the lowest 20 to 25 percent of their classes are recommended to a reading specialist who provides instruction in this program. The reading specialist, who has additional training for teaching such students, conducts a comprehensive assessment of the student's literacy needs (International Reading Association, 2000b). Instruction occurs in a small group of about five or six students, most often in a setting outside the regular classroom. Productive classes are organized to provide for ample learning opportunities, for example, for forty to forty-five minutes a day, every day of the school week, and are organized so that learners with similar requirements are grouped together.

In some cases, moderately delayed readers are taught individually. An example of such a program is Reading Recovery. Although teachers in this first-grade program describe their efforts as "preventive" rather than "remedial," this pullout program demonstrates the best features of high-quality remedial classes (Figure 10.2).

Another type of remedial program is a learning disabilities (LD) class. If the learning delay is rooted in reading problems, authorities in the reading field and in the special education discipline who are aware of current research and thinking recognize that no real differences exist between a student who has been designated as "reading delayed" (or "disabled") and one who has been labeled "learning disabled." Presently in most states, eligibility for services in an LD class and eligibility for a remedial reading program are established with the same criteria. A comparison is made between the student's current level of achievement and what should be expected of the student, given his or her intelligence level and amount of instruction. If the differences are significant, placement in either an LD class or a remedial reading program may occur. Furthermore, the causes of the difficulties in both cases are similar and multiple. The severity of the delays varies for both groups and the same instruction is required.

In recent years, there has been some emphasis on providing remedial instruction by a reading or an LD specialist within the regular classroom setting, instead of moving students to another location for that part of their school day (Walmsley & Allington, 1995). This is called an

> *Characteristics of Remedial Reading Programs*

In what ways are students who have been designated "reading delayed" (or "disabled") like those who have been labeled "learning disabled"?

FIGURE 10.2
Reading Recovery

Reading Recovery is an early intervention program designed to reduce first-grade reading failure. Developed in New Zealand in the 1970s by child psychologist Marie Clay, it was brought to the United States in the mid-1980s and is now used widely in this country (Clay, 1987; Lyons & Beaver, 1995; Pinnel, Fried, & Estice, 1990). Key characteristics of Reading Recovery are as follows:

✓ A specially trained teacher works in one-to-one instruction with first-grade students.
✓ Students selected for the program are in the lowest 20 percent of their class, based on the Reading Recovery Observational Survey.
✓ Instruction takes place in thirty-minute sessions outside the regular classroom, over a twelve- to twenty-week period.
✓ Instruction is designed to develop strategic, independent readers and emphasizes self-monitoring, searching for meaning clues, cross-checking sources of information, and self-correcting.
✓ Reading materials of increasing difficulty are used, while instructional support scaffolding is provided for the student.
✓ Reading and writing activities are closely integrated, with major emphasis on meaning construction.
✓ Daily observations and assessments note the student's use of cuing systems and self-corrections.
✓ Students' involvement in the program is discontinued when they reach the average achievement level for their class or when sixty lessons have been completed.

inclusion program. One reason this arrangement has been instituted is to promote coordination between the remedial reading program and the regular classroom teacher's reading instruction.

Whatever the special help for students with moderate delays (e.g., Title I, Reading Recovery, LD class), the program offers important assistance for the classroom teacher. However, a key point to remember is that *usually classroom teachers also provide instruction to complement and supplement* the special reading program. At times, especially with inclusion programs, the two teachers plan their instruction together, and it usually is to the student's advantage when they do so.

Clinical Reading Programs

When reading problems are *severe delays,* as is the case with Lucy, described earlier, remediation of the problem is unlikely to occur unless the student has adequate and consistent one-to-one instruction. In many school districts, this is a tall order because resources are directed to helping the majority of students, with few funds earmarked for addressing the needs of the small number of the most serious cases. In such circumstances, classroom teachers can seek help for the student in a *clinical reading program* (e.g., such as those often sponsored by universities), can lobby for greater attention to these students' needs in their school system, and can devise ways to offer instruction within their own classrooms to enhance the special clinical program. To provide supplemental instruction, you may (1) set aside a small portion of the instructional day to devote to this student; (2) supervise volunteer tutors in this effort; or (3) train other students to serve as peer tutors. Parents also may be enlisted to furnish additional support. Usually the effort is more successful if specific suggestions are supplied for parent tutoring, rather than making a more gen-eralized plea such as "Please help your child with reading each evening."

Causes of Reading Delays

When classroom teachers work with parents to ameliorate a student's reading problems, the teacher is frequently asked by the parents to explain what has caused their student's delay. Although we do not yet have the answer to this question in its entirety, research conducted over several decades has provided some clues that are useful to know. Research indicates possible causes of a reading problem, and, just as helpful, it suggests what does not contribute to delayed reading.

Two Possible Causes of Delayed Reading

Research in a number of countries has pointed to lack of **phonemic awareness** (discussed in Chapter 3 of this text) as a probable contributing factor in many students' reading delays (Lundberg, Olofsson, & Wall, 1980; Mathes & Torgesen, 2000; Smith, Simmons, & Kameenui, 1998). When students are experiencing difficulties learning letter-sound associa-tions and other phonic-analysis concepts, assessment of their phonemic awareness is often a useful step. One phonemic awareness test that has been validated with primary-grade children, the Yopp-Singer Phonemic Segmentation Test (Yopp, 1988), is described in the How To Do, along with a useful word list for administering this short test. If assessment indicates a student could benefit from instruction in this area, consult Chapter 3 of this book, where several activ-ities are described for boosting students' phonemic awareness, or refer to a published phone-mic awareness program. The recommendations presented for beginning readers work equally well for students who are struggling with reading. Many of these activities have been designed to be playful and appealing to students, which is an important consideration for students with reading delays, whose motivation for reading activities has often been depressed by their lack of success.

Another common cause of reading problems has been tagged *Matthew effects,* a designation based on the reference in the biblical New Testament chapter of Matthew that alludes to the "rich getting richer and the poor getting poorer." In literacy terms, the notion of the "rich" is meant to convey good readers who keep getting better because they read a lot, while "poor" refers to delayed readers who don't improve because the amount of reading they can do is limited by their lack of skills. For almost anything we do, we get better with practice—and reading is no

How to Do . . .

Administering the Yopp-Singer Phoneme Segmentation Test

1. Prepare the word list given below for student reading.
2. Plan to administer the test individually, allotting five to ten minutes for each student to whom you choose to administer the test.
3. To each student state, "I will say a word and I want you to break it apart. Tell me each **sound** in the word, in order. If I say *old,* you would say /o/ /l/ /d/." (Be sure to have students tell you the *sound* they hear, not the name of the letter.)
4. Before beginning the actual test, give three more practice items, using *ride, go,* and *man.*
5. Begin the test using the list of words below. An answer is correct only if the student furnishes it without teacher assistance. Tell the student when his or her answer is correct. When an answer is not correct, tell the student the correct answer before moving to the next test word. Note the number of correct responses, using teacher judgment to determine if remedial efforts are needed to teach phoneme segmentation to this student.

The Word List

dog	lay	keep	race
fine	zoo	no	three
she	job	wave	in
grew	ice	that	at
red	top	me	by
sat	do		

the Highly Effective Teacher★

on Technology and the Delayed Reader

1. Use the Internet as a resource to read about students with learning delays. The following Web site is a good place to begin: **www.ldanatl.org.**
2. Visit the Reading Recovery Web site at **www.readingrecovery.org.**
3. Use the multisensory features that interactive software provides to make reading more interesting and accessible to delayed readers, and to increase motivation to read. Some suggested titles include the following: Broderbund's *Arthur's Computer Adventure,* Renaissance Interactive Studio's *Anne of Green Gables Interactive Novel,* Broderbund's *The Tortoise and the Hare,* and Davidson's *Baba Yaga and the Magic Geese.*
4. Use interactive software that focuses on word identification strategies: Knowledge Adventure's *Reading Blaster* series or The Learning Company's *Reader Rabbit* series. Incorporate the words that students are learning into writing activities in the classroom.
5. Have students conduct Internet searches on high-interest content areas to use in writing stories that enhance motivation. Have them collect visual displays that can be incorporated into creative stories. They may use clip art collections such as those found at **www.nzwwa.com/mirror/clipart** or **www.kidsdomain.com/clip.**

exception. The Matthew-effects concept alerts us to a merciless sequence and cycle of events that frequently occur in the reading history of poor readers:

1. Some factor (often low phonemic awareness) results in slow development of word identification strategies.
2. Lack of word identification strategies results in a low volume of text reading.
3. A low volume of text reading results in failure to develop automatic word recognition.
4. Failure to develop automatic word recognition results in plodding, laborious reading.
5. Plodding, laborious reading leads to a low volume of reading.
6. A low volume of reading results in lack of development of meaning vocabulary, less background information gained, and less familiarity with narrative and informational text structures—and thus, to lowered text comprehension.

The effective teacher's answer to this unfortunate causal chain is early intervention—to stop the chain—to remediate the problem and prevent additional problems from resulting from the original one.

Other Causes of Reading Delays

EVIDENCE-BASED PRACTICE

The issues of causation are complex ones. To supplement the information on phonemic awareness and Matthew effects, see Figure 10.3 for a list of some factors that have been investigated by research. The weight of the data currently leads us to the conclusions summarized in that figure. For a thorough review of the research on this topic, see McCormick (2007).

FIGURE 10.3

Causes of Reading Delays

	Possible Cause	Not a Cause
❏ Nearsightedness		X
❏ Faulty eye movements		X
❏ Visual perception difficulties		X
❏ Severe hearing impairment	X	
❏ Poor speech articulation		X
❏ Poor motor coordination		X
❏ Lack of neurological organization		X
❏ Medically diagnosed brain damage[1]	X	
❏ Food additives in the diet		X
❏ Mixed cerebral dominance		X
❏ Refined sugar in the diet		X
❏ Sensory-integration problems		X
❏ Hereditary factors	X	
❏ Emotional problems[2]	X	
❏ Low teacher expectations	X	
❏ Home environmental conditions	X	
❏ A mismatch between instructional method and a student's preferred learning modality		X
❏ Nonstandard oral language dialect		X
❏ Lack of phonemic awareness	X	
❏ Matthew effects (i.e., reading history)	X	

[1]Such instances are rare.

[2]In most cases, the reading problem appears to be the cause of the emotional problem, rather than the result of it.

Meeting the Needs of Delayed Readers

The following ten principles can help you meet the needs of delayed readers in regular classroom settings:

1. No unusual methods or materials are necessary to provide appropriate instruction for delayed readers.
2. Insightful management of instruction is critical.
3. Appropriate matching of a student's reading level to text level is a very important consideration.
4. Determining delayed readers' strengths and weaknesses in reading necessitates accurate interpretation of assessment information.
5. Both automatic word recognition *and* adept word identification strategies are needed for reading proficiency.
6. Understanding a delayed reader's word-learning phase is central to planning effective instruction.
7. When a student's difficulties lie with comprehension, the complexity of text comprehension must be considered.
8. Content area reading presents special problems for delayed readers.
9. To adequately serve delayed readers, benign neglect must be avoided.
10. Promoting motivation is an important part of the teacher's instructional role.

The significance of each of these principles is now discussed in detail.

> *Ten Principles for Meeting the Needs of Delayed Readers in Regular Classroom Settings*

General Guidelines

Methods and Materials

Gone are the days when programs for poor readers used odd materials and curious procedures. For example, when observing any special reading program today, one should no longer see the use of visual perception exercises where students match geometric shapes and trace lines, body management programs in which pupils engage in physical activities such as walking balance beams or tossing bean bags, instruction designed to mend "defective brain processing functions," or other such bizarre proceedings once considered by some to be the hope for students with learning difficulties. Research has clearly indicated these measures provide no useful help for any type of academic learning—including reading growth.

Thus, a first important guideline for working with delayed readers is that no unusual methods or materials are needed to provide appropriate instruction for these learners. The same teaching suggestions found throughout this text for average readers can be applied to teaching delayed readers. Likewise, the same types of materials can be used—given that the materials are on the appropriate level. This holds true whether these students are mildly, moderately, or severely delayed in their reading progress.

Why do you think that the odd instructional procedures described here have failed to contribute to academic growth?

EVIDENCE-BASED PRACTICE

Management of Instructional Details

On the other hand, an equally critical principle is that while the general approaches to methods and materials need not vary from those used with average readers, special considerations to ensure insightful management of the details of instruction within those approaches is almost always necessary if delayed readers are to realize success.

Two major differences in instruction for students having difficulties with reading are related to **timing** and **pacing**. The matter of timing means these students may not be ready at the same time as others to handle certain materials and skills. Therefore, these activities should be postponed until later and substituted with others suitable to the student's present level of development. The second difference, pacing, refers to the need to adjust the rate of instruction. You may not be able to move delayed readers through a set of texts or strategies at the typical rate; rather you will need to provide multiple exposures to words, skills, strategies, and concepts, as well as many more than the usual number of opportunities for practice. Delayed readers characteristically require a good deal more time on task to master new learning. When this is sufficiently provided, good reading growth occurs (Mathes, Denton, Fletcher, Anthony, Frances, & Schatschneider, 2005).

In addition to the issues of timing and pacing, the following four guidelines are critical:

timing
students may not be ready at the same times as others to handle certain materials and skills

pacing
the need to adjust the rate of instruction; delayed readers often require a good deal more time on task to master new learning

What kinds of modeling might a teacher use for a student who is having difficulty with word identification? With comprehension of text?

➤ **Four Important Guidelines for Insightful Management of Instruction**

1. *Teachers must provide explanations that are more explicit than those typically needed for average readers.* Teacher modeling of appropriate ways to carry out a task is a technique that should be used frequently, including thinking aloud and demonstrating each new skill or strategy when it is introduced. As Gill (2000) suggests, for delayed readers "demonstrations may play a crucial role in literacy development" (p. 506). Step-by-step explanations should be offered at any time when students reach a stumbling block.

2. *Varied instruction is needed to promote generalization (i.e., transfer) of knowledge.* With an average reader, you may expect to teach a word in one setting and the student will know it in another. This is not necessarily the case with poor readers. Teach a word through flashcard exercises only, and the delayed reader may recognize the word in that setting but not in a story he or she is asked to read. Effective instruction of low-achieving readers provides for exposures to words or strategies in a variety of ways to promote transfer of learning.

3. *Delayed readers need opportunities to apply, under teacher direction, newly introduced skills and strategies.* It is ineffective to provide practice of new concepts or skills only in isolation; there also must be chances to use this information in the context of real reading material. Teacher support is needed when these first applications occur and should be removed gradually, as the student shows obvious growing control over the strategy or understanding.

4. *Review is crucial.* Important for most students, delayed readers will need review even more.

Assessment

➤ **Two Important Assessment Questions**

Two important assessment questions when working with delayed readers are (1) What are the student's approximate reading levels (both instructional and independent)? and (2) What are the student's strengths and weaknesses?

Reading Levels

Although specification of a reading level must always be viewed as an approximation of what a student can do, it is always helpful to have an estimate of the learner's instructional reading level and independent reading level. One of the most important teacher actions for leading students down the path to reading improvement is to see to it that they *read a lot*. It is not enough to merely provide instruction with reading skills and strategies; poor readers must have abundant opportunities to practice these newly learned skills in the context of real reading material, using connected text such as stories and informational articles.

Most often this practice occurs under direct teacher guidance, with the teacher present to prompt, scaffold, and assist. Under these circumstances, for practice to be most effective, the student should be reading text that is neither too difficult nor too easy. Text that is too difficult or too easy prevents the learner from fully using the new strategies. For the reader to fully utilize the developing skills and strategies, the material must be somewhat challenging—otherwise there is no need to try out the new skills. But the material also should not be so hard that the student is overwhelmed with the need to apply a new skill to every word or two—a circumstance in which both understanding and motivation are likely to break down. The material should be at the student's approximate *instructional level*.

How is word identification affected if materials are too difficult? And how might this affect comprehension?

Likewise, when the student is reading alone, consideration of the student's reading level and the approximate level of the material to be used is vital. Independent reading requires material that is quite easy for the student because no teacher is available to guide and support. This material should be at the student's approximate *independent level*.

Thus, both for direct instruction and for independent work, appropriate matching of a student's reading levels to text levels is very important. Teacher observation is one of the best ways to determine a student's levels of reading, applying to these observations the simple criteria for deciding instructional level and independent level, listed in Table 9.3 on page 266.

What are the criteria for estimating instructional and independent levels?

Strengths and Weaknesses in Reading

Information from formal and informal assessments administered to the class as a whole (which were discussed in Chapter 9) is available to classroom teachers. To answer questions about strengths and needs accurately and completely for those students who are having difficulties with reading, a bit of detective work may be necessary.

Consider the following example. Robert, a fifth grader, takes a standardized test with the rest of his classmates. He does very poorly on the section that measures knowledge of word meanings. Does this mean the teacher should place a heavy emphasis on increasing his meaning vocabulary knowledge, or did Robert do poorly on this section because his word identification skills are so poor that he could not read the words? Perhaps if only he could have read them, he would have had no difficulty specifying their meanings. To resolve this issue, as an informal diagnostic measure, the teacher-detective asks Robert to reread that section of the test orally. It should now be easy to identify the origin of Robert's reading problem. (It is easy to see that the same situation—and solution—could apply to the comprehension section of a standardized test, or to any assessment students read silently.)

A questioning attitude should apply to all test results of delayed readers, whether they are based on formal or informal measures and regardless of the skill area tested. The bottom line is that you should always ask, "Why did this student obtain these results?" and "What's really going on here?" Following leads and clues until the real needs of a student are apparent differentiates a mere test-giver from a true diagnostician.

Word Recognition and Word Identification

Word Recognition

In Chapter 4, the phrase **word recognition** was defined for you; it is those moments when students recognize a word instantly and accurately. This is also referred to as recognizing a word by sight, sight recognition, or automatic word recognition.

word recognition process of identifying a word accurately and instantly

Research and Evidence-Based Practice

Delayed Readers and Word Learning

Did You Know?

- By the time students have completed middle school, they will be required to read in excess of 80,000 different words (Adams, 1990a; Juel & Minden-Cupp, 2004)—clearly a potential problem for delayed readers because their difficulties lie more with word recognition and word identification than with any other area of literacy learning (Gough & Hillinger, 1980; McCormick, 2007; Rack, Snowling, & Olson, 1992; Spear-Swerling, 2004).

- To successfully learn and recall words by sight, students must be able to recognize and name the letters of the alphabet, have phonemic segmentation skills, and know letter-sound correspondences—thus, word recognition and word identification skills are interrelated (Ehri, 1997; Ehri & McCormick, 2004).

- One of the best predictors of successful initial reading is phonological awareness. Providing disabled readers instruction to enhance their phonological awareness furnishes an important basis for word recognition and word identification (Stanovich, 1991; Stanovich, 2004; Vellutino & Denckla, 1991).

- An important goal for teachers is to help their students develop reading fluency. Fluent reading requires automatic sight word recognition, as well as the combining of this quick, accurate recognition with comprehension processes (Fuchs et al., 2001; Spear-Swerling, 2004).

In Chapter 4, you learned that, initially, students must read words by sight because they do not yet have the concepts for applying letter-sound relationships and that, later in their development, recognizing words by sight contributes to both comprehension and fluency. But, what is more, there is evidence that students must recognize some words at sight in order to effectively learn to apply phonic analysis (see, e.g., Ehri & Wilce, 1985).

Unfortunately, automatic word recognition often does not come easily for delayed readers. In almost every case, these readers need many exposures to words—accomplished in a variety of ways—for accurate and instant recognition to occur. To do this, you may present to students the same set of words repeatedly; for example, in one lesson you may present the words through gamelike activities; in another, through board work; and, in a third, by using word sorts. In addition, you should provide exposure to these same words in spelling lessons, in writing lessons, and, most important, in the context of oral and guided silent reading lessons. In Strategies in Use: Matching Instruction to Word-Learning Phase, you will see how one teacher applied this idea of multiple exposures within multiple contexts to the sight word instruction of a delayed reader.

The How To Do box presents additional practical ideas for working with delayed readers to increase accurate, automatic word recognition. Also see sections in Chapters 3 and 4 on this topic.

Word Identification

word identification
process of using knowledge and skills, such as phonic analysis, structural analysis, or context clues, to identify unfamiliar words

During the years of literacy development all students meet words they do not yet know, and that is when **word identification** strategies must come into play. To work out the identities of unknown words, students must have at their fingertips the knowledge and the skills for applying phonic analysis, structural analysis, and, to some extent, context clues. It is fairly typical that mastering these skills and being able to apply them independently presents a major challenge for delayed readers. To meet this challenge, it is important to know what research has to say about the most successful teaching strategies for learners who are struggling with literacy progress. For example, in Chapter 4, you learned that there are a number of approaches to teaching phonics. For average readers it is likely that these can be used interchangeably or in combination with no differences in outcome. For poor readers, however, there is a good deal of research supporting the advantages of using *synthetic phonics* (also called *explicit phonics;* see How To Do . . . Letter-Sound Relationships: Teaching Implicit and Explicit Phonics, p. 99) over other approaches (Adams, 1990a; Anderson et al., 1984; Johnson & Baumann, 1984; U.S. Department of Health and Human Services, 2000). To summarize, the National Reading Panel stated that synthetic phonics—in which students are explicitly taught to turn letters into sounds and to blend them to identify printed words—is more effective with delayed readers, students with learning disabilities, and children from low socioeconomic families than approaches that are less focused (e.g., those that avoid pronunciation of sounds in isolation or that rely on incidental instruction).

Why do you think synthetic, or explicit, phonics has proved to be more successful with delayed readers?

For delayed readers, attention should be given to issues of both word recognition and word identification. Referring to information about a student's word-learning phase will cue the teacher to the relative emphasis that should be placed on each of these areas in a specific stage of development.

➤ *Characteristics of Word-Learning Phases*

Word-Learning Phases

Although students' reading delays may affect other areas of literacy learning (e.g., comprehension), more students who are struggling with reading have difficulties with word recognition and word identification than any other areas. When this is the case, it is essential that you identify the student's present word-learning phase. These phases were introduced in Chapter 4 and are summarized again in Figure 10.4 (see page 294). Answering the question "What phase of word learning is this student in?" tells you *what* to teach and *how* to teach it to this *particular student.*

What to teach and, most particularly, how to teach it, may differ from student to student—according to the student's word-learning phase. This is an important concept to understand in order to be an effective teacher of delayed readers. Making general assumptions about the needs of all students with word recognition and word identification problems—and teaching them all in generally the same way—is one reason why reading-delayed students *have failed to learn, even with instruction.*

Thus, a highly effective teacher considers the characteristics enumerated for each phase and asks for each, "Do these characteristics seem to describe this particular student who is experienc-

How to Do . . .

Some Principles and Activities for Sight-Word Instruction with Delayed Readers

1. To choose target words for sight-word instruction, select words the student will immediately encounter (today or in the next few days) in a story or an informational text to be used for reading instruction. When choosing target words, consider ones that are likely to occur frequently in other materials, as well as those important for the immediate lesson.

2. To determine which of the words in an upcoming lesson may occur often in other reading materials, consult a list of high-frequency words (one such list is printed in its entirety in Table 4.2, page 91).

3. Some high-frequency words are abstract (e.g., prepositions like *of* and *as,* conjunctions, and certain other words). Because they are abstract, they are harder to learn. In a set of target words, also include words that are easier for students to visualize and to remember (e.g., nouns like *grandmother* and *bear,* and action verbs such as *jump* and *sing*).

4. When possible, choose exactly the same words for the delayed reader's spelling lessons as those targeted for reading instruction at that time. This provides multiple exposures to the same words and does so in productive ways.

5. For delayed readers, one of the most useful ways to hasten learning and ensure recall of sight words is to use activities that require the students to *examine the internal features of the words.* This means that students look at all the individual letters and the sequence of those letters in each word to be learned. Strategies in Use: Matching Instruction to Word-Learning Phase describes creative ways one teacher met this goal. A few other of the many ways this can be accomplished are to have students spell the words with letter tiles, write the words with colored pens, spell the words orally while pointing to each letter, manipulate letter dice to form words, and guess missing letters in words through games such as Hangman. Activities that help students break the word apart and put it back together are useful.

6. When working with delayed readers, do not focus on too many words at a time. For students in the pre-alphabetic phase of word learning, a good rule of thumb is to include no more than five words in a learning set; for students in the partial-alphabetic phase, no more than ten. The higher the word-learning phase, the more words the students can successfully practice at a time—however, never overwhelm a delayed reader with large numbers of new words in a practice set. To do so will significantly delay learning time.

ing reading difficulties?" Continue asking the question until you have identified the student's most probable phase. This is a powerful type of informal teacher-observation assessment that can lead to critical decisions in planning instruction that will make a difference in whether a delayed reader progresses.

Finally, you need to consider these characteristics for their teaching implications. See the Strategies in Use for a sample of how this might be done.

Comprehension

The Complexity of Comprehension and Comprehension Instruction

A sizable number of reading-delayed students struggle with comprehension. Sometimes the needs of these students are overlooked. This happens when teachers erroneously assume a student is a "good" reader because the student demonstrates accurate word pronunciation. Although automatic word recognition certainly facilitates text comprehension, if other skills and strategies that aid understanding are not in place, accomplishing the true purpose of reading—grasping meanings, both literal and implied—will elude readers.

The real requirements of students also may go unnoticed if teachers fail to realize that it is *higher-level* comprehension tasks that present most of the confusion experienced by poor

FIGURE 10.4

Typical Characteristics of Each Word-Learning Phase

Pre-Alphabetic

- Relies heavily on context and on graphic features to read words; does not use sound cues.
- Often attempts to read words by looking only at the gross shape or length of the word.
- Often letters are not used to recognize words, but, if they are, attends only to certain ones, rather than all of them.
- Remembers a word only after many, many exposures to it and, thus, words are best learned when only a few are presented at a time.
- Knows only a limited number of sight words.

Transition to Partial-Alphabetic

- Better use of letter recognition to identify words (rather than merely attending to gross cues, such as the shape of the word).
- Some use of letter sounds emerges (usually with focus on the beginning, and maybe ending, sound—but not on all sounds in a word).
- Recognizes a few more words than when in the pre-alphabetic phase, and recognition is more often correct because of increased attention to letter (and, increasingly, to sound) cues.
- However, still depends more heavily on recognizing words at sight rather than through analysis.

Full-Alphabetic

- There is increased ability to identify unknown words through use of letter–sound relationships (commonly called "sounding out the word").
- During this phase, students progress from a slow sounding and blending of sounds to a more automatic application of this technique. As a result, from the beginning of this phase to its end, typically slow, and sometimes laborious, reading increases to a more moderately rapid rate.
- Initial uses of analogy to identify unknown words are seen (e.g., the student knows *cat, sat,* and *hat* and is able to use this knowledge—often with teacher prompting at this stage—to identify new words such as *bat* or *flat*).
- Many new words are now added to the student's repertoire as a result of sounding–blending attempts, but other words also are learned through sight memorization.
- The number of words a student can learn in a given amount of time increases.
- Word reading is more often accurate than in earlier phases, and when there are errors, fewer nonsense words are produced.

Consolidated-Alphabetic

- The student makes efficient use of predictable letter patterns (e.g., common endings such as *-ing* and *-tion* or familiar beginnings such as *pre-* and *re-*), as well as better use of letter groups that are larger than grapheme-phoneme correspondences (e.g., larger units such as the phonograms *-ake, -ate,* and *-all*).
- The student is able to decode words with multiple syllables (e.g., the word *information*).
- More words can be recognized automatically, at sight.
- Reading rate increases.

Automatic-Alphabetic

- This phase characterizes the mature, competent reader.
- This reader recognizes most words by sight.
- When an unknown word is encountered, the reader is able to select from or combine multiple word identification strategies and taps into meaning sources to aid recognition.
- The student achieves a high level of accuracy in reading.

comprehenders. Although some delayed readers do have problems with literal understandings, and literal understandings do provide an important foundation for interpretive information, a remedial program for poor readers focusing *only* on literal meanings does not recognize the complexity of comprehension or the complexity of good comprehension instruction.

Comprehension research has provided teachers with rich suggestions for meeting students' comprehension needs. Many of these suggestions are now being used in programs for average readers. Unfortunately, too often the comprehension "instruction" furnished to delayed readers consists only of teachers asking many literal questions after students have read assigned selections. As is obvious from Chapter 5, productive comprehension instruction involves active strategies and experiences that occur *before, during,* and *after* text reading—for example, PReP, reciprocal teaching, and QARs—and consists of many ways to heighten higher-level as well as literal comprehension relationships (Hall, 2006). Failure to provide these strategies will short-change the students who need rich instruction the most.

Content Area Reading

For students who have difficulty comprehending written texts, content area reading may pose special problems. There are three reasons why reading content area texts—social studies books, science books, and the like—can be especially problematic for students who have difficulty with literacy learning. First, these books are often written at a level more difficult than the level for which they are intended. It is not unusual to find fourth-grade books written at fifth-grade level or seventh-grade books written at ninth-grade level. Even taking into account that readability formulas offer only an approximation of the reading level of material, frequently teachers will find that content area texts are demanding even for the average readers in their class.

Second, much specialized vocabulary is found in content area books (Camp, 2000). Remember, the majority of delayed readers have problems with word reading skills. Combine this difficulty with the high preponderance of unfamiliar vocabulary in informational texts and you can see why it is usually necessary for teachers to preteach some words before each content area lesson.

Third, expository (i.e., informational) text has characteristics that make comprehension more challenging than understanding narrative, story-type material (Yopp & Yopp, 2000b). If there are delayed readers in your class whose problems center on gaining meaning, then it may be particularly important to use some of those rich comprehension instructional ideas available to us. For example, using schematic diagrams to illustrate (1) main and supporting ideas, (2) causes and effects, (3) sequences of events, (4) classification, and (5) problems and solutions. (Figure 10.5 on page 298 presents three examples.) You may need to try reciprocal teaching and other approaches that emphasize collaborative learning, including the use of carefully prepared study guides that students can work with in pairs to assist each other in ferreting out meanings.

If reading the content area books used in your classroom is completely beyond a student's present abilities, then *adaptations* may be required. For instance, instead of assigning text to be read, the teacher assigns graphs, pictures, and diagrams to be studied carefully. This can produce a surprising wealth of information for students who cannot decode the majority of words in a content area book. Or you may ask a student to orally read the assigned text into a tape recorder, making the tape available to any classmate who wants to supplement his or her silent reading. For the delayed reader, listening to this tape when the book proves too difficult provides an opportunity to enter into the subject-matter learning of the class.

Although adaptations may be needed in serious cases, adaptation should always be viewed as a necessary but not sufficient measure. That is, adaptation does *not* mean adjustments should be made *in place of* teaching poor readers the skills and strategies they need to know. If allowed to happen, this would be an example of **benign neglect**—that is, with kindly intentions to make accommodations to the student's problems, the teacher provides for one need but neglects another that is equally or perhaps even more crucial. Consider the following example. The class is using high-quality children's or adolescent literature as the source for their reading instruction, with the class as a whole reading the same selections. Because the books used are too difficult for one student to read, this student's "instruction" consists of a classmate reading the books aloud to the delayed learner. While that arrangement allows the student to participate in some way

the Highly Effective Teacher

➤ *Three Reasons Why Content Area Texts Pose Special Problems for Delayed Readers*

➤ *Adaptation does not mean adjustments should be made in place of teaching delayed readers the skills and strategies they need to know.*

benign neglect with some intention to accommodate a student need, the teacher neglects a more critical need

Strategies in Use

Matching Instruction to Word-Learning Phase

Matt's parents have just moved into the area and he has been in Mr. Hastings' second-grade classroom for two days. In this short time it is already apparent that Matt has not yet reached the level of reading attainment of the other students. Mr. Hastings has noted Matt's oral reading behaviors on three occasions, as well as his inability to carry out written seatwork assignments related to reading. To fine-tune these informal observations, Mr. Hastings uses Figure 10.4 in this text as a checklist, comparing the characteristics specified there to Matt's reading responses. He writes down his observations and conclusions:

- During oral reading Matt spelled out two or three of the words in the story in his attempts to read them, an indication that he is making some use of letter recognition to identify words. (Seems more consistent with transition to partial-alphabetic than pre-alphabetic.)
- Did recognize quite a few words at sight. (More consistent with transition to partial-alphabetic than pre-alphabetic.)
- Did not spontaneously attempt to sound out words, but when I prompted him, he used beginning sounds plus context clues to get some of the words he hadn't known by sight. He didn't use any other sounds in the words. (Definitely not pre-alphabetic, and more like transition to partial-alphabetic than full-alphabetic.)

- Overall analysis: Transition to partial-alphabetic phase.

With this assessment complete, Mr. Hastings plans a program for Matt. Knowing where Matt is (at the transition to partial-alphabetic phase of word learning) tells Mr. Hastings some of the things Matt is *able* to do at this point—strengths that can be capitalized on in instruction. Knowing where he needs to go next (to the full-alphabetic phase) guides Mr. Hastings in designing activities that will boost Matt into that phase. Thus, Mr. Hastings includes these objectives and activities in the program plan:

1. Use Matt's present propensity to identify words by sight to increase his sight vocabulary further. This will allow greater opportunity for connected text reading (which will increase his sight vocabulary even more, as well as help him develop letter-sound associations).
   - Choose words from stories he will read.
   - Have him practice these in a variety of ways: (1) in context (e.g., in sentences and stories); (2) so there is focus on internal features of the words (e.g., arranging magnetic letters to form the word or writing targeted words on a Magic Slate, lifting the page to correct, if needed) [*Note:* Since Matt does have control of letter recognition and has tended to use

with his or her peers, regrettably, real and important needs have been abandoned—no provision is made to help the low-achieving reader move forward from the present reading level by instructing required skills and strategies or by allowing for reading practice in materials the student can handle.

McCormick (1999) describes a similar form of benign neglect sometimes seen when teachers have the class divided into ability groups:

How can benign neglect be prevented?

> The severely delayed reader is placed for his or her reading instruction in the lowest existing reading group in the class, even though the reading level of the materials and the activities of even that group are far beyond the capabilities of the student at that time. While the student can do little more than just sit there, the rationale often given for this decision is that "they at least feel they belong, and maybe they can learn something from listening." (p. 277)

Finding it difficult to establish another reading group, the teacher hopes with all sincerity for some learning to occur for the out-of-place reader when, in actuality, little substantive good comes from sitting in on instruction that is far too difficult. In such cases, the teacher would do better to allot some time for individual attention to the much delayed student, supplemented by enrollment in a special program (e.g., remedial reading program, learning disabilities program, university-based clinical program). As yet another assist to this student's instruction, *in addition to* that provided by the classroom teacher and special teacher (reading teacher, LD teacher, etc.),

this knowledge, these important exercises also will make use of one of his present strengths.]; and (3) through use of games and manipulatives to motivate and capture attention (e.g., board games, word wheels, puzzles).

- Have him maintain a word box (in a file box), including words he knows and words he's working on. These can be used for a number of reading practice procedures, for writing activities, and as a source for his personal weekly spelling list. The cards should be filed alphabetically in the box for ease in locating them.

2. Help Matt make better use of his emerging sense of letter-sound associations.

- When he misreads a word, call attention to all of the letter sounds in the word and model blending of these. Have him repeat the sounding-blending process and say the word's name.
- Have Matt write a short story (two or three sentences) every day, allowing use of invented spellings, when necessary. [*Note:* Research (e.g., see Adams, 1990a, b) indicates that use of invented spellings can shore up transition to partial-alphabetic students' budding perceptions about letter-sound correspondences. Understanding is strengthened as they try to think of the letter to write to match a sound they hear when the word is spoken orally.] However, when Matt

writes words he has been working with in his word sets, he will be required to write the word correctly. To do this, he can find the word in his file box and simply copy it, using all of the conventional letters in the right order. [*Note:* Research (e.g., Vellutino & Denckla, 1991) also demonstrates that attending to the exact sequence of all letters in a word supports word recognition.]

- Have Matt read orally to someone every day. Use text at *his* instructional level so that he has opportunity to apply newly developing concepts about letter sounds to identify the few unknown words he encounters at this level. Matt will also reread the same story more than once over a period of days to increase his sight vocabulary, fluency, and confidence.

CRITICAL THINKING

1. What classroom arrangements can Mr. Hastings make to have time to individualize Matt's program?
2. How will Mr. Hastings know when his instruction for Matt should be changed so that it is more consistent with that needed for a student at the *full*-alphabetic phase?
3. Think through and write down one more instructional activity, not given here, that would complement the strengths or address the weaknesses of a student in the transition to partial-alphabetic phase of word learning.

tutoring likely would be very helpful. Table 10.1 on page 299 provides a description of levels of tutoring to supplement classroom and special program instruction.

Teachers of delayed readers must cautiously consider the difference between putting on Band-Aids versus curing the problem.

Motivation

One cannot expect that delayed readers will come to a classroom on the first day of school already motivated to learn. Pause a moment and think of something that *you* do not do well. Now, mentally list all the ways you have developed to avoid this activity (whether it be bowling, singing in front of others, writing a paper, or any pursuit for which you feel particularly unskilled). These musings likely will lead you to conclude that it is a natural reaction to shun activities that leave you feeling inadequate, embarrassed, or frustrated. You have to find ways to bring reading text and reading instruction together with delayed readers, even though delayed readers frequently find such involvement aversive. In short, you must identify ways to motivate these students, and assume this to be as much a part of your job as individualizing assessment, preparing a lesson on consonant sounds, or stimulating comprehension with a DR-TA lesson.

Discuss with a colleague the types of avoidance tactics you've developed in response to an activity that's aversive to you. Are there parallels with those adopted by poor readers?

FIGURE 10.5

Three Examples of Schematic Diagrams That Can Be Used to Illustrate Content Area Text Information

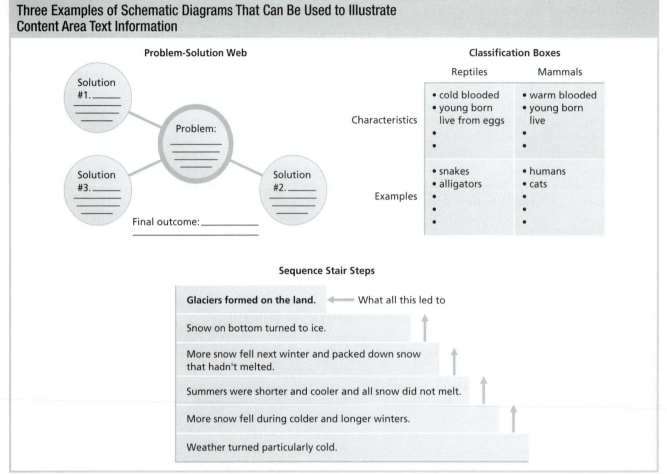

antecedents
events or actions designed to enhance motivation that precede an instructional session

Effective teachers of delayed readers plan motivational tactics around antecedents and consequences. **Antecedents** are events or actions preceding an instructional session. The following are sample antecedent events you can institute to motivate turned-off readers:

1. Select stories or informational material that matches the student's interests. If Bart is enthusiastic about soccer, find an easy-to-read book on this topic in your school library or learning center. In addition to its use for oral or silent reading practice, select words for word study from the book, choosing those that meet your current instructional objectives and, when possible, also focus on the soccer theme.

2. Select books or book-types generally popular with students of that age, at the moment. Poetry is always popular. One favorite is *Never Take a Pig to Lunch and Other Poems About the Fun of Eating* (Westcott, 1994). Children love the zany poems and illustrations in this collection (see the cover illustration in Figure 10.6, page 300). Also see Figure 10.7 (pages 301–302) for examples of high-quality children's literature that can be used to motivate primary- and middle-school age delayed readers.

3. When assigning text, give students a bona fide reason for reading it. For example, "Read this article about the science experiment we will be doing next." "Read this play aloud with Sonja because when we get into reading group we are going to take parts. This will give you a chance to figure out words ahead of time."

4. Help students write their own autobiographies; use these texts for reading instruction. This activity is especially successful with students who claim to be interested in "nothing" (usu-

> *Devise another suggestion you can plan as an antecedent to heighten motivation.*

TABLE 10.1

Tutoring Variations and Applications

Tutor	Training	Some Typical Roles in Relation to Tutoring
Reading specialists	Master's degree with specialization in reading; reading certification	In addition to small-group work with moderately delayed readers, reading specialists work individually with severely delayed readers, applying expert knowledge to problems of the most serious cases.
Learning disabilities (LD) Tutors	Graduates of special education program	Supplement efforts of LD (learning disabilities) teacher. Often LD classroom teachers provide basic literacy education, while LD tutors assist with important daily school requirements having literacy demands too great for the student (e.g., content area reading assignments).
Reading-clinic tutors	Teachers in training (undergraduate or graduate students)	Often are interns in a university program closely supervised by a professor of reading education. Delayed readers may enroll evenings and summers and frequently receive one-to-one instruction.
America Reads tutors	College students in any program, who have been provided training for tutoring	As part of a federal program for low-income college students, they are paid for tutoring young delayed readers. Training is furnished by university-level reading experts.
Paraprofessionals	Varies	Hired to assist teachers, they may have no training in the teaching of reading, or they may have a small amount of training furnished by the school or district. The assistance of paraprofessionals can be useful in helping students with assignments or in presenting reinforcement activities after teachers have provided the initial instruction.
Volunteer tutors	Varies	Although there are exceptions, most volunteers do not have teacher training. Their assistance can be helpful, however, in carrying out small segments of instruction planned by the teacher (e.g., playing a reading game to practice skills or strategy work taught by the teacher).
Parents	Varies	Enlisting a parent to tutor his or her own child at home sometimes can be successful. Such an effort often is most productive if tasks are planned in collaboration between parent and teacher and communication between the two is frequent.
Older student/ cross-class tutor	Minimal	Older students can tutor younger delayed readers. Sometimes teachers provide minimal training, and always specify the specific task. In certain cases, *older delayed readers* have tutored younger delayed readers—with reading gains made by both.
Peer tutors	Minimal	Surprising success has occurred when delayed readers have been tutored by peers. Peer tutoring works best when goals are modest (e.g., listening to a peer read and helping with words) and when assistance is exchanged. (Grace helps Rebecca with reading and then Rebecca helps Grace with math.)

ally middle school or older delayed readers)—who, like most individuals, are interested in self. Word identification practice related to phonic analysis or structural analysis can be based on vocabulary the student has used in writing (or dictating) his or her story, as can comprehension exercises. Any lesson that can accompany published texts can also be accomplished through student-authored material.

Consequences are rewards for accomplishments. They are offered after a success. Although often extrinsic motivators, the purpose of consequences is to ultimately stimulate intrinsic moti-

consequences events or actions designed to enhance motivation that follow an instructional session

FIGURE 10.6

The Cover of *Never Take a Pig to Lunch and Other Poems About the Fun of Eating*

Cover of *Never Take a Pig to Lunch and Other Poems About the Fun of Eating* selected and illustrated by Nadine Bernard Westcott. Illustration copyright © 1994 by Nadine Bernard Westcott. Reprinted by permission of Orchard Books, an imprint of Scholastic, Inc.

vation for reading and reading-related activities. The following are some types of consequences you can use:

> *Four Types of Motivating Consequences*

1. *Tangibles.* Because a delayed reader has met a predetermined reading goal, this student is given a small item, such as a paperback book or a sticker.

2. *Natural reinforcers.* An advantage is given in relation to an event that would take place in the classroom anyway. For instance, the teacher is to read poetry selections to the class from *Where the Sidewalk Ends* (Silverstein, 1974), sharing three old favorites and introducing three new poems. Because Randy has accomplished a reading goal, today he has the privilege of selecting two of the three previous favorites to be read.

3. *Knowledge of progress.* Progress may be visually demonstrated through a graph or a chart kept in a private folder for each reader. Visually demonstrating reading growth underscores for delayed readers their potential for success and does so more powerfully than merely telling them they "are doing better."

labeled praise explicitly stating why the praise is being given

4. *Praise.* A natural teacher behavior, praise is even more effective when it is **labeled praise.** That is, you explicitly state why the praise is offered—instead of simply saying, "Nice job, Shelley"—the praise might be labeled by saying, "Nice job on working out those multisyllabic words in today's story, Shelley. You really did look carefully at the prefix, root word, and suffix for each one—just like we worked on in the game yesterday."

FIGURE 10.7

Bookshelf: High-Quality Literature to Motivate Delayed Readers

Poetry Anthologies

Prelutsky, Jack. (1999). *The 20th-Century Children's Poetry Treasury*. New York: Knopf. Funny, appealing poems and those on familiar topics that research on children's poetry preferences shows to be popular. There are poems in this anthology that can be used with both elementary and middle school students. Good for reading aloud to students when time is short. Selections for this anthology were chosen by the popular Jack Prelutsky.

Westcott, Nadine, B. (1994). *Never Take a Pig to Lunch and Other Poems About the Fun of Eating*. New York: Orchard Books. Silly and fun, familiar and funny. Poems and chants selected and illustrated by Westcott. Most kids will love to hear you read aloud from this one, but many selections also are fairly easy for them to read themselves. Selected by the New York Public Library to include in a list of 100 titles for reading and sharing. *The Horn Book* says, "Sure to lure reluctant readers. It's the perfect appetizer for anyone who thinks he doesn't like poetry."

Easy-to-Read, High-Quality Books to Supplement Content Area Lessons

Greenwood, Barbara (1998). *The Last Safe House: A Story of the Underground Railroad*. Buffalo, NY: Kids Can Press, Ltd. The story of two girls, one who is an escaping slave and the other the daughter of a family who have a house on the underground railroad. These main characters appear to be about intermediate-grade age, although the text is written at approximately high third-grade level. Interspersed within short narrative chapters are informational selections about the time period. Includes an easy-to-understand glossary and a clearly prepared index for teaching about these study aids. Also good for reading aloud to students. Probably could be used suitably with students as old as seventh grade.

Gibbons, Gail. (1999). *Soaring with the Wind: The Bald Eagle*. New York: Morrow. An informational book that can be used as a substitute for reading about this topic in a content area textbook that is too difficult for a delayed reader to use effectively. While aimed at the average upper primary-grade reader, the content and format make it suitable for use with intermediate-grade or even middle school students who are having reading difficulties. Labeled diagrams, throughout, provide opportunity to teach delayed readers how to get content information from illustrations.

Paulsen, Gary (1998). *Soldier's Heart*. New York: Dell Laurel Leaf. For study of the U.S. Civil War, this novel is one to use with the older, more sophisticated middle school or high school age delayed reader. Chapters are short and the vocabulary is not difficult, but the concepts are challenging. Ideal for our many students who are good thinkers although less skilled at word recognition and word identification. A disquieting book but one that should hold interest. Paulsen has been a Newbery Honor winner three times.

Myths

Myths—replete with action, danger, malevolence, champions, threats, and monsters—are often motivating reading for turned-off readers. Try these:

Yolen, Jane. (1998). *Pegasus, the Flying Horse*. New York: Dutton Children's Books. (Beautifully illustrated by Li Ming.)

Aliki. (1994). *The Gods and Goddesses of Olympus*. New York: HarperCollins.

Beautifully Illustrated Books

Zelinsky, Paul O. (1997). *Rapunzel*. New York: Dutton Children's Books. A slightly different version of the traditional tale, both told and illustrated by Paul Zelinsky, a three-time Caldecott Award winner. This one won the Caldecott in 1998. Zelinsky illustrates the story with dramatic oil paintings.

Fleming, D. (2002). *Alphabet Under Construction*. New York: Holt. This book is appropriate for students somewhat older than those for whom alphabet books are typically targeted. The language used to describe Mouse's carpenter-like construction of each alphabet letter is relatively sophisticated. The illustrations, made with homemade paper, are charming and beautiful.

Books to Read to Middle School Students

Curtis, Christopher Paul. (1999). *Bud, Not Buddy*. New York: Delacorte Press. Realistic but unusual adventures of an African-American boy in 1936. Good humor, but exciting times also, should keep middle school students eager to hear more.

Hobbs, Will (1998). *The Maze*. New York: Avon Books. The "maze" refers to a place in the desert where 14-year-old Rick meets a bird biologist, and, as well, refers to the state of Rick's life. A runaway from a detention center, his new acquaintance helps Rick move onward and adopt positive attitudes toward coping. An engaging book. Both "Buddy," in the novel cited immediately above, and Rick are boys without a family. Comparisons could be made if both books were included in a thematic unit.

(continued)

FIGURE 10.7

Bookshelf: High-Quality Literature to Motivate Delayed Readers *(continued)*

Informational Books to Read Aloud to Students

George, Jean Craighead (1995). *Everglades.* New York: HarperCollins. Share this Smithsonian Notable Book for Children with intermediate-grade students. Combines a narrative and expository text style. Illustrated with lovely paintings by Wendell Minor.

Baldwin, Robert F. (1999). *This Is the Sea That Feeds Us.* New York: Dawn Books. A nonfiction book about the food chain in the sea, written in verse. Sidebars, in expository prose form—not verse—supply additional information about animals of the sea discussed in the rhyming text. For older primary or intermediate-grade readers.

Picture Books That Can Be Used with Older Students

Rylant, Cynthia (1996). *Whales.* New York: Scholastic. Also illustrated by Rylant, with an endnote indicating that the "paintings in this book were done with acrylics, using natural sea sponges." At times, older students respond to picture books more favorably if the text is informational rather than narrative—such as in this one. Written at approximately fourth-grade level, this book would nicely substitute for a science text on the same topic when that text is written at too difficult a level for a delayed reader.

Lester, Julius (1998). *From Slave Ship to Freedom Road.* New York: Puffin Books. Powerfully illustrated by Rod Brown. Read this one to yourself first because it's likely to evoke some emotional moments. Dramatic discussions found in this book are probably most suitable for use with older middle school or high school students.

High-Quality Informational Books to Use for Teaching Study Skills

Blackbirch Press Staff. (1999). *Kidbits.* Woodbridge, CT: Blackbirch Press. Use this one to teach students how to read graphs. Hundreds of questions that will interest most middle school students are posed and answered in graph format—with various types of graphs to learn from and about displayed across the book.

Muirden, James. (1999). *Seeing Stars.* Cambridge, MA: Candlewick Press. A good substitute for a difficult-to-read science text on this topic. Try it with middle school age delayed readers. Has a clearly prepared index for teaching use of this tool; presents an opportunity to discuss use of flow charts to communicate and understand information.

Biographies

Stanley, Diane. (2000). *Michelangelo.* New York: HarperCollins. Written for the average intermediate-grade student, this biography could be used effectively with delayed readers at the middle school level. Carefully researched facts are presented. Illustrations by the author using a style prevalent during the time period of Michelangelo's life lend authenticity.

Stanley, Diane (1999). *Joan of Arc.* New York: Morrow. Another outstanding biography written and illustrated by Stanley. (See citation immediately above.)

With consequences, the rule of thumb is to use the least intrusive consequence that will produce motivation. To do that with the list given here, start with the fourth consequence and work upward as necessary.

Motivation is learned; we, therefore, must expect to include attention to motivational issues along with other goals we target in our instructional programs. Deci (1995) identified three "C's" that provide the underpinnings for motivation. The first is *competence*; if students are skillful at a task it is more likely they will want to engage in it—thus, the basic requirement for teachers is to plan for the highest-quality instruction in needed areas. The second is *choice*; allow students to make choices among teacher-provided options. For example, you know that any one of three literature books you have found in the school library will be appropriate for Jamie's instructional level, so you let him choose which will structure his lesson for the next few days. The third is *collaboration*; when students collaborate they often are more successful—and success leads to motivation.

Final Thoughts

Some teachers have been more proficient in working with delayed readers than others. For you to become one of the highly effective teachers, in addition to adopting the ten principles to support high-quality reading instruction, consider the features of the successful Benchmark School program for at-risk learners (Gaskins, 1998).

The Benchmark curriculum has developed over many years to meet the requirements of bright but low-achieving students and, over time, has come to incorporate the following practices: (1) ongoing professional development to ensure that teachers are familiar with current literacy research; (2) generous amounts of instructional time provided to students in order for learning to develop; (3) many opportunities for connected text reading; (4) opportunities for writing to support reading; (5) special attention to strategies for reading informational text; (6) a highly developed decoding program; (7) attention to metacognitive strategies to help students learn how to learn; (8) specific instruction to aid students in controlling maladaptive, nonacademic behaviors that can impinge on learning (e.g., poor attention, lack of persistence, disorganization); and (9) programs that "are matched to where students are, proceed according to the competencies they develop, and teach explicitly what they do not figure out on their own" (p. 545).

The ten principles offered in this chapter, along with these Benchmark guidelines, offer a foundation on which student accomplishments can be built.

Summary and Classroom Applications

double entry journal

Based on what you read in Chapter 10, list solutions to the problem posed for Ms. Hernandez in the Double Entry Journal found at the beginning of this chapter. Divide your ideas into (1) instructional strategies and (2) logistical plans, adjustments, and adaptations. What other solutions would you propose that have not been offered here?

Chapter Summary

Delayed readers progress through the same steps of reading development as average readers. However, because they progress at a slower rate, there is often misunderstanding about what they potentially can and cannot do. The levels of severity of reading problems vary and influence how a regular classroom teacher arranges to meet the needs of a struggling reader. Two causes of reading problems that can be addressed by the classroom teacher are (1) lack of phonemic awareness and (2) the chain of events in which failure to ameliorate early reading problems results in additional problems, often of greater complexity. There are additional possible causes such as hereditary factors or home environment (see Figure 10.3). In these cases, the teacher has little control over the originating causes but can design instruction to meet the student's special needs.

Ten principles of highly effective instruction for poor readers were offered. Types of general approaches, activities, and materials used with delayed learners are indistinguishable from those employed with average readers. There are, however, certain specific issues that must be considered to provide beneficial programs. To address those issues, recommendations were made regarding special needs with respect to timing, pacing, explicitness of teaching, transfer of learning, and review.

In relation to assessment, teachers are encouraged to determine students' reading instructional levels and match them with reading materials—thus ensuring the most productive opportunities for literacy growth. The highly effective teacher goes beyond obvious findings from tests to obtain accurate, fine-tuned assessment information that has true potential to inform instruction for individual delayed readers. More delayed readers have difficulties with word recognition and word identification than with any of the other components of reading. Instructional objectives in such cases are to assist the student in developing automatic recognition of large numbers of words and facilitating strategies to identify unfamiliar words. Ascertaining a delayed reader's word-learning phase is a fundamental task; doing so and planning instruction to take this phase into account usually is a deciding factor between success and failure.

Many delayed readers have difficulties with comprehension, especially with higher-level comprehension tasks. Care must be taken to provide rich instruction, selecting the best approaches for these students who need them the most. Also of concern are the special comprehension-related demands of content area texts. Several suggestions for responding to these demands were presented, including, in certain circumstances, adapting requirements for

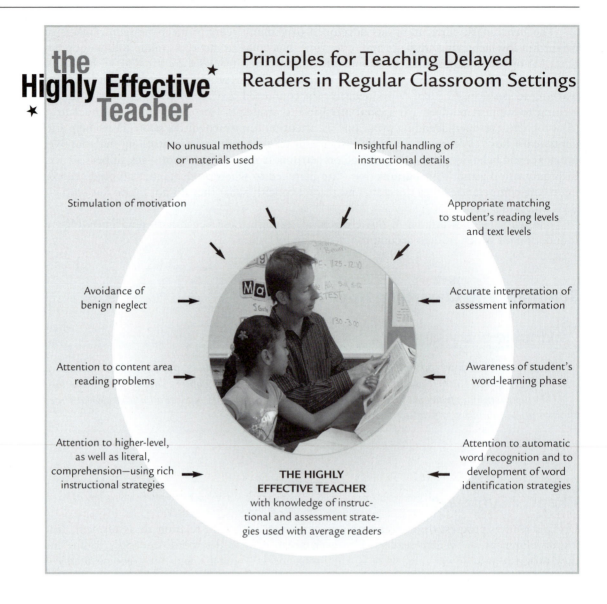

the
Highly Effective Teacher

Principles for Teaching Delayed Readers in Regular Classroom Settings

No unusual methods or materials used

Insightful handling of instructional details

Stimulation of motivation

Appropriate matching to student's reading levels and text levels

Avoidance of benign neglect

Accurate interpretation of assessment information

Attention to content area reading problems

Awareness of student's word-learning phase

Attention to higher-level, as well as literal, comprehension—using rich instructional strategies

Attention to automatic word recognition and to development of word identification strategies

THE HIGHLY EFFECTIVE TEACHER with knowledge of instructional and assessment strategies used with average readers

students with severe reading delays. Adaptations, however, should not deteriorate into benign neglect, in which well-intentioned accommodations lead to neglect of another need that is equally, if not more, critical.

Attention to motivation is a key element in planning instruction for delayed readers. It is an important part of an effective teacher's instructional responsibilities to plan for motivation.

Professional Standards and
Teacher Knowledge for Instructing Delayed Readers

Throughout this book, professional standards (International Reading Association, 2004) have been noted for preparation of highly effective teachers. These standards are especially important when working with delayed readers. It is recognized that we must provide the best literacy education for those who need it the most. Figure 10.8 denotes how Chapter 10 helps you to achieve those high standards. You can see the complete list of Standards for Reading Professionals in Appendix C.

FIGURE 10.8

Professional Standards and the Delayed Reader for Classroom Teacher Candidates

Professional Standard	Example
1. Foundational Knowledge	**Element 1.2** Articulates how teaching practices relate to reading research; e.g., knows what research has discovered about causes of reading delays and implications for instruction; knows what studies show about phases of word learning and how to apply this information to delayed readers; applies research-based strategies to comprehension instruction of delayed readers.
2. Instructional Strategies and Curriculum Materials	**Element 2.2** Plans instructional practices to accommodate developmental differences; e.g., when working with delayed readers, understands the criticality of timing, pacing, explicitness, variety, guided instruction, and review; knows adaptations meet the special demands of content area reading.
3. Assessment, Diagnosis, and Evaluation	**Element 3.2** Analyzes assessment results to place students along a developmental continuum; e.g., understands that appropriately matching a student's reading level to text level, for instructional reading and independent reading, is a critical consideration for delayed readers; recognizes the necessity to further analyze reading behaviors on formal and informal assessments to determine a delayed reader's specific strengths and weaknesses.
4. Creating a Literate Environment	**Element 4.4** Effectively implements instruction that motivates readers intrinsically and extrinsically; e.g., is familiar with literature that holds appeal for reluctant readers; understands the concepts of antecedents and consequences in relation to motivational techniques for delayed readers.
5. Professional Development	**Element 5.3** Actively engages in collaboration and dialogue with other teaching professionals; e.g., makes appropriate decisions in consultation with others regarding the programs through which a delayed reader receives his or her reading instruction (that is, through regular classroom corrective reading program only; regular classroom, plus remedial reading program taught by reading specialist, etc.); makes appropriate decisions regarding level of tutoring (if any) to supplement regular classroom instruction.

Part 2 from IRA. (2004). Professional Standards and Ethics Committee, International Reading Association. *Standards for reading professionals–revised 2003*. Reprinted with permission of the International Reading Association. All rights reserved.

Applications: Bridges to the Classroom

1. Earlier in this chapter you read a Strategies in Use section that described the thinking and actions of a teacher planning a reading program for a student who was in the partial-alphabetic phase of word learning. Examine Figure 10.4 (page 294) again and choose one of the other word-learning phases. On the basis of characteristics specified in this figure, work with a partner to plan a program for a hypothetical student who is in the developmental stage you have chosen.

2. Choose a comprehension strategy from Chapter 5 of this text. Taking into account the principles suggested for instruction of delayed readers, adapt that strategy for use with a student who is decidedly inept with higher-level comprehension tasks. Some of the recommendations you may want to consider are those related to pacing, explicit teaching, matching of reading instructional level to text, the special instructional needs when the text is expository, and motivation.

3. Devise a plan to motivate an unenthusiastic reader. Choose one of the following hypothetical students and write a plan for this student to include both antecedent events and consequences. Be specific about materials and activities you would use. Consider Deci's (1995) three "C's" in developing your plan. Your outline should account for

actions you would take over a one-month period. Select one of the following hypothetical students as the focus of your plan:

> Arnie is an eighth grader whose reading instructional level is approximately sixth-grade level. Arnie loves to draw and hates to read. He is slight in size and often teased by other boys because of his reading problems and his lack of skill in sports. His word recognition and word identification abilities have gradually developed over time, but he still lacks automatic skill in this area and reads slowly.

Shannon is a first grader who is constantly moving. Lack of attention to academic pursuits permeates her school day. Although it is April of the school year, her reading accomplishments are commensurate with that seen more typically at the beginning of first grade. Assessment by a school psychologist indicates that she has above-average intelligence. Shannon would rather do almost anything than read or write because these activities require her to sit still for too long to suit her active and outgoing nature.

Additional Research and Practice

1. Lubliner, S. (2004). **Help for struggling upper-grade elementary readers.** *The Reading Teacher, 57,* 430–438.

   This article discusses a comprehension strategy that helped three fifth-grade delayed readers. The author describes the step-by-step procedures for adopting the strategy into other classrooms. (Practice)

2. Dunston, P. J. (2007). **Instructional practices, struggling readers, and a university-based reading clinic.** *Journal of Adolescent & Adult Literacy, 50,* 328–335.

   Told through the experiences of a long-time reading teacher and clinician, this article presents many useful ideas to help classroom teachers who are working with struggling readers. (Practice)

3. Mathes, P. G., Howard, J. K., Allen, S. H., & Fuchs, D. (1998). **Peer-assisted learning strategies for first-grade readers: Responding to the needs of diverse learners.** *Reading Research Quarterly, 33,* 62–83.

   This research report details findings of a study investigating the effects of peer tutoring on the reading growth of different learner types, especially delayed readers. (Research)

CHAPTER 11

Understanding Language Diversity, Cultural Diversity, and Special Needs

Educators know how important early-childhood interactions are but may not understand that it is the <u>quality of the interaction</u>, not the language that it is carried on in, that is the critical factor.

Patton O. Tabors and Catherine E. Snow,
language educators and researchers, Harvard University

It is often easier to become outraged by injustice half a world away than by oppression and discrimination half a block from home.

Carl T. Rowan (1925–2000),
African American journalist, author, and diplomat

We all possess values that influence our attitudes and beliefs about language use, languages, and cultural groups different from our own. As you read the two brief classroom discussions that follow, explore your attitudes and feelings toward the language used and the cultural diversity of the students.

In the initial episode, the first-grade teacher (T) has put sentences from a story on strips of tagboard and has asked Lionel (C1), an African American student, to read the first sentence (Piestrup, 1973, pp. 54–55). Other students are C2, C3, and C4. The text being read aloud is identified by quotation marks.

T: This one, Lionel. This way, Lionel. Come on, you're right here. Hurry up.

C1: Dey . . .

T: Get your finger out of your mouth.

C1: Call . . .

T: Start again.

C1: Dey call, "What i' it? What is it?"

T: What's this word?

C2: Dey.

C1: Dat.

T: What is it?

C2: Dat.

C3: Dey.

C4: [Laughs]

C1: Dey.

T: Look at my tongue. They.

C1: They.

T: They. Look at my tongue [between her teeth].

C1: They.

T: That's right. Say it again.

C1:   They.

T: They. OK. Pretty good. OK, Lionel.

In the second episode, the students are native speakers of Hawaiian Creole English (Au, 1980, pp. 104–105). The central character in the story the second-grade students are reading is concerned about the outcome of using the frog he has found for bait. The teacher is identified as T and the students are identified as A, V, L, and S. The brackets show the children's overlapping speech.

T: If you're gonna use it for bait, what do you have to do with that frog? You just throw it in the water?

V: Uh-uh. (negative)

A: Put it on a hook.

T: Oh n-o-o-o! He's gonna have to stick it on a hook. (Gestures hooking something with hands, glances at S, then back to A)

L: And den go like dat, an den dat. (Gestures casting a line)

T: And throw it in the water, [and (also makes gesture of casting)]

A: [En den, en mi (ght)]

S: [The fish might come and eat it.]

A: [Da fish might come and eat it.]

What reaction do you have to these two discussions? What attitude is reflected by each teacher toward the students' home language? What effect will each interaction have on the students' comprehension and their desire to participate in group discussions?

double entry journal

Reflect on your responses to the opening classroom discussions. What would have been your reaction in these situations? In what ways do you see student diversity in the classroom as (1) an opportunity for literacy learning and (2) an obstacle to literacy instruction?

Chapter Objectives

After reading and discussing this chapter, you will be able to:

- understand the nature of linguistic and cultural diversity in the United States.
- explore eight key instructional principles and guidelines for teaching diverse learners, using a multicultural education perspective.
- develop insight into students' second-language acquisition strategies.
- understand and appreciate dialects—both standard and nonstandard English vernaculars—and understand language differences between English and Spanish and English and Chinese.

- learn instructional strategies ranging from SDAIE to read-alouds that can be effectively used to teach bilingual learners.
- recognize the learning needs of students with physical, developmental, emotional, intellectual, and other learning difficulties.
- create an instructional environment, including the use of tutors, that is conducive to reading and writing achievement of all students in your classroom.

Understanding the Impact of Diversity

diversity
an umbrella term for group differences defined by race, ethnicity, culture, language, national origin, gender, or other characteristics

Diversity will undoubtedly have an impact on your classroom. In 1996, legal immigration to the United States surged 27 percent, to 915,900 individuals. Almost 10 percent of all U.S. residents are now foreign-born, and by 2020, when today's first graders are in the workforce, the foreign-born population will number 1 in 7 people (Garcia, 1999). Whereas immigration prior to the middle of the twentieth century was primarily from Europe, the most recent immigrants are from Mexico, Asia, Latin America, the former Soviet Union, Iran, and India. You can thus expect to have students in your classroom who speak a dialect different from your own, students who are bilingual, and students who speak little or no English. You can also expect these students, along with many others born in the United States, to represent different cultures that hold different expectations for your role as teacher and for their school experiences. By 2020 it is projected that approximately 50 percent of school-age students will be youth of color (Banks, 2002).

In addition to teaching students from many cultures and with many language backgrounds, you will have students in your classroom with special needs—students with specific learning disabilities and students identified as gifted. You also will find substantial achievement diversity across your classroom. As school populations have become more diverse, educators have been given increased responsibility, by the legislature and the courts, for attempting to meet the instructional needs of all students (see Table 11.1 on page 310). As a highly effective teacher, your task is to create a supportive instructional environment that makes provisions for diverse learning needs.

➤ *Attitudes and values about teaching and learning are culture-based*

Your Beliefs and Values about Diversity

The beliefs and attitudes you hold will strongly influence your teaching; they reflect personal values that have been shaped by your life experiences. Values take the form of characteristics and behavior that you regard as right or wrong, good or bad, and appropriate or inappropriate. You need to reexamine these values given that students with cultural backgrounds and experiences different from your own may have somewhat different values. You also need to consider the beliefs you may hold about gender stereotypes. Gender bias in the classroom perpetuates social constructs and myths such as "Boys are best at math and girls are best at writing" or "Boys become doctors; girls are nurses," as one kindergarten teacher insisted (Sadker & Sadker, 1982, p. 131). Teachers must avoid stereotyping or labeling that reflects prejudice or leads to forms of discrimination.

| Have you experienced gender bias in your schooling?

Many student-related variables must be understood and accounted for if instruction is to be successful. These variables influence students' interaction, participation, and achievement. Your students' race or ethnicity and proficiency in English may directly influence their language-interaction styles, their ability to work individually or in groups, and, in turn, their academic success and self-esteem. For example, as Gallimore, Boggs, and Jordan (1974) found, Hawaiian Creole-speaking students were "manifestly competent" in home and community, where information-giving and concept development are transmitted during group conversation or verbal play but not at school, where information-sharing rules are distinctly different. Your awareness and understanding of these variables will strongly influence instructional planning and students' success in the classroom.

EVIDENCE-BASED PRACTICE

Principles and Guidelines for Teaching Diverse Learners

The eight instructional principles that follow are designed to increase your awareness of the specific learning needs of students and of your responsibility to create active learning environments for linguistically and culturally diverse students (Au, 2000; Carlo, August, McLaughlin, Snow, Dressler, Lippman, Lively, & White, 2004; Collins, 2005; Garcia, 2000; Hawkins, 2004; Jimenez, 2001; Moll, 1988; Purcell-Gates et al., 2007). To be a highly effective teacher in a diverse environment, you will need to understand the following principles:

➤ *Instructional Principles for Teaching Diverse Learners*

1. Students do not come from inferior cultures, nor do they suffer from language deficits; instead, they may possess a culture, dialect, and language that vary from your own.
2. Students' acquisition of language and literacy abilities is meaning-based as well as developmental and is best facilitated by interactive meaning construction activities.
3. It is important to learn as much as possible about your students' homes, communities, languages, and cultural backgrounds so that you can incorporate this knowledge into instructional content and interactions in the classroom.
4. It is important to create a context-rich, interactive, supportive classroom environment for language exploration and use. Creating a low-anxiety, low-risk language-learning setting (low affective filter) is also important (Krashen, 1987).
5. You can help students develop social language skills that facilitate literacy interactions both in and out of school. You must also help them develop academic and content-based literacy skills.

TABLE 11.1

A Brief Overview of Diversity Legislation and Court Decisions

Category	Year	Description
Equal Educational Opportunity	1954	In *Brown v. Board of Education of Topeka, Kansas,* the Supreme Court ruled that segregation of educational facilities was illegal (Grant & Sleeter, 1993).
	1964	The *Civil Rights Act* prohibited federal support for public institutions that segregate students on the basis of race, color, religion, or national origin.
	1964	The *Economic Opportunity Act* provided for the initiation of the Head Start, Follow-Through, and Upward Bound programs.
	1965	The *Elementary and Secondary Education Act* (ESEA), Title I provided extensive funding for compensatory education to enhance educational opportunities for African American, Hispanic American, Appalachian, and low-income students.
	1969	The *Office of Civil Rights* extended the concept of racial discrimination to include "national origin minority group children," regardless of race (Weinberg, 1977).
Second-Language and Bilingual Education	1967	The *Bilingual Education Act* (Title VII of ESEA) was the first legislation to provide federal funds earmarked for non-English speaking students (Wilson, 1993).
	1974	The *Lau v. Nichols* decision, initiated by Chinese American public school students in San Francisco, stated that schools must provide for students' language needs in order to provide equal educational opportunity (Allen, 1991).
	1981	*Castenada v. Pickard* provided for the development of a framework for determining whether school districts are in compliance with *Lau v. Nichols.*
	1994	*Reauthorization of Bilingual Educational Act* (Title VII of Improving American Schools Act, formerly ESEA) ended identification of bilingual programs as maintenance, transitional, and immersion.
	1994	*Reauthorization of Improving American Schools Act* made language-minority students eligible to receive Title I services.
	2001	*No Child Left Behind Act* mandates that all children participate in large-scale statewide assessment, including limited English proficient (LEP) students "who shall be assessed in a valid and reliable manner and provided reasonable accommodations on assessments." LEP students must be tested in English reading after thirty months of schooling. Federal funding to a school district is contingent upon student literacy growth (the student body as a whole as well as subgroups) that will reach 100 percent over a twelve-year period.
Gender Equity	1972	*Educational Amendment* (Title IX) prohibited sex discrimination in the treatment of students, including counseling, testing, financial aid, and educational activities (Banks & Banks, 1989).
	1974	*Women's Educational Equity Act* (WEEA) supported expanded programs for women in a wide variety of areas, including math, science, and technology; reduction of sex-role stereotyping in curriculum materials; increasing the number of female educational administrators; extension of educational and career opportunities to minority, disabled, and rural women; increasing educational opportunities and career aspirations for females; and encouraging more female participation in athletics.
Special Education	1974	*Public Law 93–380* provided for federal funding of state programs for students who are gifted and talented.
	1975–1990	*Public Law 94–142,* amended in 1986 (PL 99–457) and 1990 (PL 101–476), provided for mainstreaming, or the placement of students with disabilities in regular classrooms (the least restrictive instructional environment) for some or all of their day, rather than segregating them in special schools or classrooms (Smith & Luckasson, 1995).
	2001	*No Child Left Behind Act* mandates that all students will be assessed, including those with learning or other disabilities. Students with severe disabilities, but not to exceed 1 percent of the student population, will be allowed to take out-of-level tests or participate in alternative assessment forms.

6. You need to provide instructional opportunities in language use that will encourage risk-taking and will develop the understanding that individuals learn from their mistakes as they acquire a new language.

7. You need to help students build positive self-concepts by providing frequent academic and social opportunities for interactive meaning-based language use.

8. The same learning principles are at work in *all* students. For example, students with all languages and from all cultures are active theory builders and hypothesis testers. They are motivated to make sense of their world. Their language acquisition is greatly enhanced through active participation in meaning construction with their peers, teachers, and other individuals in their school and community.

These eight instructional principles are supported by Virginia Allen's (1991) conclusions based on her extensive review of research on teaching bilingual children and those who are learning English as a second language. She concludes that instruction should provide opportunities for such students to do the following:

> *Qualities of Instruction for Diverse Learners*

1. Acquire the language naturally, using the language for real purposes.
2. Receive linguistic input that is made comprehensible by a strong and supportive context.
3. Experiment with, hypothesize about, and try out language in low-anxiety settings.
4. Work with English-speaking peers on meaningful tasks that create opportunities and real reasons to talk, write, and read together.
5. Use language for a broad variety of functions, both social and academic.

Multicultural Education

A **culture** is defined by the values, symbols, interpretations, and perceptions of the members of a specific group (Banks, 1997b). In the United States, a common over-arching culture encompasses core national values, such as a strong belief in individuality. There are, however, microcultures within the national macroculture that do not share all of these beliefs to the same degree. For example, some African Americans and Hispanic Americans who have not experienced a high degree of mainstream cultural assimilation may be more group oriented. Group-oriented learners may benefit from cooperative-learning strategies in instruction.

culture
values, symbols, interpretations, and perceptions held by members of a specific group

A major goal of **multicultural education** is to adjust instructional approaches so that students from diverse cultural and ethnic groups will have equal learning opportunities. Banks (2003) emphasizes the importance of integrating curriculum content that is related to ethnic, racial, and cultural groups; developing an understanding of the way knowledge is constructed; reducing prejudice; and fostering a school culture that empowers students. These key ideas are illustrated in Figure 11.1 (page 312).

multicultural education
curriculum and instruction that acknowledges diversity and promotes equal educational opportunities

Banks' four approaches, reflecting different levels of commitment to the integration of cultural content, are shown in Figure 11.2 (page 313). The *contributions approach* (Level 1) is the traditional approach, which you probably experienced in your schooling. The major focus is on cultural heroes and holidays and specific aspects of a given culture, such as unique customs and foods. When used alone, this approach often fails to identify underlying cultural values and historical and cultural contexts.

> *Contributions Approach*

Level 2, the *additive approach*, adds content and concepts in the form of thematic units of study. A thematic unit might be developed around folktales, using the Cinderella theme (Au, 1993)—for example, by adding Steptoe's (1987) *Mufaro's Beautiful Daughters* and Louie's (1982) *Yeh Shen: A Cinderella Story from China* to the curriculum. This approach exposes students to literature of diverse cultural groups; but, when used by itself, it presents little opportunity for students to consider underlying relationships among cultures.

> *Additive Approach*

In the *transformation approach* (Level 3), relationships among cultures are examined and students consider concepts, issues, and events from the perspective of different cultural groups. This approach may incorporate literature that fosters consideration of similarities and differences between two ways of life or the changes and conflicts that occur in a society over time. The transformation approach offers opportunities to understand how our society has been changed through contributions of diverse cultures and also helps students develop pride in their own culture as they recognize these contributions.

> *Transformation Approach*

FIGURE 11.1

Banks' Dimensions of Multicultural Education

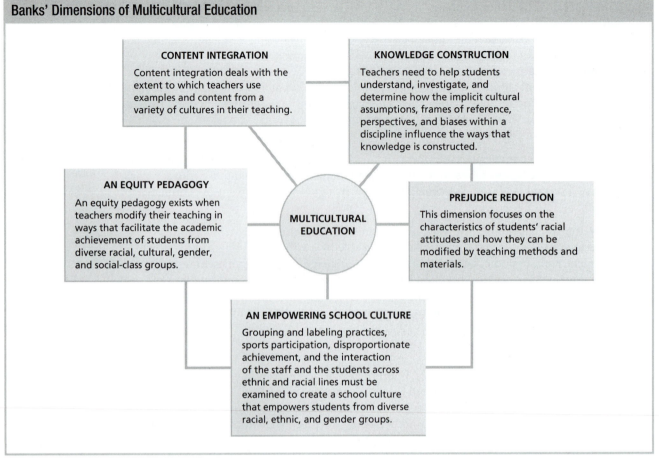

Reprinted with the author's permission from James A. Banks, *Cultural Diversity and Education: Foundations, Curriculum and Teaching* (4th ed., 2001). Boston: Allyn & Bacon, page 5.

➤ *Social-Action Approach*

Level 4, the *social-action approach*, is designed to help students gather information about social issues and problems, examine underlying values and assumptions, and propose solutions. Such goals require students to clarify their own thinking, search for new information, and consider possible actions to take. To make this approach work, you need to be willing to plan extensively, as you locate resources, examine possible issues, develop cooperative discussion groups, and become prepared to help students address controversial issues.

Language-Acquisition Strategies

➤ *Students' Language-Acquisition Strategies*

Lily Wong-Fillmore provides insight into the strategies used by 5-to 7-year-old children who are acquiring a second language (1976). She notes that they use chunks of language, such as "Gimme," "What's that?" and "My turn," that enable them to communicate before they begin to manipulate structures in the language. Young students use the following five strategies as they begin to acquire English:

1. They assume that what people are saying is related to the present situation.
2. They learn a few stock expressions and use these in their interactions.
3. They look for recurring patterns in the language.
4. They use the language forms they have acquired and make the most of them.
5. They put great effort into getting meaning across, with minimal concern for refinements.

FIGURE 11.2

Banks' Levels of Integration of Multicultural Content

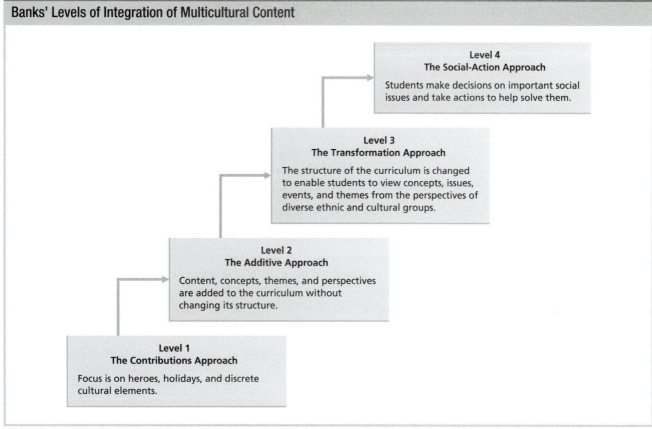

Reprinted with the author's permission from James A. Banks, *Teaching Strategies for Ethnic Studies* (7th ed., 2003). Boston: Allyn & Bacon, page 18.

Literacy Background and Linguistic Interdependence

Goodman and Goodman (1978) highlight the importance of students' background knowledge in acquiring literacy in a second language. Their study of young learners from four different language groups (Arabic, Navaho, Samoan, and Spanish) revealed that background knowledge was one of the most critical factors in successful reading and retelling of stories. The more students know about the story content, the more effective they are in reading and understanding the story. Consequently, you will need to be aware of the background knowledge that second-language students bring to your classroom and ways in which you can build on this knowledge—both through social language opportunities and skills and through academic and content-based language and literacy skills, which are crucial.

Saville-Troike (1984) studied the English language development of students in an English as a second language (ESL) class. Seven different languages were spoken by the students, who had recently arrived in the United States. Although they were able to share meaning with their peers through language formulas, gestures, and mime in social settings, this ability did not permit effective communication in the classroom setting.

Cummins (1989) proposes a language-learning framework in which students' underlying base of proficiency in their native language is used to support their learning of English (or a new second language). This cognitive base already includes an understanding of literacy concepts, logic, abstract thinking, comprehension, analysis, application, synthesis, evaluation, inference, and hypothesis, as well as **metalinguistic awareness** (self-awareness of the use of language in comprehending). Although a student's native language and English differ in surface aspects (pronunciation, grammar, vocabulary), the underlying cognitive and conceptual aspects are similar.

> How is background knowledge critical to academic success?

> **metalinguistic awareness**
> self-understanding about language functions and comprehension processes that form the basis for language learning

> *The Cummins Iceberg Metaphor for Language Competence*

According to Cummins, the student can transfer these underlying thinking processes and literacy-related skills to the acquisition of the new language. The effectiveness of this transfer depends on the learner's level of competence in his or her native language. The "iceberg" metaphor shown in Figure 11.3 illustrates Cummins's theory. The tips of the two overlapping icebergs represent the surface aspects of language competence in the student's first language (L1) and the language to be learned (L2). These tips constitute the Basic Interpersonal Communication Skills (BICS) used by the student in each language.

The submerged part that connects the two icebergs represents the learner's underlying language proficiency (literacy concepts, synthesis, inference, and metalanguage), which is used in the native language and can be transferred to English. This part of the iceberg is known as the student's Cognitive/Academic Language Proficiency (CALP). Strong support for the Cummins interdependence theory is found in Verhoeven's research (1994) with first- and second-grade students.

| What is the difference between BICS and CALP?

Development of Metalinguistic Awareness

For students, the development of metalanguage and metalinguistic awareness is an important part of acquiring a second language (Garcia, 2000). Selinker (1972) identifies this process as developing an "interlanguage," which enables the learner to create and test informal theories and hypotheses about how the new language works. Students test out their ideas by using them in communication with peers and adults. Errors reflecting language growth will result. Selinker's theory reinforces the idea that the classroom must be a psychologically safe environment for language exploration. Language-exploration errors must be valued rather than discouraged through overcorrection and peer ridicule.

EVIDENCE-BASED PRACTICE

> *Time Required for Language Proficiency*

The period of time required for students to become proficient users of English depends on their exposure to English both in and out of school, attitudes toward learning, opportunities to use the language, and proficiency in the first language, as well as developmental factors such as age. The time from initial exposure to competent use of English ranges from two to six years (Valdés, 1991; Wong-Fillmore & Valadez, 1986).

FIGURE 11.3

The Linguistic-Interdependence Model

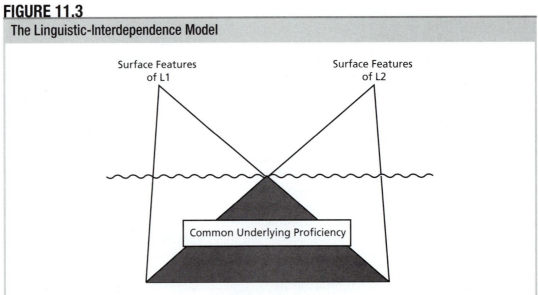

Reproduced with permission from J. Cummins. (1989). Language and literacy acquisition in bilingual contexts. *Journal of Multilingual and Multicultural Development, 10* (1), 23. Multilingual Matters Ltd., Publisher.

The Student's Language and Culture

Culture influences the language functions students use—the different oral and written language forms they regard as appropriate for different social contexts. Language forms range from casual conversation to formal presentation. They quickly learn what language forms are appropriate for different social settings and occasions, but you cannot assume that all students understand the language functions that are critical to academic success and the culture of the school. It is important to understand the close connection between language and culture as you provide for the instructional needs of your students.

Standard English Dialects

A **language** is defined by a unique group of sounds, grammatical rules, and lexical (vocabulary) elements, specific to a culture, that enables speakers to communicate with each other. These features are influenced by the language used in the home, community, and school environments. Whatever language you speak, your speech contains pronunciation, grammatical, and lexical markers that define your dialect of that language. English has regional **dialects,** many of which are considered forms of standard English, or "news broadcast" English, used in business and education. Dialects that differ from standard English, however, do not represent deficient or inferior language forms.

language
a system of phonology, grammar, and vocabulary that people in a group use to communicate with one another

dialects
variations in the phonology, grammar, and vocabulary of a language used by different groups of speakers of that language

Nonstandard English Vernaculars

In literacy development, the eventual use of standard English is an important goal, but it is not a prerequisite for literacy (Au, 1993). Standard English should not be viewed as a replacement for students' nonstandard dialects but as an alternative dialect that can be used in school and work when appropriate and necessary. Those who speak nonstandard dialects such as Black English (also known as **Black English vernacular**), Hawaiian Creole English, and Appalachian English can communicate effectively in their communities and in the classroom. You will, however, hear key phonetic and grammatical variations in their language use and oral reading. Some variations between standard English and Black English are illustrated in Tables 11.2 and 11.3 (pages 316, 317) (Labov, 1967; Ruddell, 1974).

Black English vernacular
alternative dialect of English spoken in certain African American communities

Many dialect forms, such as redundant pattern elements (e.g., "Where you at?"), will not interfere with students' comprehension. Other forms, however, such as the omission of past-tense markers, may have some effect on comprehension (Labov, 1967). For example, the absence of possessive forms, lack of future- and past-tense markers, or alternative placement of adverbs may interfere with comprehension when students first encounter the standard English forms.

Factors that Influence Second-Dialect Acquisition

Students who speak nonstandard English are able learners and should encounter little or no communication interference because of their dialect, which represents only the tip of the Cummins iceberg (surface features). Your basic instructional concern is with the submerged part of the iceberg—the development of literacy competencies. The degree to which students become completely bidialectal (able to shift easily between nonstandard and standard English) depends on a variety of factors: attitudes toward each dialect, peer and community pressures, family attitudes, and academic and economic opportunities.

When is dialect a problem and when is it not a problem?

Bilingual Learners

If **bilingual learners** (students who speak two languages with some degree of proficiency) are present in your classroom, you will have major instructional responsibility for their literacy development. Students in immigrant families comprise the majority of the bilingual population in schools, but bilingual students also come from long-established American cultures such as Navaho, Eskimo-Aleut, and Louisiana French (Portes & Rumbaut, 1990). Americans who speak Creole or other non-standard varieties of English as their first language include Hawaiian Islanders and Sea Islanders from the Carolinas.

bilingual learners
students who speak two languages with some degree of proficiency

TABLE 11.2

Examples of Pronunciation and Grammatical Differences between Standard English and Black English

Standard English Form	Black English Equivalent	The Dialect-Speaking Student May Pronounce _____ as _____.	
Initial Position			
/th/ becomes /d/		this	dis
		that	dat
/thr/ becomes /tr/		three	tree
		thrust	trust
/str/ becomes /scr/		stream	scream
		strap	scrap
Final Position			
/th/ becomes /f/		Ruth	Roof
/nt/ becomes /n/		meant	men
		bent	ben
/ng/ becomes /n/		sing	sin
/skt/ becomes /ks/		asked	axed
/sts/ becomes /s/		fists	fis
/l/ is not sounded		tool	too
		help	hep
/r/ is not sounded		four	foe
		guard	god
/d/ is not sounded		road	row

Final Position			**Grammatical Consequences**
/ft/ becomes /f/	laughed	laugh	Past tense not signaled
/md/ becomes /m/	aimed	aim	Past tense not signaled
/dz/ becomes /d/	loads	load	Agreement not signaled
/lz/ becomes /l/	holes	hole	Agreement not signaled
/ts/ becomes /t/	hits	hit	Agreement not signaled
/ks/ becomes /k/	knocks	knock	Agreement not signaled

limited English proficient (LEP) the lack of enough English to allow independent learning in classrooms where English is the language of instruction

Fluent English proficient (FEP) the presence of enough English to allow independent learning in classrooms where conversation and instruction are conducted in English

Bilingual students come to school with varying degrees of proficiency in English and may or may not be fluent and literate in their native language. Schools commonly use the following terminology to characterize bilingual students:

1. **Very limited English** speakers communicate very little, if at all, in English and use their native language (first language, or L1) as their primary means of communication.
2. **Limited English proficient (LEP)** students demonstrate some degree of oral language fluency in English. However, this fluency is insufficient for independent learning in classrooms where English is the main language of instruction. LEP students rely primarily on their native language for communication with peers, family, and community and use familiar "chunks of language" (English, or L2), mime, and gesture to function in the classroom.
3. **Fluent English proficient (FEP)** students can participate fluently in conversations and have sufficient independent control of English and literacy to participate in the predominantly English-speaking classroom.

Another term currently favored by many educators in new *English-language learners* (ELLs), a designation usually encompassing both very limited English speakers and LEP students. Although the United States Department of Education still endorses the specification "LEP," increasingly the term ELL is being adopted by school districts and by education writers.

TABLE 11.3
More Examples of Grammatical Differences between Standard English and Black English

Description	Example
Copula (or linking verbs) omitted	He tired. You playing here.
Use of *be* in place of other verb forms	They always *be* messing around. Most of the time he *be* in the house.
Absence of regular verb ending *-ed*	He pick me. He turn around.
Use of *ain't* to signal past tense of verbs; not changed in past tense	*Ain't* he finished? *Ain't* nobody see it.
Plural overgeneralization	mens, peoples, teeths, mices
Absence of plural form cued by context	two dog, several cat
Substitution of *they* for *their, you* for *your*	*They* eyes are brown. You brought it on *you* own self.
Use of *more* with adjectives in comparative form	He is *more* taller than you.
Alternative placement of adverbs, such as *mostly* and *absolutely*	That's what *mostly* we call 'em. This is a crazy world we *absolutely* livin' in.

Sentence Patterns

Omission of *do* forms in questions	How he fix that? How it taste?
Redundant pattern elements, such as *at* in "where" questions	Where you at? Where he work at?
Double negatives used with each indefinite pronoun or adverb	Nobody don't know. I ain't never had no trouble wit' none of them.
Doubling of forms	My brother he going. I didn't play with only but Wayne and Tyrone.

Major urban centers of the United States, such as Los Angeles, San Francisco, New York, Chicago, and Miami, have large percentages of language-minority students. In addition, some rural areas, particularly in the West and Southwest, have settlements of immigrant families who have recently arrived in the United States. Many of the students have acquired to some extent their native language but are limited in their English language proficiency. As these students begin to acquire English, they have several immediate needs: (1) to understand how their language differs from English in pronunciation and grammatical forms that affect meaning; (2) to acquire vocabulary, new concepts, and background knowledge related to subject-area content; and (3) to learn classroom conversational routines, classroom language concepts and the language of instruction, and meaning-construction strategies in English.

What immediate needs do LEP children have?

Spanish- and Chinese-speaking students represent a significant percentage of students with limited English proficiency in the United States. You can develop some idea of pronunciation and grammar differences between English and Spanish by examining Table 11.4 (page 318) (Ruddell, 1974, 2006; Stockwell & Bowen, 1966); differences between English and Chinese are shown in Table 11.5 (page 319) (Ruddell, 1974, 2006; San Francisco Unified School District, 1969).

Programs for New English-Language Learners

Several types of programs are provided to meet the needs of students with limited English proficiency. These include English as a second language (ESL) programs, bilingual education, and specially designed academic instruction in English (SDAIE).

How will you meet the needs of your bilingual learners? What steps would you take to develop the qualities of an effective and influential bilingual teacher?

TABLE 11.4

Language Differences between Standard English and Spanish

English Form	Spanish Equivalent	The Hispanic American Student May Pronounce _____ as _____.	
/ă/	/ĕ/ or /ŏ/	bat	bet
		hat	hot
/ĭ/	/e/	bit	beet
/ŭ/	/ē/	but	bet
/ā/	/ĕ/	late	let
/o͝o/	/o͞o/	full	fool
/b/	/p/	bar	par
/v/	/b/	vote	boat
/g/	/k/	goat	coat
/j/	/ch/	jump	chump
/th/	/s/, /t/, or /f/	thank	sank
/z/	/s/	zoo	sue

Grammatical Differences	English Form	Spanish-English Speaker
Agreement	The car runs.	The car run.
Tense	Joe said that he was ready.	Joe said that he is ready.
Use of *be*	I am five years old.	I have five years.
Negative	Joe isn't here.	Joe is no here.
	Don't come.	No come.
Pronoun omission	Is he a farmer?	Is farmer?
	Is he ready?	Is ready?
Adjective use		
Order	The red cap is pretty.	The cap red is pretty.
Comparison	It is bigger.	It more big.

TABLE 11.5
Language Differences between Standard English and Chinese

English Form	Chinese Equivalent	The Chinese American Student May Pronounce _____ as _____.	
/ā/	/ĕ/ or /ă/	bait	bet or bat
	/ŭ/	came	come
/ē/	/ĭ/	beat	bit
/ōō/	/ŏŏ/	Luke	look
/b/	/p/	rib	rip
/g/	/k/	rig	rik
/d/	/t/	rid	rit
/z/	/s/	zoo	sue
/v/	/f/	have	haf
/zh/	/s/	leisure	leaser
/th/	/d/	that	dat
/sh/	/s/	she	see
/n/	/l/	need	lead
/r/	/l/	rice	lice
		read	lead
/w/	/v/	will	vill

Grammatical Differences	English Speaker	Chinese-English Speaker
Agreement	He lives in San Francisco.	He live in San Francisco.
Tense	I am working.	I right at work.
	I had just finished watering the lawn.	I just water finish lawn.
_Be_ omitted	He is sick.	He sick.
_Be_ substituted	I was here yesterday	I at here yesterday.
Negative	I cannot go.	I no can go.
Plural	Many houses are beautiful.	Many house beautiful.
Pronoun	You have known him a long time.	You know he long time.
Preposition omitted	I live in San Francisco	I live San Francisco.
Conjunction and verb omitted	You and I are alike.	You I alike.
Question form word order	Are you going home?	You go home?
	Will you come to my house for dinner?	You tonight come I home dinner?

English as a Second Language (ESL) Programs

English as a second language (ESL) education relies heavily on an immersion approach for students with varying degrees of competency in English. ESL is usually a pull-out program in which new English-language learners (ELLs) are grouped together for instruction. In _language immersion_ (often called the sink-or-swim approach), students are taught only in English. The content is restricted to acquiring and using English language skills. Instruction may be for a limited time in special classes each day or may be extended and integrated into content areas. Language immersion is also used for English-speaking students—for example, when those students are learning Japanese.

English as a second language (ESL) education programs for students with limited English proficiency, based on English-only instruction

Bilingual Education

bilingual education
programs for bilingual learners, based on instruction in the first language and in English

Bilingual education typically provides content area instruction in students' primary language while providing literacy instruction in English during part of the school day. Students may or may not receive literacy instruction in their first language. Many schools situate their bilingual programs at the primary level (grades K–3), with the intent of bringing students into the program as early as possible so that they can make a successful transition into English-only classrooms by late second or early third grade. Other schools or districts have two-way bilingual education programs in which English-only students acquire fluency and literacy in the other language predominant in the school. Bilingual programs also exist at the intermediate level to accommodate older students with minimal English fluency. These programs require that everyone in the class have the same primary language and so are found only in schools with large concentrations of other-than-English-speaking or bilingual students who share a common native language.

Research and Evidence-Based Practice

New English-Language Learners and Literacy Development

Did You Know?

DEMOGRAPHIC INFORMATION

- Limited English proficient (LEP) students, also referred to as new English-language learners (ELLs), constitute nearly 4.6 million public school students (Abedi, Hofstetter, & Lord, 2004).

- The languages of the LEP/ELL students are represented by the following breakdown: Spanish (79 percent), Vietnamese (2 percent), Hmong (1.6 percent), Cantonese (1 percent), and Korean (1 percent). The remaining 14 percent include a wide range of languages from Russian (0.8 percent) to Romanian (0.1 percent) (Abedi, Hofstetter, & Lord, 2004; Kindler, 2002).

- In the 2000–2001 school year, LEP/ELL students were found at the following grade levels: Grades Pre-K–Grade 3, 44 percent; Grades 4–8, 35 percent; Grades 9–12, 19 percent; other, 2 percent (Kindler, 2002).

- More than half of the LEP/ELL students live in four states: California (33 percent), Texas (12 percent), Florida (6 percent), and New York (5 percent). These students represent one in four of K–12 students in California (Abedi, Hofstetter, & Lord, 2004; California Department of Education, 2000).

- Over the past fifteen years, the LEP/ELL student population has grown 105 percent compared to the overall school population growth of 12 percent (Kindler, 2002).

LITERACY DEVELOPMENT

- All children, including LEP/ELL students, learn a first language in the social-interaction context of their family structure, beginning with babbled syllables at about six months and continuing through the very rapid acquisition of vocabulary and grammar in the elementary school grades (Tabors and Snow, 2004).

- Students who have developed a strong foundation in their home language with continued support for that language through home activities such as book reading have been shown to develop skills that will later transfer to English (Snow, Burns, & Griffin, 1998).

- Students who are at-risk bilinguals may experience a home environment where parents have limited English proficiency and are unable to support language interactions, vocabulary development, and preliteracy activities in English (Snow, Burns, & Griffin, 1998).

- The early language environment of the bilingual child will have an important impact on later language and reading development (Tabors & Snow, 2004).

- Educators should encourage parents to maintain their first language at home and use it for literacy activities and everyday conversations (Tabors & Snow, 2004).

- Language-development time from initial encounter with English to fluent development ranges from two to six years (Valdés, 1991; Wong-Fillmore & Valadez, 1986).

Transitional Programs

Transitional language programs are designed to assist students in making a transition from ESL classes and bilingual programs to English-speaking classrooms. The timing of the transition depends on the type of program. When literacy is taught through the student's first language and other content is taught in English, the transition may be as short as two years. When 40 percent or more of both literacy and content area instruction is in the first language, the transition takes longer, and students frequently remain in transition classrooms through the fifth and sixth grades (Ramirez, 1992).

Maintenance Programs

The **language maintenance program** values bilingualism in a special way by providing for the continuing development of students' first language and cultural identity while teaching the second language and related cultural understandings. Maintenance programs thus preserve students' linguistic and cultural heritage while developing English fluency and social integration.

> **language maintenance program** instruction to preserve and develop the bilingual learner's first language

Two-Way Bilingual Programs

The **two-way bilingual program** has the distinct goal and potential advantage of helping all students become bilingual and bicultural. Classes consist of approximately equal numbers of standard English-speaking students and students whose first language is not English. Instructional time is equally divided between the two languages; for example, English is used during half of the class instruction time and Spanish during the other half. Research shows that students in two-way bilingual programs not only successfully develop bilingualism but also have more positive attitudes toward multicultural issues (Willis, 1994).

> **two-way bilingual program** instruction to encourage all learners to become bilingual and bicultural

Bilingual Teachers

Bilingual programs require teachers who are bilingually literate and fluent. The instructional reality for many bilingual learners, however, is that they are placed in classrooms where the teacher does not speak their native language, may not have much knowledge about their culture, and has had limited experience teaching English as a second language. The lack of bilingual teachers creates a major dilemma for all parties involved. Many states encourage teachers to increase their knowledge of second-language learning and multicultural education to gain understanding of the cultures represented by students in their schools (Figure 11.4 page 322). Teachers of bilingual learners must be able to do the following:

1. Provide a context-rich language and literacy learning environment for all students.
2. Develop concepts and language useful for participation in the school environment.
3. Build on students' experiences and background.
4. Teach learning strategies useful for constructing meaning.
5. Develop students' ability to participate in small-group interactions.
6. Adjust literacy task demands.

> ▶ *Skills for Teachers of Bilingual Learners*

Specially Designed Academic Instruction in English

Specially Designed Academic Instruction in English (SDAIE) is an instructional approach specifically designed for students with limited English proficiency. This approach applies language-acquisition principles to content area instruction (Garcia, 1999). The key purpose of SDAIE is to make information accessible to students through careful planning and scaffolding, while avoiding oversimplification of the curriculum. The four goals of SDAIE are for students to (1) learn to communicate in English, (2) learn content area material, (3) advance in higher-level thinking skills, and (4) master literacy skills (Carolo et al., 2004; Diaz-Rico & Weed, 1995).

The key instructional principles of SDAIE (Hudelson, 1989; Diaz-Rico & Weed, 1995) are as follows:

> **Specially Designed Academic Instruction in English (SDAIE)** a system of adapting classroom instruction for students with limited English proficiency

> ▶ *Instructional Principles of SDAIE*

■ Language and content are best learned through *active participation* in academic tasks.
■ The learning environment should provide a high degree of *social interaction* as activities are developed.
■ *Integration of oral and written language* in instruction will facilitate language acquisition.

FIGURE 11.4

Qualities of Highly Effective Teachers of Bilingual Learners

Effective teachers provide a context for learning:

- a caring classroom
- family-based learning
- community involvement
- a print-rich and image-rich classroom
- an experience-rich classroom
- active and interactive learning
- cooperative learning
- professional support

Effective teachers provide reading instruction specifically designed for bilingual learners:

By reading aloud in both languages, they
- model reading skills
- model the joy of reading

They use a variety of methods:
- word recognition and word identification
- question and prediction strategies
- picture and context clues
- language experience and discussion

They use a variety of materials:
- basals and children's and adolescent literature
- trade books and real-world print
- personal stories

They provide individualized reading instruction.

Effective teachers use various strategies to develop oral language:

In the first language, they provide instruction in
- the language of instruction
- meanings of academic tasks

In the first language and English, they provide instruction in
- vocabulary development
- concept and schemata development
- transfer of information and skills
- modeling of respect for both languages
- clarification of textual content

Effective teachers are sensitive to external factors:

- pressure to assimilate
- family and community communication needs
- beliefs and values about cultural preservation
- concern about potential loss of native language
- dual use of language in school and community
- influence of public opinion and media
- political, economic, and social factors
- school and district policies and practices
- student age, grade level, and development
- classroom and school composition
- teacher language, attitudes, and training
- school schedules and standardized testing

- ■ *Authentic learning* using real books and real tasks is important to increase student motivation and interest.
- ■ *Activation of prior knowledge* through classroom discussion and activities helps students connect new information to already developed knowledge schema.

Specific Classroom Strategies for Teaching Bilingual Learners

Effective strategies for teaching bilingual students are much the same as effective strategies for teaching English monolingual students. The strategy selection process is best guided by the seven conditions for optimal literacy learning presented in Chapter 3 and illustrated in Figure 11.5 (page 324).

In what sense is literacy learning collaborative?

These conditions are supported by Moll's (1988) study of Spanish-English bilingual and English monolingual classrooms. He concluded that the basis for literacy development in both groups was the belief that "both comprehension and expression are built and developed collaboratively by students and teachers through functional, relevant, and meaningful language use. Thus, a major goal of teaching is to make classrooms highly literate environments in which many language experiences can take place and different types of 'literacies' can be practiced, understood, and learned" (p. 466).

Determining Instructional Needs

It is important to discover as much as possible about the language background of your bilingual students in order to use instructional strategies effectively. Gunderson (1991) has developed a "decision heuristic"—a chart to help teachers determine students' instructional levels (Table 11.6,

How to Do . . .

A SDAIE Lesson

1. Plan instruction by developing themes. Decide on instructional objectives and what the students need to master. Organize units of study around themes.
2. Think of ways to modify lessons and bring them to life. Develop objectives for thematic content and language development. Identify high-interest visuals and manipulatives as well as concrete models to illustrate ideas. Organize material so that concepts are clearly explained.
3. Set the stage. Present a broad overview of the unit or lesson content. Initiate each lesson with a brief review of what was learned yesterday or predictions about what will happen today.
4. Preteach vocabulary and content area reading strategies. Teach words necessary for understanding the lesson or unit content. Teach strategies for reading nonfiction text.
5. Guide initial learning. Use consistent lesson formats and plans, at least initially. Find ways to animate instruction with role playing, demonstrations, realia, experiments, and activities.
6. Guide practice. Provide examples and tryouts. Demonstrate explicitly how practice activities relate to initial learning.
7. Guide independent practice. Maximize student interactions (partner pairs, groups, cooperative learning). Evaluate students using student-developed products and tests.

- **Although use of thematic units may be less critical to the literacy learning of delayed readers, many of the instructional *processes* that boost learning for LEP students also are important when working with delayed readers. These include using high-interest manipulatives, providing review, encouraging predictions, preteaching vocabulary, enhancing instruction with role playing and demonstrations, promoting cooperative learning, and furnishing *guided* initial learning and *guided* practice.**

DELAYED READER ADAPTATION

From Diaz-Rico & Weed, 1995; Hudelson, 1989.

page 324). Based on your classroom observations, you can determine a student's English oral-language proficiency (L2) by using the descriptions in the chart. Understanding students' levels of proficiency will help you select and apply appropriate instructional strategies.

Developing Background and Conceptual Knowledge

You can develop students' background and conceptual knowledge by adapting many of the instructional strategies presented in this book to meet the special needs of bilingual learners. Watson, Northcutt, and Rydell (1989) recommend the following seven principles for adapting content area instruction:

1. Adjust the language demands of the lesson. Modify speech rate and tone, use context clues extensively, and relate the discussion to students' personal experiences through analogy.
2. Build students' background knowledge by teaching the vocabulary of instruction and the vocabulary necessary to understand lesson content.
3. Develop an understanding of standard lesson formats so that students can focus on content rather than on delivery.
4. Use visuals and manipulatives that clearly and powerfully illustrate new content.
5. Use small-group cooperative-learning activities that actively involve students in meaning construction.
6. Increase wait time to enable students to construct meaning and formulate their responses in discussions.
7. Emphasize predictable questions that lead to greater involvement with content and higher-level thinking.

➤ *Guidelines for Adapting Instruction*

EVIDENCE-BASED PRACTICE

FIGURE 11.5

Optimal Conditions for Literacy Learning of Bilingual Students

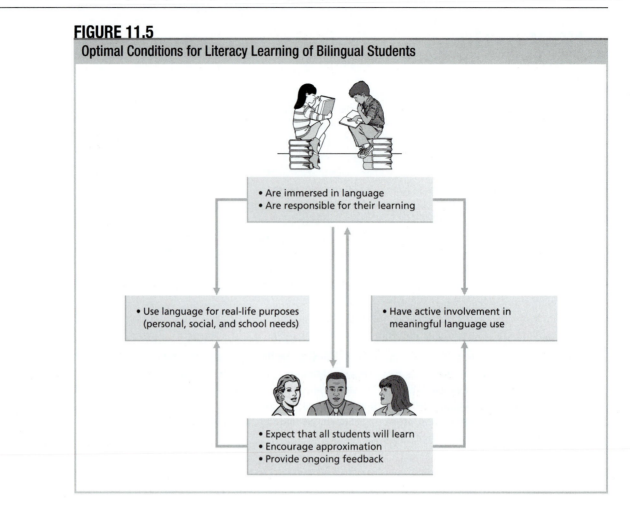

TABLE 11.6

A Decision Heuristic for Determining English Oral-Language Proficiency

Zero-Level English	Very Limited English	Limited English Proficiency (LEP)	Fluent English Proficiency (FEP)
• Does not answer yes/no questions	• Gives one-word responses to simple questions	• Responds easily to simple questions	• Speaks with ease
• Does not identify or name any objects	• Speaks in one- or two-word phrases	• Produces simple sentences	• Initiates conversations
• Understands no English	• Attempts to extend conversations	• Has difficulty elaborating when asked	• May make phonological or grammatical errors that can become fossilized; may make errors in syntactically complex utterances
• Often seems withdrawn or afraid	• Seldom initiates conversations	• Occasionally initiates conversations	• Freely and easily switches codes

L. Gunderson, *ESL Literacy Instruction: A Guidebook to Theory and Practice,* copyright © 1991, p. 26. Adapted by permission of Prentice-Hall, Englewood Cliffs, New Jersey.

Content Semantic Development and Enrichment Instruction Strategy

The Content Semantic Development and Enrichment Instruction (SDEI) strategy, presented in detail in Chapter 8 (see page 168), is a good approach to use with bilingual students. You will recall that SDEI is designed to develop new vocabulary using focus words selected from the subject-matter textbook being studied or from classroom discussions related to the text. SDEI has the added advantage of increasing bilingual students' alertness to words and providing the opportunity to develop in-depth understanding of specialized vocabulary. New content words that are unfamiliar to the bilingual student thus become targeted for students who are acquiring a new language.

Vocabulary Logs and Journals

Vocabulary logs and journals (see page 188) reinforce the background and conceptual knowledge gained through SDEI. At first, encourage students to use new vocabulary in sentence context and to illustrate the words using magazine pictures. As students become more proficient in English, they may construct formal definitions of words and check them in the dictionary. Students can develop a personal dictionary reference source for speaking, spelling, and writing.

Developing and Monitoring Meaning Construction

Some of your students will have had little opportunity to develop meaning construction and meaning monitoring strategies in their native or primary language. Strategies such as DL-TA, DR-TA, QAR, ReQuest, reciprocal teaching, and GMA can be effectively adapted for bilingual learners.

Directed Listening-Thinking Activity (DL-TA)

The advantage of the DL-TA (Stauffer, 1976) (see page 68) for LEP students is that it is presented orally and thus does not require fluent reading. Also, it relies on high-interest material with clear illustrations that assist LEP students in meaning construction. Big books with repetitive language and predictable story lines are especially valuable.

What other vocabulary-development strategies would work well with bilingual learners?

➤ *DR-TA, QAR, ReQuest, reciprocal teaching, and GMA are presented in Chapter 5.*

What multicultural literature might you select when using the DL-TA with bilingual learners?

Strategies in Use
Making Decisions about Instructional Needs

Alejandra Garcia was very concerned about Rosario, one of her new second-grade students. Using Gunderson's (1991) English oral-language proficiency categories (see Table 11.6), Alejandra determined that Rosario's English-language (L2) development was best described by the characterizations in the "Very Limited English" column. Her observations of Rosario during class and at recess confirmed this description. Fortunately, Alejandra was fluent in Spanish. She found that Rosario could easily carry on conversations and respond to questions in his native language; however, he had great difficulty conversing in English with his classmates.

Alejandra arranged for a parent conference one afternoon after school. She ascertained the following information from Rosario's mother, who spoke primarily Spanish. Rosario's family had arrived from Mexico one month before school began. He had attended school one year in Mex-

ico, where he was learning to read Spanish and was a good student. The mother indicated that Rosario liked school very much and especially his new teacher, who could explain new things about school in Spanish. She was highly supportive of her son and anxious to know how she could help him with schoolwork at home.

CRITICAL THINKING

1. What additional information would you like to have about Rosario? How would you gather this information?
2. Review the SDAIE approach explained in this chapter and then outline instructional ideas that you might use to teach Rosario in your second-grade classroom.
3. How would you use peer learning to assist Rosario's language development?

Directed Reading-Thinking Activity (DR-TA)

The DR-TA (Stauffer, 1969, 1976) (see page 132) follows the same questioning pattern as the DL-TA and has the same potential for developing predictions and inferences using higher-level thinking. Remember, however, that this strategy will have greatest application as students become fluent readers.

Question-Answer Relationships (QAR)

The value of QAR (Raphael, 1986) (see page 143) for LEP students lies in learning how to do the thinking that questions demand and how to use information sources. Thus, QAR is especially valuable in providing the thinking tools for meaning construction and monitoring. This strategy also provides immediate feedback to students; moves from short text passages to more involved text; develops thinking skills from the factual level to the interpretive, applicative, and transactive levels; and provides rich verbal context and group support that will lead to student independence.

ReQuest

ReQuest (Manzo & Manzo, 1990) (see page 147) models thinking processes for creating questions, establishing reading purpose, and building comprehension and self-monitoring responses. It can be used with individual students or small groups. ReQuest provides valuable insight into the background knowledge and reasoning processes of individual students, and it teaches them how to ask questions that enhance meaning construction.

Reciprocal Teaching

Reciprocal teaching (Palincsar & Brown, 1986) (see page 149) also uses modeling to help students develop questions and predictions. In addition, it encourages peer support and promotes independence.

Group Mapping Activity (GMA)

The GMA (Davidson, 1982) (see page 150) builds comprehension as students integrate and synthesize story ideas and concepts. A special value of GMA for LEP students is the possibility of incorporating bilingual labels as they create their own graphic representations of a story. The use of bilingual labels permits more meaningful personal interpretations of relationships among story characters, key events, and plot. The visual representations reflect students' understandings and thinking processes and reduce language fluency demands.

the Highly Effective Teacher

How might these strategies be motivational for bilingual learners?

Motivating Individual and Group Responses to Literature

Some students may find your classroom a strange (perhaps even foreign) setting. They may be encountering a new language, new interaction patterns and expectations, new classroom rules, and a room full of strangers. These factors have a strong impact on students' self-concept and their risk-taking as individuals and as learners. Your major responsibility is to provide a psychologically safe environment and to actively welcome all students' participation (Collins, 2005; Krashen, 1987). Your classroom can serve as a stable social and academic environment for their language and literacy development.

A key to this development is providing instruction that motivates individual and group responses. Using strategies such as read-alouds, Literature Response Journals, and InQuest, you can explore students' special interests to identify literature and informational books that will develop curiosity, motivation, and individual and group responses. Multicultural literature selections may be especially helpful and appropriate.

Read-Aloud Strategy

Try to provide a specific time each day for reading aloud, and select books filled with illustrations that support the plot development or informational content. You may want to supplement illustrations with visual props to enhance story interest. (See page 201, also.)

> *Strategies for using Literature-Response Journals are presented in Chapter 7.*

Literature-Response Journals

Literature-Response Journals (see page 204) provide a way for students to express their innermost thoughts, ideas, and feelings about their literature encounters and about personal topics,

Strategies in Use

A Bilingual GMA

Julie Soltis placed special emphasis on meaning interpretation with her third-grade bilingual students. About half the students were new ELLs whose pimary language was Spanish. Julie found that the GMA was a valuable strategy to help her students integrate story ideas through their drawings and language use.

Julie read the story *Borreguita and the Coyote* (Aardema, 1991) to her students, using the accompanying illustrations to develop meaning. She then asked students to map the story following GMA guidelines. After six or seven minutes, she asked each student to hold up his or her map for the class to see and invited individual students to explain how maps show relationships among the characters and events.

Julie then asked students to share their maps with peer partners and to explain why they drew them as they did. She teamed her new ELL students with English-speaking students. The student teams pooled their efforts to construct bilingual maps, using both Spanish and English for some key themes and concepts.

Julie concluded the GMA by emphasizing how the maps help in understanding story characters and events and their connections to the story plot and meaning.

CRITICAL THINKING

1. What unique features of the GMA make it a valuable strategy for teaching new ELL students?
2. How does the GMA provide a way to assess the literacy progress of new ELL students?
3. What are some advantages to students of adapting the GMA to include some bilingual labels?
4. How could other reading comprehension strategies in this book be adapted to value cultural diversity and be advantageous for new ELLs?

such as peer friendships and parent relations. The key point in developing Literature-Response Journals is to encourage students to construct meaning based on their personal interactions and transactions with text. Your written responses to students' journal writing subsequently motivate them and encourage them to continue to express their ideas and communicate with you.

Literature Circles

Literature circles, discussed in Chapter 7 (page 207), can be used to encourage students' thinking and authentic language use that is motivated by high-interest literature. This instructional strategy relies on discussion in groups of five or six students who assume different discussion roles, such as discussion leader, summarizer, and illustrator. The degree of your involvement will vary depending on the students' oral-language proficiency. For discussion groups in which students have very limited English proficiency, you will need to model the role of discussion leader and invite student participation through strategic and high-interest questions. Students who are fluent English proficient can assume various discussion roles much earlier and carry out meaningful and stimulating discussions about their literature selections. As student responsibilities increase in literature circle discussions, each student's role, role definition, and student identification should be placed on chart paper for easy reference. After students in each literature-circle complete discussion of their text, they will need to decide how best to share their book with students in other literature circles.

Literature circles can be used successfully with bilingual students at various grade levels, including first grade (Martinez-Roldan & Lopez-Robertson, 2000).

Investigative Questioning Procedure (InQuest)

Group and individual responses can also be motivated through use of InQuest (Shoop, 1986) (see page 210), which encourages students to play story character and investigative-reporter roles and participate in interviews about the central story character and key story events. InQuest can increase the comfort level of LEP students as they learn the question-and-response format for interactions.

How to Do . . .

Read-Alouds with Bilingual Learners

1. Identify literature, poetry, or expository writing that relates to your students' interests and, if possible, cultural backgrounds. When possible, use books written in two languages, and read aloud in both languages. If your students are literate in their primary language, consider inviting one or more of them to coread a dual-language book with you: Page by page, you read the English text, while the students read the text written in the other language.

DELAYED READER
ADAPTATION

   ■ **Reading aloud to students who lack English proficiency can provide opportunity for delayed readers to serve as peer tutors; that is, the English-proficient delayed reader reads selections to students who are just learning oral and written English, using materials at the delayed reader's independent-reading level. Experience has shown that both students show improved achievement as a result of this activity.**

2. Use a predominantly aesthetic instructional stance, emphasizing identification with key characters and eliciting positive attitudes toward the content. Involving students in selecting books is consistent with an aesthetic stance. The objective is to encourage motivation, high interest, and response.
3. Familiarize yourself with the story, identify the tones of the moods and feelings you wish to create, and complete a practice reading.
4. Think of the background knowledge and new concepts that may need to be explained before the story is presented. Also consider the individual and group responses you wish to develop during and after the story, such as creating sound effects or predicting story outcome. At the conclusion of the story, you might use a GMA followed by discussion between peer partners, or you might ask students to create a new ending for the story.
5. Establish an atmosphere and comfort level for story-reading time. For example, follow a ritual such as ringing a special bell to announce reading time. Make sure children are seated comfortably and can easily see any illustrations.
6. Read the story, using voice intonation (and visual aids) to help create story characters, setting, mood, and plot development. Use a reading pace that matches the visualization of the story, and let your enthusiasm for the story be evident. Use question prompts that capture the gist of the story rather than specific details, and provide sufficient wait time for responses.

Using Multicultural Literature and Multicultural Thematic Units

➤ *Benefits of Using Multicultural Literature*

The use of multicultural and multiethnic literature is valuable for all students (Au, 1993):

1. Students of diverse backgrounds feel pride in their own identity and heritage.
2. Students of diverse backgrounds learn about each other and the cultural diversity and complexity of American society.
3. All students gain more complete and balanced views of the historical forces that shape American cultural and ethnic diversity.
4. All students can explore issues of equality and social justice.

➤ *Guidelines for creating integrated thematic units are presented in Chapter 8.*

In addition, use of multicultural and multiethnic literature can greatly increase students' motivation to read, write, and respond to literature by enhancing their identification, catharsis, and insight as readers.

A central instructional goal is to encourage reader response through identification with story characters, through personal interpretation, and especially through connections to students' personal life experiences.

The books in the starter lists in Figures 11.6, 11.7, 11.8, and 11.9 (pages 330–333) have been selected on the basis of the four values of multicultural/multiethnic literature identified earlier. These selections focus on Asian American, African American, Hispanic American, and Native

the Highly Effective Teacher★

on Technology and Teaching Culturally Diverse Learners

1. Involve parents and the larger community in your classroom by sharing what your students are learning. You may want to have the class publish a newsletter. They can use a word-processing program such as Broderbund's *The Amazing Writing Machine*. You could also publish a class Web page at **www.actden.com/fp/**. Another resource for creating Web pages is available at **www.yahooligans.com**.

2. Create a class book. Have each student create a character representing his or her cultural heritage and history, or the cultural heritage of a fictional character the student is interested in. Use the Internet to research information about students' countries of origin or interest. Create a storyline that involves diversity and values that are important in different cultures. For example, you could create a book based on myths or celebrations. Share this book with other classrooms.

3. Visit the Web site **www.harwich.edu/depts/lmcelm/cinderlsnpln.htm;** click on 6, "Cinder" Tales: Cinderella Travels Our World; and follow the WebQuest for the "Cinder" Tales. This quest begins with exploration of different "Cinder" tales from different cultures, encourages students to understand why the Cinder tales are important to our human society today, and ends with creating a new Cinderella story to be shared with the class.

4. Establish pen pals with students around the world. Participate in an e-mail exchange at **www.epals.com/** and click on ePALS Classroom Exchange with students from different countries to learn about their lives and cultures.

5. Participate in the Underground Railroad Project at **www.education-world.com/a_curr/curr195.shtml**.

American cultural/ethnic groups, respectively; each entry includes an appropriate age range for reading. Figure 11.10 (page 334) lists general references, which provide further resources.

Understanding Students with Special Needs

Regardless of grade level, students in your classroom will exhibit achievement variability. Students who are achieving significantly above the norm or below their potential will require special instruction under your direction; additional support may be available from programs and specialists in your school or school district. For example, suppose you find a fifth- or sixth-grade student of normal intelligence reading at a second- or third-grade level. The immediate problem will be how to design your instruction to meet the special needs of this student. A related issue is the possibility of obtaining additional professional support; the student may have a disability that requires special education services. Federal categories of disability include learning disabilities, mental retardation, serious emotional disturbance, autism, hearing impairment, visual impairment, deafness, blindness, speech and language disorders, and orthopedic impairments.

Students with Disabilities

Commonly occurring disabilities are identified in special education as **high-incidence disabilities.** The Individuals with Disabilities Education Act (IDEA) lists the following categories of high-incidence disabilities (their frequency of occurrence in all students under IDEA follows in

high-incidence disabilities
disabilities that occur with relatively high frequency and permit mainstreaming into regular classrooms

FIGURE 11.6

Bookshelf: Asian American Literature

Brown, T. (1991). *Lee Ann: The Story of a Vietnamese-American Girl*. New York: Putnam. Ages 6–8.

Bunting, E. (2001). *Jin Woo*. New York: Clarion Books. Ages 6–9.

Choi, S. N. (1991). *Year of Impossible Goodbyes*. Boston: Houghton Mifflin. Ages 9–12.

Coerr, E., & Young E. (1993). *Sadako*. New York: Putnam. Ages 9–12.

Ishii, M. (1987). *The Tongue-Cut Sparrow*. New York: Dutton. Ages 7–9.

Kajikawa, K. (2000). *Yoshi's Feast*. (Y. Heo. Illus.). New York: Dorling Kindersley. Ages 7–10.

Levin, E. (1989). *I Hate English!* New York: Scholastic. Ages 7–9.

Lin, G. (2001). *Dim Sum for Everyone*. New York: Knopf. Ages 6–9.

Lipp, F. (2001). *The Caged Birds of Phnom Penh*. New York: Holiday House. Ages 7–9.

Lord, B. Bao (1984). *In the Year of the Boar and Jackie Robinson*. New York: Harper. Ages 7–9.

Morimoto, J. (1990). *My Hiroshima*. New York: Viking. Ages 8–10.

Nhuong, H. Q. (1982). *The Land I Lost: Adventures of a Boy in Vietnam*. New York: Harper. Ages 9–12.

Pak, S. (2003). *Sumi's First Day of School Ever*. New York: Viking. Ages 6–9.

Park, F., & Park, G. (1998). *My Freedom Trip: A Child's Escape from North Korea*. Honesdale, PA: Boyds Mills Press. Ages 9–12.

Riecheck, J. (1994). *Japanese Boys' Festival*. Chicago: Children's Press. Ages 6–12.

Ringgold, F. (1993). *Dinner at Aunt Connie's House*. New York: Hyperion. Ages 6–8.

Snyder, D. (1988). *The Boy of the Three-Year Nap*. Boston: Houghton Mifflin. Ages 7–9.

Uchida, Y. (1971). *Journey to Topaz*. New York: Scribner's. Ages 9–12.

Wong, J. S. (2002). *Apple Pie 4th of July*. San Diego: Harcourt. Ages 6–9.

Yee, P. (1990). *Tales from Gold Mountain: Stories of the Chinese in the New World*. New York: Macmillan. Ages 8–10.

Yep, L. (1975). *Dragonwings*. New York: Harper. Ages 9–12.

——. (1977). *Child of the Owl*. New York: Harper. Ages 12–young adult.

——. (1991). *Tongues of Jade*. New York: HarperCollins. Ages 8–12.

——. (1994). *The Ghost Fox*. New York: Scholastic. Ages 9–12.

——. (Ed.). (1995). *American Dragons: Twenty-Five Asian American Voices*. New York: Trophy Press. Ages 9–12.

---

parentheses): learning disabilities, exhibited by a significant difference between ability and school achievement (51.3 percent); speech deviations that interfere with communication and cause the speaker distress, or language impairments, exhibited through impaired or poorly developed comprehension and use of symbol systems (22.9 percent); and emotional disturbance, described by inability to build and maintain satisfactory interpersonal relationships with peers and teachers (8.4 percent) (Friend & Bursuck, 1996, p. 151). Students with high-incidence disabilities tend to be mainstreamed into regular classrooms. You will have these students in your classroom, and you will play a critical role in their reading and literacy education.

Less common disabilities are defined as **low-incidence disabilities.** Students with low-incidence disabilities, who make up about 20 percent of students with disabilities in schools, usually receive some type of special education services, beginning in their early years. Low-incidence disabilities include mental retardation; multiple disabilities; hearing and visual impairments; orthopedic impairments, such as spina bifida; and other health impairments, such as cerebral palsy, AIDS, deafness, blindness, autism (impairments in communication, learning, and reciprocal social interactions), and traumatic brain injury.

Although students with low-incidence disabilities will also benefit from participation in your classroom, you will need additional information about their disability to assist you in structuring their literacy education, and you will need to work closely with special education professionals in your school or school district.

Special Education and Inclusion

Special education is prescribed by law and covers a broad range of services, such as psychological testing and speech therapy, provided in a variety of educational placements. The placement of students in special education programs is directed by legislation that calls for the

---

low-incidence disabilities
disabilities that occur with relatively low frequency and require special knowledge in structuring literacy instruction

▶ *Every class you teach will likely include one or more students with high-incidence disabilities.*

special education
educational programs and related services mandated by law for students with special needs

FIGURE 11.7

Bookshelf: African American Literature

Aardema, V. (1975). *Why Mosquitoes Buzz in People's Ears*. New York: Dial. Ages 5–7.

Adoff, A. (1973). *Black Is Brown Is Tan*. New York: Harper. Ages 8–10.

Armstrong, W. H. (1969). *Sounder*. New York: Harper. Ages 9–12.

Birtha, B. (2006). *Grandmama's Pride*. New York: Albert Whitman. Ages 9–12.

Carew, J. (1980). *Children of the Sun*. New York: Little, Brown. Ages 6–8.

Clifton, L. (1988). *Everett Anderson's Goodbye*. New York: Holt. Ages 5–7.

Collier, J., & Collier, C. (1981). *Jump Ship to Freedom*. New York: Delacorte. Ages 9–12.

Cummings, P. (2002). *Ananse and the Lizard*. New York: Henry Holt. Ages 7–10.

Davis, O. (1982). *Langston: A Play*. New York: Delacorte. Ages 8–10.

Feelings, M. (1974). *Jambo Means Hello: Swahili Alphabet Book*. New York: Dial. Ages 6–8.

Flournoy, V. (1985). *The Patchwork Quilt*. New York: Dial. Ages 5–7.

Fox, P. (1973). *The Slave Dancer*. New York: Bradbury. Ages 9–12.

Giovanni, N. (2006). *Rosa*. New York: Henry Holt. Ages 9–12.

Greenfield, E. (1988). *Under the Sunday Tree*. New York: Harper. Ages 6–10.

———. (1989). *Nathaniel Talking*. New York: Black Butterfly. Ages 6–10.

Greenwood, B. (1998). *The Last Safe House: A Story of the Underground Railroad*. Buffalo, NY: Kids Can Press. Ages 9–12.

Grimes, N. (2002). *Talkin' about Bessie: The Story of Aviator Elizabeth Coleman*. (E. B. Lewis, Illus.). New York: Orchard Books. Ages 9–11.

Hamilton, V. (1974). *M. C. Higgins, the Great*. New York: Macmillan. Ages 9–12.

———. (1985). *The People Could Fly: American Black Folktales*. New York: Knopf. Ages 7–9.

———. (1990). *Cousins*. New York: Philomel. Ages 9–12.

Hesse, K. (2001). *Witness*. New York: Scholastic. Ages 12–Young Adult.

Hoffman, M. (1991). *Amazing Grace*. New York: Dial. Ages 6–8.

Howard, E. G. (1991). *Aunt Flossie's Hats*. New York: Clarion. Ages 8–10.

Hurmence, B. (1982). *A Girl Called Boy*. New York: Clarion. Ages 9–12.

Joseph, L. (1991). *A Wave in Her Pocket: Stories from Trinidad*. New York: Clarion. Ages 7–9.

Lester, J. (1987). *The Tales of Uncle Remus: The Adventures of Brer Rabbit*. New York: Penguin Books. Ages 7–9.

———. (1998). *Black Cowboy, Wild Horses: A True Story*. New York: Dial. Ages 9–12.

Littlesugar, A. (2002). *Freedom School, Yes*. New York: Philomel. Ages 7–9.

McDermott, G. (1972). *Anansi the Spider: A Tale from the Ashanti*. New York: Holt. Ages 7–9.

Martin, A. (2001). *Belle Teal*. New York. Scholastic. Ages 12–Young Adult.

McKissack, P., & McKissack, F. (1989). *A Long Hard Journey: The Story of the Pullman Porter*. New York: Walker. Ages 8–10.

Meltzer, M. (1984). *The Black Americans: A History in Their Own Words: 1619–1983*. New York: Crowell. Ages 12–young Adult.

Myers, D. M. (2007). *Harlem Summer*. New York: Scholastic. Ages 14–Young Adult.

Myers, W. D. (1991). *Now Is Your Time: The African-American Struggle for Freedom*. New York: Harper. Ages 9–12.

Patterson, L. (1989). *Martin Luther King, Jr. and the Freedom Movement*. New York: A Maker of American Books, Facts on File. Ages 11–young adult.

Polacco, P. (1992). *Mrs. Katz and Tush*. New York: Bantam. Ages 7–12.

Ringgold, F. (1991). *Tar Beach*. New York: Crown. Ages 6–8.

Steptoe, J. (1987). *Mufaro's Beautiful Daughters*. New York: Lothrop. Ages 7–9.

Tate, E. E. (1995). *A Blessing in Disguise*. New York: Delacorte. Ages 8–10.

Taylor, M. D. (1976). *Roll of Thunder, Hear My Cry*. New York: Dial. Ages 9–12.

Turner, G. T. (1989). *Take a Walk in Their Shoes*. New York: Cobblehill. Ages 9–12.

Uhlberg, M. (2006). *Dad, Jackie, and Me*. New York: Peachtree. Ages 6–9.

Weik, M. H. (1966). *The Jazz Man*. New York: Atheneum. Ages 6–8.

Woodson, J. (2003). *Locomotion*. New York: Putnam. Ages 12–Young Adult.

Yarbrough, C. (1979). *Cornrows*. New York: Coward-McCann. Ages 6–8.

FIGURE 11.8

Bookshelf: Hispanic American Literature

Aardema, V. (1991). *Borreguita and the Coyote*. New York: Knopf. Ages 6–8.

Ada, A. F. (2003). *I Love Saturdays y domingos*. New York: Atheneum. Ages 5–8.

Anzaldua, G. (1995). *Prietita and the Ghost Woman*. San Francisco: Children's Book Press. Ages 9–12.

Buchanan, K. (1994). *This House Is Made of Mud. Esta Casa Esta Hecha de Lodo*. Flagstaff, AZ: Northland Publishing. Ages 7–9.

Carlson, L. M. (1994). *Cool Salsa—Bilingual Poems on Growing Up Latino in the United States*. New York: Fawcett Juniper. Ages 10–12.

Carlson, L. M., & Ventura, C. L. (Eds.). (1990). *Where Angels Glide at Dawn: New Stories from Latin America*. New York: Lippincott. Ages 12–young adult.

Delacre, L. (1989). *Arroz con Leche: Popular Songs and Rhymes from Latin America*. New York: Scholastic. Ages 6–10.

Ets, M. H., & Labastida, A. (1959). *Nine Days to Christmas: A Story of Mexico*. New York: Viking. Ages 6–8.

Garza, C. L. (1996). *In My Family—En Mi Familia*. San Francisco: Children's Book Press. Ages 7–12.

Gerson, M. J. (2001). *Fiesta femenina: Celebrating Women in Mexican Folktale*. (M. C. Gonzalez, Illus.). New York: Barefoot Books. Ages 11–young adult.

Haseley, D. (1991). *Ghost Catcher*. New York: Harper. Ages 6–8.

Herrera, J. F. (2001). *The Upside Down Boy, El nino de cabeza*. San Francisco: Children's Book Press. Ages 6–8.

Hinojosa, F. (1984). *The Old Lady Who Ate People*. Boston: Little, Brown. Ages 6–8.

Krumgold, J. (1953). *And Now Miguel*. New York: Crowell. Ages 8–10.

Mangurian, D. (1979). *Children of the Incas*. New York: Macmillan. Ages 8–10.

Martin. A. (2001). *Belle Teal*. New York: Scholastic. Ages 12–Young Adult.

Meyer, C., & Gallenkamp, C. (1985). *The Mystery of the Ancient Maya*. New York: Atheneum. Ages 8–10.

Mora, P. (1997). *Tomas and the Library Lady*. New York: Knopf. Ages 9–12.

Ramirez, M. R. (1995). *The Little Ant: La Hormiga Chiquita*. New York: Rizzoli. Ages 5–7.

Rice, D. (2001). *Crazy loco*. New York: Dial Books. Ages 12–Young Adult.

Rohmer, H. (1989). *Uncle Nacho's Hat*. New York: Children's Book Press. Ages 6–8. (English-Spanish).

Ryan, P. M. (2000). *Esperanza Rising*. New York: Scholastic. Ages 9–12.

Soto, G. (1990). *Baseball in April and Other Stories*. New York: Harcourt Brace Jovanovich. Ages 9–12.

Smothers, E. F. (2003). *The Hard-times Jar*. New York: Farrar, Straus, & Giroux. Ages 6–9.

Winter, J. (2003). *Nino's Mask*. New York: Dial Books. Ages 6–9.

Zubizarreta, R., Rohmer, H., & Schecter, D. (1991). *The Woman Who Outshone the Sun*. New York: Children's Book Press. Ages 6–8. (English-Spanish).

least restrictive environment (LRE)
educational placement for each exceptional student that allows maximum integration into the general education classroom

least restrictive environment (LRE) for students. This clause is interpreted to mean that students are best served in instructional settings in which they can most effectively learn alongside their peers and that they cannot be educated in segregated settings just because it is more convenient (Hallahan & Kauffman, 2000).

This legislation has significantly changed the role of the classroom teacher in educating students with special needs. More and more, such students are mainstreamed into general education classes; self-contained special education classrooms are becoming the exception. Approximately one-third of students with disabilities are placed in regular classrooms, while another one-third attend regular classes but receive some assistance in pull-out programs and resource rooms. Approximately one-fourth of students with special needs attend separate special education classes for about 50 percent of the school day, and a much smaller number (about 5 percent) attend separate schools. Only about 1 percent of students with severe disabilities are educated in residential facilities (Friend & Bursuck, 1996, pp. 66–67).

inclusion
integration or mainstreaming of students with special needs into general education programs with their nondisabled peers

Inclusion refers to the integration of students with disabilities into general education classrooms with their nondisabled peers. Special education support and services are used as needed to maintain the students in regular classrooms. The terms *inclusion* and *mainstreaming* are used interchangeably in many educational settings. Advocates of full inclusion, however, distinguish between these two terms because they oppose pull-out programs and resource rooms and believe that students with disabilities should be educated on a full-time basis with regular students.

FIGURE 11.9

Bookshelf: Native American Literature

Aliki. (1976). *Corn Is Maize: The Gift of the Indians.* New York: Crowell. Ages 6–8.

Ancona, G. (1993). *Powwow.* New York: Harcourt Brace. Ages 9–12.

Aveni, A. (2006). *The First Americans: The Story of Where They Came From and Who They Became.* New York: Scholastic. Ages 9–12.

Baker, O. (1981). *Where the Buffaloes Begin.* New York: Warner. Ages 7–9.

Baylor, B. (1975). *The Desert Is Theirs.* New York: Scribner's. Ages 7–9.

———. (1976). *Hawk, I'm Your Brother.* New York: Scribner's. Ages 8–10.

———. (1981). *A God on Every Mountain Top: Stories of Southwest Indian Mountains.* New York: Scribner's. Ages 8–10.

Bealer, A. (1972). *Only the Names Remain: The Cherokees and the Trail of Tears.* New York: Little, Brown. Ages 9–12.

Bierhorst, J. (1987). *Doctor Coyote: A Native American Aesop's Fables.* New York: Macmillan. Ages 7–9.

———. (Ed.). (1982). *The Whistling Skeleton: American Indian Tales of the Supernatural.* New York: Four Winds. Ages 7–9.

Bruchac, J. (2000). *Sacajawea.* San Diego: Silverwhistle.

Bruchac, J., & Bruchac, J. (2001). *How Chipmunk Got His Stripes.* (J. Areugo & A. Dewey, Illus.). New York: Dial. Ages 7–10.

Cohen, C. L. (1988). *The Mud Pony.* New York: Scholastic. Ages 6–8.

dePaola, T. (1983). *The Legend of the Bluebonnet.* New York: Putnam. Ages 6–8.

Driving Hawk Horse Sneve, V. (1989). *Dancing Tepees: Poems of American Indian Youth.* New York: Holiday. Ages 9–12.

Duval, J. D. (1994). *The Chumash.* Chicago: Children's Press. Ages 9–12.

Ekoomiak, N. (1990). *Arctic Memories.* New York: Holt. Ages 9–12. (English-Inuktitut).

Freedman, R. (1988). *Buffalo Hunt.* New York: Holiday. Ages 9–12.

George, J. C. (1972). *Julie of the Wolves.* New York: Harper-Collins. Ages 9–12.

———. (1997). *Julie's Wolf Pack.* New York: HarperCollins. Ages 9–12.

Goble, P. (1978). *The Girl Who Loved Wild Horses.* New York: Bradbury. Ages 6–8.

———. (1991). *Iktomi and the Buffalo Skull.* New York: Orchard. Ages 7–9.

Highwater, J. (1977). *Anpao: An American Indian Odyssey.* Philadelphia: Lippincott. Ages 9–12.

———. (1986). *I Wear the Morning Star.* New York: Harper. Ages 9–12.

Keegan, M. (1991). *Pueblo Boy: Growing Up in Two Worlds.* New York: Cobblehill. Ages 7–9.

Kennard, E. A. (2000). *Field Mouse Goes to War/Tusan homichi tuwvota.* (F. Kabotie, Illus.). Walnut Creek, CA: Kiva. Ages 7–10.

Martin, B., & Archambault, J. (1987). *Knots on a Counting Rope.* Boston: Little, Brown. Ages 6–8.

McKinley, M. E. K. (1997). *The Secret of the Eagle Feathers.* New York: Steck-Vaughn. Ages 9–12.

McLellan, J., & McLellan, M. (2002). *Nanabosho Grants a Wish.* (L. Swampy, Illus.). Winnipeg, Canada: Pemmican. Ages 8–11.

O'Dell, S. (1960). *Island of the Blue Dolphins.* New York: Dell. Ages 9–12.

———. (1988). *Black Star, Bright Dawn.* Boston: Houghton Mifflin. Ages 9–12.

Robinson, G. (1982). *Raven the Trickster: Legends of the North American Indians.* New York: Atheneum. Ages 8–10.

Seattle, Chief. (1991). *Brother Eagle, Sister Sky.* New York: Dial. Ages 6–10.

Secakuku, W. (2003). *Meet Mindy: A Native Girl from the Southwest.* Hillsboro, OR: Beyond Words. Ages 9–12.

Speare, E. G. (1983). *The Sign of the Beaver.* Boston: Houghton Mifflin. Ages 8–10.

Stein, R. C. (1993). *The Trail of Tears.* Chicago: Children's Press. Ages 9–12.

Steptoe, J. (1984). *The Story of Jumping Mouse.* New York: Lothrop. Ages 7–9.

Tayac. G. (2002). *Meet Naiche: A Native Boy from the Chesapeake Bay Area.* Hillsboro, OR: Beyond Words. Ages 9–12.

Toye, W. (1977). *The Loon's Necklace.* New York: Oxford. Ages 7–9.

Your Beliefs and Values about Students' Abilities and Disabilities

Your beliefs about and attitudes toward exceptional students will influence your instruction of these students. It is important to examine your experiences and assumptions about achievement, intelligence, mental illness, physical disabilities, giftedness, and other aspects of individual variability. Do you tend to assume that low achievement is always a result of lack of effort, lack of motivation, bad attitude, or low IQ? If so, you may be wrong. Research on students who experience great difficulty in reading achievement revealed the following (McCormick, 2007, pp. 418–419):

- Their problems often result from multiple and different causes.
- They are found in all intelligence ranges, but most have average intelligence.

> ➤ *Characteristics of Students with Reading Difficulties*

FIGURE 11.10

Bookshelf: Multicultural Literature—General Reference and Resource Books

Barchers, S. I. (2000). *Multicultural Folktales: Readers Theatre for Elementary Students.* Englewood, CO: Teacher Ideas Press.

Cullinan, B. E. (Ed.). (1993). *Fact and Fiction: Literature Across the Curriculum.* Newark, DE: International Reading Association.

Esbenson, B. (1996). *Echoes for the Eye: Poems to Celebrate Patterns in Nature.* New York: HarperCollins.

Gonzalez, R. (1998). *Touching the Fire: Fifteen Poets of Today's Latino Renaissance.* New York: Doubleday.

Harris, V. J. (Ed.). (1992). *Teaching Multicultural Literature in Grades K–8.* Norwood, MA: Christopher-Gordon Publishers.

Kruse, G. M., & Horning, K. T. (1991). *Multicultural Literature for Children and Young Adults: A Selected Listing of Books 1980–1990 by and about People of Color.* Madison, WI:

Cooperative Children's Book Center, University of Wisconsin, Department of Public Instruction, Madison, Wisconsin.

Lindgren, M. V. (Ed.). (1991). *The Multicolored Mirror: Cultural Substance in Literature for Children and Young Adults.* Fort Atkinson, WI: Cooperative Children's Book Center, Highsmith Press.

Norton, D. E., & Norton, S. E. (2003). *Through the Eyes of a Child: An Introduction to Children's Literature* (6th ed.). Upper Saddle River, NJ: Merrill/Prentice Hall.

Raines, S. C. (1994). *Story Stretchers for the Primary Grades.* Mt. Rainier, MD: Gryphon House.

Young, T. A. (Ed.). (2004). *Happily Ever After: Sharing Folk Literature with Elementary and Middle School Students.* Newark, DE: International Reading Association.

- They *do* have the desire to learn to read, although their overt behaviors often belie that fact.
- They are habitually demoralized, believing they *cannot* learn to read.
- They usually require one-to-one instruction.
- They can learn to read.

EVIDENCE-BASED PRACTICE

You also should examine your beliefs and values about categories of disability. As a highly effective teacher, you need the information, attitudes, and strategies that will help all your students succeed.

multidisciplinary team (MDT)
a group of education professionals who meet to make decisions about individual students' needs for special education services

individualized education program (IEP)
an instructional program developed specifically for an individual student with special educational needs

▶ *Seven Components of an IEP*

Your Role in Planning and Adapting Instruction for Students with Special Needs

Students are qualified for special education services and placement through the efforts of a **multidisciplinary team (MDT)**, which includes you as the classroom teacher. In addition, the team consists of a representative of the local educational agency, such as the school principal; the special education teacher; the student's parents or guardians; and, depending on the student's need, a professional from relevant services, such as the psychologist, occupational therapist, or speech and language specialist. The multidisciplinary team has two purposes: first, to determine whether the student has a disability; second, to develop an **individualized education program (IEP)** for the student.

The IEP identifies key areas of student need, including special accommodations to be made in your classroom and special education services to be provided. In many schools, this plan is often prepared in the spring for the next school year, giving you an opportunity to examine the IEP and prepare for an incoming student with special needs. The IEP has seven components (Friend & Bursuck, 1996):

1. *Present level of functioning*—provides detailed information on the student's achievement and social functioning
2. *Annual goals*—develops expectations in the form of annual goals
3. *Measurable, short-term instructional objectives*—provides descriptions of instructional and other steps needed to achieve the annual goals
4. *Date of initiation and duration of service*—specifies dates for beginning specialized services and how long the services will be provided
5. *Services needed*—outlines what specialized services the student needs and who is responsible for providing them

6. *Strategies for evaluation*—specifies how progress toward the short-term and annual goals will be measured

7. *Transition plan*—outlines strategies to ensure that transition will be made to the next educational or adult life step (applies to some students as young as fourteen and to all students who are sixteen years old or older)

The IEP requires time and energy on the part of the multidisciplinary team, but it can be valuable in helping you clarify learning expectations for your student and for yourself.

Friend and Bursuck (1996, pp. 21–29) have developed a strategy to assist teachers in accommodating students with special needs in general education classrooms. The INCLUDE strategy (shown in the How to Do) is, for the most part, self-explanatory and can be easily applied to reading and literacy instruction for special needs students.

Principles and Guidelines for Teaching Students with Special Needs

Like the INCLUDE strategy, the following instructional principles will help you meet the special needs of students who are experiencing reading and learning difficulties:

- Search for the underlying causes of achievement variation. Low achievement and reading difficulties do not occur suddenly but develop over a long period of time and have multiple causes that include ineffective instruction, different home and school expectations, little home support and encouragement, and, in some cases, disabilities that interfere with learning.
- Carefully observe your students' responses to identify behavior suggesting special learning needs. For example, a student who asks to have questions repeated or is consistently unable to follow oral directions or pay attention may have a hearing problem or attention deficit disorder.
- Understand the importance of active learning that is meaning-based and of high interest to low-achieving students. Create an instructional environment that uses rich context and authentic learning activities relevant to the students' lives.
- Encourage risk-taking in learning and create a psychologically safe environment that supports the understanding that people can learn from their mistakes. Many low-achieving students lack the confidence to pursue new ideas, are afraid to "try on" new ideas, and feel that persistence on a task is futile, as they cannot learn.
- Adapt the instructional strategies that you have found successful for whole-class and large-group discussions to small-group, peer-partner, and individual learning situations.

How to Do . . .

The INCLUDE Strategy

1. **I**dentify classroom environmental, curricular, and instructional demands.
2. **N**ote student learning strengths and needs.
3. **C**heck for potential areas of student success.
4. **L**ook for potential problem areas.
5. **U**se information gathered to brainstorm adaptations.

- **In Chapter 10 and in the How To Dos throughout this book, adaptations for delayed readers are given. The majority of these adaptations also are suitable for use with many special education students, especially learning-disabled students, whose problems primarily relate to reading.**

6. **D**ecide which adaptations to implement.
7. **E**valuate student progress.

DELAYED READER ADAPTATION

- Provide praise and encouragement for the small successful steps that build confidence and literacy growth over time. You will find that accepting approximation—rather than insisting on perfection—and providing positive feedback on success will be of great value in teaching all students.
- Create high expectations for the special needs student and for yourself, to foster self-confidence and learning. It is important, however, that these expectations be realistic and built into your instructional plan and evaluation process.
- Apply known learning principles to adjust and adapt your instructional program to meet students' special learning needs. Remember that your personal observations, instructional knowledge, insight, and patience will be your most valuable resources in meeting these needs.
- Involve parents, discussing with them your observations, instructional plans for both school and home, and any special support planned by special education professionals to assist in diagnosing and addressing their students' special learning needs.
- Become informed about student variability, services provided by reading and special education specialists, and the school district's procedures for maintaining students and referring students for special education and support services.

How can other instructional strategies described in this book be adapted for students with reading difficulties?

Ideas for Adapting Instruction

Academic achievement in students varies tremendously, and it is important to take this into account in your language and literacy instruction. If a student with special needs is always struggling to catch up with faster-learning classmates, he or she is likely to get discouraged and experience motivation and achievement difficulties. By contrast, a pupil whose learning rate is very fast may be completely frustrated in a classroom that provides only for traditional "three group" instruction. Therefore, it is important that you make every effort to understand the special learning needs of your students—from the learning disabled to the gifted—in order to adjust your teaching and instructional strategies to meet those needs.

How might literature by and about students with disabilities foster social acceptance?

Figure 11.11 (page 337) contains a starter list of children's literature that you will find helpful for your special needs students. Many of these books are appropriate for all students in your classroom. Your goals are to help students with special needs gain self-understanding and build a positive self-concept and, at the same time, to foster social acceptance by peers. Keep in mind, however, that students should not be required to read materials that parallel specific conditions or traumatic events in their lives.

Students with Emotional Disturbances

It is often difficult to determine whether a student's emotional adjustment is the source of difficulty in his or her reading and literacy progress or if the literacy difficulty has contributed to the emotional state. The features presented in Figure 11.12 (page 338) are characteristic of students who are experiencing emotional disturbance and emotional adjustment difficulty.

Some learners with emotional problems read without difficulty and even use reading as an escape from their problems. Others demonstrate significant adjustment problems when confronted with reading and other literacy tasks. Frequently, repeated failure in the classroom and inadequate provision for instructional needs produce high-level frustration and anxiety.

Negative parental attitudes toward school can contribute to a student's learning difficulty. It is important to be alert to evidence that she or he may be experiencing excessive pressure from parents to achieve, continuous conflict between parents, overprotection, abuse, or other emotionally disturbing home influences. Such home environments can contribute significantly to a student's anxieties and uncertainties and can interfere with a positive concept of self. Should such evidence be present, it is your responsibility to arrange a parent conference, make a referral, or report the possible abuse.

Poor social adjustment with peers or a personality conflict with you can threaten a student's emotional stability and literacy achievement. You should provide a sympathetic, supportive

FIGURE 11.11

Bookshelf: Literature for Special Needs Students and Their Classmates

Speech, Vision, or Hearing Impairment

Alexander, S. H. (2000). *Do You Remember the Color Blue?* East Rutherford, NJ: Viking. Ages 10–13.

Andrews, J. F. (1992). *Hasta leugo, San Diego.* Washington, DC: Gallaudet University Press. Ages 9–12.

Brown, A., & Forsberg. G. (1989). *Lost Boys Never Say Die.* New York: Delacorte Press. Ages 9–12.

Corrigan, K. (1984). *Emily, Emily.* Toronto: Annick Press. Ages 8–10.

Gragg, V. (1998). *What Is an Audiogram?* Washington, DC: Gallaudet University Press. Ages 9–12.

Levine, E. S. (1974). *Lisa and Her Soundless World.* New York: Human Sciences. Ages 6–8.

Little, J. (1972). *From Anna.* New York: Harper. Ages 9–12.

Peterson, J. W. (1984). *I Have a Sister. My Sister Is Deaf.* New York: Harper & Row. Ages 8–12.

Raskin, E. (1968). *Spectacles.* New York: Atheneum. Ages 6–9.

White, E. B. (1970). *The Trumpet of the Swan.* New York: Harper & Row. Ages 10–12.

Yolen, J. (1977). *The Seeing Stick.* New York: Crowell. Ages 10–12.

Physical Disabilities

Burnett, F. H. (1910). *The Secret Garden.* Philadelphia: Lippincott. Ages 10–young adult.

Butler, B. (1993). *Witch's Fire.* New York: Dutton. Ages 9–12.

Brown, T. (1984). *Someone Special, Just Like You.* New York: Holt. Ages 6–8.

Greenfield, E., & Revia, A. (1981). *Alesia.* New York: Philomel. Ages 12–young adult.

Krementz, J. (1992). *How it Feels to Live with a Physical Disability.* New York: Simon & Schuster.

Riskin, M. L. (1981). *Apple Is My Sign.* Boston: Houghton Mifflin. Ages 10–young adult.

Robinet, H. G. (1980). *Ride the Red Cycle.* Boston: Houghton Mifflin. Ages 7–11.

Rogers, F. (2000). *Let's Talk About It: Extraordinary Friends.* New York: Family Communications/Putnam's Sons. Ages 5–8.

Roy, R, (1985). *Move Over, Wheelchairs Coming Through!* Boston: Houghton Mifflin. Ages 6–12.

Mental Retardation

Anderson, R. (1989). *The Bus People.* New York: Henry Holt. Ages 8–10.

Byars, B. (1970). *Summer of the Swans.* New York: Viking. Ages 10–12.

Clifton, L. (1980). *My Friend Jacob.* New York: Dutton. Ages 5–7.

Gilson, J. (1980). *Do Bananas Chew Gum?* New York: Lothrop, Lee & Shepard. Ages 9–11.

Hermes, P. (1983). *Who Will Take Care of Me?* New York: Harcourt Brace Jovanovich. Ages 6–10.

Kamien, J. (1979). *What If You Couldn't . . . ? A Book About Special Needs.* New York: Scribner's. Ages 8–12.

Lasker, J. (1974). *He's My Brother.* Chicago: Whitman. Ages 5–8.

Pulver, R. (1999). *Way to Go, Alex!* (E. Wolf, Illus.). Morton Grove, IL: Whitman. Ages 7–9.

Shyer, M. F. (1988). *Welcome Home, Jellybean.* New York: Aladdin. Ages 9–12.

Wartski, M. C. (1979). *My Brother Is Special.* New York: Westminster. Ages 10–12.

Emotional Disturbances

Baylor, B. (1974). *Everybody Needs a Rock.* New York: MacMillan. Ages 6–8.

Blue, R. (1980). *Wishful Lying.* New York: Human Science Press. Ages 6–9.

Cohen, M. (1967). *Will I Have a Friend?* New York: Collier-Macmillan. Ages 6–8.

Jonness, A. (1990). *Families: A Celebration of Diversity, Commitment, and Love.* Boston: Houghton Mifflin. Ages 6–12.

Kroll, S. (1981). *Friday the 13th.* New York: Holiday House. Ages 5–7.

Sheehan, C. (1981). *The Colors That I Am.* New York: Human Science Press. Ages 7–9.

Viorst, J. (1972). *Alexander and the Terrible, Horrible, No Good, Very Bad Day.* New York: MacMillan. Ages 6–10.

Wimann, E. (1982). *It Takes Brains.* New York: Atheneum. Ages 10–12.

Giftedness

Aliki. (1984). *Feelings.* New York: Greenwillow.

Base, G. (1988). *The Eleventh Hour: A Curious Mystery.* New York: Abrams. Ages 10–12.

Fitzgerald, J. D. (1967). *The Great Brain.* New York: Dell. Ages 8–12.

Fitzhugh, L. (1964). *Harriet the Spy.* New York: Dell. Ages 8–12.

Greenwald. S. (1987). *Alvin Webster's Surefire Plan for Success (and How It Failed).* Boston: Little, Brown. Ages 9–12.

Lewis, C. S. (1950). *The Lion, the Witch, and the Wardrobe.* New York: MacMillan. Ages 10–young adult.

Lowry, L. (1979). *Anastasia Krupnik.* New York: Bantam. Ages 8–12.

Sadler, M. (1992). *Alistair's Time Machine.* New York: Simon & Schuster. Ages 5–8.

Warren, S. (1987). *Being Gifted: Because You're Special from the Rest.* New York: Trillium. Ages 4–7.

FIGURE 11.12
Signs of Possible Emotional Adjustment Difficulty in School

- Few or no friends
- Problems with family relations
- Problems with relationships with teachers
- Hyperactive behavior, indicated by excessive movement
- Aggression toward self and others
- Impulsivity
- Immature social skills
- Feelings of depression and unhappiness
- Withdrawal into self
- Anxiety or fearfulness
- Ideas of suicide expressed
- Distractibility or inability to pay attention for a length of time comparable to that of peers

From Smith, Deborah Deutsch, and Luckasson, Ruth. *Introduction to Special Education: Teaching in an Age of Challenge*, 2/e. Published by Allyn & Bacon, Boston, MA. Copyright © 1995 by Pearson Education. Reprinted by permission of the publisher.

classroom environment and set clear expectations about peer interactions and about social boundaries in teacher-student relationships. The following suggestions will help you teach students with emotional and behavioral disorders (Smith & Luckasson, 1995, p. 322):

> *Suggestions for Working with Students with Emotional and Behavioral Disorders*

1. Establish clear rules for the class.
2. Role-play and practice the rules with the students.
3. Reinforce individual students when they follow a rule.
4. Provide fair and realistic consequences for following and not following rules.
5. Foster cooperation and friendship by using cooperative learning techniques to teach students how to work in small groups.
6. Communicate regularly with students' parents or caretakers.
7. Teach students to negotiate and mediate conflict.
8. Keep up-to-date records on behavior changes, especially during changes in medication.
9. Find at least one opportunity each day to praise students.
10. Learn to carefully observe and listen to students.

Students Who Are Gifted

What are your beliefs and values regarding giftedness?

Students identified as gifted and talented possess learning characteristics that allow rapid acquisition of literacy skills or expressive communication skills. These students often have special educational needs. Gifted learners frequently exhibit a cluster of intellectual abilities and personality traits, such as exceptional verbal reasoning, curiosity, creativity, strong internal motivation, and the ability to apply background knowledge rapidly to integrate new relationships and ideas. These students often are high achievers and capable of learning and retaining knowledge easily. They often are self-critical, socially mature, persistent, individualistic, and capable as leaders.

Gifted students do have difficulties in school, however. Potential problem areas deserve careful consideration as you plan your instruction. You may need to adjust your attitude toward gifted students' creative and individualistic responses and involve them in cooperative activities to develop their tolerance of others. You also will need to challenge these students, going beyond the planned curriculum to broaden their literacy and intellectual growth.

The following suggestions will help you design literacy instruction for gifted learners and for all students in your classroom (Smith & Luckasson, 1995):

➤ *Suggestions for Working with Gifted Learners*

1. Encourage students to become independent learners who pursue topics of high personal interest.
2. Initiate small-group cooperative-learning activities to develop social interchange skills and tolerance for the thinking of others.
3. Enrich units of study with guest speakers, field trips, demonstrations, and interest centers.
4. Watch for signs of boredom and provide intellectual stimulation through cooperative-learning and problem-solving discussions involving interpretive, applicative, and transactive thinking.
5. Create a psychologically safe classroom environment where novel ideas can be discussed and accepted.
6. Develop instructional interactions and activities that use questions to generate application of higher-level thinking skills.
7. Teach and foster the use of independent library and research skills.

Using Tutors to Assist in Meeting Student Needs

Under your direction, tutors can serve as a second set of eyes, hands, and ears for you and can make all the difference for students with reading and writing difficulties. The following ideas on the effective use of tutors are applicable to instructional needs of students from diverse backgrounds as well as special education. In addition, tutors can be very helpful to you in working with delayed readers, as discussed in Chapter 10.

Tutoring can also play an important role in early reading acquisition, which is of paramount importance if students are to succeed academically. Unless basic reading skills are well developed by the end of third grade, students are likely to experience academic difficulty in the later grades. Stanovich (2004) identifies this phenomenon as the "Matthew Effect"—the rich get richer and the poor get poorer.

The following ideas apply to peer tutoring, cross-age tutoring, and adult volunteer assistance. It is important that you select tutors carefully, provide training, and develop clear directions and expectations for their role (Topping, 1998).

It is also important to consider your instructional objectives and match tutors' or volunteers' competencies with the learning experiences leading to those outcomes: What role do you expect tutors to play in instruction? How will they operate in your classroom? How will you match tutors to your students? Will you use older peers or adult volunteers? Will they work with individual students or small groups? You also will need to take into account the personal characteristics of both tutor and student (Friend & Bursuck, 1996). Individual characteristics that are important to consider as you select and assign potential tutors are identified in Figure 11.13.

As you prepare peer or adult volunteer tutors, you will need to develop clear expectations of their role in relation to your responsibility as the teacher. This understanding will help avoid

FIGURE 11.13
Important Characteristics of Peer and Adult Volunteer Tutors

1. Ability to convey a friendly and supportive attitude to others
2. Ability to treat others in a respectful manner rather than as inferior or deficient
3. Awareness that other individuals differ in background knowledge and rate of learning
4. Desire and motivation to help others
5. Ability to relate to others and offer leadership and guidance to them in a learning situation
6. Ability to work with an individual or a small group in a learning situation
7. Skill in communicating and relating to you, the classroom teacher

conflicts about decision making, time allocation, and assignments. At the same time, you must be prepared to assign responsibility, provide clear directions, have materials ready for tutoring, and spend some time following up the tutoring or small-group session.

The dynamics of small-group instruction differ from one-to-one instructional relationships. Tutors must be sensitive to comfortable pacing and different expectation levels and must be able to handle a dominant or aggressive group member. Tutors also need to be consistent and fair in their responses, to listen to the students' ideas and respond to them appropriately, and to provide praise and positive feedback. You will find that one of the most effective training approaches for tutors is having them observe you in your own work with your students. First, provide an overview of what you plan to do in a lesson; then, model instruction as you conduct the lesson. Afterward, provide an opportunity to discuss what you did. For example, tutors might learn how to listen and respond to a student reading orally, help a pupil select and use a library book, record a student's dictation describing a field trip, or assist a learner with a writing assignment. If tutors have frequent opportunities to question, to understand their role, and to contribute, they will have higher morale and be more effective.

> *Suggestions for Peer Tutoring*

the Highly Effective Teacher

Teaching Culturally Diverse Learners and Students with Special Needs

Skills in Adapting Instruction
- developing background knowledge
- monitoring meaning construction
- motivating literature response
- using multicultural materials and themes
- using assistive technology

Application of Programs, Services, and Resources
- multicultural education
- multicultural and inclusive literature
- bilingual education and SDAIE
- special education
- IEPs and multi-disciplinary teams
- tutoring and parental involvement

Knowledge of Students and Their Instructional Needs
- cultural and literacy backgrounds
- proficiency in the first language
- proficiency in English
- level of metalinguistic awareness
- areas of ability, disability, and exceptionality
- motivations, purposes, and goals

Knowledge of Self
- beliefs and values about cultural/ethnic diversity
- beliefs and values about languages and dialects
- beliefs and values about gender
- beliefs and values about abilities and disabilities

As Friend and Bursuck (1996) note, "Peer tutoring outcomes are influenced by many factors, including the type of material being practiced, the age and sex of the students involved, and the level of achievement and amount of training the tutors and tutees have" (p. 461). Keep in mind the following tips for fostering successful peer tutoring:[1]

1. Many aspects of the school curriculum are amenable to instruction and practice via peer and cross-age tutoring.
2. A student of any age may be either the tutor or the tutee; the older student does not necessarily have to be the tutor.
3. Peer and cross-age tutors are often high achievers, but an achiever at any level might serve equally well as a tutor. More important than actual ability is the tutor's ability to teach without making value judgments about the tutee.
4. Same-sex partners work best in both cross-age and peer tutoring, especially for older students.
5. Tutors should be trained both in how to interact with their tutees and in how to present content to them and record their learning.
6. Tutoring can influence both cognitive and affective objectives for students.

Summary and Classroom Applications

double entry journal

Review your responses in the Double Entry Journal at the beginning of this chapter. How would you change your responses on the basis of information in this chapter? What other opportunities and obstacles do student diversity and variability present to you now? What will your plan be for overcoming the obstacles you foresee?

Chapter Summary

Your students will reflect language and cultural diversity, group differences in race and ethnicity, and individual differences in ability. Diversity, in all its forms, influences teaching and literacy learning in the classroom.

Multicultural education involves the integration of cultural content, attention to students' knowledge base, and creation of a classroom culture based on equity. The framework developed by Banks (1997b) emphasizes different levels of commitment to the integration of ethnic content in your curriculum and instruction, from the contributions approach to the social-action approach.

Second-language acquisition requires literacy background knowledge, metalinguistic awareness, and a psychologically safe language-learning environment. Students

in your classroom may speak a nonstandard English dialect or may be bilingual. Students with limited English proficiency participate in bilingual education programs. You must determine the instructional needs of your students and be able to apply the Specially Designed Academic Instruction in English (SDAIE) approach. It is also necessary to adopt key literacy strategies—such as the SDEI, DL-TA, reciprocal teaching, and read-alouds—as well as to use multicultural/multilingual literature and thematic units.

Your class will include students with different levels of ability and achievement and with special learning needs as a result of learning disabilities, emotional disturbance, giftedness, and other exceptionalities. While students with disabilities may receive special education and related

[1]From M. Friend and W. Bursuck, *Including Students with Special Needs: A Practical Guide for Classroom Teachers.* Copyright © 1996 by Allyn & Bacon. Adapted by permission. Tips from Rekrut, Martha D. (1994, February). Peer and cross-age tutoring: The lessons of research. *Journal of Reading, 37* (5), 356–362.

services, most are placed in general education classrooms to be educated alongside their nondisabled peers. You will participate in planning and implementing IEPs and adapting instruction for these students. The INCLUDE strategy will assist you in designing instruction for your special needs students so that meaning construction and active learning are the centerpieces of your teaching. You can also be expected to be involved in the selection and training of peer and adult volunteer tutors to provide additional instructional support in your classroom.

Applications: Bridges to the Classroom

1. Reread the two brief classroom discussions at the beginning of this chapter. What effect do teacher sensitivity and understanding of language and cultural diversity have on students' motivation to learn? What principles of instruction would you apply in these cases to ensure that literacy learning takes place?

2. Study the overview of legislation and court decisions on diversity (see Table 11.1, page 310). How will each influence you and the students in your classroom? What effect will each have on your teaching?

3. Arrange to observe an elementary classroom where nonstandard-English speakers or bilingual children are represented. Observe one child during reading and writing instruction. Briefly describe the student's proficiency in English. How does the student respond to and communicate with the teacher? With other students? How does the teacher communicate with the student? How would you describe his or her attitude toward learning and classroom instruction? How would you describe the teacher's attitude toward the student and her or his progress? Discuss your observations with a class partner.

4. Review the guidelines for using the Specially Designed Academic Instruction in English (SDAIE) approach. Iden-

tify a high-interest story appropriate for the grade level (and developmental reading level) of greatest interest to you. Based on this story, outline an instructional plan for bilingual students with limited English proficiency using the SDAIE guidelines. Share your plan with classmates, and add it to your teaching portfolio.

5. Identify and review multicultural literature that you would like to use with your students. For one selection, develop a lesson plan using the read-aloud strategy. Test your plan by arranging a classroom visit to implement your strategy with a small group of students. What insights do you derive from their responses? How would you change your plan for a second presentation? Add additional lesson plans for using multicultural literature to your portfolio.

6. Develop interview questions about teaching students with special needs in the general education classroom. With a partner, interview teachers and administrators in a school near you. How are special education, mainstreaming, and inclusion implemented in that school? What roles do special educators, classroom teachers, and reading specialists play in literacy instruction for students with special needs?

Professional Standards and
Teacher Knowledge for Understanding Language Diversity, Cultural Diversity, and Special Needs

The standards listed in Figure 11.14 (page 343) are the major standards for reading professionals found in the International Reading Association's *Standards for Reading Professionals— Revised 2003* (2004). The classroom teacher–candidate standards are developed with examples for each. After examining these standards, ask yourself, "How well equipped am I to meet these standards?" You can see the complete list of Standards for Reading Professionals in Appendix C.

FIGURE 11.14

Professional Standards and Understanding of Language Diversity, Cultural Diversity, and Special Needs for Classroom Teacher Candidates

Professional Standard	Example
1. Foundational Knowledge	**Element 1.3** Demonstrates knowledge of language development and reading acquisition and the variations related to cultural and linguistic diversity; e.g., describes key principles for teaching diverse learners; based on observations of student's oral language, determines level of English oral language proficiency; uses observational information on LEP students to plan and create appropriate instruction.
2. Instructional Strategies and Curriculum Materials	**Element 2.2** Uses a wide range of instructional practices, approaches, and methods for learners from differing cultural and linguistic backgrounds; e.g., demonstrates effective use of instructional strategies, ranging from SDAIE and SDEI to read-alouds and GMA to teach bilingual learners; shows how to adapt classroom strategies such as literature circles using multicultural literature and multicultural thematic units; implements the INCLUDE strategy to accommodate students with special instructional needs.
3. Assessment, Diagnosis, and Evaluation	**Element 3.4** Communicates results of assessments to students, parents, colleagues, and administrators; e.g., interprets a student's reading and language development profile from observations and various assessments, ranging from quick notes on reading and language interactions to running records and achievement tests; effectively communicates these interpretations to parents, colleagues, and administrators; uses portfolio assessment and interprets reading and language achievement progress to students, parents, and the school community.
4. Creating a Literate Environment	**Element 4.2** Uses a large supply of books, technology-based information to meet student needs from a wide range of cultural and linguistic backgrounds; e.g., selects and effectively uses children's literature from various cultural, linguistic, and special needs backgrounds to meet the interests and needs of students; articulates and explains the research, theory, and evidence-based rationale supporting the importance of a literate classroom environment for LEP students.
5. Professional Development	**Element 5.1** Displays positive dispositions related to reading and the teaching of reading; e.g., creates and demonstrates positive and caring attitudes toward all students in the classroom; builds on positive strengths of students and engages them in high-interest stories and discussions; works with tutors, parents, and the school community to promote positive attitude and home support of reading and literacy development.

Part 2 from IRA. (2004). Professional Standards and Ethics Committee, International Reading Association. *Standards for reading professionals—revised 2003.* Reprinted with permission of the International Reading Association. All rights reserved.

Additional Research and Practice

1. Drucker, M. J. (2003). **What reading teachers should know about ESL learners.** *The Reading Teacher, 57* (1), 22–29.

   This discussion provides an insightful overview of suggestions for adapting eleven instructional strategies for effective use with English-language learners who are at different levels of language proficiency. (Practice)

2. Martinez-Roldan, C. M., & Lopez-Robertson, J. M. (2000). **Initiating literature circles in a first-grade bilingual classroom.** *The Reading Teacher, 53* (4), 270–281.

   This article explores the use and value of literature discussions with first-grade bilingual students and reveals how they learn to talk about books and make book connections. (Practice)

3. Carlo, M. S., August, D., McLaughlin, B., Snow, C. E., Dressler, C., Lippman, D. N., Lively, T. J., & White, C. E. (2004). **Closing the gap: Addressing the vocabulary needs of English-language learners in bilingual and mainstream classrooms.** *Reading Research Quarterly, 39,* 188–215.

   This study was designed to test the effect of an English vocabulary enrichment intervention that combined direct word instruction with instruction in word-learning strategies for ELL students. The results indicate that the instruction was effective in increasing depth of vocabulary knowledge, multiple meanings, and reading comprehension. (Research)

CHAPTER 12

Examining Instructional Approaches to and the Organization and Management of Literacy Learning

Get in touch with what you believe about teaching and learning.
Your belief system provides the foundation for everything you do.
But always keep the door open for new ideas and insights.

Dorothy S. Strickland,
literacy educator and State of New Jersey Professor of Reading at Rutgers University

The Internet and other continuously emerging information and
communication technologies will be central to literacy . . . if we
hope to prepare all students for the literacy futures they deserve.

Donald J. Leu,
literacy and technology educator, University of Connecticut
Charles K. Kinzer,
literacy and technology educator, Teachers College, Columbia University

Angela Lee has taught third grade at Oak Grove school for three years. Although her reading instruction relies on a basal reader adopted by her school district, she has modified the basal approach by incorporating features of the literature-based and language-based approaches.

On a crisp Monday morning in November, she introduces her third graders to John Steptoe's (1987) African folktale *Mufaro's Beautiful Daughters*. The teacher's guide for the basal reader program recommends using a Directed Reading Activity (DRA), but Angela decides that a Directed Reading-Thinking Activity (DR-TA) will work better.

Angela launches her lesson by asking students to place their closed texts on their desks. She reads the story's title to them and asks, "With a title like that, what do you think this story will be about?" Following discussion, she tells the students to open their books and read to a stop-point at the bottom of the second page. This part of the text reveals the different character traits of Mufaro's daughters, Nyasha (warm and caring) and Manyara (cold and self-absorbed). "What do you think will happen next?" she asks. The DR-TA is successful.

Angela goes on to explain about the Caldecott Medal that Steptoe received for the beautiful illustrations of his story. She invites students to write about their favorite illustrations in their reading logs and then to share the reasons for their choices with a partner.

Angela considers other follow-up activities. She could have the students use their observations as a basis for developing concept webs to contrast Nyasha's and Manyara's character traits. She also could discuss folktales as a literary genre and invite her students to share folktales from their family's cultural heritage.

double entry journal

What follow-up activities would you recommend to Angela? How might you incorporate features and elements of the three main approaches to literacy instruction? How might you incorporate a technology-based approach?

Chapter Objectives

After reading and discussing this chapter, you will be able to:

- articulate instructional beliefs that cross a wide continuum from phonics and the basal reader to literature-based and language-based programs.

- understand the basal reader approach, including underlying beliefs, instructional components, organization and management, and how to adapt the approach to meet students' needs.

- understand the literature-based approach, including underlying beliefs, identification of core readings, organization and management, and how to adapt the approach to meet individual needs.

- understand the language-based approach, including underlying beliefs, implementation, organization and management, and how to adapt the program to meet student needs.

- know how to evaluate instructional approaches and supplementary programs with the help of an evaluation checklist.

- integrate technology-based instruction into your classroom by comprehending underlying beliefs, instructional uses, classroom integration, and evaluation of software to meet the needs of your students.

Understanding Instructional Approaches and Management

EVIDENCE-BASED PRACTICE

The use of instructional approaches and programs in elementary classrooms has changed as a result of new understandings about language and literacy-learning processes and highly effective teaching practices (Gunning, 2008). These new understandings relate to (1) the complexities of literacy processes, (2) how children acquire and develop language literacy, (3) social and language interactions in classrooms, and (4) interrelationships between literacy processes and subject-area learning. Instructional approaches must reflect these new understandings in order to meet students' literacy needs.

A Bottom-Up–Top-Down Instructional Continuum

It is helpful to think of instructional approaches as extending along a continuum (Figure 12.1) from a bottom-up philosophy to a top-down philosophy. The *bottom-up philosophy* places emphasis on teaching a predetermined scope and sequence of skills in areas such as word identification

FIGURE 12.1

An Instructional Continuum of Beliefs about Reading and Literacy Development

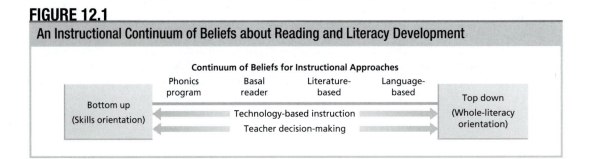

and comprehension. In contrast, the *top-down philosophy* stresses situating all literacy instruction within the context of natural learning events and giving attention to skills as needs arise.

As a highly effective teacher, you may have to make critical decisions in choosing a designated approach, and in many cases, modifying it to achieve a balanced reading program. It is important to realize that there is no "perfect method" in reading instruction. The key to high-level achievement is the highly effective teacher and the adjustment of instructional methodology to meet the needs of your students (Allington & McGill-Franzen, 2004; Brown et al., 2004; Langer, 2004; Ruddell, 2004).

the ★ Highly Effective Teacher ★

EVIDENCE-BASED PRACTICE

The Basal Reader Approach

As you may recall, the basal reader approach is the instructional approach most widely used for literacy development in the United States. According to current estimates, basal readers are the chief instructional tool in 75 to 85 percent of elementary classrooms. During the 1970s and early 1980s, some fifteen publishers produced basal readers. Today, however, this number has been reduced to about four publishers—Harcourt Brace, Houghton Mifflin, Open Court, and Scott Foresman—because of corporate consolidation, acquisitions, and mergers. The total investment required to produce a complete basal reading program is estimated to range from $20 million to $50 million. These costs include editorial and author costs; permissions fees (paid to reprint

Research and Evidence-Based Practice

Instructional Approaches, Effective Teaching, and Literacy Learning

Did You Know?

- The basal reader, literature-based, and language-based approaches are used in over 75 to 85 percent of the classrooms across the United States. The majority of classrooms use the basal reader approach (Chall & Squire, 1991).

- The classic First Grade Studies involved twenty-seven research centers and revealed that combined approaches using both systematic phonics as well as emphasis on connected reading and meaning produced superior results (Bond & Dykstra, 1967).

- Students' ability to recognize and name capital letters and small letters of the alphabet at the beginning of first grade has been found to be the best predictor of reading success. This finding supports the importance of understanding print awareness, letter-sound relationships, and early literacy development, regardless of the instructional approach (Adams, 1990b; Dykstra, 1968).

- Fluency instruction, such as repeated reading or paired reading, with students from the late preprimer level to the late second-grade level has been shown to increase reading achievement (Kuhn & Stahl, 2004; Schwanenflugel et al., 2006.

- Primary-grade teachers identified as influential and highly effective teachers, in contrast to noninfluential and less effective teachers, have been found to place a higher degree of emphasis (82 percent vs. 30 percent) on interpretive-type discussion questions and reach successful closure and resolution (96 percent vs. 57 percent) in instructional episode discussions with their students, leading to higher comprehension achievement (Ruddell, 2004).

- The use of highly interactive and transactional discussion strategies with low-achieving students has been shown to result in a richer, more personalized understanding of stories, greater awareness of strategic reading, and increase in reading achievement (Brown, Pressley, Van Meter, & Schuder, 2004; McIntyre et al., 2006; Palinscar & Brown, 1986).

- In some of the First Grade Studies, greater variation was found between different teachers' classrooms than between the kinds of reading programs used. This finding clearly supports the importance of effective teaching, regardless of the instructional approach used (Bond & Dykstra, 1967; Dykstra, 1968).

published stories); and expenditures for product research and field testing, promotion and sales training, printing and binding, and distribution and warehousing of the initial printing runs.

Underlying Beliefs and Assumptions about Literacy Learning in the Basal Reader Approach

The basal reader approach to developing students' literacy is based on the following beliefs and assumptions:

What are the five main elements of the DRA?

- Students' acquisition and development of fluent literacy is best accomplished by progressing through a systematic, predetermined sequence of skills, taught in conjunction with carefully selected short narrative and expository texts.
- Students acquire and develop fluent literacy as they become increasingly proficient in word identification, vocabulary, comprehension, language knowledge, content area reading, and independent reading.
- Materials for developing students' literacy need to be selected from high-quality literature and presented in an ordered sequence of difficulty to support their growing literacy competence.
- Lessons for fostering students' literacy development should rely heavily on the Directed Reading Activity (DRA).
- Students acquire and develop fluent literacy best by learning in small groups organized according to proficiency and matched to reading materials of comparable difficulty.

Instructional Components of the Basal Reader Approach

➤ Basal reader programs rely on a scope and sequence of skills

The instructional components of a basal reader are conceptualized and designed by a team composed of respected individuals in literacy education and publishing-house editors. This team directs the philosophy and plan for development and identifies literature and content area selections for the student text, based on general themes. These themes might range from "families" and "friendship" in the early grades to "memories" and "machines" in the intermediate grades. Selections in the student reader are analyzed to ensure a consistent level of difficulty at each grade level. Stories and content area selections often are custom written to follow a predetermined scope and sequence of skills, vocabulary, and thematic unit plan. A teacher's guide, student workbook, and other supplementary materials are developed in a similar fashion, based on lesson plans for the predetermined skill sequence for instructional strands such as word identification, vocabulary, comprehension, literature, and content area reading strategies. The entire process of publishing a basal reading program requires from three to five years.

What literature or content area themes might appeal to these students? What themes would appeal to the students that you teach?

The Teacher's Guide

The teacher's guide is a critical part of the basal reader approach and is designed to assist the teacher in the teaching process. A planning guide for the story *Ramona and Her Father* (Cleary, 1977) from the third-grade teacher's guide *Diamond Cove* (Farr & Strickland, 1997) appears in Figure 12.2 (page 350). This story and several other fiction, nonfiction, and poetry selections comprise Theme 3, called "Exploring Challenges." This theme focuses on solving problems by meeting challenges in a creative way. Each selection is linked to reading, integrating language arts, and learning through literature. A wide range of ideas are presented for curriculum integration, strategies and skills to be taught, and suggested resources to use (including practice books and media resources). A wide range of skills are emphasized, including comprehension, vocabulary, and word identification.

Lesson Plans and Annotated Student Text

The lesson plan for each selection in the student text contains a detailed story summary, an overview of the lesson, and specific suggestions for each part of the lesson, following the DRA strategy. Most teacher's guides contain not only teaching suggestions but also annotated reduced-size facsimiles of pages from the student text and print supplements. The lesson plan for the first step of the DRA (activating prior knowledge and building background by introducing new vocabulary and concepts) for *Ramona and Her Father* is shown in Figure 12.3 (page 351).

> *Basal reader programs are prescribed in detail in teacher's guides.*

The Student Workbook

The student workbook, or practice book, provides reinforcing activities for the skills taught in the lesson. Figure 12.4 (page 352) shows a page from the student's edition of the workbook for *Ramona and Her Father*. The activities are designed to develop vocabulary. A facsimile of this page also appears in the teacher's guide in reduced size for quick reference.

Grade-Level and Reading-Level Organization

Basal readers traditionally had grade designations, but these designations have been replaced by reading levels referenced to grades. The goal is to place students at the reading level most appropriate for them, regardless of grade level. Students' success depends directly on the classroom teacher's understanding of appropriate reading levels for individual children, as well as on the school district's willingness to order materials based on the teacher's recommendation.

the Highly Effective Teacher

What is the significance of reading-level designations?

Organization and Management of the Basal Reading Classroom

Grouping by proficiency or ability level is a major component of basal reading instruction. Basal reading classrooms usually have three or four reading groups, each of which is using a different text or working in a different part of a text in the basal series. Group instruction is teacher-led; therefore, the classroom must be organized so that the teacher can work with one group of children in a designated area while the rest of the class works independently. Figure 12.5 (page 353) shows a classroom arrangement for basal reading instruction.

Reading Group Instructional Area

Locate the reading group instructional area away from other work areas. Use a table large enough to allow everyone to sit comfortably, without crowding, with books and writing materials. Arrange the table so that the students sit with their backs to the rest of the room and you sit facing the room. This arrangement directs group members' voices away from the other students, reducing noise, and increases the feeling of intimacy between you and the group you're teaching. Also, by facing the room, you can monitor and manage the rest of the class more easily.

The basal reading group instructional area should be near a chalkboard for your convenience when teaching vocabulary and word identification. In primary classrooms, a pocket chart placed on an easel is also useful for displaying vocabulary on word cards in this area. Finally, the reading group area should contain a bookcase, storage closet, or bin to house the basal readers and related materials. Storing basals in a central location rather than in students' desks helps preserve them. This is a good place to store supplies of paper and writing utensils for mapping and other writing activities. You may also want to keep your teacher's guide here, as well as visuals,

How does the basal reading classroom account for instructional effectiveness?

FIGURE 12.2

A Teacher's Planning Guide for a Story

MEETING INDIVIDUAL NEEDS

Flexible Grouping

RAMONA AND HER FATHER T631–T668

	BELOW-LEVEL READERS	ABOVE-LEVEL READERS	ESL	BILINGUAL
I READING AND RESPONDING Build Concepts and Vocabulary Strategic Reading Response Corner	**BEFORE** students read the selection, introduce Key Words (p. T635). **TEACHER-LED GROUP** **WHILE** reading the selection, use the Guiding the Reading pages of the *Intervention Strategies Manual* (p. 142). **TEACHER-LED GROUP**	**BEFORE** reading the selection, have students complete the *Practice Book* (p. 86). **INDEPENDENT** **AFTER** students read the selection, have them choose and complete a Response activity (p. T650). **COOPERATIVE GROUPS**	**BEFORE** students read the selection, use the Introducing the Literature pages of the *Sheltered English/ESL Manual* (pp. 94–96). **TEACHER-LED GROUP**	**INSTEAD OF** reading the selection in the anthology, have students read the translation in the appropriate *Anthology Translation Booklet.* **INDEPENDENT** **INSTEAD OF** completing the Vocabulary Strategies, have Spanish-speaking students read *Camila come cuentos* in CIELO ABIERTO. **INDEPENDENT/ PAIRS**
2 INTEGRATING LANGUAGE ARTS Idea Bank Writer's Workshop Grammar Spelling Vocabulary Workshop	**DURING** the Writer's Workshop, review the *Language Handbook* (pp. 48–50). **TEACHER-LED GROUP** **AFTER** the Writer's Workshop, students may use the Bright Ideas tool in *The Amazing Writing Machine* to find descriptive words (p. T656). **INDEPENDENT/ PAIRS**	**DURING** the Writer's Workshop, students may refer to the *Language Handbook* (pp. 48–50). **INDEPENDENT** **AFTER** the Grammar lesson, have students complete the *Practice Book* (p. 88) with less-fluent partners. **PAIRS**	**DURING** the Idea Bank, model and guide the completion of the Writer's *Magazine* (pp. 90-91). **TEACHER-LED GROUP** **AFTER** the Grammar lesson, have students describe something that they did yesterday or that they will do tomorrow or later (T659). **TEACHER-LED GROUP**	**INSTEAD OF** completing the Writer's Workshop, use CIELO ABIERTO *Teacher's Handbook* page 63 to have students write a poem. **INDEPENDENT** **INSTEAD OF** completing the Grammar lesson, use page 11 in *Camila come cuentos Teacher's Guide.* **TEACHER-LED GROUP**
3 LEARNING THROUGH THE LITERATURE Direct Skills Instruction Integrated Curriclum Reading Trade Books Theme Project	**WHILE** others are working in groups, use the *Intervention Strategies Manual* Phonics lesson (pp. 144-145). **TEACHER-LED GROUP**	**AFTER** the skill lesson, have students write paragraphs in which they make judgments about Ramona's work, attitude, or behavior. (p. T663) **INDEPENDENT** **WHILE** others are working on the Theme Project, provide students with Project Cards 32–36 so that they can work at their own pace. (p. T670). **COOPERATIVE GROUPS**	**AFTER** the skill lesson, model and guide the completion of the *Practice Book* (p. 90). **TEACHER-LED GROUP** **WHILE** others are working in groups, students may make and read the Take-Home Book *No Problem.* **INDEPENDENT**	**WHILE** others are working in groups, Chinese-speaking students can read *Daddy Doesn't Go to Work* in the *Multi-Language Library.* **INDEPENDENT** **WHILE** others are working in groups, have students complete the ongoing cross-curricular project. See *Camila come cuentos Teacher's Guide* page 2. **COOPERATIVE GROUPS**

Exploring Challenges   T481

Excerpts from *Signatures: Diamond Cove*, Grade 3, Book 2, Teacher's Edition, T481, copyright © 1997 by Harcourt, Inc., reprinted by permission of the publisher.

FIGURE 12.3

A Teacher's Guide Page on Developing Concepts and Vocabulary

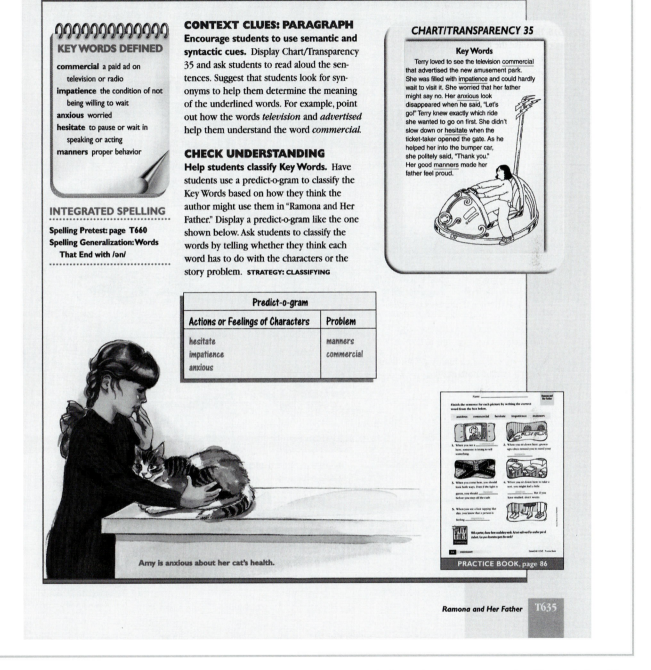

VOCABULARY STRATEGIES

KEY WORDS DEFINED

commercial a paid ad on television or radio

impatience the condition of not being willing to wait

anxious worried

hesitate to pause or wait in speaking or acting

manners proper behavior

INTEGRATED SPELLING

Spelling Pretest: page T660

Spelling Generalization: Words That End with /ən/

CONTEXT CLUES: PARAGRAPH

Encourage students to use semantic and syntactic cues. Display Chart/Transparency 35 and ask students to read aloud the sentences. Suggest that students look for synonyms to help them determine the meaning of the underlined words. For example, point out how the words *television* and *advertised* help them understand the word *commercial*.

CHECK UNDERSTANDING

Help students classify Key Words. Have students use a predict-o-gram to classify the Key Words based on how they think the author might use them in "Ramona and Her Father." Display a predict-o-gram like the one shown below. Ask students to classify the words by telling whether they think each word has to do with the characters or the story problem. **STRATEGY: CLASSIFYING**

CHART/TRANSPARENCY 35

Key Words

Terry loved to see the television commercial that advertised the new amusement park. She was filled with impatience and could hardly wait to visit it. She worried that her father might say no. Her anxious look disappeared when he said, "Let's go!" Terry knew exactly which ride she wanted to go on first. She didn't slow down or hesitate when the ticket-taker opened the gate. As he helped her into the bumper car, she politely said, "Thank you." Her good manners made her father feel proud.

Predict-o-gram	
Actions or Feelings of Characters	**Problem**
hesitate	manners
impatience	commercial
anxious	

Amy is anxious about her cat's health.

PRACTICE BOOK, page 86

Ramona and Her Father   T635

FIGURE 12.4

Student Workbook Page for Vocabulary Development

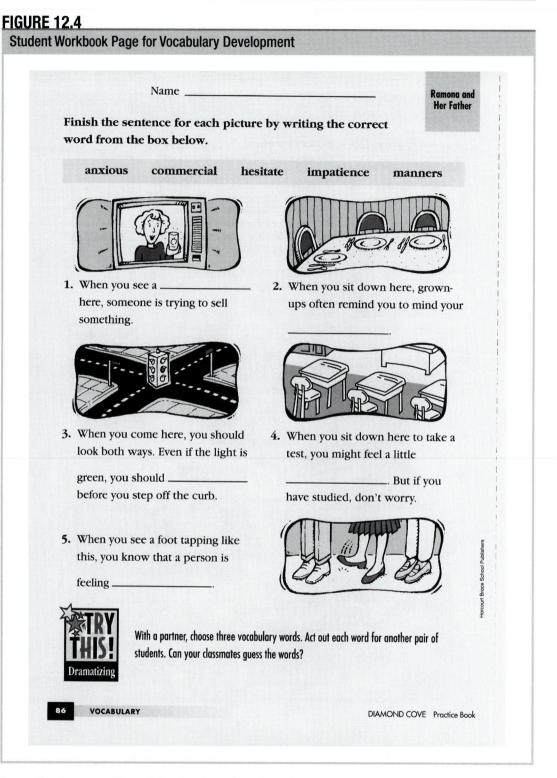

Name _____

Ramona and Her Father

Finish the sentence for each picture by writing the correct word from the box below.

| anxious | commercial | hesitate | impatience | manners |

1. When you see a _____ here, someone is trying to sell something.

2. When you sit down here, grown-ups often remind you to mind your _____.

3. When you come here, you should look both ways. Even if the light is green, you should _____ before you step off the curb.

4. When you sit down here to take a test, you might feel a little _____. But if you have studied, don't worry.

5. When you see a foot tapping like this, you know that a person is feeling _____.

TRY THIS! Dramatizing

With a partner, choose three vocabulary words. Act out each word for another pair of students. Can your classmates guess the words?

Harcourt Brace School Publishers

86 VOCABULARY

DIAMOND COVE Practice Book

Excerpts from *Signatures: Diamond Cove*, Practice Book, Student Edition, Grade 3–2, copyright © 1997 by Harcourt, Inc., reprinted by permission of the publisher.

FIGURE 12.5

Physical Organization of the Basal Reading Classroom

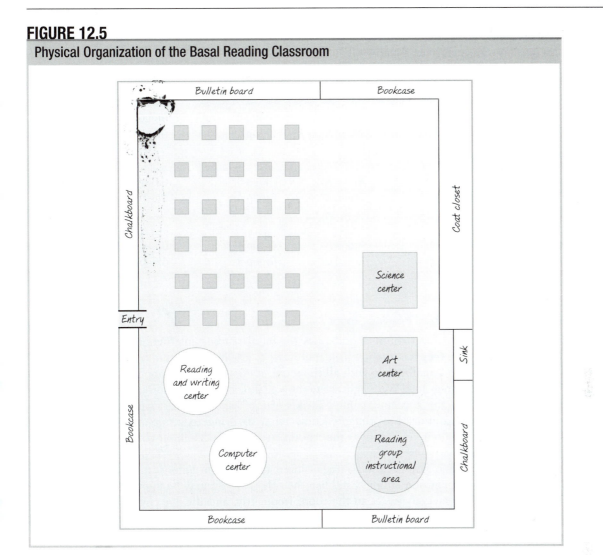

several books from which basal selections have been drawn, related literature, and perhaps some puppets or other dramatic props.

Scheduling Reading Groups

Most basal reading instruction occurs at a designated time during the class day (usually in the morning). The length of time and the time of day allotted to reading instruction may be determined at the school or district level or by teachers. Reading instruction may be part of a larger language arts block, or it may be separated from spelling and writing instruction.

Once you have established a time block for basal reading instruction and your reading groups, you need to decide how you will schedule your groups into the time block. It is not necessary to meet with each group every day. If you attempt to do so, you will find that you do not have enough time to finish the lesson! Arrange the schedule so that you have one or more extended periods with each group every week. Table 12.1 (page 354) shows how you might schedule reading groups by starting with a different group each week. In this way, you have two forty-five-minute meetings with two groups each week and one forty-five-minute period with one. For example, while you are working with Group A on Monday from 9:15 to 10:00, Groups B and C will need assignment and direction on individual or small-group projects. Although not perfect, this arrangement does give you sufficiently long blocks of time for extended and elaborated discussions. There are other ways basal reading instructional blocks can be scheduled; use your imagination to make the schedule work for you and your instructional goals.

Should you meet with every reading group every day?

TABLE 12.1
Scheduling Basal Reading Groups—A Three-Week Cycle

	Monday	Tuesday	Wednesday	Thursday	Friday
Week 1					
9:15–10:00	Group A	Group C	Group B	Group A	Group C
10:00–10:30	Group B	Group A	Group C	Group B	Journals
Week 2					
9:15–10:00	Group B	Group A	Group C	Group B	Group A
10:00–10:30	Group C	Group B	Group A	Group C	Journals
Week 3					
9:15–10:00	Group C	Group B	Group A	Group C	Group B
10:00–10:30	Group A	Group C	Group B	Group A	Journals

the **Highly Effective Teacher**

In what noninterruptive, nonverbal ways can you respond to student behavior?

➤ *Negative Effects of Ability Grouping*

the **Highly Effective Teacher**

Routines and Rules for Basal Reading Groups

Early in the year, establish routines and rules for basal reading instruction and have students rehearse them. Later, they will require little monitoring. The first important routine is getting students to and from the small group with all the required materials and supplies. Determine a signal to call students to group. You might write the schedule on the board every morning and then quietly announce at the appointed time "Tarik's group" or "Alejandra's group." Spend some time clarifying the routine. Let students know what to bring to group, the deportment you expect, and what to do upon arrival at the reading group table. Then see to it that the routine is followed consistently.

During group time, you need to be free of interruptions from other students who have questions or want to tell you something. Establish the rule that you may be interrupted during reading group only for emergencies. Scan the room frequently, and use eye contact, small gestures, facial expressions, or silent speech as needed, without interrupting group interaction. Scanning also alerts you to a student who may need your immediate attention.

Effects of Ability Grouping

Ability grouping has a stigmatizing effect on students and may exacerbate status and self-esteem issues that are already present in your classroom (Strickland, 1994/1995). However neutral the reading group names may seem and no matter how careful you are to give equal instruction to all groups, students will know early on who's in the "high" reading group and who's in the "low" group. In schools with immigrant students and students who are learning English as a second language, an additional unfortunate effect is that these students tend to be grouped together in the low reading group or segregated into a group by themselves.

One way to reduce the negative effects of ability grouping is to alternate basal reading instruction with literature-based instruction, in which students self-select reading groups on the basis of the books they choose to read. This gives them opportunities to cross basal reading group lines. Another method is to have project groups at another time during the day. Here, students group themselves according to interest or some criterion other than reading ability. Instituting cross-ability groupings is important in helping students understand and appreciate the many strengths of their peers.

Strengths and Limitations of the Basal Reader Approach

The basal reader approach offers the distinct advantage of an instructional program with preselected and developed skill strands already prepared for the classroom. This program includes literature (usually excerpts from full-length stories) and expository selections in a student text. Extended suggestions for teaching the selection are provided in a teacher's guide and follow a DRA instructional pattern. Workbooks and various supplementary materials support and reinforce the development of the preselected reading material and skills. This approach thus affords significant savings in teacher time.

The basal approach also limits the range of literature and expository material children are exposed to and the range of instructional strategies teachers use. Heavy reliance on the DRA strategy circumscribes children's approach to reading and the way they think about reading as a process. Skill development activities in the supplements tend to follow a uniform pattern and thus can become boring busywork for students. The basal approach also tends to promote between-group ability grouping, a kind of tracking.

Adapting Basal Reading Programs to Meet Students' Needs

The key to using the basal reader approach effectively is adapting the program to meet the instructional needs of students, rather than adhering strictly to the teacher's guide (Fawson & Reutzel, 2000). Begin by familiarizing yourself thoroughly with the program. Carefully read the literature and expository selections in the student text, and ask yourself the following questions: "Will my students find this story interesting?" "How can I introduce this selection effectively?" "Is this selection taken from a full-length story? If so, can I make the full-length story available to students who would enjoy reading it in its entirety? Or would I rather teach the full-length story?" Carefully examine the teacher's guide and be selective in identifying the activities you wish to use. The authors of the teacher's guide do not know your students' specific needs. You have the *freedom and responsibility* to select only those activities you believe will work well with your students.

Also examine the student workbook and supplementary program activities. You have full control over the use of these activities with your students. Going beyond busywork and time fillers, the activities should develop and reinforce important lesson concepts. Use only those activities that support your instructional goals and students' needs; eliminate those that do not. If you use the preselected vocabulary, think carefully about your students and the words you believe they already know, as well as words not in the preselected list that they may need to know. Remember, you have the knowledge, ability, responsibility, and control to adapt the basal reading program to fit your own philosophy and meet the instructional needs of your students.

The Literature-Based Approach

Wide variation exists in literature-based programs. In some classes, literature-based instruction is predominantly large group: Everyone reads the same literary work, discusses it in a large group led by the teacher, and completes follow-up activities. In other classrooms, literature-based instruction is a combination of individualized and small group. Students read a book by sections, complete worksheets, and then meet in small groups to discuss the story, using the worksheets to guide discussion. Other classrooms have highly individualized literature-based programs in which every student reads a self-selected book. This chapter considers literature-based programs revolving around reading-response groups, which were introduced in Chapter 7 (page 205). The teacher identifies eight to ten core books and obtains multiple copies (five to ten) of each. Students decide which book they wish to read and thus which group they wish to join. With teacher guidance, the groups read the books in sections and meet to discuss their reading and responses. The teacher monitors individual and group progress and maintains records documenting each student's literacy development.

Underlying Beliefs and Assumptions about Literacy Learning in the Literature-Based Approach

Literature-based instruction relies on the following beliefs and assumptions about literacy learning:

- Students acquire and develop fluent literacy by reading and responding to complete literary works of high quality.
- Students read and respond avidly to literature that interests them, even when the difficulty of the literary works exceeds their apparent ability level.

---

the ★ **Highly Effective Teacher** ★

What do you like best (and least) about the basal approach?

How would converting a DRA to a DR-TA change a basal lesson? What kinds of assessment best fit basal reader programs?

How does the reading-response-group strategy work?

- Students do not need to understand every word of text in order to construct full, rich meaning for that text.
- As active theory builders and hypothesis testers, students can acquire all the requisite language and literacy skills for competent reading and writing as they progress through works of literature that interest them.
- In the event that specific skills are needed for students' literacy development, these skills should be taught in the context of that immediate need.

Identifying Core Readings

Core literature selections are generally identified by a committee of teachers representing various grade levels, although in some schools teachers may be able to make their own choices. A core selection is a full-length children's or adolescent book deemed to be of exceptional quality and identified as meeting a literature-based instructional goal. The teacher committee may be at the school site level or the school district level and should include at least one elementary or middle school librarian. Reaching a consensus on the core selections is the first important step in launching the literature-based approach.

Many factors guide the selection of core literature.

The process of identifying core selections is guided by the teachers' and librarians' experiences—relating to developmental interest and motivation—in using literature with students at various grade levels. It is important that all major literary genres be represented in the core selections (see Chapter 7 page 183). A balance also needs to be achieved among old favorites such as folktales and fables, literature classics that have stood the test of time, and the most recent modern fiction and expository works. Care must be taken to include in the core collection fair and accurate representations of many kinds of human diversity and variability, including gender and exceptionality (see Chapter 11 pages 328–334; page 337). In addition, the collection must provide for a range of difficulty levels, particularly at the upper-primary and intermediate and middle school grades, where a wider achievement range is to be expected.

Although core books are designated for specific grade levels, students should not be barred from reading a book on that basis. Eight to ten titles should be available per grade level, and teachers may use any titles they wish beyond the core books. Five to ten copies of each title are necessary for reading-response group instruction. Note that if ten core books have been identified for your grade and you desire to have ten copies of each, you will need to order one hundred books. Costs can be reduced by ordering paperbacks.

Implementing the Literature-Based Approach

Instructional stances and strategies for literature instruction need to be carefully selected.

The major instructional goals and objectives of a literature-based program range from fostering high motivation to read and developing new concepts to understanding the power of language to convey human experiences and reinforcing the development of reading skills and strategies (McMahon & Raphael, 1997). It is important to take into account the core selection being used as you decide whether to implement a predominantly aesthetic or efferent stance. Instructional strategies to be used with the core selections also deserve careful consideration. The reading-response-group approach is highly recommended, with teacher-designed prompts guiding group discussion. Transferring to a literature-based approach can be a problem in school districts that previously used a basal reader approach because teachers tend to simply transfer basal practices (the DRA strategy) to the reading of literature; in effect, they "basalize" the literature selections. As you use the core literature selections, it is important to consider the many strategies available to you in addition to the DRA.

Which teaching strategies in this book are appropriate for literature-based instruction?

Organization and Management of the Literature-Based Classroom

What kinds of assessment best fit literature-based programs?

The three physical requirements for literature-based classrooms are:

1. A reading and literature center in which to store the many books and other reading matter that such a program needs

2. Flexible floor space, to allow students to move in and out of reading-response groups and to give response groups the room they need so that members can converse without interference from other groups

3. Working areas and materials and props for developing end-of-book productions

Figure 12.6 (see below) suggests one possible arrangement for a literature-based classroom.

The Reading Center

The reading center is the heart of the literature-based classroom. It houses the classroom library, with many kinds of interesting and enjoyable books. In addition to the core books, the library should have literature classics as well as lighter works, comic books, magazines, reference books, joke books, and anything else students like to read. The reading center should make a clear statement about the value you place on books and the enjoyment students can expect in their encounters with books. After their use in the reading-response groups, core books should be made available for individual checkout. Make sure to add titles that complement the core book collection's topics and authors. For example, if your response groups will be reading *Ira Sleeps Over* (Waber, 1972), include other books about children's fears, frustrations, and security objects, such as *Everybody Needs a Rock* (Baylor, 1974), *Frederick* (Lionni, 1967), and *Goodnight Moon* (Brown, 1947). Also try to stock all the titles in a series.

What are some sources of books for the reading center?

FIGURE 12.6

Physical Organization of the Literature-Based Classroom

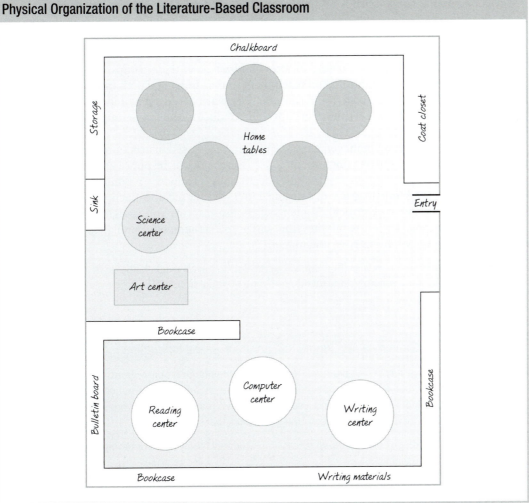

Flexible Floor Space

The literature-based classroom requires lots of space and comfortable furniture and needs to be flexible to accommodate various activities. One idea is to have movable desks that students can arrange into reading response groups and then rearrange into other formations for other class activities. Another idea is to assign students to tables according to their response groups. Students might also move their chairs into circles for group work. The ideal situation is to have sufficient table centers in the room—at the reading center, listening center, and writing center—so that they can leave their assigned seats and relocate to a center for reading-response-group discussion. Leave as much room as possible between groups so that talking noise from one group does not disturb other working groups. Avoid having groups meet at tables or centers where work in progress is on display.

Routines and Rules for Literature-Based Instruction

Two management issues are prominent in literature-based instruction. The first is twofold: scheduling the reading-response groups and then moving students into and out of the groups in a manner that minimizes wasted time and confusion. Many teachers using the literature-based approach simply apply the time designated for reading or language arts to reading-response-group activities (Table 12.2 see below).

Anytime everyone in the classroom is moving about simultaneously, the possibility exists for disruptions and conflicts. Students playfully push and shove, trip each other, punch and poke, and shoot baskets into the trash can. Sometimes, this can escalate into rowdiness and out-of-control behavior, making it necessary for you to use precious instructional time for crowd control. Rules and routines help prevent this problem and safeguard students from possible injury or harm.

A good routine to establish is to announce when each reading-response group should move to its discussion area. Give one group time to settle in before announcing the next. Early in the year, make clear what materials students should bring to their response groups and your expectations for deportment en route. Consistently give focus instructions ("Create a map that shows the mood of your story.") either before or after children go to their groups. Also choose the signals you will use to focus attention, and teach them to the students. Focus instructions, prompts, and signals will thus become part of the routine. If they are practiced and monitored early in the year, transitions to and from response groups and conduct within the groups will become easy, trouble-free routines.

The second challenging management issue in literature-based instruction is ensuring that students engage in rich, productive, high-quality discussions in their response groups. What can you do to keep response groups on track and educationally productive? Bonnie Raines (1991), a teacher in a third- and fourth- grade class using a literature-based approach, found that clear discussion task directions were critical. Some teachers use rotating role assignments to help guide and focus discussion. The following literature-circle role assignments similar to those developed in Chapter 7 will be helpful in role assignment:

> *Discussion leader* develops questions and keeps the discussion on track; helps shy students respond and ensures that the more talkative students do not control discussion; makes sure task is completed.

TABLE 12.2

Organization of the Language Arts Period for Literature-Based Instruction

9:15–9:20	*Focus, discussion prompts:* Teacher guides reading-response-group discussion by focusing attention (create a group map that shows the mood of your story) or using response prompts (as a group, find a section of today's reading that everyone in the group likes, and jot down some reasons the group likes that section).
9:20–9:50	*Reading-response-group discussion:* Students follow focus or prompt as major topic of discussion.
9:50–10:15	*Whole class sharing:* The essence of each group's discussion is shared with class.
10:15–10:30	*Journal writing:* Students reflect on and record responses to their reading and discussion.

Literary reporter identifies key words or short passages that create outstanding imagery.

Timer keeps track of time; makes sure the discussion is moving on schedule.

Illustrator provides a graphic summary of the piece.

Connector helps connect the text world to the students' real world.

Summarizer ensures that key student ideas are captured; provides a final summary of the selection.

> ➤ *Students need training and practice in discussion-group roles.*

If you want to use these or other role assignments in your reading-response groups, you will need to prepare students for the roles. In her study of response groups, Raines (1991) found that because of inexperience, discussion leaders sometimes asked questions that interrupted the flow of discussion and limited, rather than extended, elaboration of ideas.

> ➤ *Using Tape Recorders*

You can monitor small-group discussions in a number of ways to assess students' group growth and literacy development. You can listen in from a distance, or you can briefly join each group each day. However, your presence in the group will change the group dynamic and may reduce students' spontaneity. Adult aides and volunteers also need to know how to sit in with groups without taking over. Raines distributed a tape recorder to each group so that the students could tape their discussions. She then listened regularly to the tapes and gave students feedback on the quality of their discussions and their group process.

Because end-of-unit tests and other evaluation events are not built into the literature-based approach, evaluation procedures also become a management issue. You will need to choose, develop, and maintain an evaluation system based on observation that yields productive information about students' literacy development. Record the books students read, the productions they participate in, and the reading and writing skills they acquire, as identified by your school district for their grade level.

> How can you keep track of students' literacy development in the literature-based approach?

Strengths and Limitations of the Literature-Based Approach

The literature-based approach gives teachers the greatest freedom in the selection both of literature and of strategies for carrying out instructional goals. The reading center becomes a resource for instruction and provides opportunities for students to develop reading interests and reading skills.

> ➤ *The literature-based approach provides freedom but requires commitment.*

Literature-based instruction carries significant responsibility and requires a high level of teacher commitment. It takes time and energy to establish instructional goals; identify appropriate literature selections; select, create, or adapt instructional strategies; and then implement the program with students. You must possess in-depth knowledge of children's literature, children's interests and motivation, and instructional stances and strategies. Furthermore, you must know how to build bridges between students and books. The literature-based approach assumes that word identification and recognition and other skills will be developed through literature or through a supplementary program. Finally, the implementation of a literature-based approach requires curriculum support from the school principal and financial support from the school district.

Adapting the Literature-Based Approach to Meet Program Needs

If you, for any reason, are unable to implement a full-fledged literature-based approach, you can adapt the literature-based approach for use with basal programs (Fawson & Reutzel, 2000). Begin by building a collection of literature based on the excerpts used in your basal reading program. For example, if an excerpt is used from *Julie of the Wolves* (George, 1972), locate or purchase a paperback copy of the book for your reading center, and encourage students to explore the characters and plot in depth. Also add books that engage the internal motivations of readers, and augment content area topics with children's and adolescent literature. For example, make it possible for children to explore the American Revolution through the eyes of Johnny Tremain (*Johnny Tremain,* Forbes, 1943); to live with Jeanne Wakatsuki in the Manzanar internment camp during World War II (*Farewell to Manzanar,* Houston & Houston, 1973); to experience the hopes and fears of Anne Frank (*Anne Frank: The Diary of a Young Girl,* Frank, 1967); or to enjoy the dreams of Cassie Louise Lightfoot, a young African-American girl living in New York City (*Tar Beach,* Ringgold, 1991).

the Highly Effective Teacher

> ➤ *Basal reader programs can be adapted to include literature-based instruction.*

Strategies in Use

Developing Planning Webs for Literature-Based Instruction

Ricardo Morris uses a literature-based approach in his second-grade classroom. He is developing lessons for a unit based on one of the core books in his literature collection, *Ira Sleeps Over* (Waber, 1972), which he thinks the students really will enjoy. Most of them have experienced nighttime fears, and the main character in the story conquers those fears through friendship.

Ricardo's first goal is to introduce students to the seven literary elements (character, setting, mood/tone, plot, point of view, theme, and genre), which will require a lot of concept development. Immediately, he can think of a million things to do, and he realizes he will have to choose carefully his question prompts, discussion topics, and classroom activities. As an initial guide to lesson planning, Ricardo sketches the planning web, showing the seven literary elements.

Another important goal is to connect the liter-

acy unit with other content areas. Ricardo and his colleagues in the school have made a commitment to providing a curriculum that is as thematically integrated as possible. The planning web showing interdisciplinary content reflects Ricardo's ideas for linking the literature selection to other subjects. He also makes a note to explore the possibility of using "fear" as an interdisciplinary theme—the students could study effects on heart rate and pupil size in science. Ricardo will talk to Colin and Nan about this during their team meeting.

Ricardo also double-checks the state standards for second-grade literacy learning. He designs another planning web for teaching reading and language arts skills.

Ricardo used the following letter code to show the type of activity he planned to use: I = introduction to the story; T = through the story; and B = beyond the story.

PLANNING WEB: LITERARY ELEMENTS   Example

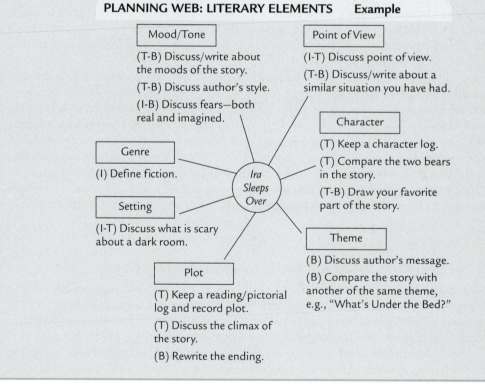

Mood/Tone
(T-B) Discuss/write about the moods of the story.
(T-B) Discuss author's style.
(I-B) Discuss fears—both real and imagined.

Point of View
(I-T) Discuss point of view.
(T-B) Discuss/write about a similar situation you have had.

Genre
(I) Define fiction.

Setting
(I-T) Discuss what is scary about a dark room.

Ira Sleeps Over

Character
(T) Keep a character log.
(T) Compare the two bears in the story.
(T-B) Draw your favorite part of the story.

Theme
(B) Discuss author's message.
(B) Compare the story with another of the same theme, e.g., "What's Under the Bed?"

Plot
(T) Keep a reading/pictorial log and record plot.
(T) Discuss the climax of the story.
(B) Rewrite the ending.

PLANNING WEB: INTERDISCIPLINARY CONTENT   Example

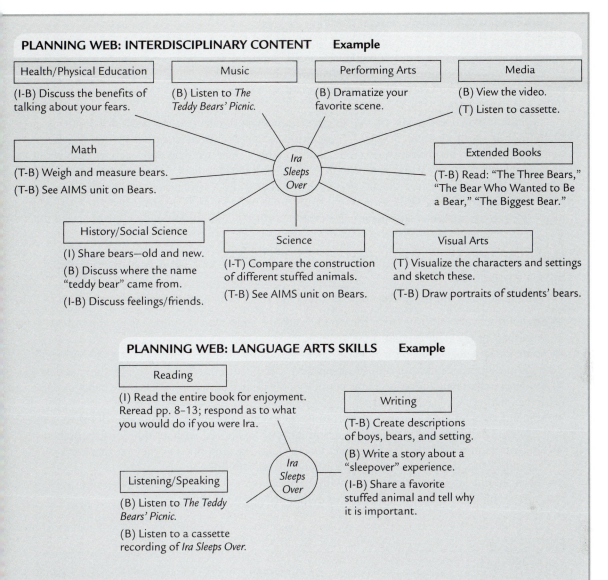

Health/Physical Education	Music	Performing Arts	Media
(I-B) Discuss the benefits of talking about your fears.	(B) Listen to *The Teddy Bears' Picnic*.	(B) Dramatize your favorite scene.	(B) View the video. (T) Listen to cassette.

Math
(T-B) Weigh and measure bears.
(T-B) See AIMS unit on Bears.

Ira Sleeps Over

Extended Books
(T-B) Read: "The Three Bears," "The Bear Who Wanted to Be a Bear," "The Biggest Bear."

History/Social Science
(I) Share bears—old and new.
(B) Discuss where the name "teddy bear" came from.
(I-B) Discuss feelings/friends.

Science
(I-T) Compare the construction of different stuffed animals.
(T-B) See AIMS unit on Bears.

Visual Arts
(T) Visualize the characters and settings and sketch these.
(T-B) Draw portraits of students' bears.

PLANNING WEB: LANGUAGE ARTS SKILLS   Example

Reading
(I) Read the entire book for enjoyment. Reread pp. 8–13; respond as to what you would do if you were Ira.

Ira Sleeps Over

Writing
(T-B) Create descriptions of boys, bears, and setting.
(B) Write a story about a "sleepover" experience.
(I-B) Share a favorite stuffed animal and tell why it is important.

Listening/Speaking
(B) Listen to *The Teddy Bears' Picnic*.
(B) Listen to a cassette recording of *Ira Sleeps Over*.

Planning webs reprinted with permission of Cooperative County Course of Study, 1989–1994. California Association of County Superintendents of Schools.

CRITICAL THINKING

1. What are some benefits of using planning webs in literature-based instruction? How could you use planning webs with the other approaches to literacy instruction?

2. What specific objectives or performance outcomes would you develop for each of Ricardo's goals?

3. How would you change Ricardo's planning web for interdisciplinary content to reflect a theme of friendship? a theme of fears?

4. Why does Ricardo have to be concerned with the state's framework for skills instruction?

5. How can Ricardo best coordinate his classroom observations and assessments of students' progress toward all three goals?

The Language-Based Approach

The language-based approach, introduced in Chapter 1, considers reading and writing skills as highly interrelated and best developed in the social context of the classroom. The primary goal is to develop students' active meaning construction through both reading and writing. This close connection between writing and reading as process is evident in Atwell's "What authors do" list (Figure 12.7 see below).

Specific instructional goals of the language-based approach focus on skill development in such areas as word identification and recognition, comprehension, vocabulary, oral language, written expression, literature, study skills, and thinking processes. The approach to developing these skills differs significantly from the preselected skill development found in the basal reader approach. In the language-based classroom, the teacher is the instructional decision-maker who plans the goals and objectives, creates the learning environment, and designs instruction that will foster skills in the authentic social context of the classroom (Church, 1994; Gavelek et al., 2000).

Underlying Beliefs and Assumptions about Literacy Learning in the Language-Based Approach

The language-based approach rests on the following beliefs and assumptions:

- Students actively seek to extend their own language and literacy abilities as they interact with their physical and social environments.
- Students' language and literacy development is socially mediated through on-going interactions and transactions with other learners and with proficient language and literacy models.
- Students acquire and develop fluent literacy as they participate and use literate behaviors in active, naturalistic learning events.
- Students transfer language and literacy abilities to, and reintegrate them with, all other learning. Language and literacy instruction must be integrated with all other instruction.
- Students acquire and develop language, literacy, and learning skills as they participate in learning events that incorporate language and literacy abilities.
- When specific language and literacy skills are needed for continuing development, these skills should be taught in the context of authentic learning events.

FIGURE 12.7

What Authors Do

Writers:

- Rehearse: develop an idea, perhaps make notes or lists or try different leads
  - Draft one and read, revise, confer
    - (Maybe) draft two and read, revise, confer . . .
      - Decide the content is set
        - Polish: final word choices, clarification, tightening
          - Final, formal editing for conventions
            - Peer editing, if you wish
              - Submit to an outside editor (e.g., the teacher)
                - Create a final copy
                  - Proofread
                    - Publish

Reprinted by permission from *In the Middle: New Understandings About Writing, Reading, and Learning,* 2/e by Nancie Atwell. Copyright © 1998 by Nancie Atwell. Published by Heinemann, a division of Reed Elsevier Inc., Portsmouth, NH. All rights reserved.

Implementing the Language-Based Approach

Instructional strategies in the language-based approach must engage student background knowledge and help students actively construct meaning using relevant literacy events in the social context of the classroom. These strategies are meaning process–driven rather than content–driven. The content, however, must be relevant to the background knowledge, cognitive and social development, age, and interests of students. Literature and informational books are a valuable resource, and language-based instruction may be developed around specific pieces of literature. Peer reading, reading-response groups, writing workshop, theme cycles, and project-based writing are all consistent with the language-based philosophy.

> *The language-based approach is meaning process–driven.*

Classroom events of all kinds provide contexts for reading and writing—writing to pen pals on the Internet, planning a field trip, publishing a classroom newsletter, or conducting a student-initiated investigation into a local or a regional issue. Any event relevant to the lives of your students is a potential vehicle for literacy instruction. At the same time, language-based instruction requires careful attention to planning and fulfillment.

> What events are used for literacy instruction in the language-based approach?

Organization and Management of the Language-Based Classroom

Language-based instruction requires considerable teacher-developed organization and input, because there is no one right way to construct a language-based classroom. There are no instructional algorithms or pat answers, no scope and sequence charts, and no teacher's guides. Most language-based classrooms are bustling with activity in centers or project areas stocked with materials for literacy—books, magazines, paper, writing utensils, staplers, paper clips, paste, tape, word processors, and other reading and writing materials. Figure 12.8 (page 364) suggests a floor plan for a language-based classroom.

> Why do language-based classrooms sometimes seem noisy or chaotic?

Language-based classrooms often resemble classrooms for early and beginning readers, because this approach requires similar accommodations for movement and activity, exploration, and the hustle-bustle of productions, constructions, and projects. The room layout must provide for clearly defined pathways, plenty of storage space, a ready water supply, and lots of space where children can spread out and work without crowding one another. One or more computers and a printer are important resources in language-based classrooms.

Large Blocks of Writing Time

Activity- and project-based instruction requires large blocks of time for students to engage in extended exploration and sharing. As you can see from the daily class schedule in Table 12.3 (page 365), language-based classroom days pivot around three large blocks of working time. In the example, three focused activities occupy these blocks of time: theme-cycle projects (8:35–9:30), writing workshop (10:30–11:30), and activity time (12:50–1:50). When students are given forty-five minutes to an hour to work in groups or individually, the work must have definition, specific goals and plans, and accountability throughout. The schedule will need to be adjusted for different age and grade levels, different activities, and even different days. For example, larger blocks of time may be needed when students are bringing their projects to a close, and very young students may need smaller blocks of time to work effectively in groups.

> *Language-based approaches work best with block scheduling.*

Reflections, Feedback, and Goal Setting

Surrounding the large blocks of working time should be short, to-the-point discussions of what groups are planning to accomplish and have accomplished each day. These status-of-the-group or status-of-the-class roll calls are guided by questions such as "What are your plans for today?" and "Where are you in that planning now?" and are recorded in the Discussion Record Form (see Figure 8.6, page 232). Slightly longer reflection periods following group work give groups and individuals an opportunity to monitor their progress ("What did we accomplish today?") and share with other students and the teacher what they've found in their research or specific problems they're encountering. Analytical discussions of this kind increase students' ability to self-monitor their progress and develop their planning and strategic inquiry skills. They also keep you informed of students' progress for purposes of assessment.

> How can you keep track of student progress in a language-based classroom?

FIGURE 12.8

Physical Organization of the Language-Based Classroom

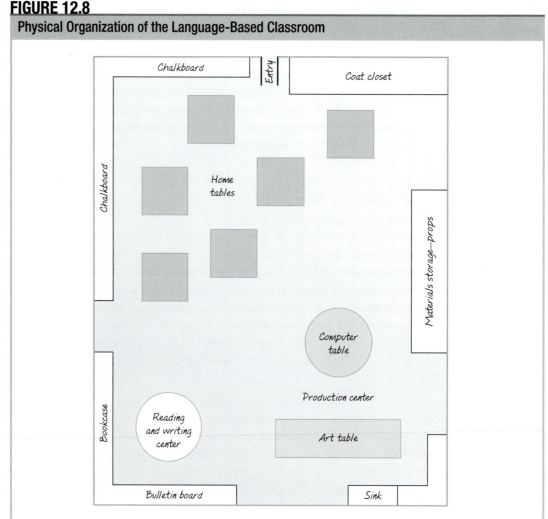

the
**Highly
Effective
Teacher**

| What does it
mean to be
consistent?

➤ *In language-
based classrooms,
exploration and
self-directed
inquiry are of
paramount
importance.*

Creating the Environment for Learning

One of the great advantages of the language-based approach is that students' interests and self-determined inquiry questions and concerns are the central focus of what goes on in the classroom. Thus, their natural curiosity and need to know help guide activity in the classroom in positive and productive ways. Keep in mind, however, that natural curiosity and inquiry will not overcome a capricious or chaotic environment. Students require a certain amount of order and stability to function well. You, as the teacher, are responsible for seeing that an orderly and stable environment exists in your classroom, by carefully planning instruction and by maintaining rules and routines that permit active learning.

You also create a stable classroom environment through consistency, which means that you respond to students today just as you did yesterday and will tomorrow; and that whatever the rules and routines are, you follow them today as you did yesterday and will tomorrow. Research provides ample evidence (for better or for worse) that children readily adapt to any teaching style as long as they can depend on its constancy.

The learning environment in a language-based classroom, where exploration and self-directed inquiry are of paramount importance, must be accepting of missteps and mistakes. Inappropriate decisions and behavior must be dealt with and then forgotten so that language-based learning can move forward.

TABLE 12.3

Organization of the Classroom Day for the Language-Based Approach

8:15–8:30	*Attendance, opening, poetry/song.*
8:30–8:35	*Status-of-the-group roll call—theme cycle units:* Check with each group leader about plans for the day and what the group expects to accomplish.
8:35–9:30	*Theme-cycle projects:* Each group is engaged in inquiry and research on the topic and issues selected.
9:30–9:45	*Projects meeting—whole class:* Groups discuss accomplishments of the day, assistance they need, and plans for tomorrow.
9:45–10:15	*Book clubs:* Small groups and partners gather to share good books. Special-interest groups (e.g., comic book collectors, mystery buffs) are encouraged.
10:15–10:30	*Snack, recess.*
10:30–10:45	*Writing workshop mini-lesson, status-of-the-class roll call.*
10:45–11:30	*Writing time, conferences.*
11:30–11:50	*Sharing time, Author's Chair.*
11:50–12:30	*Lunch, recess.*
12:30–12:50	*Story time:* Read to students.
12:50–1:50	*M, T, Th, F—Activity centers:* Groups engage in problem solving involving math, science, social studies, art, or language arts. Children work in two centers each day.
	W—Library.
1:50–2:15	*M, W—Music.*
	T, Th, F—Physical education.
2:15–2:45	*M, W—Recess 2:15–2:30; free activity 2:30–2:45.*
	T, Th, F—Free activity: Students read, write in journals, share a book or some writing with a friend, do follow-up project work, listen to music, or use the art center.
2:45–3:10	*End-of-day reflections:* Whole group shares a story/song.
3:10	*Dismissal.*

Fostering Independence

In the language-based classroom, students need to become increasingly independent in planning and directing their own learning. The most powerful lessons in independence occur when they observe you as you use questioning and thinking strategies for self-direction. Through example, you teach students that "What am I doing?" and "Where am I going with it?" are important questions to ask in the process of reaching one's goal. Just as important are conversations in which you guide groups through reflective problem solving ("Now what are you going to do about that?") and brainstorming ("What if you . . . ?") to seek possible solutions to a problem. Students will rapidly adopt the self-directed problem-solution processes you model.

Strengths and Limitations of the Language-Based Approach

Like the literature-based approach, the language-based approach provides broad instructional freedom for teachers. Both novice and expert teachers encounter language-based approaches in university-based teacher education and master's programs.

the★
**Highly
Effective
Teacher**
★

How do
language-based
routines foster
reflection and
problem solving?

> *Language-based programs can be adapted to include instruction in word identification skills.*

A limitation of the language-based approach is the need for block scheduling, which school districts may not be able or willing to accommodate. Another limitation of the language-based approach is one of its greatest strengths: the teacher commitment required to create and implement this approach in the classroom (Church, 1994). Time, energy, teaching experience, and a thorough knowledge of language and literacy development are critical to creating and implementing a successful language-based program. Teachers also need to be able to target specific skills for development as needed in the context of students' authentic reading and writing activities (Strickland, 1994/1995). Careful observation and record keeping are required to know which students need what skills instruction.

Adapting the Language-Based Approach

Your commitment to creating and implementing a language-based classroom may be limited because of time and instructional preparation constraints, lack of administrative support, or a variety of other reasons. These limitations need not hinder you from using the meaning-construction philosophy of the language-based approach in your teaching. Understanding the interrelationships of reading, writing, speaking, listening, and thinking—as well as the role of background knowledge and experiences, social interactions, and reader-writer transactions with text—remains critical to your students' literacy development.

> *Basal reader programs can be adapted to include student-directed components of the language-based approach.*

For example, assume that you are using a basal reader approach but want to incorporate aspects of a language-based approach. To that end, you have the option of retaining, decreasing, or even eliminating parts of the basal instructional program. For example, you might use the reading selections in the basal reader but introduce a language-based emphasis by forming reading-response groups and allowing each group to construct its own themed unit, for which students choose the selections they wish to read. These experiences then could be connected to writing development through Literature-Response Journals or the writing workshop. Many opportunities exist to alter and shape instructional experiences and to emphasize or deemphasize aspects of skill development with your students.

Evaluation of Instructional and Supplementary Programs

Whatever instructional approach you use, the evaluation and selection of instructional materials can have a major impact on your teaching. Most instructional programs today are selected by teacher committees, which hold the power to choose materials and make adoption recommendations. Imagine yourself in this role, and ask "What do I look for in evaluating publisher- produced programs being considered for adoption in my school or school district?" You must be able to identify key criteria that can be used in this process, such as those listed in Table 12.4 (page 368).

> What textbooks have been adopted in your state for the grade levels you plan to teach?

The textbook adoption process varies from state to state and district to district across the nation. About half the states, including California and Texas, use State Department of Education criteria and adopt new textbooks on a cycle of every five to six years. The remaining states, including Ohio and Illinois, are known as "open territory" states. Although they may offer general recommendations, they leave discussions about the adoption process and the adoption cycle to local school districts. Publishers are closely attuned to this process and often encourage school districts to pilot instructional programs at various grade levels shortly in advance of the adoption cycle. Publishers also lobby teachers, curriculum coordinators, administrators, and State Department of Education personnel.

> **supplementary programs**
> reading instruction programs that focus on a particular skill, enrichment, or a specific area

Many programs are published each year to supplement reading instruction. **Supplementary programs,** which usually are narrow in focus, are basically of three types, designed to meet perceived special needs. The first type is a program in a discrete skill area such as phonics, study skills, or comprehension. The second is a program designed for enrichment, exemplified by activities based on specific literature selections. The third is a program designed for a specific area, such as bilingual, gifted, or special education. These supplementary programs usually follow a workbook format and include a brief teacher's guide. Some programs, however, are in kit form and have audiotape and videotape materials, and include DVDs, CD-ROMs, and Web-based activities.

How to Do . . .

Designing a Comprehensive Instructional Program through Adaptation

Adapting the Basal Reader Approach

1. Reject components of the program that do not meet your students' instructional needs and interests.
2. Selectively interrelate reading, writing, speaking, listening, and thinking and problem solving.
3. Add opportunities for social interactions, reading response, reader-writer transactions with text, and writing workshop.
4. Allow students to choose reading selections. Add opportunities for self-directed thematic learning.
5. Provide authentic contexts for skill instruction (e.g., teach skills in the context of literature).
6. Build a classroom collection of full-length basal literature and selections of interest to children. Selectively develop and incorporate literature-based thematic units.
7. Add opportunities for block-scheduled and technology-based learning.

Adapting the Literature-Based Approach

1. Add opportunities to learn word recognition and identification and other skills through systematic approaches. Selectively incorporate vocabulary development.
2. Add opportunities for student-directed exploration and integration of reading, writing, speaking, listening, and thinking and problem solving.
3. Add opportunities for block-scheduled and technology-based learning.

Adapting the Language-Based Approach

1. Selectively incorporate some high-interest basal reading materials or supplementary programs.
2. Add structured opportunities for skill instruction and vocabulary development.
3. Develop the classroom literature collection, and incorporate literature-based thematic units.

■ **Individualize the delayed reader's program by selecting from the elements of each program type (basal, literature-based, language-based) that best match the student's *most critical* needs. The basis of these decisions should be assessments and observations. Several delayed readers in your class may have overlapping needs; if instruction is matched to these needs, then you are individualizing instruction even if it is carried out with more than one student. It is important to place the delayed reader in material at his or her instructional (*not* frustration) level; otherwise, progress is unlikely to occur despite other learning activities that you provide.**

DELAYED READER ADAPTATION

You will need to exercise care in selecting a supplementary program, as they vary greatly in the quality of the activities. The following are some key questions you need to ask in this selection process:

■ Do the instructional objectives of the program meet my students' needs? Your answer should be based on careful examination of the student materials.
■ Are the activities presented in an attractive and appealing format that teaches, reinforces skills, and requires meaning construction on the part of my students? If activities are developed in a formulaic manner requiring little thinking, they will not stimulate student growth.
■ Can the program be integrated with ease into the main instructional approach I am currently using?
■ How does the cost of the program compare to the cost of other instructional materials that would be of value in my classroom? For example, should I spend the money on this supplementary program or buy more paperback literature selections? Is the program cost-effective enough to warrant sacrificing some of these other materials?

the Highly Effective Teacher

➤ *Guidelines for Selecting Supplementary Programs*

TABLE 12.4

Instructional Program Evaluation Checklist

Evaluator _____   Date _____

Name of Program _____

Title(s) of Level(s) _____

Recommended Grade Level _____

Specific Materials Examined: Teacher Manual _____, Student Text _____,

Workbook _____, Other Material _____

Criteria	Poor		Rating		Outstanding
1. Informed philosophy (word identification? comprehension? engagement? meaning-based?)	1	2	3	4	5
2. Evidence of research and theory base	1	2	3	4	5
3. Range of objectives (beginning literacy, comprehension, vocabulary, literature and reader response, word identification, writing, reading and writing across content, technology)	1	2	3	4	5
4. Range of needs and interests provided for by instructional strategies and activities	1	2	3	4	5
5. Quality of literature and informational selections, cultural and ethnic diversity, gender role models, and other forms of diversity	1	2	3	4	5
6. Potential of materials and activities, including the Internet, for developing motivation and interest	1	2	3	4	5
7. Quality and ease of use of teacher's guide	1	2	3	4	5
8. Recognition of importance of informal observation and ongoing evaluation	1	2	3	4	5
9. Adaptability of program to your instructional philosophy	1	2	3	4	5
10. Potential of program to be used effectively	1	2	3	4	5

Total ratings for program_____

Summary observations:

You will find that a number of supplementary programs, including those offered in disk or CD-ROM formats, can indeed enhance special areas of your reading program.

Technology-Based Instruction

In the twenty-first century, technology will have an increasing influence on classroom instruction (Leu et al., 2004; Smolin & Lawless, 2003; Sutherland-Smith, 2002; Wepner et al., 2000). Technology-rich environments can and will provide the means for students to work cooperatively on computers and the Internet, using theme-based projects; to enter a multitude of contexts and content research through computer-based reading and writing; and to engage in a variety of conversations on the Internet and through e-mail (Coiro & Dobler, 2007; Leu & Leu, 2000; Leu et al., 2004).

How to Do . . .

Evaluation of Instructional Programs

1. Is it the philosophy of the program to integrate reading and writing processes with meaning-centered strategies and activities that encourage active meaning construction on the part of students?

2. Does the program reflect the latest theories and research on literacy development?

3. Do the objectives of the program account for important areas of literacy development, including beginning reading and writing, comprehension, vocabulary, literature and reader response, word recognition and identification, writing, and reading and writing across content areas?

4. Are the objectives of the program clearly developed through instructional strategies and activities that are appropriate and suitable for a range of students' needs and interests?

5. Does the program include high-quality literature and informational material that will appeal to students? Is the literature altered to provide for a lower readability level, or is it the original text? Are any full-length original stories and illustrations presented in the material? Do the literature selections reflect cultural and ethnic diversity? varied gender role models? other kinds of diversity?

6. Do the materials and instructional activities hold potential for developing students' motivation and interest?

7. Are the teacher's guides written clearly and in a format that can be used with ease? Do they contain annotated pages from the student text? from the workbook?

8. Does the program recognize the importance of informal observation and ongoing evaluation of individual students? Are parts of the program adaptable to portfolio assessment?

9. Is the program organized in such a way that you can adapt it to your own instructional philosophy by selecting units or unit portions instead of following the program lesson by lesson and unit by unit to the end, as prescribed by the publisher?

10. Do you believe that you can use the program effectively and integrate it into your own instructional approach?

- **Supplementary materials for delayed readers vary widely in quality. In addition to the questions posed for all programs, ask (a) Does the program furnish much opportunity for the delayed reader to read in regular, connected text (in addition to specific skills and strategy work)? (b) Is the material suitable for the delayed reader's maturity level (in terms of topic, print size, and pictures)? (c) Is the material a good choice for initial learning, or is it better for practice? (d) Is the material designed correctly? Does it really teach or merely test?**

DELAYED READER ADAPTATION

Over the past decade, more and more classrooms and homes have acquired access to computers, the Internet, and e-mail. Over an eight-year period, from 1994 to 2002, Internet access in classrooms increased dramatically from 3 percent to 92 percent (National Center for Educational Statistics, 2003).

A recent study sponsored by the Henry J. Kaiser Family Foundation (Kopytoff, 2004) found that 96 percent of all students between the ages of 8 and 18 have been online at least once. This finding was in contrast to a U.S. Department of Education Study in 2001 that indicated that only 60 percent of students had used the Internet.

By 2004, almost 75 percent of all homes reported that Internet access was available (Coiro & Dobler, 2007). The more recent Kaiser study indicates that home access to the Internet has increased; however, the level of access varies by ethnic group. While 80 percent of Caucasian families have Internet access at home, only 67 percent of Hispanic American families and 61 percent of African American families have similar access. The effect on student use of the Internet is striking. Ninety-four percent of students age 12 to 17 who had Internet access reported that they used the Internet for school-related research (Lenhart, Simon, & Graziano, 2001).

You probably will have several computers available in your classroom or school to supplement your reading and writing instruction. With access to technology and the Internet, the key issue you will confront is deciding how to integrate computer use into the curriculum with the instructional approaches and strategies that meet the varied needs and interests of your students (Carroll, 2004; Leu & Leu, 2000; Leu et al., 2004; Smolin & Lawless, 2003; Sutherland-Smith, 2002).

Underlying Beliefs and Assumptions about Computer-Based Literacy Learning

In making decisions about how to use technology, you must consider the underlying rationale for doing so. Carroll (2004) identifies two basic reasons for using technology in literacy development: It contributes to the development of children's ability to (1) reflect on language and (2) consider multiple meaning perspectives.

> *Ability to Reflect on Language*

The development of the ability to reflect on language occurs as children attempt to make sense of language and interact with different forms of print, which include the graphic features of print, the alphabetic principle, spelling, and orthographic structure. Throughout the process of language development (see Chapter 2 pages 39–43), students change or adjust current hypotheses to accommodate new knowledge. These adjustments come about as they reflect on language. In reading, adjustment happens as the student reads a word and realizes that it doesn't make sense; in writing, it occurs as a student reads aloud what he or she has written and realizes that the words have not captured the intended meaning.

As students write, they begin to try to match the print meanings and graphics in a more precise manner, and they begin to experience the tensions that exist between intended meanings and those articulated through symbolic forms (Carroll, 2004). At these moments, students are searching for some sort of equivalence—that is, trying to create and use symbols that capture their intended meaning. This also happens as they reflect on language, trying to understand the role of language in their own lives and how to use these growing understandings.

> *Ability to Develop Multiple Perspectives*

The development of the ability to use multiple perspectives to express meaning is facilitated as students begin to use a number of different symbol systems, including art, music, dance, numbers, drama, and language. Learning to think about ideas from a variety of perspectives and to express ideas in a variety of forms is a critical part of the development of higher-level thinking. It is important that students be able to consider multiple meaning perspectives for the purpose of increasing their ability to construct full, rich meaning from text and to create and express their own understandings.

The benefits of computer-based technology use in literacy instruction are expressed by the following five principles (Carroll, 1997).

> *Principles for Using Technology in Literacy Instruction*

1. Technology can assist students in moving easily among and across symbol systems to construct meaning. As students engage in the social construction of meaning, they often make use of a variety of symbol systems. Access to computer-based technology gives them the opportunity to freely explore and manipulate different systems, such as print, illustrations, and art. This, in turn, enhances reflection on these systems and understanding of the ways in which different forms of expression represent meaning (Carroll, 2004). In addition, the teacher is able to see how sense making is occurring from the student's point of view and can use this knowledge to inform her or his own instructional goals for particular students.

> *Authoring Software*

   Software that allows students to move between making symbols with artistic tools (such as paintbrushes, different design patterns, or clip-art icons) and with word-processing tools (such as the keyboard, different fonts, picture rotations, and letter stamps) facilitates the process of authorship. In addition to using drawing and letters and words, a student can use music and mathematical expressions and can explore dimensions of shape, line, color, and form. The student as author can manipulate different forms of symbolic representation and reflect on these representations to discover other ways to express meaning.

2. Technology can serve as an engaging resource that encourages experimentation and meaning construction within different contexts of learning. The use of technology can promote and sustain students' interest in literacy activities (Carroll, 2004; Coiro & Dobler, 2007). School purposes and instructional stances often change the flavor of a young student's initial experiences with print. An emphasis on the literal and efferent instructional stance (which focuses

on the retention of specific bits of information), rather than on an aesthetic and higher-level thinking stance, may take the pleasure out of reading and writing. If the student is unable to make personal connections with what he or she is reading or writing and does not become engaged in the process, much of the intrinsic motivation to pursue reading and writing activities becomes lost.

▶ *Technology and Intrinsic Motivation*

A great variety of software programs embed reading, writing, and critical-thinking activities in multisensory scenarios of high interest to students. For the younger student, talking picture books—software that replicates paper books on the computer screen, usually with the addition of speech feedback and animation—can be a valuable resource in literacy development. The student is given the choice of having the entire book read aloud or selecting different words to be pronounced. Some programs contain options enabling the student to explore and construct meaning from the text in many different ways; for example, he or she might hear music by clicking on a particular part of an illustration or obtain new information by clicking on window shutters. Talking picture books provide a multitude of visual, semantic, syntactic, and phonic cues at a high level of engagement (De Jong & Bus, 2004).

▶ *Talking Picture Books*

The Internet may be used by the student who already is reading, to search out and pursue specific areas of interest in depth. Online, students can find pictures, music, movies, articles, maps—a great variety of resources that otherwise would not be readily available to them. E-mail and Web sites can be used to communicate with others who are knowledgeable about topics of mutual interest.

▶ *The Internet*

This independent pursuit of self-selected areas of interest can have a powerful effect on learning. Knowledge is constructed through multiple perspectives as learners become aware that there are many ways to access information and to use language.

3. Technology can support a cooperative-learning environment. Used in a cooperative-learning environment, technology can provide for collaborative, student-centered, project-based activities and encourage shared authority (Carroll, 2004; Coiro & Dobler, 2007). The teacher is seen as a facilitator of knowledge to assist students in the construction of meaning, rather than as a transmitter of knowledge (Molinelli, 2000).

▶ *Cooperative Learning and Exploration*

Using technology as a means of peer-mediated exploration frees the student from depending on the teacher as the sole source of information and permits exploration of multiple viewpoints. For example, collaborative writing on the computer provides a context in which students can increase their awareness of language and writing. As they work collaboratively to develop understanding of how language works, they are forced to make what they know explicit. This occurs as they talk to each other about what they are writing, and it enhances their ability to reflect on language and consider another person's perspective.

In the cooperative-learning environment, students pursue avenues of inquiry independently. They can search the Web and CD-ROM encyclopedias to gain access to information that is not easily available to them in a traditional classroom setting. They might access historical documents, full-length literary classics, photographs of art in museums, or videotapes of an archaeological expedition. They might visit the sites of the National Geographic Society, the Library of Congress, or NASA's Challenger Space Center. These resources can then be incorporated into collaborative writing events. As students pursue areas of inquiry that are of high interest to them personally, their sense of involvement in and ownership of literacy processes increases.

4. Technology can provide a means for popular culture to become part of the classroom learning experiences by fostering the development of critical-thinking skills using authentic resources. Technology can connect a student's personal life experiences with classroom experiences. The development of a peer culture, which is based on elements of popular culture, is an important part of a child's experience. The use of technology facilitates the integration of the out-of-school, popular culture with instructional experiences. Popular culture includes characters and events based on movies, television, and sports. Students can make use of these authentic resources in technology-based reading and writing experiences and beginning research.

▶ *Popular Peer Culture and Other Authentic Resources*

5. Technology can provide opportunities for a students to engage in three key processes—inquiry, authorship, and ownership—that enhance their ability to reflect on language and

▶ *Inquiry, Authorship, and Ownership*

consider multiple perspectives. The process of inquiry is facilitated because technology provides a medium through which students are able to easily explore a wide variety of contexts. Technology facilitates the process of authorship by enabling them to express meaning in new ways (see further discussion of authorship under principle 1; Weston & Ingram, 1997). And it facilitates the process of ownership by allowing students to make choices and to create personally meaningful expressions as they interact within a wide range of multisensory literacy contexts. Multimedia programs, PowerPoint presentation software, and Web site authoring tools involve students in all three processes.

Instructional Uses of Technology in Students' Literacy Development

Technology-based instruction can serve a number of important functions in literacy development. In addition to playing the role of tutor in special skill areas such as word recognition and identification, vocabulary, and comprehension development, the computer can be the instructional medium for activities such as story writing, researching, e-mailing, and Web authoring. A wide variety of instructional software and Web sites are available (Carroll, 2004; Taylor, 2004; Wepner, Valmont, & Thurlow, 2000). Some programs merely resemble worksheets found in basal or supplementary workbooks. Although computerized worksheets evaluate students' answers and provide feedback, the worksheets themselves may be almost as boring on the computer screen as in print. However, some highly structured drill-and-skill software is useful for some students with special needs. A number of programs and Web sites that can support literacy instruction and have action appeal are listed in Figure 12.9.

FIGURE 12.9
Examples of Instructional Software

Reading Emphasis

Reading Blaster (Davidson & Associates). Emphasis ranges from letter recognition to antonyms and synonyms. In games in which words have been stolen from Earth, the child's task is to recover the stolen words.

Writing Advantage (Innovative Software Corporation). Multiple approaches are used to teach vocabulary. Lessons are adjusted based on student progress.

Beginning Reading (BrightStar). Emphasis is on word construction from word parts and use of context.

Mercer Mayer's Just Grandma and Me (Living Books: A Random House-Broderbund Company). This CD-ROM incorporates sound effects, music, humor, and animation into an interactive story experience for young children to enjoy in English, Spanish, and Japanese.

Writing Emphasis

Kidworks 2 (Davidson & Associates). Designed for the primary grades, this program combines word processing with a paint program. It also has speech capabilities for reading students' stories aloud.

Kid Pix 2 (Broderbund Software). This software gives children access to both artistic tools and word processing tools, including paintbrushes, drawing pencils, clip-art icons, keyboard fonts, letter stamps, and editing functions.

Orly's Draw a Story (Broderbund Software). Students create drawings that are incorporated into the scenes and stories on the screen and become animated.

Storybook Theatre (Sunburst). Students create multimedia stories using project suggestions and a collection of photographs, sounds, and text.

Storybook Weaver (MECC). Graphics and word processing tools assist students in developing illustrated text.

Reading and Writing Emphasis: Web Sites

www.ed.gov/pubs/CompactforReading/tablek.html
 Contains school-home links and reading and literacy skills activities for beginning levels. Can download a section or individual activities.

www.starfall.com/
 Creative Web site to assist in reading and literacy instruction. Interactive books with sound are available.

www.theschoolbell.com/Links/Dolch/Dolch.html; click on the Dolch Kit.
 Many practice games and activities are available to help students learn the Dolch word list of 220 high-frequency words that should be recognized at sight to increase reading fluency.

www.manatee.k12.fl.us/sites/elementary/palmasola/rcompindex1.htm
 Early literacy level reading workshop for parents and teachers that begins with phonemic awareness and a variety of games and stories.

FIGURE 12.10

Example of a CD-ROM Screen Page from *Mud Puddle*

🔊 Her mother
picked her up,
took off all her
clothes and
dropped her into a
tub of water.
🔊 She scrubbed
Jule Ann till she
was red all over.

Mud Puddle

Used with permission from Dreamcatcher Interactive Inc.

A valuable asset to your classroom is a **CD-ROM** (compact disk–read only memory) drive. As the name suggests, this hardware reads information stored on a disk that cannot be overwritten. Electronic books such as Mercer Mayer's *Just Grandma and Me* and *Mud Puddle* from Dreamcatcher Interactive Inc. are available in CD-ROM format (Figure 12.10). These books can be used interactively by students, who click on "hot spots" that provide responses. For example, clicking on a knothole in a tree may cause a squirrel to peek out and run around the tree trunk (Willis, Stephens, & Matthew, 1996). This type of interaction provides high interest for students (De Jong & Bus, 2004). CD-ROM applications also include resource texts such as the *New Grolier Multimedia Encyclopedia,* which incorporates the twenty-one volumes of the *Academic American Encyclopedia* and eight thousand photographs and illustrations along with video clips and sounds (Merrill et al., 1996). Electronic encyclopedias add great interest for the beginning researcher.

The Internet consists of all the computers around the world that are connected to one another at any given time (Leu & Leu, 2000). With a desktop computer, monitor, and telephone line, you can connect your classroom to the world. Increasingly, schools are wiring classrooms to the school district's main computer and then linking up with the World Wide Web through telephone or cable. Software programs known as Web browsers let you conduct a topic search or go directly to a specific site by typing in the address. You can send an e-mail message to anyone in the world, acquire information, communicate with others who share a similar interest, download new software, conduct a video conference, or publish a page on the Web for your school or your class.

Once your classroom is connected to the Internet, you will find the addresses in Figure 12.11 (page 376) of value (Leu & Leu, 2000). This list is only the beginning. You and your students will find many exciting places to go on the Internet and will discover many ways to integrate this valuable resource into your curriculum.

CD-ROM
compact disk–read only memory; a type of disk containing information that can be read but not overwritten

➤ *Electronic Books and Encyclopedias*

➤ *With a computer, monitor, and telephone line, you can connect your classroom to the world.*

Strategies in Use

Connecting Technology and Literacy

Joan Laurel's fourth-grade students are working on an interdisciplinary thematic unit titled "Celebrations and Carbonation." Joan's plan is to use her classroom computers and the school's Internet connection to study the topic of bubbles from a variety of perspectives. She designed this thematic unit to incorporate several curriculum areas, including science, social studies, mathematics, art, music, and language arts. She felt that bubbles would fascinate budding scientists and inspire student poets at the same time. She integrated this unit into a larger theme of multicultural celebrations. The whole class unit-ending project will be designing a Web page.

This morning, Joan divides her class into two groups—the Scientific Observers and the Creative Story Writers. After moving the class outdoors, she asks the groups to observe her blowing bubbles. Group members focus on this event as either scientists or story writers. They return to the classroom to discuss their observations.

The Scientific Observers try to figure out why bubbles pop.

"I think they pop when they hit something in the air," says Ben.

"I don't think so," Ellen replies. "There has to be something larger than air particles that would make them pop."

Ben and Ellen decide to log on to the Internet to do a keyword search for scientific experiments with bubbles. They begin at the Web site of the children's science museum in their area.

Joan's class has been corresponding by e-mail with keypals in New Hampshire who are also working on carbonation. Deborah, Michael, and Janine decide to brainstorm a list of possible explanations of why bubbles pop and send it to their friends in New Hampshire to get their reactions. Together, they will propose theories and experiments to try to figure out the scientific principles that explain why bubbles pop.

Maria joins the Scientific Observers group and suggests that they use the multimedia CD-ROM encyclopedia to check on the ideas they have developed so far (evaporation, dirt, and gravity). While Michael and Janine are e-mailing, Deborah and Maria begin their own investigation. Ben and Ellen continue browsing the Internet for more information.

The information gathered by the group is typed into their learning log, which they update on the computer at the end of each day. Joan reviews a printout of their log updates after school.

Meanwhile, the Creative Story Writers are making use of a software program that provides artistic tools and word-processing functions. Four students

Integrating Technology in Your Classroom

As you integrate use of the Internet into your classroom, you will find that scheduling computer time for students will be important. This can be accomplished through a simple schedule, with days of the week across the top and times of the day down the left margin. Children's names or names of partner teams can then be entered into the appropriate time slots.

To make effective use of technology in your classroom, you will need to become familiar with the resources available to you (De Jong & Bus, 2004; Leu & Leu, 2000; Taylor, 2004). As you become familiar with these resources, you can decide how technology can support your instructional goals (Carroll, 2004; Coiro & Dobler, 2007; Leu & Leu, 2000; Wepner, Valmont, & Thurlow, 2000). For example, if you are preparing a unit on a particular topic— tornadoes and hurricanes, bats, California Missions, the United Nations—you will be able to search a variety of databases, documents, and images to develop the unit and guide student explorations. You also can communicate online with other teachers to share ideas and resources.

➤ *You must decide how technology can support your instructional goals.*

Evaluating Software Programs

A major issue in integrating technology is how to select software to use with your students. The key questions discussed earlier with respect to the selection of supplementary programs apply to the selection of computer software. Features that are unique to software selection include com-in this group pair up in order to work collaboratively, while Samantha and Beth each choose to work alone.

Joan has noticed that sometimes Beth is hesitant to begin writing. Joan previously downloaded a list of books and videos on the topic of bubbles and found five of them in the school library, including a talking picture book. She brings them to Beth and suggests that she might want to look at them. "I saw this video at my friend Laura's house," Beth exclaims. "It's about a magician who blows bubbles in his show!" She is eager to find out more.

Samantha decides to draw bubbles on the screen and add background music. She selects a lively melody and fills the screen with small, softly brushed bubbles. Samantha is totally absorbed in what she is doing and doesn't seem to notice when some of the other children gather around her.

Lois and Joyce decide to write a play about bubbles. They visit a Web site they found previously when researching a new movie they were curious about; it shows them how scripts are written. They print out this information and work at Joyce's after school.

Les and Jerry want to write an adventure story about a bubble that escapes from the bubble factory. Les types the following sentence on the screen: "The bubble that was inside was left by himself and he was so lost that he asked the other one what to do."

"Who is he talking to, Les?" Jerry asks. "I don't understand who is lost."

"You know—the first one!" Les says.

"Les, *you* know who. But when I read this, I don't. You have to give them names or something to tell them apart."

"Okay," Les agrees. The boys continue their collaboration.

From Carroll, 1997.

CRITICAL THINKING

1. How are the technology-based instructional experiences in Joan's classroom developing students' ability to reflect on language and take multiple perspectives in constructing meaning?
2. How are inquiry, authorship, and ownership developed through these experiences?
3. How does technology-based instruction help Joan address students' individual strengths and needs?
4. How does Joan's technology-based unit stimulate internal reader motivations and higher-level thinking?
5. How does this technology-based unit provide practice in cooperative learning, problem solving, and reading and writing for a variety of purposes in authentic contexts?

patibility with your classroom computer, memory capacity required for the software to work properly, difficulty of keyboard use, and level of user-friendliness.

In selecting software, you also need to take into account a variety of important instructional and student-related issues. The checklist in Table 12.5 (see page 377) will help you identify important questions to consider in evaluating software. You may also want to check the Web site at www.economics.semo.edu/kidscomp/ for more details on software evaluation. Using the evaluation checklist in Table 12.5, you can identify the strengths and weaknesses of any given software program and determine what software to order for your reading and writing program.

the Highly Effective Teacher

➤ *A System for Rating Software*

Summary and Classroom Applications

double entry journal

Which approach to literacy instruction appeals to you the most? Where does it fit on the bottom-up–top-down continuum shown in Figure 12.1? What are the reasons for your choice? How would you use the Internet as part of your program?

FIGURE 12.11
Selected Internet Addresses for Classroom Use

Connecting Student Keypals

Good Keypal Site: ePALS Classroom Exchange.
　　http://epals.com/
Intercultural E-Mail Classroom Connections: Links to partners from different countries.
　　www.stolaf.edu/network/iecc/

Projects

Kid Projects: A place to visit projects at a variety of age levels.
　　http://telenaut.com/gst/
　　Click on Global Show-n-Tell Museum.
　　www.kids-space.org/
　　Click on Wings.

Educational Focus

A wide range of lesson plans on current topics.
　　www.nytimes.com/
　　Click on www.nytimes.com/learning/.
Early childhood Internet resources.
　　www.kiddyhouse.com/Early/earlykids.html
　　Click on LT Technologies.

Special Interest Focus Areas

NASA Aerospace Education Services Program: Emphasis on science, technology, and space.
　　www.okstate.edu/aesp/AESP.html/
The Exploratorium: Great location for science, fun, and learning.
　　www.exploratorium.edu/
Official Web site of the Olympic movement.
　　www.olympic.org/uk/indes_uk.asp/

Chapter Summary

The three major instructional approaches (basal reader, literature-based, and language-based) have different underlying beliefs and assumptions, implementations, organization and management, strengths and limitations, and classroom adaptations.

The basal reader approach requires that the classroom be organized to permit the teacher to conduct small-group reading instruction while the rest of the class works independently. Reading groups may meet with the teacher every day or every other day to allow for more in-depth discussion and interaction. Rules and routines guide students in transitions to and from reading group spaces. Negative status and self-esteem issues resulting from ability grouping may be reduced by cross-ability grouping for other activities.

The literature-based approach is built around a selection of core books and requires a well-stocked reading and literature center, flexible floor space in which reading-response groups can meet, and working areas and materials for development of end-of-book productions. Routines are useful for moving students into and out of reading-response groups and getting their attention when groups are meeting. Developing clear discussion task goals and assigning group roles are ways to increase the quality of response-group discussions.

The language-based approach centers around large blocks of time when students are engaged in self-directed projects and group activities. Language and literacy learning occur as a natural part of the projects and activities. Frequent opportunities to engage in short goal-setting and reflection activities provide guidance for students in their exploration and inquiry projects. Rules and routines assist in creating a stable and orderly environment, which gives students freedom to work and fosters independence.

Instructional programs and supplemental programs

TABLE 12.5

Instructional Software Evaluation Checklist

Evaluator _____ Date _____

Name of Software _____

Recommended Grade Level _____

Nature of Software (Indicate one or more):

Word Identification _____ Comprehension _____ Vocabulary _____

Research and Study Skills _____ Literature _____ Writing _____

Other (Describe) _____

Specific Materials Examined: Software _____ Guide _____

Other Support Material _____

	Rating				
Evaluation Questions	Low				High
1. Are the skills and content appropriate for your instructional purposes and curriculum?	1	2	3	4	5
2. Is the skill development and/or content of high interest and meaning-based?	1	2	3	4	5
3. Will the content engage your students and provide for discovery of new concepts?	1	2	3	4	5
4. Is the software interactive, and does it require active thinking and responses?	1	2	3	4	5
5. Is the program free of gender, racial, and socioeconomic bias?	1	2	3	4	5
6. Can the software be used independently and with ease?	1	2	3	4	5
7. Are the instructions clear?	1	2	3	4	5
8. Can students enter and exit the software easily?	1	2	3	4	5
9. Can students set their own pace and stop and start at various points in the software?	1	2	3	4	5
10. Can the software be used with more than one student?	1	2	3	4	5
11. Is the length of time required to complete the software appropriate for your classroom?	1	2	3	4	5
12. Are color, graphics, and sound used effectively to engage active student interest?	1	2	3	4	5

you are considering adopting require careful evaluation. This process is critical if you are to select an instructional program that fits your instructional philosophy and that of your school. You should participate actively in textbook and literature selection. Supplementary materials, such as phonics supplements, need to match your instructional beliefs and curriculum.

The instructional use of technology in the classroom has immense potential value for you and your students. Computer-based technology is an important and rapidly expanding area, and your familiarity with computers, software, CD-ROMs, and the Internet will prove a valuable resource for your reading, writing, and content area teaching.

the Highly Effective Teacher

on Technology and Instructional Approaches

1. If you are considering how the three different instructional approaches meet the needs of your students, you may find that keeping an electronic journal is a helpful tool. Record various research and practice articles that discuss the pros and cons of basal, literature-based, and language-based approaches.

2. Think about how to adapt a basal lesson by extending or modifying the questions in the teacher's guide to meet your specific instructional goals. Use Internet resources, such as The Global Schoolhouse at **www.gsh.org/** or Teacher CyberGuides at **www.sdcoe.k12.ca.us/score/stella/ stellatg.html.**

3. Allow your students to explore books and topics of personal interest using both software and the Internet within a literature-based approach. For example, they might visit the many Harry Potter Web sites developed around the popular series by author J. K. Rowling. Some sites to begin with are the following: **www.scholastic.com/harrypotter/home. asp, www.bloomsbury.com/ harrypotter/,** and **www.jkrowling.com.** This will encourage students to view literature as a resource to be shared, discussed, and written about within the larger community.

4. Have your students visit The Reading Zone of the Internet Public Library at **www.ipl. org/youth/lapage.html,** where they can ask a variety of questions, share their own writing, and read or listen to stories. Choose a topic that you are teaching thematically from the language-based approach and have the students do research on this theme.

Professional Standards and Teacher Knowledge for Instructional Approaches to and the Organization and Management of Literacy Learning

Figure 12.12 (page 380) identifies the five major standard areas related to instructional approaches with specific elements and examples for the classroom teacher candidate (International Reading Association, 2004). Again, check your professional knowledge of instructional approaches against these standards. You can see the complete list of Standards for Reading Professionals in Appendix C.

Applications: Bridges to the Classroom

1. Obtain a copy of a recently published basal reader, teacher's guide, and workbook for a grade level that interests you. Read one of the stories, and examine the teaching recommendations and student activities. Select the recommendations and activities that you believe would be most effective. Create a lesson plan, using a strategy described in this book to introduce and develop the story. Add your plan to your teaching portfolio.

2. Assume that you are using a literature-based approach and identify one high-interest children's or adolescent book you wish to use. Create planning webs like the examples shown in "Strategies in Use: Developing Planning Webs for Literature-Based Instruction." Include a planning web for incorporating instructional technology in your literature-based lesson plan. Add the planning webs to your portfolio.

3. Visit a language-based classroom. Design a checklist of instructional features and strategies that you expect to find, and record your observations on it. How does the teacher take advantage of authentic learning tasks and

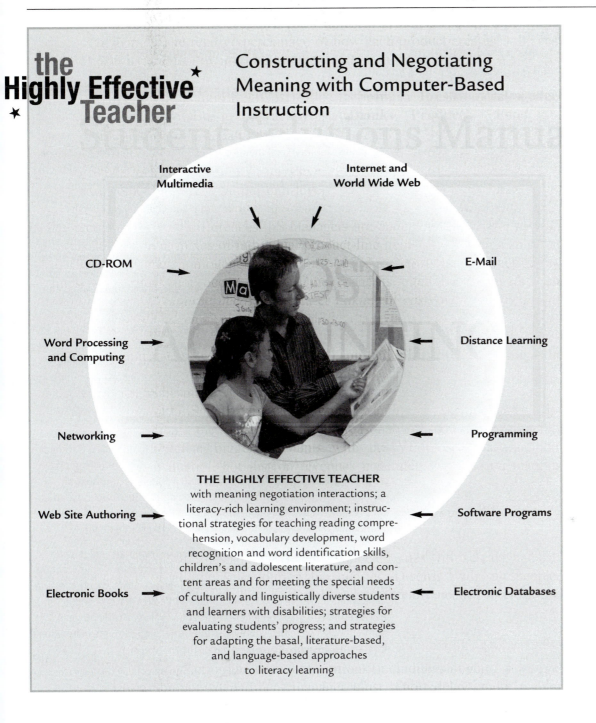

the Highly Effective Teacher

Constructing and Negotiating Meaning with Computer-Based Instruction

Interactive Multimedia

Internet and World Wide Web

CD-ROM

E-Mail

Word Processing and Computing

Distance Learning

Networking

Programming

Web Site Authoring

Software Programs

Electronic Books

Electronic Databases

THE HIGHLY EFFECTIVE TEACHER
with meaning negotiation interactions; a literacy-rich learning environment; instructional strategies for teaching reading comprehension, vocabulary development, word recognition and word identification skills, children's and adolescent literature, and content areas and for meeting the special needs of culturally and linguistically diverse students and learners with disabilities; strategies for evaluating students' progress; and strategies for adapting the basal, literature-based, and language-based approaches to literacy learning

social contexts as instructional opportunities? Solicit the teacher's views on the advantages and limitations of the language-based approach.

4. For the instructional approach of your choice, create a daily schedule of activities, a diagram of the physical organization of the classroom, and an annotated list of the literacy materials and equipment you wish to have in the classroom. Compare your schedule, classroom organization, and list of materials with those of classmates who have chosen the same instructional approach.

5. With a partner, explore the Internet and determine how this resource can be used for a topical or thematic unit of

study that students can undertake independently in small groups. What print support will you provide to guide students' explorations and follow up on their learning? Include in your plan a list of Web and e-mail addresses students should use and a flow chart showing the sequence they should follow. What information will students record and in what form? How will students collaborate, and what products will they create? How can you use their Internet activities to meet your instructional goals and objectives?

FIGURE 12.12

Professional Standards and Instructional Approaches to and Organization and Management of Literacy Learning

Professional Standard	Example
1. Foundational Knowledge	**Element 1.1** Demonstrates knowledge of psychological, sociological, and linguistic foundations of reading and writing processes and instruction; e.g., knows foundational theories that support the selection and use of instructional approaches in the classroom; applies these foundations to adapt an instructional approach to meet a range of student needs.
2. Instructional Strategies and Curriculum Materials	**Element 2.3** Uses a wide range of curriculum materials in effective reading instruction for learners at different stages of development and from different cultural and linguistic backgrounds; e.g., plans for a range of curriculum materials and instructional programs, including use of the Internet, to meet a wide range of student needs; uses evidence-based rationale to guide selections of materials to accommodate developmental, cultural, and linguistic student differences.
3. Assessment, Diagnosis, and Evaluation	**Element 3.3** Uses assessment information to plan, evaluate, and revise effective instruction to meet a wide range of student needs; e.g., can use assessment results to select instructional materials and approaches for all students within an assessment/evaluation/instruction cycle; understands and can select children's literature from different cultural backgrounds to use in the instructional cycle.
4. Creating a Literate Environment	**Element 4.2** Uses a large supply of books, technology-based information, and nonprint materials representing multiple levels, broad interests, and cultural and linguistic backgrounds; e.g., selects books, technology-based information, and nonprint materials representing multiple levels, interests, and cultural and linguistic backgrounds; articulates research and theory that supports the instructional use of books, information, and materials to meet a wide range of student needs.
5. Professional Development	**Element 5.3** Works with colleagues to observe, evaluate, and provide feedback on each other's practice; e.g., actively engages in collaboration and dialogue with other teachers and reading specialists to obtain recommendations and advice on instructional approaches and technology, and organization and management of instruction to meet a wide range of instructional needs; may conduct action research to evaluate instructional approaches designed to meet specific student needs.

Part 2 from IRA. (2004). Professional Standards and Ethics Committee, International Reading Association. *Standards for reading professionals—revised 2003.* Reprinted with permission of the International Reading Association. All rights reserved.

Additional Research and Practice

1. Shamir, A. & Korat, O. (2006). How to select CD-ROM storybooks for young children: The teacher's role. *The Reading Teacher, 59,* 532–543.

   This article describes the potential benefit that electronic storybooks can hold for students. Emphasis, however, is placed on the importance of selecting the software. An excellent evaluation checklist and an example evaluation procedure using this checklist is developed. (Practice)

2. Smolin, L. I., & Lawless, K. A. (2003). Becoming literate in the technological age: New responsibilities and tools for teachers. *The Reading Teacher, 56* (6), 570–577.

   This excellent article identifies technological, visual, and information literacies to enable students to make meaning from a variety of texts and explores specific tools and Internet connections that are immediately available to help teachers accomplish this task. (Practice)

3. Freppon, P. A., & Dahl, K. L. (1998). Balanced instruction: Insights and considerations. *Reading Research Quarterly, 33* (2), 240–251.

   This discussion explores the nature of balanced reading instruction and identifies key implications for classroom practice. (Research and Practice)

Continuing Your Professional Growth as a Highly Effective and Influential Literacy Teacher

*Why teach? Why did Prometheus steal fire only to turn
around and give it away? There is an inherent generosity in the
human spirit—one of its faces is the face of the teacher.*

Michael Crichton, (1942–),
American writer

If you plan for a decade, plant a tree. If you plan for a century, teach the children.

Anonymous

Cindy Hayes and Jolene Merriwether are the first teachers in Mary Engles Elementary School to take advantage of the long-awaited block scheduling. The new daily schedule allows for greater flexibility in unit and lesson planning and also allows much more time for cooperative teaching and other collaborations.

The two fifth-grade teachers have met almost daily since before the start of school to plan a five-week integrated thematic unit on written communication and how this form of communication has developed and changed over the centuries. Cindy and Jolene will co-teach the unit, each contributing in her areas of special interest and academic strength.

"Here's an idea for a science and technology tie-in," Jolene explains to Cindy. "I thought of it last night and ran it past two of my K–8 science partners on the Internet. They liked it and gave me even more ideas. I wish we could do this all the time. Anyway, we have the kids do observations and experiments on the history and technology of writing. There are tons of things they can do here. They can examine writing under magnifiers, play with invisible ink, decode pictographs from photographs, compare the various writing instruments used over the past two centuries using our CD-ROM encyclopedia, and—listen to this—they can use the draw program to print and write on the computer. Agnes, one of my science partners, says our kids can send the results of their writing experiments and observations to her kids and vice versa. Our district is in the same network as hers."

"Hold it a sec," Cindy interrupts. "This all sounds great, Jo, but remember what we decided: Content area tie-ins should have a strong literacy component. I think we need to spend more time selecting literature for this theme, both informational books and stories. I saw a book the kids will love on Egyptian hieroglyphics, but we need a lot more. We also need to attend to reference skills and develop ideas to help beginning researchers. Also, we want to be working with vocabulary development and advanced word identification skills on roots and prefixes. I know what you mean, though: It is exciting. I keep thinking about a social studies angle: The kids compose a group letter and send it out in a bottle—a far cry from sending a letter to Agnes's classroom in a single keystroke."

"Hey, that could be a science tie-in!" Jolene exclaims. "They could find out how a message goes through a computer

September 20, 2005

Dear _____(parent's name)_____,

I am looking forward to working with (student's name) this year. As we begin our new school year, I would like to tell you about a special unit that another teacher, (teacher's name), and I will be teaching together. The theme of the unit is written communication, and the idea is to integrate the curriculum around this theme. Students will be writing, reading about writing, and learning about the development of writing over the centuries. They will be applying mathematics, science, and technology to the theme of written communication.

We are really excited about this special unit, which is based on the new block schedule that will run for five weeks, starting October 18. To make it work, though, we need your help. We know that you are busy, but we hope to make it possible for you to contribute in some way. To give you an idea and to help you get ready, a list is enclosed showing you the kinds of assistance we'll be asking for from parents, family members, and others in the community.

More information on the special unit will be coming soon. In the meantime, please call or e-mail if you have any questions or suggestions. We welcome any ideas you have for teaching materials or learning experiences for the written communication unit.

Sincerely,

_____(name)_____   _____(room no.)_____

_____(teacher's e-mail address and school telephone no.)_____

and arrives on the screen of a keypal's computer, and they could find out how a message follows tides and currents. Wow, that could be big!"

"Speaking of big," Cindy says, "I'm worried about whether we can really do all this. We have to figure out how we'll schedule our team teaching and whose classroom we'll be in for what. Also, we're going to have to choreograph individual, small-group, and large-group instruction, and I think we're going to need some help. Let's talk to Dan about getting classroom assistants. And let's see if we can get parents really involved too."

The two teachers settle down to focus on a specific task—developing a letter to send home to parents to alert them to the upcoming unit. They come up with the letter on this page.

Jolene and Cindy spend the rest of the week developing the list of needs for parent involvement in the special unit.

"Let's ask if they can write in a language other than English," Cindy suggests. "They could come and demonstrate the writing in the classroom, or they could send a sample of the writing to school with their child. What do you think?"

"Great idea. And it would be great to have someone who works with computers to explain how electronic messages travel. We'll also definitely need somebody who knows something about the way the river runs, in order to send a message in a bottle. Otherwise, it'll probably wash up on a levee someplace."

"Then there's basic classroom help, like helping with the science experiments and reading aloud and listening to the kids read and showing them how to use reference materials and . . ."

"Yup, it's endless! But there are so many parents who have no hope of participating during school hours. What can they do?"

"Hmmmm. That'll take some thought, but they can always support the unit at home by monitoring homework. They can donate different kinds of written communication that the kids can bring to school as exhibits. The kids could create their own learning center with those items and write about them. Also, parents might enjoy decoding an encrypted message at home with their kids."

"I'll bet there are tons of things if we really think about it. It's just as important for the families to be involved as it is for us to get help with the unit . . ."

Jolene and Cindy are enriching themselves, their students, and students' families through a professional collaboration calling for a lot of dedication, study, and creativity. Planning an integrated thematic unit and learning how to co-teach that unit effectively are benchmarks in their development as professional educators. In the process, they are growing as effective and influential teachers.

double entry journal

In your opinion, what are your areas of strength and weakness as a reading teacher? In what ways are you (or will you be) an effective and influential teacher? What do you feel you need to know and do to grow as an effective teacher?

Chapter Objectives

After reading and discussing this chapter, you will be able to:

- understand the nature of professional change and teacher characteristics, differences between novice and expert teachers, and the importance of understanding your personal teaching style.
- explore ways to develop your personal and professional support network in your school.
- understand the important role of your past influential teachers, peer and mentor teachers, the school principal and staff, and the school's parents and community in developing your classroom support network.
- develop key strategies useful in building professional connections through school district staff

development, professional organizations, Internet resources, and continued professional growth both within and outside of your school district.

- grasp the importance of professional reflection on your teaching by examining your teaching strengths, understanding areas where additional strength is needed, and planning goal-setting actions (including professional standards), which will help you become a highly effective literacy teacher.

Processes of Professional Development

Like Cindy and Jolene, teachers everywhere anticipate the opening of the school year by planning for instruction and preparing to meet students for the first time. Even after years of teaching experience, you will anticipate the first day of school with both excitement and anxiety. As a new teacher, you will be asking yourself lots of questions: "What will the new students be like?" "Will I be prepared to teach them effectively?" "What help and support will there be to assist me in my teaching?" "What instructional materials will be available for my teaching?" "Will I find other teachers to share ideas with and confide in?" "Will my principal be supportive of me and my teaching ideas?" These questions are natural and mark the beginning stage of your professional growth as a teacher.

The discussion in this text has provided the foundation for your professional growth by equipping you with the following:

> *Foundations of Professional Growth*

- Instructional principles critical to creating rich language and literacy environments for students with varied language and cultural backgrounds
- Learning theories, including the understanding that the driving motivations underlying students' language and literacy development are social interaction and the search for meaning
- A wide range of instructional strategies and approaches to use in teaching and evaluating reading and writing skills for all students

You will learn much more from experience, and you will encounter many new instructional ideas in years to come.

> *Experience is still the best teacher.*

A Model of Change

As you strive to become an effective literacy teacher, you will need to reflect on the change process (Dole, 2004). Change can be seen as a three-stage process (Ruddell & Sperling, 1988; Ruddell & Williams, 1972):

1. Confronting a new idea
2. Resisting but examining the idea
3. Negotiating and adapting the idea to your belief system

You will observe and experience this process as you enter your school for the first time, examine textbooks that have already been adopted, review school policy for handling discipline problems, and attend your first inservice workshop. When you encounter ideas and strategies that are not consistent with your own instructional knowledge or belief system, you will participate in the change process as you struggle to understand, evaluate, and adapt those ideas (Poglinco & Bach, 2004). In California, difficulty in adjusting to the demands of change is a factor in the decision to leave teaching for approximately 30 percent of all teachers who leave after their first two years and for 20 percent of those who leave within five to seven years.

Initial resistance is common as teachers confront new and different strategies or situations. A significant number of curriculum projects and potentially valuable innovations fail at the "resisting but examining" stage of change because of teachers' lack of understanding of the dynamics of change (Hendricks-Lee, Soled, & Yinger, 1995). Collaborative efforts among teachers, principals, and curriculum personnel facilitate change by providing opportunities for everyone's concerns to be voiced and addressed. After the "negotiating and adapting" stage of the process, teachers need support in launching and using the new idea or program.

How can change cause problems for you as a teacher? Why?

▶ *Reasons for Resistance to Change*

Five Factors in the Acceptance of Change

Studies of the change process in education (Quatroche, Bean, & Hamilton, 2001; Rogers, 1983; Ruddell & Sperling, 1988; Sashkin & Egermeier, 1993) provide strong evidence that a new idea is most quickly incorporated into practice when it has one or more of the following five features:

1. The new idea has a distinct advantage over an alternative instructional approach or strategy the teacher is currently using.
2. The change is compatible with the teacher's knowledge and beliefs.
3. The innovation is not too complex and does not require an exhaustive intellectual effort.
4. The teacher can try it out or observe it in practice and make judgments and decisions about it.
5. The teacher has an opportunity to commit to, modify, or reject the new idea.

These five features describe a user-friendly approach to change and help explain why teachers tend to readily accept the basal reader approach. This approach incorporates reading material, skillbooks, and teacher's guides with detailed instructional guidelines. Because the basal reader approach is often representative of how teachers themselves learned to read, it is likely to be at least partly compatible with their instructional beliefs. Often the publisher or the district sponsors inservice workshops to explain and assist in installing the program, offers opportunities for pilot demonstration trials and observations in selected classrooms, and encourages teacher involvement in and commitment to program selection.

Awareness of the five factors conducive to accepting change can help you make decisions. For example, if you wish to incorporate the basal reader, literature-based, or language-based approach in your classroom instruction, you will need to determine the distinct advantage of the approach, its instructional complexity, and how it relates to your beliefs and values (Ruddell, 2002; Santa, 1997). Ideally, you should have opportunities to observe the approach in use in other classrooms and to try it out before committing to it. Instructional change also requires a strong desire on the part of the teacher for change and supportive leadership by the principal or team leader.

How can the factors in accepting change help you make decisions about change in your school?

Links between Change and Teacher Characteristics and Beliefs

Additional insight into the relationship between the instructional change process and teachers' characteristics and beliefs is found in the research literature (Anders et al., 2000; Hoffman & Pearson, 2000; Rogers et al., 2006; Santa, 1997; Taylor et al., 2005). One study (Ruddell & Sperling, 1988; Ruddell & Williams, 1972) identifies four descriptors predictive of a teacher's degree of willingness to explore new instructional ideas or curriculum changes. These descriptors and the corresponding potential for change are presented in Table 13.1 (page 385). As you examine each descriptor and its related characteristics, determine which ones most closely fit your perception of yourself as a teacher.

TABLE 13.1
Teacher Descriptors and Characteristics and the Change Process

| Teacher Descriptor | Teacher Characteristics | | | | Change Process | |
	Communications with Students and Teacher Peers	Perception of Self in Relation to Peers	Management Style; Motivation	Problem-Solution Approach	Openness to New Ideas	Potential for Change
1. Supportive-Productive	Open; two-way; seeking clarification and resolution	Equal	Cooperatively determined action, praise; high motivation	Intellectually curious; self-confident; open to consultation, internal locus of control; positive, high expectations	High	High
2. Supportive-Nonproductive	Partially open; defensive; self-deprecating; suggesting feelings of inadequacy	Inferior	Assigned action, praise, admonition; moderate to low motivation	Expresses little curiosity; relies heavily on work and support of others; external locus of control; moderate to low expectations	Moderate	Low
3. Nonsupportive-Productive	Partially open; defensive of personal beliefs; verbally aggressive; exhibiting little concern for ideas of others	Superior	Use of authority, admonition; moderate to low motivation	Expresses little curiosity; rejects others' ideas and provokes others; internal locus of control; moderate expectations	Low	Low
4. Nonsupportive-Nonproductive	Closed; defensive; hostile; conflictual	Inferior; rejected	Use of authority, reprimand; very low motivation	Expresses little or no curiosity; is overwhelmed by problem; external locus of control; low expectations	Very low	Very low

Adapted from Ruddell & Sperling, 1988, Table 2, p. 324.

Based on the information in Table 13.1, you might predict that *supportive-productive teachers* are self-starters and early innovators in educational change. These teachers are open to new ideas and willing to work cooperatively and passionately toward the new ideas they embrace. *Supportive-nonproductive teachers* are likely to give "lip service" to innovation and hold only moderate potential for change. They need substantial support—in the form of creativity and implementation energy—from other teachers, the principal, and the curriculum innovator.

Nonsupportive-productive teachers have low potential for change because of their tendency to respond, "I've already got the answer." These teachers believe in the superiority of their own instructional approach. They can play an important role in the change process, however, by

Which descriptor in Table 13.1 best describes you?

venting emotions, reducing tensions, and forcing other teachers to examine carefully the reasoning behind the proposed innovations.

Nonsupportive-nonproductive teachers also have very low potential for change, often expressed in the view "I've seen it before, and it doesn't work." These teachers tend to be closed to curriculum change, although change sometimes can be initiated effectively through peer demonstration teaching and peer pressure.

Developing a Personal Teaching Style

As you move from novice to expert teacher, you will develop a distinctive teaching style defined by the way you plan and direct instruction and interact with students. Your style will be influenced strongly by your prior knowledge and beliefs about teaching and students and by your

Research and Evidence-Based Practice

How Expert and Influential Teachers Develop and How They Teach

Did you Know?

FACTORS INFLUENCING THEIR DEVELOPMENT

- Their beliefs and teaching effectiveness are shaped and influenced by views held by (a) their parents and family and (b) highly effective and influential teachers they have encountered in their own schooling (Ruddell, 2006; Ruddell & Greybeck, 1995; Ruddell & Kern, 1986; Ruddell & Unrau, 2004b).

- Parents of influential teachers valued education and the joy of learning, and they encouraged goal setting, held high expectations, and provided a home environment that encouraged the development of aesthetic sensitivity (Ruddell & Greybeck, 1995; Ruddell & Kern, 1986).

- Their effectiveness is also influenced by their personal identification as a teacher, which drives a desire to becoming highly effective (Ruddell, 2006; Ruddell & Greybeck, 1995; Ruddell & Kern, 1986; Ruddell & Unrau, 2004b).

- Many influential teachers describe themselves much as they describe their former influential teachers in terms of characteristics and classroom performance, including personal characteristics, quality of instruction, and attitude toward the subject (Ruddell, 2004; Ruddell & Kern, 1986).

HOW THEY TEACH

- They stimulate students' interest and motivation by demonstrating their own enthusiasm and by engaging students in the thought processes of intellectual inquiry

that they use in their own teaching (Ruddell, 2006; Ruddell & Greybeck, 1995; Ruddell & Kern, 1986; Ruddell & Unrau, 2004b).

- They maintain high standards and have a genuine concern and respect for individual students (Ruddell & Greybeck, 1995; Ruddell & Unrau, 2004b).

- Like expert dancers or gymnasts, they draw on a reservoir of mastered strategies that enable them to identify a problem and mentally apply an integrated set of principles to develop a solution, in contrast to the novice teacher who struggles with problem identification and possible solutions (Ruddell & Greybeck, 1995; Woolfolk, 1995).

- They develop near-automatic teaching routines they can apply in their classroom (e.g., taking roll, distributing material), which free their mental and physical energy for focusing on student problems and progress (Woolfolk, 1995).

- They use an elaborate system of knowledge for understanding students' responses and problems (Woolfolk, 1995).

- Expert teachers are aware of their own thinking processes as they arrive at possible solutions and are highly effective in implementing these solutions with their students (Ruddell, 2006; Ruddell & Greybeck, 1995; Ruddell & Unrau, 2004b; Taylor et al., 2005; Woolfolk, 1995).

Corroborative support for many of these key features is found in the work of Ashton-Warner (1963); Ayers & Shubert (1994); Beidler (1986); Bloom (1982); Kridel, Bullough, & Shaker (1996); Ladson-Billings (1994); Sturtevant (1996); and Perl & Wilson (1986).

How does the performance of an expert teacher differ from that of a novice teacher? What is your plan for your professional development as an influential teacher?

knowledge of content, teaching strategies, and instructional procedures (Hoffman & Pearson, 2000; Rogers et al., 2006). You can begin to identify your personal style as soon as you start considering the ways you teach, plan, organize your classroom, and provide instruction.

As you express your thoughts about your teaching style, you will reveal your personal metaphors for teaching (Morrison, 1997). If, for example, you see your classroom as a "workplace" and yourself as "manager," you may begin to think of your students as workers. You may focus your instruction on task-based behavior in a quiet, smooth-functioning, and well-managed classroom. In contrast, if you perceive your classroom as an "active learning center," you are likely to view your students as learners with special needs and emphasize teacher-student and student-student interactions (Hendricks-Lee, Soled, & Yinger, 1995).

What are your metaphors for students, the teaching process, and your role as a teacher?

Your personal metaphors for yourself and your role as a teacher will evolve as you develop professionally. Morrison (1997) provides an excellent example of the way a novice teacher's metaphor for classroom management shifted as she gained experience in the classroom:

> When I began student teaching, my metaphor for classroom management was a river. Now I believe that management is like [being] a gardener. . . . [The teacher] needs to be able to . . . provide a nurturing, healthy, learning environment. . . . [Teachers] also need to guide or direct, but you need to specially do things for each child and with each need. You have to be careful not to crush or damage the child (like a flower). You need to tend to each child and be alert to all needs. (p. 14)

As your teaching style develops, partly in response to your reflections and experiences, so too will your teaching metaphors.

How would you describe your teaching style?

Your Personal and Professional Support Network

During the early weeks of the school year, you will find yourself totally immersed in your classroom, as you get to know your students, become familiar with your new reading and writing curriculum (as well as other curricula), and try to stay a step ahead in instructional preparation. You will find the following types of support of great value during this time and over the course of the school year:

➤ Sources of Teaching Support

- Influential and effective teachers in your past
- Your background knowledge and skills
- Effective peer and mentor teachers
- School administrators and staff
- Students' parents and members of the local community

the **Highly Effective Teacher**

Influential and Highly Effective Teachers in Your Past

In Chapter 1 (page 2), you were asked to identify teachers who influenced you in your own schooling from kindergarten through college. Reflect again on your memories of these teachers, and visualize them individually in terms of the following characteristics and behaviors:

■ Personal characteristics, including energy, commitment, passion, flexibility, and expectations of self

■ Understanding of student potential and learner expectations, including their ability and willingness to adjust instruction to meet students' needs

■ Attitude toward content and skills instruction, exhibited in their enthusiasm and ability to generate intellectual excitement in students

■ Concern for students' life adjustment, exhibited through personal attention to students' academic progress and personal problems

■ Ability and willingness to make instructional content relevant to students, use a strategy-oriented approach, and engage students in a process of intellectual discovery

> *How did you respond in Chapter 1 to questions about your effective and influential teachers? How did your responses compare to the information in Figure 13.1?*

Your former highly effective teachers are likely to be important role models for you as you assume full responsibility in your classroom. You will find yourself asking "How would (your highly effective teacher) have presented this lesson (or handled this difficult situation)?" Your reflections should extend to teachers you regarded as ineffective or detrimental to your educational experience. Why were these teachers ineffective? What negative features should you guard against in your own teaching? Figure 13.1 (page 389) presents a more detailed summary of the characteristics of highly effective and influential teachers, describing their actions before, during, and after instruction.

Your Background Knowledge and Skills

Shaped and influenced by years of schooling, your professional knowledge and your beliefs and values about education are an important support resource. Your professional preparation, ranging from theory and methods courses to field experiences and practice teaching, will provide an important information base. You will know, for example, the abilities and interests of primary- and intermediate-grade students, reading and writing development approaches and strategies, and the culture of the school. This background will prove valuable in your teaching. You will discover that past educational experiences have left you with a rich hidden reservoir of ideas that you can use effectively to direct instruction. You may even find yourself returning to class notes, course projects, and texts used in your teacher-preparation program as you develop a successful problem-solving approach to teaching.

Highly Effective Peer and Mentor Teachers

Even before the first day of school, you should begin your search to identify individuals who can serve as highly effective peer teachers (and friends). These potential peer teachers exist in every school. You will recognize them as friendly and outgoing, energetic and enthusiastic, intellectually curious, and open to consultation. They have developed a successful track record of teaching and are willing to share their ideas, resources, and wisdom.

What will you look for in a highly effective peer teacher?

Your goal is to find a teacher who possesses an instructional belief system and philosophy compatible with your own. Initial contact with teachers will occur just before the beginning of the school year, during room preparation and introductory teacher meetings. Take these opportunities to introduce yourself and to find out about the other teachers' beliefs about teaching and approaches to reading and writing instruction. Room preparation will provide clues to their sensitivity to individual needs and their learning expectations for their students. For example, a teacher's instructional philosophy may be revealed by the use of bulletin boards to display student work, desk arrangements that encourage peer interaction, and an attractive and inviting reading and literature center. This is a good time to talk with highly effective peers about the students who attend the school; the instructional programs and approaches used in the school; the reputation, leadership style, and level of support of the principal; and your professional and personal interests.

FIGURE 13.1

The Highly Effective and Influential Literacy Teacher: A Summary

Highly Effective and Influential Teacher Characteristics

- shares authority to encourage student thinking, responsibility, interaction, and ownership of learning
- understands the role of instructional stance in setting the purpose of instruction
- understands the importance of internal reader motivation
- understands the importance of authentic meaning construction
- understands the importance of text and task in negotiating and constructing meaning
- understands the importance of sources of authority and sociocultural meanings in meaning construction
- is sensitive to individual students' backgrounds, needs, motivations, and aptitudes
- holds appropriate and high expectations for learning
- believes in professional development and understands the need for change
- has an open, supportive, and productive approach to teaching

Highly Effective and Influential Teacher Actions *before* Instruction and *during* Beginning Instruction

- creates an effective literacy learning environment
- establishes objectives, goals, and expected outcomes
- develops clear purposes
- plans for successful resolution of instructional episodes
- encourages the creation of an active and interactive community of learners

- selects and activates students' prior knowledge, experiences, beliefs, and schemata
- focuses reader intention and develops reader motivation
- activates students' processing strategies for meaning construction
- mobilizes students' attitudes and values
- activates students' self-monitoring strategies for comprehension
- chooses among the four levels of meaning construction strategies
- takes an aesthetic instructional stance

Highly Effective and Influential Teacher Actions *during* and *after* Instruction

- applies in-depth knowledge of reading and writing processes
- acts as an instructional decision maker
- orchestrates instruction using a problem-solving approach
- provides task engagement resources
- provides authentic literacy-learning contexts
- engages students in active literacy learning
- interacts with students to negotiate meaning of text
- uses higher-level thinking questions in meaning negotiation
- encourages students to construct meaning together
- uses clearly formulated instructional strategies
- provides monitoring and feedback
- uses verbal feedback that encourages active thinking
- encourages intellectual discovery by posing, exploring, and resolving problems

From R. B. Ruddell (1997a). Researching the influential literacy teacher: Characteristics, beliefs, strategies, and new research directions. In C. K. Kinzer, K. A. Hinchman, D. J. Leu (Eds.), *Inquiries in Literacy, Theory and Practice: 46th Yearbook of the National Reading Conference.* Chicago: National Reading Conference (pp. 37–53).

Highly effective peer teachers will play an important support role as the school year progresses. These teachers will become your in-house consultants, providing valuable information on the operation and organization of the school, the nature of the curriculum, and the expectations of the principal and the parents, as well as answers to a multitude of questions that will arise throughout the year. One great benefit of having such a relationship is the opportunity to share ideas and search for solutions to any problems that you may be experiencing. Highly effective peer teachers not only help you guard against isolation in your classroom but also help you overcome feelings of depression or anxiety that can sometimes arise from the heavy demands of teaching.

You may have the opportunity to work with a mentor teacher, assigned to you in your first year of teaching. If so, you will need to develop a collaborative relationship with this master teacher, who will play much the same role as a highly effective peer teacher.

> *Mentor teachers, like effective peers, can help you develop successful problem-solving strategies.*

School Principal and Staff

The principal of your school is empowered by the superintendent of schools to assume direct responsibility for instructional and administrative leadership. The principal's effectiveness, however, will depend to a great extent on his or her stance toward instruction and administrative duties. Strong evidence (Cunningham & Allington, 1999; Ruddell & Sperling, 1988) suggests that a successful principal has the following characteristics:

> **Characteristics of Successful Principals**

- Believes and expects that every student will achieve
- Demonstrates consultative leadership with teachers and involves teachers in open, process-oriented change and innovation in the school curriculum
- Participates actively in inservice workshops and project training sessions
- Legitimizes and empowers teachers to work toward improved teaching effectiveness, innovation, and change
- Develops a positive school atmosphere that is orderly without being oppressive
- Exhibits enthusiasm and optimism toward the important role of the school in educating and changing the lives of children

> How might you encourage your principal to become involved in your classroom?

You will gradually come to know the principal and his or her beliefs and philosophy about language and literacy development and the curriculum in general. As you do, you can convey your instructional beliefs and philosophy through your teaching and think of ways you can involve the principal in your classroom (Vogt & Shearer, 2003).

The principal's administrative and instructional duties include evaluating your teaching during your beginning years, based on both informal and formal visits to your classroom. Informal visits will acquaint the principal with your teaching style, your classroom, and your students before the first formal evaluation. The principal also plays an important role in decision making that will affect your classroom. When the principal is ready to make decisions ranging from what instructional supplies to provide throughout the year to what books and resource materials to purchase with end-of-year monies, you should have your wish list ready.

> **Your Professional Support Network**

Most principals are very supportive of inservice and continuing education for their teachers. Again, your knowledge and understanding of the principal's educational beliefs and priorities will be of value. For example, a principal who is interested in cooperative learning or a computer-based approach might make it possible for you to attend a reading or literacy conference to learn about implementing such a program in your classroom. The principal often influences the allocation and funding of professional development days and can serve as an advocate of your continued professional growth.

Your support network also will include other professionals in your school and school district, such as the librarian, reading specialist, and special education teachers who are working with your special needs students. You may have a team leader for the grade level you teach. A curriculum coordinator may work with you on new instructional programs. Meeting and working with these individuals will help you expand your professional support network.

Your Students' Parents

Parents are important participants in their students' literacy development and can be of great help to you throughout the school year (Burgess, Hecht, & Logan, 2002). It is important to develop contact with parents early in the school year. Parents can become partners in your instructional program, although their desire and availability to work with you in the classroom will vary widely. Some parents are anxious about visiting the school either because of personal negative experiences with schooling or because of a belief that they are not welcome in the school environment. Work schedules of both one- and two-parent families often prevent direct participation. Your contact with these parents will occur for the most part during scheduled parent-teacher conferences. These conferences should be designed to reduce parents' anxiety about the school, communicate your high interest in their child, and help them understand that they are indeed welcome in your classroom as partners in their child's educational development.

> Chapter 9 offers guidelines for conducting parent conferences.

> Chapters 10 and 11 offer guidelines for working with tutors and parent volunteers.

Initiate parent participation by designing and distributing a parent-volunteer checklist such as the one in Figure 13.2 (page 391). Your checklist should reflect your instructional program and plans for parent involvement. You might keep the volunteer response sheets in a folder called "Parent Resources" to consult as you plan instruction. It is important when working with parent volunteers that you provide guidelines and explain your philosophy of teaching and your expectations of volunteers.

FIGURE 13.2
Parent-Volunteer Checklist Information

Name _____

Child's Name _____

Phone _____

I would like to help in the following ways:

1. Working directly with students on classroom learning
   - _____ listening to students read
   - _____ taking dictation of students' stories or poems
   - _____ assisting students as they do assigned work
   - _____ assisting students with technology and Internet projects
   - _____ going on short school field-trip walks
   - _____ going on day-long field trips
   - _____ working with students as they use computers

2. Assisting a small group or individual students with a project
   - _____ arts or crafts
   - _____ drama (plays, puppets)
   - _____ creative writing
   - _____ music
   - _____ storytelling and children's literature
   - _____ photography, filmmaking, or videotaping
   - _____ sharing an interest or a hobby (please describe) _____
   - _____ other _____

3. Assisting with large school projects
   - _____ carnival, fiesta, or special event
   - _____ fund-raising
   - _____ student council
   - _____ school newspaper
   - _____ collecting or preparing instructional materials or props
   - _____ other _____

4. Schoolwide tasks
   - _____ library assistance
   - _____ office assistance
   - _____ making phone calls
   - _____ school advisory committee
   - _____ other _____

I will be able to participate at school on the following days at the following times:

Day: M   T   W   TH   F   Any day

Time: Morning _____ Afternoon _____ After School _____

I cannot participate in your classroom on a regular basis but would be available for special events._____

_____Signature

Your School's Community

What kind of partnership might you initiate with a business near your school?

The community in which your school is located offers many educational resources and additional potential members of your professional support network. You might develop partnerships with other schools, fraternal organizations, government agencies, local businesses, or a nearby college or university. Roles of partners might range from volunteer tutoring to sponsoring educational projects. Local businesses often are interested in developing good community relations and, at the same time, improving education for students in the community. Many large companies have public relations officers who look for opportunities to get involved in their local schools. Community-school collaborations provide opportunities for authentic tasking and service learning.

Professional Connections for Reading and Writing Teachers

Continued professional development is essential for improving your teaching. As you work toward your goal of becoming a highly effective teacher, be alert to possible professional connections and opportunities to continue your education. For example, you might participate in inservice workshops, join a professional association, and network on the Internet.

Staff Development in Your School District

You will find a variety of opportunities available in your local school district for exploring new instructional ideas, approaches, and materials. Staff development generally includes inservice sessions on particular topics or skills, often with the goal of motivating you to apply the information in your classroom, and regular staff meetings to discuss important instructional concerns in your school or district.

How to Do . . .

Parent Classroom Participation

1. Describe your instructional program, and explain how it develops literacy in students.
2. Invite parents to observe or to lead instructional experiences involving their children.
3. Develop parents' understanding of ways to provide educational support at home for their students.

DELAYED READER ADAPTATION

■ **Don't underestimate the effectiveness of relatively uncomplicated help from parents. Research has shown that students who are read aloud to on a regular basis develop a larger, more sophisticated knowledge of word meanings and demonstrate greater comprehension because of growth in background knowledge—and that the effect is especially strong for delayed readers. Asking parents to read aloud to delayed readers *every day* is a hassle-free form of help.**

4. Schedule parents to assist you in the classroom and during special school events such as field trips.
5. Give parents tips on tutoring and leading instruction, such as the following:
   ■ Be consistent.
   ■ Be alert to children's responses, and respond to them.
   ■ Encourage active participation by working with their children.
   ■ Work toward approximation of a skill or concept—not perfection.
   ■ Give feedback and praise.
   ■ Don't pry or betray confidences.
   ■ Follow through on promises.
6. Follow up on parents' participation and contributions with feedback and thanks or recognition.

Strategies in Use   Initiating Partnerships

Cindy Hayes and Jolene Merriwether, introduced at the beginning of this chapter, researched possible links between the community and the classroom to support their integrated thematic unit on written communication. They each arranged a formal partnership and proposed it in writing to their principal, who presented it to the district superintendent and the school board.

Cindy's plan linked volunteers from two sources to her fifth-grade classroom: tenth graders from the nearby high school, who got credit for community service, and insurance underwriters from a local corporation, who received work release time for volunteerism. During the five weeks of the special unit, these volunteers worked one-on-one with students on reading and writing for an hour a day. The plan included two training sessions to ensure that the volunteers would learn about the unit and know how to support student learning appropriately.

Jolene's partnership involved a donation of time and material from a local printer, who agreed to print a book of the children's writings for the unit. Each family would receive a free copy of the book. In addition, the printing company would host field trips to show the fifth graders the printing process. The county newspaper ran a full-page story, including photographs, on the printer's contribution.

CRITICAL THINKING

1. What other partnerships might Cindy and Jolene consider?
2. What kind of integrated thematic unit might you be interested in teaching? What literacy goals and activities would be involved? How would those goals and activities relate to the world outside of the classroom and school?
3. What kinds of school-community partnerships might contribute to your unit? How would you go about developing these partnerships?
4. Would you enjoy co-teaching your unit with a colleague? What might be some of the advantages and disadvantages of cooperative teaching?

> *Inservice Workshops*

Inservice sessions can provide a valuable professional experience. For example, a back-to-school professional day at the beginning of the school year in one school district focused on "Developing Comprehension and Higher-Level Thinking through the Literature Program." After a keynote speaker introduced the topic, speakers developed related topics, including "Literature and Thinking Processes in the Primary Grades" and "Using Children's Literature to Enrich Social Studies and Science Teaching." Teachers were invited to attend subsessions on the topics of greatest interest to them. Many school districts offer inservice workshops during early release days throughout the year to address concerns such as eliminating gender bias in the literacy classroom and learning to use technology for instruction. An after-school inservice workshop might be scheduled for just your school at the request of your principal and a representative committee of teachers who reflect your needs and those of other teachers.

Inservice professional development across the country is increasingly being conducted through coaching ("Coaches, controversy, consensus," 2004; Dole, 2004; Poglinco & Bach, 2004). This process is frequently directed by experienced and highly trained teachers who provide instructional support, instructional feedback, and materials for classroom teachers. Most often, coaching takes two forms. The first is in-class modeling and observations to assist the classroom teacher in becoming more effective. For example, a literacy coach might demonstrate the use of the DR-TA and a GMA and show how to combine these two strategies, working directly with students in the teacher's classroom. This experience would be followed with the coach helping the classroom teacher plan the use of these strategies, observe the teacher introducing them, and provide feedback on how to improve the instructional effectiveness, using the strategies. The second form is a carefully planned group-developed series of inservice activities led by a coach. These activities would take place over a period of several weeks or months. This form of inservice is most effective if the coach can do follow-up work with individual teachers to ensure implementation, respond to questions, and provide feedback.

Staff-development projects that continue over the school year provide ongoing contact with the instructional leader—generally a principal, a literacy coach, a school literacy specialist, or an outside curriculum innovator. A staff-development project usually focuses on an area of major concern at the local or district level. For example, a problem might be addressed by school or area specialists, teaching demonstrated by highly successful teachers, or materials collaboratively developed or adapted to meet students' instructional needs. Other possible goals of ongoing staff development in a school or district include the adoption of new reading or literature textbooks; development of a new instructional approach, such as a literature-based approach; and design of a new evaluation approach, such as portfolio assessment.

Some professional organizations provide support for the creation and planning of professional development projects. One example of such support is found in the Gertrude Whipple Professional Development Grant, sponsored by the International Reading Association. This grant provides monetary support up to $5,000 to be awarded to a member of the International Reading Association to assist the development of professional-growth projects, production of high-quality materials, sponsorship of professional meetings and workshops for teachers, and support for conducting these professional experiences. Guidelines for developing a proposal for the Whipple Grant may be obtained by contacting the International Reading Association (for address see the following discussion) or e-mailing gcasey@reading.org.

Professional Organizations for Teachers

One hallmark of the effective teacher is knowledge and understanding of the most recent thinking and instructional ideas in the field. One way this knowledge and awareness can be developed is through participation in professional reading and literacy organizations such as the International Reading Association and the National Council of Teachers of English.

The **International Reading Association (IRA)** has over one thousand local reading councils throughout the United States, its territories, and Canada, plus affiliates in approximately thirty other countries. IRA councils sponsor local and national speakers on a wide variety of reading and literacy topics, and your attendance at, and participation in, these events will be welcomed. Most state councils also hold a large statewide meeting each year. The IRA produces *The Reading Teacher*, a journal for preschool and elementary teachers, emphasizing instructional approaches and strategies that reflect the latest thinking in the field (nine issues per year). This journal also reviews children's and adolescent books, professional books, evaluation approaches, and research. For teachers at the middle school, secondary, and post-secondary levels, the IRA also publishes *The Journal of Adolescent and Adult Literacy*.

Reading Online is the IRA's new electronic journal, serving literacy educators at all levels (www.readingonline.org). If you are a member of the IRA and subscribe to *The Reading Teacher*, *Journal of Adolescent and Adult Literacy*, or *Reading Research Quarterly*, you can access the journal online as well as receive your print copy of the journal by mail ("A new world of online resources," 2004). The value of the electronic version of these journals is found in ease of access in locating articles of most interest and of most use to you. You will also find a new *Reading Today* daily section that offers news updates about literacy in general and the activities of the IRA. In addition, you can go online and share ideas about various issues in reading. These electronic forms are made available through the IRA Web site at www.reading.org, clicking on those sites that you wish to search.

The IRA sponsors an annual convention and regional conferences, held in different parts of the United States and Canada. A World Reading Congress is convened in even-numbered years in a foreign country. The publication division of the IRA publishes professional books about current concerns and issues in the field. You can obtain information on membership, the council closest to your teaching location, and IRA publications by contacting the IRA.

International Reading Association
800 Barksdale Road
P.O. Box 8139
Newark, DE 19714–8139

What ongoing staff-development projects might your school conduct?

the **Highly Effective Teacher**

International Reading Association (IRA) a professional organization for literacy teachers and researchers at all instructional levels

800–336-READ
Fax: 302–731–1057
Web site: www.reading.org

The **National Council of Teachers of English (NCTE)** has members throughout the United States and Canada and provides leadership in encouraging the integration of language arts skills. The NCTE publishes *Language Arts* for elementary school teachers and *Voices from the Middle* for middle-grade teachers (both eight issues per year). These journals emphasize theory and instructional practices and strategies and include reviews of children's and adolescent literature, professional books, and research. The NCTE publication for secondary English teachers is *The English Journal*.

The NCTE holds a major convention each year, as well as regional and state conferences. Information on membership and publications can be obtained by contacting the NCTE:

National Council of Teachers of English
1111 West Kenyon Road
Urbana, IL 61801–1096
800–369-NCTE
Fax: 217–328–9645
Web site: www.ncte.org

Both the IRA and the NCTE conduct research, award grants for literacy projects, and give service and recognition awards to individual teachers.

> **National Council of Teachers of English (NCTE)** a professional organization for literacy and language arts teachers and researchers at all grade levels

Internet Resources for Teachers

Through the Internet, you can be connected in a few seconds to a tremendous variety of literacy resources. Web sites that may be of interest to you include the following:

> ▶ *Sample these Web sites. See Chapter 12 for more suggestions.*

Educational Resources Information Center (ERIC): Digests, lesson plans, information on conferences, databases, and question-answering services
www.eric.ed.gov

The following list of sites suggests the great variety of Internet resources for pre-K–8 literacy teachers:

Library of Congress
www.lcweb.loc.gov

Proliteracy Worldwide
www.literacyvolunteers.org
Click on Find a Program.

ERIC Clearinghouse on Reading, English, and Communication
http://reading.indiana.edu

Continuing Education for Teachers

As you begin your teaching career, you should carefully consider continuing your professional growth through credit provided by your school district and through colleges and universities in your area. Most school districts provide credit toward increases in the salary ladder through workshops and course offerings during the school year or summer.

Explore the higher education certificate or degree programs for teachers in your area. Your state or school district might reimburse you if you pursue continuing-education goals through summer courses. Most master's programs require twenty-four to thirty-six units of credit for completion. Some programs require the completion of a thesis on a specific aspect of reading and literacy development, while others require a comprehensive examination. Many M.A. and M.Ed. programs can be completed in one year of full-time study or two years of part-time study combined with one or two summer sessions.

> What postgraduate courses, certificates, and degrees for teachers are honored in the state or district where you plan to teach? What professional advantages do they offer?

Some professional development courses for teachers are offered on television or online through the Internet. You can find online courses and telecourses by doing a keyword search by university or network name.

Today, many teacher education programs and school districts base teacher evaluations on portfolios teachers maintain. A critical element to include in such portfolios is evidence of attendance at conferences, staff development meetings, and university courses (Temple, Ogle, Crawford, & Freppon, 2008).

The Role of Professional Reflection

How do your responses to the Reflective Teaching Checklist relate to your self-assessment in Table 1.3?

➤ *Ongoing professional reflection and problem solving is the key to becoming an effective and influential teacher.*

Take a few moments to reflect on your own teaching experiences. Perhaps you have been involved in tutoring, student teaching, or substitute teaching, or maybe you hold the responsibility of a full-time classroom teacher. On the basis of your reflections, identify your strengths and areas you wish to improve to increase your teaching effectiveness. Use the checklist in Table 13.2 (page 397) to assist you in this self-assessment.

Once you have identified the effective-teacher characteristics and reading and literacy areas that represent your greatest strengths, reflect on the factors that contributed to your development of those strengths. After identifying the areas that you believe need the most improvement, think of actions you can take or a plan you can formulate to increase your effectiveness in these areas (Taylor et al., 2005).

This process of professional reflection and planning will become a process of personal change as you confront, examine, and adapt ideas to increase your teaching effectiveness. Your desire to participate in this process stems from your self-confidence, internal motivations, and high personal standards—all characteristics of the supportive-productive teacher discussed earlier in this chapter. These characteristics and the reflection/goal-setting action cycle will help you to become a highly effective teacher.

Summary and Classroom Applications

double entry journal

How do your reflections on the self-assessment in Table 13.2 (page 397) compare with what you wrote in the Double Entry Journal at the beginning of the chapter? Use this information to write three immediate and three long-term goals for your professional development as a highly effective teacher.

Chapter Summary

Becoming a highly effective and influential teacher requires continued professional growth. Professional growth involves change, which is a three-stage process of encountering new ideas, resisting but carefully reflecting on these ideas, and adapting ideas to your belief system. Research on the change process in education reveals that new ideas are more readily put into practice when they hold perceived advantages over alternatives, are compatible with beliefs, are not too complex, can be observed, and are subject to teacher approval rather than imposed by others. Understanding the change process will be of

value as you encounter a wide range of innovative practices in your teaching.

Teachers described as supportive-productive are open to new ideas and to working cooperatively toward idea innovation. These teachers are early innovators and contrast distinctly with nonsupportive-nonproductive teachers, who show little interest in new ideas and are basically closed to professional change.

Research indicates that highly effective teachers believe that key factors influencing their beliefs and teaching effectiveness include parents and family, former

TABLE 13.2

Reflective Teaching Checklist

	Teaching Strengths	Teaching Emphasis Desired
Highly Effective Teacher Characteristics		
1. Personal characteristics (lots of energy, caring, high self-expectations)		
2. Learner potential (understanding of student needs, learning expectations)		
3. Attitude toward teaching (enthusiasm, intellectual excitement)		
4. Life adjustment (concern for academic and personal problems)		
5. Quality of instruction (use of personally relevant material, orientation toward strategy, engagement of students in intellectual discovery)		
Reading and Literacy Areas*		
1. Highly effective and influential literacy teacher instruction		
2. Reading and literacy process		
3. Early reading and literacy development		
4. Word recognition and identification		
5. Reading comprehension		
6. Vocabulary development		
7. Literature, reader response, and engagement		
8. Content area literacy		
9. Assessment of reading and literacy development		
10. Teaching the delayed reader		
11. Language, diversity, cultural diversity, and special needs		
12. Instructional approaches and organization and management of literacy instruction		
13. Continued professional development		

*These thirteen areas correspond to each chapter of this text.

influential teachers, and personal identification as a teacher, which drives the strong desire to become a highly effective teacher. Examination of differences between novice and expert teachers suggests that teaching effectiveness is enhanced by the use of near-automatic instructional strategies and routines and a system of knowledge for understanding students' responses.

Your personal and professional support network will include past highly effective teachers, who shaped your personal belief system; peer and mentor teachers, who will be of great value as you enter a new school and class-room; and school administrators, who can be helpful in providing instructional suggestions and financial support for your classroom. Your own background knowledge—developed through years of schooling, your professional development program, and your teaching experience—provides an important information base for your teaching. Finally, your support network should include parents. Efforts to involve parents in your classroom might range from reporting on a student's progress at scheduled conferences to enlisting parent volunteers to assist you in literacy instruction.

the Highly Effective Teacher

on Technology and Professional Support Networks

1. You may want to broaden your perspective by incorporating the larger world community into your classroom. For example, you may want to visit Egypt and travel along the Nile River at **www.memphis.edu/egypt,** and click on Color Tour of Egypt. Another idea is to have your students participate in The Hunger Site at **www.thehungersite. com,** a United Nations project where food is donated by sponsors each time someone visits the site, or travel to the Wright Brothers Aeroplane and Museum of Aviation at **www.first-to-fly.com** and explore the developement of aviation. On the basis of these sites, you could incorporate a diverse range of themes into your instruction, such as hunger, tolerance, globalism, economics, human rights, and geography.

2. Use the Internet as a source of professional support. The following Web sites will provide a wide range of ideas and options that can be explored and adapted to your classroom:

The Global Schoolhouse
www.gsh.org

Thinkport—Maryland Public Television
www.thinkport.org

PBS Teacher Source
www.pbs.org/teachersource

EdWeb E-Mail Discussion Lists is devoted to education only with background information about lists and is located at **www. edwebproject.org/lists.html.**

3. As a highly effective teacher, you may want to participate in professional education organizations and subscribe to professional journals. Many of these organizations have ongoing forums for discussion and provide mentoring as well. Using e-mail, you are able to continue discussions that were begun at conferences and share your professional concerns, thoughts, and opinions with others in your field.

Participation in school district staff-development projects and workshops enhances professional development. New ideas and teaching practices based on the most recent theories and research are readily available through professional organizations such as the International Reading Association and the National Council of Teachers of English. A rich resource is the Internet. As your classroom experience develops and your professional interests become more focused, you should consider continuing education through summer courses and advanced-degree programs at your local college or university.

The process of professional change leading to highly effective teaching requires that you reflect on your teaching, take risks as you try out new ideas, and tolerate your mistakes. Self-fulfillment and professional pride will be the rewards for your successes. It is important to remember that becoming a highly effective teacher means becoming a lifelong learner.

Applications: Bridges to the Classroom

1. Interview a veteran teacher about changes in curriculum and instruction at his or her school. How did the teacher and others in the school respond to the changes? What issues were involved? What were the results? Analyze the teacher's account in terms of the model of change presented in this chapter, the key factors that influence change, and the links between teacher characteristics and change. What are the elements of effective change in the classroom and school?

2. With classmates, observe first-year or student teachers, and compare their teaching performance with that of highly effective and influential teachers. Record and discuss your findings. What advice might you give the novices to help them on their path to becoming highly effective literacy teachers?

3. Begin to develop a personal and professional support network now, as a student in your teacher-education program,

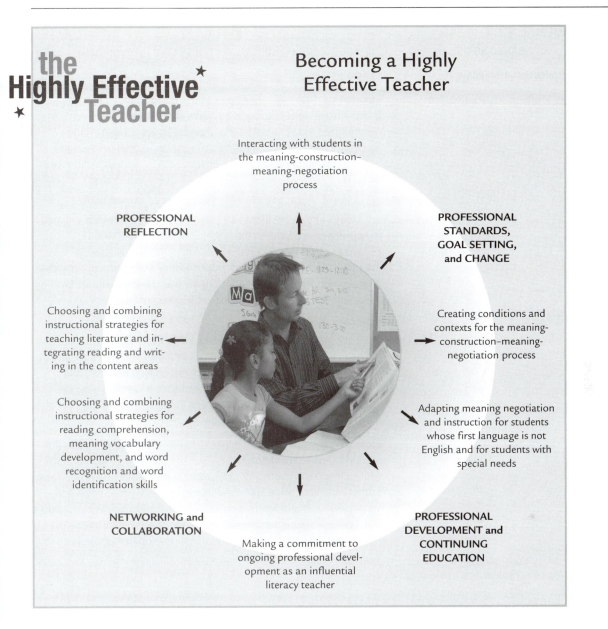

the
Highly Effective ★
★ Teacher

Becoming a Highly Effective Teacher

Interacting with students in the meaning-construction–meaning-negotiation process

PROFESSIONAL REFLECTION

PROFESSIONAL STANDARDS, GOAL SETTING, and CHANGE

Choosing and combining instructional strategies for teaching literature and integrating reading and writing in the content areas

Creating conditions and contexts for the meaning-construction–meaning-negotiation process

Choosing and combining instructional strategies for reading comprehension, meaning vocabulary development, and word recognition and word identification skills

Adapting meaning negotiation and instruction for students whose first language is not English and for students with special needs

NETWORKING and COLLABORATION

PROFESSIONAL DEVELOPMENT and CONTINUING EDUCATION

Making a commitment to ongoing professional development as an influential literacy teacher

Professional Standards and
Teacher Knowledge on Continued Professional Growth

Specific professional standard elements for Standard 5, Professional Development, are found in Figure 13.3 (page 400) (International Reading Association, 2004). This figure differs from the professional standards figures in previous chapters because here we focus only on Standard 5. Examine the four elements in this standard and complete a brief assessment of your progress toward meeting these professional standards. You can see the complete list of Standards for Reading Professionals in Appendix C.

FIGURE 13.3

Professional Standards and Teacher Knowledge on Continued Professional Development

Professional Standard	Example
5. Professional Development*	**Element 5.1** Displays caring and positive disposition related to reading and the teaching of reading; e.g., works with families, colleagues, and communities to support students' learning by encouraging parent classroom participation, creating partnerships with fellow teachers and the community, and developing joint school-community literacy projects.
	Element 5.2 Continues to pursue the development of professional knowledge and dispositions; e.g., identifies specific questions related to knowledge and skills in the teaching of reading and writing; possesses strategies for finding answers to those questions; is informed about important professional issues and is an active member of professional literacy organizations such as the International Reading Association or the National Council of Teachers of English.
	Element 5.3 Works with colleagues to observe, evaluate, and provide feedback on each other's practice; e.g., engages in collaboration and dialogue with other teachers, reading specialists, and literacy coaches to obtain recommendations and advice on teaching practices and ideas; articulates the evidence base related to these recommendations; conducts research to better understand literacy instruction as part of his or her professional collaboration.
	Element 5.4 Participates in, initiates, implements, and evaluates professional development programs; e.g., participates individually and with colleagues in professional development experiences such as local school and districtwide staff-development projects; articulates personal classroom and local school professional-knowledge needs; works with fellow professionals, including the principal, reading specialist, and literacy coach to initiate professional-development projects.

*For additional examples of Standard 5, Professional Development, see the Professional Standards and Teacher Knowledge figures in Chapters 1 and 3 through 12.

Part 2 from IRA. (2004). Professional Standards and Ethics Committee, International Reading Association. *Standards for reading professionals—revised 2003*. Reprinted with permission of the International Reading Association. All rights reserved.

and formulate a plan for establishing school connections during your first year as a teacher. Keep your action plan in your professional portfolio. Note especially the characteristics you will look for in peer and mentor teachers, school administrators, parents, and resource people in the community. Also include a working plan and timetable for your continuing professional development as a teacher.

4. Attend a monthly meeting of the local reading council in your area and an annual state conference sponsored by the International Reading Association or the National Council of Teachers of English. (Be sure to inquire about a student discount on registration and membership fees.) Keep a log of your conference experiences, including notes on the presentations and exhibits you attended and the people you met. How might you participate more actively in professional meetings in the future?

5. Review the Highly Effective Teacher feature at the end of each chapter and the information highlighted by the Highly Effective Teacher symbols throughout the book. Incorporate this information into an essay on your personal thoughts about being a highly effective literacy teacher. Share your ideas with a friend, and add your essay to your teaching portfolio. How might you use your ideas to prepare for interviews for your first job?

Additional Research and Practice

1. Cunningham, P. M., & Allington, R. L. (1999). *Classrooms that work: They can all read and write.* New York: Longman.

   This hands-on paperback provides excellent ideas for improving literacy instruction, and the last chapter, "Beyond the Classroom: Things Worth Fighting For," identifies fourteen thought-provoking issues that deserve educators' close attention. (Practice)

2. Dole, J. A. (2004). The changing role of the reading specialist in school reform. *The Reading Teacher, 57* (5), 462–471.

   This carefully developed article provides a clear picture of the evolution of the reading specialist's role from that of working only with students to supporting teachers as coach and mentor in their professional development. The impor-tance of teaching demonstrations and modeling of lessons by the reading coach is emphasized through real classroom examples. (Practice)

3. Taylor, B. M., Pearson, D. P., Peterson, D. S., & Rodriguez, M. C. (2005). The CIERA School Change Framework: An evidence-based approach to professional development and school reading improvement. *Reading Research Quarterly, 40,* 40–69.

   This article describes a carefully planned school reform effort designed to improve reading instruction. Higher level questioning by teachers was found to be positively related to students' reading growth. Teachers in schools that were successful in implementing the reform framework were found to change their teaching toward more high-level questions. (Research)

Newbery Medal Books

The John Newbery Medal has been awarded annually since 1922 under the supervision of the American Library Association's Association for Library Service to Children. It is presented to the author of the work judged to be the most distinguished contribution to children's literature published in the United States during the previous year. One or more Honor Books are also chosen. Winners must be residents or citizens of the United States. This distinguished list of books will be of help to you in building reading interest and motivation with your elementary and middle school students.

Go to www.ala.org/ala/alsc/awardsscholarships/literaryawds/literaryrelated.htm and click on ALA/Literary and Related Awards and then John Newbery Medal home page to find the most recent Newbery Medal winners and abstracts of these books. Then click on Past Newbery Medal and Honor Books, 1922–Present, to find the entire list of Medal Winners and Honor books.

1922
The Story of Mankind by Hendrik Willem van Loon (Liveright)

Honor Books
Cedric the Forester by Bernard Marshall (Appleton)
The Golden Fleece and the Heroes Who Lived before Achilles by Padraic Colum (Macmillan)
The Great Quest by Charles Hawes (Little, Brown)
The Old Tobacco Shop by William Bowen (Macmillan)
Windy Hill by Cornelia Meigs (Macmillan)

1923
The Voyages of Doctor Dolittle by Hugh Lofting (Lippincott)

1924
The Dark Frigate by Charles Hawes (Atlantic/Little, Brown)

1925
Tales from Silver Lands by Charles Finger (Doubleday)

Honor Books
Dream Coach by Anne Parrish (Macmillan)
Nicholas by Anne Carroll Moore (Putnam)

1926
Shen of the Sea by Arthur Bowie Chrisman (Dutton)

Honor Book
Voyagers by Padraic Colum (Macmillan)

1927
Smoky, the Cowhorse by Will James (Scribner's)

1928
Gayneck, the Story of a Pigeon by Dhan Gopal Mukerji (Dutton)

Honor Books
Downright Dencey by Caroline Snedeker (Doubleday)
The Wonder Smith and His Son by Ella Young (Longmans)

1929
The Trumpeter of Krakow by Eric P. Kelly (Macmillan)

Honor Books
The Boy Who Was by Grace Hallock (Dutton)
Clearing Weather by Cornelia Meigs (Little, Brown)
Millions of Cats by Wanda Gág (Coward)
Pigtail of Ah Lee Ben Loo by John Bennett (Longmans)
Runaway Papoose by Grace Moon (Doubleday)
Tod of the Fens by Elinor Whitney (Macmillan)

1930
Hitty, Her First Hundred Years by Rachel Field (Macmillan)

Honor Books
Daughter of the Seine by Jeanette Eaton (Harper)
Jumping-Off Place by Marian Hurd McNeely (Longmans)
Little Blacknose by Hildegarde Swift (Harcourt)

Pran of Albania by Elizabeth Miller (Doubleday)
Tangle-Coated Horse and Other Tales by Ella Young (Longmans)
Vaino by Julia Davis Adams (Dutton)

1931
The Cat Who Went to Heaven by Elizabeth Coatsworth (Macmillan)

Honor Books
The Dark Star of Itza by Alida Malkus (Harcourt)
Floating Island by Anne Parrish (Harper)
Garram the Hunter by Herbert Best (Doubleday)
Meggy Macintosh by Elizabeth Janet Gray (Doubleday)
Mountains Are Free by Julia Davis Adams (Dutton)
Ood-Le-Uk the Wanderer by Alice Lide and Margaret Johansen (Little, Brown)
Queer Person by Ralph Hubbard (Doubleday)
Spice and the Devil's Cake by Agnes Hewes (Knopf)

1932
Waterless Mountain by Laura Adams Armer (Longmans)

Honor Books
Boy of the South Seas by Eunice Tietjens (Coward)
Calico Bush by Rachel Field (Macmillan)
The Fairy Circus by Dorothy P. Lathrop (Macmillan)
Jane's Island by Marjorie Allee (Houghton Mifflin)
Out of the Flames by Eloise Lownsbery (Longmans)

*Truce of the Wolf and Other Tales of
Old Italy* by Mary Gould Davis
(Harcourt)

1933
Young Fu of the Upper Yangtze by
Elizabeth Lewis (Winston)

Honor Books
Children of the Soil by Nora Burglon
(Doubleday)
The Railroad to Freedom by Hildegarde
Swift (Harcourt)
Swift Rivers by Cornelia Meigs (Little,
Brown)

1934
Invincible Louisa by Cornelia Meigs
(Little, Brown)

Honor Books
ABC Bunny by Wanda Gág (Coward)
Apprentice of Florence by Anne Kyle
(Houghton Mifflin)
Big Tree of Bunlahy by Padraic Colum
(Macmillan)
The Forgotten Daughter by Caroline
Snedeker (Doubleday)
Glory of the Seas by Agnes Hewes
(Knopf)
New Land by Sarah Schmidt (McBride)
Swords of Steel by Elsie Singmaster
(Houghton Mifflin)
Winged Girl of Knossos by Erik Berry
(Appleton)

1935
Dobry by Monica Shannon (Viking)

Honor Books
Davy Crockett by Constance Rourke
(Harcourt)
Day on Skates by Hilda Van Stockum
(Harper)
Pageant of Chinese History by Elizabeth
Seeger (Longmans)

1936
Caddie Woodlawn by Carol Ryrie Brink
(Macmillan)

Honor Books
All Sail Set by Armstrong Sperry
(Winston)
The Good Master by Kate Seredy
(Viking)
Honk, the Moose by Phil Strong (Dodd)
Young Walter Scott by Elizabeth Janet
Gray (Viking)

1937
Roller Skates by Ruth Sawyer (Viking)

Honor Books
Audubon by Constance Rourke
(Harcourt)
The Codfish Musket by Agnes Hewes
(Doubleday)
Golden Basket by Ludwig Bemelmans
(Viking)
Phebe Fairchild: Her Book by Lois
Lenski (Stokes)
Whistler's Van by Idwal Jones
(Viking)
Winterbound by Margery Bianco
(Viking)

1938
The White Stag by Kate Seredy (Viking)

Honor Books
Bright Island by Mabel Robinson
(Random House)
On the Banks of Plum Creek by Laura
Ingalls Wilder (Harper)
Pecos Bill by James Cloyd Bowman
(Little, Brown)

1939
Thimble Summer by Elizabeth Enright
(Rinehart)

Honor Books
Hello the Boat! by Phyllis Crawford
(Holt)
*Leader by Destiny: George Washington,
Man and Patriot* by Jeanette Eaton
(Harcourt)
Mr. Popper's Penguins by Richard and
Florence Atwater (Little, Brown)
Nino by Valenti Angelo (Viking)
Penn by Elizabeth Janet Gray (Viking)

1940
Daniel Boone by James Daugherty
(Viking)

Honor Books
Boy with a Pack by Stephen W. Meader
(Harcourt)
By the Shores of Silver Lake by Laura
Ingalls Wilder (Harper)
Runner of the Mountain Tops by Mabel
Robinson (Random House)
The Singing Tree by Kate Seredy
(Viking)

1941
Call It Courage by Armstrong Sperry
(Macmillan)

Honor Books
Blue Willow by Doris Gates (Viking)
The Long Winter by Laura Ingalls
Wilder (Harper)
Nansen by Anna Gertrude Hall
(Viking)
Young Mac of Fort Vancouver by Mary
Jane Carr (Crowell)

1942
The Matchlock Gun by Walter D.
Edmonds (Dodd)

Honor Books
Down Ryton Water by Eva Roe Gaggin
(Viking)
George Washington's World by
Genevieve Foster (Scribner's)
*Indian Captive: The Story of Mary
Jemison* by Lois Lenski (Lippincott)
Little Town on the Prairie by Laura
Ingalls Wilder (Harper)

1943
Adam of the Road by Elizabeth Janet
Gray (Viking)

Honor Books
Have You Seen Tom Thumb? by Mabel
Leigh Hunt (Lippincott)
The Middle Moffat by Eleanor Estes
(Harcourt)

1944
Johnny Tremain by Esther Forbes
(Houghton Mifflin)

Honor Books
Fog Magic by Julia Sauer (Viking)
Mountain Born by Elizabeth Yates
(Coward)
Rufus M. by Eleanor Estes (Harcourt)
These Happy Golden Years by Laura
Ingalls Wilder (Harper)

1945
Rabbit Hill by Robert Lawson (Viking)

Honor Books
Abraham Lincoln's World by Genevieve
Foster (Scribner's)
The Hundred Dresses by Eleanor Estes
(Harcourt)
*Lone Journey: The Life of Roger
Williams* by Jeanette Eaton (Harcourt)
The Silver Pencil by Alice Dalgliesh
(Scribner's)

1946
Strawberry Girl by Lois Lenski
(Lippincott)

Honor Books
Bhimsa, the Dancing Bear by Christine
Weston (Scribner's)
Justin Morgan Had a Horse by
Marguerite Henry (Rand McNally)
The Moved-Outers by Florence Crannell
Means (Houghton Mifflin)
New Found World by Katherine Shippen
(Viking)

1947
Miss Hickory by Carolyn Sherwin Bailey
(Viking)

Honor Books
The Avion My Uncle Flew by Cyrus
Fisher (Appleton)
Big Tree by Mary and Conrad Buff
(Viking)
The Heavenly Tenants by William
Maxwell (Harper)
The Hidden Treasure of Glaston by
Eleanore Jewett (Viking)
Wonderful Year by Nancy Barnes
(Messner)

1948
The Twenty-One Balloons by William
Pène du Bois (Viking)

Honor Books
*The Cow-Tail Switch and Other West
African Stories* by Harold Courlander
(Holt)
Li Lun, Lad of Courage by Carolyn
Treffinger (Abingdon)
Misty of Chincoteague by Marguerite
Henry (Rand McNally)
Pancakes-Paris by Claire Huchet Bishop
(Viking)
*The Quaint and Curious Quest of
Johnny Longfoot* by Catherine
Besterman (Bobbs)

1949
King of the Wind by Marguerite Henry
(Rand McNally)

Honor Books
Daughter of the Mountains by Louise Rankin (Viking)
My Father's Dragon by Ruth S. Gannett (Random House)
Seabird by Holling C. Holling (Houghton Mifflin)
Story of the Negro by Arna Bontemps (Knopf)

1950
A Door in the Wall by Marguerite de Angeli (Doubleday)

Honor Books
The Blue Cat of Castle Town by Catherine Coblentz (Longmans)
George Washington by Genevieve Foster (Scribner's)
Kildee House by Rutherford Montgomery (Doubleday)
Song of the Pines by Walter and Marion Havighurst (Winston)
Tree of Freedom by Rebecca Caudill (Viking)

1951
Amos Fortune, Free Man by Elizabeth Yates (Dutton)

Honor Books
Abraham Lincoln, Friend of the People by Clara Ingram Judson (Follett)
Better Known as Johnny Appleseed by Mabel Leigh Hunt (Lippincott)
Gandhi, Fighter without a Sword by Jeanette Eaton (Morrow)
The Story of Appleby Capple by Anne Parrish (Harper)

1952
Ginger Pye by Eleanor Estes (Harcourt)

Honor Books
Americans before Columbus by Elizabeth Baity (Viking)
The Apple and the Arrow by Mary and Conrad Buff (Houghton Mifflin)
The Defender by Nicholas Kalashnikoff (Scribner's)
The Light at Tern Rocks by Julia Sauer (Viking)
Minn of the Mississippi by Holling C. Holling (Houghton Mifflin)

1953
Secret of the Andes by Ann Nolan Clark (Viking)

Honor Books
The Bears of Hemlock Mountain by Alice Dalgliesh (Scribner's)
Birthdays of Freedom, Vol. I by Genevieve Foster (Scribner's)
Charlotte's Web by E. B. White (Harper)
Moccasin Trail by Eloise McGraw (Coward)
Red Sails to Capri by Ann Weil (Viking)

1954
And Now Miguel by Joseph Krumgold (Crowell)

Honor Books
All Alone by Claire Huchet Bishop (Viking)

Hurry Home Candy by Meindert DeJong (Harper)
Magic Maize by Mary and Conrad Buff (Houghton Mifflin)
Shadrach by Meindert DeJong (Harper)
Theodore Roosevelt, Fighting Patriot by Clara Ingram Judson (Follett)

1955
The Wheel on the School by Meindert DeJong (Harper)

Honor Books
Banner in the Sky by James Ullman (Lippincott)
Courage of Sarah Noble by Alice Dalgliesh (Scribner's)

1956
Carry On, Mr. Bowditch by Jean Lee Latham (Houghton Mifflin)

Honor Books
The Golden Name Day by Jennie Lindquist (Harper)
Men, Microscopes, and Living Things by Katherine Shippen (Viking)
The Secret River by Marjorie Kinnan Rawlings (Scribner's)

1957
Miracles on Maple Hill by Virginia Sorensen (Harcourt)

Honor Books
Black Fox of Lorne by Marguerite de Angeli (Doubleday)
The Corn Grows Ripe by Dorothy Rhoads (Viking)
The House of Sixty Fathers by Meindert DeJong (Harper)
Mr. Justice Holmes by Clara Ingram Judson (Follett)
Old Yeller by Fred Gipson (Harper)

1958
Rifles for Watie by Harold Keith (Crowell)

Honor Books
Gone-Away Lake by Elizabeth Enright (Harcourt)
The Great Wheel by Robert Lawson (Viking)
The Horse Catcher by Mari Sandoz (Westminster)
Tom Paine, Freedom's Apostle by Leo Gurko (Crowell)

1959
The Witch of Blackbird Pond by Elizabeth George Speare (Houghton Mifflin)

Honor Books
Along Came a Dog by Meindert DeJong (Harper)
Chucaro: Wild Pony of the Pampa by Francis Kalnay (Harcourt)
The Family under the Bridge by Natalie Savage Carlson (Harper)
The Perilous Road by William O. Steele (Harcourt)

1960
Onion John by Joseph Krumgold (Crowell)

Honor Books
America Is Born by Gerald W. Johnson (Morrow)
The Gammage Cup by Carol Kendall (Harcourt)
My Side of the Mountain by Jean Craighead George (Dutton)

1961
Island of the Blue Dolphins by Scott O'Dell (Houghton Mifflin)

Honor Books
America Moves Forward by Gerald W. Johnson (Morrow)
The Cricket in Times Square by George Selden (Farrar)
Old Ramon by Jack Schaefer (Houghton Mifflin)

1962
The Bronze Bow by Elizabeth George Speare (Houghton Mifflin)

Honor Books
Belling the Tiger by Mary Stolz (Harper)
Frontier Living by Edwin Tunis (World)
The Golden Goblet by Eloise McGraw (Coward)

1963
A Wrinkle in Time by Madeleine L'Engle (Farrar)

Honor Books
Men of Athens by Olivia Coolidge (Houghton Mifflin)
Thistle and Thyme by Sorche Nic Leodhas (Holt)

1964
It's Like This, Cat by Emily Cheney Neville (Harper)

Honor Books
The Loner by Ester Wier (McKay)
Rascal by Sterling North (Dutton)

1965
Shadow of a Bull by Maia Wojciechowska (Atheneum)

Honor Books
Across Five Aprils by Irene Hunt (Follett)

1966
I, Juan de Pareja by Elizabeth Borten de Trevino (Farrar)

Honor Books
The Animal Family by Randall Jarrell (Pantheon)
The Black Cauldron by Lloyd Alexander (Holt)
The Noonday Friends by Mary Stolz (Harper)

1967
Up a Road Slowly by Irene Hunt (Follett)

Honor Books
The Jazz Man by Mary H. Weik
  (Atheneum)
The King's Fifth by Scott O'Dell
  (Houghton)
Zlateh the Goat and Other Stories by
  Isaac Bashevis Singer (Harper)

1968
*From the Mixed-Up Files of Mrs. Basil E.
  Frankweiler* by E. L. Konigsburg
  (Atheneum)

Honor Books
The Black Pearl by Scott O'Dell
  (Houghton Mifflin)
The Egypt Game by Zilpha Keatley
  Snyder (Atheneum)
The Fearsome Inn by Isaac Bashevis
  Singer (Scribner's)
*Jennifer, Hecate, Macbeth, William
  McKinley, and Me, Elizabeth* by E. L.
  Konigsburg (Atheneum)

1969
The High King by Lloyd Alexander
  (Holt)

Honor Books
To Be a Slave by Julius Lester (Dial)
*When Sheemiel Went to Warsaw and
  Other Stories* by Isaac Bashevis Singer
  (Farrar)

1970
Sounder by William H. Armstrong
  (Harper)

Honor Books
Journey Outside by Mary Q. Steele
  (Viking)
*The Many Ways of Seeing: An
  Introduction to the Pleasures
  of Art* by Janet Gaylord Moore
  (World)
Our Eddie by Sulamith Ish-Kishor
  (Pantheon)

1971
Summer of the Swans by Betsy Byars
  (Viking)

Honor Books
Enchantress from the Stars by
  Sylvia Louise Engdahl
  (Atheneum)
Knee-Knock Rise by Natalie Babbitt
  (Farrar)
Sing Down the Moon by Scott O'Dell
  (Houghton Mifflin)

1972
Mrs. Frisby and the Rats of NIMH by
  Robert C. O'Brien (Atheneum)

Honor Books
Annie and the Old One by Miska Miles
  (Atlantic/Little, Brown)
The Headless Cupid by Zilpha Keatley
  Snyder (Atheneum)
Incident at Hawk's Hill by Allan W.
  Eckert (Little, Brown)
The Planet of Junior Brown by Virginia
  Hamilton (Macmillan)
The Tombs of Atuan by Ursula K. Le
  Guin (Atheneum)

1973
Julie of the Wolves by Jean Craighead
  George (Harper)

Honor Books
Frog and Toad Together by Arnold Lobel
  (Harper)
The Upstairs Room by Johanna Reiss
  (Crowell)
The Witches of Worm by Zilpha Keatley
  Snyder (Atheneum)

1974
The Slave Dancer by Paula Fox
  (Bradbury)

Honor Book
The Dark Is Rising by Susan Cooper
  (McElderry)

1975
M. C. Higgins, the Great by Virginia
  Hamilton (Macmillan)

Honor Books
Figgs and Phantoms by Ellen Raskin
  (Dutton)
My Brother Sam Is Dead by James
  Lincoln Collier and Christopher
  Collier (Four Winds)
The Perilous Gard by Elizabeth Marie
  Pope (Houghton Mifflin)
Philip Hall Likes Me, I Reckon Maybe
  by Bette Greene (Dial)

1976
The Grey King by Susan Cooper
  (McElderry)

Honor Books
Dragonwings by Laurence Yep
  (Harper)
The Hundred Penny Box by Sharon
  Bell Mathis (Viking)

1977
Roll of Thunder, Hear My Cry by
  Mildred D. Taylor (Dial)

Honor Books
Abel's Island by William Steig (Farrar)
A String in the Harp by Nancy Bond
  (McElderry)

1978
Bridge to Terabithia by Katherine
  Paterson (Crowell)

Honor Books
Anpao: An American Indian Odyssey by
  Jamake Highwater (Lippincott)
Ramona and Her Father by Beverly
  Cleary (Morrow)

1979
The Westing Game by Ellen Raskin
  (Dutton)

Honor Book
The Great Gilly Hopkins by Katherine
  Paterson (Crowell)

1980
*A Gathering of Days: A New England
  Girl's Journal, 1830–32* by Joan W.
  Blos (Scribner's)

Honor Book
*The Road from Home: The Story of an
  Armenian Girl* by David Kherdian
  (Greenwillow)

1981
Jacob Have I Loved by Katherine
  Paterson (Crowell)

Honor Books
The Fledgling by Jane Langton
  (Harper)
A Ring of Endless Light by Madeleine
  L'Engle (Farrar)

1982
*A Visit to William Blake's Inn: Poems for
  Innocent and Experienced Travelers* by
  Nancy Willard (Harcourt)

Honor Books
Ramona Quimby, Age 8 by Beverly
  Cleary (Morrow)
*Upon the Head of the Goat: A
  Childhood in Hungary, 1939–1944* by
  Aranka Siegal (Farrar)

1983
Dicey's Song by Cynthia Voigt
  (Atheneum)

Honor Books
The Blue Sword by Robin McKinley
  (Greenwillow)
Doctor De Soto by William Steig
  (Farrar)
Graven Images by Paul Fleischman
  (Harper)
Homesick: My Own Story by Jean Fritz
  (Putnam)
Sweet Whispers, Brother Rush by
  Virginia Hamilton (Philomel)

1984
Dear Mr. Henshaw by Beverly Cleary
  (Morrow)

Honor Books
The Sign of the Beaver by Elizabeth
  George Speare (Houghton Mifflin)
A Solitary Blue by Cynthia Voigt
  (Atheneum)
Sugaring Time by Kathryn Lasky
  (Macmillan)
The Wish Giver by Bill Brittain
  (Harper)

1985
The Hero and the Crown by Robin
  McKinley (Greenwillow)

Honor Books
Like Jake and Me by Mavis Jukes
  (Knopf)
The Moves Make the Man by Bruce
  Brooks (Harper)
One-Eyed Cat by Paula Fox (Bradbury)

1986
Sarah, Plain and Tall by Patricia
  MacLachlan (Harper)

Honor Books
*Commodore Perry in the Land of the
  Shogun* by Rhoda Blumberg (Lothrop)
Dogsong by Gary Paulsen (Bradbury)

1987
The Whipping Boy by Sid Fleischman
(Greenwillow)

Honor Books
A Fine White Dust by Cynthia Rylant
(Bradbury)
On My Honor by Marion Dane Bauer
(Clarion)
*Volcano: The Eruption and Healing of
Mount St. Helens* by Patricia Lauber
(Bradbury)

1988
Lincoln: A Photobiography by Russell
Freedman (Clarion)

Honor Books
After the Rain by Norma Fox Mazer
(Morrow)
Hatchet by Gary Paulsen (Bradbury)

1989
Joyful Noise: Poems for Two Voices by
Paul Fleischman (Harper)

Honor Books
*In the Beginning: Creation Stories from
Around the World* by Virginia
Hamilton (Harcourt)
Scorpions by Walter Dean Myers
(Harper)

1990
Number the Stars by Lois Lowry
(Houghton Mifflin)

Honor Books
Afternoon of the Elves by Janet Taylor
Lisle (Orchard)
Shabanu: Daughter of the Wind by
Suzanne Fisher Staples (Knopf)
The Winter Room by Gary Paulsen
(Orchard)

1991
Maniac Magee by Jerry Spinelli (Little,
Brown)

Honor Book
The True Confessions of Charlotte Doyle
by Avi (Orchard)

1992
Shiloh by Phyllis Reynolds Naylor
(Atheneum)

Honor Books
*Nothing but the Truth: A Documentary
Novel* by Avi (Orchard)
*The Wright Brothers: How They
Invented the Airplane* by Russell
Freedman (Holiday House)

1993
Missing May by Cynthia Rylant
(Orchard)

Honor Books
*The Dark-Thirty: Southern Tales of the
Supernatural* by Patricia McKissack
(Knopf)
Somewhere in the Darkness by Walter
Dean Myers (Scholastic)
What Hearts by Bruce Brooks
(HarperCollins)

1994
The Giver by Lois Lowry (Houghton
Mifflin)

Honor Books
Crazy Lady! by Jane Leslie Conly
(HarperCollins)
Dragon's Gate by Laurence Yep
(HarperCollins)
Eleanor Roosevelt: A Life of Discovery
by Russell Freedman (Clarion)

1995
Walk Two Moons by Sharon Creech
(HarperCollins)

Honor Books
Catherine, Called Birdy by Karen
Cushman (Clarion)
The Ear, the Eye and the Arm by Nancy
Farmer (Orchard/Richard Jackson)

1996
The Midwife's Apprentice by Karen
Cushman (Clarion)

Honor Books
What Jamie Saw by Carolyn Coman
(Front Street)
*The Watsons Go to Birmingham—
1963* by Christopher Paul Curtis
(Delacorte)
Yolonda's Genius by Carol Fenner
(McElderry/Simon & Schuster)
The Great Fire by Jim Murphy
(Scholastic)

1997
The View from Saturday by E. L.
Konigsburg (Jean Karl/Atheneum)

Honor Books
A Girl Named Disaster by Nancy Farmer
(Richard Jackson/Orchard)
Moorchild by Eloise Jarvis McGraw
(McElderry)
The Thief by Megan Whalen Turner
(Greenwillow)
Belle Prater's Boy by Ruth White
(Farrar)

1998
Out of the Dust by Karen Hesse
(Scholastic)

Honor Books
Ella Enchanted by Gail Carson Levine
(HarperCollins)
Lily's Crossing by Patricia Reilly Giff
(Delacorte)
Wringer by Jerry Spinelli (HarperCollins)

1999
Holes by Louis Sachar (Frances Foster)

Honor Book
A Long Way from Chicago by Richard
Peck (Dial)

2000
Bud, Not Buddy by Christopher Paul
Curtis (Delacorte)

Honor Books
Getting Near to Baby by Audrey
Couloumbis (Putnam)

Our Only May Amelia by Jennifer L.
Holm (HarperCollins)
26 Fairmount Avenue by Tomie dePaola
(Putnam)

2001
A Year Down Under by Richard Peck (Dial)

Honor Books
Hope Was Here by Joan Bauer (G. P.
Putnam's Sons)
Because of Winn-Dixie by Kate
DiCamillo (Candlewick Press)
Joey Pigza Loses Control by Jack Gantos
(Farrar, Straus, and Giroux)
The Wanderer by Sharon Creech (Joanna
Cotler Books/HarperCollins)

2002
A Single Shard by Linda Sue Park
(Clarion Books/Houghton Mifflin)

Honor Books
Everything on a Waffle by Polly Horvath
(Farrar Straus Giroux)
Carver: A Life in Poems by Marilyn
Nelson (Front Street)

2003
Crispin: The Cross of Lead by Avi
(Hyperion Books for Children)

Honor Books
The House of the Scorpion by Nancy
Farmer (Atheneum)
Pictures of Hollis Woods by Patricia
Reilly Giff (Random House/Wendy
Lamb Books)
Hoot by Carl Hiaasen (Knopf)
A Corner of the Universe by Ann M.
Martin (Scholastic)
Surviving the Applewhites by Stephanie S.
Tolan (HarperCollins)

2004
*The Tale of Despereaux: Being the Story
of a Mouse, a Princess, Some Soup,
and a Spool of Thread* by Kate
DiCamillo, illustrated by Basil Ering
(Candlewick Press)

Honor Books
Olive's Ocean by Kevin Henkes
(Greenwillow Books)
*An American Plague: The True and
Terrifying Story of the Yellow Fever
Epidemic of 1793* by Jim Murphy
(Clarion Books)

2005
Kira-Kira by Cynthia Kadohata
(Atheneum Books for Young
Readers/Simon & Schuster)

Honor Books
Al Capone Does My Shirts by Gennifer
Choldenko (G.P. Putnam's Sons/a
division of Penguin Young Readers
Group)
*The Voice That Challenged a Nation:
Marian Anderson and the Struggle for
Equal Rights* by Russell Freedman
(Clarion Books/Houghton Mifflin)
Lizzie Bright and the Buckminister Boy
by Gary D. Schmidt (Clarion
Books/Houghton Mifflin)

2006

Criss Cross by Lynne Rae Perkins (Greenwillow Books/HarperCollins)

Honor Books

Whittington by Alan Armstrong, illustrated by S. D. Schindler (Random House)

Hitler Youth: Growing Up in Hitler's Shadow by Susan Campbell Bartoletti (Scholastic)

Princess Academy by Shannon Hale (Bloomsbury Children's Books)

Show Way by Jacqueline Woodson, illustrated by Hudson Talbott (G.P. Putnam's Sons)

2007

The Higher Power of Lucky by Susan Patron, illustrated by Matt Phelan (Simon & Schuster/Richard Jackson)

Honor Books

Penny from Heaven by Jennifer L. Holm (Random House)

Hattie Big Sky by Kirby Larson (Delacorte Press)

Rules by Cynthia Lord (Scholastic)

Caldecott Medal Books

The Randolph Caldecott Medal, named in honor of the nineteenth-century illustrator of children's books, is awarded annually under the supervision of the Association for Library Service to Children of the American Library Association. It is awarded to the illustrator of the most distinguished children's book published in the United States in the previous year. Usually, one or more Honor Books are also chosen. The award is limited to residents or citizens of the United States. This delightful list of books will be of high interest to your students and valuable in your reading instruction.

Go to www.ala.org/ala/alsc/awardsscholarships/literaryawds/literaryrelated.htm and click on ALA/Literary and Related Awards and then Randolph Caldecott Medal home page to find the most recent Caldecott Medal winners and abstracts of these books. Then click on Past Caldecott Medal and Honor Books, 1938–Present, to find the entire list of Medal Winners and Honor books.

1938
Animals of the Bible by Helen Dean Fish, illustrated by Dorothy P. Lathrop (Lippincott)

Honor Books
Four and Twenty Blackbirds by Helen Dean Fish, illustrated by Robert Lawson (Stokes)
Seven Simeons by Boris Artzybasheff (Viking)

1939
Mei Li by Thomas Handforth (Doubleday)

Honor Books
Andy and the Lion by James Daugherty (Viking)
Barkis by Clare Newberry (Harper)
The Forest Pool by Laura Adams Armer (Longman)
Snow White and the Seven Dwarfs by Wanda Gág (Coward)
Wee Gillis by Munro Leaf, illustrated by Robert Lawson (Viking)

1940
Abraham Lincoln by Ingri and Edgar Parin D'Aulaire (Doubleday)

Honor Books
The Ageless Story by Lauren Ford (Dodd)
Cock-a-Doodle Doo by Berta and Elmer Hader (Macmillan)
Madeline by Ludwig Bemelmans (Viking)

1941
They Were Strong and Good by Robert Lawson (Viking)

Honor Books
April's Kittens by Clare Newberry (Harper)

1942
Make Way for Ducklings by Robert McCloskey (Viking)

Honor Books
An American ABC by Maud and Miska Petersham (Macmillan)
In My Mother's House by Ann Nolan Clark, illustrated by Velino Herrera (Viking)
Nothing at All by Wanda Gág (Coward)
Paddle-to-the-Sea by Holling C. Holling (Houghton Mifflin)

1943
The Little House by Virginia Lee Burton (Houghton Mifflin)

Honor Books
Dash and Dart by Mary and Conrad Buff (Viking)
Marshmallow by Clare Newberry (Harper)

1944
Many Moons by James Thurber, illustrated by Louis Slobodkin (Harcourt)

Honor Books
A Child's Good Night Book by Margaret Wise Brown, illustrated by Jean Charlot (Scott)
Good Luck Horse by Chin-Yi Chan, illustrated by Plao Chan (Whittlesey)
The Mighty Hunter by Berta and Elmer Hader (Macmillan)
Pierre Pigeon by Lee Kingman, illustrated by Arnold E. Bare (Houghton Mifflin)
Small Rain: Verses from the Bible, selected by Jessie Orton Jones, illustrated by Elizabeth Orton Jones (Viking)

1945
Prayer for a Child by Rachel Field, illustrated by Elizabeth Orton Jones (Macmillan)

Honor Books
The Christmas Anna Angel by Ruth Sawyer, illustrated by Kate Seredy (Viking)
In the Forest by Marie Hall Ets (Viking)
Mother Goose, illustrated by Tasha Tudor (Walck)
Yonie Wondernose by Marguerite de Angeli (Doubleday)

1946
The Rooster Crows (Traditional Mother Goose), illustrated by Maud and Miska Petersham (Macmillan)

Honor Books
Little Lost Lamb by Golden MacDonald, illustrated by Leonard Weisgard (Doubleday)
My Mother Is the Most Beautiful Woman in the World by Becky Reyher, illustrated by Ruth C. Gannett (Lothrop)
Sing Mother Goose by Opal Wheeler, illustrated by Marjorie Torrey (Dutton)
You Can Write Chinese by Kurt Wiese (Viking)

1947
The Little Island by Golden MacDonald, illustrated by Leonard Weisgard (Doubleday)

Honor Books
Boats on the River by Marjorie Flack, illustrated by Jay Hyde Barnum (Viking)

Pedro, the Angel of Olvera Street by Leo Politi (Scribner's)
Rain Drop Splash by Alvin Tresselt, illustrated by Leonard Weisgard (Lothrop)
Sing in Praise: A Collection of the Best Loved Hymns by Opal Wheeler, illustrated by Marjorie Torrey (Dutton)
Timothy Turtle by Al Graham, illustrated by Tony Palazzo (Welch)

1948

White Snow, Bright Snow by Alvin Tresselt, illustrated by Roger Duvoisin (Lothrop)

Honor Books

Bambino the Clown by George Schreiber (Viking)
McElligot's Pool by Dr. Seuss (Random House)
Roger and the Fox by Lavinia Davis, illustrated by Hildegard Woodward (Doubleday)
Song of Robin Hood, edited by Anne Malcolmson, illustrated by Virginia Lee Burton (Houghton Mifflin)
Stone Soup by Marcia Brown (Scribner's)

1949

The Big Snow by Berta and Elmer Hader (Macmillan)

Honor Books

All Around the Town by Phyllis McGinley, illustrated by Helen Stone (Lippincott)
Blueberries for Sal by Robert McCloskey (Viking)
Fish in the Air by Kurt Wiese (Viking)
Juanita by Leo Politi (Scribner's)

1950

Song of the Swallows by Leo Politi (Scribner's)

Honor Books

America's Ethan Allen by Stewart Holbrook, illustrated by Lynd Ward (Houghton Mifflin)
Bartholomew and the Oobleck by Dr. Seuss (Random House)
The Happy Day by Ruth Krauss, illustrated by Marc Simont (Harper)
Henry Fisherman by Marcia Brown (Scribner's)
The Wild Birthday Cake by Lavinia Davis, illustrated by Hildegard Woodward (Doubleday)

1951

The Egg Tree by Katherine Milhous (Scribner's)

Honor Books

Dick Whittington and His Cat by Marcia Brown (Scribner's)
If I Ran the Zoo by Dr. Seuss (Random House)
The Most Wonderful Doll in the World by Phyllis McGinley, illustrated by Helen Stone (Lippincott)
T-Bone, the Baby Sitter by Clare Newberry (Harper)

The Two Reds by Will (William Lipkind), illustrated by Nicolas (Nicolas Mordvinoff) (Harcourt)

1952

Finders Keepers by Will (William Lipkind), illustrated by Nicolas (Nicolas Mordvinoff) (Harcourt)

Honor Books

All Falling Down by Gene Zion, illustrated by Margaret Bloy Graham (Harper)
Bear Party by William Pène du Bois (Viking)
Feather Mountain by Elizabeth Olds (Houghton Mifflin)
Mr. T. W. Anthony Woo by Marie Hall Ets (Viking)
Skipper John's Cook by Marcia Brown (Scribner's)

1953

The Biggest Bear by Lynd Ward (Houghton Mifflin)

Honor Books

Ape in a Cape by Fritz Eichenberg (Harcourt)
Five Little Monkeys by Juliet Kepes (Houghton Mifflin)
One Morning in Maine by Robert McCloskey (Viking)
Puss in Boots by Charles Perrault, illustrated by Marcia Brown (Scribner's)
The Storm Book by Charlotte Zolotow, illustrated by Margaret Bloy Graham (Harper)

1954

Madeline's Rescue by Ludwig Bemelmans (Viking)

Honor Books

A Very Special House by Ruth Krauss, illustrated by Maurice Sendak (Harper)
Green Eyes by A. Birnbaum (Capitol)
Journey Cake, Ho! by Ruth Sawyer, illustrated by Robert McCloskey (Viking)
The Steadfast Tin Soldier by Hans Christian Andersen, illustrated by Marcia Brown (Scribner's)
When Will the World Be Mine? by Miriam Schlein, illustrated by Jean Charlot (Scott)

1955

Cinderella, or the Little Glass Slipper by Charles Perrault, illustrated by Marcia Brown (Scribner's)

Honor Books

Book of Nursery and Mother Goose Rhymes, illustrated by Marguerite de Angeli (Doubleday)
The Thanksgiving Story by Alice Dalgliesh, illustrated by Helen Sewell (Scribner's)
Wheel on the Chimney by Margaret Wise Brown, illustrated by Tibor Gergely (Lippincott)

1956

Frog Went A-Courtin', retold by John Langstaff, illustrated by Feodor Rojankovsky (Harcourt)

Honor Books

Crow Boy by Taro Yashima (Viking)
Play with Me by Marie Hall Ets (Viking)

1957

A Tree Is Nice by Janice May Udry, illustrated by Marc Simont (Harper)

Honor Books

Anatole by Eve Titus, illustrated by Paul Galdone (McGraw-Hill)
Gillespie and the Guards by Benjamin Elkin, illustrated by James Daugherty (Viking)
Lion by William Pène du Bois (Viking)
Mr. Penny's Race Horse by Marie Hall Ets (Viking)
1 Is One by Tasha Tudor (Walck)

1958

Time of Wonder by Robert McCloskey (Viking)

Honor Books

Anatole and the Cat by Eve Titus, illustrated by Paul Galdone (McGraw-Hill)
Fly High, Fly Low by Don Freeman (Viking)

1959

Chanticleer and the Fox, adapted from Chaucer, illustrated by Barbara Cooney (Crowell)

Honor Books

The House That Jack Built by Antonio Frasconi (Harcourt)
Umbrella by Taro Yashima (Viking)
What Do You Say, Dear? by Sesyle Joslin, illustrated by Maurice Sendak (Scott)

1960

Nine Days to Christmas by Marie Hall Ets and Aurora Labastida, illustrated by Marie Hall Ets (Viking)

Honor Books

Houses from the Sea by Alice E. Goudey, illustrated by Adrienne Adams (Scribner's)
The Moon Jumpers by Janice May Udry, illustrated by Maurice Sendak (Harper)

1961

Baboushka and the Three Kings by Ruth Robbins, illustrated by Nicholas Sidjakov (Parnassus)

Honor Books

Inch by Inch by Leo Lionni (Astor-Honor)

1962

Once a Mouse by Marcia Brown (Scribner's)

Honor Books

The Day We Saw the Sun Come Up by Alice E. Goudey, illustrated by Adrienne Adams (Scribner's)

The Fox Went Out on a Chilly Night, illustrated by Peter Spier (Doubleday)
Little Bear's Visit by Else Holmelund Minarik, illustrated by Maurice Sendak (Harper)

1963

The Snowy Day by Ezra Jack Keats (Viking)

Honor Books

Mr. Rabbit and the Lovely Present by Charlotte Zolotow, illustrated by Maurice Sendak (Harper)
The Sun Is a Golden Earring by Natalia M. Belting, illustrated by Bernarda Bryson (Holt)

1964

Where the Wild Things Are by Maurice Sendak (Harper)

Honor Books

All in the Morning Early by Sorche Nic Leodhas, illustrated by Evaline Ness (Holt)
Mother Goose and Nursery Rhymes, illustrated by Philip Reed (Atheneum)
Swimmy by Leo Lionni (Pantheon)

1965

May I Bring a Friend? by Beatrice Schenk de Regniers, illustrated by Beni Montresor (Atheneum)

Honor Books

A Pocketful of Cricket by Rebecca Caudill, illustrated by Evaline Ness (Holt)
Rain Makes Applesauce by Julian Scheer, illustrated by Marvin Bileck (Holiday House)
The Wave by Margaret Hodges, illustrated by Blair Lent (Houghton Mifflin)

1966

Always Room for One More by Sorche Nic Leodhas, illustrated by Nonny Hogrogian (Holt)

Honor Books

Hide and Seek Fog by Alvin Tresselt, illustrated by Roger Duvoisin (Lothrop)
Just Me by Marie Hall Ets (Viking)
Tom Tit Tot by Evaline Ness (Scribner's)

1967

Sam, Bangs & Moonshine by Evaline Ness (Holt)

Honor Books

One Wide River to Cross by Barbara Emberley, illustrated by Ed Emberley (Prentice-Hall)

1968

Drummer Hoff by Barbara Emberley, illustrated by Ed Emberley (Prentice-Hall)

Honor Books

The Emperor and the Kite by Jane Yolen, illustrated by Ed Young (World)

Frederick by Leo Lionni (Pantheon)
Seashore Story by Taro Yashima (Viking)

1969

The Fool of the World and the Flying Ship, retold by Arthur Ransome, illustrated by Uri Shulevitz (Farrar)

Honor Books

Why the Sun and the Moon Live in the Sky by Elphinstone Dayrell, illustrated by Blair Lent (Houghton Mifflin)

1970

Sylvester and the Magic Pebble by William Steig (Windmill/Simon & Schuster)

Honor Books

Alexander and the Wind-Up Mouse by Leo Lionni (Pantheon)
Goggles! by Ezra Jack Keats (Macmillan)
The Judge by Harve Zemach, illustrated by Margot Zemach (Farrar)
Pop Corn & Ma Goodness by Edna Mitchell Preston, illustrated by Robert Andrew Parker (Viking)
Thy Friend, Obadiah by Brinton Turkle (Viking)

1971

A Story, a Story by Gail E. Haley (Atheneum)

Honor Books

The Angry Moon by William Sleator, illustrated by Blair Lent (Atlantic/Little, Brown)
Frog and Toad Are Friends by Arnold Lobel (Harper)
In the Night Kitchen by Maurice Sendak (Harper)

1972

One Fine Day by Nonny Hogrogian (Macmillan)

Honor Books

Hildilid's Night by Cheli Durán Ryan, illustrated by Arnold Lobel (Macmillan)
If All the Seas Were One Sea by Janina Domanska (Macmillan)
Moja Means One by Muriel Feelings, illustrated by Tom Feelings (Dial)

1973

The Funny Little Woman, retold by Arlene Mosel, illustrated by Blair Lent (Dutton)

Honor Books

Anansi the Spider, adapted and illustrated by Gerald McDermott (Holt)
Hosie's Alphabet by Hosea, Tobias, and Lisa Baskin, illustrated by Leonard Baskin (Viking)
Snow White and the Seven Dwarfs, illustrated by Nancy Eckholm Burkert (Farrar)
When Clay Sings by Byrd Baylor, illustrated by Tom Bahti (Scribner's)

1974

Duffy and the Devil, retold by Harve Zemach, illustrated by Margot Zemach (Farrar)

Honor Books

Cathedral by David Macaulay (Houghton Mifflin)
Three Jovial Huntsmen by Susan Jeffers (Bradbury)

1975

Arrow to the Sun by Gerald McDermott (Viking)

Honor Books

Jambo Means Hello by Muriel Feelings, illustrated by Tom Feelings (Dial)

1976

Why Mosquitoes Buzz in People's Ears by Verna Aardema, illustrated by Leo and Diane Dillon (Dial)

Honor Books

The Desert Is Theirs by Byrd Baylor, illustrated by Peter Parnall (Scribner's)
Strega Nona, retold and illustrated by Tomie de Paola (Prentice-Hall)

1977

Ashanti to Zulu: African Traditions by Margaret Musgrove, illustrated by Leo and Diane Dillon (Dial)

Honor Books

The Amazing Bone by William Steig (Farrar)
The Contest, retold and illustrated by Nonny Hogrogian (Greenwillow)
Fish for Supper by M. B. Goffstein (Dial)
The Golem by Beverly Brodsky McDermott (Lippincott)
Hawk, I'm Your Brother by Byrd Baylor, illustrated by Peter Parnall (Scribner's)

1978

Noah's Ark, illustrated by Peter Spier (Doubleday)

Honor Books

Castle by David Macaulay (Houghton Mifflin)
It Could Always Be Worse by Margot Zemach (Farrar)

1979

The Girl Who Loved Wild Horses by Paul Goble (Bradbury)

Honor Books

Freight Train by Donald Crews (Greenwillow)
The Way to Start a Day by Byrd Baylor, illustrated by Peter Parnall (Scribner's)

1980

Ox-Cart Man by Donald Hall, illustrated by Barbara Cooney (Viking)

Honor Books

Ben's Trumpet by Rachel Isadora (Greenwillow)
The Garden of Abdul Gasazi by Chris Van Allsburg (Houghton Mifflin)
The Treasure by Uri Shulevitz (Farrar)

1981
Fables by Arnold Lobel (Harper)

Honor Books
The Bremen Town Musicians, retold and
    illustrated by Ilse Plume (Doubleday)
*The Grey Lady and the Strawberry
    Snatcher* by Molly Bang (Four Winds)
Mice Twice by Joseph Low (McElderry)
Truck by Donald Crews (Greenwillow)

1982
Jumanji by Chris Van Allsburg
    (Houghton Mifflin)

Honor Books
On Market Street by Arnold Lobel,
    illustrated by Anita Lobel
    (Greenwillow)
Outside Over There by Maurice Sendak
    (Harper)
*A Visit to William Blake's Inn: Poems for
    Innocent and Experienced Travelers* by
    Nancy Willard, illustrated by Alice and
    Martin Provensen (Harcourt)
Where the Buffaloes Begin by Olaf
    Baker, illustrated by Stephen Gammell
    (Warner)

1983
Shadow by Blaise Cendrars, illustrated
    by Marcia Brown (Scribner's)

Honor Books
A Chair for My Mother by Vera B.
    Williams (Greenwillow)
When I Was Young in the Mountains by
    Cynthia Rylant, illustrated by Diane
    Goode (Dutton)

1984
*The Glorious Flight: Across the Channel
    with Louis Blériot* by Alice and Martin
    Provensen (Viking)

Honor Books
Little Red Riding Hood, retold and
    illustrated by Trina Schart Hyman
    (Holiday House)
Ten, Nine, Eight by Molly Bang
    (Greenwillow)

1985
Saint George and the Dragon by
    Margaret Hodges, illustrated by Trina
    Schart Hyman (Little, Brown)

Honor Books
Hansel and Gretel, retold by Rika Lesser,
    illustrated by Paul O. Zelinsky (Dodd)
Have You Seen My Duckling? by Nancy
    Tafuri (Greenwillow)
The Story of Jumping Mouse, retold and
    illustrated by John Steptoe (Lothrop)

1986
The Polar Express by Chris Van Allsburg
    (Houghton Mifflin)

Honor Books
King Bidgood's in the Bathtub by Audrey
    Wood, illustrated by Don Wood
    (Harcourt)
The Relatives Came by Cynthia Rylant,
    illustrated by Stephen Gammell
    (Bradbury)

1987
Hey, Al by Arthur Yorinks, illustrated by
    Richard Egielski (Farrar)

Honor Books
Alphabatics by Suse MacDonald
    (Bradbury)
Rumpelstiltskin by Paul O. Zelinsky
    (Dutton)
*The Village of Round and Square
    Houses* by Ann Grifalconi (Little,
    Brown)

1988
Owl Moon by Jane Yolen, illustrated by
    John Schoenherr (Philomel)

Honor Books
*Mufaro's Beautiful Daughters: An
    African Tale* by John Steptoe
    (Lothrop)

1989
Song and Dance Man by Karen
    Ackerman, illustrated by Stephen
    Gammell (Knopf)

Honor Books
The Boy of the Three-Year Nap by
    Dianne Snyder, illustrated by Allen Say
    (Houghton Mifflin)
Free-Fall by David Wiesner (Lothrop)
Goldilocks and the Three Bears by James
    Marshall (Dial)
Mirandy and Brother Wind by Patricia C.
    McKissack, illustrated by Jerry
    Pinkney (Knopf)

1990
*Lon Po Po: A Red-Riding Hood Story
    from China*, translated and illustrated
    by Ed Young (Philomel)

Honor Books
Bill Peet: An Autobiography by Bill Peet
    (Houghton Mifflin)
Color Zoo by Lois Ehlert (Lippincott)
Hershel and the Hanukkah Goblins by
    Eric Kimmel, illustrated by Trina
    Schart Hyman (Holiday House)
The Talking Eggs by Robert D. San
    Souci, illustrated by Jerry Pinkney
    (Dial)

1991
Black and White by David Macaulay
    (Houghton Mifflin)

Honor Books
*"More More More," Said the Baby: 3
    Love Stories* by Vera B. Williams
    (Greenwillow)
Puss in Boots by Charles Perrault,
    translated by Malcolm Arthur,
    illustrated by Fred Marcellino
    (Farrar)

1992
Tuesday by David Wiesner (Clarion)

Honor Book
Tar Beach by Faith Ringgold (Crown)

1993
Mirette on the High Wire by Emily
    Arnold McCully (Putnam)

Honor Books
Seven Blind Mice by Ed Young
    (Philomel)
*The Stinky Cheese Man and Other Fairly
    Stupid Tales* by Jon Scieszka,
    illustrated by Lane Smith (Viking)
Working Cotton by Sherley Anne
    Williams, illustrated by Carole Byard
    (Harcourt)

1994
Grandfather's Journey by Allen Say
    (Houghton Mifflin)

Honor Books
Owen by Kevin Henkes (Greenwillow)
Peppe, the Lamplighter by Elisa Bartone
    (Lothrop)
Raven by Gerald McDermott
    (Harcourt)
In the Small, Small Pond by Denise
    Fleming (Holt)
Yo! Yes? by Chris Raschka (Orchard)

1995
Smoky Night by Eve Bunting, illustrated
    by David Diaz (Harcourt)

Honor Books
Swamp Angel by Anne Isaacs, illustrated
    by Paul O. Zelinsky (Dutton)
John Henry by Julius Lester, illustrated
    by Jerry Pinkney (Dial)
Time Flies by Eric Rohmann (Crown)

1996
Officer Buckle and Gloria by Peggy
    Rathmann (Putnam)

Honor Books
Alphabet City by Stephen T. Johnson
    (Viking)
Zin! Zin! Zin! A Violin by Lloyd Moss
    (Simon & Schuster)
The Faithful Friend by Robert D. San
    Souci, illustrated by Brian Pinkney
    (Simon & Schuster)
Tops & Bottoms, adapted and illustrated
    by Janet Stevens (Harcourt)

1997
Golem by David Wisniewski
    (Clarion)

Honor Books
Hush! A Thai Lullaby by Minfong Ho,
    illustrated by Holly Meade
    (Kroupa/Orchard)
The Graphic Alphabet by Neal Porter,
    illustrated by David Pelletier (Orchard)
The Paperboy by Dav Pilkey
    (Jackson/Orchard)
Starry Messenger by Peter Sis (Foster/
    Farrar)

1998
Rapunzel by Paul O. Zelinsky (Dutton)

Honor Books
The Gardener by Sarah Stewart and
    David Small (Farrar)
*There Was an Old Lady Who Swallowed
    a Fly* by Simms Taback (Viking)
Harlem: A Poem by Walter Dean
    Myers and Christopher Myers
    (Scholastic)

1999

Snowflake Bentley by Jacqueline Briggs Martin, illustrated by Mary Azarian (Houghton)

Honor Books

Duke Ellington: The Piano Prince and the Orchestra by Andrea Davis Pinkney, illustrated by Brian Pinkney

No, David! by David Shannon (Scholastic)

Snow by Uri Shulevitz (Farrar)

Tibet Through the Red Box by Peter Sis (Frances Foster)

2000

Joseph Had a Little Overcoat by Simms Taback (Viking)

Honor Books

A Child's Calendar by John Updike, illustrated by Trina Schart Hyman (Holiday House)

Sector 7 by David Wiesner (Clarion Books)

When Sophie Gets Angry—Really, Really, Angry by Molly Bang (Scholastic)

The Ugly Duckling by Hans Christian Andersen, adapted by Jerry Pinkney, illustrated by Jerry Pinkney (Morrow)

2001

So You Want to Be President? by Judith St. George, illustrated by David Small (Philomel)

Honor Books

Casey at the Bat by Ernest Thayer, illustrated by Christopher Bing (Handprint)

Click, Clack, Moo: Cows that Type by Doreen Cronin, illustrated by Betsy Lewin (Simon and Schuster)

Olivia by Ian Falconer (Atheneum)

2002

The Three Pigs by David Wiesner (Clarion/Houghton Mifflin)

Honor Books

The Dinosaurs of Waterhouse Hawkins by Barbara Kerley, illustrated by Brian Selznick (Scholastic)

Martin's Big Words: The Life of Martin Luther King, Jr. by Doreen Rappaport, illustrated by Bryan Collier (Jump at the Sun/Hyperion)

The Stray Dog by Marc Simont (HarperCollins)

2003

My Friend Rabbit by Eric Rohmann (Roaring Book Press/Millbrook Press)

Honor Books

The Spider and the Fly by Mary Howitt, illustrated by Tony DiTerlizzi (Simon & Schuster Books for Young Readers)

Hondo & Fabian by Peter McCarty (Holt)

Noah's Ark by Jerry Pinkney (SeaStar Books, a division of North-South Books)

2004

The Man Who Walked Between the Towers by Mordecai Gerstein (Roaring Brook Press/Millbrook Press)

Honor Books

Ella Sarah Gets Dressed by Margaret Chodos-Irvine (Harcourt)

What Do You DO with a Tail Like This? by Steve Jenkins and Robin Page (Houghton Mifflin)

Don't Let the Pigeon Drive the Bus by Mo Willems (Hyperion)

2005

Kitten's First Full Moon by Kevin Henkes (Greenwillow Books/HarperCollins Publishers)

Honor Books

The Red Book by Barbara Lehman (Houghton Mifflin Company)

Coming on Home Soon illustrated by E. B. Lewis, written by Jacqueline Woodson (G.P. Putnam's Sons/Penguin Young Readers Group)

Knuffle Bunny: A Cautionary Tale illustrated and written by Mo Willems (Hyperion Books for Children)

2006

The Hello Goodbye Window illustrated by Chris Raschka, written by Norton Juster (Michael di Capua Books/Hyperion Books for Children)

Honor Books

Rosa illustrated by Brylan Collier, written by Nikka Giovanni (Henry Holt and Company)

Zen Shorts illustrated and written by Jon J. Muth (Scholastic Press)

Hot Air: The (Mostly) True Story of the First Hot-Air Balloon Ride illustrated and written by Marjorie Priceman. (An Anne Schwartz Book/Atheneum Books for Young Readers/Simon & Schuster)

Song of the Water Boatman and Other Pond Poems illustrated by Beckie Prange, written by Joyce Sidman (Houghton Mifflin Company)

2007

Flotsam by David Wiesner (Clarion)

Honor Books

Gone Wild: An Endangered Animal Alphabet by David McLimans (Walker)

Moses: When Harriet Tubman Led Her People to Freedom illustrated by Kadir Nelson, written by Carole Boston Weatherford (Hyperion/Jump at the Sun)

Standards for Reading Professionals—Revised 2003

Standards and Criteria for Judging Performance

As newly graduated reading professionals enter the field, they must demonstrate the performances essential for meeting the reading instructional needs of all students. In essence, they must give evidence of meeting the standards presented in this document. The five standards are:

1. Candidates have knowledge of the foundations of reading and writing processes and instruction.
2. Candidates use a wide range of instructional practices, approaches, methods, and curriculum materials to support reading and writing instruction.
3. Candidates use a variety of assessment tools and practices to plan and evaluate effective reading instruction.
4. Candidates create a literate environment that fosters reading and writing by integrating foundational knowledge, use of instructional practices, approaches and methods, curriculum materials, and the appropriate use of assessments.
5. Candidates view professional development as a career-long effort and responsibility.

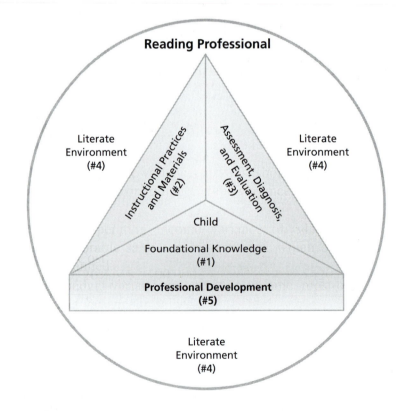

Part 2 from IRA. (2004). Professional Standards and Ethics Committee, International Reading Association. *Standards for reading professionals—revised 2003.* Reprinted with permission of the International Reading Association. All rights reserved.

For each of these standards, the matrix that follows describes performance criteria for judging whether preparation programs produce candidates who are competent to meet the instructional needs of their students. Each of the standards has three or four elements that make up the standard. Within the matrix, the performance criteria for each category of professional are listed for each element of the standard. As noted before, with the exception of administrators, the criteria are cumulative. The criteria for administrators are independent of the previous categories because administrators' responsibilities are primarily to provide leadership, supervision, and support for reading professionals, and thus require an independent set of performances and criteria.

The five standards can be visualized as a tetrahedron (see figure) with the reading professional at the apex and professional development as the base. The three faces of the tetrahedron are foundational knowledge, use of instructional practices and materials, and use of assessment tools. These three combine to create a literate environment that fosters reading and writing. The tetrahedron rests solidly on the base of professional development that begins with excellent initial preparation and continues with a commitment to lifelong career learning.

Standard 1: Foundational Knowledge

Candidates have knowledge of the foundations of reading and writing processes and instruction. As a result, candidates:

Element	Paraprofessional Candidates	Classroom Teacher Candidates (plus previous level)	Reading Specialist/ Literacy Coach Candidates (plus previous 2 levels)	Teacher Educator Candidates (plus previous 3 levels)	Administrator Candidates
1.1 Demonstrate knowledge of psychological, sociological, and linguistic foundations of reading and writing processes and instruction.	Know and apply elements from learning theory.	Know foundational theories related to practices and materials they use in the classroom.	Refer to major theories in the foundational areas as they relate to reading. They can explain, compare, contrast, and critique the theories.	Know a wide range of theories and how they relate to a range of classroom practices and materials. They can summarize empirical evidence related to these foundational theories. They conduct and publish research and contribute to the development of the knowledge base.	Know basic learning theory. They recognize well-grounded applications of the foundational knowledge in the classroom.
1.2 Demonstrate knowledge of reading research and histories of reading.	N/A	Recognize historical antecedents to contemporary reading methods and materials. They articulate how their teaching practices relate to reading research.	Summarize seminal reading studies and articulate how these studies impacted reading instruction. They can recount historical developments in the history of reading.	Articulate specific knowledge bases in their particular area of research and study.	Know general patterns in the history of reading, reading research, methods, and materials.
1.3 Demonstrate knowledge of language development and reading acquisition and the variations related to cultural and linguistic diversity.	Can articulate developmental aspects of oral language and its relationship to reading and writing. They can also summarize the developmental progression of reading acquisition and the variations related to cultural and linguistic diversity.	Can describe when students are meeting developmental benchmarks. They know when to consult other professionals for guidance.	Identify, explain, compare, and contrast the theories and research in the areas of language development and learning to read.	Synthesize information across the knowledge of learning theories and teaching. They can explain the connection between theories and practices.	Articulate developmental aspects of oral language and its relationship to reading and writing. They can also summarize the developmental progression of reading.

Standard 1: Foundational Knowledge *(continued)*

Candidates have knowledge of the foundations of reading and writing processes and instruction. As a result, candidates:

Element	Paraprofessional Candidates	Classroom Teacher Candidates (plus previous level)	Reading Specialist/ Literacy Coach Candidates (plus previous 2 levels)	Teacher Educator Candidates (plus previous 3 levels)	Administrator Candidates
I.4 Demonstrate knowledge of the major components of reading (phonemic awareness, word identification and phonics, vocabulary and background knowledge, fluency, comprehension strategies, and motivation) and how they are integrated in fluent reading.	List and define the major components of reading (phonemic awareness, word identification and phonics, vocabulary and background knowledge, fluency, comprehension strategies, and motivation).	Explain how the components (phonemic awareness, word identification and phonics, vocabulary and background knowledge, fluency, comprehension strategies, and motivation) are integrated during fluent reading. They can articulate the research that grounds their practice. They identify students' strengths and weaknesses in relation to the various components.	Are able to determine if students are appropriately integrating the components (phonemic awareness, word identification and phonics, vocabulary and background knowledge, fluency, comprehension strategies, and motivation) in fluent reading.	Articulate and synthesize information about the major components (phonemic awareness, word identification and phonics, vocabulary and background knowledge, fluency, comprehension strategies, and motivation) and explicate how the components are related to instructional practices and materials.	Explain how the components (phonemic awareness, word identification and phonics, vocabulary and background knowledge, fluency, comprehension strategies, and motivation) are integrated during fluent reading. They can articulate the research that grounds their practice.

Standard 2: Instructional Strategies and Curriculum Materials

Candidates use a wide range of instructional practices, approaches, methods, and curriculum materials to support reading and writing instruction. As a result, candidates:

Element	Paraprofessional Candidates	Classroom Teacher Candidates (plus previous level)	Reading Specialist/ Literacy Coach Candidates (plus previous 2 levels)	Teacher Educator Candidates (plus previous 3 levels)	Administrator Candidates
2.1 Use instructional grouping options (individual, small-group, whole-class, and computer based) as appropriate for accomplishing given purposes.	Use a variety of instructional grouping options selected by and supervised by a classroom teacher or reading specialist.	Match instructional grouping options to specific instructional purposes that take into account developmental, cultural, and linguistic differences among students. They model and scaffold procedures so that students learn to work effectively. They provide an evidence-based rationale for their selections.	Support classroom teachers and paraprofessionals in their use of instructional grouping options. They help teachers select appropriate options. They demonstrate the options and explain the evidence-based rationale for changing configurations to best meet the needs of all students.	Prepare and coach preservice candidates and inservice teachers to use instructional grouping options. They provide the candidates with opportunities to select, use, and practice the options.	Evaluate, support, and coach teachers' use of instructional grouping options for specific purposes based on their appropriateness for those purposes and for accommodating cultural and linguistic differences among their students.
2.2 Use a wide range of instructional practices, approaches, and methods, including technology-based practices, for learners at different stages of development and from different cultural and linguistic backgrounds.	Use a wide range of instructional practices, approaches, and methods, including technology-based practices, that are selected and supervised by a classroom teacher or reading specialist.	Plan for the use of a wide range of instructional practices, approaches, and methods, including technology-based practices. Their selections are guided by an evidence-based rationale and accommodate the developmental, cultural, and linguistic differences of their students.	Support classroom teachers and paraprofessionals in the use of a wide range of instructional practices, approaches, and methods, including technology-based practices. They help teachers select appropriate options and explain the evidence base for selecting practices to best meet the needs of all students. They demonstrate the options in their own teaching and in demonstration teaching.	Prepare and coach preservice candidates and inservice teachers to use a wide range of instructional practices, approaches, and methods, including technology-based practices. They provide strong evidence-based rationales for selecting appropriate options. They provide candidates with opportunities to select, to provide evidence-based rationales for their selections, and to use and practice a wide range of instructional practices, methods, and approaches.	Evaluate, support, and coach teachers' use of a wide range of instructional practices, approaches, and methods, including technology-based practices, for specific purposes based on their appropriateness for those purposes and for accommodating developmental, cultural, and linguistic differences among their students. They ensure that teachers' selections are supported by an evidence-based rationale.

Standard 2: Instructional Strategies and Curriculum Materials *(continued)*

Candidates use a wide range of instructional practices, approaches, methods, and curriculum materials to support reading and writing instruction. As a result, candidates:

Element	Paraprofessional Candidates	Classroom Teacher Candidates (plus previous level)	Reading Specialist/ Literacy Coach Candidates (plus previous 2 levels)	Teacher Educator Candidates (plus previous 3 levels)	Administrator Candidates
2.3 Use a wide range of curriculum materials in effective reading instruction for learners at different stages of reading and writing development and from different cultural and linguistic backgrounds.	Use a wide range of curriculum materials selected by a classroom teacher or reading specialist.	Plan for the use of a wide range of curriculum materials. Their selections are guided by an evidence-based rationale and accommodate the developmental, cultural, and linguistic differences of their students.	Support classroom teachers and paraprofessionals in the use of a wide range of curriculum materials. They help teachers select appropriate options and explain the evidence base for selecting practices to best meet the needs of all students. They demonstrate the options in their own teaching and in demonstration teaching.	Prepare and coach preservice candidates and inservice teachers to use a wide range of instructional materials. They provide strong evidence-based rationales for selecting appropriate options. They provide candidates with opportunities to select, to provide evidence-based rationales for their selections, and to use and practice a wide range of instructional practices.	Evaluate, support, and coach teachers' use of a wide range of curriculum materials for specific purposes based on their appropriateness for those purposes and for accommodating developmental, cultural, and linguistic differences among their students. They ensure that teachers' selections are supported by an evidence-based rationale.

Standard 3: Assessment, Diagnosis, and Evaluation

Candidates use a variety of assessment tools and practices to plan and evaluate effective reading instruction. As a result, candidates:

Element	Paraprofessional Candidates	Classroom Teacher Candidates (plus previous level)	Reading Specialist/ Literacy Coach Candidates (plus previous 2 levels)	Teacher Educator Candidates (plus previous 3 levels)	Administrator Candidates
3.1 Use a wide range of assessment tools and practices that range from individual and group standardized tests to individual and group informal classroom assessment strategies, including technology-based assessment tools.	Administer scripted formal and informal assessments and technology-based assessment under the direction of certified personnel.	Select and administer appropriate formal and informal assessments, including technology-based assessments. They understand the requirements for technical adequacy of assessments and can select technically adequate assessment tools. They can interpret the results of these tests and assessments.	Compare and contrast, use, interpret, and recommend a wide range of assessment tools and practices. Assessments may range from standardized tests to informal assessments and also include technology-based assessments. They demonstrate appropriate use of assessments in their practice, and they can train classroom teachers to administer and interpret these assessments.	Prepare and coach preservice candidates and inservice teachers to administer and interpret assessments appropriate for selected purposes. They interpret and critique technical aspects of assessments. They can articulate what makes up an effective assessment plan.	Understand the role of assessment in the delivery of excellent reading instruction. Working with reading professionals, they can develop appropriate building- and districtwide assessment plans.
3.2 Place students along a developmental continuum and identify students' proficiencies and difficulties.	N/A	Compare, contrast, and analyze information and assessment results to place students along a developmental continuum. They recognize the variability in reading levels across children in the same grade and within a child across different subject areas. They can identify students' proficiencies and difficulties. They recognize the need to make referrals for appropriate services.	Support the classroom teacher in the assessment of individual students. They extend the assessment to further determine proficiencies and difficulties for appropriate services.	Prepare and coach preservice candidates and inservice teachers to place students along a developmental continuum. They ground this preparation in research.	Know the range of students' reading performance in their building or under their control and know how this range relates to the broader student population. They provide support for an effective assessment plan.

Standard 3: Assessment, Diagnosis, and Evaluation *(continued)*

Candidates use a variety of assessment tools and practices to plan and evaluate effective reading instruction. As a result, candidates:

Element	Paraprofessional Candidates	Classroom Teacher Candidates (plus previous level)	Reading Specialist/ Literacy Coach Candidates (plus previous 2 levels)	Teacher Educator Candidates (plus previous 3 levels)	Administrator Candidates
3.3 Use assessment information to plan, evaluate, and revise effective instruction that meets the needs of all students, including those at different developmental stages and those from different cultural and linguistic backgrounds.	N/A	Analyze, compare, contrast, and use assessment results to plan, evaluate, and revise effective instruction for all students within an assessment/evaluation/ instruction cycle.	Assist the classroom teacher in using assessment to plan instruction for all students. They use in-depth assessment information to plan individual instruction for struggling readers. They collaborate with other education professionals to implement appropriate reading instruction for individual students. They collect, analyze, and use schoolwide assessment data to implement and revise school reading programs.	Prepare and coach preservice candidates and inservice teachers to use assessments to plan and revise effective instruction for all students within an assessment instruction cycle. They acknowledge and understand the research supporting different perspectives regarding assessment and instruction.	Support professional uses of assessment data.
3.4 Communicate results of assessments to specific individuals (students, parents, caregivers, colleagues, administrators, policymakers, policy officials, community, etc.).	N/A	Interpret a student's reading profile from assessments and communicate the results to the student, parents, caregivers, colleagues, and administrators.	Communicate assessment information to various audiences for both accountability and instructional purposes (policymakers, public officials, community members, clinical specialists, school psychologists, social workers, classroom teachers, and parents).	Prepare and coach preservice candidates and inservice teachers to be able to communicate for various audiences (policymakers, public officials, community members, classroom teachers, and parents).	Communicate assessment information to various audiences for accountability. They understand how assessment should be used for instructional purposes and demonstrate the ability to use it for the benefit of student growth and development. They can articulate to the public what makes up an effective assessment plan.

Standard 4: Creating a Literate Environment

Candidates create a literate environment that fosters reading and writing by integrating foundational knowledge, use of instructional practices, approaches and methods, curriculum materials, and the appropriate use of assessments. As a result, candidates:

Element	Paraprofessional Candidates	Classroom Teacher Candidates (plus previous level)	Reading Specialist/ Literacy Coach Candidates (plus previous 2 levels)	Teacher Educator Candidates (plus previous 3 levels)	Administrator Candidates
4.1 Use students' interests, reading abilities, and backgrounds as foundations for the reading and writing program.	Assist the teacher and reading specialist in gathering information on students' interests and cultural and linguistic backgrounds. They can use appropriate technology to collect this information.	Collect information about children's interests, reading abilities, and backgrounds. They use this information when planning instruction. They select materials and help students select materials that match their reading levels, interests, and cultural and linguistic backgrounds. They can use technology to gather and to use this information in instructional planning. They can articulate the research base that grounds their practice.	Assist the classroom teacher and paraprofessional in selecting materials that match the reading levels, interests, and cultural and linguistic background of students.	Prepare and coach preservice candidates and inservice teachers in gathering information relevant to creating a literate environment. They demonstrate how to level materials, assess the cultural and linguistical appropriateness and match materials to student interest. They demonstrate the development of instructional plans based on students' interests and cultural and linguistic backgrounds. They can use technology to enhance these processes.	Support the professional staff in designing curriculum based on students' interests, reading abilities, and cultural and linguistic backgrounds. They can articulate the research that grounds their practice.
4.2 Use a large supply of books, technology-based information, and nonprint materials representing multiple levels, broad interests, and cultural and linguistic backgrounds.	Assist students in selecting books, technology-based information, and nonprint materials that are appropriate for them.	Select books, technology-based information, and nonprint materials representing multiple levels, broad interests, and cultural and linguistic backgrounds. They can articulate the research that grounds their practice.	Assist the classroom teacher in selecting books, technology-based information, and nonprint materials representing multiple levels, broad interests, and cultural and linguistic backgrounds.	Prepare and coach preservice candidates and inservice teachers in the selection of books, technology-based information, and nonprint materials representing multiple levels, broad interests, and cultural and linguistic backgrounds.	Support the professional staff in selecting books, technology-based information, and nonprint materials representing multiple levels, broad interests, and cultural and linguistic backgrounds. They can articulate the research that grounds their practice.

Standard 4: Creating a Literate Environment *(continued)*

Candidates create a literate environment that fosters reading and writing by integrating foundational knowledge, use of instructional practices, approaches and methods, curriculum materials, and the appropriate use of assessments. As a result, candidates:

Element	Paraprofessional Candidates	Classroom Teacher Candidates (plus previous level)	Reading Specialist/ Literacy Coach Candidates (plus previous 2 levels)	Teacher Educator Candidates (plus previous 3 levels)	Administrator Candidates
4.3 Model reading and writing enthusiastically as valued lifelong activities.	Read aloud enthusiastically and fluently when reading to students.	Model and share the use of reading and writing for real purposes in daily life. They use think-alouds to demonstrate good reading and writing strategies. They can articulate the research that supports modeling think-alouds and read-alouds to students.	Demonstrate and model reading and writing for real purposes in daily interactions with students and education professionals. Assist teachers and paraprofessionals to model reading and writing as valued lifelong activities.	Prepare and coach preservice candidates and inservice teachers to model and share the use of reading and writing for real purposes in daily life. They demonstrate the process of think-alouds. They model how to read aloud enthusiastically and fluently.	Participate and support the professional staff in modeling reading and writing enthusiastically as valued lifelong activities.
4.4 Motivate learners to be lifelong readers.	Support students' choices of reading materials.	Effectively plan and implement instruction that motivates readers intrinsically and extrinsically. They are aware of children's literature, interests, and reading levels of students in their class and can select appropriate text. They assist children in discovering reading for personal purposes. They can provide an evidence-based rationale for their practice.	Use methods to effectively revise instructional plans to motivate all students. They assist classroom teachers in designing programs that will intrinsically and extrinsically motivate students. They demonstrate these techniques and they can articulate the research base that grounds their practice.	Prepare and coach preservice candidates and inservice teachers in the use of effective motivational reading techniques.	Support the professional staff in designing intrinsic and extrinsic motivational programs.

Standard 5: Professional Development

| | | | Reading Specialist/ | | |
Element	Paraprofessional Candidates	Classroom Teacher Candidates (plus previous level)	Literacy Coach Candidates (plus previous 2 levels)	Teacher Educator Candidates (plus previous 3 levels)	Administrator Candidates
		Candidates view professional development as a career-long effort and responsibility. As a result, candidates:			
5.1 Display positive dispositions related to reading and the teaching of reading.	Know the importance of confidentiality, and respect students and their cultural and linguistic backgrounds. They care for the well-being of students and believe that all students can learn.	Ensure that all individuals project ethical and caring attitudes in the classroom. They work with families, colleagues, and communities to support students' learning.	Articulate the theories related to the connections between teacher dispositions and student achievement.	Articulate the research base related to the connections between teacher dispositions and student achievement.	Ensure that there is an ethical learning context for reading instruction that respects students, families, teachers, colleagues, and communities.
5.2 Continue to pursue the development of professional knowledge and dispositions.	Study specific aspects of reading/instruction as recommended by teachers, reading specialists, and/or principals with whom they work. They demonstrate a curiosity and interest in the area of knowledge, skills, and dispositions related to reading and writing instruction.	Identify specific questions related to knowledge, skills, and/or dispositions related to their teaching of reading and writing. They plan specific strategies for finding answers to those questions. They carry out those plans and articulate the answers derived. They indicate knowledge of and are members of some professional organizations related to reading and writing. They are informed about important professional issues and are effective advocates with administrators; school boards; and local, state, and federal policymaking bodies.	Conduct professional study groups for paraprofessionals and teachers. Assist classroom teachers and paraprofessionals in identifying, planning, and implementing personal professional development plans. Advocate to advance the professional research base to expand knowledge-used practices.	Read, compare, and contrast articles in professional journals and other publications. They regularly participate in professional conferences. They conduct research and write for appropriate purposes. They prepare and coach preservice candidates and inservice teachers to conduct teacher action research.	Support teachers and reading specialists to develop their professional knowledge, skills, and dispositions. They provide information about opportunities for teachers and reading specialists to engage in professional development.

Standard 5: Professional Development *(continued)*

Candidates view professional development as a career-long effort and responsibility. As a result, candidates:

Element	Paraprofessional Candidates	Classroom Teacher Candidates (plus previous level)	Reading Specialist/ Literacy Coach Candidates (plus previous 2 levels)	Teacher Educator Candidates (plus previous 3 levels)	Administrator Candidates
5.3 Work with colleagues to observe, evaluate, and provide feedback on each other's practice.	N/A	Actively engage in collaboration and dialogue with other teachers and reading specialists to obtain recommendations and advice on teaching practices and ideas. They can articulate the evidence base related to these recommendations. They may conduct action research as a part of these collaborations.	Positively and constructively provide an evaluation of their own or others' teaching practices. Assist classroom teachers and paraprofessionals as they strive to improve their practice.	Read related research studies and use reflection as they actively engage in dialogue with other professionals in observation, evaluation, and feedback activities.	Encourage and facilitate collaboration and dialogue among professional personnel.
5.4 Participate in, initiate, implement, and evaluate professional development programs.	N/A	Participate individually and with colleagues in professional development experiences.	Exhibit leadership skills in professional development. They plan, implement, and evaluate professional development efforts at the grade, school, district, and/or state level. They are cognizant of and can identify and describe the characteristics of sound professional development programs. They can articulate the evidence base that grounds their practice.	Prepare and coach the reading specialist to plan, implement, and evaluate professional development efforts at the grade, school, district, and state levels. They also participate in professional development through the national level.	Provide opportunities for school staff to attend professional development programs. They bring consultants to school and district level for sustained professional development.

References for Children's and Adolescent Literature, Technology, and Teacher Resources

Teacher Resources

Literacy Content Area	Location	Page
Concept-Development Books	Figure 3.5	57
Wordless Storybooks	Figure 3.6	58
Picture Storybooks	Figure 3.7	58
Big Books	Figure 3.8	59
Alphabet Books	Figure 3.9	61
Poetry Anthologies Useful for Developing Rime and Phonemic Awareness	Figure 3.11	63
Books Rich in Imagery	Figure 3.15	68
Internal Reader Motivation	Items 1 through 6	191
Children's Books Classified for Easy Reference	Table 7.1	193
Poetry Anthologies for the Classrooom	Figure 7.1	196
Reference Works for Choosing Children's and Adolescent Literature	Figure 7.3	197
Teachers' and Students' Favorite Books for the Classroom Reading Center	Table 7.2	200
Children's Literature to Read Aloud	Figure 7.5	202
Books Appropriate for Developing Notetaking	Figure 8.7	239
High-Quality Literature to Motivate Delayed Readers	Figure 10.7	301–302
Asian American Literature	Figure 11.6	330
African American Literature	Figure 11.7	331
Hispanic American Literature	Figure 11.8	332
Native American Literature	Figure 11.9	333
Multicultural Literature—General Reference and Resource Books	Figure 11.10	334
Literature for Special Needs Students and Their Classmates	Figure 11.11	337
Examples of Instructional Software	Figure 12.9	372
Selected Internet Addresses for Classroom Use	Figure 12.11	376
Internet Resources for Teachers	International Reading Association, National Council of Teachers of English, Others	394–395
Newbery Medal Books	Appendix A	403
Caldecott Medal Books	Appendix B	409

General References

"A new world of online resources" (2004, August/September). *Reading Today, 22* (1), 1.

Abrahamson, R. F. (1979). *Children's favorite picture storybooks: An analysis of structure and reading preferences* (ERIC Documents Reproduction Service No. ED 174 977).

Abedi, J., Hofstetter, C. H., & Lord, C. (2004). Assessment accommodations for English language learners: Implications for policy-based empirical research. *Review of Educational Research, 74* (1), 1–28.

Abrahamson, R. F., & Shannon, P. (1983). A plot structure analysis of favorite picture books. *Reading Teacher, 37,* 44–48.

Abt-Perkins, D., & Gomez, M. L. (1993). A good place to begin: Examining our personal perspectives. *Language Arts, 70* (3), 193–202.

Adams, J., & Collins, A. (1985). A schema-theoretic view of reading. In H. Singer & R. B. Ruddell (Eds.), *Theoretical models and processes of reading* (3rd ed., pp. 404–425). Newark, DE: International Reading Association.

Adams, M. J. (1990a). *Beginning to read: Thinking and learning about print.* Cambridge, MA: MIT Press.

———. (1990b). *Beginning to read: Thinking and learning about print: A summary.* Urbana-Champaign: University of Illinois, Center for the Study of Reading.

———. (1994). Modeling the connections between word recognition and reading. In R. B. Ruddell, M. R. Ruddell, & H. Singer (Eds.), *Theoretical models and processes of reading* (4th ed., pp. 838–863). Newark, DE: International Reading Association.

———. (2004). A theory of reading: From eye fixations to comprehension. In R. B. Ruddell & N. J. Unrau (Eds.), *Theoretical models and processes of reading* (5th ed., pp. 1,219–1,243). Newark, DE: International Reading Association.

Adams, M. J., Bereiter, C., Hirshberg, J., & Anderson, V. (1995). *Reading and writing connection: Collection for Young Scholars* (p. 86). New York: McGraw-Hill.

Afflerbach, P. (1993). Report cards and reading. *The Reading Teacher, 46* (6), 458–465.

Alexander, P. A., & Jetton, T. L. (2000). Learning from text: A multidimensional and developmental perspective. In M. L. Kamil, P. B. Mosenthal, P. D. Pearson, & R. Barr (Eds.), *Handbook of reading research: Volume III* (pp. 285–310). Mahwah, NJ: Lawrence Erlbaum.

Allen, R. V. (1976). *Language experiences in communication.* Boston: Houghton Mifflin.

Allen, V. G. (1991). Teaching bilingual and ESL children. In J. Flood, J. M. Jensen, D. Lapp, & J. R. Squire (Eds.), *Handbook of research on teaching the English language arts* (pp. 356–364). New York: Macmillan.

Alexander, P. A., & Fox, E. (2004). A historical perspective on reading research and practice. In R. B. Ruddell & N. J. Unrau (Eds.), *Theoretical models and processes of reading* (5th ed., pp. 33–68). Newark, DE: International Reading Association.

Allington, R., Guice, S., Michelson, N., Baker, K., & Li, S. (1996). Literature-based curricula in high-poverty schools. In M. F. Graves, P. van den Broek, & B. M. Taylor (Eds.), *The first R: Every child's right to read* (pp. 73–96). New York: Teachers College Press.

Allington, R. L., & Cunningham, P. M. (1996). *Schools that work: Where all children read and write.* New York: HarperCollins College Publishers.

Allington, R. L., & McGill-Franzen, A. (2004). Looking back, looking forward: A conversation about teaching reading in the 21st century. In R. B. Ruddell & N. J. Unrau (Eds.), *Theoretical models and processes of reading* (5th ed., pp. 5–32). Newark, DE: International Reading Association.

Almasi, J. F. (1995). The nature of fourth graders' sociocognitive conflicts in peer-led and teacher-led discussions of literature. *Reading Research Quarterly, 30,* 314–351.

Altwerger, B., & Flores, B. (1991). Theme cycles: An overview. In K. S. Goodman, L. B. Bird, & Y. M. Goodman (Eds.), *The whole language catalog.* New York: Macmillan.

Ambe, E. B. (2007). Inviting reluctant adolescent readers into the literacy club: Some comprehension strategies to tutor individuals or small groups of reluctant readers. *Journal of Adolescent & Adult Literacy, 50,* 632–638.

Anders, P. L., Hoffman, J. V., & Duffy, G. G. (2000). Teaching teachers to teach reading: Paradigm shifts, persistent problems, and challenges. In M. L. Kamil, P. B. Mosenthal, P. D. Pearson, & R. Barr (Eds.), *Handbook of reading research: Volume III* (pp. 719–742). Mahwah, NJ: Lawrence Erlbaum.

Anderson, R. C. (2004). Role of the reader's schema in comprehension, learning, and memory. In R. B. Ruddell & N. J. Unrau (Eds.), *Theoretical models and processes of reading* (5th ed., pp. 594–606). Newark, DE: International Reading Association.

Anderson, R. C., & Freebody, P. (1981). Vocabulary knowledge. In J. T. Guthrie (Ed.), *Comprehension and teaching: Research reviews* (pp. 77–117). Newark, DE: International Reading Association.

———. (1985). Vocabulary knowledge. In H. Singer & R. B. Ruddell (Eds.), *Theoretical models and processes of reading* (3rd ed., pp. 343–371). Newark, DE: International Reading Association.

Anderson, R. C., Hiebert, E. H., Scott, J. A., and Wilkinson, I. A. G. (1984). *Becoming a nation of readers.* Washington, DC: National Institute of Education.

———. (1985). *Becoming a nation of readers: The report of the Commission on Reading.* Washington, DC: National Institute of Education.

Anderson-Inman, L., Horney, M. A., Chen, D.-T., & Lewin, L. (1994). Hypertext literacy: Observations from the electrotext project. *Language Arts, 71* (4), 279–287.

Andrade, H. G. (2000). Using rubrics to promote thinking and learning. *Educational Leadership, 57,* 13–18.

Anonymous (1978). *Influential Teacher Research Project.* Berkeley, CA: University of California.

Applebee, A. (1973). *The spectator role: Theoretical and developmental studies of ideas about and responses to literature with special reference to four age levels.* Unpublished doctoral dissertation, University of London, London, England.

———. (1978). *The child's concept of story.* Chicago: University of Chicago Press.

———. (1991). Environments for language teaching and learning: Contemporary issues and future directions. In J. Flood, J. M. Jensen, D. Lapp, & J. R. Squire (Eds.), *Handbook of research on teaching the English language arts* (pp. 549–556). New York: Macmillan.

Armstrong, T. (1994). *Multiple intelligences in the classroom.* Alexandria, VA: Association for Supervision and Curriculum Development.

Ashton-Warner, S. (1963). *Teacher.* London: Virgo Press.

Atwell, N. (1984). Writing and reading literature from the inside out. *Language Arts, 61,* 240–252.

———. (1991). *Coming to know: Writing to learn in the intermediate grades.* Portsmouth, NH: Heinemann.

———. (1998). *In the middle: New understandings about writing, reading, and learning.* Portsmouth, NH: Heinemann.

Au, K. H. (1980). Participation structures in a reading lesson with Hawaiian children: Analysis of a culturally appropriate instructional event. *Anthropology and Educational Quarterly, 11* (2), 91–115.

———. (1993). *Literacy instruction in multicultural settings.* New York: Harcourt Brace Jovanovich.

———. (2000). A multicultural perspective on policies for improving literacy achievement: Equity and excellence. In M. L. Kamil, P. B. Mosenthal, P. D. Pearson, & R. Barr (Eds.), *Handbook of reading research: Volume III* (pp. 835–851). Mahwah, NJ: Lawrence Erlbaum.

Avery, C. S. (1991). Organizing for whole language. In Y. M. Goodman, W. J. Hood, & K. S. Goodman (Eds.), *Organizing for whole language* (pp. 58–64). Portsmouth, NH: Heinemann.

Ayers, W., & Shubert, W. H. (1994). Teacher lore: Learning about teaching from teachers. In T. Shanahan (Ed.), *Teachers thinking, teachers knowing* (pp. 105–121). Urbana, IL: National Council of Teachers of English.

Baker, L., & Wigfield, Q. (1999). Dimensions of children's motivation for reading and their relations to reading activity and reading achievement. *Reading Research Quarterly, 34,* 452–477.

Ball, E. W., & Blachman, B. A. (1991). Does phoneme awareness training in kindergarten make a difference in early word recognition and developmental spelling? *Reading Research Quarterly, 26,* 49–66.

Baloche, L., & Platt, T. J. (1993). Sprouting magic beans: Exploring literature through creative questioning and cooperative learning. *Language Arts, 70* (4), 264–271.

Banks, J. A. (1997a). Approaches to multicultural curriculum reform. In J. A. Banks & C. A. M. Banks (Eds.), *Multicultural education: Issues and perspectives* (3rd ed., pp. 229–250). Boston: Allyn & Bacon.

———. (1997b). Multicultural education: Characteristics and goals. In J. A. Banks & C. A. M. Banks (Eds.), *Multicultural education: Issues and perspectives* (3rd ed., pp. 3–31). Boston: Allyn & Bacon.

———. (2002). *An introduction to multicultural education.* Boston: Allyn & Bacon.

———. (2003). Teaching literacy for social justice and global citizenship. *Language Arts, 81* (1), 18–19.

Banks, J. A., & Banks, C. A. M. (1989). *Multicultural education.* Boston: Allyn & Bacon.

Barchers, S. I. (2000). *Multicultural folktales: Readers theatre for elementary students.* Englewood, CO: Teacher Ideas Press.

Barone, T., Eeds, M., & Mason, K. (1995). Literature, the disciplines, and the lives of elementary school children. *Language Arts, 72* (1), 30–38.

Barr, R., Kamil, M. L., Mosenthal, P. B., & Pearson, P. D. (1991). *Handbook of reading research: Vol. II.* New York: Longman.

Barrentine, S. J. (1996). Engaging with reading through interactive read-alouds. *The Reading Teacher, 50* (1), 36–43.

Baugh, A. C. (1957). *A history of the English language.* New York: Appleton-Century-Crofts.

Baumann, J. F., & Bergeron, B. (1993). Story-map instruction using children's literature: Effects on first graders' comprehension of central narrative elements. *Journal of Reading Behavior, 25,* 407–437.

Baumann, J. F., Clymer, T., Grant, C., Hiebert, E. H., Indrisano, R., Johnson, D. D., Juel, C., Paratore, J. R., Pearson, P. D., Raphael, T. E., Toth, M. D., & Venezky, R. L. (1993). *Leaving footprints.* Needham, MA: Silver Burdett Ginn.

Baumann, J. F., Hoffman, J. V., Moon, J., & Duffy-Hester, A. M. (1998). Where are teachers' voices in the phonics/whole language debate? Results from a survey of U.S. elementary classroom teachers. *The Reading Teacher, 51,* 636–650.

Beach, J. D. (1983). Teaching students to write informational reports. *Elementary School Journal, 84,* 213–220.

Bean, T. W. (2000). Reading in the Content Areas: Social Constructivist Dimensions. In M. L. Kamil, P. B. Mosenthal, P. D. Pearson, & R. Barr (Eds.), *Handbook of reading research: Volume III* (pp. 629–644). Mahwah, NJ: Lawrence Erlbaum.

Bear, D. R., & Templeton, S. (1998). Explorations in developmental spelling: Foundations for learning and teaching phonics, spelling, and vocabulary. *The Reading Teacher, 52* (3), 222–242.

Beck, I. L., & McCaslin, E. S. (1978). *An analysis of dimensions that affect the development of code-breaking ability in eight beginning reading programs* (LRDC Report No. 1978/6). Pittsburgh, PA: University of Pittsburgh Learning Research and Development Center.

Beck, I. L., & McKeown, M. G. (1991). Conditions of vocabulary acquisition. In R. Barr, M. L. Kamil, P. Mosenthal, & P. D. Pearson (Eds.), *Handbook of reading research: Vol. II* (pp. 787–814). New York: Longman.

Beck, I. L., McKeown, M. G., Hamilton, R. L., & Kucan, L. (1997). *Questioning the author: An approach for enhancing student engagement with text.* Newark, DE: International Reading Association.

Beck, I. L., Perfetti, C. A., & McKeown, M. G. (1982). The effects of long-term vocabulary instruction on lexical access and reading comprehension. *Journal of Educational Psychology, 74,* 506–521.

Becker, W. C., & Gersten, R. (1982). A follow-up of Follow-Through: The later effects of the direct instruction model on children in fifth and sixth grades. *American Educational Research Journal, 19,* 75–92.

Beidler, P. G. (Ed.). (1986). Distinguished teachers on effective teaching. *New Directions for Teaching and Learning. 28* (Winter), 51–61.

Berghoff, B. (1993). Moving towards aesthetic literacy in the first grade. In D. J. Leu & C. K. Hinzer (Eds.), *The 42nd yearbook of the National Reading Conference* (pp. 217–226). Rochester, NY: National Reading Conference.

Betts, E. A. (1946). *Foundations of reading instruction.* New York: American Book.

Blachman, B. A. (2000). Phonological awareness. In M. L. Kamil, P. B. Mosenthal, P. D. Pearson, & R. Barr (Eds.), *Handbook of reading research: Volume III* (pp. 483–502). Mahwah, NJ: Lawrence Erlbaum.

Blachowicz, C. L. Z., & Fisher, P. (2000). Vocabulary instruction. In M. L. Kamil, P. B. Mosenthal, P. D. Pearson, & R. Barr (Eds.), *Handbook of reading research: Volume III* (pp. 503–523). Mahwah, NJ: Lawrence Erlbaum Associates.

Blachowicz, C. L. Z., Fisher, P. J. L., Ogle, D., Watts-Taffe, S. (2006). Vocabulary: Questions from the classroom. *Reading Research Quarterly, 41,* 524–539.

Blachowicz, C. L. Z., & Lee, J. J. (1991). Vocabulary development in the whole literacy classroom. *The Reading Teacher, 45* (3), 188–195.

Black, A., & Stave, A. M. (2007). *A comprehensive guide to readers theatre.* Newark, DE: International Reading Association.

Black, P., & William, D. (1998). Assessment and classroom learning. *Assessment in Education: Principles, Policy, and Practice, 5* (1), 7–74.

Blake, M. (1990). Learning logs in the upper elementary grades. In N. Atwell (Ed.), *Coming to know: Writing to learn in the intermediate grades* (pp. 53–60). Portsmouth, NH: Heinemann.

Block, C. C. (1997). *Teaching the language arts.* Boston: Allyn & Bacon.

Block, C. C., & Pressley, M. (2001). *Comprehension instruction: Research-based best practices.* New York: Guilford.

Bloom, B. S. (1982). The master teachers. *Phi Delta Kappan, 63* (10), 664–669, 715.

Bloome, D. (1991). Anthropology and research on teaching the English language arts. In J. Flood, J. M. Jensen, D. Lapp, & J. R. Squire (Eds.), *Handbook of research on teaching the English language arts* (pp. 46–56). New York: Macmillan.

Bloome, D., & Bailey, F. (1992). Studying language and literacy through events, particularities, and intertextuality. In R. Beach, J. Green, M. Kamil, & T. Shanahan (Eds.), *Multidisciplinary perspectives on literacy research* (pp. 181–210). Urbana, IL: National Council of Teachers of English.

Bond, G. I., & Dykstra, R. (1967, summer). The cooperative research program in first-grade reading instruction. *Reading Research Quarterly, 2* (4), 5–142.

Bownas, J., McClure, A. A., & Oxley, P. (1998). Bringing the rhythm of poetry into the classroom. *Language Arts, 75* (1), 48–55.

Britton, J., Burgess, T., Martin, N., McLeod, A., & Rosen, H. (1975). *The development of writing abilities.* London: Macmillan Education.

Brown, A. (1985). Metacognition: The development of selective attention strategies for learning from texts. In H. Singer & R. B. Ruddell (Eds.), *Theoretical models and processes of reading* (3rd ed., pp. 501–526). Newark, DE: International Reading Association.

Brown, A. L., Palincsar, A. M., & Armbruster, B. B. (2004). In R. B. Ruddell & N. J. Unrau (Eds.), *Theoretical models and processes of reading* (5th ed., pp. 780–809). Newark, DE: International Reading Association.

Brown, H., & Cambourne, B. (1987). *Read and retell.* Portsmouth, NH: Heinemann.

Brown, R. (1973). *First language: The early stages.* Cambridge, MA: Harvard University Press.

Brown, R., Pressley, M., Van Meter, P., & Schuder, T. (2004). In R. B. Ruddell & N. J. Unrau (Eds.), *Theoretical models and processes of reading* (5th ed., pp. 998–1039). Newark, DE: International Reading Association.

Brozo, W. G., & Simpson, M. L. (2007). *Content literacy for today's adolescents.* Upper Saddle River, NJ: Merrill Prentice Hall.

Bruner, J. S. (1990). *Acts of meaning.* Cambridge, MA: Harvard University Press.

Bruning, R., & Schweiger, B. M. (1997). Integrating science and literacy experiences to motivate student learning. In J. T. Guthrie & A. Wigfield (Eds.), *Reading engagement: Motivating readers through integrated instruction* (pp. 149–167). Newark, DE: International Reading Association.

Bryant, P., & Bradley, L. (1985). *Children's reading problems.* New York: Oxford University Press.

Burgess, S. A. (1985). Reading but not literate: The child-read survey. *School Library Journal, 31,* 27–30.

Burgess, S. R., Hecht, S. A., & Logan, C. J. (2002). Relations of the home literacy environment (HLE) to the development of reading-related abilities: A one-year longitudinal study. *Reading Research Quarterly, 37* (4), 408–426.

Burns, B. (1998). Changing the classroom climate with literature circles. *Journal of Adolescent & Adult Literacy, 42* (2), 1998.

Buss, K., & Karnowski, L. (2000). *Reading and writing: Literary genres.* Newark, DE: International Reading Association.

Bussie, A. M., Chittenden, E. A., Amarel, M., & Klausner, E. (1985). *Inquiry into meaning: An investigation of learning to read.* Hillsdale, NJ: Erlbaum.

California Commission on Teacher Credentialing. (1992). *Success for beginning teachers: The California new teacher project 1988–1992.* Sacramento: California State Department of Education.

California State Department of Education. (1989). *California Assessment Portfolio Project.* Sacramento, CA: Author.

California State Department of Education. (2000). *California demographics data.* Retrieved February 2003 from www.cde.ca.gov/demographics.

Calkins, L. M. (1983). *Lessons from a child.* Portsmouth, NH: Heinemann.

———. (1986). *The art of teaching writing.* Portsmouth, NH: Heinemann.

———. (1991). *Living between the lines.* Portsmouth, NH: Heinemann.

Cambourne, B. (1984). Basic conditions for language development. Paper presented at the meeting of the 10th National Australian Reading Association Conference, Sydney, Australia.

———. (1994). The rhetoric of "The Rhetoric of Whole Language." *Reading Research Quarterly, 29* (4), 330–333.

———. (1995). Toward an educationally relevant theory of literacy learning: Twenty years of inquiry. *The Reading Teacher, 49* (3), 182–190.

Cambourne, B., & Turbill, J. (1987). *Coping with chaos.* Portsmouth, NH: Heinemann.

Camp, D. (2000). It takes two: Teaching with twin texts of fact and fiction. *The Reading Teacher, 53,* 400–408.

Carlisle, J. F., & Stone, C. A. (2005). Exploring the role of morphemes in word reading. *Reading Research Quarterly, 40,* 428–449.

Carolo, M. S., August, D., McLaughlin, B., Snow, C. E., Dressler, C., Lippman, D. N., Lively, R. J., & White, C. E. (2004). Closing the gap: Addressing the vocabulary needs of English-language learners in bilingual and mainstream classrooms. *Reading Research Quarterly, 39,* 188–206.

Carr, E., & Ogle, D. (1987). K-W-L Plus: A strategy for comprehension and summarization. *Journal of Reading, 30,* 626–631.

Carroll, M. (1997). Using computers in the classroom. Unpublished manuscript, University of California at Berkeley.

Carroll, M. (2004). *Cartwheels on the keyboard: Computer-based literacy instruction in an elementary classroom.* Newark, DE: International Reading Association.

Casteel, C. P., & Isom, B. A. (1994). Reciprocal processes in science and literacy learning. *The Reading Teacher, 47* (7), 538–545.

Cazden, C. B. (1965). Environmental assistance to the child's acquisition of grammar. Unpublished doctoral dissertation, Harvard University, Cambridge, MA.

———. (1968). The acquisition of noun and verb inflections. *Child Development, 39,* 433–448.

———. (1994). What is sharing time for? In A. H. Dyson & C. Genishi (Eds.), *The need for story: Cultural diversity in classroom and community* (pp. 72–79). Urbana, IL: National Council of Teachers of English.

Chall, J. S. (1967/1983). *Learning to read: The great debate.* New York: McGraw-Hill.

———. (2000). *The academic achievement challenge: What really works in the classroom?* New York: Guilford Press.

Chall, J. S., & Squire, J. R. (1991). The publishing industry and textbooks. In R. Barr, M. L. Kamil, P. Mosenthal, & P. D. Pearson (Eds.), *Handbook of reading research: Vol. II* (pp. 120–146). New York: Longman.

Chard, N. (1990). How learning logs change teaching. In N. Atwell (Ed.), *Coming to know: Writing to learn in the intermediate grades* (pp. 61–68). Portsmouth, NH: Heinemann.

Chihank, J. (1999). Success is in the details: Publishing to validate elementary authors. *Language Arts, 76* (6), 491–498.

Chomsky, C. S. (1969). *The acquisition of syntax in children from 5 to 10.* Cambridge, MA: MIT Press.

———. (1979). Approaching reading through invented spelling. In L. B. Resnick & P. A. Weaver (Eds.), *Theory and practice of early reading* (pp. 43–65). Hillsdale, NJ: Erlbaum.

Christian-Smith, L. K. (1993). *Texts of desire: Essays on fiction, femininity and schooling.* London: Falmer.

Church, S. M. (1994). Is whole language really warm and fuzzy? *The Reading Teacher, 47* (5), 362–370.

Ciardiello, A. V. (1998). Did you ask a good question today? Alternative cognitive and metacognitive strategies. *Journal of Adolescent and Adult Literacy, 42* (3), 210–219.

———. (2003). "To wander and wonder": Pathways to literacy and inquiry through question finding. *Journal of Adolescent and Adult Literacy, 47* (3), 228–239.

Clay, M. M. (1967). The reading behavior of five-year-old-children: A research report. *New Zealand Journal of Educational Studies, 2,* 11–31.

———. (1975). *What did I write?* Portsmouth, NH: Heinemann.

———. (1979). *Concepts about print test.* Portsmouth, NH: Heinemann.

———. (1983). Getting a theory of writing. In B. M. Kroll & G. Wells (Eds.), *Explorations in a development of writing* (pp. 259–284). New York: Wiley.

———. (1985). *The early detection of reading difficulties: A diagnostic survey with recovery procedures.* Portsmouth, NH: Heinemann.

———. (1987). Implementing Reading Recovery: Systemic adaptations to an educational innovation. *New Zealand Journal of Educational Studies, 22* (1), 55–58.

———. (1993). *An observation survey of early literacy achievement.* Portsmouth, NH: Heinemann.

Cleary, B. (1996). *My own two feet: A memoir.* New York: Avon Books.

Cleland, J. V. (1999). We can charts: Building blocks for student-led conferences. *The Reading Teacher, 52* (6), 588–595.

"Coaches, controversy, consensus" (2004, April/May). *Reading Today, 21* (5), 1, 18.

Cochran-Smith, M., Kahn, J., & Paris, C. L. (1988). In J. L. Hoot & S. B. Silvern (Eds.), *Writing with computers in the early grades* (pp. 43–74). New York: Teachers College Press.

Coiro, J., & Dobler, E. (2007). Exploring the online reading comprehension strategies used by sixth-grade skilled readers to search for and locate information on the Internet. *Reading Research Quarterly, 42,* 2007.

Coley, J. D., DePinto, T., Craig, S., & Gardner, R. (1993). From college to classroom: Three teachers' accounts of their adaptations of reciprocal teaching. *The Elementary School Journal, 94,* 255–266.

Collier, V. P. (1989, April). Academic achievement, attitudes, and occupations among graduates of two-way bilingual classes. Paper presented at the annual meeting of the American Education Research Association, San Francisco.

Collins, M. F. (2005). ESL preschoolers' English vocabulary acquisition from storybook reading. *Reading Research Quarterly, 40,* 406–408.

Collins, P. J. (1990). Bridging the gap. In N. Atwell (Ed.), *Coming to know: Writing to learn in the intermediate grades* (pp. 17–31). Portsmouth, NH: Heinemann.

Come, B., & Fredericks, A. D. (1995). Family literacy in urban schools: Meeting the needs of at-risk children. *The Reading Teacher, 48* (7), 566–570.

Consuelo, Sr. M. (1967). What do first graders like to read? *Catholic School Journal, 67,* 42–43.

Cooper, J. D., & Pikulski, J. J. (1996). *Hello/Share Literacy Activity Book* (p. 144), Boston: Houghton Mifflin.

———. (2005). *Horizons: Smart solutions.* Teacher's edition (pp. 367Y–367Z). Boston: Houghton Mifflin.

Cooter, R. B., Jr. (1991). Storytelling in the language arts classroom. *Reading Research and Instruction, 30* (2), 71–76.

Cote, N., & Goldman, S. R. (2004). Building representations of informational text: Evidence from children's think-aloud protocols. In R. B. Ruddell & N. J. Unrau (Eds.), *Theoretical models and processes of reading* (5th ed., pp. 660–683). Newark, DE: International Reading Association.

Cox, B. E., Fang, Z, & Otto, B. W. (2004). Preschoolers' developing ownership of literate register. In R. B. Ruddell & N. J. Unrau (Eds.), *Theoretical models and processes of reading* (5th ed., pp. 281–312). Newark, DE: International Reading Association.

Crosby, M. (1964). *Curriculum development for elementary schools in a changing society.* Boston: D.C. Heath.

Cudd, E. T., & Roberts, L. L. (1993/1994). A scaffolding technique to develop sentence sense and vocabulary. *The Reading Teacher, 47* (4), 346–349.

Cullinan, B., Harwood, K., & Galda, L. (1983). The reader and the story: Comprehension and response. *Journal of Research and Development in Education, 16,* 29–37.

Cullinan, B. E. (1992). *Read to me: Raising kids who love to read.* New York: Scholastic.

———. (Ed.). (1993). *Fact and fiction: Literature across the curriculum.* Newark, DE: International Reading Association.

Cummins, J. (1989). Language and literacy acquisition in bilingual contexts. *Journal of Multilingual and Multicultural Development, 10* (1), 17–31.

Cunningham, P. M. (1991). *Phonics they use: Words for reading and writing.* New York: Longman.

———. (2005). *Phonics they use: Words for reading and writing* (4th ed.). Boston: Allyn & Bacon.

Cunningham, P. M., & Allington, R. L. (1999). *Classrooms that work: They can all read and write.* New York: Longman.

Cunningham, P. M., & Cunningham, J. W. (1987). Content area reading-writing lessons. *The Reading Teacher, 40,* 506–512.

Daiute, C. (1993). Youth genres and literacy: Links between sociocultural and developmental theories. *Language Arts, 70* (5), 403–416.

Dale, E., & Chall, J. S. (1948). A formula for predicting readability. *Educational Research Bulletin, 27,* 11–20, 37–54.

Damon, W. (1984). Peer education: The untapped potential. *Journal of Applied Developmental Psychology, 5,* 331–343.

Dana, C., & Rodriquez, M. (1992). TOAST: A system to study vocabulary. *Reading Research and Instruction, 31* (4), 78–84.

Danielewicz, J. M. (1984). Developmental differences between children's spoken and written language. Unpublished manuscript, University of California, Berkeley.

Danner, F. W. (1976). Children's understanding of intersentence organization in the recall of short descriptive passages. *Journal of Educational Psychology, 68,* 174–183.

Davidson, J. L. (1978, April). Mapping: A dynamic extension of the DR-TA. Paper presented at the meeting of the IRA Language-Experience Special Interest Group, San Antonio, TX.

———. (1982). The group mapping activity for instruction in reading and thinking. *Journal of Reading, 26,* 52–56.

Davis, F. B. (1944). Fundamental factors in reading comprehension. *Psychometrika, 9,* 185–197.

———. (1968). Research in comprehension in reading. *Reading Research Quarterly, 3,* 499–545.

Deci, E. L. (1995). *Why we do what we do: The dynamic of personal autonomy.* New York: Putnam.

Denton, P. J., Ciancio, D. J., & Fletcher, J. M. (2006). Validity, reliability, and utility of the Observation Survey of Early Literacy Achievement. *Reading Research Quarterly, 41,* 8–34.

Denver, B., & Leedham, L. (1992, November). Stevens Creek portfolio project: Apple Classrooms of Tomorrow. Paper presented at the meeting of the California Reading Association, San Diego, CA.

Depree, H., & Iversen, S. (1994). *Early literacy in the classroom: A new standard for young readers.* Bothell, WA: Wright Group Publishing.

DeJong, M. T., & Bus, A. G. (2004). The efficacy of electronic books in fostering kindergarten children's emergent story understanding. *Reading Research Quarterly, 29,* 378–393.

DeStefano, J. S. (1978). *Language, the learner and the school.* New York: Wiley.

DeVilliers, J. G., & DeVilliers, P. A. (1973). A cross-sectional study of the development of grammatical morphemes in child speech. *Journal of Psycholinguistic Research, 2,* 267–278.

DeVries, R. (1997). Piaget's social theory. *Educational Researcher, 26* (2), 4–17.

Díaz-Rico, L. T., & Weed, K. A. (1995). *The crosscultural, language, and academic development handbook.* Boston: Allyn & Bacon.

Dickinson, D. K., & Smith, M. W. (1994). Long-term effects of preschool teachers' book readings on low-income children's vocabulary and story comprehension. *Reading Research Quarterly, 29* (2), 104–122.

Dolch, E. W. (1936). A basic sight vocabulary. *The Elementary School Journal, 36,* 456–460.

Dole, J. A. (2004), The changing role of the reading specialist in school reform. *The Reading Teacher, 57, 5,* 462–471.

Dole, J. A., Brown, K. J., & Trathen, W. (1996). The effects of strategy instruction on the comprehension performance of at-risk students. *Reading Research Quarterly, 31* (1), 62–88.

Dowhower, S. L. (1999). Supporting a strategic stance in the classroom: A comprehension framework for helping teachers help students to be strategic. *The Reading Teacher, 52* (7), 672–688.

Doyle, W., & Carter, K. (1984). Academic tasks in classrooms. *Curriculum Inquiry, 14,* 129–149.

Drucker, M. J. (2003). What reading teachers should know about ESL learners. *The Reading Teacher, 57* (1), 22–29.

Drum, P. A., & Konopak, B. C. (1987). Learning word meanings from written context. In M. G. McKeown & M. E. Curtis (Eds.), *The nature of vocabulary acquisition* (pp. 73–87). Hillsdale, NJ: Erlbaum.

Duffy, G. G., & Hoffman, J. V. (1999). In pursuit of an illusion: The flawed search for a perfect method. *The Reading Teacher, 53* (1), 10–16.

Duffy-Hester, A. M. (1999). Teaching struggling readers in elementary school classrooms. *The Reading Teacher, 52,* 480–495.

Duke, N. K., & Bennett-Armistead, V. S. (2003). *Reading and writing informational text in the primary grades: Research-based practices.* New York: Scholastic Teaching Resources.

Duke, N. K., Purcell-Gates, V., Hall, L. A., & Tower, C. (2007). Authentic literacy activities for developing comprehension and writing. *The Reading Teacher, 60,* 244–355.

Dunston, P. J. (2007). Instructional practices, struggling readers, and a university-based reading clinic. *Journal of Adolescent & Adult Literacy, 50,* 328–334.

Durkin, D. (1966). *Children who read early.* New York: Teachers College Press.

———. (1978–1979). What classroom observations reveal about reading comprehension instruction. *Reading Research Quarterly, 15,* 481–533.

Durr, W. (1973). Computer study of high frequency words in popular trade journals. *The Reading Teacher, 27,* 37–42.

Duthie, C. (1994). Nonfiction: A genre study for the primary classroom. *Language Arts, 71* (8), 588–595.

Dykstra, R. (1968). Summary of the second-grade phase of the Cooperative Research Program in Primary Reading Instruction. *Reading Research Quarterly, 4,* 49–71.

Dyson, A. H. (1982). Reading, writing, and language: Young children solve the written language puzzle. *Language Arts, 59,* 829–839.

———. (1984). Learning to write/learning to do school: Emergent writers' interpretations of school literacy tasks. *Research in the Teaching of English, 18,* 233–265.

———. (1988). Negotiating among multiple worlds: The space/time dimensions of young children's composing. *Research in the Teaching of English, 22* (4), 355–390.

———. (1991). Viewpoints: The word and the world—reconceptualizing written language development or do rainbows mean a lot to little girls? *Research in the Teaching of English, 25* (1), 97–123.

———. (1995). Writing children: Reinventing the development of childhood literacy. *Written Communication, 12* (1), 4–46.

———. (1998). Folk processes and media creatures: Reflections on popular culture for literacy educators. *The Reading Teacher, 51* (5), 392–402.

———. (2000). On reframing children's words: The perils, promises, and pleasures of writing children. *Research in the Teaching of English, 34* (3), 352–367.

———. (2004). Writing in a sea of voices: Oral language in, around, and about writing. In R. B. Ruddell & N. J. Unrau (Eds.), *Theoretical models and processes of reading* (5th ed., pp. 146–162). Newark, DE: International Reading Association.

Dyson, A. H., & Freedman, S. W. (1991). Writing. In J. Flood, J. M. Jensen, D. Lapp, & J. R. Squire (Eds.), *Handbook of research on teaching the English language arts* (pp. 754–774). New York: Macmillan.

Education Week. (2000). Quality counts 2000. *Education Week, 19* (18), 72–75.

Edwards, P. A. (1996). Creating sharing time conversations: Parents and teachers work together. *Language Arts, 73* (5), 344–349.

Eeds, M., & Wells, D. (1989). Grand conversations: An exploration of meaning construction in literature study groups. *Research in the Teaching of English, 23*, 4–29.

Ehri, L. (1997). Learning to read and learning to spell are one and the same, almost. In C. Perfetti, L. Rieben, & M. Fayol (Eds.), *Learning to spell: Research, theory, and practice across languages* (pp. 237–269). Mahwah, NJ: Erlbaum.

Ehri, L. C. (1991). Development of the ability to read words. In R. Barr, M. L. Kamil, P. Mosenthal, & P. D. Pearson (Eds.), *Handbook of reading research: Volume II* (pp. 383–417). New York: Longman.

Ehri, L. C., & McCormick, S. (2004). Phases of word learning: Implications for instruction with delayed and disabled readers. In R. B. Ruddell & N. J. Unrau (Eds.), *Theoretical models and processes of reading* (5th ed., pp. 365–389). Newark, DE: International Reading Association.

Ehri, L. C., Nunes, S. R., Willows, D. M., Shuster, B. V., Yaghoub-Zadeh, Z. & Shanahan, T. (2001). Phonemic awareness instruction helps children learn to read: Evidence from the National Panel's meta-analysis. *Reading Research Quarterly, 36*, 250–287.

Ehri, L. C., & Wilce, L. S. (1985). Movement into reading: Is the first stage of printed word learning visual or phonetic? *Reading Research Quarterly, 20*, 163–179.

Encisco, P. E. (1994). Cultural identity and response to literature: Running lessons from Maniac Magee. *Language Arts, 71* (7), 524–533.

Erickson, F. (1982). Taught cognitive learning in its immediate environments: A neglected topic in the anthropology of education. *Anthropology & Education Quarterly, 13*, 148–180.

Ernst, K. (1994). Writing pictures, painting words: Writing in an artists' workshop. *Language Arts, 71* (1), 44–52.

Ervin, S. M., & Miller, W. R. (1963). Language development. In H. Stevenson (Ed.), *The 62nd yearbook of the National Society for the Study of Education* (pp. 108–143). Chicago: University of Chicago Press.

Evans, K. S. (1995). Teacher reflection as a cure for tunnel vision. *Language Arts, 72* (4), 266–271.

Falk, B., & Ort, S. (1998). Sitting down to score: Teacher learning through assessment. *Phi Delta Kappan, 80*, 59–64.

Farnan, N. (1992). Promoting connections between reader and text: A reader response approach. *The California Reader, 25*, 6–8.

Farr, R. (1992). Putting it all together: Solving the reading assessment puzzle. *The Reading Teacher, 46*, 26–37.

Farr, R., & Beck, M. (1991). Evaluating language development: Formal methods of assessment. In J. Flood, J. M. Jensen, D. Lapp, & J. R. Squire (Eds.), *Handbook of research on teaching the English language arts* (pp. 489–501). New York: Macmillan.

Farstrup, A. E., & Samuels, S. J. (2002). *What research has to say about reading instruction* (3rd ed.). Newark, DE: International Reading Association.

Fawson, P. C., & Reutzel, D. R. (2000). But I only have a basal: Implementing guided reading in the early grades. *The Reading Teacher, 54* (1), 84–97.

Feeley, J. T. (1981). What do our children like to read? *NJEA Review, 54* (8), 26–27.

Ferreiro, E. (1978). What is written in a written sentence? A developmental answer. *Journal of Education, 160*, 25–39.

———. (1986). The interplay between information and assimilation in beginning literacy. In W. H. Teale & E. Sulzby (Eds.), *Emergent literacy: Writing and reading* (pp. 15–49). Cambridge, UK: Cambridge University Press.

Fielding, L. G., Anderson, R. C., & Pearson, P. D. (January 1990). *How discussion questions influence children's story understanding* (Tech. Rep. No. 490). Urbana: University of Illinois, Center for the Study of Reading.

Flesch, R. (1955). *Why Johnny can't read.* New York: Harper & Row.

Flint, A. S. (2000). Escapists, butterflies, and experts: Stance alignment in literary texts. *Language Arts, 77* (6), 522–531.

Flitterman-King, S. (1988). The role of the response journal in active reading. *The Quarterly of the National Writing Project and the Center for the Study of Writing, 10*, 4–11.

Forman, E. A., & Cazden, C. B. (2004). Exploring Vygotskian perspectives in education: The cognitive values of peer interaction. In R. B. Ruddell & N. J. Unrau (Eds.), *Theoretical models and processes of reading* (5th ed., pp. 163–186). Newark, DE: International Reading Association.

Forrest, D. L., & Waller, T. B. (1979, March). Cognitive and metacognitive aspects of reading. Paper presented at the meeting of the Society of Research in Child Development, San Francisco.

Fortescue, C. M. (1994). Using oral and written language to increase understanding of math concepts. *Language Arts, 71* (8), 576–580.

Fractor, J. S., Woodruff, M. C., Martinez, M. G., & Teale, W. H. (1993). Let's not miss opportunities to promote voluntary reading: Classroom libraries in the elementary school. *The Reading Teacher, 46* (6), 476–484.

Frank, C. R., Dixon, C. N., & Brandts, L. R. (2001). Bears, trolls, and pagemasters: Learning about learners in book clubs. *The Reading Teacher, 54* (5), 448–462.

Fraser, C., Bellugi, U., & Brown, R. (1963). Control of grammar in imitation comprehension and production. *Journal of Verbal Learning and Verbal Behavior, 2*, 121–135.

Freeman, E. B., Martinez, M., Yokata, J., and Templte, C. A. (2006). *Children's books in children's hands: An introduction to their literature.* Boston: Allyn & Bacon.

Freppon, P. A., & Dahl, K. L. (1998). Balanced instruction: Insights and considerations. *Reading Research Quarterly, 33* (2), 240–251.

Fresch, M. J. (1995). Self-selection of early literacy learners. *The Reading Teacher, 49* (3), 220–227.

Fresch, M. J. (Ed.) (2008). *Read the past to inform the future: A historical perspective on current reading practices.* Newark, DE: International Reading Association.

Friend, M., & Bursuck, W. (1996). *Including students with special needs: A practical guide for classroom teachers.* Boston: Allyn & Bacon.

Frith, U. (1985). Beneath the surface of developmental dyslexia. In K. E. Patterson, J. C. Marshall, & M. Coltheart (Eds.), *Surface dyslexia* (pp. 301–330). London: Erlbaum.

Fromkin, V., & Rodman, R. (1993). *An introduction to language* (5th ed.). Fort Worth, TX: Harcourt Brace Jovanovich.

Fry, E. (1977a). *Elementary reading instruction.* New York: McGraw-Hill.

———. (1977b). Fry's readability graph: Clarification, validity, and extension to level 17. *Journal of Reading, 21,* 242–252.

———. (2004). Phonics: A large phoneme-grapheme frequency count revised. *Journal of Literacy Research, 36* (1), 83–96.

Fry, E. B. (2004). *The vocabulary teacher's book of lists.* San Francisco, CA: Jossey-Bass.

———. (2006). *The reading teacher's book of lists* (5th ed.). San Francisco, CA: Jossey-Bass.

Fuchs, L. S., Fuchs, D., Hosp, M. K., & Jenkins, J. R. (2001). Oral reading fluency as an indicator of reading competence: A theoretical, empirical, and historical analysis. *Scientific Studies of Reading, 5,* 239–256.

Galda, L., Ash, G. E., & Cullinan, B. E. (2000). Children's literature. In M. L. Kamil, P. B. Mosenthal, P. D. Pearson, & R. Barr (Eds.), *Handbook of reading research: Volume III* (pp. 361–379). Mahwah, NJ: Lawrence Erlbaum.

Galda, L., & Beach, R. (2004). Response to literature as cultural activity. In R. B. Ruddell & N. J. Unrau (Eds.), *Theoretical models and processes of reading* (5th ed., pp. 852–869). Newark, DE: International Reading Association.

Galda, L., Bisplinghoff, B. A., Pellegrini, A. D., & Stahl, S. (1995). Sharing lives: Reading, writing, talking, and living in a first-grade classroom. *Language Arts, 72* (5), 334–339.

Galda, L., Cullinan, B. E., & Strickland, D. S. (1993). *Language, literacy and the child.* New York: Harcourt Brace Jovanovich.

Gallagher, M. C., Goudvis, A., & Pearson, P. D. (1988). Principles of organizational change. In S. J. Samuels & P. D. Pearson (Eds.), *Changing school reading programs: Principles and case studies* (pp. 11–39). Newark, DE: International Reading Association.

Gallimore, R., Boggs, J. W., & Jordan, C. (1974). *Culture, behavior and education: A study of Hawaiian-Americans.* Beverly Hills, CA: Sage Publications.

Gambrell, L. B. (1996). Creating classroom cultures that foster reading motivation. *The Reading Teacher, 50* (1), 14–25.

Gambrell, L. B., & Almsi, J. F. (1996). *Lively discussions! Fostering engaged reading.* Newark, DE: International Reading Association.

Garcia, E. (1999). *Student cultural diversity: Understanding and meeting the challenge.* Boston: Houghton Mifflin.

Garcia, G. E. (2000). Bilingual children's reading. In M. L. Kamil, P. B. Mosenthal, P. D. Pearson, & R. Barr (Eds.), *Handbook of reading research: Volume III* (pp. 813–834). Mahwah, NJ: Lawrence Erlbaum.

Garcia, T., & Pintrich, P. R. (1994). Regulating motivation and cognition in the classroom: The role of self-schemas and self-regulatory strategies. In D. H. Schunk & B. J. Zimmerman (Eds.), *Self-regulation of learning and performance: Issues and educational applications* (pp. 127–153). Hillsdale, NJ: Erlbaum.

Gardner, H. (1993). *Multiple intelligences: The theory in practice.* New York: Basic Books.

Gaskins, I. W. (1998). There's more to teaching at-risk and delayed readers than good reading instruction. *The Reading Teacher, 51,* 534–547.

Gaskins, I. W., Anderson, R. C., Pressley, M., Cunicelli, E., & Satlow, E. (1993). Six teachers' dialogue during cognitive process instruction. *The Elementary School Journal, 93,* 277–304.

Gaskins, I. W., Ehri, L. C., Cress, C., O'Hara, C., & Donnelly, K. (1997a). Procedures for word learning: Making discoveries about words. *The Reading Teacher, 50,* 312–327.

———. (1997b). Analyzing words and making discoveries about the alphabetic system: Activities for beginning readers. *Language Arts, 74* (3), 172–184.

Gavelek, J. R., & Raphael, T. E. (1996). Changing talk about text: New roles for teachers and students. *Language Arts, 73* (3), 182–192.

Gavelek, J. R., Raphael, T. E., Biondo, S. M., & Wang, D. (2000). Integrated literacy instruction. In M. L. Kamil, P. B. Mosenthal, P. D. Pearson, & R. Barr (Eds.), *Handbook of reading research: Volume III* (pp. 587–607). Mahwah, NJ: Lawrence Erlbaum.

Gee, J. P. (2004). Reading as situated language: A sociocognitive perspective. In R. B. Ruddell & N. J. Unrau (Eds.) *Theoretical models and processes of reading* (5th ed., pp. 929–953). Newark, DE: International Reading Association.

Genishi, C., & Dyson, A. H. (1984). *Language assessment in the early years.* Norwood, NJ: Ablex.

Gentile, L. M., & McMillan, M. M. (1987). *Stress and reading difficulties: Research, assessment and intervention.* Newark, DE: International Reading Association.

Gibson, E. J., Gibson, J. J., Pick, A. D., & Osser, H. A. (1962). A developmental study of the discrimination of letter-like forms. *Journal of Comparative and Psychological Psychology, 55,* 674–691.

Gill, S. R. (2000). Reading with Amy: Teaching and learning through reading conferences. *The Reading Teacher, 53,* 500–509.

Gillet, J. W., & Temple, C. (1990). *Understanding reading problems: Assessment and instruction* (3rd ed.). Boston: Allyn & Bacon.

Giorgis, C., & Peterson B. (1996). Teachers and librarians collaborate to create a community of learners. *Language Arts, 73,* 477–482.

Glushko, R. J. (1979). The organization and activation of orthographic knowledge in reading aloud. *Journal of Experimental Psychology: Human Perception and Performance, 5,* 674–691.

———. (1981). Principles for pronouncing print: The psychology of phonography. In A. M. Lesgold & C. A. Perfetti (Eds.), *Interactive processes in reading* (pp. 61–84). Hillsdale, NJ: Erlbaum.

Goldenberg, C. (1993). Instructional conversations: Promoting comprehension through discussion. *The Reading Teacher, 46* (4), 316–326.

Goldenhersh, B. L. (1992). *Read it with bookmarks.* Belleville, IL: Classroom Catalyst Press.

Gomez, M. L., Graue, M. E., & Bloch, M. N. (1991). Reassessing portfolio assessment: Rhetoric and reality. *Language Arts, 68* (8), 620–628.

Goodlad, J. I. (1983). *A place called school: Prospects for the future.* New York: McGraw-Hill.

———. (1984). *A place called school: Prospects for the future.* New York: McGraw-Hill.

Goodman, K., & Goodman, Y. (1978). *Reading of American children whose language is a stable rural dialect of English or a language other than English* (NIE-C-00-3-0087). Washington, DC: U.S. Department of Health, Education and Welfare.

Goodman, K. S. (1994). Deconstructing the rhetoric of Moorman, Blanton, and McLaughlin: A response. *Reading Research Quarterly, 29* (4), 340–347.

Goodman, Y. M. (1972). Qualitative reading miscue analysis for teacher training. In R. E. Hodges & E. H. Rudorf (Eds.), *Language and learning to read: What teachers should know about language* (pp. 160–166). Boston: Houghton Mifflin.

———. (1991a). What is whole language? In K. S. Goodman, L. B. Bird, & Y. M. Goodman (Eds.), *The whole language catalog* (pp. 4–5). Santa Rosa, CA: American School Publishers.

———. (1991b). Informal methods of evaluation. In J. Flood, J. M. Jensen, D. Lapp, & J. R. Squire (Eds.), *Handbook of research on teaching the English language arts* (pp. 502–509). New York: Macmillan.

Goodman, Y. M., & Goodman, K. S. (1994). To err is human: Learning about language processes by analyzing miscues. In R. B. Ruddell, M. R. Ruddell, & H. Singer (Eds.), *Theoretical models and processes of reading* (4th ed., pp. 104–123). Newark, DE: International Reading Association.

———. (2004). To err is human: Learning about language processes by analyzing miscues. In R. B. Ruddell & N. J. Unrau (Eds.), *Theoretical models and processes of reading* (5th ed., pp. 620–639). Newark, DE: International Reading Association.

Goodman, Y. M., Hood, W. J., & Goodman, K. S. (1991). *Organizing for whole language.* Portsmouth, NH: Heinemann.

Goodman, Y. M., Watson, D. J., & Burke, C. L. (1987). *Reading miscue inventory.* New York: Richard C. Owen Publishers.

Gough, P. B., Juel, C., & Roper-Schneider, D. (1983). A two-stage model of initial reading acquisition. In J. A. Niles & L. A. Harris (Eds.), *Searches for meaning in reading/language processing and instruction* (pp. 207–211). Rochester, NY: National Reading Conference.

Gough, P. B., & Hillinger, M. L. (1980). Learning to read: An unnatural act. *Bulletin of the Orton Society, 30,* 179–196.

Gould, J. S. (1996). A constructivist perspective on teaching and learning in the language arts. In C. T. Fosnot (Ed.), *Constructivism: Theory, perspectives, and practice* (pp. 92–103). New York: Teachers College, Columbia University.

Graham, S. A. (1986). Assessing reading preferences: A new approach. *New England Reading Association Journal, 21,* 8–12.

Grande, A. (1965). Authentic existence and the teaching of literature. Unpublished doctoral dissertation, University of Pittsburgh, Pittsburgh, PA.

Grant, C. A., & Sleeter, C. E. (1993). Race, class, gender, and disability in the classroom. In J. A. Banks & C. A. M. Banks (Eds.), *Multicultural education: Issues and perspectives* (2nd ed., pp. 48–68). Boston: Allyn & Bacon.

Graves, D. (1982, December). Let's take another look at the development of young writers. Paper presented at the National Reading Conference, Clearwater Beach, FL.

Graves, D. H. (1983). *Writing: Teachers and children at work.* Portsmouth, NH: Heinemann.

———. (1990). *Discover your own literacy.* Portsmouth, NH: Heinemann.

Graves, M. F. (1987). The roles of instruction in fostering vocabulary development. In M. G. McKeown & M. E. Curtis (Eds.), *The nature of vocabulary acquisition* (pp. 165–184). Hillsdale, NJ: Erlbaum.

———. (2000). A vocabulary program to complement and bolster a middle-grade comprehension program. In B. M. Taylor, M. F. Graves, & P. van den Broek (Eds.), *Reading for meaning: Fostering comprehension in the middle grades* (pp. 116–135). Newark, DE: International Reading Association.

Graves, M. F., & Slater, W. H. (1987, April). The development of reading vocabularies in rural disadvantaged students, inner-city disadvantaged students, and middle-class suburban students. Paper presented at the annual meeting of the American Educational Research Association, Washington, DC.

Gray, W. S., & Arbuthnot, M. A. (1947). *Days and deeds.* Chicago: Scott, Foresman.

Greenlee, A. A., Monson, D. L., & Taylor, B. M. (1996). The lure of series books: Does it affect appreciation for recommended literature? *The Reading Teacher, 50* (3), 216–225.

Griffith, P. L., & Olson, M. W. (1992). Phonemic awareness helps beginning readers break the code. *The Reading Teacher, 45,* 516–523.

Gross, C. H. (1989). An inservice presentation of a literature-based integrated unit for teaching content-area reading. Unpublished manuscript, University of California, Berkeley.

Guillaume, A. M. (1998). Learning with text in the primary grades. *The Reading Teacher, 51* (6), 476–486.

Gunderson, L. (1991). *ESL literacy instruction: A guidebook to theory and practice.* Englewood Cliffs, NJ: Prentice-Hall.

Gunning. T. (1998). *Best books for beginning readers.* Boston: Allyn & Bacon.

Gunning, T. G. (2008). *Creating literacy instruction for all students* (6th ed.). Boston: Allyn & Bacon.

Guszak, F. J. (1967). Teacher questioning and reading. *The Reading Teacher, 21,* 227–234.

Guthrie, J. T., & McCann, A. D. (1997). Characteristics of classrooms that promote motivations and strategies for learning. In J. T. Guthrie & A. Wigfield (Eds.), *Reading engagement: Motivating readers through integrated instruction* (pp. 128–148). Newark, DE: International Reading Association.

Guthrie, J. T., Van Meter, P., McCann, A. D., Wigfield, A., Bennett, L., Poundstone, C. C., Rice, M. E., Faibisch, F. M., Hunt, B., & Mitchell, A. M. (1996). Growth of literacy engagement: Changes in motivations and strategies during concept-oriented reading instruction. *Reading Research Quarterly, 31* (3), 306–332.

Guthrie, J. T., Wigfield, A., Metsala, J. L., & Cox, K. E. (2004). Motivational and cognitive predictors of text comprehension. In R. B. Ruddell & N. J. Unrau (Eds.), *Theoretical models and processes of reading* (5th ed., pp. 929–953). Newark, DE: International Reading Association.

Hacker, D. J. (2004). Self-regulated comprehension during reading. In R. B. Ruddell & N. J. Unrau (Eds.), *Theoretical models and processes of reading* (5th ed., pp. 755–579). Newark, DE: International Reading Association.

Haggard, M. R. (1980). Vocabulary acquisition during elementary and post-elementary years: A preliminary report. *Reading Horizons, 21,* 61–69.

———. (1989). Instructional strategies for developing student interest in content area subjects. In D. Lapp, J. Flood, & N. Farnan (Eds.), *Content area reading-learning: Instructional strategies* (pp. 70–88). Englewood Cliffs, NJ: Prentice-Hall.

Hall, L. A. (2006). Anything but lazy: New understandings about struggling readers, teaching, and text. *Reading Research Quarterly, 41,* 424–426.

Hallahan, D. P., & Kauffman, J. M. (2000). *Exceptional learners: Introduction to special education.* Boston: Allyn & Bacon.

Halliday, M. A. K. (1973). *Explorations in the functions of language.* London, UK: Edward Arnold.

———. (1978). *Language as social semiotic.* London, UK: Edward Arnold.

———. (1993). Towards a language-based theory of learning. *Linguistics and Education, 5,* 93–116.

Hamlin, T. (1982). American reading materials: A selective reflector. In E. M. Sheridan (Ed.), *Sex stereotypes and reading: Research and strategies* (pp. 49–63). Newark, DE: International Reading Association.

Hancock, M. (1992). Literature Response Journals: Insights beyond the printed page. *Language Arts, 69,* 36–42.

Hancock, M. R. (1993). Exploring and extending personal response through literature journals. *The Reading Teacher, 46* (6), 466–474.

Hanna, P. R., Hanna, J. S., Hodges, R. E., and Rudorf, E. H. (1966). *Phoneme grapheme correspondences as cues to spelling improvement.* Washington, DC: Department of Health, Education, and Welfare.

Hansen, J. (1981). The effects of inference training and practice on young children's reading comprehension. *Reading Research Quarterly, 16,* 321–417.

Hardy, M., Stennett, R., & Smythe, P. (1974). Development of auditory and visual language concepts and relationship to instructional strategies in kindergarten. *Elementary English, 51,* 525–532.

Harris, P. (1989). First grade children's constructs of teacher-assigned reading tasks in a whole language classroom. Unpublished doctoral dissertation, University of California, Berkeley.

Harris, P., Trezise, J., & Winser, W. N. (2004). Where is the story?: Intertextual reflections on literacy research and practices in the early school years. *Research in the Teaching of English, 38,* 250–261.

Harris, S. (1996). Bringing about change in reading instruction. *The Reading Teacher, 49* (8), 612–618.

Harris, V. J. (Ed.). (1992). *Teaching multicultural literature in grades K–8.* Norwood, MA: Christopher-Gordon Publishers.

Harste, J. C. (1994). Literacy as curricular conversations about knowledge, inquiry, and morality. In R. B. Ruddell, M. R. Ruddell, & H. Singer (Eds.), *Theoretical models and processes of reading* (4th ed., pp. 1220–1242). Newark, DE: International Reading Association.

Harste, J. C., Burke, C. L., & Woodward, V. A. (1982). Children's language and world: Initial encounters with print. In J. Langer & M. T. Smith-Burke (Eds.), *Reader meets author: Bridging the gap* (pp. 105–131). Newark, DE: International Reading Association.

Harste, J. C., & Short, K. G. (1988). *Creating classrooms for authors.* Portsmouth, NH: Heinemann.

Harste, J. C., Woodward, V. A., & Burke, C. L. (1984). *Language stories and literacy lessons.* Portsmouth, NH: Heinemann.

Hauschildt, P. M., & McMahon, S. I. (1996). Reconceptualizing "resistant" learners and rethinking instruction: Risking a trip to the swamp. *Language Arts, 73* (8), 576–586.

Hawkins, M. R. (2004). Researching English language and literacy development in schools. *Educational Researcher, 33* (3), 14–25.

Hearne, B. (1990). *Choosing books for children.* New York: Dell.

Heath, S. B. (1982a). Questioning at home and at school: A comparative study. In G. Spindler (Ed.), *Doing the ethnography of schooling* (pp. 105–131). New York: Holt, Rinehart & Winston.

———. (1982b). What no bedtime story means: Narrative skills at home and school. *Language and Society, 2,* 49–76.

———. (1983). *Ways with words: Language, life and work in communities and classrooms.* Cambridge, UK: Cambridge University Press.

Heffernan, L. (2004). *Critical literacy and writer's workshop: Bring purpose and passion to student writing.* Newark, DE: International Reading Association.

Heimlich, J. E., & Pittelman, S. D. (1986). *Semantic mapping: Classroom applications.* Newark, DE: International Reading Association.

Henderson, E., & Beers, J. (Eds.). (1980). *Developmental and cognitive aspects of learning to spell.* Newark, DE: International Reading Association.

Hendricks-Lee, M. S., Soled, S. W., & Yinger, R. J. (1995). Sustaining reform through teacher learning. *Language Arts, 72* (4), 288–292.

Hernandez, H. (1989). *Multicultural education: A teacher's guide to content and process.* Columbus, OH: Merrill.

Hiebert, E. H. (1996). Creating and sustaining a love of literature . . . and the ability to read it. In M. F. Graves, P. van den Broek, & B. M. Taylor (Eds.), *The first R: Every child's right to read* (pp. 15–36). New York: Teachers College Press.

———. (1999). Test matters in learning to read. *The Reading Teacher, 52* (6), 552–566.

Hiebert, E. H., & Hutchison, T. A. (1991). Research directions: The current state of alternative assessments for policy and instructional uses. *Language Arts, 68* (8), 662–668.

Hiebert, E. H. & Martin, L. A. (2004). The texts of beginning reading instruction. In R. B. Ruddell & N. J. Unrau (Eds.), *Theoretical models and processes of reading* (5th ed., pp. 390–411). Newark, DE: International Reading Association.

Hiebert, E. H., & Taylor, B. M. (2000). Beginning reading instruction: Research on early interventions. In M. L. Kamil, P. B. Mosenthal, P. D. Pearson, & R. Barr (Eds.), *Handbook of reading research: Volume III* (pp. 455–482). Mahwah, NJ: Lawrence Erlbaum.

Hillman, J. (1999). *Discovering children's literature.* Upper Saddle River, NJ: Prentice-Hall.

Hoffman, J., & Pearson, P. D. (2000). Reading teacher education in the next millennium: What your grandmother's teacher didn't know that your granddaughter's teacher should. *Reading Research Quarterly, 35* (1), 28–44.

Hoffman, J. V., Roser, N. L., & Battle, J. (1993). Reading aloud in classrooms: From the modal toward a "model." *The Reading Teacher, 46* (6), 496–503.

Hohn, W., Ball, E. W., & Blachman, B. A. (1991). Does phoneme awareness training in kindergarten make a difference in early word recognition and developmental spelling? *Reading Research Quarterly, 26,* 49–66.

Hohn, W., & Ehri, L. C. (1983). Do alphabet letters help prereaders acquire phonemic segmentation skill? *Journal of Educational Psychology, 75,* 752–762.

Holdaway, D. (1979). *The foundations of literacy.* New York: Ashton Scholastic.

Huck, C., Hepler, S., Hickman, J., & Kiefer, B. (2001). *Children's literature in the elementary school.* Boston: McGraw-Hill.

Huck, S. C. (1976). *Children's literature in the elementary school* (3rd ed.). New York: Holt, Rinehart & Winston.

Hudelson, S. (1989). Teaching English through content-area activities. In P. Rigg & V. Allen (Eds.), *When they don't all speak English.* Urbana, IL: National Council of Teachers of English.

Huey, E. B. (1908/1968). *The psychology and pedagogy of reading.* Cambridge, MA: MIT Press.

Hunt, K. W. (1970). Syntactic maturity in school children and adults. *Monographs of the Society for Research in Child Development, 35,* 57–83.

Hunt, L. C. (1971). Six steps to the individualized reading program (IRP). *Elementary English, 48,* 27–32.

Ingham, J. (1982). Middle school children's responses to E. Blyton in "The Bradford book flood experience." *Journal of Research in Reading, 5,* 43–56.

International Reading Association. (1992). *Kids' favorite books.* Newark, DE: Author.

———. (1999a). High-stakes assessments in reading: A position statement of the International Reading Association. *The Reading Teacher, 53* (3), 257–263.

———. (1999b). Teachers' choices for 1999. *The Reading Teacher, 53* (3), 249–255.

———. (2000a). Making a difference means making it different: Honoring children's rights to excellent reading instruction. Newark, DE: Author.

———. (2000b). Teaching all children to read: The roles of the reading specialist. *Journal of Adolescent and Adult Literacy, 44,* 99–104.

———. (2004). *Standards for reading professionals, revised 2003.* Newark, DE: International Reading Association.

Invernizzi, M., Juel, C., & Rosemary, C. A. (1996/1997). A community volunteer tutorial that works. *The Reading Teacher, 50* (4), 304–311.

Invernizzi, M. A., Abouzeid, M. P., & Bloodgood, J. W. (1997). Integrated word study: Spelling, grammar, and meaning in the language arts classroom. *Language Arts, 74* (3), 185–192.

Jacobs, L. B. (1965). Telling stories to young children. In L. B. Jacobs (Ed.), *Using literature with young children* (pp. 15–20). New York: Teachers College Press.

Jenkins, J. R., Matlock, B., & Slocum, T. A. (1989). Two approaches to vocabulary instruction: The teaching of individual word meanings and practice in deriving word meaning from context. *Reading Research Quarterly, 24,* 215–235.

Jewell, T. A., & Pratt, D. (1999). Literature discussions in the primary grades: Children's thoughtful discourse about books and what teachers can do to make it happen. *The Reading Teacher 52* (8), 842–850.

Jimenez, R. T. (2001). "It's a difference that changes us": An alternative view of the language and literacy learning needs of Latina/o students. *The Reading Teacher, 54* (8), 736–746.

Johns, J. (1972). Children's concepts of their reading and their reading achievement. *Journal of Reading Behavior, 4,* 56–57.

———. (2005). *Basic reading inventory* (3rd ed.). Dubuque, IA: Kendall/Hunt.

Johnson, D. D., & Baumann, J. F. (1984). Word identification. In P. D. Pearson (Ed.), *Handbook of reading research* (pp. 583–608). New York: Longman.

Johnson, D. D., Toms-Bronowski, S., & Pittelman, S. D. (1981). *A review of trends in vocabulary research and the effects of prior knowledge on instructional strategies for vocabulary acquisition* (Program Report No. 95). Madison, WI: Wisconsin Center for Education Research.

Johnson, M. S., Kress, R. A., & Pikulski, J. J. (1987). *Informal reading inventories* (2nd ed.). Newark, DE: International Reading Association.

Johnson, N. M., & Ebert, M. J. (1992). Time travel is possible: Historical fiction and biography—passport to the past. *The Reading Teacher, 45,* 488–495.

Johnston, F. R. (1998). The reader, the text, and the task: Learning words in first grade. *The Reading Teacher, 51* (8), 666–675.

Juel, C. (1983). The development of mediated word identification. *Reading Research Quarterly, 18,* 306–327.

———. (1991). Beginning reading. In R. Barr, M. L. Kamil, P. Mosenthal, & P. D. Pearson (Eds.). *Handbook of reading research: Volume II* (pp. 759–788). New York: Longman.

———. (1996). What makes literacy tutoring effective? *Reading Research Quarterly, 31* (3), 268–289.

Juel, C., & Minden-Cupp, C. (2000). One down and 80,000 to go: Word recognition instruction in the primary grades. *The Reading Teacher, 53* (4), 332–335.

———. (2004). Learning to read words: Linguistic units and instructional strategies. In R. B. Ruddell & N. J. Unrau (Eds.), *Theoretical models and processes of reading* (5th ed., pp. 313–364). Newark, DE: International Reading Association.

Just, M. A., & Carpenter, P. A. (1987). *The psychology of reading and language comprehension.* Boston: Allyn & Bacon.

Kamhi, A. B. (1992). Response to historical perspective: A developmental language perspective. *Journal of Learning Disabilities, 25,* 48–52.

Kamil, M. L., Mosenthal, P. B., Pearson, P. D., & Barr, R. (Eds.). (2000). *Handbook of reading research: Volume III.* Mahwah, NJ: Lawrence Erlbaum.

Kane, S. (1998). The view from the discourse level: Teaching relationships and text structure. *The Reading Teacher, 42* (2), 182–184.

Kantor, R., Green, J., Bradley, M., & Lin, L. (1992). The construction of schooled discourse repertoires: An interactional sociolinguistic perspective on learning to talk in preschool. *Linguistics and Education, 4,* 131–172.

Kelly, G. (1955). *The psychology of personal constructs.* New York: W. W. Norton.

Kennedy, C. (2005). *A family of poems, my favorite poetry for children.* New York: Hyperion.

Kessels, J. P. A. M., & Korthagen, F. A. J. (1996). The relationship between theory and practice: Back to the classics. *Educational Researcher, 25* (3), 17–22.

Kibby, M. W. (1995). The organization and teaching of things and the words that signify them. *Journal of Adolescent & Adult Literacy, 39* (3), 208–223.

Kieffer, R. D., & Morrison, L. S. (1994). Changing portfolio process: One journey toward authentic assessment. *Language Arts, 71* (6), 411–418.

Kindler, A. L. (2002). *Survey of the states' limited English proficient students and available educational programs and services, 2000–2001 summary report.* Washington, DC: National Clearinghouse for English Language Acquisition and Language Instruction Educational Programs.

King, R. (1995). Teacher's revisiting. *Language Arts, 72* (3), 188–191.

Kintsch, W. (2004). The construction-integration model of text comprehension and its implications for instruction. In R. B. Ruddell & N. J. Unrau (Eds.), *Theoretical models and processes of reading* (5th ed., pp. 1270–1328). Newark, DE: International Reading Association.

Kita, J. (1979, November). Children's conceptions of reading and writing. Paper presented at the annual meeting of the National Reading Conference, San Antonio, TX.

Klingner, J. K., & Vaughn, S. (1999). Promoting reading comprehension, content learning and English acquisition through collaborative strategic reading (CSR). *The Reading Teacher, 52* (7), 738–747.

Kong, A., & Fitch, E. (2002/2003). Using book club to engage culturally and linguistically diverse learners in reading, writing, and talking about books. *The Reading Teacher, 56* (4), 352–362.

Kooy, M. (2003). Riding the coattails of Harry Potter: Readings, relational learning, and revelations in book clubs. *Journal of Adolescent and Adult Literacy, 47* (2), 136–145, 2003.

Kopytoff, V. (2004, September 17). Digital divide of kids narrows. *San Francisco Chronicle,* pp. C1, C6.

Krashen, S. D. (1987). *Principles and practice in second language acquisition.* Englewood Cliffs, NJ: Prentice-Hall.

Kridel, C., Bullough, R. V., & Shaker, P. (Eds.). (1996). *Teachers and mentors: Profiles of distinguished twentieth-century professors of education.* New York: Garland Publishing, Inc.

Kruse, G. M., & Horning, K. T. (1991). *Multicultural literature for children and young adults: A selected listing of books 1980–1990 by and about people of color.* Madison: Cooperative Children's Book Center,

University of Wisconsin, Department of Public Instruction.

Kucera, C. A. (1995). Detours and destinations: One teacher's journey into an environmental writing workshop. *Language Arts, 72* (3), 179–187.

Kucera, H., & Francis, W. N. (1967). *Computational analysis of present-day American English.* Providence, RI: Brown University Press.

Kuhn, M. R., & Stahl, S. A. (2004). Fluency: A review of developmental and remedial practices. *Theoretical models and processes of reading* (5th ed., pp. 412–453). Newark, DE: International Reading Association.

Labov, W. (1967). Some sources of reading problems for Negro speakers of nonstandard English. In Alexander Frazier (Ed.), *New directions in elementary English* (pp. 143–153). Champaign, IL: National Council of Teachers of English.

Ladson-Billings. G. (1994). *The dreamkeepers: Successful teachers of African American children.* San Francisco: Jossey-Bass.

———. (1995). Toward a theory of culturally relevant pedagogy. *American Educational Research Journal, 32* (3), 465–491.

Lamme, L. L., & Hysmith, C. (1991). One school's adventure into portfolio assessment. *Language Arts, 68* (8), 629–640.

Landy, S. (1977). Why Johnny can read . . . but doesn't. *Canadian Library Journal, 34,* 379–387.

Langer, J. A. (1981). From theory to practice: A prereading plan. *Journal of Reading, 25,* 2.

———. (1982). Facilitating text processing: The elaboration of prior knowledge. In J. Langer & M. Smith-Burke (Eds.), *Reader meets author/Bridging the gap* (pp. 149–162). Newark, DE: International Reading Association.

———. (1994). A response-based approach to reading literature. *Language Arts, 71* (3), 203–211.

———. (2004). Beating the odds: Teaching middle and high school students to read and write well. In R. B. Ruddell & N. J. Unrau (Eds.), *Theoretical models and processes of reading* (5th ed., pp. 1040–1082). Newark, DE: International Reading Association.

Langer, J. A., & Applebee, A. N. (1987). *How writing shapes thinking* (NCTE Research Report No. 22). Urbana, IL: National Council of Teachers of English.

Langer, J. A., Applebee, A. N., Mullis, I. V. S., & Foertsch, M. A. (1990). *Learning to read in our nation's schools: Instruction and achievement in 1988 at grades 4, 8, and 12.* Princeton, NJ: Educational Testing Service.

Law, B., & Eckes, M. (1990). *The more-than-just-surviving handbook.* Winnipeg, Canada: Peguis.

Leal, D. J. (1993). The power of literary peer-group discussions: How children collaboratively negotiate meaning. *The Reading Teacher, 47* (2), 114–120.

Lebo, H. (2003). *The UCLA Internet report: Surveying the digital future, year three.* Los Angeles: UCLA Center for Communications Policy.

Lehman, B. A., & Scharer, P. L. (1996). Reading alone, talking together: The role of discussion in developing literary awareness. *The Reading Teacher, 50* (1), 26–35.

Lehr, S., & Thompson, D. L. (2000). The dynamic nature of response: Children reading and responding to *Maniac Magee and The Friendship. The Reading Teacher, 53* (6), 480–493.

Lenhart, A., Simon, M., & Graziano, M. (2001). *The Internet and education: Findings of the Pew Internet & American life project.* Retrieved December 13, 2003, from www.pewinternet.org/reports/toc.asp?Report-39.

Lenski, S. D., Ehlers-Zavala, F. Daniel, M. C., & Sun-Irminger, X. (2006). Profiles in comprehension. *The Reading Teacher, 60,* 24–34.

Leppanen, U., Niemi, P., Aunola, K., & Nurmi, J. E. (2004). Development of reading skills among pre-school and primary school pupils. *Reading Research Quarterly, 39,* 72–93.

Leu, D. J., Kinzer, C. K., Corio, J. L., & Cammack, D. W. (2004). Toward a theory of new literacies emerging from the internet and other information and communication technologies. In R. B. Ruddell & N. J. Unrau (Eds.), *Theoretical models and processes of reading* (5th ed., pp. 1570–1613). Newark, DE: International Reading Association.

Leu, D. J., Jr., & Kinzer, C. K. (1999). *Effective literacy instruction.* Columbus, OH: Prentice-Hall.

———. (2000). *Teaching with the Internet: Lessons from the classroom* (3rd ed.). Norwood, MA: Christopher-Gordon.

Leu, D. J., Jr., & Leu, D. D. (2000). *Teaching with the Internet: Lessons from the classroom.* Norwood, MA: Christopher-Gordon.

Levin, H. (1963). *A basic research program on reading* (Cooperative Research Project No. 639). Ithaca, NY: Cornell University.

Lima, C. W. (2006). *A to zoo: Subject access to children's picture books* (7th ed.). Westport, CT: Libraries Unlimited.

Lindgren, M. V. (Ed.). (1991). *The multicolored mirror: Cultural substance in literature for children and young adults.* Fort Atkinson, WI: Cooperative Children's Book Center, Highsmith Press.

Lindsay, M. R. (1969). A descriptive exploration of the growth and development of spontaneous oral vocabulary of elementary school children. Unpublished doctoral dissertation, University of California, Berkeley.

Lipson, E. R. (2004). The New York Times *parent's guide to the best books for children.* New York: Times Books.

Lipson, M. Y., Valencia, S. W., Wixon, K. K., & Peters, C. W. (1993). Teaching: Integration to improve teaching and learning. *Language Arts, 70* (4), 252–263.

Loban, W. D. (1976). *Language development: Kindergarten through grade twelve.* Urbana, IL: National Council of Teachers of English.

Long, T. W., & Gove, M. K. (2003). How engagement strategies and literature circles promote critical response in a fourth-grade urban classroom. *The Reading Teacher, 57* (4), 350–361.

Lubliner, S. (2004). Help for struggling upper-grade elementary readers. *The Reading Teacher, 57,* 430.

Lukens, R. J. (1995). *A critical handbook of children's literature* (5th ed.). Glenview, IL: Scott, Foresman.

Lundberg, I., Olofsson, A., & Wall, A. (1980). Reading and spelling skills in the first school years predicted from phonemic awareness skills in kindergarten. *Scandinavian Journal of Psychology, 21,* 159–173.

Lunsford, S. H. (1997). "And they wrote happily ever after": Literature-based mini-lessons in writing. *Language Arts, 74* (1), 42–48.

Lynch, P. (1986). *Using big books and predictable books.* Richmond Hill, Ontario: Scholastic-TAB.

Lynch-Brown, C., & Tomlinson, C. M. (1993). *Essentials of children's literature.* Boston: Allyn & Bacon.

Lyons, C. A., & Beaver, J. (1995). Reducing retention and learning disability placement through reading recovery: An educationally sound, cost-effective choice. In R. L. Allington & S. A. Walmsley (Eds.), *No quick fix: Rethinking literacy programs in America's elementary schools* (pp. 116–136). Newark, DE: International Reading Association.

Mansell, J., Evans, M. A., & Manilton-Hulak, L. (2005). Developmental changes in parents' use of miscue feedback during shared book reading, *40,* 294–317.

Many, J. E. (2004). The effect of reader stance on students' personal understanding of literature. In R. B. Ruddell & N. J. Unrau (Eds.), *Theoretical models and processes of reading* (5th ed., pp. 914–928). Newark, DE: International Reading Association.

Manzo, A. V. (1969). The ReQuest procedure. *Journal of Reading, 13,* 123–126.

Manzo, A. V., & Manzo, U. (1990). *Content area reading: A heuristic approach.* Columbus, OH: Merrill.

Marks, M., Pressley, M., Coley, J. D., Craig, S., Gardner, R., DePinto, T., & Rose, W. (1993). Three teachers' adaptations of reciprocal teaching in comparison to traditional reciprocal teaching. *The Elementary School Journal, 94,* 267–283.

Martinez, M. G., & Roser, N. L. (1991). Children's responses to literature. In J. Flood, J. M. Jensen, D. Lapp, & J. R. Squire (Eds.), *Handbook on research on teaching the English language arts* (pp. 643–654). New York: Macmillan.

Martinez, M., Roser, N. L., & Strecker, S. (1998/1999). "I never thought I could be a star." A readers theatre ticket to fluency. *The Reading Teacher, 52* (4), 326–334.

Martinez, M. G., & Teale, W. H. (1993). Teacher storybook reading style: A comparison of six teachers. *Research in the Teaching of English, 27* (2), 175–199.

Martinez-Roldan C. M., & Lopez-Robertson, J. M. (2000). Initiating literature circles in a first-grade bilingual classroom. *The Reading Teacher 53* (4), 270–281.

Mason, J. M. (1984). Early reading from a developmental perspective. In P. D. Pearson, R. Barr, M. L. Kamil, & P. Mosenthal (Eds.), *Handbook of reading research* (pp. 508–543). New York: Longman.

Mason, J. M., Herman, P. A., & Au, K. H. (1991). Children's developing knowledge of words. In J. Flood, J. M. Jensen, D. Lapp, & J. R. Squire (Eds.), *Handbook of research on teaching the English language arts* (pp. 721–731). New York: Macmillan.

Mathes, P. G., Denton, C. A., Fletcher, J. M., Anthony, J. L., Frances, D. J., & Schatschneider, C. (2005). The effects of theoretically different instruction and student characteristics on the skills of struggling readers. *Reading Research Quarterly, 40,* 148–182.

Mathes, P. G., Howard, J. K., Allen, S. H., & Fuchs, D. (1998). Peer-assisted learning strategies for first-grade readers: Responding to the needs of diverse learners. *Reading Research Quarterly, 33,* 62–83.

Mathes, P. G., Simmons, D. C., & Davis, B. I. (1992). Assisted reading techniques for developing reading fluency. *Reading Research and Instruction, 31* (4), 70–77.

Mathes, P. G., & Torgesen, J. K. (2000). A call for equity in reading instruction for all students: A response to Allington and Woodside-Jiron. *Educational Researcher, 29,* 4–14.

Mathewson, G. C. (2004). Model of attitude influence upon reading and learning to read. In R. B. Ruddell & N. J. Unrau (Eds.), *Theoretical models and processes of reading* (5th ed., pp. 1431–1461). Newark, DE: International Reading Association.

Maxim, D. (1990). Beginning researchers. In N. Atwell (Ed.), *Coming to know: Writing to learn in the intermediate grades* (pp. 3–16). Portsmouth, NH: Heinemann.

McCarthy, D. A. (1954). Language development in children. In L. Carmichael (Ed.), *Manual of child psychology* (pp. 492–630). New York: Wiley.

McCormick, S. (1992). Disabled readers' erroneous responses to inferential questions: Description and analysis. *Reading Research Quarterly, 27,* 54–77.

———. (1999). Severely delayed readers in clinical programs. *Advances in Reading/Language Research, 6,* 273–289.

———. (2003). *Instructing students who have literacy problems* (4th ed.), Upper Saddle River, NJ: Merrill/Prentice Hall.

———. (2007). *Instructing students who have literacy problems* (5th ed.). Columbus: Prentice Hall.

McCracken, R. A. (1971). Initiating sustained silent reading. *Journal of Reading, 14,* 521–524, 582–583.

McCracken, R. A., & McCracken, M. J. (1978). Modeling is the key to sustained silent reading. *The Reading Teacher, 31,* 406–408.

McGee, L. M., Courtney, L., & Lomax, R. (1994). Supporting first graders' responses to literature: An analysis of teachers' roles in grand conversations. In C. K. Kinzer & D. J. Leu (Eds.), *Multidimensional aspects of literacy research, National Reading Conference,* pp. 517–526. Chicago: National Reading Conference.

McGinley, W., & Kamberelis, G. (1996). Maniac Magee and Ragtime Tumpie: Children negotiating self and world through reading and writing. *Research in the Teaching of English, 30,* 75–113.

McGuinness, D., McGuinness, C., & Donohue, J. (1995). Phonological training and the alphabet principle: Evidence for reciprocal causality. *Reading Research Quarterly, 30* (4), 830–852.

McIntyre, E., Kyle, D. W., & Moore, G. H. (2006). A primary-grade teacher's guidance toward small-group dialogue. *Reading Research Quarterly, 41,* 36–66.

McKeown, M. B. & Beck, I. L. (1988) Learning vocabulary: Different ways for different goals. *Remedial and Special Education, 9,* 42–52.

———. (2003). Taking advantage of read-alouds to help children make sense of decontextualized language. In A. Van Kleeck, S. A. Stahl, & E. B. Bauer (Eds.). *On reading books to children* (pp. 159–176). Mahwah, NJ: Erlbaum.

McKeown, M. B., Beck, I. L., Omanson, R. C., & Pople, M. T. (1985). Some effects of the nature and frequency of vocabulary instruction on the knowledge and use of words. *Reading Research Quarterly, 20,* 522–535.

McLaughlin, M. W., & Marsh, D. D. (1978). Staff development and school change. *Teachers College Record, 80* (1), 69–94.

McLeod, R. G. (1997, April 20). Immigrant numbers highest in California. *San Francisco Chronicle,* p. A14.

McMahon, S. I., & Raphael, T. E. (Eds.) (1997). *The book club connection: Literacy learning and classroom talk.* Newark, DE: International Reading Association.

McMahon, S. I., Raphael, T., Goatley, V., & Pardo, L. (1997). *The book club connection: Literacy learning and classroom talk.* New York: Teachers College Press. Newark, DE: International Reading Association.

McNeil, J. D. (1987). *Reading comprehension: New directions for classroom practice* (3rd ed.). Glenview, IL: Scott Foresman.

Meehan, P. (1997/1998). Beyond a chocolate crunch bar: A teacher examines her philosophy of teaching reading. *The Reading Teacher, 51* (4), 314–324.

Meeks, J. W., & Morgan, R. F. (1978). Classroom and the Cloze procedure: Interaction in imagery. *Reading Horizons, 18,* 261–264.

Menyuk, P. (1963). Syntactic structures in the language of children. *Child Development, 34,* 407–422.

———. (1984). Language development and reading. In J. Flood (Ed.), *Understanding reading comprehension* (pp. 101–121). Newark, DE: International Reading Association.

———. (1991). Linguistics and teaching the language arts. In J. Flood, J. M. Jensen, D. Lapp, & J. R. Squire (Eds.), *Handbook of research on teaching the English language arts* (pp. 24–29). New York: Macmillan.

Merrill, P. F., Hammons, K., Vincent, B. R., Reynolds, P. L., Christensen, L., & Tolman, M. N. (1996). *Computers in education.* Boston: Allyn & Bacon.

Meyer, B. J. F., & Freedle, R. (1979). *The effects of different discourse types on recall.* Princeton, NJ: Educational Testing Service.

Meyer, B. J. F., & Poon, L. W. (2004). Effects of structure strategy training and signaling on recall of text. In R. B. Ruddell & N. J. Unrau (Eds.), *Theoretical models and processes of reading* (5th ed., pp. 810–851). Newark, DE: International Reading Association.

Miller, P. J., & Mehler, R. A. (1994). The power of personal storytelling in families and kindergartens. In A. H. Dyson & C. Genishi (Eds.), *The need for story: Cultural diversity in classroom and community* (pp. 39–54). Urbana, IL: National Council of Teachers of English.

Miller, W. R. (1967). Language acquisition and reading. Unpublished manuscript, University of California, Berkeley.

Miller, W. R., & Ervin, S. (1964). The development of grammar in child language. *Monographs of the Society for Research in Child Development, 92,* 9–34.

Milner, E. (1951). A study of the relationship between reading readiness in grade one schoolchildren and patterns of parent-child interaction. *Child Development, 22,* 95–112.

Molinelli, P. (2000). "Kind of like jazz": Reader stance, shared authority, and identity in a twelfth-grade English course. Unpublished doctoral dissertation, University of California, Berkeley.

Moll, L. C. (1988). Some key issues in teaching Latino students. *Language Arts, 65* (5), 465–472.

———. (1992). Literacy research in community and classrooms: A sociocultural approach. In R. Beach, J. L. Green, M. L. Kamil, & T. Shanahan (Eds.), *Multidisciplinary perspectives on literacy research* (pp. 211–244). Urbana, IL: National Council of Teachers of English.

———. (1994). Literacy research in community and classrooms: A sociocultural approach. In R. B. Ruddell, M. R. Ruddell, & H. Singer (Eds.), *Theoretical models and processes of reading* (pp. 179–207). Newark, DE: International Reading Association.

Monson, D. L., & Sebesta, S. (1991). Reading preferences. In J. Flood, J. M. Jensen, D. Lapp, & J. R. Squire (Eds.), *Handbook of research on teaching the English language arts* (pp. 664–673). New York: Macmillan.

Moore, D. W., & Moore, S. A. (1986). Possible sentences. In E. K. Dishner, T. W. Bean, J. E. Readence, & D. W. Moore (Eds.), *Reading in the content areas: Improving classroom instruction* (2nd ed., pp. 174–179). Dubuque, IA: Kendall/Hunt.

Moorman, G. B., Blanton, W. E., & McLaughlin, T. (1994). The rhetoric of whole language. *Reading Research Quarterly, 29* (4), 308–329.

Morris, D. (1993). The relationship between children's concept of word in text and phoneme awareness in learning to read: A longitudinal study. *Research in the Teaching of English, 27* (2), 133–154.

Morrison, G. S. (1997). *Teaching in America.* Boston: Allyn & Bacon.

Morrow, L. M. (1991). Promoting voluntary reading. In J. Flood, J. M. Jensen, D. Lapp, & J. R. Squire (Eds.), *Handbook of research on teaching the English language arts* (pp. 681–690). New York: Macmillan.

———. (1993). *Literacy development in early years.* Boston: Allyn & Bacon.

Morrow, L. M., & Gambrell, L. B. (2000). *Literature-based reading instruction.* In M. L. Kamil, P. B. Mosenthal, P. D. Pearson, & R. Barr (Eds.),

Handbook of reading research: Volume III (pp. 563–586). Mahwah, NJ: Lawrence Erlbaum.

Morrow, L. M., Kuhn, M. R., Schwanenflugel, P. J. (2007). The family literacy program. *The Reading Teacher, 60,* 322–333.

Morrow, L. M., Pressley, M., Smith, J. K., & Smith, M. (1997). The effect of a literature-based program integrated into literacy and science instruction with children from diverse backgrounds. *Reading Research Quarterly, 32* (1), 54–76.

Morrow, L. M., Tracey, D. H., Woo, D. G., & Pressley, M. (1999). Characteristics of exemplary first-grade literacy instruction. *The Reading Teacher, 52* (5), 462–476.

Moss, B. (2004). Teaching expository text structures through information trade book retellings. *The Reading Teacher, 57* (8), 710–718.

Moss, J. F. (1996). *Teaching literature in the elementary school: A thematic approach.* Norwood, MA: Christopher-Gordon.

Moss, J. F., & Fenster, M. F. (2002). *From literature to literacy: Bridging learning in the library and the primary grade classroom.* Newark, DE: International Reading Association.

Mullis, I. V. S., Campbell, J. R., & Farstrup, A. E. (1993). *NAEP 1992 reading report card for the nation and the states.* Washington, DC: U.S. Department of Education, Office of Educational Research and Improvement.

Murphy, S., & Smith, M. A. (1991). *Writing portfolios: A bridge from teaching to assessment.* Markham, Ontario, Canada: Pippen Publishing.

Murphy, S. B. (1988, February). The problem with reading tasks: Watching children learn. Paper presented at the Eastern Educational Research Association, Miami Beach, FL.

Mydnas, S. (1993, June 24). Immigration opposition grows. *San Francisco Chronicle,* p. A3.

Myers, M., & Paris, S. (1978). Children's metacognitive knowledge about reading. *Journal of Educational Psychology, 70,* 680–690.

Nagy, W. E. (1988). Teaching vocabulary to improve reading comprehension. Newark, DE: International Reading Association.

Nagy, W. E., Anderson, R. C., & Herman, P. A. (1987). Learning word meanings from context during normal reading. *American Educational Research Journal, 24,* 237–270.

Nagy, W. E., & Herman, P. A. (1987). Breadth and depth of vocabulary knowledge: Implications for acquisition and instruction. In M. G. McKeown & M. E. Curtis (Eds.), *The nature of vocabulary acquisition* (pp. 19–35). Hillsdale, NJ: Erlbaum.

Nagy, W. E., Herman, P. A., & Anderson, R. C. (1985). Learning words from context. *Reading Research Quarterly, 20,* 233–253.

Nagy, W. E., & Scott, J. A. (2004). Vocabulary processes. In R. B. Ruddell & N. J. Unrau (Eds.), *Theoretical models and processes of reading* (5th ed., pp. 574–593). Newark, DE: International Reading Association.

Nation, K., & Hulme, D. (1997). Phonemic segmentation, not onset-rime segmentation, predicts early reading and spelling skills. *Reading Research Quarterly, 32,* 154–167.

National Assessment of Educational Progress. (1997). *NAEP 1997 Trends in academic progress.* Washington, DC: National Center for Educational Statistics.

National Center for Educational Statistics. (2003). *The nation's report card: Reading highlights 2003.* Washington, DC: U.S. Department of Education.

National Commission on Teaching & America's Future (1996). *What matters most: Teaching for America's future.* New York: Teachers College, Columbia University (Summary Report, September 1996).

National Reading Panel, Report of the. Teaching children to read: An evidence-based assessment of the scientific research literature on reading and its implications for reading instruction (2000). National Institute of Child Heath and Human Development. (NIH Publication No. 00–4769). Washington, DC: U.S. Government Printing Office.

Nelson, C. S. (1994). Historical literacy: A journey of discovery. *The Reading Teacher, 47* (7), 552–556.

Nelson, R. C. (1966). Children's poetry preferences. *Elementary English, 43,* 247–251.

Nikola-Lisa, W. (1997). Sound and sense in children's picturebooks. *Language Arts, 74* (3), 168–171.

No Child Left Behind Act of 2001, U.S. Public Law PL 107-110, 107th Congress, 1st session, 8 January 2002.

Norton, D. E., & Norton, S. E. (2003). *Through the eyes of a child: An introduction to children's literature* (6th ed.). Upper Saddle River, NJ: Merrill/Prentice Hall.

Nurss, J. R. (1979). Assessment of readiness. In G. E. MacKinnon & T. G. Waller (Eds.), *Reading research: Advances in theory and practice, Vol. 12* (pp. 31–62). New York: Academic Press.

Nystrand, M. (1999, Spring). The contexts of learning: Foundations of academic achievement. *English update: A newsletter from the Center on English Learning and Achievement,* pp. 2, 8.

O'Connor, R. E., Notari-Syverson, A., & Vadasy, P. F. (1998). *Ladders to literacy.* Baltimore: Paul H. Brookes Publishing.

O'Donnell, R. C., Griffin, W. J., & Norris, R. C. (1967). *Syntax of kindergarten and elementary school children: A transformational analysis.* Champaign, IL: National Council of Teachers of English.

O'Flahavan, J. (1989). An exploration of the effects of participant structure upon literacy development in reading group discussion. Doctoral dissertation, University of Illinois, Champaign.

Ogbu, J. U. (1983). Literacy and schooling in subordinate cultures: The case of Black Americans. In D. P. Resnick (Ed.), *Literacy in historical perspective* (pp. 129–153). Washington, DC: Library of Congress.

Ogle, D. (2004, May). *Essentials for effective content area reading.* Paper presented to the International Reading Association, Reno, NV.

Olness, R. (2007). *Using literature to enhance content area instruction.* Newark, DE: International Reading Association.

Olshansky, B. (1994). Making writing a work of art: Image-making within the writing process. *Language Arts, 71* (5), 350–356.

Osborne, A. B., & DiMattia, P. (1994). The IDEA's least restrictive environment mandate: Legal implications. *Exceptional Children, 61,* 6–14.

Ovando, C. J. (1988). Language diversity and education. In J. A. Banks & C. A. M. Banks (Eds.), *Multicultural education: Issues and perspectives* (pp. 208–227). Boston: Allyn & Bacon.

Palincsar, A. S. (1984). The quest for meaning from expository text: A teacher-guided journey. In G. G. Duffy, L. R. Roehler, & J. M. Mason (Eds.), *Comprehension instruction: Perspectives and suggestions.* New York: Longman.

Palincsar, A. S., & Brown, A. L. (1986). Interactive teaching to promote independent learning from text. *The Reading Teacher, 39,* 771–777.

Palmer, B. C., & Brooks, M. A. (2004). Reading until the cows come home: Figurative language and reading comprehension. *Journal of Adolescent and Adult Literacy, 47* (5), 370–378,

Pappas, C. C. (2006). The information book genre: Its role in integrated science literacy research and practice. *Reading Research Quarterly, 41,* 226–250.

Patterson, L., Santa, C. M., Short, K. G., & Smith, K. (Eds.). (1993). *Teachers are researchers: Reflection and action.* Newark, DE: International Reading Association.

Pearson, P. D. (1996). Reclaiming the center. In M. F. Graves, P. van den Broek, & B. M. Taylor (Eds.), *The first R: Every child's right to read* (pp. 259–274). New York: Teachers College Press.

Pearson, P. D., & Camperell, K. (1994). Comprehension of text structures. In R. B. Ruddell, M. R. Ruddell, & H. Singer (Eds.), *Theoretical models and processes of reading* (4th ed., pp. 448–468). Newark, DE: International Reading Association.

Pearson, P. D., & Fielding, L. (1991). Comprehension instruction. In R. Barr, M. L. Kamil, P. Mosenthal, & P. D. Pearson (Eds.), *Handbook of reading research, Volume II* (pp. 815–860). New York: Longman.

Pearson, P. D., Hiebert, E. H., & Kamil, M. L. (2007). Vocabulary assessment: What we know and what we need to learn. *Reading Research Quarterly, 41,* 282–296.

Pearson, P. D., Roehler, L., Dole, J., & Duffy, G. (1992). Developing expertise in reading comprehension. In S. J. Samuels & A. E. Farstrup (Eds.), *What research has to say about reading instruction* (2nd ed., pp. 145–199), Newark, DE: International Reading Association.

Pellowski, A. (1987). *The family storytelling handbook: How to use stories, anecdotes, rhymes, handkerchiefs, paper, and other objects to enrich your family traditions.* New York: Macmillan.

Perfetti, C. A., & Zhang, S. (1996). What it means to learn to read. In M. F. Graves, P. van den Broek, & B. M. Taylor (Eds.), *The first R: Every child's right to read* (pp. 37–61). New York: Teachers College Press.

Perl, S., & Wilson, N. (1986). *Through teachers' eyes: Portraits of writing teachers at work.* Portsmouth, NH: Heinemann.

Peterson, S. (1996). The principal's request: A missed opportunity for dialogue. *The Reading Teacher, 50* (1), 44–48.

Piaget, J. (1952). *The origins of intelligence in children.* New York: International University Press.

———. (1967). The genetic approach to the psychology of thought. In J. P. DeCecco (Ed.), *The psychology of language, thought and instruction.* New York: Holt, Rinehart & Winston.

Piaget, J., & Inhelder, B. (1969). *The psychology of the child.* New York: Basic Books.

Pick, A. D. (1965). Improvement of visual and tactual form discrimination. *Journal of Experimental Psychology, 69,* 331–339.

Piestrup, A. M. (1973). Black dialect interference and accommodation of reading instruction in first grade (Monographs of the Language-Behavior Research Laboratory, No. 4). Berkeley: University of California.

Pinnel, G. A., Fried, M. D., & Estice, R. M. (1990). Reading recovery: Learning how to make a difference. *The Reading Teacher, 43,* 282–295.

Pittelman, S. D., Heimlich, J. E., Berglund, R. L., & French, M. P. (1991). *Semantic feature analysis.* Newark, DE: International Reading Association.

Poglinco, S. M., Bach, A. J. (2004). The heart of the matter: Coaching as a vehicle for professional development. *Phi Delta Kappan, 85* (5), 398–400.

Portes, A., & Rumbaut, R. G. (1990). *Immigrant America: A portrait.* Berkeley: University of California Press.

Powell, W. R. (1970). Reappraising the criteria for interpreting informal reading inventories. In J. DeBoer (Ed.), *Reading diagnosis and evaluation.* Newark, DE: International Reading Association.

Prenn, M. C., & Honeychurch, J. C. (1990). Enhancing content area learning through expressive writing. In N. L. Cecil (Ed.), *Literacy in the '90s* (pp. 114–121). Dubuque, IA: Kendall/Hunt.

Pressley, M. (2000). What should comprehension instruction be the instruction of? In M. L. Kamil, P. B. Mosenthal, P. D. Pearson, & R. Barr (Eds.), *Handbook of reading research: Volume III* (pp. 545–561). Mahwah, NJ: Lawrence Erlbaum.

Pressley, M., & Afflerbach, P. (1995). *Verbal protocols of reading: The nature of constructively responsive reading.* Hillsdale, NJ: Erlbaum.

Pressley, M., & Forrest-Pressley, D. (1985). Questions and children's cognitive processing. In A. C. Graesser & J. B. Black (Eds.), *The psychology of questions* (pp. 277–296). Hillsdale, NJ: Erlbaum.

Purcell-Gates, V. (1988). Lexical and syntactic knowledge of written narrative held by well-read-to kindergartners and second graders. *Research in the Teaching of English, 22* (21), 128–160.

———. (1996). Stories, coupons, and the *TV Guide:* Relationships between home literacy experiences and emergent literacy knowledge. *Reading Research Quarterly, 31* (4), 406–428.

———. (2000). Family literacy. In M. L. Kamil, P. B. Mosenthal, P. D. Pearson, & R. Barr (Eds.), *Handbook of reading research: Volume III* (pp. 853–870). Mahwah, NJ: Lawrence Erlbaum.

Purcell-Gates, V., Duke, N. K., & Martineau, J. A. (2007). Learning to read and write genre-specific text: Roles of authentic experience and explicit teaching. *Reading Research Quarterly, 42,* 8–45.

Pyles, T. (1964). *The origins and development of the English language.* New York: Harcourt Brace Jovanovich.

Quatroche, D. J., Bean, R. M., Hamilton, R. L. (2001). The role of the reading specialist: A review of research. *The Reading Teacher, 55* (3), 282–294.

Rack, J. P., Snowling, M. J., & Olson, R. K. (1992). The nonword reading deficit in developmental dyslexia: A review. *Reading Research Quarterly, 27,* 28–53.

Raines, B. (1991). Response and collaboration in literature discussion groups: A two-year study of an intermediate grade classroom. Master's thesis, Sonoma State University, Rohnert Park, CA.

Raines, S. C. (1994). *Story stretchers for the primary grades.* Mt. Rainier, MD: Gryphon House.

Raines, S. C., & Canady, R. J. (1991). *More story stretchers.* Mt. Rainier, MD: Gryphon House.

Ramirez, J. D., & Merino, B. J. (1990). Classroom talk in English immersion, early-exit & late-exit transitional bilingual education programs. In R. Jacobson & C. Faltis (Eds.), *Language distribution issues in bilingual schooling.* Cleveland, OH: Multilingual Matters.

Ramirez, M. (1992, winter/spring). Executive summary, final report: Longitudinal study of structured English immersion strategy, early-exit and late-exit transitional bilingual education programs for language-minority children. *Bilingual Research Journal, 16* (1, 2), 1–62.

Raphael, T. E. (1982). Question-answering strategies for children. *The Reading Teacher, 36,* 186–190.

———. (1986). Teaching question-answer relationships, revisited. *The Reading Teacher, 39,* 516–523.

Raphael, T. E., & McMahon, S. I. (1994). Book club: An alternative framework for reading instruction. *The Reading Teacher, 48* (2), 102–116.

Rasinski, T. (2000). Speech does matter in reading. *The Reading Teacher, 54* (2), 146–151.

Rasinski, T. & Padak, N. (2000). *Effective reading strategies: Teaching children who find reading a challenge* (2nd ed.). Columbus, OH: Merrill.

Read, C. (1971). Preschool children's knowledge of English phonology. *Harvard Educational Review, 41,* 1–34.

———. (1975). *Children's categorization of speech sounds in English.* Champaign, IL: National Council of Teachers of English.

Reid, J. (1966). Learning to think about reading. *Educational Research, 9,* 56–62.

Rekrut, M. D. (1994). Peer and cross-age tutoring: The lessons of research. *Journal of Reading, 37* (5), 356–362.

Reutzel, D. R., & Larsen, N. S. (1995). Look what they've done to the real children's books in the new basal readers! *Language Arts, 72* (7), 495–507.

Reutzel, D. R., Larson, C. M., & Sabey, B. L. (1995). Dialogical books: Connecting content, conversation, and composition. *The Reading Teacher, 49* (2), 98–109.

Richardson, V. (Ed.). (1994). *Teacher change and the staff development process: A case in reading instruction.* New York: Teachers College Press.

Richgels, D. J., Poremba, K. J., & McGee, L. M. (1996). Kindergarteners talk about print: Phonemic awareness in meaningful contexts. *The Reading Teacher, 49* (8), 632–642.

Rief, L. (1990). Finding the value in evaluation: Self-assessment in a middle school classroom. *Educational Leadership, 47,* 24–29.

Ringgold, F. (1991). *Tar beach.* New York: Crown.

Rogers, C. (1961). *On becoming a person.* Boston: Houghton Mifflin.

Rogers, E. (1983). *Diffusions of innovations.* New York: The Free Press.

Rogers, T., Marshall, E., & Tyson, C. A. (2006). Dialogic narratives of literacy, teaching, and schooling: Preparing literacy teachers for diverse settings. *Reading Research Quarterly, 41,* 202–223.

Rose, D. H., & Meyer, A. (1994). The role of technology in language arts instruction. *Language Arts, 71* (4), 290–294.

Rosenblatt, L. M. (1985). The transactional theory of literary work: Implications for research. In C. R. Cooper (Ed.), *Researching response to literature and the teaching of literature: Points of departure* (pp. 33–53). Norwood, NJ: Ablex.

———. (1988). *Writing and reading: The transactional theory* (Report No. 13). Berkeley: University of California, Center for the Study of Writing.

———. (1991). Literature—S.O.S.! *Language Arts, 68,* 444–448.

Rosenblatt, L. M. (2004). The transactional theory of reading and writing. In R. B. Ruddell & N. J. Unrau (Eds.), *Theoretical models and processes of reading* (5th ed., pp. 1363–1398). Newark, DE: International Reading Association.

Rosenshine, B., & Meister, C. (1992). The use of scaffolds for teaching higher-level cognitive strategies. *Educational Leadership,* April, 26–33.

Roser, N. L. & Keehn, S. (2002). Fostering thought, talk, and inquiry: Linking literature and social studies. *The Reading Teacher, 55,* (5), 416–426.

Routman, R. (1991). *Invitations.* Portsmouth, NH: Heinemann.

Row, B. H. (1968). Reading interests of elementary school pupils in selected schools in Muscogee County, Georgia. Unpublished doctoral dissertation, Auburn University, Montgomery, AL.

Ruddell, M. R. (1988). Developing critical thinking with the directed reading-thinking activity. *The Reading Teacher, 41,* 526–533.

———. (1993). *Teaching content reading and writing.* Boston: Allyn & Bacon.

Ruddell, R. B. (1974). *Reading-language insruction: Innovative practices.* Englewood Cliffs, NJ: Prentice-Hall.

———. (1978). Developing comprehension abilities: Implications from research for an instructional framework. In S. J. Samuels (Ed.), *What research has to say about reading instruction* (pp. 109–120). Newark, DE: International Reading Association.

———. (1991, December). A study of the effect of reader motivation and comprehension development on students' reading comprehension achievement in influential and noninfluential teachers' classrooms. Paper presented at the National Reading Conference, Palm Springs, CA.

———. (1995). Those influential literacy teachers: Meaning negotiators and motivation builders. *The Reading Teacher, 48,* 454–463.

———. (1997). Researching the influential literacy teacher: Characteristics, beliefs, strategies, and new research directions. In C. K. Kinzer, K. A. Hinchman, & D. J. Leu (Eds.), *Inquiries in literacy theory and practice: 46th Yearbook of the National Reading Conference* (pp. 37–53). Chicago, IL: National Reading Conference.

———. (2002). *Teaching children to read and write: Becoming an effective literacy teacher* (3rd ed.). Boston: Allyn & Bacon.

———. (2004). Researching the influential literacy teacher: Characteristics, beliefs, strategies, and new research directions. In R. B. Ruddell & N. J. Unrau (Eds.), *Theoretical models and processes of reading* (5th ed., pp. 979–997). Newark, DE: International Reading Association.

———. (2006). *Teaching children to read and write: Becoming an effective literacy teacher* (4th ed.). Boston: Allyn & Bacon.

Ruddell, R. B., Draheim, M., & Barnes, J. (1990). A comparative study of the teaching effectiveness of influential and noninfluential teachers and reading comprehension development. In J. Zutell & S. McCormick (Eds.), *The 39th yearbook of the National Reading Conference* (pp. 153–163). Chicago: National Reading Conference.

Ruddell, R. B., & Greybeck, B. (1995, April). Meaning negotiation and meaning construction strategies used by influential teachers in content area instruction. Paper presented at the meeting of the American Educational Research Association, San Francisco, CA.

Ruddell, R. B., & Haggard, M. R. (1986). *Thinking about reading: Level C.* Cleveland, OH: Modern Curriculum Press.

———. (1987). *Thinking about reading, series 2: Level E.* Cleveland, OH: Modern Curriculum Press.

Ruddell, R. B., & Harris, P. (1989). A study of the relationship between influential teachers' prior knowledge and beliefs and teaching effectiveness: Developing higher-order thinking in content areas. In S. McCormick & J. Zutell (Eds.), *The 38th yearbook*

of the National Reading Conference (pp. 461–472). Chicago: National Reading Conference.

Ruddell, R. B., & Kern, R. B. (1986). The development of belief systems and teaching effectiveness of influential teachers. In M. P. Douglas (Ed.), *Reading: The quest for meaning* (pp. 133–150). Claremont, CA: Claremont Graduate School Yearbook.

Ruddell, R. B., & Kinzer, C. K. (1982). Test preferences and competencies of field educators. In J. Niles & L. A. Harris (Eds.), *New inquiries in reading research and instruction* (pp. 196–199). Clemson, SC: National Reading Conference.

Ruddell, R. B., Monson, D. L., & Sebesta, S. L. (1981). *Wingspan, Teacher's edition.* Boston: Allyn & Bacon.

Ruddell, R. B., & Sperling, M. (1988). Factors influencing the use of literacy research by the classroom teacher: Research review and new directions. In J. E. Readence & R. S. Baldwin (Eds.), *Dialogues in literacy research* (pp. 319–329). Chicago: National Reading Conference.

Ruddell, R. B., & Unrau, N. J. (2004a). Reading as a meaning-construction process: The reader, the text, and the teacher. In R. B. Ruddell & N. J. Unrau (Eds.), *Theoretical models and processes of reading* (5th ed., pp. 1462–1523). Newark, DE: International Reading Association.

———. (2004b). The role of responsive teaching in focusing reader intention and developing reader motivation. In R. B. Ruddell & N. J. Unrau (Eds.), *Theoretical models and processes of reading* (5th ed., pp. 954–978). Newark, DE: International Reading Association.

Ruddell, R. B., & Williams, A. (1972). *A research investigation of a literacy teaching model: Project DELTA* (EPDA Project No. 005262). Washington, DC: Department of Health, Education and Welfare, Office of Education.

Rumelhart, D. E. (1981). Schemata: The building blocks of cognition. In J. T. Guthrie (Ed.), *Comprehension and teaching: Research reviews.* Newark, DE: International Reading Association.

Rumelhart, D. E., & Ortony, A. (1977). The representation of knowledge in memory. In R. C. Anderson, R. J. Spiro, & W. E. Montague (Eds.), *Schooling and the acquisition of knowledge.* Hillsdale, NJ: Erlbaum.

Rupley, W. H., Logan, J. W., & Nichols, W. D. (December 1998–January 1999). Vocabulary instruction in a balanced reading program. *The Reading Teacher, 52,* 336–346.

Russell, D. H. (1970). Reading and mental health: Clinical approaches. In R. Ruddell (Ed.), *The dynamics of reading* (pp. 207–229). Waltham, MA: Ginn.

Sadker, D., & Sadker, M. (1982). *Sex equity handbook for schools.* New York: Longman.

Salinger, T., & Chittenden, E. (1994). Analysis of an early literacy portfolio: Consequences for instruction. *Language Arts, 71* (6), 446–452.

———. (1996). Howling in the wind: Academics try to change classroom reading instruction. In M. F. Graves, P. van den Broek, & B. M. Taylor (Eds.), *The first R:*

Every child's right to read (pp. 120–130). New York: Teachers College Press.

Samuels, S. J. (1979). The method of repeated reading. *The Reading Teacher, 32,* 403–408.

———. (1997). The method of repeated readings. *The Reading Teacher, 50* (5), 376–381.

———. (2004). Toward a theory of automatic information processing in reading. In R. B. Ruddell & N. J. Unrau (Eds.), *Theoretical models and processes of reading* (5th ed., pp. 1127–1148). Newark, DE: International Reading Association.

San Francisco Unified School District (1969, summer). Problems in teaching English to Chinese-speaking students. Unpublished manuscript.

Santa, C. M. (1997). School change and literacy engagement: Preparing teaching and learning environments. In J. T. Guthrie & A. Wigfield (Eds.), *Reading engagement: Motivating readers through integrated instruction* (pp. 218–233). Newark, DE: International Reading Association.

Sashkin, M., & Egermeier, J. (1993). *School change models and processes: A review and synthesis of research and practice.* Washington, DC: OERI, U.S. Department of Education.

Saville-Troike, M. (1984). What really matters in second language learning for academic achievement. *TESOL Quarterly, 18,* 199–220.

Schallert, D. L. (1991). The contribution of psychology to teaching the language arts. In J. Flood, J. M. Jensen, D. Lapp, & J. R. Squire (Eds.), *Handbook of research on teaching the English language arts* (pp. 30–39). New York: Macmillan.

Schank, R., & Abelson, R. (1975). *Knowledge structures.* Hillsdale, NJ: Erlbaum.

Schmidt, P. R., Gillen, S., Zollo, T. C., & Stone, R. (2002). Literacy learning and scientific inquiry: Children respond. *The Reading Teacher, 55* (6), 534–548.

Schunk, D. H. (1991) Self-efficacy and academic motivation. *Educational Psychologist, 26,* 207–231.

———. (1994). Self-regulation of self-efficacy and attributions in academic settings. In D. H. Schunk & B. J. Zimmerman (Eds). *Self-regulation of learning and performance: Issues and educational applications* (pp. 75–99). Hillsdale, NJ: Erlbaum.

Schwanenflugel, P. J., & Akin, C. E. (1994). Developmental trends in lexical decisions for abstract and concrete words. *Reading Research Quarterly, 29* (3), 250–264.

Schwanenflugel, P. J., Kuhn, M. R., Strauss, G. P., Morris, R. D. (2006). Becoming a fluent and automatic reader in the early elementary school years. *Reading Research Quarterly, 41,* 496–522.

Seiter, E. (1995). *Sold separately: Children and parents in consumer culture.* New Brunswick, NJ: Rutgers University Press.

Selinker, L. (1972). Interlanguage. *International Review of Applied Linguistics, 10,* 209–231.

Senechal, M., & Cornell, E. H. (1993). Vocabulary acquisition through shared reading experiences. *Reading Research Quarterly, 28* (4), 360–374.

Shamir, A. & Korat, O. (2006). How to select CD-ROM storybooks for young children: The teacher's role. *The Reading Teacher, 59,* 532–543.

Shanahan, T. (2001). Phonemic awareness instruction helps children learn to read: Evidence from the National Panel's meta-analysis. *Reading Research Quarterly, 36,* 250–287.

Shanahan, T., Mulhern, M., & Rodriguez-Brown, F. (1995). Project FLAME: Lessons learned from a family literacy program for linguistic minority families. *The Reading Teacher, 48* (7), 586–593.

Shanahan, T., & Neuman, S. B. (1997). Literacy research that makes a difference. *Reading Research Quarterly, 32* (2), 202–210.

Shanklin, N. K. (1982). *Relating reading and writing: Developing a transitional model of the writing process.* Bloomington, IN: Monographs in Teaching and Learning, School of Education, Indiana University.

Shepard, L. A. (2004). The role of assessment in a learning culture. In R. B. Ruddell & N. J. Unrau (Eds.), *Theoretical models and processes of reading* (5th ed., pp. 1614–1635). Newark, DE: International Reading Association.

Shoop, M. (1986). InQuest: A listening and reading comprehension strategy. *The Reading Teacher, 39,* 660–674.

Shores, J. H. (1954). Reading interests and informational needs of children in grades four to eight. *Elementary English, 31,* 493–500.

Shu, H., Anderson, R. C., & Zhang, H. (1995). Incidental learning of word meanings while reading: A Chinese and American cross-cultural study. *Reading Research Quarterly, 30* (1), 76–95.

Shuy, R. W. (1973). Some relationships of linguistics to the reading process. In T. Clymer & R. B. Ruddell (Eds.), *Teacher's edition of how it is nowadays* (pp. 22–24). Boston: Ginn.

Siegel, M. (1994, April). The curricular possibilities of transmediation: Strategy framework and metaphor. In C. Panofsky (Chair): Vygotsky and beyond: Semiotic mediation and its significance for literacy teaching and performance. Symposium conducted at the meeting of the American Educational Research Association, New Orleans, LA.

Signatures: Rhythm and rhyme practice book: Teacher's edition. (1996). (p. 59). Orlando, FL: Harcourt Brace.

Silvaroli, N., & Wheelock, W. H. (2004). *Classroom reading inventory* (9th ed.). New York: McGraw-Hill.

Sinatra, R., Beaudry, J. S., Stahl-Gemake, J., & Guastello, E. F. (1990). Combining visual literacy, text understanding, and writing for culturally diverse students. *Journal of Reading, 33,* 612–617.

Singer, H. (1980). Active comprehension: From answering to asking questions. In C. M. McCullough (Ed.), *Inchworm, inchworm: Persistent problems in reading education* (pp. 222–232). Newark, DE: International Reading Association.

Slavin, R. E. (1995). Cooperative learning and intergroup relations. In J. A. Banks & C. A. M. Banks (Eds.), *Handbook of research on multicultural education* (pp. 628–634). New York: Macmillan.

Sloyer, S. (1982). *Readers Theatre: Story dramatization in the classroom.* Urbana, IL: National Council for Teachers of English.

Smallwood, B. A. (1991). *The literature connection: A read aloud guide for multicultural classrooms.* Reading, MA: Addison-Wesley.

Smith, B. O., & Orlosky, D. E. (1974). Educational change: Its origins and characteristics. In R. B. Ruddell, E. J. Ahern, E. Hartson, & J. Taylor (Eds.), *Resources in reading-language instruction* (pp. 64–69). Englewood Cliffs, NJ: Prentice-Hall.

Smith, D. D., & Luckasson, R. (1995). *Introduction to special education: Teaching in an age of challenge.* Boston: Allyn & Bacon.

Smith, F. (1981). Demonstrations, engagement and sensitivity: A revised approach to language learning. *Language Arts, 58,* 103–112.

Smith, J. (1991). DISKovery: Goin' wild in hypercard. *Language Arts, 68* (8), 674–680.

Smith, J. L., & Johnson, H. (1994). Models for implementing literature in content studies. *The Reading Teacher, 48* (3), 198–209.

Smith, N. B. (1974). *American reading instruction.* Newark, DE: International Reading Association.

———. (2002). *American reading instruction.* Newark, DE: International Reading Association.

Smith, S. B., Simmons, D. C., & Kameenui, E. J. (1998). Phonological awareness: Research bases. In D. C. Simmons, & E. J. Kameenui (Eds.), *What research tells us about children with diverse learning needs: Bases and basics* (pp. 61–127). Marwah, NJ: Erlbaum.

Smolin, L. I., & Lawless, K. A. (2003). Becoming literate in the technological age: New responsibilities and tools for teachers. *The Reading Teacher, 56* (6), 570–577.

Snow, C. E., Burns, M. S., & Griffin, P. (Eds.), (1998). *Preventing reading difficulties in young children.* Washington, DC: National Academy Press.

Sobul, D. (1994, February). Strategies to meet the goals of SDAIE. Paper presented at California Association for Bilingual Education, San Jose.

Soderbergh, R. (1977). *Reading in early childhood: A linguistic study of a preschool child's gradual acquisition of reading ability.* Washington, DC: Georgetown University Press.

Solomon, G. (1992). The computer as electronic doorway: Technology and the promise of empowerment. *Phi Delta Kappan, 74* (4), 327–329.

Spache, G. (1953). A new readability formula for primary-grade reading materials. *Elementary School Journal, 53,* 410–413.

Spear-Swerling, L. (2004). A road map for understanding reading disability and other reading problems: Origins, prevention and intervention. In R. B. Ruddell & N. J. Unrau (Eds.), *Theoretical models and processes of reading* (5th ed., pp. 517–573). Newark, DE: International Reading Association.

Spiegel, D. L. (1992). Blending whole language and systematic direct instruction. *The Reading Teacher, 46* (1), 38–44.

———. (1996). The role of trust in reader-response groups. *Language Arts, 73* (5), 332–339.

———. (1998). Silver bullets, babies, and bath water: Literature response groups in a balanced literacy program. *The Reading Teacher, 52* (2), 114–124.

Spiro, R. J. (2004). Principled pluralism for adaptive flexibility in teaching and learning. In R. B. Ruddell & N. J. Unrau (Eds.), *Theoretical models and processes of reading* (5th ed., pp. 654–659). Newark, DE: International Reading Association.

Spiro, R. J., Coulson, R. L., Feltovich, P. J., & Anderson, D. K. (2004). Cognitive flexibility theory: Advanced knowledge acquisition. In R. B. Ruddell & N. J. Unrau (Eds.), *Theoretical models and processes of reading* (5th ed., pp. 640–653). Newark, DE: International Reading Association.

Squire, R. J. (1989, May). Research on reader response and the national literature initiative. Paper presented at the International Reading Association Convention, Atlanta, GA.

Squires, D. & Bliss, T. (2004) Teacher visions: Navigating beliefs about literacy learning. *The Reading Teacher, 57* (8), 756–763,

Stahl, S. A., Duffy-Hester, A. M., & Stahl, K. A. D. (1998). Everything you wanted to know about phonics (but were afraid to ask). *Reading Research Quarterly, 33* (3), 338–355.

Stainback, S., & Stainback, W. (1992). *Curriculum consideration in inclusive classrooms: Facilitating learning for all students.* Baltimore: Paul Brooks.

Standards for Reading Professionals—Revised 2003 (2004). Newark, DE: International Reading Association.

Stahl, K. A. D. (2004), Proof, practice, and promise: Comprehension strategy instruction in the primary grades. *The Reading Teacher, 57* (7), April, 2004.

Stanovich, K. E. (1991). Word recognition: Changing perspectives. In R. Barr, M. L. Kamil, P. Mosenthal, & P. D. Pearson (Eds.), *Handbook of reading research: Volume II* (pp. 418–452). New York: Longman.

———. (2004). Matthew effects in reading: Some consequences of individual differences in the acquisition of literacy. In R. B. Ruddell & N. J. Unrau (Eds.), *Theoretical models and processes of reading* (5th ed., pp. 454–516). Newark, DE: International Reading Association.

Stauffer, R. G. (1969). *Directing reading maturity as a cognitive process.* New York: Harper & Row.

———. (1976). *Teaching reading as a thinking process.* New York: Harper & Row.

Steele, J. L., & Meredith, K. (1991). Standardized measures of reading achievement for placement of students in Chapter I and learning disability programs: A nationwide survey of assessment practices. *Reading Research and Instruction, 30* (2), 17–31.

Stevenson, J. (1990). Transitions: Incorporating a new style of teaching and assessment into the elementary classroom. Unpublished master's thesis, University of California, Berkeley.

Stockwell, R. B., & Bowen, J. D. (1966). *The sounds of English and Spanish.* Chicago: University of Chicago Press.

Stokes, S. M. (1997). Curriculum for Native American students: Using Native American values. *The Reading Teacher, 50* (7), 576–584.

Stoll, D. R. (1997). *Magazines for kids and teens.* Newark, DE: International Reading Association.

Strickland, D. S. (1994/1995). Reinventing our literacy programs: Books, basics, balance. *The Reading Teacher, 48* (4), 294–302.

Strickland, D. S., & Feeley, J. T. (1991). The learner develops: Development in the elementary school years. In J. Flood, J. M. Jensen, D. Lapp, & J. R. Squire (Eds.), *Handbook of research on teaching the English language arts* (pp. 286–302). New York: Macmillan.

Strickland, D. S., & Morrow, L. M. (1989). *Emerging literacy: Young children learn to read and write.* Newark, DE: International Reading Association.

———. (2000). *Beginning reading and writing.* New York: Teachers College Press.

Strommen, L. T., & Mates, B. F. (1997). What readers do: Young children's ideas about the nature of reading. *The Reading Teacher, 51* (2), 98–107.

Sturtevant, E. G. (1996). Lifetime influences on the literacy-related instructional beliefs of experienced high school history teachers: Two comparative case studies. *Journal of Literacy Research, 28* (2), 227–257.

Sulzby, E. (1985). Children's emergent reading of favorite storybooks: A developmental study. *Reading Research Quarterly, 20,* 458–481.

———. (1991). The development of the young child and the emergence of literacy. In J. Flood, J. M. Jensen, D. Lapp, & J. R. Squire (Eds.), *Handbook of research on teaching the English language arts* (pp. 273–285). New York: Macmillan.

Sulzby, E., & Teale, W. (1991). Emergent literacy. In R. Barr, M. L. Kamil, P. B. Mosenthal, & P. D. Pearson (Eds.), *Handbook of reading research, Volume II* (pp. 727–757). New York: Longman.

Sutherland-Smith, W. (2002). Weaving the literacy web: Changes in reading from page to screen. *The Reading Teacher, 55,* 662–669.

Sweet, A. P. (1993). *State of the art: Transforming ideas for teaching and learning to read* (GPO Document No. 065–000–00620–1). Washington, DC. Department of Education, Office of Education Research and Improvement.

Taba, H. (1965). The teaching of thinking. *Elementary English, 42,* 534–542.

Tabors, P. O., & Snow, C. E. (2004). Young bilingual children and early literacy development. In R. B. Ruddell & N. J. Unrau (Eds.), *Theoretical models and processes of reading* (5th ed., pp. 240–267). Newark, DE: International Reading Association.

Taylor, B. M., Pearson, P. D., Peterson, D. S. & Rodriguez, M. C. (2005). The CIERA School Change Network: An evidence-based approach to professional development and school reading improvement. *Reading Research Quarterly, 40,* 40–68.

Taylor, B. M., Pressley, M., & Pearson, P. D. (2002). Research supported characteristics of teachers and schools that promote reading achievement. In B. M.

Taylor & P. D. Pearson (Eds.), *Teaching reading* (pp. 361–374). Mahwah, NJ: Erlbaum.

Taylor, B., Short, R., Shearer, B., & Frye, B. (1995). First-grade teachers provide early reading intervention in the classroom. In R. L. Allington & S. A. Walmsley (Eds.), *No quick fix: Rethinking literacy programs in America's elementary schools* (pp. 159–176). Newark, DE: International Reading Association.

Taylor, B., Strait, J., & Medo, M. A. (1994). Early intervention in reading: Supplemental instruction for groups of low-achieving students provided by first-grade teachers. In E. H. Hiebert & B. M. Taylor (Eds.), *Getting reading right from the start* (pp. 107–122). Boston: Allyn & Bacon.

Taylor, B. M. (1996). Looking beyond ourselves to help all children learn to read. In M. F. Graves, P. van den Broek, & B. M. Taylor (Eds.), *The first R: Every child's right to read* (pp. 62–69). New York: Teachers College Press.

Taylor, E. (2004). *Taylor's educational internet connections.* Las Vegas Valley, CA: Elaine Taylor & KT Graphics.

Taylor, W. L. (1953). Cloze procedures: A new tool for measuring readability. *Journalism Quarterly, 30,* 360–368.

Teale, W. H., & Sulzby, E. (1989). Emergent literacy: New perspectives. In D. S. Strickland & L. M. Morrow (Eds.), *Emerging literacy: Young children learn to read and write* (pp. 1–15). Newark, DE: International Reading Association.

Temple, C., & Gillet, J. W. (1989). *Language arts: Learning processes and teaching practices* (2nd ed.). Glenview, IL: Scott, Foresman.

Temple, C., Ogle, D., Crawford A., & Freppon, P. (2008). *All children read: Teaching literacy in today's diverse classrooms* (2nd ed.). Boston: Allyn & Bacon.

Templin, M. C. (1957). *Certain language skills in children.* Minneapolis: University of Minnesota Press, Institute of Child Welfare Monographs.

Thomas, K. J. (1986). The Directed Inquiry Activity: An instructional procedure for content reading. In E. K. Dishner, T. W. Bean, J. E. Readence, & D. W. Moore (Eds.), *Reading in the content areas* (2nd ed., pp. 278–281). Dubuque, IA: Kendall/Hunt.

Thompson, A. (1990). Thinking and writing in learning logs. In N. Atwell (Ed.), *Coming to know: Writing to learn in the intermediate grades.* Portsmouth, NH: Heinemann.

Thorndike, E. L., & Lorge, I. (1944). *The teacher's book of 30,000 words.* New York: Teachers College Press.

Tierney, R. J. (1998). Literacy assessment reform: Shifting beliefs, principled possibilities, and emerging practices. *The Reading Teacher, 51* (5), 374–390.

Tierney, R. J., Carter, M. A., & Desai, L. E. (1991). *Assessment in the reading-writing classroom.* New York: Christopher-Gordon Publishers.

Tierney, R. J., & Readence, J. E. (2000). *Reading strategies and practices: A compendium* (5th ed.). Boston: Allyn & Bacon.

Tierney, R. J., Readence, J. E., & Dishner, E. K. (1990). *Reading strategies and practices: A compendium.* Boston: Allyn & Bacon.

———. (1995). *Reading strategies and practices: A compendium* (4th ed). Boston: Allyn & Bacon.

Topping, K. (1998). Effective tutoring in America Reads: A reply to Wasik. *The Reading Teacher, 52* (1), 42–50.

Trace, A. (1961). *What Ivan knows that Johnny doesn't.* New York: Random House.

Trelease, J. (2006). *The new read-aloud handbook* (6th ed.). New York: Penguin.

Trieman, R. (1985). Onsets and rimes as units of spoken syllables: Evidence from children. *Journal of Experimental Psychology, 39,* 161–181.

Tuttle, F. B., Jr. (1991). Teaching the gifted. In J. Flood, J. M. Jenson, D. Lapp, & J. R. Squire (Eds.), *Handbook of research on teaching English and the language arts* (pp. 372–379). New York: Macmillan.

Tway, E. (1991). The elementary school classroom. In J. Flood, J. M. Jensen, D. Lapp, & J. R. Squire (Eds.), *Handbook of research on teaching the English language arts* (pp. 425–437). New York: Macmillan.

Underwood, T. (1998). The consequences of portfolio assessment: A case study. *Educational Assessment, 5,* 147–194.

U.S. Department of Education. (2003). *National assessment of educational progress.* Retrieved July 16, 2004, from http://nces.ed.gov/nationsreportcard/reading/results.

U.S. Department of Health and Human Services. (2000). *Report of the National Reading Panel: Teaching children to read.* (NIH Publication No. 00-4769). Washington, DC: Author.

Valdés, G. (1991). *Bilingual minorities and language issues in writing: Toward profession-wide responses to a new challenge* (Tech. Rep. No. 54). Berkeley: University of California Center for the Study of Writing.

Valencia, S. (1990). A portfolio approach to classroom reading assessment: The whys, whats, and hows. *The Reading Teacher, 43* (4), 338–340.

Valencia, S. W. (2000, November). Assessment that makes a difference: Improving teaching and learning. Paper presented to the California Reading Association, Anaheim, CA.

Valencia, S. W., & Au, K. H. (1997). Portfolios across educational contexts: Issues of evaluation, professional development, and system validity. *Educational Assessment, 4,* 1–35.

Valencia, S. W., & Wixon, K. K. (2000). Policy-oriented research on literacy standards and assessment. In M. L. Kamil, P. B. Mosenthal, P. D. Pearson, & R. Barr (Eds.), *Handbook of reading research, Volume III* (pp. 909–935). Mahwah, NJ: Erlbaum.

Valencia, S. W., & Wixon, K. (2004). Literacy policy and policy research that make a difference. In R. B. Ruddell & N. J. Unrau (Eds.), *Theoretical models and processes of reading* (5th ed., pp. 69–93). Newark, DE: International Reading Association.

van den Broek, P. (1996). On becoming literate: The many sources of success and failure in reading. In M. F. Graves, P. van den Broek, & B. M. Taylor (Eds.), *The first R: Every child's right to read* (pp. 189–196). New York: Teachers College Press.

Vandergrift, K. (1965). Reading aloud to young children. In L. B. Jacobs (Ed.), *Using literature with young children* (pp. 11–14). New York: Teachers College Press.

Vandervelden, M. C., & Siegel, L. S. (1995). Phonological recoding and phoneme awareness in early literacy: A developmental approach. *Reading Research Quarterly, 30* (4), 854–875.

Vaughn, C. L. (1990). Knitting writing: The Double-Entry Journal. In N. Atwell (Ed.), *Coming to know: Writing to learn in the intermediate grades.* Portsmouth, NH: Heinemann.

Vaughn, S., Bos, C. S., & Schumm, J. S. (1997). *Teaching mainstreamed, diverse, and at-risk students in the general education classroom.* Boston: Allyn & Bacon.

Veatch, J. (1968). How to teach reading with children's books. New York: Citation Press.

Vellutino, F. R., & Denckla, M. B. (1991). Cognitive and neuropsychological foundations of word identification in poor and normally developing readers. In R. Barr, M. L. Kamil, P. Mosenthal, & P. D. Pearson (Eds.), Handbook of reading research, Volume II (pp. 571–608). New York: Longman.

Vellutino, F. R., & Scanlon, D. B. (1987). Phonological coding, phonological awareness, and reading ability: Evidence from longitudinal and experimental study. *Merrill Palmer Quarterly, 33,* 321–363.

Venezky, R. L. (1991). The development of literacy in the industrialized nations of the West. In R. Barr, M. L. Kamil, P. Mosenthal, & P. D. Pearson (Eds.), *Handbook of reading research: Vol. II* (pp. 46–67). New York: Longman.

Venezky, R. L., & Massaro, D. W. (1979). The role of orthographic regularity in word recognition. In L. Resnick & P. Weaver (Eds.), *Theory and practice of early reading* (pp. 85–107). Hillsdale, NJ: Erlbaum.

Verhoeven, L. T. (1994). Transfer in bilingual development: The linguistic interdependence hypothesis revisited. *Language Learning, 44,* 381–415.

Villaume, S. K., Worden, T., Williams, S., Hopkins, L., & Roseblatt, C. (1994). Five teachers in search of a discussion. *Language Arts, 47,* 480–489.

Vintz, R., Gordon, E., Hamilton, G., Lamontagne, J., & Lundgren, B. (2000). *Becoming (other)wise: Enhancing critical reading perspectives.* Portland, ME: Calendar Islands.

Vogt, M. (1991). An observation guide for supervisors and administrators: Moving toward integrated reading/language arts instruction. *The Reading Teacher, 45* (3), 206–211.

Vogt, M. E., & Shearer, B. A. (2003). *Reading specialists in the real world.* Boston: Allyn & Bacon.

Vygotsky, L. S. (1962/1986). *Thought and language.* Cambridge, MA: MIT Press.

———. (1978). *Mind in society.* Cambridge, MA: Harvard University Press.

Wadsworth, B. J. (1971). *Piaget's theory of cognitive development.* New York: David McKay.

Walker, C. M. (1979). High frequency word list for grades 3 through 9. *The Reading Teacher, 32,* 802–812.

Waldbart, A., Meyers, B., & Meyers, J. (2006). Invitations to families in an early literacy support program. *The Reading Teacher, 59,* 774–785.

Walmsley, S. A. (1992). Reflections on the state of elementary literature instruction. *Language Arts, 69,* 508–514.

Walmsley, S. A., & Allington, R. L. (1995). Redefining and reforming instructional support programs for at-risk students. In R. L. Allington & S. A. Walmsley (Eds.), *No quick fix: Rethinking literacy programs in America's elementary schools* (pp. 19–46). Newark, DE: International Reading Association.

Walpole, S. (1998/1999). Changing texts, changing thinking: Comprehension demands of new science textbooks. *The Reading Teacher, 52* (4), 358–369.

Wang, J. H., & Guthrie, J. T. (2004). Modeling the effects of intrinsic motivation, extrinsic motivation, amount of reading, and past reading achievement on text comprehension between U.S. and Chinese students. *Reading Research Quarterly, 39,* 162–184.

Ward, M. C. (1971). *Them children: A study in language learning.* New York: Holt, Rinehart and Winston.

Watson, D. L., Northcutt, L., & Rydell, L. (1989). Teaching bilingual students successfully. *Educational Leadership, 46,* 59–61.

Weinberg, M. (1977). *A chance to learn: The history of race and education in the United States.* Cambridge, MA: Harvard University Press.

Wells, G. (1999). *Dialogic inquiry: Toward a sociocultural practice and theory of education.* New York: Cambridge University Press.

Wepner, S. B., Valmont, W. J., & Thurlow, R. (2000). *Linking literacy and technology: A guide for K–8 classrooms.* Newark, DE: International Reading Association.

Wertsch, J. V. (1981). The concept of activity in Soviet psychology. In J. V. Wertsch (Ed.), *The concept of activity in Soviet psychology* (pp. 3–36). Armonk, NY: M. E. Sharpe, Inc.

Weston, N., & Ingram, J. H. (1997). Whole language and technology: Opposites, or opposites in harmony? *Educational Horizons, 75* (2), 83–89.

Whaley, J. F. (1981). Story grammar and reading instruction. *The Reading Teacher, 34,* 762–771.

White, T. G. (2005). Effects of systematic and strategic analogy-based phonics on grade 2 students' word reading and reading comprehension. *Reading Research Quarterly, 40,* 234–251.

Wigel, D. J., Martin, S. S., & Bennett, K. K. (2005). Ecological influences of the home and child-care center on preschool-age children's literacy development. *Reading Research Quarterly, 40,* 204–230.

Willinsky, J. (1994). Theory and meaning in whole language: Engaging Moorman, Blanton, and McLaughlin. *Reading Research Quarterly, 29* (4), 334–339.

Willis, J. W., Stephens, C., & Matthew, K. I. (1996). *Technology, reading, and language arts.* Boston: Allyn & Bacon.

Willis, S. (1994). Teaching language-minority students: Role of native-language instruction is debated. *Update, 36* (5), 1, 4–6.

Wilson, C. (1993). The relative influence of language versus minority status on the educational achievement of language minority students: A review of the literature. Unpublished manuscript, University of California, Division of Language and Literacy, Berkeley.

Winograd, K., & Higgins, K. M. (1994/1995). Writing, reading, and talking mathematics: One interdisciplinary possibility. *The Reading Teacher, 48* (4), 310–318.

Wixon, K. (1979). Miscue analysis: A critical review. *Journal of Reading Behavior, 11,* 163–175.

Wolf, D. P., & Reardon, S. F. (1996) Access to excellence through new forms of student assessment. In J. B. Baron & D. P. Wolf (Eds.), *Performance-based assessment: Challenges and possibilities* (pp. 1–31). Chicago: University of Chicago Press.

Wolfson, B. J., Manning, G., & Manning, M. (1984). Revisiting what children say their reading interests are. *Reading World, 24,* 4–10.

Wong-Fillmore, L. W. (1976). The second time around: Cognitive and social strategies in second language acquisition. Unpublished doctoral dissertation, Stanford University, Stanford, CA.

Wong-Fillmore, L. W., & Valadez, C. (1986). Teaching bilingual learners. In M. C. Wittrock (Ed.), *Handbook of research on teaching* (pp. 648–685). New York: Macmillan.

Wood, D., Bruner, J., & Ross, G. (1976). The role of tutoring in problem solving. *Journal of Child Psychology and Psychiatry, 17,* 89–100.

Woods, M. L., & Moe, A. J. (2007). *Analytical reading inventory, 7th edition.* Upper Saddle River, N.J.: Prentice Hall.

Woolfolk, A. E. (1995). *Educational psychology.* Boston: Allyn & Bacon.

Writing yellow pages: For students and teachers. (1988). Nashville: Incentive.

Yopp, H. K. (1988). The validity and reliability of phonemic awareness tests. *Reading Research Quarterly, 23,* 159–177.

———. (1992). Developing phonemic awareness in young children. *The Reading Teacher, 45,* 696–703.

Yopp, H. K., & Yopp, R. H. (2000a). Supporting phonemic awareness development in the classroom. *The Reading Teacher, 54,* 2, 130–143.

Yopp, R. H., & Yopp, H. K. (2000b). Sharing informational text with young children. *The Reading Teacher, 53* (5), 410–423.

Young, T. A. (Ed.). (2006). *Happily ever after: Sharing folk literature with elementary and middle school students.* Newark, DE: International Reading Association.

Zinsser, W. (1988). *Writing to learn.* New York: Harper & Row.

Name and Subject Index

Key terms and concepts and the page numbers on which they appear are in **boldface**. Personal names in **bold-face** indicate authors of professional publications. Those names not in boldface are authors of children and juvenile literature books.

A

Aardema, V., 200, 327, 331, 332
Abedi, J., 320
Ability grouping, 354
Accommodation, cognitive
    development and, 40
**Achievement tests, 20, 269–270,
    272–273**
Active learning, 162–165
Active participation, 321
Active thinking, 123, 125
Activity centers, 76
Ada, A. F., 332
Adams, A., 191
Adams, M. J., 26, 60, 92, 96, 97,
    98, 99, 291, 292
Adaptation, 295
    cognitive development and, 40
Additive approach to multicultural
    education, 311, 313
Adoff, A., 331
Aesthetic appreciation, 191
Aesthetic stance, 189, 190, 204
Affixes, 111–112
Afflerbach, P., 221
African American literature, 331
Agard, J., 61
Agenbroad, L. D., 191
Ahlberg, A., 58
Akin, C. E., 160
Alexander, P. A., 17, 92, 123
Alexander, S., 191
Alexander, S. H., 337
Alexander and the Wind-up Mouse
    (Lionni), 130–131, 194
Aliki, 68, 301, 333, 337
Allard, H., 200, 209
Allen, V. G., 311
Allington, R. L., 10, 17, 90, 285,
    347, 390
Almasi, J. F., 192, 197
Alphabet books, 61, 74
Alphabetical organization, 180
Alphabetic principle, 87

Alphabets. *See also* Letter
    recognition
    displaying, 61
    letter recognition, 60–61
Altwerger, B., 243
American Library Association, 199
America Reads tutors, 299
Analytical Reading Inventory
    (Woods & Moe), 259
Analytic phonics, 97, 99
Ancona, G., 333
Anders, P. L., 384
Anderson, D. K., 7, 41
Anderson, R., 337
Anderson, R. C., 7, 26, 28, 96, 99,
    125, 139, 160, 284, 292
Andrade, H. G., 253
Andrews, J. F., 337
Angelou, M., 68
Anno, M., 58
Anonymous, 6
Antecedents, 298–299
Anthologies, 62–63, 193, 301
Anthony, J. L., 289
Anticipation, in writing instruction,
    229
Antonyms, 172
Anzaldua, G., 332
Applebee, A., 8, 197
Applicative level of thinking,
    125–126, 127, 140
Approximation
    assessment of, 252
    encouraging, 12, 51–52
Arbuthnot, M. A., 16
Archambault, J., 61, 333
Archbold, R., 239
Are You My Mother? (Eastman),
    54
Armbruster, B. B., 123, 192, 347
Armstrong, A., 239
Armstrong, W. H., 331
Art, expression through, 63–64
Art centers, 76

Ash, G. E., 196–197
Ashman, L., 200
Asian American literature, 330
Assessment, 79
    achievement tests, 20
    authentic, 252–253
    basal readers and, 355
    bias in, 252–253
    classroom-based, 251–252
    classroom observation and,
        254–264
    communicating with parents
        about, 275–277, 278
    of delayed readers, 290–291
    of early literacy, 79, 80–81
    formal, 269–275
    Informal Reading Inventory for,
        259, 267
    information sources for, 254, 255
    interest inventories, 254–257
    language-based approach and,
        363
    of literacy development, 250–281
    in literature-based approach, 11
    miscue analysis in, 259–261, 262
    observational, 79
    opposing views of, 270, 273
    portfolio, 234, 264–269, 272
    principles of, 251–253
    of print awareness, 57
    professional standards and, 5,
        279–280, 420–421
    purpose of, 79
    Reading Achievement Inventory
        for, 257–258
    of reading level, 263–264, 265
    of response to literature, 212, 213
    role of in instruction, 251
    running records in, 261, 263, 264
    standards' influence on, 20
    of students with special needs, 335
    technology and, 275
    test result interpretation in,
        274–275

Photo Credits: